A RESOURCE GUIDE FOR TEACHING: K-12

THIRD EDITION

RICHARD D. KELLOUGH

California State University, Sacramento

Merrill
an imprint of Prentice Hall
Upper Saddle River, New Jersey   *Columbus, Ohio*

Library of Congress Cataloging-in-Publication Data

Kellough, Richard D. (Richard Dean)
   A resource guide for teaching : K–12 / Richard D. Kellough.
      p.   cm.
   Includes bibliographical references and indexes.
   ISBN 0-13-022510-X
      1. Teaching Problems, exercises, etc.   2. Classroom management-
   -United States Problems, exercises, etc.   I. Title.
   LB1025.3.K45   2000
   371.102—dc21   99-41104
                                                          CIP

Editor: Debra A. Stollenwerk
Developmental Editor: Gianna M. Marsella
Editorial Assistant: Penny S. Burleson
Production Editor: Mary Harlan
Design Coordinator: Karrie Converse-Jones
Photo Coordinator: Anthony Magnacca
Text Design and Project Coordination: Carlisle Publishers Services
Cover Designer: Paul Isaacs
Cover Art: ©SuperStock, Inc.
Production Manager: Pamela D. Bennett
Director of Marketing: Kevin Flanagan
Marketing Manager: Meghan Shepherd
Marketing Coordinator: Krista Groshong

This book was set in New Baskerville by Carlisle Communictions, Ltd. and was
printed and bound by Banta Company/Harrisonburg. The cover was printed by
Banta Company/Harrisonburg.

©2000, 1997 by Prentice-Hall, Inc.
Pearson Education
Upper Saddle River, New Jersey 07458

All rights reserved. No part of this book may be reproduced, in any form or by any
means, without permission in writing from the publisher.

Earlier edition ©1994 by Macmillan Publishing Company

Photo Credits:
Scott Cunningham/Merrill: 1, 73, 98, 125, 157, 247, 263, 327;
KS Studios/Merrill: 205, 282; Anthony Magnaccas/Merrill: 9, 23, 28, 135, 146, 184,
185, 217, 224, 235, 262, 263, 328, 384; Barbara Schwartz/Merrill: 70, 91, 341;
Tom Watson/Merrill: 17; Anne Vega/Merrill: 26, 103, 121, 154

Printed in the United States of America

10 9 8 7 6 5 4 3 2 1

ISBN: 0-13-022510-X

Prentice-Hall International (UK) Limited, *London*
Prentice-Hall of Australia Pty. Limited, *Sydney*
Prentice-Hall of Canada, Inc., *Toronto*
Prentice-Hall Hispanoamericana, S. A., *Mexico*
Prentice-Hall of India Private Limited, *New Delhi*
Prentice-Hall of Japan, Inc., *Tokyo*
Prentice-Hall (Singapore) Pte. Ltd., *Singapore*
Editora Prentice-Hall do Brasil, Ltda., *Rio de Janeiro*

To my parents, Mayme and Stanley Kellough,
in celebration of their 65th wedding anniversary.
This book has resulted from their unwavering love, care, and devotion
to the importance of family and to the value of education.

Foreword

Congratulations! You have chosen the most frustrating, satisfying, perplexing, inspiring, fatiguing, energizing, stressful, and rewarding of professions: teaching. You will experience moments of despair, days of euphoria, times of exhilaration, and states of confusion. This resource guide is intended to see you through both the good times and the bad. Employing the knowledge and the practices contained in this guide will maximize the possibilities of the positives outweighing the negatives.

One of the factors contributing to the dichotomy between the stresses and the satisfactions of teaching is the ambiguity of rewards—there is little immediate and direct feedback that would indicate that you are doing an outstanding job as a teacher. You often will not know if a lesson went well, if students have learned, or if your instructional strategies were appropriate. Indicators of your success are often elusive, and the few shreds of evidence you might collect disclose very little about what you should do next. While you probably will be externally evaluated by others, such as a supervising teacher or an administrator, autonomous professionals increasingly assume responsibility for assessing their own efficacy. The rewards of being an effective teacher must therefore be sought from within. Ultimately, you must judge your excellence for yourself according to a set of internal criteria and values.

As you look forward to a career in education, then, how will you assess yourself as an educator? What will be said of you on that remote date when you retire? What shall serve as your measures of success in your chosen profession? On what creative achievements will you proudly affix your signature?

Your contemplation of such visions and values may be obscured by your initial concerns about classroom life. Your highest priorities now seem occupied with developing classroom management techniques, establishing positive relationships with your students and colleagues, covering the content, and creatively using your limited resources of time, space, and energy. As you master these essential skills of classroom survival, however, you also may wish to take some time to ponder such larger questions, as they will provide professional meaning, sharpen your philosophical beliefs, and refine your personal values with which to evaluate your own achievements in your life mission.

Teaching is variously referred to as an act of mercy, a performing art, a moral craft, and a science. Teachers have been compared to artisans, bureaucrats, managers, laborers, artists, assembly-line workers, physicians, and mechanics. Whatever metaphor you employ, teaching is a cooperative, intellectual process of decision making. The work of teaching is the application of your powerful intellect to both the science and the artistry of instruction.

As a professional, you will find yourself working in three arenas: the classroom, the school, and the community. As a skillful, collaborative, autonomous, and concerned professional decision maker, you will assume responsibility for managing the knowledge, selecting the content, creating the instructional strategies, designing the assessment techniques, and engaging in all the curriculum decisions that orchestrate the complex implementation of effective learning. You will take responsibility for assuring your own continued learning and intellectual growth, for collaborating with your colleagues as you plan, coach, teach, and learn with other members of your instructional team, and for educating and networking with the larger school and professional communities.

The information in this resource guide will serve as a starting place for working in these three arenas. What follows is intended to provoke an internal, ongoing, and lifelong dialogue within yourself and in interaction with others as you journey along the pathways of your career. It is designed to provide you with some high standards for assessing your growth and development in your various roles as an authentic educator in the three arenas of professional life.

THE CLASSROOM ARENA

While this resource guide contains much valuable information about learning, you will translate it into action through interaction with students and colleagues. Professional teachers learn from experience. They grow and change throughout their careers. Each lesson you teach is an experiment. You will plan, conduct, and reflect on each lesson. From such analysis, you will synthesize and apply new knowledge about teaching and learning to other lessons, other content areas, and other life situations. Through such daily practice, you will continue to learn more about learning. You will produce new meaning by combining such knowledge with practice.

Through workshops, advanced course work, coaching, and training; through the acquisition of further knowledge by reading and study; and through collaboration with and role modeling of significant and more experienced colleagues, you will be in a continual learning mode. You will be a learner among learners.

One criterion by which you may judge your own excellence as a professional, therefore, is the degree to which you are continuing to learn throughout your life. You will want to hold yourself accountable for your continued growth in the skills, performances, and habits of mind that are prerequisite to effective teaching. If teaching is an intellectual process of instructional decision making, you will want to assess your own capacity to reflect on practice, analyze your lessons, synthesize meaning from each experience, prescribe alternatives, and modify your own instructional behavior accordingly.

Human beings are made to be different. Diversity is the basis of biological survival. Each of us has a different genetic structure; unique facial features; a distinguishing thumbprint; a distinctive signature; a diverse background of knowledge, experience, and culture; and a preferred way of gathering, processing, and expressing information. We even have a singular frequency in which we vibrate. Since you, your students, other staff members at your school, and parents and community members strive to exert their individuality, you will be in a constant state of flux as you adapt to changing situations, personalities, styles, cultures, philosophies, languages, values, innovations, and societal problems. One of your greatest assets as a teacher will be your ability to adapt.

Another measure of your excellence as a teacher, therefore, will be your increasing capacity to manage constructively, teach toward, and enhance the complexity and diversity of the classroom. You will want to assess continually how you are becoming better able to value the richness and diversity within and among your students, your colleagues, and your community.

THE COLLEGIAL ARENA

We do not become smarter or better at what we do without a healthy and continued dose of collegial practice. Your professional development will be a function of the collegiality and self-reflection made possible through your interaction with others. As you continually grow toward greater efficacy, flexibility, consciousness, and artistry, you will increasingly focus your energies and attention on greater interdependence with your colleagues and community. You will design and seize numerous opportunities for collaborative communicating, problem solving, and decision making with your colleagues.

As individuals engage in problem solving, communicating, and coaching with each other, multiple perspectives and points of view are expressed. This creates a healthy dissonance in the group. The group and the individuals grow as such tensions are reduced, discrepancies resolved, alternatives weighed, options selected, and consequences explored. As you gain experience together, you increasingly select, integrate, and develop more intricate and harmonious patterns of group behavior. Over time, you will shift from thinking in terms of "my kids, my lesson, my room" toward "our kids, our school, our goals, our vision, and our community."

You may wish to evaluate your own professional excellence by examining your increased ability to create and discuss ideas that contribute to the group's thinking that surpasses individual efforts. Excellence in your group interactions will be measured by your ability to contribute to group consensus, to listen to others with understanding and empathy, to be able to assume another's point of view, and to lend your resources to achieving the greater good.

THE COMMUNITY ARENA

Once you perceive that interdependent relationship between you and the broader community, your context for learning and contributing will expand even further. With this wider perspective, you will focus on the school, the profession, the community, and the society as a whole. You may hear yourself asking such questions of major magnitude as:

- What is the purpose of schooling?
- What will the next generation of teachers be like?
- What is the role of schooling from a global perspective?
- How will schools address issues of social conditions, interdependence, and cultural diversity?
- How can I contribute to the profession and to society?
- What leadership can I best provide?

You may find yourself conducting research, obtaining grants, contributing to and writing your own publications, pursuing higher degrees, and presenting staff development programs for your own and other schools. You may also become active in professional associations and voluntarily take responsibility for solving troublesome school and community problems.

You may find yourself playing a variety of roles: mentor, teacher in residence, coach, lead teacher, master teacher, member of a leadership team, facilitator for community participation, organizational member of professional groups, and networker with other teachers, schools, and community agencies that all serve the same clients—your students.

Thus, as you reflect on your career, you will want to assess your excellence in terms of the degree to which you are assuming an expanded role as a contributing and influential member of the larger community.

Throughout your career, you will never lose sight of your ultimate purpose for being a teacher—the students. The career you have chosen is unique in that those with whom you come in contact will leave you in a better condition than when they came to you. In your charge will be the statespeople, parents, teachers, leaders, decision makers, students, and workers of the twenty-first century. You have assumed an awesome responsibility.

As Alan Kay stated, "The best way to predict the future is to invent it."[1] If you want a future that is much more thoughtful, vastly more cooperative, greatly more compassionate, and a lot more loving, then *you* will have to invent it, because the future is in your schools and classrooms today.

Arthur L. Costa, Ed.D.
Kalaheo, Hawaii

---

[1]Kay, A. "The Best Way to Predict the Future Is to Invent It," keynote presentation at the annual conference of the Association for Supervision and Curriculum Development, San Francisco, 1990.

Preface

The purpose of *A Resource Guide for Teaching: K–12* is to provide a practical, concise, criterion-referenced, performance-based, mastery learning model for college or university students who are preparing to become competent teachers. Others who find it useful are experienced teachers who desire to continue developing their skills and curriculum specialists and school administrators who desire to have available for reference purposes a current, practical, and concise book of methods and resources about teaching.

NEW TO THIS EDITION

Major changes for this edition include:

- *Outstanding practices and exemplary school programs.* Despite the blue ribbon commissions, authors, and politicians that vilify what they perceive as the failures of public school education in this country, thousands of committed teachers, administrators, parents, and community representatives struggle daily, year after year, to provide youth with a quality education. So that readers can learn about or visit exemplary schools and programs, many are recognized and identified by name throughout this text.
- *Instructional scenarios and classroom vignettes.* Found throughout the text (see, for example, Figures 1.5 and 2.1), these serve as additional springboards for class discussion.
- *Increased emphasis on interweaving multimedia with lessons and learning* (see Chapter 10). See, for example, the many figures of recommended sites on the Internet—for example Figures 1.3 and 1.6 (Chapter 1), 8.3 (Chapter 8) and 10.2 (Chapter 10) as well as the recommended Web sites mentioned throughout.
- *Increased emphasis on community service learning.* To reflect the concerted efforts throughout the nation to help students at all grade levels to connect academic learning, personal growth, and a sense of civic respon-

sibility, this edition of the resource guide identifies many sample projects, especially in Chapters 1 and 8.

Other changes include:

For Part I

Chapter 1 is shorter, and the content of Chapters 1 and 2 has been rearranged. Some exercises of Chapter 1 of the previous edition have been omitted from this edition, and some new exercises have been added, such as Exercises 4.1 and 4.4. Case studies were added to Chapter 4.

For Part II

Part II consists of two rather than four chapters. Chapter 5 is about planning curriculum and its content, and Chapter 6 is about planning the actual units of instruction. This edition places increased emphasis on the use of interdisciplinary thematic instruction with examples of interdisciplinary projects (Chapters 5 and 6).

For Part III

Part III now consists of four rather than five chapters. New is a presentation of more than one hundred ideas for motivating lessons, interdisciplinary teaching, transcultural studies, community service learning, and student projects (Chapter 8). There is emphasis on connecting the levels of thinking (Chapter 9) with the phases of instruction and of decision making (Chapter 3), the levels of cognition (Chapter 5), and the levels of questioning (Chapter 7). Increased emphasis is also focused on the use of visual and technological tools as a means for students to access information and to make sense out of it (Chapter 10).

For Part IV

Many sample checklists and scoring rubrics for use in assessment have been added. A new section titled "Professional Development Through Reflection and Self-Assessment" has been added to Chapter 12.

ORGANIZATION OF THIS EDITION

Developmental components are involved in becoming a competent teacher. This book is organized around four developmental components: *why*—the rationale to support the components that follow; *what*—what you will be teaching; *how*—how you will do it; and *how well*—how well you are doing it. These are represented by the four parts of the book. Each part is introduced with the goals of the chapters that follow and with reflective thoughts relevant to topics addressed in its chapters. The following visual map illustrates how these four developmental elements are divided:

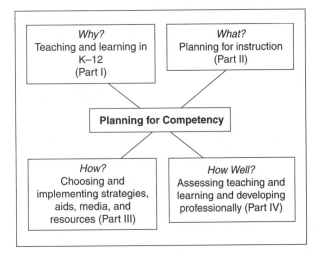

Each chapter, in turn, begins with a brief introduction to that chapter, followed by its major learning objectives.

Throughout, I provide information useful for a teacher who is a decision maker. You will find frequent exercises for practicing the handling of concepts in ways that are facilitative of metacognitive thinking. All exercises require you to deal in some descriptive, analytical, or self-reflective manner with text concepts and actual practice. Most of the exercises are adaptable for cooperative/collaborative group processing.

Part I: Orientation to Teaching and Learning

The four chapters of Part I reflect the *why* component, the reality and challenge of K–12 public school classroom teaching today. They present an overview of that reality and challenge, along with specific guidelines for meeting the challenge. Regardless of their individual differences, all students must have equal opportunity to participate and learn in the classroom. Beginning in the first chapter, this belief is reflected throughout this resource guide, sometimes in a very direct fashion and other times more discursively. This attention to details in showing an overall sensitivity to diversity is intended to model not only my belief but

also the many ways in which a classroom teacher can be inclusive. Chapter 1 presents an introductory review of the descriptions and challenges of school organization. Chapter 2 focuses on the unique and varied characteristics and developmentally appropriate ways of working with students. Chapter 3 reflects the expectations, responsibilities, and behaviors that are characteristic of competent and effective teachers. To teach young people effectively, you must recognize, appreciate, and understand your students and be able to establish and maintain a safe and supportive classroom learning environment. Guidelines for accomplishing that are presented in Chapter 4.

Part II: Curriculum and Planning for Instruction

Effective teaching is performance based and criterion referenced. This resource guide is constructed in this manner. Because I believe that teaching, indeed living, must allow for serendipity, encourage the intuitive, and foster the most creative aspects of one's thinking, we cannot always be specific about what children will learn as a result of our instruction. Hence, the occasional ambiguity must be expected. The two chapters in Part II reflect this planning, or the *what* component.

Chapter 5 provides a focus on curriculum, on the rationale for planning and selecting the content of the curriculum; provides information about the national, state, and local documents that guide content selection; and describes preparing goals and objectives and using them in planning.

Chapter 6 is intended to be the major draw on your time and attention as you use this resource guide to become a competent classroom teacher. The chapter presents detailed information and step-by-step guidelines for integrating the learning, selecting developmentally appropriate learning activities, and preparing instructional units and lessons.

Part III: Choosing and Implementing Instructional Strategies, Aids, Media, and Resources

Although it is very difficult to predict what youth of today will need to know to be productive citizens in the middle of the twenty-first century, it is my belief that they will always need to know how to learn, how to read, how to communicate effectively and work together cooperatively, and how to think productively. I believe young people need skills in how to gain knowledge and how to process information, and they need learning experiences that foster effective communication and productive, cooperative behaviors. I hope all students feel good about themselves, about others, and about their teachers, schools, and communities. I emphasize the importance of helping students to develop those skills, feelings, and attitudes. All teachers share in the responsibility for teaching skills in reading, writing, thinking, working cooperatively, and communicating effectively. This responsibility is reflected throughout this book.

The appropriate teaching methods for reaching these goals are those that incorporate thoughtful planning, acceptance of the uniqueness of each individual, honesty, trust, sharing, risking, collaboration, communication, and cooperation. Furthermore, I believe students best learn these skills and values from teachers who model the same. This book is faithful to that hope and to that end.

Part III presents the *how* component in four chapters, but that component cannot be as cleanly separated from the *what* component of Part II or the *how well* component of Part IV as this organization might seem to imply. In reality, you will need to refer to this second half of the resource guide before you complete your instructional plans started during your study of Part II.

Chapter 7 begins Part III by focusing your attention on one significantly important teaching and learning strategy—questioning—with an emphasis on the encouragement of questions formulated and investigated by students.

Chapter 8 presents guidelines for grouping students, using project-centered teaching, assignments and homework, ensuring classroom equity, and writing across the curriculum. Chapter 8 ends with an annotated listing of more than 100 motivational strategies and ideas for lessons, interdisciplinary teaching, transcultural studies, and student projects, a section you may find useful for years to come.

Chapter 9 presents guidelines for using teacher talk, demonstrations, direct teaching of thinking, discovery and inquiry, and educational games. Throughout the book, but particularly in Chapter 10, you find emphasis on the importance of students using visual and technological tools to access information and to make sense of it.

Part IV: Assessment and Continuing Professional Development

In two chapters, Part IV addresses the fourth component of teaching and learning—*how well* the students are learning and how well the teacher is teaching. Although separated in this resource guide for reasons of organizational clarity, the assessment component of teaching and learning is an integral and ongoing component of the total curriculum.

Chapter 11 focuses attention on the assessment of what students know or think they know preceding, during, and following the instructional experience. To complete your instructional planning (Chapter 6) you will necessarily be referring to the content of Chapter 11. Chapter 11 also provides practical guidelines for parent-teacher collaboration and for grading and reporting student achievement.

Chapter 12, the final chapter, focuses on how well you are doing—the assessment of teaching effectiveness. In addition, it provides guidelines that you will find useful during your student teaching, for finding a teaching position, and for continued professional growth after you are employed as a teacher. These guidelines—as with this resource guide in general—will be useful as references for years beyond a methods course.

FEATURES OF THE TEXT

To achieve professional competency, you need guided learning, guided practice, productive feedback, encouragement, and positive reinforcement. To provide the resources and encouragement to make you an effective and confident teacher, this resource guide is organized with the following features.

- **A strong, current, and broad research base.** This is evidenced by the footnotes throughout the text, which are arranged at the bottom of text pages for your immediate reference and clarification.
- **Advance organizers.** The four parts, along with their goals and reflective thoughts at the beginning of each part, and the objectives found at the beginning of each chapter serve as advance organizers; that is, they establish a mind-set.
- **Exercises for active learning.** Exercises within each chapter require you to deal in some descriptive, analytical, or self-reflective manner with text concepts and actual practice. Each is designed to (1) encourage continual assessment and reflection on your progress in understanding and skill development for teaching, and (2) involve you in collaborative and cooperative learning. Since some exercises necessitate a school visit, an early review of the exercises will allow you to plan your visits and work schedule. In fact, because certain exercises build upon previous ones or suggest that help be obtained from teachers in the field, it is advised that all exercises be reviewed at the beginning of your course. Because it is unlikely that the more than 50 exercises found in this book could be (or should be) completed in a one-semester course, your class must decide which exercises will be done.
- **Perforated pages** for easy removal of the exercises. Exercises and other forms that are likely to be removed for use begin on new pages so that they can be removed without disturbing text.

- **Performance assessment.** Assessment of your developing competencies is encouraged by micro peer teaching exercises found in Chapters 7 (Exercise 7.7), 9 (Exercises 9.2), and 12 (Exercise 12.2).
- **Situational case studies, instructional scenarios and teaching vignettes, and questions for class discussion.** For extended class discussions, situational case studies are presented in Chapter 4. Teaching vignettes and instructional scenarios are distributed in several locations, such as "Interdisciplinary thematic instruction at West Salem Middle School" (Chapter 1), "Using the theory of learning capacities and multilevel instruction" (Chapter 2), and "A teachable moment" (Chapter 6). Questions for Class Discussion appear at the end of each chapter.
- **Outstanding practices and exemplary programs.** To help you gain further insight or to visit exemplary programs, schools recognized as having exemplary programs are identified throughout the text.
- **Resources and guidelines.** Useful resources and detailed guidelines appearing throughout the text are current, useful, practical, research based, and tested.
- **For further reading.** At the conclusion of each chapter are additional sources, both current and classic, to deepen and broaden your understanding of particular topics.
- **Glossary and index.** The text concludes with a glossary of terms, a name index, and a subject index. Care has been taken to assure that the subject index and table of contents are thorough for ease of cross-reference.

ACKNOWLEDGMENTS

I would never have been able to complete this book had it not been for the valued help of many individuals: former students in my classes and teachers who have shared their experiences with me; administrators and colleagues who have talked and debated with me, and authors and publishers who have graciously granted permission to reprint materials and who are acknowledged in the book. To each I offer my warmest thanks.

Although I take full responsibility for any errors or omissions in this book, I am deeply appreciative to others for their cogent comments and important contributions that led to the development of this third edition. I express my appreciation to the reviewers: Ronald J. Anderson, Texas A & M International; Allan F. Cook, University of Illinois, Springfield; Claire B. Gallagher, Monmouth University; Janet Handler, Mount Mercy College; Nancy W. Hazlewood, Trevecca Nazarene University; and Scott Popplewell, Ball State University. In addition I wish to acknowledge those who reviewed earlier versions: George Belden, North Georgia College; John Cannon, University of Nevada; Leigh Chairelott, Bowling Green State University; Noble Corey, Indiana State University; Judith Costello, Regis College; Ann Dorsey, University of Cincinnati; Edward W. Holmes, Towson State University; Elizabeth Simons, Kansas State University; and David R. Stronck, California State University. A special thank you goes to Arthur L. Costa for writing the foreword to this book.

I also express my deepest admiration and appreciation to the highly competent professionals at Merrill/Prentice Hall with whom I have had a long and rewarding relationship, especially to Senior Editor Debbie Stollenwerk, whose professional knowledge and talent, bright confidence, positive demeanor, and sense of humor helped make writing this new edition more enjoyable.

I am indeed indebted and grateful to all the people in my life, now and in the past, who have interacted with me and reinforced what I have known since the days I first began my career in teaching: teaching is the most rewarding profession of all.

R. D. K.

To the Student

In preparing this book, I saw my task *not* as making the teaching job easier for you—effective teaching is never easy—but as improving your teaching effectiveness and providing relevant guidelines and current resources. You may choose from these resources and build upon what works best for you. Nobody can tell you what will work with your students; you will know them best. I do share what I believe to be the best of practice, the most useful of recent research findings, and the richest of experiences. The following paragraphs highlight statements that present my beliefs and explain how they are embraced in this resource guide.

The best learning occurs when the learner actively participates in the process, which includes having ownership in both the process and the product of the learning. Consequently, this resource guide is designed to engage your hands and your mind in learning about effective teaching. For example, rather than finding a chapter devoted to an exposition of the important topic of cooperative learning, in each chapter *you* will become involved in cooperative and collaborative learning. In essence, via the exercises found in every chapter, you will practice cooperative learning, talk about it, practice it some more, and finally, through the process of doing it, learn a great deal about it. This resource guide *involves* you in cooperative learning.

The best strategies for learning about teaching model the very strategies used in exemplary teaching. As you will learn, integrated learning is the cornerstone of effective teaching, and that is a premise upon which this resource guide is designed.

To be most effective, any teacher, regardless of grade level and subject, must use an eclectic style in teaching. Rather than focusing your attention on particular "models of teaching," I emphasize the importance of an eclectic model, one in which you select and integrate the best from various instructional approaches. For example, sometimes you will want to use a direct, expository approach, perhaps by a minilecture, but more often you will want to use an indirect, social-interactive, or student-centered approach, perhaps through project-based learning. This resource guide provides guidelines that will help you both to decide which approach to use at a particular time and to develop your skill in using specific approaches.

Learning should be active, pleasant, fun, meaningful, and productive. My desire is to present this book in an enthusiastic, positive, and cognitive-humanistic way, in part by providing rich experiences in social-interactive learning. How this is done is perhaps best exemplified by the active learning exercises found throughout the book. Exercises have been developed to assure that you become an active participant in learning the methods and procedures that are most appropriate in facilitating the learning of active, responsive students.

Teaching skills can be learned. In medicine, certain knowledge and skills must be learned and developed before the student physician is licensed to practice with patients. In law, certain knowledge and skills must be learned and developed before the law student is licensed to practice in a courtroom. So it is in teacher preparation: knowledge and skills must be learned and developed before the teacher candidate is licensed to practice the art and science of teaching young people. I would never allow just any person to treat my child's illness or to defend me in a legal case; the professional education of teachers is no less important! Receiving a professional education specifically on how to teach young students is absolutely necessary, and certain aspects of that education must precede any interaction with students if teachers are to become truly competent professionals.

Brief Contents

Contents

Part I

ORIENTATION TO TEACHING AND LEARNING

Part I responds to your needs concerning:

- The realities of public school classroom teaching today and the diversity of students and types of schools
- Development of a personal instructional strategies repertoire
- Developmentally appropriate instructional practices
- An effective, safe, and supportive classroom environment
- Expectations, responsibilities, competencies, and fundamental teaching behaviors of a classroom teacher
- Home, school, and community connections
- Selected legal guidelines for the classroom teacher
- Productive ways to start the school year
- Creation of your professional resources file
- The teacher as a reflective decision maker
- Development of a teaching style

REFLECTIVE THOUGHTS

Exemplary schools are those that are rooted in celebrating and building upon the diverse characteristics and needs of students. To become and to remain exemplary, they must be in a continual mode of inquiry, reflection, and change.

All students—regardless of gender, social class, and ethnic or cultural characteristics—must have an equal opportunity to participate and to learn in the classroom.

To hold high, although not necessarily identical, expectations for all learners is to promote respect for diversity.

A caring and responsive learning environment has as its sole purpose that of helping all students to make the transitions necessary to succeed in school and in life.

During one school year, you will make literally thousands of decisions, many of which can and will affect the lives of children for years to come. You may view this as an awesome responsibility, which it is.

Like intelligences, teaching style is neither absolutely inherited nor fixed. Your teaching style will change, develop, and emerge throughout your career.

Rather than being controlled by classroom events, the competent teacher is in control of classroom events.

To be most effective, learning must be enjoyable for students; it cannot be enjoyable when a teacher consistently acts like a marine drill sergeant.

Chapter 1

Teaching and Learning in Today's Schools

You have probably begun reading this book because you are interested in a career in teaching. Whether you are in your early twenties and starting your first career, or older and in the process of beginning a new career, this book is for you; that is, it is for any person interested in becoming a competent classroom teacher.

If you are now in a program of teacher preparation, then perhaps near the completion of the program you will be offered your first teaching contract. If that happens, you will be excited, eager to sign the contract and begin your new career. After the initial excitement, you will have time to reflect. Many questions will then begin to form in your mind. If in a multiple-school district, to which school will I be assigned? Will it be a traditional school or will it be a *magnet school,* that is, a school that specializes in a particular area of the curriculum, such as the visual and performing arts, or science, mathematics, and technology, or international studies?[1] (Magnet schools occur at all levels: elementary, middle, and high school. The North Dade Center for Modern Languages, for example, is a public elementary magnet school that focuses on international studies and provides students with the opportunity to become bilingual, biliterate, and multicultural.) Or a *partnership school* that has entered into a partnership agreement with community business and industry to link school

studies with the workplace?[2] Or a *tech prep* high school that combines academic and vocational programs?[3] Or an *International Baccalaureate school* with a curriculum approved by the International Baccalaureate Organization (IBO), a worldwide nonprofit educational foundation founded in the 1960s and based in Switzerland?[4] Or a *full-service school* offering quality education and comprehensive social services all under one roof?[5]

It could also be a *charter school,* "an autonomous educational entity operating under a charter, or contract, that has been negotiated between the organizers, who create and operate the school, and a sponsor, who

---

[1]See K. Checkley, "Magnet Schools: Designed to Provide Equity and Choice," *Education Update* 39(2):1, 3, 8 (March 1997).

[2]Some schools belong to the National Network of Partnership 2000 Schools. For information, contact the Center on School, Family, and Community Partnerships, The Johns Hopkins University, 3506 North Charles Street, Baltimore, MD 21216. Phone 410-516-8807 or Fax 410-516-8890. See also W. Johnson et al., "Texas Scholars," *Phi Delta Kappan* 79(10):781–783 (June 1998) about the Texas Scholars Program adopted by the Texas Business and Education Coalition.

[3]See, for example: S. Corwin, "Tech Prep—an Education That Really Works," *Educational Horizons* 73(4):181–186 (Summer 1995); and L. D. Anderson, "Implementing the Technology Preparation (Tech-Prep) Curriculum," *Journal of Technology Studies* 21(1):48–58 (Winter/Spring 1995).

[4]IBO offers a Primary Years Program for students aged 3 to 12, a Middle Years Program for students 11 to 16 years old, and a Diploma Program for students in the final two years of secondary school. See IBO's site on the Internet at <http://www.ibo.org>.

[5]See J. G. Dryfoos, "Full-Service Schools," *Educational Leadership* 53(7):18–23 (April 1996).

oversees the provisions of the charter?"[6] Since the first in Minnesota in 1991, charter school legislation has been passed in at least 34 states and the District of Columbia and Puerto Rico, reflecting a general dissatisfaction with centralized state or district control, bureaucratic inflexibility, and uneven progress in student performance.

Another option is an *ungraded school* with *multiage classrooms,* known also as mix-aged or nongraded, where children, usually of primary grades, are grouped in classes without grade-level designations and with more than a one-year age span.[7] Or perhaps it might be another type or a combination of these, such as a *charter-magnet school.*[8]

Will it be a school that has its start in the fall, as is traditional, or will it be a year-round school? (In just ten years, from 1985 to 1995, the number of schools in the United States that changed to a year-round program increased from only about 400 in sixteen states to more than 2,200 in thirty-seven states.) What specific grade levels will I have? Which subjects will I be responsible for teaching? Will I be a member of a teaching team? What supervision and advisory responsibilities might I have? What will the students be like? How can I prepare for students I know nothing about? What will their parents or guardians be like? What textbooks will I use, and when can I expect to see them? Will I be using a multimedia program? How *can* I prepare when there are so many unanswered questions? What school district policies do I need to learn about now? What support services can I expect? How extensive are the school's rules and regulations? Is there a dress code or uniform requirement for the students? Will there be an orientation meeting where I can obtain answers to some of my questions?

Those questions and many others are often the focus of long, concentrated thinking by beginning teachers. To guide you through this initial experience and to help answer some of your questions, this chapter offers a first glimpse into today's world of classroom teaching. This chapter and the three that follow in Part I provide a basis for your planning and selecting learning activities presented in subsequent chapters. Enjoy your quest toward becoming the best classroom teacher you can be.

Upon completion of this first chapter you should be able to

1. Define and differentiate *elementary school, middle school,* and *high school.*
2. Describe essential characteristics that characterize a school as being exemplary.
3. Describe similarities and differences between the exemplary middle school and the traditional junior high school.
4. Describe the purposes and characteristics of the "school-within-a-school" concept.
5. Demonstrate understanding of the term *developmentally appropriate.*
6. Describe current trends, problems, and issues in American public school education.

ORIENTATION

Rapid and dramatic changes occurring throughout modern society, combined with what has been learned in recent years about intelligence and learning, are reflected in the equally rapid and dramatic changes occurring in today's public schools. The school in which you soon will be teaching may bear little resemblance to the school of your childhood in its curriculum, its student body, its methods of instruction, or its physical appearance. From the moment you set foot onto a school campus during this program for teacher preparation and later when you obtain your first paid teaching job, you will want to keep your sensory input channels wide open to learn as much as you can about the school, its organization, its students, and its support staff. Although it is only the beginning to your learning about teaching, this resource guide offers information and resources you will want to refer to time and again, long after the initial course for which it is used is over.

Orientation Meetings: Start of the School Year

As a beginning teacher, you will likely be expected to participate in orientation meetings designed to help you get off to a good beginning. Some school districts start the school year with a districtwide orientation, whereas others schedule on-site orientations at each school. Many school districts do both, with perhaps a districtwide morning meeting followed by school on-site meetings in the afternoon. Such meetings provide you the opportunity to meet other teachers and estab-

---

[6]L. A. Mulholland and L. A. Bierlein, *Understanding Charter Schools,* Fastback 383 (Bloomington, IN: Phi Delta Kappa Educational Foundation, 1995), p. 7. See also the theme issue, "The Charter School Movement," in the March 1998 *Phi Delta Kappan,* Volume 79, number 7, and the several articles about charter schools in the October 1998 issue of *Educational Leadership,* Volume 56, number 2. Connect to charter school home pages via the United States Charter School Web site at <http://www.uscharterschools.org/>. For additional information and for a copy of the *National Charter School Directory,* contact the Center for Education Reform (CER) at 800-521-2118, e-mail to cerdc@aol.com, or see the web site at <http://edreform.com/reserach/css9697.htm>.

[7]See, for example, B. A. Miller, "A Basic Understanding of Multiage Grouping," *School Administrator* 53(1):12–17 (January 1996), and H. J. McLaughlin, et al., "Crossing the Grade Level Gap: Research on Multiage Grouping," *Middle School Journal* 30(3):55–58 (January 1999).

[8]For example, the Natomas Charter School (Natomas School District, Sacramento, CA) is a magnet performing and fine arts academy with grades 7–12.

lish new collegial friendships and professional relationships. Of course, the scheduling and planning of orientation meetings will vary district by district and school by school. The objectives for all orientation meetings, however, should be similar to those in the following paragraphs.

You should become familiar with the district's (or school's) written statement of its beliefs and goals—its *statement of mission*—and what that statement means to the people affiliated with the district or school. See sample missions statements shown in Figure 1.1.

You will be encouraged to become familiar with the policies of the school and district. Numerous policies often cover a wide range. Various policies relate procedures for injuries of students at school; natural disasters, such as earthquakes and severe storms; allowing students to take prescribed medications; finding non-prescribed drugs, other controlled substances, and weapons; parking on campus; leaving campus during the school day; class conduct; school programs, field trips, and parties in the classroom; grading practices; completing absentee and tardy forms; sending students to the office; and chaperoning and sponsoring student activities. These are just a few examples.

You will learn about the myriad forms that teachers must fill out. There are forms for injuries at school, for textbook loans, for key loans, for attendance and tardies, for student academic grade deficiencies, for

Figure 1.1 Sample mission statements reprinted by permission.

- The mission of Jackie Carden Elementary School (Fort Worth, TX; grades K–6; available on-line <http://www.flash.net/~jcelem/mis.html>, April 11, 1998) is to provide students with a positive, challenging, and rewarding educational environment so that all students will become productive citizens.

- The mission of Honey Creek Community Charter School (Ann Arbor, MI; ages 5–11; available on-line <http://isd.wash.k12.mi.us/~hcreek/mission.html>, April 21, 1998) is to provide an education of the whole child, to integrate the different aspects of children's learning and lives so as to make them fuller and more meaningful. Honey Creek Community school offers an integrated, theme- and project-based curriculum which draws on experiences at home, in the school, and in the larger community, and which encourages parents and other community members to participate in the school and share their expertise. The interaction among students, teachers, family members, and community members is designed to allow students to view their learning from a variety of different perspectives and, in the process, to learn to develop their own views while simultaneously developing an understanding of their local and global communities and ecosystems, and learning to participate more meaningfully in them.

- It is the mission of O. E. Dunckel Middle School (Farmington Hills, MI; grades 6–8; available on-line <http://www.farmington.k12.mi.us/FPS/schools/dunckel/index.html>, April 11, 1998) to provide a positive learning environment challenging all students to become successful lifelong learners and positive contributors to a changing society.

- It is the mission of Antelope Union High School (Wellton, AZ; grades 9–12; available on-line <http://www.primenet.com/~antelope/handbook/mission.htm>, April 9, 1998) to create a safe learning environment where students learn to be responsible, thoughtful, self-reliant, productive citizens capable of adapting to and competing in a rapidly changing world community.

- It is the mission of Irvington High School (Fremont, CA; grades 9–12; available on-line <http://www.irvington.org/info/profile.html>, April 9, 1998) to prepare students for a self-fulfilling future—to succeed in citizenship, in higher education, in their careers, and in achieving their individual goals . . . We believe that: all students can learn and deserve the opportunity to achieve their fullest potential; students need to master basic skills and develop the ability to think critically; students learn in different ways; the school must preserve, transmit, and help clarify ethical, cultural, and social views; the school must recognize that every student is an individual with a unique set of academic and nonacademic strengths and needs; the school, the parents, and the community serve as partners in the educational process.

sponsoring student activities, for field trips, and for referrals of students for misbehavior, to name just a few.

You will learn about the approved curriculum that defines what teachers are to teach and what students are to learn. This means that you must familiarize yourself with the courses of study, curriculum guides, resource units, teacher's manuals, student textbooks, media programs, and supplementary materials—all of which should reflect the school's mission statement and approved curriculum. You will learn about the school or district plan for monitoring, assessing, and supervising implementation of the curriculum; about available resource materials and equipment; and about procedures for reserving and using them on certain dates.

You will learn about the school library/media resource center, its personnel, and its procedures, and you will meet district and school personnel and become familiar with the many services that support you in the classroom. You will meet campus security personnel, resource officers, and other ancillary personnel and learn about their functions and locations.

When not in meetings you will have time to prepare your assigned classroom(s) for instruction.

As a student in a program for teacher preparation, you may be expected to participate in an orientation meeting at your college or university. The meeting may be held at the beginning of the program and/or just before the beginning of your field experiences. Perhaps this meeting will be a function of one of your college or university courses. You will receive your school assignment, the name of the school and the school district, the school's location, the date when you should report to that assignment, the name of your cooperating teacher(s), the grade level(s), the subject(s), and perhaps the name of your college or university supervisor. You will probably be encouraged to follow many of the objectives discussed in the preceding paragraphs and to meet other teacher candidates.

When you arrive at your assigned school and after introductions have been made, you should begin to become familiar with the school campus and the way that the school is organized. Walk around the campus, perhaps with a copy of the school map, and learn the location of your classroom. Also locate the nearest restrooms for girls, boys, and faculty men or women. You may be loaned one or several keys—one for the classroom, one for the faculty restroom, and perhaps one for a faculty workroom. Become familiar with such areas as the teacher's workroom, the faculty room, and the faculty lunch room (which may or may not be a single area—a large comprehensive high school may have several faculty rooms scattered about the campus).

Thoroughly investigate the campus environment. Where do students eat their lunches? Is there a multipurpose room used for lunch and for educational purposes? Is there a school nurse? Where is the nurse's room? When is the nurse available? Where is the nearest first-aid and emergency equipment? How do you notify maintenance personnel quickly and efficiently? Where are the written procedures for fire drills and other emergencies? Where is information about the school's emergency warning system? Is there a plan posted in a conspicuous place for all to see? Where are the various administrative offices? Where are the counseling and guidance offices? Is there an office of student activities? Where are the library, the media center, the resources room, gymnasium(s), and the auditorium? Where are textbooks stored, and how are they checked out and distributed? Where is the attendance office? Are there resource specialists, and if there are, what are their functions and where are their offices?

At an orientation session, you may meet the grade level or department chairperson or the team leader and members of that team. How can you discover where those persons are to be found at various times during the school day? Where are teaching materials and laboratory supplies kept, and how do you obtain them? Have you located your faculty mailbox and the place to check in or out when you arrive at school or leave at the end of the day? What procedures do you follow if you are absent because of illness or if you know you are going to be late? Do you have the necessary phone numbers? Not least in importance, if you drive a vehicle to school, where do you park? Otherwise, what is the best local transportation available for getting to and from school each day?

After becoming familiar with the school campus and obtaining answers to some of your more urgent questions, you will want to focus your attention on the various school schedules and particularly your own teaching schedule.

The School Calendar Year: Conventional and Year-Round

School years vary from state to state, from district to district, and from school to school. Most school years begin in mid- to late-August or early-September and continue through late-May or mid-June. However, to accommodate more students without a significant increase in capital costs and to better sustain student learning, an increasing number of schools are eliminating the traditional long summer break by switching to *year-round education (YRE),* which, by the way, has been around for more than half a century.[9] Whether the school follows a year-round schedule or not, for teachers and students in the United States the school year still approximates 180 days.

In a school with year-round operation, a teacher might teach for three-quarters of the year and be off for one-quarter or teach in a 45/15 program, which means nine weeks of school (45 days) "on track" followed by three weeks of school (15 days) "off track" throughout the year. Nearly 70 percent of YRE schools use the 45/15 plan.[10] In 45/15 arrangements, teachers and students are on tracks, referred to as A Track, B Track, and so on, with starting and ending times that vary depending on the track and time of year. At any one time there is always at least one track on vacation. "Intersession" programs may be held during off-track time, at which time students might participate in special classes for remediation or enrichment.

Beginning about 8:00 A.M. the school day lasts until about 3:00 or 4:00 P.M. During hot summer months, some schools begin earlier, say at 7:15 A.M., and end around 2:00 P.M. District and state laws vary, but generally teachers are expected to be in the classroom no less than 15 minutes prior to the start of school and to remain in their classrooms no less than 15 minutes after final dismissal of students.

Drawing upon studies of adolescent sleep patterns and the need to find ways to deal with crowded schools or to cut transportation expenses by reducing the number of busses and drivers needed, some schools recently have begun experimenting with modified starting times. For example, students at Kerr Middle School (Elk Grove, CA) have a 9:20 A.M. start. At North Salem High School (Salem, OR), students can opt for either a 12:20 P.M.–7:30 P.M. school day or for the traditional times.

Teaching Teams

Traditionally, elementary school teachers taught their groups of children in their self-contained classrooms for most of the school day and secondary school teachers taught their subject disciplines as often as seven or eight times each day to as many groups of students. At all levels, teachers taught in their assigned classrooms while fairly isolated from other teachers and school activities—not unlike the parallel play of preschool children, that is, playing side-by-side but not really together. In some schools, that is still the case. Increasingly, however, at all levels, teachers are finding themselves members of a collaborative **teaching team** in which several teachers work together to reflect, plan, and implement a curriculum for a common cohort of students. (*Note:* A distinction must be made between teaching teams and team teaching; **team teaching** refers to two or more teachers simultaneously providing instruction to students in the same classroom. Members of a teaching team may participate in team teaching.)

The teaching team may comprise only a few teachers, for example, all third grade teachers of a particular elementary school, or the tenth and eleventh grade teachers of history and English at a particular high school, or the teachers who teach the same cohort of seventh grade students in English/reading/language arts and in history/social studies/geography at a middle level school. They may meet periodically to plan a curriculum and learning activities around a common theme. Sometimes teaching teams comprise one teacher each from English/reading/language arts (known also as *literacy*), history/social studies/geography, mathematics, and science. These four areas are known as the **core curriculum.** In addition to teachers of the core subjects, specialty-area teachers may be part of the team, including teachers of physical education, the visual and performing arts, and even special education teachers and at-risk specialty personnel or school counselors. As a visiting or continuing member of this interdisciplinary team organization (ITO), a team may invite a community-resource person (see, for example, the vignette in Figure 1.5). Because the core and specialty subjects cross different disciplines of study, these teams are commonly called *interdisciplinary teaching teams,* or simply **interdisciplinary teams.**

The School-within-a-School Concept

An interdisciplinary teaching team and its common cohort of students is referred to as the **school-within-a-school** (also called *village, pod, academy, family, house,* or sometimes just plain *team*), where each team of teachers is assigned each day to the same cohort of students for a *common block of time.* Within this block of time, teachers on the team are responsible for the many professional decisions necessary, such as how school can be made *developmentally responsive,* or most meaningful, to students' lives, what specific responsibilities each teacher has each day, what guidance activities need to

[9]See, for example, M. McCord, "Bursting at the Seams: Financing and Planning for Rising Enrollments," *School Business Affairs* 63(6):20–23 (June 1997); B. P. Venable, "A School for All Seasons," *Executive Educator* 18(7):24–27 (July 1996); C. C. Kneese, "Review of Research on Student Learning in Year-Round Education," *Journal of Research and Development in Education* 29(2):60–72 (Winter 1996); J. Curry et al., *Year-Round Schools Evaluation, 1996–97* (Austin, TX: Publication Number 96.10, Austin Independent School District, 1997); B. Prohm and N. Baenen, "Are Year-Round, Multi-Track Elementary Schools Effective? An Analysis of Schools in Wake County, North Carolina," *ERS Spectrum* 14(2):42–47 (Spring 1996); and, N. R. Brekke, *Year-Round Education: Does It Cost More?* (Madison, WI: Consortium for Policy Research in Education, 1997).

[10]W. D. Gee, "The Copernican Plan and Year-Round Education: Two Ideas That Work Together," *Phi Delta Kappan* 78(10):795 (June 1997).

be implemented, which students need special attention, and how students will be grouped for instruction. Members of such a team become "students of their students" and thereby build the curriculum and instruction around their students' interests, perspectives, and perceptions. Because they "turn on" learning, the school and its classrooms become exciting places to be and to learn. (In contrast, "symptoms of turned-off learning include students' seeming inability to grasp concepts, to exert effort, or to display enthusiasm; repeated lateness or absence; boredom; and work that is sloppy or of poor quality.")[11]

The school-within-a school concept helps students make important and meaningful connections among disciplines. It also provides them with both peer and adult group identification, which provides an important sense of belonging. In some schools, using an arrangement called **looping** (also referred to as *multiyear grouping, multiyear instruction, multiyear placement,* and *teacher-student progression*), the cohort of students and teachers remain together as a group for several or for all the years a student is at that school. Looping is used at all levels of schooling, but especially in the primary grades and in some middle schools.[12]

The advantages of being a member of a teaching team in a school-within-a-school environment are numerous. For example, the combined thinking of several teachers creates an expanded pool of ideas, enhances individual capacities for handling complex problems, and provides intellectual stimulation and emotional support. The synergism of talents produces an energy that has a positive impact on the instructional program. A beginning teacher who joins a team has the benefit of support from more experienced teammates. When a team member is absent, other members of the team work closely with the substitute, resulting in less loss of instructional time for students. More and better planning for students occurs as teachers discuss, argue, and reach agreement on behavioral expectations, curriculum emphasis, instructional approaches, and materials.[13]

Common Planning Time

For an interdisciplinary team to plan effectively and efficiently, members must meet together frequently. This is best accomplished when they share a *common planning time,* a minimum of four hours a week. This means that in addition to each member's daily preparation time (discussed in the next section), members of a team share a common planning time to plan curriculum and to discuss the progress and needs of individual students within the cohort.[14]

Each team assigns a member to be team facilitator, or lead teacher. The lead teacher organizes the meetings and facilitates discussions during the common planning time. Usually, this teacher also acts as a liaison with the administration to assure that the team has the necessary resources to put its plans into action. A team's lead teacher (or another member designated by the team) may also serve on the school leadership team, a group of teachers, administrators, and sometimes students designated by the principal or elected by the faculty (and student body) to assist in the leadership of the school. Sometimes, in lieu of a traditional site principal, the school leadership team *is* the leadership for the school.[15]

Teachers' Daily Schedules

Reflecting the educational goals and objectives and the needs and interests of the children, the elementary school teacher's daily schedule will differ depending on the program, the ages of the children involved, whether the program is full or half day (as might be the case with kindergarten), and whether it continues year-round. As you might suspect, there is a tremendous variation in the amount of time spent on different subjects in elementary schools. Because many teachers today use a holistic approach to teaching and learning that emphasizes the interdisciplinary nature of meaningful learning rather than departmentalized learning, it is quite difficult to generalize about how much time is actually spent on any given discipline.

Children tend to feel more secure when the daily schedule is routine and is posted. However, teaching children is never predictable. Even the best of daily schedules will be modified by the impulsive nature and spontaneous interests of children. Although every teacher should have clear goals and objectives and a routine that students can rely on from day to day, effective teachers consider and build upon the interests, experiences, and spontaneous nature of their students.

---

[11]The phrases "students of their students" and "turn on learning" are borrowed from C. A. Grant and C. E. Sleeter, *Turning on Learning* (Upper Saddle River, NJ: Prentice Hall, 1989), p. 2.

[12]See, for example, A. Pyle, "In the Loop," *Middle Ground* 1(1):15 (August 1997); K. Rasmussen, "Looping—Discovering the Benefits of Multiyear Teaching," *Education Update* 40(2):1, 3–4 (March 1998); C. Forsten et al., *Looping Q&A: 72 Practical Answers to Your Most Pressing Questions* (Peterborough, NJ: Crystal Springs Books, 1997); and D. L. Burke, *Looping: Adding Time, Strengthening Relationships* (Champaign, IL: ED414098, ERIC Clearinghouse on Elementary and Early Childhood Education, 1997).

[13]R. J. McCarthy, *Initiating Restructuring at the School Site,* Fastback 324 (Bloomington, IN: Phi Delta Kappa Educational Foundation, 1991), p. 11.

---

[14]See, for example, A. C. Howe and J. Bell, "Factors Associated with Successful Implementation of Interdisciplinary Curriculum Units," *Research in Middle Level Education Quarterly* 21(2):39–52 (Winter 1998).

[15]See, for example, D. Barnett et al., "A School Without a Principal," *Educational Leadership* 55(7):48–49 (April 1998).

For a teaching team to plan effectively and efficiently, members must meet together frequently. This is best accomplished when they share a common planning time where they can plan curriculum and discuss the progress and needs of individual students within the cohort.

For many middle level and high school teachers, the school day consists of the traditional seven or eight periods, each period lasting about 50 minutes. This traditional schedule includes teaching three or four classes before lunch and three or four following lunch. One of these periods is a *preparation period,* referred to sometimes as the conference or planning period. Most teachers are quite busy during their preparation periods, reading and grading student papers, preparing class materials, meeting in conferences, or preparing instructional tools.

Nontraditional Scheduling

To maximize the learning time, to allow for more instructional flexibility, and to accommodate common planning time for teachers, an increasing number of schools, kindergarten through high school, are using some form of **block scheduling.** Block scheduling means that, for at least part of the school day, or part of the week, blocks of time ranging from 70 to 140 or more minutes replace the traditional structure of 50-minute-long classes. The possible variations are nearly limitless.[16]

For example, for some secondary schools, the school year consists of three 12-week trimesters, and each school day is divided into five 70-minute-long class periods. Such a schedule is referred to as a *5 × 7 block plan.* Some schools use a *4 × 4 block plan,* whereby students take four 85- to 90-minute-long *macroperiods* (or *macroclasses*) each day, each semester.[17] Other schools use an A-B, or *alternating day block plan,* where classes meet every other day for the entire school year for 90-minute blocks.[18]

Using macroperiods lengthens the time each day students are in a course, simultaneously reducing the number of courses taken at one time. The extended period, or macroperiod, allows the teacher to supervise and assist students with assignments and project work and with their reading, writing, thinking, and study skills. Macroperiods provide more time for interactive and interdisciplinary thematic instruction that might otherwise be difficult or impossible to accomplish in shorter class periods.

---

[16]For a description of a program called *parallel block scheduling* and its successful use in grades K–5, see M. Delany et al., "Parallel Block Scheduling Spells Success," *Educational Leadership* 55(4):61–63 (December 1997/January 1998). See also H. J. Hopkins and R. L. Canady, "Integrating the Curriculum with Parallel Block Bock Scheduling," *Principal* 76(4):28–31 (March 1997).

[17]See, for example, D. W. Mutter et al., "Evaluation of 4 × 4 Block Schedules," *ERS Spectrum* 15(1):3–8 (Winter 1997).

[18]See, for example, M. D. DiRocco, "How an Alternating-Day Schedule Empowers Teachers," *Educational Leadership* 56(4):82–84 (December 1998/January 1999).

BLOCK SCHEDULING: ADVANTAGES
AND DISADVANTAGES

Consistently reported in the research of schools using block scheduling—where students and teachers work together in longer but fewer classes at a time—are: (1) greater satisfaction among teachers and administrators and (2) improvement in both the behavior and the learning of students. Students do more writing, pursue issues in greater depth, enjoy classes more, feel more challenged, and gain deeper understandings. In addition, teachers get to know the students better and are therefore able to respond to a student's needs with greater care.

Other reported benefits of the block plans over a traditional seven- or eight-period daily schedule include

1. In one school year the total hours of instruction are significantly greater.
2. Each teacher teaches fewer courses during a semester and is responsible for fewer students; therefore, student-teacher interaction is more productive and the school climate is positive with fewer discipline problems.
3. Because planning periods are longer, there is more time for teachers to plan and to interact with parents.

In evaluations of schools using block scheduling, Carroll found more course credits completed, equal or better mastery and retention of material, and a significant reduction in suspension and dropout rates.[19] Most teachers using block scheduling report they accomplish more in each class session.[20]

There are also benefits to taxpayers. During one school year teachers teach more courses and potentially more students, thereby decreasing the number of faculty needed. In addition, fewer textbooks are needed. For example, instead of all eleventh graders taking history for an entire year, half of them take it the first semester and half the second, thereby reducing the number of textbooks needed by one-half.

Block scheduling arrangements often produce serendipitous benefits. For example, students may not have to carry as many books and may go to their lockers fewer times a day to exchange textbooks and materials between blocks. In many schools, except perhaps in physical education and vocational education, student lockers are not used at all. Also, the reduction of bells ringing from as many as eight times a day to perhaps only two or three times a day or not at all creates less disturbance.

Because students are not roaming halls for three to five minutes five or six times a day, teachers can more easily supervise unstructured time and thereby have better control over portions of the unplanned and subtle message systems within schools, referred to as the *hidden curriculum.* The messages of the hidden curriculum are the school climate, the feelings projected from the teacher and other adults to students and from the students to one another, not only in classrooms but before and after school, at social events, and in the halls, restrooms, and other areas of the school that are not monitored as closely as the individual classrooms.

Nontraditional school schedules are not without their problems. Problems that sometimes arise from block scheduling are: (1) content coverage in a course may be less than that which was traditionally covered; (2) there may be a mismatch between content actually covered and that expected by state mandated tests and the dates those tests are given to students; and (3) community relations problems may occur when students are out of school and off campus at nontraditional times.

Using a *modified block schedule,* some schools have successfully combined schedules, thus satisfying teachers who prefer block scheduling and those who prefer a traditional schedule. A modified block schedule can provide both traditional 40-minute periods (sometimes called *split-block periods*) that meet daily (sometimes preferred especially by teachers of mathematics[21] and foreign languages) and longer blocks. A modified block schedule provides seven or eight 45- or 40-minute periods per day along with alternate longer blocks. In a modified block schedule all students might start the day with a 30- or 40-minute first period, which serves as a homeroom or advisor/advisee time. From there, some students continue the morning attending traditional-length periods while others move into a morning block class. Throughout the day, teachers and students may pass from block classes to those of traditional length or vice versa.

Some schools use a *flexible block schedule.* The daily schedule is a seven-period day with all seven classes meeting on Monday. Periods one through four meet for 75 minutes, while periods five through seven meet for 30 minutes. Periods one through four meet for 105

[19]J. M. Carroll, "Organizing Time to Support Learning," *The School Administrator* 51(3):26–28, 30–33 (March 1994). See also the December 1995 "Report Study of the Four-Period Schedule for Anoka-Hennepin District No. 11," from the Center for Applied Research and Educational Improvement, College of Education and Human Development, University of Minnesota, Internet site at <http://carei.coled.umn.edu/blockscheduling/research/REPORTs. HTM>, and T. L. Shortt and Y. V. Thayer, "Block Scheduling Can Enhance School Climate," *Educational Leadership* 56(4):76–81 (December 1998/January 1999).

[20]R. Jones, "Wake Up," *Executive Educator* 17(8):14–18 (August 1995).

[21]See, for example, S. L. Kramer, "What We Know About Block Scheduling and Its Effects on Math Instruction, Part II," *NASSP* (National Association of Secondary School Principals) *Bulletin* 81(587):69–82 (March 1997).

minutes each on Tuesdays and Thursdays, and periods five through seven meet for 120 minutes each on Wednesdays and Fridays. A 30-minute period, perhaps for advisory or for independent research, is held at the same time each day, perhaps the first thing in the morning or after lunch.

In short, there is little doubt that longer blocks of instructional time with students are a positive factor contributing to students' meaningful learning, especially when combined with some form of year-round education and the use of interdisciplinary thematic instruction.

Striving to Present Quality Education for All Students

Nontraditional scheduling is part of the effort to restructure schools to deliver quality education for all students. The curriculum of a *quality education school* is one seen by students as having meaning and usefulness in their lives and is delivered by activity-oriented instruction (see Chapter 8). Rather than dictating procedures, ordering students to work, and berating them when they do not, the teachers in a quality school provide a stimulating learning environment and are seen by students as being encouraging and helpful.

Sometimes it may appear that more energy is devoted to organizational change (*how* the curriculum is delivered) than to school curriculum (*what* is taught). However, as discussed in Chapter 5, the two are inseparable. School organization has a direct effect on what students learn; if it didn't, educators wouldn't be spending so much valuable time trying to restructure their schools to effect the most productive (and cost-effective) delivery of the curriculum. Exemplary schools establish and maintain a climate of constant modification and are in a continual process of inquiry, reflection, and change.

Organizational changes are often referred to as *school restructuring,* a term that has a variety of connotations, including site-based management, collaborative decision making, school choice, personalized learning, integrated curricula, and collegial staffing. School restructuring has been defined as "activities that change fundamental assumptions, practices, and relationships, both within the organization and between the organization and the outside world, in ways leading to improved learning outcomes."[22] No matter how they define the term, educators agree on the following point: the design and functions of schools should reflect the needs of young people of the twenty-first century rather than a nineteenth century factory model.

Exemplified by efforts mentioned in the preceding discussions, the movement to year-round operation and the redesigning of schools into "houses" represents a movement that is becoming increasingly common across the country. With this redesign, the intention is that schools will better address the needs and capabilities of each unique student. To that end, a number of specific trends are shown in Figure 1.7 (page 22). As a teacher in the twenty-first century, you will undoubtedly help accomplish many of those changes.

Middle Schools and Junior High Schools

When you receive your state teaching credentials, you may or may not be certified to teach at the middle school level. In some states an elementary school credential certifies a person to teach in any grade, kindergarten through grade 8. In some states a secondary school credential certifies a person to teach a particular subject at any grade level, kindergarten through grade twelve. In other states such a credential qualifies a person to teach only grades seven through twelve. At least thirty-three states provide a middle school teaching credential to candidates who have successfully completed a program specifically designed to prepare teachers for that level.

At this point you should note that there are two sometimes quite different types of schools, both of which may be called middle schools. One is the traditional junior high school with perhaps a few minor changes, such as changing its name to "middle school." The second is the exemplary middle school, which is, as shown in Table 1.1, quite different from the traditional junior high school. To understand the significance of what has become known as the **middle school concept,** certain background information may prove helpful.

EVOLUTION OF THE MIDDLE SCHOOL
CONCEPT AND PHILOSOPHY

Used historically from about 1880, the term *junior high school* most commonly refers to schools having grades seven and eight or grades seven, eight, and nine, in which a program is designed to approximate the type of education commonly found in traditional high schools. Thus, a junior high school might be considered a "not-quite-yet-but-trying-to-be" high school. Students graduating from a junior high school often would then move on to a *senior high school.*

The term *middle school* gained favor as a result of the movement away from the concept of "junior" high school. Reasons for the reorganization away from the concept of junior high school and the adoption of a middle school education include: (1) to provide a program specifically designed for students of the 10 to 14 age group, (2) to set up a more effective transition between the elementary school and the high school,

---

[22]D. T. Conley, "Restructuring: In Search of a Definition," *Principal* 72(3):12 (January 1993).

Table 1.1   Summary of Differences between Middle Schools and Traditional Junior High Schools.

Characteristic	Junior High School	Middle School
Most common grade-span organization	7–8 or 7–9	6–8
Scheduling	Traditional 50-minute periods, six-period day	Flexible, usually block
Subject organization	Departmentalized	Integrated and thematic; interdisciplinary, usually language arts, math, science, and social studies
Guidance/counseling	Separate sessions with counselor on individual basis or as needed; full-time counselors	Advisor–advisee relationship between teacher and student in homeroom or home base
Exploratory curriculum	Electives by individual choice	Common "wheel" of experiences for all students
Teachers	Subject-centered; grades 7–12 certification	Interdisciplinary teams; student-centered; grades K–8 or 6–8 certification
Instruction	Traditional; lecture, skills, and repetition	Thematic units; discovery techniques; study skills
Athletics	Interscholastic sports emphasizing competition	Intramural programs emphasizing participation

and (3) to move ninth graders to the high school or, as has happened in some school districts in recent years, to a location designed solely for ninth graders, known as a *ninth grade center*.[23,24]

Although any combination of grades five through nine may be included in a middle school, the trend and the most common configuration is grades six through eight. The trend of including sixth graders and excluding ninth graders is a reflection of the recommendation of the National Middle School Association in its official position paper, *This We Believe*.[25] The trend continues. For example, in California the number of middle schools that include sixth graders doubled during the decade from 1987 to 1997. Grades six to eight are now the most common grade span inclusion of middle schools in that state.

The term *middle level education* identifies school organizations based on a philosophy that incorporates curricula and instructional practices specifically designed to meet the needs of students ages 10 to 14.

This philosophy is referred to as the *middle school concept*. The notion that greater and more specific attention should be given to the special needs of young adolescents became known as the *middle school movement*. Basic to the movement is the belief that middle school teachers need specialized training to work most effectively with young adolescents.

School Restructuring and Students at Risk

Although the focus in Chapter 2 is on specifics of working with particular groups of students, it is appropriate at this time to say a few words about school restructuring efforts and at-risk students. "At risk" is the term educators use when referring to students who have a high probability of not finishing formal schooling. Categories of factors that cause a student to be at risk are:[26]

- academic failure—exemplified by low grades, academic failure, absences, low self-esteem
- family instability—exemplified by moving, separation, divorce
- family socioeconomic situation—exemplified by low income, negativism, lack of education
- family tragedy—exemplified by parent illness or death, health problems
- personal pain—exemplified by alcohol and other drug use, physical and psychological abuse, suspension from school

---

[23]K. Brooks and F. Edwards, *The Middle School in Transition: A Research Report on the Status of the Middle School Movement* (Lexington: College of Education, University of Kentucky, 1978).

[24]See, for example, the story of Oregon City High School, a ninth-grade-only school since 1990, in C. Paglin and J. Fager, *Grade Configuration: Who Goes Where?* (Portland, OR: Northwest Regional Educational Laboratory, 1997), pp. 29–31; the West Orange High School (Orlando, FL) Ninth Grade Center, opened in 1993, on the Internet at <http://mac.ae10.ocps.k12.fl.us/sch/hwo/9TH/INDEX.HTM>; and the Scott County Schools (Georgetown, KY) Ninth Grade Center, opened in 1996, on the Internet at <http://www.scott.k12.ky.us/9th/8thhistory.html>.

[25]National Middle School Association, *This We Believe* (Columbus, OH: Author, 1982, reissued in 1995).

[26]P. L. Tiedt and I. M. Tiedt, *Multicultural Teaching: A Handbook of Activities, Information, and Resources,* 5th ed. (Boston: Allyn and Bacon, 1999), p. 35.

Many students, at any one time, have risk factors from more than one of these categories. It has been estimated that by year 2020, the majority of students in American public schools will be at risk.[27] A nontraditional school schedule alone, without quality, personalized attention to each student, may be of no value in addressing the needs of students who are at risk of not finishing school. (See discussions about working with at-risk students in Chapter 2, "There Are Success Stories" in Chapter 4, and "strategies for personalizing the instruction" in Chapter 8) In addition, visit the home page of The National Institute on the Education of At-Risk Students at <http://www.ed.gov/offices/OERI/At-Risk/>.)

Today's movement to transform schools into caring and responsive learning environments has as its sole purpose that of helping all students, and especially those at risk, to make the transitions necessary to succeed in school and in life.

Responsive Practices for Helping All Students Succeed in School

Because of the enormous diversity of students, the advantage from using a combination of practices concurrently is usually greater to help all students succeed in school than is the gain from using any single practice. The reorganization of schools and the restructuring of school schedules represent only two aspects of efforts to help all students to make successful transitions.

Other important responsive practices (including attitudes) are (1) a perception, shared by all teachers and staff, that all students can learn when they are given adequate support, although not all students need the same amount of time to learn the same thing, (2) high, although not necessarily identical, expectations for all students, (3) personalized and individualized attention, adult advocacy, scheduling and learning plans to help students learn in a manner by which they best learn (research clearly points out that achievement increases, students learn more, and students enjoy learning and remember more of what they have learned when individual learning styles and capacities are identified and accommodated; learning style traits that significantly discriminate between students who are at risk of dropping out of school and students who perform well discussed in sections on "learning modalities" and "learning styles" in Chapter 2), (4) engagement of parents and guardians as partners in their child's education, (5) extra time and guided attention to basic skills, such as those of thinking, writing, and

reading rather than on rote memory, (6) specialist teachers and smaller classes, (7) peer tutoring and cross-age coaching, and (8) attention and guidance in the development of coping skills.

THE FUNDAMENTAL CHARACTERISTIC OF EXEMPLARY EDUCATION

Wherever and however the students are housed, and regardless of other responsive practices, in the end it is the dedication, commitment, and nature of the understanding of involved adults—the teachers, administrators, bus drivers, cooks, grounds crew, security staff, custodial staff, and support personnel—that remains the incisive element. That, in my opinion, is the fundamental characteristic of exemplary public education—that is, to celebrate and build upon the diverse characteristics and needs of students. That, in fact, is the title of Chapter 2 of this resource guide.

Committed Teachers

Public school teachers represent myriad individual personalities, which are perhaps impossible to capture in generalizations. Let us imagine that a teaching colleague mentions that Andi Rogers in room 17 is a "fantastic teacher," "one of the best teachers in the district," "super," and "magnificent." What might be some of the characteristics you would expect to see in Andi's teaching behaviors? (Teacher responsibilities and behaviors are the topic of Chapter 3.)

We can expect Andi to (1) be understanding of and committed to the school's statement of philosophy or mission, (2) know the curriculum and how best to teach it, (3) be enthusiastic, motivated, and well organized, (4) show effective communication and interpersonal skills, (5) be willing to listen to the students and to risk trying their ideas, and (6) be warm, caring, accepting, and nurturing about all students.

Students of all ages need teachers who are well organized and who know how to establish and manage an active and supportive learning environment (the topic of Chapter 4), even with its multiple instructional demands. Students respond best to teachers who provide leadership and who enjoy their function as role models, advisors, mentors, and reflective decision makers.

Reflective Decision Making

Whether you are a teacher of kindergarten children or of high school seniors or of students in between, during any school day you will make hundreds of nontrivial decisions, many of them instantaneously. In addition, you will have already made many decisions in preparation for the teaching day. During one school

---

[27]R. J. Rossi and S. C. Stringfield, "What We Must Do for Students Placed at Risk," *Phi Delta Kappan* 77(1):73–76 (September 1995). See also the several related articles in the theme issue, "The Changing Lives of Children," *Educational Leadership* Volume 54, number 7 (April 1997).

year a teacher makes literally thousands of decisions, many of which can and will affect the lives of her or his students for years to come. This may seem to be an awesome responsibility; indeed it is.

Initially, of course, you will make errors in judgment, but you will also learn that children are fairly resilient and that experts are available who can guide you to help ensure that the students are not harmed severely by your mistakes. You can learn from your errors. Keep in mind that the sheer number of decisions you make each day will mean that not all will be the best decisions that could have been made had you had more time and better resources for planning.

GOOD TEACHING IS AS MUCH AN ART AS IT IS A SCIENCE

Although pedagogy is based on scientific principles, good classroom teaching is as much an art as it is a science. Few rules apply to every teaching situation. In fact, decisions about the selection of content, instructional objectives and materials, teaching strategies, a teacher's response to student misbehavior, and the selection of techniques for assessment of the learning experiences are all the result of subjective judgments.

Although many decisions are made at a somewhat unhurried pace when you are planning for your instruction, many others will be made intuitively and *tout de suite*. Once the school day has begun, there is rarely time for making carefully thought-out judgments. At your best, you base your decisions on your teaching style, which, in turn, is based on your knowledge of school policies, pedagogical research, the curriculum, and the unique characteristics of the students in your classroom. You will also base your decisions on instinct, common sense, and reflective judgment. The better your understanding and experience with schools, the curriculum, and the students, and the more time you give for thoughtful reflection, the more likely it will be that your decisions will result in students meeting the educational goals. You will reflect upon, conceptualize, and apply understandings from one teaching experience to the next. As your understanding about your classroom experiences accumulate, your teaching will become more routinized, predictable, and refined. The topic of reflective decision making is presented more fully in Chapter 3; to learn more about the reality of teaching, complete Exercise 1.1.

EXERCISE 1.1 CONVERSATION WITH A CLASSROOM TEACHER

INSTRUCTIONS: The purpose of this exercise is to interview one or more teachers, perhaps one who is relatively new to the classroom and one who has been teaching for ten years or more. Use the following questions. You may duplicate blank copies of this form. Share the results with others in your class.

1. Name and location of school _____

_____

2. Grade span of school _____

3. Date of interview _____

4. Name and grade level (and/or subject) of interviewee _____

_____

5. In which area(s) of the school's curriculum do you work? _____

_____

6. Why did you select teaching as a career? _____

_____

_____

_____

_____

_____

7. Why are you teaching at this grade level? _____

_____

_____

_____

_____

_____

8. What preparation or training did you have? _____

_____

_____

_____

_____

_____

9. What advice about preparation can you offer? _____

_____

_____

_____

EXERCISE 1.1 (*continued*)

10. What do you like most about teaching? _____

_____

_____

_____

_____

_____

11. What do you like least about teaching? _____

_____

_____

_____

_____

_____

12. What is the most important thing to know to be an effective classroom teacher? _____

_____

_____

_____

_____

_____

13. What other specific advice do you have for those of us entering teaching at this level? _____

_____

_____

_____

_____

_____

The Principal Can Make a Difference

As a new or visiting member of the faculty, one of your tasks is to become familiar with the administrative organization of your school and district.

One person significantly responsible for the success of any school is its principal. What are the characteristics of an effective school principal? See Figure 1.2.

Perhaps foremost is that the principal has a vision of what a quality school is and strives to bring that vision to life. School improvement is the effective principal's constant theme.

The principal establishes a climate in which teachers and students share the responsibility for determining the appropriate use of time and facilities. Because exemplary educators believe in the innate potential of

Figure 1.2 Key characteristics of the exemplary school principal.

- Admonishes behaviors rather than personalities.
- Advocates a school of problem solvers rather than of blamers and faultfinders.
- Assures a base of community support for the school, its students, its faculty, and its mission.
- Emphasizes the importance of making everyone feel like a winner.
- Encourages people when they have made a mistake to say "I'm sorry," rather than making them feel compelled to cover their mistakes.
- Ensures that school policies are closely and collaboratively defined and clearly communicated.
- Ensures that staff and students receive proper and timely recognition for their achievements.
- Ensures that teachers' administrative chores and classroom interruptions are limited only to those that are critically important to student learning and effective functioning of the school.
- Establishes a climate in which teachers and students share the responsibility for determining the appropriate use of time and facilities.
- Follows up promptly on recommendations, concerns, and complaints.
- Fosters professional growth and development for teachers, with opportunities for visitations, demonstrations, conferences, workshops, and projects.
- Has a vision of what an exemplary school is and strives to bring that vision to life.
- Involves teachers, parents, and students in decision making and goal setting.
- Is an advocate for teachers and students.
- Is positive in her or his outlook.
- Keeps everyone well informed of events and of successes.
- Spends time each day with students.

The exemplary school principal has a vision of what a quality school is and strives to bring that vision to life.

every student, instead of dumbing down standards and expectations, they modify the key variables of time, grouping, and instructional strategies to help individual students achieve mastery (see Chapter 8). That task is nearly impossible without a supportive, knowledgeable, and positive thinking school principal.[28] (Sometimes, instead of having a school principal, the responsibility traditionally held by the person in that position is shared by a site-based management team or site council.)[29]

In addition to the school principal there will be vice or assistant principals, and persons with specific responsibilities and oversight functions, such as student activities, school discipline and security, transition programs, and curriculum and instruction. Some large schools have the school site principal plus persons designated as grade level principals.[30] Sometimes teachers who are department chairpersons, or designated team leaders, may also serve administrative functions. However, the principal is (or should be) the person with the final responsibility for everything that happens at the school. Where principals used to debate whether they were leaders or managers, today there is no debate: to be most effective, the principal must be both.

TELECOMMUNICATIONS NETWORKS, MEMBERS OF THE COMMUNITY, AND PARENT ORGANIZATIONS: VEHICLES FOR OBTAINING AND SHARING IDEAS AND INFORMATION

Today's exemplary educators are making major efforts to enhance the connections between the home, school, and local and global communities to promote the success of all students.

Home and School Connections

It is well known that parental involvement in their child's education can have a positive impact on their child's achievement at school. For example, when parents of at-risk students get involved, children benefit with more consistent attendance at school, more positive attitudes and actions, better grades, and higher test scores.

Although not all schools have a parent organization, when school principals were given a list of community groups or organizations and asked to assess the influence

each group had exerted on their school, the group that had the most influence was the parent-teacher organization (PTO) or parent-teacher association (PTA).[31] In recognition of the positive effect that parent and family involvement has on student achievement and success, in 1997 the National PTA published *National Standards for Parent/Family Involvement Programs.*[32]

Many schools have adopted formal policies about home and community connections. These policies usually emphasize that parents should be included as partners in the educational program, that teachers and administrators will inform parents about their child's progress, the school's family involvement policy, and any programs in which family members can participate. Some schools are members of the National Network of Partnership 2000 Schools. Efforts to foster parent and community involvement are as varied as the people who participate and include (a) student-teacher-parent contracts and assignment calendars, sometimes available via the school's web page on the Internet, (b) home visitor programs, (c) involvement of community leaders in the classroom as mentors, aides, and role models,[33] (d) newsletters, workshops,[34] and electronic hardware and software for parents to help their children, (e) homework hotlines, (f) regular phone calls[35] and personal notes home about a student's progress, and (g) involvement of students in community service learning.[36]

Community Service Learning

Through service learning students can learn and develop through active participation in thoughtfully organized and curriculum-connected experiences that meet community needs. (See Figure 1.3 for Internet sources of additional information and descriptions of community service projects; examples of service learning projects are described in the final section of Chapter 8.)

[28]B. J. Omotani and L. Omotani, "Expect the Best," *Executive Educator* 18(8):27, 31 (March 1996).

[29]See, for example, D. Barnett et al., "A School Without a Principal," *Educational Leadership* 55(7):48–49 (April 1998).

[30]For example, housing approximately 1,300 students First Colony Middle School (Sugar Land, TX) has, in addition to its school site principal, principals for each grade level, 6–8.

[31]J. W. Valentine et al., *Leadership in Middle Level Education. Vol. 1: A National Survey of Middle Level Leaders and Schools* (Reston, VA: National Association of Secondary School Principals, 1993), p. 98.

[32]See P. Sullivan, "The PTA's National Standards," *Educational Leadership* 55(8):43–44 (May 1998). For a copy of the standards contact the National PTA, 330 N. Wabash Ave., Chicago, IL 60611-3690. Phone 312-670-6782; Fax 312-670-6783.

[33]See, for example, the "Hand in Hand" web page at <http://www.handinhand.org>.

[34]See, for example, T. Whiteford, "Math for Moms and Dads," *Educational Leadership* 55(8):64–66 (May 1998).

[35]See, for example, C. Gustafson, "Phone Home," *Educational Leadership* 56(2):31–32 (October 1998).

[36]See C. Bodinger-deUriarte et al., *A Guide to Promising Practices in Educational Partnerships* (Washington, DC: ED392980, U.S. Government Printing Office, 1996), and the articles in the May 1998 theme issue, "Engaging parents and the community in school," of *Educational Leadership*, Volume 55, number 8.

Community members, geographic features, buildings, monuments, historic sites, and other places in a school's geographic area constitute one of the richest instructional laboratories that can be imagined. To take advantage of this accumulated wealth of resources and to build school-community partnerships, you should start a file of community resources once you are hired by a school. For instance, you might include files about the skills of the students' parents and other family members, noting which ones could be resources for the study occurring in your classroom. You might also include files on various resource people who could speak to the class, on free and inexpensive materials, sites for field trips, and what other communities of teachers, students, and adult helpers have done.

It is a good idea to start your professional resources file now, and keep it going throughout your professional career; for guidelines, see Figure 1.4. Many resource ideas and sources are mentioned and listed throughout this resource guide.

Figure 1.3 Internet sources on community service learning.

- *Big Dummy's Guide to Service-Learning* at <http://www.fiu.edu/time4chg/Library/bigdummy.html>
- *Links for Service-Learning* at <http://www.bbrook.k12.nj.us/servlink.htm>
- *National Service-Learning Cooperative Clearinghouse* at <http://www.nicsl.coled.umn.edu>

Telecommunications Networks

Teachers are increasingly turning to the Internet to guide their students toward becoming autonomous thinkers, effective decision makers, and life-long learners and to make their classrooms more student-centered, collaborative, interdisciplinary, and interactive. See, for example, the vignette in Figure 1.5. Webs of connected computers allow teachers and students from around the world to reach each other directly and gain access to quantities of information previously unimaginable. Students using networks learn and develop new inquiry and analytical skills in a stimulating environment and gain an increased appreciation of their role as world citizens. Sample web sites and addresses are shown in Figure 1.6; others are indicated throughout this guide, including Figures 8.3 (especially for subject-specific sites) and 10.2 (especially for sites about materials and technology). For a sample lesson plan illustrating student use of the Internet, see Figure 6.12 (Chapter 6).

THE EMERGENT OVERALL PICTURE

Certainly, no facet of education receives more attention from the media, causes more concern among parents and teachers, or gets larger headlines than that of a decline (factual or fanciful) in students' achievement in the public schools. Reports are issued, polls taken, debates organized, and blue-ribbon commissions are formed. Community members write letters to local editors about it, news editors devote editorial space to it, television anchors comment about it, and documentaries and specials focus on it in full color. We read, "Students Play Catch-Up on Basic Skills," "U.S. Students

Figure 1.4 Beginning your professional resources file.

A professional resource file is a project you can begin now and continue throughout your professional career. Begin your resources file either on a computer database program or on color-coded file cards that list (1) name of resource, (2) how and where to obtain the resource, (3) description of how to use the resource, and (4) evaluative comments about the resource.

Organize the file in a way that makes the most sense to you now. Cross-reference or color-code your system to accommodate the following categories of instructional aids and resources:

- Articles from print sources
- Compact disc titles
- Computer software titles
- Field trip destinations
- Games
- Guest speakers and other community resources
- Internet resources
- Media catalogs
- Motivational ideas
- Pictures, posters, graphs

- Resources to order
- Sources of free and inexpensive materials
- Student worksheets
- Test items
- Thematic units and ideas
- Unit and lesson plans and ideas
- Videocassette titles
- Videodisc titles
- Miscellaneous

Figure 1.5   Vignette: Interdisciplinary thematic instruction at West Salem Middle School.

What began as an isolated, single-grade, telecommunications-dependent project for sixth graders at West Salem Middle School (Wisconsin) eventually developed into a longer-term cross-grade interdisciplinary program of students and adults working together to design and develop a local nature preserve. Sixth graders began their adventure by interacting with explorer Will Steger as he led the International Arctic Project's first training expedition. Electronic on-line messages, via the Internet, allowed students to receive and send messages to Will and his team in real time. Students delved into the Arctic world, researching the physical environment and the intriguing wildlife, reading native stories and novels about survival, keeping their own imaginary expedition journals, learning about the impact of industrialized society on the Arctic, and conversing with students from around the world. But something very important was missing—a connection between the students' immediate environment and the faraway Arctic.

West Salem Middle School's focus became the local 700-acre Lake Neshonoc, an impound of the LaCrosse River, a tributary of the Mississippi. Although many students had enjoyed its recreational opportunities, they had never formally studied the lake. The Neshonoc Partners, a committee of parents, community leaders, teachers, students, and environmentalists, was established to assist in setting goals, brainstorming ideas, and developing the program for a year's study of the lake. Right from the start, students showed keen interest in active involvement in the project. A second committee, involving parents, students, and the classroom teacher, met during lunch time on a weekly basis to allow for more intensive discussions about the lake and the overall project.

The team of sixth grade teachers brainstormed ideas to further develop an interdisciplinary approach to the study of Lake Neshonoc. Special activities, including an all-day "winter survival" adventure, gave students a sense of what the real explorers experience. Students learned about hypothermia, winter trekking by cross-country skiing, and building their own snow caves.

For several weeks, students learned about the ecosystem of Lake Neshonoc through field experiences led by local environmentalists and community leaders. Guest speakers told their stories about life on the lake and their observations about the lake's health. Student sketchbooks provided a place to document personal observations about the shoreline, water testing, animal and plant life, and the value of the lake. From these sketchbooks, the best student creations were compiled to create books to share electronically with students with similar interests in schools from Russia, Canada, Missouri, South Carolina, Nevada, Wisconsin, and Washington, DC. The opportunity to share findings about their local watershed sparked discussions about how students can make a difference in their own community. Comparative studies gave students a chance to consider how other watersheds are impacted by humans and nature.

West Salem students worked with the local County Parks and Recreation Department to assist in developing a sign marking the new county park where the nature sanctuary will reside. Students brainstormed design ideas and then constructed a beautiful redwood sign with the help of a local technical educational teacher. Today the sign is a symbol of the partnership that has been established between the students and the community. It is a concrete reminder that together we can work for the common good of the community and the environment. Students celebrated the study of the lake with a closure. Will Steger, along with community leaders, parents, school board members, and staff, commended the students for what is sure to be the start of a long and enduring relationship—a partnership created out of common respect and appreciation for the value of our ecosystem.

Source: J. Wee, "The Neshonoc Project: Profiles in Partnership," *World School for Adventure Learning Bulletin* (Fall 1993):2–3. Adapted by permission.

Lag Behind Other Nations," and so on. What initiated this attention that began more than a quarter-century ago and continues today? I am not sure, but it has never been matched in its political interest and participation, and it has affected and continues to affect both the public schools and programs in higher education that are directly or indirectly related to teacher preparation and certification.[37]

In response to the reports, educators, corporations and local business persons, and politicians acted. Around the nation, their actions resulted in:

• Changes in standards for teacher certification. For example, model standards describing what prospective teachers should know and be able to do to receive a teaching license were prepared and released in 1992 by the Interstate New Teacher Assessment and Support Consortium (INTASC), a project of the Council of Chief State School Officers (CCSSO), in a document titled *Model Standards for Beginning Teacher Licensing and Development*. Representatives of at least 36 states and professional associations—including the National Education Association (NEA), the American Federation of Teachers (AFT), the American Association of Colleges for Teacher Education (AACTE), and the

---

[37]See, for example, G. I. Maeroff (Ed.), *Imaging Education: The Media and School in America* (New York: Teachers College Press, 1998).

Figure 1.6 Sample Internet sites for teachers and students.

- *Classroom Connect* <http://www.wentworth.com>. Resources for teachers; links to schools.
- *Coucil of the Great City Schools* <http://cgcs.org>. Descriptions of programs and projects in large urban schools.
- *Education links* <http://www.execpc.com/~dboals/k–12.html>. K–12 education links.
- *Education World* <http://www.education-world.com>. Electronic version of *Education Week*.
- *ENC* <http://www.enc.org>. Eisenhower National Clearinghouse for Mathematics and Science.
- *FedWorld* <http://www.fedworld.gov>. Access to information from government agencies.
- *GEM, the Gateway to Educational Materials* <http://www.thegateway.org/index.html>. National government's effort to provide access to Internet-based educational materials.
- *GlobaLearn* <http://www.globalearn.org/>. Students interact with remote expedition teams.
- *Global Schoolnet Foundation* <http://www.gsn.org/>. Global resources and links.
- *GLOBE* (Global Learning and Observations to Benefit the Environment) *Program* <http://www.globe.gov>. An international environmental science and education partnership.
- *Homeschool Resources* <http://mint.net~caronfam/links.htm>.
- *HomeworkCentral* <http://www.homeworkcentral.com>. For lesson plans and subject research.
- *Kathy Schrock's Guide for Educators* <http://www.capecod.net/schrockguide/> for resources and information on education.
- *Library of Congress* <http://lcweb.loc.gov/homepage/lchp.html>. National Digital Library life history manuscripts from the WPA Federal Writers' Folklore Project, Civil War photographs, early motion pictures, legal information, and research sources.
- *ClubMid* <http://www.ClubMid.phschool.com>. Middle grades network.
- *MiddleWeb* <http://www.middleweb.com/>. Focuses on middle schools.
- *National Consortium for School Networking* <http://cosn.org>.
- *Novagate reference site* <http://www.novagate.com/novasurf/onlinereference.html>.
- *Study Web* <http://www.studyweb.com>. Place for students and teachers to research topics.
- *Teachers Helping Teachers* <http://www.pacificnet.net/~mandel/>.
- *Teacher Talk* <http://education.indiana.edu/cas/tt/tthmpg.html>. Mostly for middle school and high school teachers.
- *21st Century Teachers* <http://www.21ct.org>. Teachers for teachers exchange.
- *United Nations' CyberSchool Bus* <http://www.un.org/Pubs/CyberSchoolBus/>. Curriculum units and projects, databases on U.N. member states, and global trends.
- *United States Department of Education* <http://www.ed.gov/index.html>.
- *Virtual Reference Desk, for Educators* <http://thorplus.lib.purdue.edu/reference/>.
- *Yahoo's Education Index* <http://www.yahoo.com/Education/tree.html>.

National Council for the Accreditation of Teacher Education (NCATE)—comprise the group. The standards are performance-based and revolve around a common core of principles of knowledge and skills that cut across disciplines. The INTASC standards were developed to be compatible with the National Board for Professional Teaching Standards (NBPTS).[38] Specifically addressing middle level instruction, in 1997 the NBPTS released eleven categories of standards for certification as a Middle Childhood/Generalist. Those categories are (1) knowledge of students, (2) knowledge of content and curriculum, (3) learning environment, (4) respect for diversity, (5) instructional resources, (6) meaningful applications of knowledge, (7) multiple paths of knowledge, (8) assessment, (9) family involvement, (10) reflection, and (11) contributions to the profession.[39]

- Emphasis on education for cultural diversity and ways of teaching language minority students.
- Emphasis on helping students make effective transitions from one level of schooling to the next and from school to life, with an increased focus on helping students make connections between what is being learned and real life, and connections between subjects in the curriculum and between academics and vocations.

---

[38]For copies of the INTASC document, contact CCSSO, One Massachusetts Ave. NW, Suite 700, Washington, DC 20001, 202-408-5505, http://www.ccsso.org.

[39]Access the standards via Internet <http://www.nbpts.org/nbpts/standards/mc-gen.html>. You may want to compare the 11 standards of the NBPTS document with the 22 competencies that are identified in Chapter 3 of this resource guide and with the 22 "components of professional practice" in C. Danielson, *Enhancing Professional Practice: A Framework for Teaching* (Alexandria, VA: Association for Supervision and Curriculum Development, 1996).

- Emphasis on rising test scores, reducing dropout rates (that is, the rate of students who do not complete high school or receive the equivalent degree), increasing instructional time, and changing curricula.
- Federally enacted Goals 2000: Educate America Act and the development of national education standards for all major subject areas (see Chapter 5).
- Formation of school-home-community connections.
- New "basics" required for a high school diploma.
- School restructuring to provide more meaningful curriculum options.

Key Trends and Practices Today

Key trends and practices today are listed in Figure 1.7.

Problems and Issues That Plague the Nation's Schools

Major problems and issues plague our nation's schools, some of which are shown in Figure 1.8. Some of these are discussed in subsequent chapters (see index for topic locations). Perhaps you and members of your class can identify other issues and problems facing our nation's schools.[40]

---

[40]See D. R. Walling (Ed.), *Hot Buttons: Unraveling 10 Controversial Issues in Education* (Bloomington, IN: Phi Delta Kappa International, 1997).

SUMMARY

In beginning to plan for developing your teaching competencies, you have read an overview of today's schools and of the characteristics of some of the adults who work there, of trends and practices, and of problems and issues that continue to plague our nation's schools. That knowledge will be useful in your assimilation of the content explored in chapters that follow, beginning in the next chapter with the characteristics of young people, the ways they learn, and strategies to use to work effectively with them.

Despite the many blue ribbon commissions, writers, and politicians that have criticized and continue to vilify the failures of public school education, thousands of committed teachers, administrators, parents, and members of the community struggle daily, year after year, to provide students with a quality education. Throughout the remaining chapters of this text many exemplary schools and school programs are recognized and identified by name.

QUESTIONS FOR CLASS DISCUSSION

1. How would you be able to tell if you were at an exemplary school? Describe at least three characteristics of an exemplary elementary school, middle school, or high school. Is it possible for a traditional school to also be an exemplary school? Explain why or why not.

Figure 1.7 Key trends and practices in today's schools.

- Dividing the student body and faculty into smaller groups, called the house concept, and using nontraditional scheduling and interdisciplinary teaching teams
- Eliminating curriculum tracking and instead providing meaningful curriculum options with multiple pathways for academic success
- Facilitating students' social skills as they interact, relate to one another, solve meaningful problems, and develop relationships and peaceful friendships
- Facilitating the developing of students' values as related to their families, the community, and schools
- Holding high expectations, although not necessarily the same expectations, for all students by establishing goals and assessing results against those goals
- Integrating the curriculum, especially with the language arts, and introducing reading, thinking, and writing across the curriculum
- Involving communities in the schools by developing community learning centers, involving parents and guardians in school decision making
- Involving students in self-assessment
- Making multicultural education work for all students
- Providing students with the time and opportunity to think and be creative, rather than simply memorizing and repeating information
- Redefining giftedness to include nonacademic and traditional academic abilities
- Using heterogeneous grouping and cooperative learning, peer coaching, and cross-age tutoring as instructional strategies
- Using the Internet in the classroom as a communication tool and learning resource
- Using occupations to contextualize learning and instruction to vitalize a school-to-work transition

A critical problem in schools today is the scarcity of minority teachers to serve as effective role models for an increasing percentage of minority students.

Figure 1.8   Problems and issues that plague the nation's schools.

- A demand for test scores and statistics that can be used to judge schools and their principals
- Continuing controversy over books and their content
- Continuing, long-running controversy over values, morality, and sexuality education
- Controversy created by the concept of teaching less content but teaching it better
- Controversy over the development of a national curriculum with national assessments
- Continued controversy over traditional ability grouping or tracking
- Environmental air quality of schools
- Identification and development of programs that recognize, develop, and nurture talents in all our young people at all levels of education[41]
- Retention in grade versus social promotion[42]
- Scarcity of teachers of color to serve as role models for minority students[43]
- School security and the related problem of weapons, crime, violence, and drugs on school campuses and in school neighborhoods[44]
- Sexual harassment of students, mostly from other students but sometimes from school employees
- Shortage of qualified teachers[45]
- Teaching and assessing for higher-order thinking skills
- The education of teachers to work effectively with students who may be too overwhelmed by personal problems to focus on learning and to succeed in school
- The number of students at risk of dropping out of school, especially Hispanics among whom the dropout rate remains unchanged for more than twenty years, at around 30 percent.[46]

---

[41]See, for example, J. Fulkerson and M. Horvich, "Talent Development: Two Perspectives," and J. VanTassel-Baska, "The Development of Academic Talent," both in *Phi Delta Kappan* 79(10):756–759 and 760–763 (respectively) (June 1998).

[42]See, for example, K. Kelly, "Retention vs. Social Promotion: Schools Search for Alternatives," *The Harvard Education Letter* 15(1):1–3 (January/February 1999).

[43]M. S. Lewis, *Supply and Demand of Teachers of Color* (Washington, DC: ED390875, ERIC Clearinghouse on Teaching and Teacher Education, 1996). See also "The Need for Minority Teachers" in P. R. Rettig and M. Khodavandi, *Recruiting Minority Teachers: The UTOP Program,* Fastback 436 (Bloomington, IN: Phi Delta Kappa Educational Foundation, 1998), pp. 13–21.

[44]Intended to alert parents to the warning signs exhibited by troubled children is *Early Warning–Time Response: A Guide to Safe Schools.* Written by the National Association of School Psychologists and released in August 1998, the guide is available free by calling 877-4ED-PUBS or from the Internet at <http://www.ed.gov/offices/OSERS/OSEP/earlywrn.html>.

[45]See, for example, R. M. Ingersoll, "The Problem of Out-of-Field Teaching," *Phi Delta Kappan* 79(10):773–776 (June 1998).

[46]National Center for Education Statistics, *Mini-Digest of Education Statistics 1996* (Washington, DC: Office of Educational Research and Improvement, U.S. Department of Education, 1997), p. 37.

2. In some schools, ungraded, mixed-age classrooms are used as an alternative to retaining students in grade. Research the literature about the pros and cons of this approach, and report your finding to your class.

3. Identify at least six differences between the exemplary middle school and the traditional junior high school.

4. From your point of view, what societal influences affect today's youth? Are crime, gangs, drugs, and images of professional athletes and musicians among those influences? Explain the effects.

5. When students are dismissed from school in mid-afternoon, where do they go? Do they go home? For most children, is a parent or other adult guardian present when they arrive home from school? Is there a national problem here that needs to be, or is being, addressed?

6. It is estimated that approximately a half-million children are being kept out of the public schools and taught at home, perhaps double the number that were home-schooled just a decade ago. Why do you suppose so many parents are choosing to keep their children out of school? Should there be concerns about the quality of education and socialization for children when schooled at home? Some school districts are reaching out to home-schooling parents and offering services such as textbooks, library privileges, and testing. What do you think about the trend toward home schooling and its effects on children? Describe how schools in your geographic area are cooperating with home schooling.

7. Confronted by serious problems in some of the nation's public schools and reflected in a growth in the number of children being taught at home or in private schools, some people advocate shifting financial support and authority for schools from the public to the private sector, which would mark a radical change in American education. Organize a class debate on this question: Is there still a need in this country for public schools?

8. Express your opinion on the following statement: It is not important that a child might complete his or her elementary school education without ever having had a male or an ethnic minority teacher.

9. From your current observations and field work as related to this teacher preparation program, clearly identify one specific example of educational practice that seems contradictory to exemplary practice or theory as presented in this chapter. Present your explanation for the discrepancy.

10. Do you have other questions generated by the content of this chapter? If you do, list them along with ways answers might be found.

FOR FURTHER READING

Battista, M. T. "The Mathematical Miseducation of America's Youth: Ignoring Research and Scientific Study in Education." *Phi Delta Kappa* 80(6):425–433 (February 1999).

Black, S. "Learning on the Block." *American School Board Journal* 185(1):32–34 (January 1998).

Carnegie Council on Adolescent Development. *Great Transitions: Preparing Adolescents for a New Century.* Washington, DC: Author, 1995.

Gallagher, J. "Teaching in the Block." *Middle Ground* 2(3):10–15 (February 1999).

Kohn, L. "Quest High School's Mission and the 'Fully Functioning Person.'" In Freiberg, H. J. (Ed.). *Perceiving, Behaving, Becoming: Lessons Learned.* Alexandria, VA: Association for Supervision and Curriculum Development, 1999.

Kommer, D. "Is it Time to Revisit Multiage Teams in the Middle Grades?" *Middle School Journal* 30(3):28–32 (January 1999).

Lucas, S. R. *Tracking Inequality: Stratification and Mobility in American High Schools.* New York: Teachers College Press, 1999.

Maeroff, G. I. (Ed.). *Imaging Education: The Media and Schools in America.* New York: Teachers College Press, 1998.

Nolan, F. "Ability Grouping Plus Heterogeneous Grouping: Win-Win Schedules." *Middle School Journal* 29(5):14–19 (May 1998).

Oakes, J., and Wells, A. S. "Detracking for High Student Achievement." *Educational Leadership* 55(6):38–41 (March 1998).

Olson, L. "The New Basics in School-to-Work." *Educational Leadership* 55(6):50–53 (March 1998).

Sarason, S. B. *Charter Schools: Another Flawed Educational Reform?* New York: Teachers College Press, 1998.

Seed, A. "Free at Last: Making the Most of the Flexible Block Schedule." *Middle School Journal* 29(5):20–21 (May 1998).

Siegel, J. "Harlem Knights." *Teacher Magazine* X(2):30–34 (October 1998).

Smith, D. G., et al. "Flexing the Middle School Block Schedule by Adding Non-Traditional Core Subjects and Teachers to the Interdisciplinary Team." *Middle School Journal* 29(5):22–27 (May 1998).

Treffinger, D. J. "From Gifted Education to Programming for Talent Development." *Phi Delta Kappan* 79(10):752–755 (June 1998).

Wahlstrom, K. L. "The Prickly Politics of School Starting Times." *Phi Delta Kappan* 80(5): 345–347 (January 1999).

Walling, D. R. (Ed.). *Hot Buttons: Unraveling 10 Controversial Issues in Education.* Bloomington, IN: Phi Delta Kappa International, 1997.

Wang, M. C., et al. *Building Educational Resilience.* Fastback 430. Bloomington, IN: Phi Delta Kappa Educational Foundation, 1998.

Chapter 2

Celebrating and Building upon the Diverse Characteristics and Needs of Youth: The Nature of the Challenge

The bell rings, and the students enter your classroom, a kaleidoscope of personalities, all peerless and idiosyncratic, each a packet of energy, with different focuses, experiences, dispositions, learning capacities, and proficiencies in use of the English language. What a challenge it is to understand and teach thirty or so unique individuals all at once for six hours a day, five days a week, 180 days a year! What a challenge it is today to be a public school classroom teacher. To prepare yourself for this challenge, consider the following information about the diverse characteristics and needs of youth, for it is well known that the academic achievement of young people depends greatly upon how well their other developmental needs are understood and satisfied.

Specifically, upon completion of this chapter you will be able to

1. Demonstrate an understanding of the developmental characteristics of youth and their implications for appropriate practice.
2. Demonstrate an understanding of the significance of the concepts of learning modalities, learning styles, and learning capacities and of their implications for appropriate practice.
3. Demonstrate an understanding of the three-phase learning cycle and types of learning activities that might occur in each phase.
4. Demonstrate an awareness of appropriate curriculum options and instructional practices for specific groups of learners.
5. Demonstrate your developing knowledge of practical ways of attending to students' individual differences while working with a cohort of students.

DIMENSIONS OF THE CHALLENGE

At any age young people differ in many ways: physical characteristics, interests, home life, intellectual ability, learning capacities, motor ability, social skills, aptitudes and talents, language skills, experience, ideals, attitudes, needs, ambitions, hopes, and dreams. Having long recognized the importance of these individual differences, educators have made many attempts to develop systematic programs of individualized and personalized instruction. In the 1920s there were the "programmed" workbooks of the Winetka Plan. The 1960s brought a multitude of plans, such as IPI (Individually Prescribed Instruction), IGE (Individually Guided Education), and PLAN (Program for Learning in Accordance with Needs). The 1970s saw the development and growth in popularity of individual learning packages and the Individualized Education Program (IEP) for students with special needs. Although some of these efforts did not survive the test of time, others met with more success; some have been refined and are still being used. Today, for example, some schools report success using IEPs for all students, not only those with special needs.

Furthermore, for a variety of reasons (e.g., learning styles and learning capacities, modality preferences, information-processing habits, motivational factors, and physiological factors) all persons learn in their own ways and at their own rates. Interests, backgrounds, innate and acquired abilities, and a myriad of other influences shape how and what a person will learn. From any particular learning experience no two persons ever learn exactly the same thing.

At any age young people differ in many ways: physical characteristics, interests, home life, intellectual ability, learning capacities, motor ability, social skills, aptitudes and talents, language skills, experience, ideals, attitudes, needs, ambitions, hopes, and dreams.

The Classroom in a Nation of Increasing Diversity

Central to the challenge is the concept of multicultural education, the recognition and acceptance of students from a variety of backgrounds. The goal of this concept is to provide schooling so that all young people—male and female students, exceptional students, and students who are members of diverse racial, ethnic, and cultural groups—have equal opportunity to achieve academically.[1]

The variety of individual differences among students requires that teachers use teaching strategies and tactics that accommodate those differences. To most effectively teach students who are different from you, you need skills in (1) establishing a classroom climate in which all students feel welcome and where they can learn and are supported in doing so (the topic of Chapter 4), (2) techniques that emphasize cooperative and social-interactive learning and de-emphasize competitive learning (topics of Chapters 8 and 9), (3) building upon students' learning styles, capacities, and modalities, and (4) strategies and techniques that have proven successful for students of specific differences. The final two skills are the topic of this chapter.

To help you meet the challenge, a wealth of information is available. As a licensed teacher you are expected to know it all, or at least to know where you can find all necessary information and to review it when needed. Certain information you have stored in memory will surface and become useful at the most unex-

pected times. While concerned about all students' safety and physical well-being, you will want to remain sensitive to each student's attitudes, values, social adjustment, emotional well-being, and cognitive development. You must be prepared not only to teach one or more subjects but also to do it effectively with students of different cultural backgrounds, diverse linguistic abilities, and different learning styles and with young people who have been identified as having special needs. It is indeed a challenge! The statistics that follow make even more clear the scope of this challenge.

The traditional two-parent, two-child family now constitutes only about 6 percent of U.S. households. Approximately one-half of American children will spend some years being raised by a single parent. Between one-third and one-fourth of U.S. children go home after school to places devoid of adult supervision. On any given day, it is estimated that as many as 300,000 children have no place at all to call home.

By the year 2050, the nation's population is predicted to reach 383 million (from 1998's approximately 252 million), a population boom that will be led by Hispanics and Asian Americans. Although by then minority youths in the school-age population throughout the United States will average close to 40 percent, a steady increase in interracial marriages and interracial babies may challenge today's conceptions of multiculturalism and race.[2]

The United States truly is a multilingual, multiethnic, multicultural country. Of students of ages 5 to 7, approximately one out of every six speak a language

---

[1]J. A. Banks and C. A. McGee Banks, eds., *Multicultural Education: Issues and Perspectives* (Boston: Allyn & Bacon, 1989), 1.

[2]L. Baines, "Future Schlock," *Phi Delta Kappan* 78(7):497 (March 1997).

other than English at home. Many of those students have only limited proficiency in the English language (i.e., conversational speaking ability only). In many large school districts, as many as one hundred languages are represented, with as many as twenty or more different primary languages found in some classrooms. An increasing ethnic, cultural, and linguistic diversity is affecting schools all across the country, not only the large urban areas but also traditionally homogeneous suburbs and small rural communities.

The overall picture that emerges is a rapidly changing, diverse student population that challenges teaching skills. Teachers who traditionally have used direct instruction (see Chapter 6) as the dominant mode of instruction have done so with the assumption that their students were relatively homogeneous in terms of experience, background, knowledge, motivation, and facility with the English language. However, no such assumption can be made today in classrooms of such cultural, ethnic, and linguistic diversity. As a classroom teacher for the twenty-first century, you must be knowledgeable and skilled in using teaching strategies that recognize, celebrate, and build upon that diversity. In a nutshell, that is your challenge.

STYLES OF LEARNING AND IMPLICATIONS FOR TEACHING

Classroom teachers who are most effective are those who adapt their teaching styles and methods to their students, using approaches that interest the students, that are neither too easy nor too difficult, that match the students' learning styles and learning capacities, and that are relevant to students' lives. This adaptation process is further complicated because each student is different from every other one. All have varying interests, abilities, backgrounds, and learning styles and capacities. As a matter of fact, not only do young people differ from one another, but each student can change to some extent from one day to the next. What appeals to a student today may not have the same appeal tomorrow. Therefore, you need to consider both the nature of students in general (for example, methods appropriate for a particular third grade class are unlikely to be the same as those that work best for a group of ninth graders) and each child in particular. Since you probably have already experienced a recent course in the psychology of learning, what follows is only a brief synopsis of knowledge about learning.

Brain Laterality

How a person learns is, in part, related to differences in the left and right hemispheres of the brain. This theory is sometimes referred to as *brain laterality* or *brain hemisphericity*. Verbal learning, logical and convergent thinking, and the academic cognitive processes are dominated by the left cerebral hemisphere, while affective, intuitive, spatial, emotional, divergent thinking, and visual elements are dominated by the right cerebral hemisphere. Some learners are oriented toward right cerebral hemisphere learning and others toward the left. This means that some students learn better through verbal interactions while many others learn through visual, kinesthetic, and tactile involvement. However, in a healthy person the two hemispheres are inextricably interactive, regardless of whether a person is dealing with words, numbers, music, or art.[3]

When teachers integrate the disciplines, use a variety of teaching strategies to engage more of the sensory input channels, and help students connect what is being learned with real-life situations, the instruction is more likely to be teaching to both hemispheres.

Learning Modalities

Learning modality refers to *the sensory portal* (or input channel) by which a student prefers to receive sensory reception (modality preference), or the actual way a student learns best (modality adeptness). Some students prefer learning by seeing, a *visual modality;* others prefer learning through instruction from others (through talk), an *auditory modality;* while many others prefer learning by doing and being physically involved, the *kinesthetic modality,* and by touching objects, the *tactile modality.* A student's modality preference is not always that student's modality strength.

While primary modality strength can be determined by observing students, it can also be mixed and can change as the result of experience and intellectual maturity. As one might suspect, modality integration (i.e., engaging more of the sensory input channels, using several modalities at once or staggered) has been found to contribute to better achievement in student learning. We will return to this concept in Part II of this resource guide.

Because many young people neither have a preference nor a strength for auditory reception, K–12 teachers should severely limit their use of the lecture method of instruction; in other words, don't rely primarily on formal teacher talk. Furthermore, instruction that uses a singular approach, such as auditory (e.g., talking to the students), cheats students who learn better another way. This difference can affect student achievement. For example, a teacher who only talks to the students or uses

---

[3]See G. Salomon, "Of Mind and Media," *Phi Delta Kappan* 78(5):375–380 (January 1997), and J. Abbott, "To Be Intelligent," and C. R. Pool, "Maximizing Learning: A Conversation with Renate Nummela Caine," *Educational Leadership* 54(6):6–10 and 11–15 (respectively) (March 1997).

As a general rule, most K–12 students are not strong auditory learners. For most of them, sitting and listening is difficult. By preference and by adeptness, students learn best when mentally and physically engaged.

discussions day after day is shortchanging the education of students who are kinesthetic and visual learners.

Finally, if a teacher's verbal communication conflicts with his or her nonverbal messages, students can become confused, and this too can affect their learning. And when there is a discrepancy between what the teacher says and what that teacher does, the teacher's nonverbal signal will win every time. For instance, a teacher who has just finished a lesson on the conservation of energy and does not turn off the room lights upon leaving the classroom for lunch has, by modeling inappropriate behavior, created cognitive disequilibrium and sabotaged the real purpose for the lesson. Actions do speak louder than words![4]

As a general rule, most young people prefer and learn best by touching objects, by feeling shapes and textures, by interacting with each other, and by moving things around. In contrast, learning by sitting and listening is difficult for many of them. At one elementary school, after discovering that nearly two-thirds of their students were either tactile or kinesthetic learners, teachers and administrators grouped the students according to their modality strengths and altered reading instruction schedules every three weeks so that each group had opportunities to learn at the best time of day. As a result, student behavior, learning achievement, and attitudes improved considerably.[5]

Some learning style traits significantly discriminate between students who are at risk of not finishing school and students who perform well. Students who are underachieving and at risk need (a) frequent opportunities for mobility, (b) options and choices, (c) a variety of instructional resources, environments, and sociological groupings rather than routines and patterns, (d) opportunities to learn during late morning, afternoon, or evening hours rather than in the early morning, (e) informal seating rather than wooden, steel, or plastic chairs, (f) low illumination, because bright light contributes to hyperactivity, and (g) tactile/visual introductory resources reinforced by kinesthetic (i.e., direct experiencing and whole-body activities)/visual resources or introductory kinesthetic/visual resources reinforced by tactile/visual resources.[6]

Regardless of the grade level and subject(s) you intend to teach, an effective approach is to use strategies that integrate the modalities. When well designed, thematic units and project-based learning incorporate modality integration. In conclusion then, when teaching any group of students of mixed learning abilities, modality strengths, language proficiency, and cultural backgrounds, integrating learning modalities is a must for the most successful teaching.

Learning Styles

Related to learning modality is **learning style,** which can be defined as independent forms of knowing and processing information. While some students may be

---

[4]T. L. Good and J. E. Brophy, *Looking in Classrooms* (New York: Longman, 1997), p. 131.

[5]P. Stone, "How We Turned Around a Problem School," *Principal* 72(2):34–36 (November 1992). See also B. G. Barron et al., "Effects of Time of Day Instruction on Reading Achievement of Below Grade Readers," *Reading Improvement* 31(1): 59–60 (Spring 1994).

[6]R. Dunn, *Strategies for Educating Diverse Learners,* Fastback 384 (Bloomington, IN: Phi Delta Kappa Educational Foundation, 1995), p. 9.

comfortable with beginning their learning of a new idea in the abstract (visual or verbal symbolization), most need to begin with the concrete (learning by doing). Many students prosper while working in groups, while others prefer to work alone. Some are quick in their studies, whereas others are slow, methodical, cautious, and meticulous. Some can sustain attention on a single topic for a long time, becoming more absorbed in their study as time passes. Others are slower starters and more casual in their pursuits but are capable of shifting with ease from subject to subject. Some can study in the midst of music, noise, or movement, whereas others need quiet, solitude, and a desk or table. The point is this: students vary in not only their skills and preferences in the way knowledge is received, but also in how they mentally process that information once it has been received. This latter is a person's style of learning.

CLASSIFICATIONS OF LEARNING STYLES

It is important to note that learning style is not an indicator of intelligence, but rather an indicator of how a person learns. Although there are probably as many types of learning styles as there are individuals, David Kolb describes two major differences in how people learn: how they perceive situations and how they process information.[7] On the basis of perceiving and processing and earlier work by Carl Jung on psychological types,[8] Bernice McCarthy has described four major learning styles, presented in the following paragraphs.[9]

The *imaginative learner* perceives information concretely and processes it reflectively. Imaginative learners learn well by listening and sharing with others, integrating the ideas of others with their own experiences. Imaginative learners often have difficulty adjusting to traditional teaching, which depends less on classroom interactions and students' sharing and connecting of their prior experiences. In a traditional classroom, the imaginative learner is likely to be an at-risk student.

The *analytic learner* perceives information abstractly and processes it reflectively. The analytic learner prefers sequential thinking, needs details, and values what experts have to offer. Analytic learners do well in traditional classrooms.

The *common sense learner* perceives information abstractly and processes it actively. The common sense learner is pragmatic and enjoys hands-on learning. Common sense learners sometimes find school frustrating unless they can see immediate use to what is being learned. In the traditional classroom the common sense learner is likely to be a learner who is at risk of not completing school, of dropping out.

The *dynamic learner* perceives information concretely and processes it actively. The dynamic learner also prefers hands-on learning and is excited by anything new. Dynamic learners are risk takers and are frustrated by learning if they see it as being tedious and sequential. In a traditional classroom the dynamic learner also is likely to be an at-risk student.

The Three-Phase Learning Cycle

To understand conceptual development and change, researchers in the 1960s developed a Piaget-based theory of learning where students are guided from concrete, hands-on learning experiences to the abstract formulations of concepts and their formal applications. This theory became known as the *three-phase learning cycle*.[10] Long a popular strategy for teaching science, the learning cycle can be useful in other disciplines as well.[11] The three phases are (1) the *exploratory hands-on phase,* where students can explore ideas and experience assimilation and disequilibrium that lead to their own questions and tentative answers, (2) the *invention* or *concept development phase,* where, under the guidance of the teacher, students invent concepts and principles that help them answer their questions and reorganize their ideas (that is, the students revise their thinking to allow the new information to fit), and (3) the *expansion* or *concept application phase,* another hands-on phase in which students try out their new ideas by applying them to situations that are relevant and meaningful to them. During application of a concept the learner may discover new information that causes a change in the learner's understanding of the concept being applied. Thus, as discussed further in Chapter 9, the process of learning is cyclical.[12]

Recent interpretations or modifications of the three-phase cycle include McCarthy's 4MAT.[13] With

---

[7]D. A. Kolb, *Experiential Learning: Experience as the Source of Learning and Development* (Upper Saddle River, NJ: Prentice Hall, 1984).

[8]C. G. Jung, *Psychological Types* (New York: Harcourt Brace, 1923).

[9]See B. McCarthy, "A Tale of Four Learners: 4MAT's Learning Styles," *Educational Leadership* 54(6):47–51 (March 1997).

[10]See R. Karplus, *Science Curriculum Improvement Study,* Teacher's Handbook (Berkeley: University of California, 1974).

[11]See, for example: A. Colburn and M. P. Clough, "Implementing the Learning Cycle," *Science Teacher* 64(5):30–33 (May 1997); E. A. Kral, "Scientific Reasoning and Achievement in a High School English Course," *Skeptical Inquirer* 21(3):34–39 (May/June 1997); A. C. Rule, *Using the Learning Cycle to Teach Acronyms, a Language Arts Lesson* (ED383000, 1995); and, J. E. Sowell, "Approach to Art History in the Classroom," *Art Education* 46(2):19–24 (March 1993).

[12]The three phases of the learning cycle are comparable to the three levels of thinking, described variously by others. For example, in Elliot Eisner's *The Educational Imagination* (Macmillan, 1979), the levels are referred to as "descriptive," "interpretive," and "evaluative."

[13]For information about 4MAT, contact Excel, Inc., 23385 W. Old Barrington Road, Barrington, IL 60010, 847-382-7272, or at 6322 Fenworth Ct., Agoura Hills, CA 91301, 818-879-7442, or via the Internet at <http://www.excelcorp.com/4mataboutlong.html>.

the 4MAT system developed by McCarthy, teachers employ a learning cycle of instructional strategies to try to reach each student's learning style. As McCarthy describes the cycle, learners

> sense and feel, they experience, then they watch, they reflect, then they think, they develop theories, then they try out theories, they experiment. Finally, they evaluate and synthesize what they have learned in order to apply it to their next similar experience. They get smarter. They apply experience to experiences.[14]

In this process they are likely to be using all four learning modalities.

The *constructivist learning theory* suggests learning is a process involving the active engagement of learners who adapt the educative event to fit and expand their individual world view (as opposed to the behaviorist pedagogical assumption that learning is something done to learners)[15] and to accentuate the importance of student self-assessment. In support of that theory, some variations of the learning cycle include a fourth phase of assessment. However, because I believe that assessment of what students know or think they know should be a continual process, permeating all three phases of the learning cycle, I reject any treatment of assessment as a self-standing phase.

Learning Capacities: The Theory of Multiple Intelligences

In contrast to learning styles, Gardner introduced what he calls *learning capacities* exhibited by individuals in differing ways.[16] Originally and sometimes still referred to as *multiple intelligences* or *ways of knowing*, capacities thus far identified are:

- *Bodily/kinesthetic:* ability to use the body skillfully and to handle objects skillfully
- *Interpersonal:* ability to understand people and relationships
- *Intrapersonal:* ability to assess one's emotional life as a means to understand oneself and others
- *Logical/mathematical:* ability to handle chains of reasoning and to recognize patterns and orders
- *Musical:* sensitivity to pitch, melody, rhythm, and tone
- *Naturalist:* ability to draw on materials and features of the natural environment to solve problems or fashion products

- *Verbal/linguistic:* sensitivity to the meaning and order of words
- *Visual/spatial:* ability to perceive the world accurately and to manipulate the nature of space, such as through architecture, mime, or sculpture

As discussed earlier, and as implied in the presentation of McCarthy's four types of learners, many educators believe that many students who are at risk of not completing school are those who may be dominant in a cognitive learning style that is not in synch with traditional teaching methods. Traditional methods are largely of McCarthy's analytic style: information is presented in a logical, linear, sequential fashion. Traditional methods also reflect three of the Gardner types: verbal/linguistic, logical/mathematical, and intrapersonal. Consequently, to better synchronize methods of instruction with learning styles, some teachers and schools have restructured the curriculum and instruction around Gardner's learning capacities[17] or around Sternberg's Triarchic Theory.[18]

Sternberg identifies seven metaphors for the mind and intelligence (geographic, computational, biological, epistemological, anthropological, sociological, and systems) and proposes a theory of intelligence consisting of three elements: analytical, practical, and creative.[19]

See the sample classroom scenario shown in Figure 2.1. Internet resources on learning styles and multiple intelligences are shown in Figure 2.2.

From the preceding information about learning styles you must realize at least two facts:

1. *Intelligence is not a fixed or static reality, but can be learned, taught, and developed.* This concept is important for students to understand too. When students understand that intelligence is incremental, something that is developed through use over time, they tend to be more motivated to work at learning than when they believe intelligence is a fixed entity.[20]

2. *Not all students learn and respond to learning situations in the same way.* A student may learn differently according to the situation or according to the student's ethnicity, cultural background, or socioeconomic status.[21] A teacher who, for all students, uses only one style

---

[14]B. McCarthy, "Using the 4MAT System to Bring Learning Styles to Schools," *Educational Leadership* 48(2):33 (October 1990).

[15]R. DeLay, "Forming Knowledge: Constructivist Learning and Experiential Education," *Journal of Experiential Education* 19(2):76–81 (August/September 1996).

[16]For Gardner's distinction between "learning style" and "intelligences," see: H. Gardner, "Multiple Intelligences: Myths and Messages," *International Schools Journal* 15(2):8–22 (April 1996) and the many articles in the "Teaching for Multiple Intelligences" theme issue of *Educational Leadership* Volume 55, number 1 (September 1997).

[17]For example, see G. Gallagher, "Multiple Intelligences," *Middle Ground* 1(2):10–12 (October 1997).

[18]See, for example, L. English, "Uncovering Students' Analytic, Practical, and Creative Intelligences: One School's Application of Sternberg's Triarchic Theory," *School Administrator* 55(1):28–29 (January 1998).

[19]See R. J. Sternberg, "Teaching and Assessing for Successful Intelligence," *School Administrator* 55(1):26–27, 30–31 (January 1998).

[20]L. B. Resnick and L. E. Klopfer, *Toward the Thinking Curriculum: Current Cognitive Research* (Alexandria, VA: 1989 ASCD Yearbook, Association for Supervision and Curriculum Development, 1989), p. 8.

[21]See P. Guild, "The Culture/Learning Style Connection," *Educational Leadership* 51(8):16–21 (May 1994).

In one fourth grade classroom, during one week of a six-week thematic unit on weather, students were concentrating on learning about the water cycle. For this study of the water cycle, with the students' help the teacher divided the class into several groups of three to five students per group. While working on six projects simultaneously to learn about the water cycle:

- One group of students designed, conducted, and repeated an experiment to discover the number of drops of water that can be held on one side of a new one-cent coin versus the number that can be held on the side of a worn penny
- Working in part with the first group, a second group designed and prepared graphs to illustrate the results of the experiments of the first group
- A third group of students created and composed the words and music of a song about the water cycle
- A fourth group incorporated their combined interests in mathematics and art to design, collect the necessary materials, and create a colorful and interactive bulletin board about the water cycle
- A fifth group read about the water cycle in materials they researched from the Internet and various libraries
- A sixth group created a puppet show about the water cycle.

  On Friday, after each group had finished, the groups shared their projects with the class.

Figure 2.1 Classroom Vignette: Using the theory of learning capacities (multiple intelligences) and multilevel instruction.

Figure 2.2 Internet resources on learning styles and multiple intelligences.

- ERIC link to multiple intelligences resources at <http://www.indiana.edu/~eric_rec/ieo/bibs/multiple.html>
- Howard Gardner's Project Zero web site at <http://pzweb.harvard.edu/HPZpages/Whatsnew.html>
- Resources on learning styles at <http://www.d.umn.edu/student/loon/acad/strat/lrnsty.html>

of teaching, or who teaches to only one or a few styles of learning, day after day is short-changing those students who learn better another way. As emphasized by Rita Dunn, when students do not learn the way we teach them, then we must teach them the way they learn.[22]

MEETING THE CHALLENGE: RECOGNIZING AND PROVIDING FOR STUDENT DIFFERENCES

From research and practical experience have come a variety of instructional techniques that make a difference. First consider the following general guidelines, most of which are discussed in further detail in later chapters as designated.

Instructional Practices That Provide for Student Differences: General Guidelines

To provide learning experiences that are consistent with what is known about ways of learning and knowing, consider the recommendations that follow and refer to them during the preactive phase of your instruction (discussed in Chapter 3).

- As frequently as is appropriate, and especially for skills development, plan the learning activities so they follow a step-by-step sequence from concrete to abstract (see "The Learning Experiences Ladder" in Chapter 6).
- Collaboratively plan with students challenging and engaging classroom learning activities and assignments (see Chapters 5 and 6 and others).
- Concentrate on using student-centered instruction by using project-centered learning, discovery, and inquiry strategies, simulations, and role-play (Chapters 8 and 9).
- Establish multiple learning centers within the classroom (Chapter 8).
- Maintain high expectations, although not necessarily identical, for every student; establish high standards and teach toward them without wavering (throughout).
- Make learning meaningful by integrating learning with life, academic with vocational, and helping each student successfully make the transitions from one level of learning to the next, one level of schooling to the next, and from school to life (throughout).
- Provide a structured learning environment with regular and understood procedures (Chapter 4).

---

[22]Dunn, *Strategies for Educating Diverse Learners,* p. 30.

- Provide ongoing and frequent monitoring of individual student learning (formative assessment) (Chapters 3, 4, 11, and others).
- Provide variations in meaningful assignments, with optional due dates and based on individual student abilities and interests (Chapters 5 and 8).
- Use direct instruction to teach to the development of observation, generalization, and other thinking and learning skills (Chapter 9).
- Use reciprocal peer coaching and cross-age tutoring (Chapter 8).
- Use multilevel instruction (See Figure 2.1 and Chapter 3).
- Use interactive computer programs and multimedia (Chapter 10).
- Use small-group and cooperative learning strategies (Chapter 8).

Because social awareness is such an important and integral part of a student's experience, exemplary school programs and much of their practices are geared toward some type of social interaction. Indeed, learning is a social enterprise among learners and their teachers. Although many of today's successful instructional practices rely heavily on social learning activities and interpersonal relationships, each teacher must be aware of and sensitive to individual student differences. For working with specific learners, consider the guidelines that follow and refer back to these guidelines often during your preactive phase of instruction.

Recognizing and Working with Students with Disabilities

Students with disabilities (also referred to as *exceptional students* and *special-needs students*) include those with disabling conditions or impairments in any one or more of the following categories: mental retardation, hearing, speech or language, visual, emotional, orthopedic, autism, traumatic brain injury, other health impairment, or specific learning disabilities. To the extent possible, students with special needs must be educated with their peers in the regular classroom. Public Law 94-142, the Education for All Handicapped Children Act (EAHCA) of 1975, mandates that all children have the right to a free and appropriate education and to nondiscriminatory assessment. (Public Law 94-142 was amended in 1986 by P.L. 99-457 and in 1990 by P.L. 101-476 at which time its name was changed to Individuals with Disabilities Education Act–IDEA; it was also amended in 1997 by P.L. 105-17.) Emphasizing normalizing the educational environment for students with disabilities, this legislation requires provision of the least-restrictive environment (LRE) for these students. A LRE is an environment that is as normal as possible.

Students identified as having special needs may be placed in the regular classroom for the entire school day, called *full inclusion* (as is the trend[23]). Those students may also be in a regular classroom the greater part of the school day, called *partial inclusion,* or only for designated periods. Although there is no single, universally accepted definition of the term, *inclusion* is the concept that students with disabilities should be integrated into general education classrooms regardless of whether they can meet traditional academic standards.[24] (The term *inclusion* has largely replaced use of an earlier and similar term, mainstreaming.) As a classroom teacher you will need information and skills specific to teaching learners with special needs who are included in your classes.

Generally speaking, teaching students who have special needs requires more care, better diagnosis, greater skill, more attention to individual needs, and an even greater understanding of the students. The challenges of teaching students with special needs in the regular classroom are great enough that to do it well you need specialized training beyond the general guidelines presented here. At some point in your teacher preparation you should take one or more courses on working with special-needs learners in the regular classroom.

When a student with special needs is placed in your classroom, your task is to deal directly with the differences between this student and other students in your classroom. To do this, you should develop an understanding of the general characteristics of different types of special-needs learners, identify the student's unique needs relative to your classroom, and design lessons that teach to different needs at the same time, called **multilevel teaching,** or **multitasking,** as exemplified in Figure 2.1. Remember that just because a student has been identified as having one or more special needs does not preclude that person from being gifted or talented.

Congress stipulated in P.L. 94-142 that an Individualized Educational Program (IEP) be devised annually for each special-needs child. According to that law, an IEP is developed for each student each year by a team that includes special education teachers, the child's parents or guardians, and the classroom teachers. The IEP contains a statement of the student's present educational levels, the educational goals for the year, specifications for the services to be provided and the extent

---

[23]See, for example, M. L. Yell, "The Legal Basis of Inclusion," *Educational Leadership* 56(2):70–73 (October 1998). For information about education law as related to special education students, see the web site at <http://www.access.digex.net/~edlawinc/>.

[24]E. Tiegerman-Farber and C. Radziewicz, *Collaborative Decision Making: The Pathway to Inclusion* (Upper Saddle River, NJ: Merrill/Prentice Hall, 1998), p. 12–13.

to which the student should be expected to take part in the regular education program, and the evaluative criteria for the services to be provided. Consultation by special and skilled support personnel is essential in all IEP models. A consultant works directly with teachers or with students and parents. As a classroom teacher, you may play an active role in preparing the specifications for the special-needs students assigned to your classroom, and assume a major responsibility for implementing the program.

GUIDELINES FOR WORKING
WITH SPECIAL-NEEDS STUDENTS
IN THE REGULAR CLASSROOM

Although the guidelines represented by the paragraphs that follow are important for teaching all students, they are especially crucial for working with special-needs students.

Familiarize yourself with exactly what the special needs of each learner are. Privately ask the special-needs student whether there is anything he or she would like you to know about that learner and that you specifically can do to facilitate his or her learning.

Adapt and modify materials and procedures to the special needs of each student. For example, a student who has extreme difficulty sitting still for more than a few minutes will need planned changes in learning activities. When establishing student seating arrangements in the classroom, give preference to students according to their special needs. Try to incorporate into lessons activities that engage all learning modalities: visual, auditory, tactile, and kinesthetic. Be flexible in your classroom procedures. For example, allow the use of tape recorders for note taking and test taking when students have trouble with the written language.

Provide high structure and clear expectations by defining the learning objectives in behavioral terms (discussed in Chapter 5). Teach students the correct procedures for everything (Chapter 4). Break complex learning into simpler components, moving from the most concrete to the abstract, rather than the other way around. Check frequently for student understanding of instructions and procedures and for comprehension of content. Use computers and other self-correcting materials for drill and practice and for provision of immediate and private feedback to the student.

Develop your "withitness" (discussed in Chapters 3 and 4), which is your awareness of everything that is going on in the classroom, at all times, monitoring students for signs of restlessness, frustration, anxiety, and off-task behaviors. Be ready to reassign individual learners to different activities as the situation warrants. Established classroom learning centers (discussed in Chapter 8) can be a big help.

Have all students maintain assignments for the week or some other period of time in an assignment book or in a folder that is kept in their notebooks. Post assignments in a special place in the classroom and frequently remind students of assignments and deadlines.

Maintain consistency in your expectations and in your responses. Special-needs learners, particularly, can become frustrated when they do not understand a teacher's expectations and when they cannot depend on a teacher's reactions.

Plan interesting activities to bridge learning, activities that help the students connect what is being learned with their real world. Learning that connects what is being learned with the real world helps to motivate students and keep them on task.

Plan questions and questioning sequences and write them into your lesson plans (discussed in Chapters 6 and 7). Plan questions that you ask special-needs learners so that they are likely to answer them with confidence. Use signals to let students know you are likely to call on them in class (e.g., prolonged eye contact or mentioning your intention to the student before class begins). After asking a question, give the student adequate time to think and respond. Then, after the student responds, build upon the response to indicate that the student's contribution was accepted as being important.

Provide for and teach toward student success. Offer students activities and experiences that ensure each individual student's success and mastery at some level. Use of student portfolios (discussed in Chapters 5 and 11) can give evidence of progress and help in building student confidence and self-esteem.

Provide guided or coached practice. Provide time in class for students to work on assignments and projects. During this time, you can monitor the work of each student while looking for misconceptions, thus ensuring that students get started on the right track (discussed in Chapter 6).

Provide help in the organization of students' learning. For example, give instruction in the organization of notes and notebooks. Have a three-hole punch available in the classroom so students can put papers into their notebooks immediately, thus avoiding disorganization and their loss of papers. During class presentations use an overhead projector with transparencies; students who need more time can then copy material from the transparencies. Ask students to read their notes aloud to each other in small groups, thereby aiding their recall and understanding and encouraging them to take notes for meaning rather than for rote learning. Encourage and provide for peer support, peer tutoring or coaching, and cross-age teaching (Chapter 8). Ensure that the special-needs learner is included in all class activities to the fullest extent possible.[25]

---

[25]See L. Farlow, "A Quartet of Success Stories: How to Make Inclusion Work," *Educational Leadership* 53(5):51–55 (April 1996) and other articles in the theme issue on "Students With Special Needs."

Recognizing and Working with Students of Diversity and Differences

Quickly determine the language and nationality groups represented by the students in your classroom. A major problem for recent immigrant children and for some ethnic groups is learning a second (or third or fourth) language. While in many schools it is not uncommon for more than half the students to come from homes where the native language is not English, standard English is a necessity in most communities of this country if a person is to become vocationally successful and enjoy a full life. Learning to communicate reasonably well in English can take an immigrant student at least a year and probably longer; some authorities say three to seven years. By default, then, an increasing number of teachers are teachers of English language learning. Helpful to the success of teaching students who have limited proficiency in English (LEP) are the demonstration of respect for students' cultural backgrounds, long-term teacher-student cohorts (such as, for example, in looping), and the use of active and cooperative learning.[26]

Numerous programs are specially designed for working with English as a second language (ESL) learners. Most use the acronym LEP with five number levels, from LEP 1 that designates non-English-speaking, although the student may understand single sentences and speak simple words or phrases in English, to LEP 5, sometimes designated FEP (fluent English proficient), for the student who is fully fluent in English, although the student's overall academic achievement may still be less than desired because of language or cultural differences.[27]

Some schools use a "pullout" approach, in which part of the student's school time is spent in special bilingual classes and the rest of the time the student is placed in regular classrooms. In some schools, LEP students are placed in academic classrooms that use a simplified or "sheltered" English approach. Regardless of the program, specific techniques recommended for teaching ESL students include:

- Allowing more time for learning activities than one normally would.
- Allowing time for translation by a classroom aide or by a classmate and allowing time for discussion to clarify meaning, encouraging the students to transfer into English what they already know in their native language.

- Avoiding jargon or idioms that might be misunderstood. See the scenario that follows.

A HUMOROUS SCENARIO RELATED TO IDIOMS

A teachable moment

While Lina, a third grade student, was reciting she had a little difficulty with her throat (due to a cold) and stumbled over some words. The student teacher jokingly commented, "That's okay Lina, you must have a horse in your throat." Quickly, Monique, an Hispanic student asked, "How could she have a horse in her throat?" The teacher ignored Monique's question. Missing this teachable moment, she continued with her planned lesson.

- Dividing complex or extended language discourse into smaller, more manageable units.
- Giving directions in a variety of ways.
- Giving special attention to key words that convey meaning and writing them on the board.
- Reading written directions aloud and then writing the directions on the board.
- Speaking clearly and naturally but at a slower than normal pace.
- Using a variety of examples and observable models.
- Using simplified vocabulary but without talking down to students.[28]

ADDITIONAL GUIDELINES FOR WORKING WITH LANGUAGE-MINORITY STUDENTS

While they are becoming literate in the English language, LEP students can learn the same curriculum in the various disciplines as native English-speaking students. Although the guidelines presented in the following paragraphs are important for teaching all students, they are especially important when working with language-minority students.

Present instruction that is concrete and includes the most direct learning experiences possible. Use the most concrete (least abstract) forms of instruction (Chapter 6).

Build upon (or connect with) what the students already have experienced and know. Building upon what students already know, or think they know, helps them to connect their knowledge and construct their understandings.

Encourage student writing. One way is by using student journals (see Chapters 8 and 11). Two kinds of journals are appropriate when working with LEP students: dialogue journals and response journals. Dialogue journals are used for students to write anything that is on their minds, usually on the right page. Teachers, parents,

---

[26]See P. Berman et al., *School Reform and Student Diversity, Volume II: Case Studies of Exemplary Practices for LEP Students* (Berkeley, CA: National Center for Research on Cultural Diversity and Second Language Learning, 1995).

[27]D. R. Walling, *English as a Second Language: 25 Questions and Answers,* Fastback 347 (Bloomington, IN: Phi Delta Kappa Educational Foundation, 1993), p. 12–13.

[28]Walling, *English as a Second Language: 25 Questions and Answers,* p. 26.

and classmates then respond on the left page, thereby "talking with" the journal writers. Response journals are used for students to write (record) their responses to what they are reading or studying.[29]

Help students learn the vocabulary. Assist the LEP students in learning two vocabulary sets: the regular English vocabulary needed for learning and the new vocabulary introduced by the subject content. For example, while learning science a student is dealing with both the regular English language vocabulary and the special vocabulary of science.

Involve parents or guardians or older siblings. Students whose primary language is not English may have other differences about which you will also need to become knowledgeable. These differences are related to culture, customs, family life, and expectations. To be most successful in working with language minority students, you should learn as much as possible about each student. To this end it can be valuable to solicit the help of the student's parent, guardian, or even an older sibling. Parents (or guardians) of new immigrant children are usually truly concerned about the education of their children and may be very interested in cooperating with you in any way possible. In a study of eight schools recognized for their exemplary practices with language-minority students, the schools were noted for being "parent friendly," that is, for welcoming parents in a variety of innovative ways.[30]

Plan for and use all learning modalities. As with teaching children in general, in working with language-minority students in particular you need to use multisensory approaches, learning activities that involve students in auditory, visual, tactile, and kinesthetic learning activities.

Use small group cooperative learning. Cooperative learning strategies are particularly effective with language-minority students because they provide opportunities for students to produce language in a setting that is less threatening than is speaking before the entire class.

Use the benefits afforded by modern technology. For example, computer networking allows the language-minority students to write and communicate with peers from around the world and to participate in "publishing" their classroom work (Chapters 5 and 10).

ADDITIONAL GUIDELINES FOR WORKING WITH STUDENTS OF DIVERSE BACKGROUNDS
To be compatible with, and be able to teach, students who come from backgrounds different from yours, you need to believe that, given adequate support, all students *can* learn, regardless of gender, social class, physical characteristics, language, and ethnic or cultural backgrounds. You also need to develop special skills that include those in the following guidelines, each of which is discussed in detail in other chapters. To work successfully and most effectively with students of diverse backgrounds, you should:

- Build the learning around students' individual learning styles. Personalize learning for each student, much like what is done by using the IEP with special-needs learners. Involve students in understanding and in making important decisions about their own learning, so that they feel ownership (i.e., a sense of empowerment and connectedness) of that learning.
- Communicate positively with every student and with the student's parents or guardians, learning as much as you can about the student and the student's culture, and encouraging family members to participate in the student's learning. Involve parents, guardians, and other members of the community in the educational program so that all have a sense of ownership and responsibility and feel positive about the school program.
- Establish and maintain high expectations, although not necessarily the same expectations, for each student. Both you and your students must understand that intelligence is not a fixed entity, but a set of characteristics that—through a feeling of "I can" and with proper coaching—can be developed.
- Teach to individuals by using a variety of strategies to achieve an objective or by using a number of different objectives at the same time (multilevel teaching).
- Use techniques that emphasize collaborative and cooperative learning and de-emphasize competitive learning.

Recognizing and Working with Students Who Are Gifted

Historically, educators have used the term *gifted* when referring to a child with identified exceptional ability in one or more academic subjects. The term *talented* typically referred to a child with exceptional ability in one or more of the visual or performing arts.[31] Today, however, the terms often are used interchangeably, which is how they are used for this resource guide.

Sometimes in the regular classroom gifted students are neglected.[32] At least part of the time, it is

[29]See K. M. Johns and C. Espinoza, *Mainstreaming Language Minority Children in Reading and Writing*, Fastback 340 (Bloomington, IN: Phi Delta Kappa Educational Foundation, 1992).

[30]C. Minicucci et al., "School Reform and Student Diversity," *Phi Delta Kappan* 77(1):77–80 (September 1995).

[31]See the discussion in G. Clark and E. Zimmerman, "Nurturing the Arts in Programs for Gifted and Talented Students," *Phi Delta Kappan* 79(10):747–751 (June 1998).

[32]See, for example, J. F. Feldhusen, "Programs for the Gifted Few or Talent Development for the Many?" *Phi Delta Kappan* 79(10):735–738 (June 1998).

likely to be because no single method is accepted to identify these students. For placement in special classes or programs for the gifted and talented, school districts traditionally have used grade point averages and standard intelligence quotient (IQ) scores. On the other hand, because IQ testing measures linguistic and logical/mathematical aspects of giftedness (refer to the discussion earlier in this chapter on learning capacities), it does not account for others and thus gifted students sometimes are unrecognized. They also are sometimes among the students most at risk of dropping out of school.[33] It is estimated that between 10 and 20 percent of school dropouts are students who are in the range of being intellectually gifted.[34]

To work most effectively with gifted learners, their talents first must be identified. This can be done by using tests, rating scales, and auditions and by observations in the classroom, on the playground, and from knowledge about the student's personal life. With those information sources in mind, here is a list of indicators of superior intelligence:[35]

- Ability to extrapolate knowledge to different circumstances
- Ability to manipulate a symbol system
- Ability to reason by analogy
- Ability to take on adult roles at home, such as managing the household and supervising siblings, even at the expense of school attendance and achievement
- Ability to think logically
- Ability to use stored knowledge to solve problems
- Creativity and artistic ability
- Leadership ability and an independent mind
- Resiliency, or the ability to cope with school while living in poverty with dysfunctional families
- Strong sense of self, pride, and worth
- Understanding of one's cultural heritage

To assist you in understanding gifted students who may or may not have yet been identified as being gifted, here are some types of students and the kinds of problems to which they may be prone, that is, personal behaviors that may identify them as being gifted but academically disabled, bored, and alienated.

- *Antisocial* students, alienated by their differences from peers, may become bored and impatient troublemakers.

- *Creative, high achieving* students often feel isolated, weird, and depressed.
- *Divergent thinking* students can develop self-esteem problems when they provide answers that are logical to them but seem unusual and off-the-wall to their peers. They may have only a few peer friends.
- *Perfectionists* may exhibit compulsive behaviors because they feel as though their value comes from their accomplishments. When their accomplishments do not live up to expectations—their own, their parents', or their teachers—anxiety and feelings of inadequacy arise. When other students do not live up to the gifted student's high standards, alienation from those students is probable.
- *Sensitive* students who also are gifted may become easily depressed because they are more aware of their surroundings and of their differences.
- *Students with special needs* may be gifted. Attention deficit disorder, dyslexia, hyperactivity, and other learning disorders sometimes mask giftedness.
- *Underachieving* students can also be gifted students but fail in their studies because they learn in ways that are seldom or never challenged by classroom teachers. Although often expected to excel in everything they do, most gifted students can be underachievers in some areas. Having high expectations of themselves, underachievers tend to be highly critical of themselves and may develop a low self-esteem. They can become indifferent and even hostile.[36]

Curriculum Tracking: Not a Viable Option

All students, not only those who have been identified as gifted, need a challenging academic environment. Although grouping and tracking students into classes based on interest and demonstrated ability is still widely practiced (such as reading groups, grade level retention, and special education placement in the early grades; college bound and non-college bound curriculum tracks in secondary school), an overwhelming abundance of sources in the literature adamantly opposes the homogeneous grouping of students according to ability, or *curriculum tracking,* as it has long been known. Grouping and tracking do not seem to increase overall achievement of learning, but they do promote inequity.[37]

Although many, perhaps most, research studies lead one to conclude that tracking as has been traditionally practiced should be discontinued because of

---

[33]C. Dixon, L. Mains, and M. J. Reeves, *Gifted and At Risk,* Fastback 398 (Bloomington, IN: Phi Delta Kappa Educational Foundation, 1996), p. 7.

[34]S. B. Rimm, "Underachievement Syndrome: A National Epidemic," in N. Colangelo and G. A. Davis (Eds.), *Handbook of Gifted Education,* 2d ed. (Needham Heights, MA: Allyn & Bacon, 1997), p. 416.

[35]S. Schwartz, *Strategies for Identifying the Talents of Diverse Students,* ERIC/CUE Digest, Number 122 (New York: ED410323, ERIC Clearinghouse on Urban Education, May 1997).

[36]Adapted from Dixon, Mains, and Reeves, *Gifted and At Risk,* p. 9–12. By permission of the Phi Delta Kappa Educational Foundation.

[37]See J. Oakes et al., "Equity Lessons from Detracking Schools," Chapter 3 (pp. 43–72) of A. Hargreaves (Ed.), *Rethinking Educational Change With Heart and Mind* (Alexandria, VA: ASCD 1997 Yearbook, Association for Supervision and Curriculum Development, 1997).

- Advisory programs and adult advocacy relationships for every student
- Allowing a student to attend a high school class while still in middle school or to attend college classes while still in high school
- Allowing a student to skip a traditional grade level, thereby accelerating the time a student passes through the grades
- Community service learning from intermediate grades through high school
- Cooperative learning in the classroom
- Curriculum compacting
- Extra effort to provide academic help
- High expectations for all students
- Individualized educational plans and instruction
- Integrating new technologies into the curriculum
- Interdisciplinary teaming and thematic instruction
- Mid-year promotions
- Nongraded or multiage grouping
- Peer and cross-age teaching
- Personal problems assistance provision on campus
- Problem-centered learning
- Second opportunity recovery strategies
- Specialized schools and flexible block schedules
- Within-class and across discipline student-centered projects

Figure 2.3   Multiple pathways to success: productive ways of attending to student differences, of providing a more challenging learning environment, and of stimulating the talents and motivation of each student.

its discriminatory and damaging effects on students, many schools continue to use it. Direct examples are counseling students into classes according to evidence of ability and the degree of academic rigor of the program. Tracking also results indirectly by designating certain classes and programs as "academic" or "accelerated" and others as "non-academic" or "standard" and allowing students some degree of latitude to choose, either partly or wholly, from one or the other.

Meaningful Curriculum Options: Multiple Pathways to Success

Because of what we now know about learning and intelligence, the trend today is to assume that each student, to some degree and in some area of learning and doing, has the potential for giftedness and to provide sufficient curriculum options, or multiple pathways, so each student can reach those potentials. Clearly, achievement in school increases and students learn more and enjoy learning and remember more of what they have learned when individual learning capacities, styles, and modalities are identified and accommodated.[38]

To provide relevant curriculum options, a trend is to eliminate from the school curriculum what have traditionally been the lower and general curriculum tracks and instead provide curriculum options to try to assure success for all students. Most experts agree that schools should be organized around nontracked, the-

matic programs of student design to prepare all students for entry ultimately into both higher education and high-skill employment through intellectually rigorous practical education.

While attempting to diminish the discriminatory and damaging effects on students believed to be caused by tracking and homogeneous ability grouping, educators have devised and are refining numerous other seemingly more productive ways of attending to student differences, of providing a more challenging but supportive learning environment, and of stimulating the talents and motivation of each student. Because the advantage gained from using a combination of responsive practices concurrently is generally greater than is the gain from using any singular practice, in many instances in a given school the practices overlap and are used simultaneously. These practices are shown in Figure 2.3, and most are discussed in various places of this resource guide. Check the index for topic locations.

ADDITIONAL GUIDELINES FOR WORKING WITH GIFTED STUDENTS
When working in the regular classroom with a student who has special gifts and talents, you are advised to:

- Emphasize skills in critical thinking, problem solving, and inquiry.
- Identify and showcase the student's special gift or talent.
- Involve the student in selecting and planning activities, encouraging the development of the student's leadership skills.

---

[38]Dixon, Mains, and Reeves, *Gifted and At Risk*, p. 21.

- Use curriculum compacting, a process that allows a student who already knows the material to pursue enriched or accelerated study.[39] Plan and provide optional and voluntary enrichment activities. Learning centers, special projects, and computer and multimedia activities are excellent tools for provision of enriched learning activities.

- Plan assignments and activities that challenge students to the fullest of their abilities. This does *not* mean overloading them with homework or giving identical assignments to all students (see "tiered assignments" in Chapter 7). Rather, carefully plan so that the students' time spent on assignments and activities is quality time on meaningful learning.

- Provide in-class seminars for students to discuss topics and problems that they are pursuing individually or as members of a learning team.

- Provide independent and dyad learning opportunities. Gifted and talented students often prefer to work alone or with another gifted student.

- Use preassessments (diagnostic evaluation) for reading level and subject content achievement so that you are better able to prescribe objectives and activities for each student.

- Work with individual students in some planning of their own objectives and activities for learning.

Recognizing and Working with Students Who Take More Time but Are Willing to Try

Students who are slower to learn typically fall into one of two categories: (1) those who try to learn but simply need more time to do it, and (2) those who do not try, referred to variously as underachievers or recalcitrant or reluctant learners. Practices that work well with students of one category are often not those that work well with those of the second, which makes life difficult for a teacher of thirty students, half who try and half who don't. It is worse still for a teacher of a group of thirty students, some who try but need time, one or two who are academically talented, a few LEP students, and several who not only seem unwilling to try but who are also disruptive in the classroom.

Remember that just because a student is slow to learn doesn't mean that the student is less intelligent; some students just take longer, for any number of reasons. The following guidelines may be helpful when working with a slow student who has indicated a willingness to try:

- Adjust the instruction to the student's preferred learning style, which may be different from yours and from other students in the group.

- Be less concerned with the amount of content coverage than with the student's successful understanding of content that is covered.

- Discover something the student does exceptionally well, or a special interest, and try to build on that.

- Emphasize basic communication skills, such as speaking, listening, reading, and writing, to ensure that the student's skills in these areas are sufficient for learning the intended content.

- Help the student learn content in small sequential steps with frequent checks for comprehension.

- If necessary, help the student to improve his or her reading skills, such as pronunciation and word meanings.

- If using a single textbook, be certain that the reading level is adequate for the student; if it is not, then for that student use other more appropriate reading materials.

- Maximize the use of in-class, on-task work and cooperative learning, with close monitoring of the student's progress. Avoid relying much on successful completion of traditional out-of-class assignments unless you can supply coached guidance to the student in the classroom.

- Vary the instructional strategies, using a variety of activities to engage the visual, verbal, tactile, and kinesthetic modalities.

- When appropriate, use frequent positive reinforcement, with the intention of increasing the student's self-esteem.

Recognizing and Working with Recalcitrant Learners

For working with recalcitrant learners you can use many of the same guidelines from the preceding list, except that you should understand that the reasons for these students' behaviors may be quite different from those for the other category of slow learners. Slower-learning students who are willing to try may be slow because of their learning style or because of genetic reasons, or a combination of the two. But they can and will learn. Recalcitrant learners, on the other hand, may be generally quick and bright thinkers but reluctant even to try because of a history of failure, a history of boredom with school, a poor self-concept, severe personal problems that distract from school, or any variety and combination of reasons, many of which are psychological in nature.

Whatever the case, you need to know that a student identified as being a slow or recalcitrant learner might, in fact, be quite gifted or talented in some way; however, because of personal problems, he or she may have a history of increasingly poor school attendance, poor attention to schoolwork, poor self-confidence, and an attitude problem. Consider the following guidelines when working with recalcitrant learners:

---

[39]See, for example, J. J. Gallagher, "Accountability for Gifted Students," *Phi Delta Kappan* 79(10):739–742 (June 1998).

- As the school year begins, learn as much about each student as you can. Be cautious in how you do it, though, because many of these students will be suspicious of any interest you show in them. Be businesslike, trusting, genuinely interested, and patient. A second caution: although you learn as much as possible about each student, what has happened in the past is history. Use that information not as ammunition, something to be held against the student, but as insight to help you work more productively with the student.
- Avoid lecturing to these students; it won't work.
- Early in the school term, preferably with the help of adult volunteers (e.g., professional community members as mentors have worked well at helping change students' attitudes from rebellion to hope, challenge, and success), work out an individual education program (IEP) with each student.
- Engage students in learning by using interactive media, such as the Internet.
- Engage students in active learning with real-world problem solving and perhaps community service projects.
- Forget about trying to "cover the subject," concentrating instead on students learning some things well. A good procedure is to use thematic teaching and divide the theme into short segments. Because school attendance for these students is sometimes sporadic, try to individualize their assignments so that they can pick up where they left off and move through the course in an orderly fashion even when they have been absent excessively. Try to assure some degree of success for each student.
- Help students develop their studying and learning skills, such as concentrating, remembering, and comprehending. Mnemonics, for example, is a device these students respond to positively; they are often quick to create their own mnemonic systems (see Chapter 8).
- If using a single textbook, see if the reading level is appropriate; if it is not, discard the book for that student and select other more appropriate reading materials.
- Make sure your classroom procedures and rules are understood at the beginning of the school term and be consistent about enforcing them.
- Maximize the use of in-class, on-task work and cooperative learning, with close monitoring of the student's progress. Do not rely on successful completion of traditional out-of-class assignments unless the student gets coached guidance from you before leaving your classroom.
- Use simple language in the classroom. Be concerned less about the words the students use and the way they use them and more about the ideas they are expressing. Let students use their own idioms without carping too much on grammar and syntax. Always take care, though, to use proper and professional English yourself.
- When appropriate, use frequent positive reinforcement, with the intention of increasing the student's sense of personal worth. When using praise for reinforcement, however, try to praise the deed rather than the student (see discussion of praise, encouragement, and reinforcement in Chapters 4 and 7).

Teaching toward Positive Character Development

In what appears to be a cycle, arising first in the 1930s, again in the late '60s, and now today, interest is high in the development of students' values, especially those of honesty, kindness, respect, and responsibility. Today this interest is in what some refer to as *character education*. Whether defined as ethics, citizenship, moral values, or personal development, character education has long been part of public education in this country.[40] Stimulated by a perceived need to act to reduce students' antisocial behaviors and to produce more respectful and responsible citizens, many schools and districts today are developing curricula in character education with the ultimate goal of "developing mature adults capable of responsible citizenship and moral action."[41]

You can teach toward positive character development in two general ways (both of which are discussed further in Chapters 3, 4, and 5): by providing a conducive classroom atmosphere where students actively and positively share in decision making and by being a model that students can proudly emulate. Acquiring knowledge and developing understanding can enhance the learning of attitudes. Nevertheless, changing an attitude is often a long and tedious process, requiring the commitment of the teacher and the school, assistance from the community, and the provision of numerous experiences that will guide students to new convictions. Here are some specific practices, most of which are, as indicated, discussed further in later chapters:

- Build a sense of community in the school and in the classroom, with shared goals, optimism, cooperative efforts, and clearly identified and practiced procedures for reaching those goals (see Chapter 4).
- Collaboratively plan with students action- and community-oriented projects that relate to curriculum themes; solicit parent and community members to assist in projects (see Chapters 1, 5, 8, and others).

---

[40]See K. Burrett and T. Rusnak, *Integrated Character Education*, Fastback 351 (Bloomington, IN: Phi Delta Kappa Educational Foundation, 1993).

[41]Burrett and Rusnak, *Integrated Character Education*, p. 15.

Figure 2.4 Selected resources on character education.

- Character Education Institute, 8918 Tesoro Drive, San Antonio, TX 78217 (800-284-0499).
- Developmental Studies Center, 111 Deerwood Place, San Ramon, CA 94583 (415-838-7633).
- Ethics Resource Center, 1120 G Street NW, Washington, DC 20005 (202-434-8465).
- Jefferson Center for Character Education, 202 S. Lake Avenue, Pasadena, CA 91101 (818-792-8130).
- Josephson Institute of Ethics, 310 Washington Boulevard, Marina Del Rey, CA 90292 (310-306-1868).

- Teach students to negotiate; practice and develop skills in conflict resolution, skills such as empathy, problem solving, impulse control, and anger management.[42]
- Have students research and present by advocating a particular stance on a controversial issue[43] (see Chapter 8).
- Share and highlight anchor examples of class and individual cooperation in serving the classroom, school, and community (throughout).
- Make student service projects visible in the school and community[44] (Chapter 5).
- Promote higher-order thinking about value issues through the development of skills in questioning (Chapters 7 and 9).

- Sensitize students to issues and teach skills of conflict resolution through role play, simulations, and creative drama (Chapter 9).

Resources on character education are shown in Figure 2.4. When compared with traditional instruction, one characteristic of exemplary instruction today is the teacher's encouragement of dialogue among students in the classroom to discuss and to explore their own ideas. Modeling the very behaviors we expect of teachers and students in the classroom is, as was emphasized in the preface, a constant theme throughout this resource guide. One purpose of Exercise 2.1 is, in a similar fashion, to start that dialogue. Complete that exercise now.

---

[42]See D. W. Johnson and R. T. Johnson, *Reducing School Violence Through Conflict Resolution* (Alexandria, VA: Association for Supervision and Curriculum Development, 1995).

[43]See Chapter 11 of Johnson and Johnson, *Reducing School Violence Through Conflict Resolution.*

[44]See J. Van Til, "Facing Inequality and the End of Work," *Educational Leadership* 54(6):78–81 (March 1997).

EXERCISE 2.1: REFLECTING UPON MY OWN SCHOOL EXPERIENCES

INSTRUCTIONS: The purpose of this exercise is to share with others in your class your reflections on your own elementary and secondary school experiences.

1. What school(s) did you attend, where, and when? Were they public or private?

_____

_____

_____

_____

2. What do you remember most from your elementary and secondary school experiences?

_____

_____

_____

_____

3. What do you remember most about your teachers? _____

_____

_____

_____

_____

4. What do you remember most about the other students? _____

_____

_____

_____

_____

5. What do you remember most about your overall school life? _____

_____

_____

_____

_____

6. What grade (or class) do you specifically recall with fondness? Why? _____

_____

_____

_____

_____

EXERCISE 2.1 (*continued*)

7. What grade (or class) would you particularly like to forget? Why? _____

_____

_____

_____

_____

8. What do you recall about peer and parental pressures? _____

_____

_____

_____

_____

9. What do you recall about your own feelings during those years? _____

_____

_____

_____

_____

10. Is there any other aspect of your life as an elementary or secondary school student you wish to share with

others? _____

_____

_____

_____

_____

SUMMARY

As a classroom teacher you must acknowledge that students in your classroom have different ways of receiving information, processing that information, and knowing and constructing their knowledge. These differences are unique and important; as you will learn in Part II of this resource guide, they are central considerations in curriculum development and instructional practice.

You must try to learn as much as you can about how each student learns and processes information. But because you can never know everything about each student, the more you dialogue with your colleagues, vary your teaching strategies, and assist students in integrating their learning, the more likely you are to reach more of the students more of the time. In short, to be an effective classroom teacher you should: (1) learn as much about your students and their preferred styles of learning as you can, (2) develop an eclectic style of teaching that is flexible and adaptable, and (3) integrate the disciplines, thereby helping students make bridges or connections between their lives and all that is being learned.

QUESTIONS FOR CLASS DISCUSSION

1. Explain why knowledge of learning styles, learning capacities, and teaching styles is or should be important to you.
2. Colleen, a social studies teacher, has a class of thirty-three eighth graders, who during her lecture, teacher-led discussion, and recitation lessons are restless and inattentive, creating for her a problem in classroom management. At Colleen's invitation, the school psychologist tests the students for learning modality and finds that of the thirty-three students, twenty-nine are predominately kinesthetic learners. Of what value is this information to Colleen? Describe what, if anything, Colleen should try as a result of this information.
3. What concerns you most about teaching the diversity of students you are likely to have in a classroom? Share those concerns with others in your class. Categorize your group's concerns. Access an Internet teacher bulletin board to see what kinds of problems classroom teachers are currently concerned about. Are block scheduling, thematic instruction, grading, group learning, and classroom management high in frequency of concern? Are the concerns of teachers as expressed on the Internet similar to yours? As a class, devise a plan and time line for attempting to ameliorate your concerns.

4. Give an example of how and when you would use multilevel instruction. Of what benefit is its use to students? To teachers? What particular skills must a teacher have to implement multilevel instruction effectively?
5. Explain why the use of curriculum tracking and homogeneous grouping are discouraged by many educators and researchers. What strategies are recommended in the place of traditional tracking?
6. Prepare an argument either for or against the following statement and present your argument to your classmates: Since teaching about citizenship, ethics, and moral values are unavoidable, a school should plan and do it well.
7. It is estimated that approximately one of every five children ages 6 to 11 in the United States are living in poverty. Explain any relevance that this may have for you as a classroom teacher.
8. Describe any prior concepts you held that changed as a result of your experiences with this chapter. Describe the changes.
9. From your current observations and field work as related to this teacher preparation program, clearly identify one specific example of educational practice that seems contradictory to exemplary practice or theory as presented in this chapter. Present your explanation for the discrepancy.
10. Do you have other questions generated by the content of this chapter? If you do, list them along with ways answers might be found.

FOR FURTHER READING

Armstrong, T. *Awakening Genius in the Classroom.* Alexandria, VA: Association for Supervision and Curriculum Development, 1998.

Baker, J. C., and Martin, F. G. *A Neural Network Guide to Teaching.* Fastback 431. Bloomington, IN: Phi Delta Kappa Educational Foundation, 1998.

Brandt, R. *Powerful Learning.* Alexandria, VA: Association for Supervision and Curriculum Development, 1998.

Choate, J. S., and Rakes, T. A. *Inclusive Instruction for Struggling Readers.* Fastback 434. Bloomington, IN: Phi Delta Kappa Educational Foundation, 1998.

Clark, G., and Zimmerman, E. "Nurturing the Arts in Programs for Gifted and Talented Students." *Phi Delta Kappan* 79(10):747–751 (June 1998).

Fogarty, R. "The Intelligence-Friendly Classroom." *Phi Delta Kappan* 79(9):655–657 (May 1998).

Gonzalez, M. L.; Huerta-Macias, A.; and Tinajero, J. V. (Editors). *Educating Latino Students: A Guide to Successful Practice.* Lancaster, PA: Technomic, 1998.

Jensen, E. *Teaching With the Brain in Mind.* Alexandria, VA: Association for Supervision and Curriculum Development, 1998.

Kovalik, S., and Olsen, K. D. "The Physiology of Learning—Just What Does Go On in There?" *Schools in the Middle* 7(4):32–37 (March/April 1998).

Loveless, T. *The Tracking and Ability Grouping Debate.* Washington, DC: Thomas B. Fordham Foundation, 1998.

Smutney, J. F. *Gifted Girls.* Fastback 427. Bloomington, IN: Phi Delta Kappa Educational Foundation, 1998.

Sweet, S. S. "A Lesson Learned About Multiple Intelligences." *Educational Leadership* 56(3):50–51 (November 1998).

Tiegerman-Farber, E. M. *Collaborative Decision-Making: The Pathway to Inclusion.* Upper Saddle River, NJ: Merrill/Prentice Hall, 1998.

Williams, C. W., and Hounshell, P. B. "Enabling the Learning Disabled." *Science Teacher* 65(1):29–31 (January 1998).

Chapter 3

The Expectations, Responsibilities, and Facilitating Behaviors of a Classroom Teacher

The primary expectation of any teacher is to facilitate student learning. As a classroom teacher your professional responsibilities will extend well beyond the ability to work effectively in a classroom from approximately 8:00 A.M. until mid-afternoon. In this chapter, you will learn about the many responsibilities you will assume and the competencies and behaviors necessary for fulfilling them. Four categories of responsibilities and twenty-two competencies are identified.

The four categories are (1) responsibility as a reflective decision maker, (2) commitment to children and to the profession, (3) noninstructional responsibilities, and (4) instructional responsibilities and fundamental teaching behaviors. As these categories and the twenty-two competencies are presented, you are guided through the reality of these expectations as they exist for today's classroom teacher.

Specifically, upon completion of this chapter you should be able to

1. Describe the decision-making and thought-processing phases of instruction and the types of decisions you must make during each.
2. Describe the importance of the concept of locus of control and its relationship to your professional responsibilities.
3. Demonstrate your understanding of the depth and breadth of the responsibilities of being a classroom teacher.
4. Demonstrate an understanding of the concept of *meaningful learning.*
5. Compare and contrast the two phrases, *hands-on* and *minds-on learning.*

6. Contrast teacher use of praise and of encouragement, and describe situations in which each is more appropriate.
7. Demonstrate the concept of multilevel instruction and how you would use multilevel instruction in your teaching.
8. Compare and contrast teacher facilitating behaviors with instructional strategies.
9. Demonstrate your growing understanding of the concept of teaching style and its relevance to classroom instruction.
10. Demonstrate your understanding of the importance of reflection to the process of constructing skills and understandings.

THE TEACHER AS A REFLECTIVE DECISION MAKER

During any single school day you will make hundreds, perhaps thousands, of decisions. Some decisions will have been made prior to meeting your students for instruction, others will be made during the instructional activities, and yet still others are made later as you reflect on the instruction for that day. Let's now consider further these decision-making and thought-processing phases of instruction.

Decision-Making Phases of Instruction

Instruction can be divided into four decision-making and thought-processing phases: (1) the planning or *preactive phase,* (2) the teaching or *interactive phase,*

(3) the analyzing and evaluating or *reflective phase,* and (4) the application or *projective phase.*[1]

The preactive phase consists of all those intellectual functions and decisions you will make prior to actual instruction. This includes decisions about the goals and objectives, homework assignments, identification of what children already know and can do, appropriate learning activities, questions to be asked (and possible answers), and the selection and preparation of instructional materials.

The interactive phase includes all the decisions made during the immediacy and spontaneity of the teaching act. This includes maintaining student attention, questions to be asked, types of feedback given to the children, and ongoing adjustments to the lesson plan. Decisions made during this phase are likely to be more intuitive, unconscious, and routine than those made during the planning phase.

The reflective phase is the time you will take to reflect on, analyze, and judge the decisions and behaviors that occurred during the interactive phase. It is during reflection that you make decisions about student learning, student grades, feedback given to parents, and adjustments on what to teach next.

As a result of this reflection, decisions are made to use what was learned in subsequent teaching actions. At this point, you are in the projective phase, abstracting from your reflection and projecting your analysis into subsequent teaching behaviors.

Reflection, Locus of Control, and Teacher Responsibility

During the reflective phase, teachers have a choice of whether to assume full responsibility for the instructional outcomes or whether to assume responsibility for only the positive outcomes of the planned instruction while placing the blame for the negative outcomes on outside forces (e.g., parents and guardians, society in general, peers, other teachers, administrators, textbooks). Where the responsibility for outcomes is placed is referred to as locus of control.

Just because a teacher thinks that he or she is a competent teacher doesn't mean it is so. If many of a teacher's students are not learning, then that teacher is not competent. In the words of the late Madeline Hunter, "To say that I am an effective teacher and acknowledge that my students may not be learning, is the same as saying I am a great surgeon but most of my patients die."[2] Teachers who are intrinsically motivated and competent tend to assume full responsibility for instructional outcomes, regardless of whether or not the outcomes are as intended from the planning phase.

Now, further your understanding by completing Exercises 3.1 and 3.2.

---

[1]See A. L. Costa, *The School as a Home for the Mind* (Palatine, IL: Skylight Publishing, 1991), pp. 97–106.

[2]In R. A. Villa and J. S. Thousands, Eds., *Creating an Inclusive School* (Alexandria, VA: Association for Supervision and Curriculum Development, 1995), p. 36.

EXERCISE 3.1 THE TEACHER AS REFLECTIVE DECISION MAKER

INSTRUCTIONS: The purpose of this exercise is to learn more about the nature of the decisions and the decision-making process used by teachers. To accomplish this, you are to observe one teacher for one hour during that teacher's teaching. Tabulate as accurately as possible the number of decisions the teacher makes during that time period, and then share the results with your classmates. Obtain permission from a cooperating teacher by explaining the purpose of your observations. You will need to have a follow-up discussion with the cooperating teacher regarding your tabulations. A follow-up thank you letter is appropriate.

School, teacher, and class observed: _____

1. Use the following format for your tabulations. You may first want to make your tabulations on a separate blank sheet of paper and then organize and transfer those tabulations to this page. Tabulate and identify each decision. To tabulate the decisions made before and after instruction, confer with the teacher after class.

DECISION MADE BEFORE INSTRUCTION

Examples:
- objectives of lesson
- amount of time to be devoted to particular activities
- classroom management procedures

DECISIONS MADE DURING INSTRUCTION

Examples:
- called on Roberta to answer a question
- teacher remained silent until students in back corner got quiet
- talked with tardy student

DECISIONS MADE AFTER INSTRUCTION

Examples:
- to review a particular concept tomorrow
- to arrange a conference with Sean to talk with him about his hostility in class
- to make a revision in Friday's homework assignment

2. What was the total number of decisions made by this teacher

before instruction?_____   during instruction?_____   after instruction?_____

Compare your results with those of others in your class.

☞

EXERCISE 3.1 (*continued*)

3. Did you observe any evidence that this teacher assumed full responsibility for the learning outcomes of this class session? Describe the evidence.

4. What percentage of all decisions by this teacher

   were planned?_____   were spontaneous?_____

5. Did you share your results of this exercise with the cooperating teacher? His or her reaction?

6. Your conclusions from this exercise?

EXERCISE 3.2 THE PREACTIVE PHASE OF INSTRUCTION

INSTRUCTIONS: Mentally rehearsing your actions before meeting the students is absolutely essential for effective teaching and learning. The purpose of this exercise is to stress the importance of clearly and fully thinking about what you will do and say in the classroom, to demonstrate how mental rehearsal of a lesson can identify possible problems. Follow these steps:

1. Select a grade level you are currently teaching or that you would like to teach._____

   _____

2. Objective of lesson: Students will design a name tag for their desks during a 20-minute time frame.
3. *Without looking ahead at step 4,* on a separate paper write a lesson plan for this activity. (Although you have not yet learned the details of lesson planning, outline the steps you would follow and things you would say to your students to accomplish the objective of step 2.)
4. Now, to analyze the thoroughness of your preactive thinking, respond to the following questions.

   4.1. Are materials listed in your plan? _____

   4.2. Are those materials readily available in your classroom? _____

   4.3. Will paper or tagboard need to be pre-cut? _____

   4.4. How large can the name tags be? _____

   4.5. How and where will they be attached to each desk? _____

   _____

   4.6. Should they be flat or three-dimensional? _____

   4.7. Do you have markers or crayons or are the students expected to have them? _____

   _____

   4.8. Will students need scissors? _____

   4.9. Do you have left-handed scissors available if needed? _____

   4.10. Should name tags have first name, last name, last initial? _____

   4.11. Can other words or designs be added? _____

   4.12. When and how will materials be distributed? Collected? _____

   _____

   4.13. What plan do you have for absent or tardy students? _____

   _____

5. Share the results of your steps 1–4 with others in your class. Did members of your class come up with other questions relevant and necessary to the preplanning for this instructional period? If so, share them with the rest of the class.

Conclusion: A teacher who practices thorough preactive planning should have planned answers for each of these questions.

TEACHING STYLE

Teaching style is the way teachers teach, which includes their distinctive mannerisms complemented by their choices of teaching behaviors and strategies. A teacher's style affects the way that teacher presents information and interacts with students. The manner and pattern of those interactions with students clearly determines a teacher's effectiveness in promoting student learning, positive attitudes about learning, and students' self-esteem.

A teacher's style is determined by the teacher's personal characteristics (especially the teacher's own learning style), experiences, and knowledge of research findings about how young people learn. Teaching style can be altered, intentionally or unintentionally, as a result of changes in any of these three areas.

While there are other ways to label and describe teaching styles, we shall consider two contrasting styles—the *traditional* and *facilitating* styles (see Table 3.1)—to emphasize that although today's teacher must use aspects from each (that is, be eclectic in style choice), there must be a strong inclination toward the facilitating style.

Multilevel Instruction

As emphasized in the preceding chapter, students in your classroom have their own independent ways of knowing and learning. It is important to try to attend to how each student best learns and to where each student is developmentally, that is, to individualize both the content and methods of learning. In essence, although perhaps not as detailed as those prepared for special education students, at various times during the school year you will be devel-

oping individual educational programs (IEPs) for each student. These may be prepared in collaboration with members of your teaching team. To accomplish this individual teaching, you can use multilevel instruction (known also as multitasking). As explained in Chapter 2 (see Figure 2.1), multilevel instruction is when individual students and groups of students are working at different tasks to accomplish the same objective or at different tasks to accomplish different objectives.

When integrating student learning, as you will be learning in Part II of this guide, multitasking is an important and useful, perhaps even necessary, strategy. Project-centered teaching (discussed in Chapter 8) is an instructional method that easily allows for the provision of multilevel instruction. Multilevel teaching occurs when several levels of teaching and learning are going on simultaneously. For example, while some students may be working independently of the teacher—that is, within the facilitating mode—others may be receiving direct instruction—that is, more within the traditional mode.

The Theoretical Origins of Teaching Styles and Their Relation to Constructivism

Constructivist teaching and the integration of curriculum are not new to education. The importance of constructivism and curriculum integration approaches are found, for example, in the writings of John Dewey,[3] Arthur W. Combs,[4] and Jean Piaget.[5]

---

[3] J. Dewey, *How We Think* (Boston: Heath, 1933).
[4] A. W. Combs (Ed.), *Perceiving, Behaving, and Becoming: A New Focus for Education* (Arlington, VA: 1962 ASCD Yearbook, Association for Supervision and Curriculum Development, 1962).
[5] J. Piaget, *Science of Education and the Psychology of the Child* (New York: Orion, 1970).

Table 3.1 A Contrast of Two Teaching Styles

Characteristic	Traditional Style	Facilitating Style
Teacher	Autocratic	Democratic
	Curriculum-centered	Student-centered
	Direct	Indirect
	Dominative	Informal
	Formal	Inquiring
	Informative	Interactive
	Prescriptive	Reflective
Classroom	Teacher-centered	Student-centered
	Linear (seats facing front)	Grouped or circular
Instructional modes	Abstract learning	Concrete learning
	Teacher-centered discussion	Discussions
	Lectures	Peer and cross-age coaching
	Competitive learning	Cooperative learning
	Some problem solving	Problem solving
	Teacher demonstrations	Student inquiries
	From simple to complex	Starting with complex tasks and using instructional scaffolding and dialogue
	Transmission of information from teacher to students	Reciprocal teaching, using dialogue between teacher and students and between students and students

Instructional styles are deeply rooted in certain theoretical assumptions about learners and their development. Although it is beyond the scope of my intent for this resource guide to explore deeply those assumptions, three major theoretical positions with research findings, each of which is based on certain philosophical and psychological assumptions, suggest different ways of working with children. The theoretical positions are described in the next three paragraphs.

Tied to the theoretical positions of *romanticism-maturationism* is the assumption that the learner's mind is neutral-passive to good-active, and the main focus in teaching should be the addition of new ideas to a subconscious store of old ones. Key persons behind these theories include Jean J. Rousseau and Sigmund Freud; key instructional strategies include classic lecturing with rote memorization.

Tied to the theoretical position of *behaviorism* is the assumption that the learner's mind is neutral-passive with innate reflexes and needs, and the main focus in teaching should be on the successive, systematic changes in the learner's environment to increase the possibilities of desired behavior responses. Key persons behind these theories include John Locke, B. F. Skinner, A. H. Thorndike, Robert Gagné, and John Watson; key instructional strategies include practice and reinforcement as in workbook drill activities and programmed instruction.

Tied to the theoretical position of *cognitive-experimentalism* (including *constructivism*) is the assumption that the learner is a neutral-interactive purposive individual in simultaneous interaction with physical and biological environments. The main focus in teaching should be on facilitating the learner's gain and construction of new perceptions that lead to desired behavioral changes and ultimately to a more fully functioning individual. Key persons are John Dewey, Lev Vygotsky, Jerome Bruner, Jean Piaget, and Arthur W. Combs; key instructional strategies include discovery, inquiry, project-centered teaching, cooperative and social-interactive learning, and integrated curriculum.

It is my opinion that with a diversity of students, to be most effective a teacher must be eclectic, but with a strong emphasis toward cognitive-experimentalism-constructivism because of its divergence in learning and the importance given to learning as a change in perceptions. An effective approach is to use at appropriate times the best of strategies and knowledgeable instructor behaviors, regardless of whether individually they can be classified within any style dichotomy, such as direct vs. indirect, formal vs. informal, traditional vs. progressive, or didactic vs. facilitative.

Now, to further your understanding of styles of teaching, complete Exercises 3.3 and 3.4. After you finish those exercises, we review the category of commitment and professionalism.

EXERCISE 3.3 USING OBSERVATION OF CLASSROOM INTERACTION TO ANALYZE ONE TEACHER'S STYLE*

INSTRUCTIONS: The purpose of this exercise is to visit a classroom to observe and identify a teacher's instructional style. Be certain to obtain permission and to explain to the teacher that you are observing, not evaluating, teaching style. The host teacher may be interested in discussing with you the results of your observation. A follow-up thank-you letter is appropriate.

Observe the teacher's behavior at one-minute intervals for a period of ten minutes, and tabulate the appropriate item on the following chart. Continue this for the entire class meeting.

Class, grade level, and school visited _____

_____

_____

Date of visit _____

	Minute										
	1	2	3	4	5	6	7	8	9	10	Total
Traditional Teacher Behaviors *Prescribing:* Giving advice or directions, being critical or evaluative, offering judgments											
Informing: Giving information, lecturing, interpreting											
Confronting: Directly challenging students											

Traditional behaviors total _____

Facilitating Teacher Behaviors *Relaxing:* Releasing tension, using humor											
Mediating: Asking for information, being reflective, encouraging self-directed problem solving											
Supporting: Approving, confirming, validating, listening											

Facilitating behaviors total _____

Total traditional behaviors divided by total facilitating behaviors (T/F ratio) _____

Conclusions about the teacher's style _____

_____

_____

_____

_____

_____

_____

_____

_____

*Adapted from J. Heron, *Six Category Intervention Analysis* (Guildford, England: Centre of Adult Education, University of Surrey, 1975).

☞

EXERCISE 3.3 (*continued*)

_____

_____

_____

_____

_____

_____

_____

Did you discuss your observations with the teacher? _____

_____

_____

_____

_____

_____

_____

EXERCISE 3.4 USING A QUESTIONNAIRE TO DEVELOP A PROFILE AND A STATEMENT ABOUT MY OWN EMERGING TEACHING STYLE

INSTRUCTIONS: The purpose of this exercise is to help you clarify and articulate your own assumptions about teaching and learning. You will develop a profile of your emerging teaching style and from that a statement representative of your current thinking and philosophy about teaching and learning. Proceed with the following five steps.

Step 1. Read each of the 50 statements and rate your feelings about each, giving a *1* if you strongly agree, a *2* if you are neutral, and a *3* if you strongly disagree.

Remember: 1 = strongly agree; 2 = neutral; 3 = strongly disagree

_____ 1. Most of what children learn, they learn on their own.

_____ 2. Children should be concerned about other students' reactions to their work in the classroom.

_____ 3. An important part of schooling is learning to work with others.

_____ 4. Children learn more by working on their own than by working with others.

_____ 5. Children should be given opportunities to participate actively in class planning and implementation of lessons.

_____ 6. In an effective learning environment, grades are inappropriate.

_____ 7. Children enjoy working in a classroom that has clearly defined learning objectives and assessment criteria.

_____ 8. I favor teaching methods and classroom procedures that maximize student independence to learn from their own experiences.

_____ 9. Most of what children learn is learned from other children.

_____ 10. Children should be concerned with getting good grades.

_____ 11. An important part of teaching and learning is learning how to work independently.

_____ 12. In the classroom, the teacher should not be contradicted or challenged by a student.

_____ 13. Interchanges between children and a teacher can provide ideas about content better than those found in a textbook.

_____ 14. For children to get the most out of a class, they must be aware of the primary concerns and biases of the teacher.

_____ 15. Students should not be given high grades unless clearly earned.

_____ 16. Learning should help the learner to become an independent thinker.

_____ 17. Most of what children learn is learned from their teachers.

_____ 18. A teacher who makes children do things they don't want to do is an ineffective teacher.

*Adapted from William H. Berquist and Steve R. Phillips, *A Handbook for Faculty Development* (Washington, DC: The Council for Independent Colleges, June 1975), 25–27.

EXERCISE 3.4 (*continued*)

_____ 19. Learning takes place most effectively under conditions in which children are in competition with one another.

_____ 20. A teacher should try to persuade students that particular ideas are valid and exciting.

_____ 21. To do well in school, children must be assertive.

_____ 22. Facts in textbooks are usually accurate.

_____ 23. I favor the use of teaching methods and classroom procedures that maximize student and teacher interaction.

_____ 24. Most of what children learn is learned from books.

_____ 25. A teacher who lets children do whatever they want is incompetent.

_____ 26. Students can learn more by working with an enthusiastic teacher than by working alone.

_____ 27. I favor the use of teaching methods and classroom procedures that maximize student learning of basic subject matter content.

_____ 28. Ideas of other students are useful for helping a student understand the content of lessons.

_____ 29. A student should study what the teacher says is important and not necessarily what is important to that student.

_____ 30. A teacher who does not motivate student interest in subject content is incompetent.

_____ 31. An important part of education is learning how to perform under testing and evaluation conditions.

_____ 32. Children can learn more by sharing their ideas than by keeping their ideas to themselves.

_____ 33. Teachers tend to give students too many assignments that are trivial.

_____ 34. Ideas contained in the textbook should be the primary source of the content taught.

_____ 35. Children should be given high grades as a means of motivating them and increasing their self-esteem.

_____ 36. The ideas a student brings into a class are useful for helping the child to understand subject content.

_____ 37. Students should study what is important to them and not necessarily what the teacher claims is important.

_____ 38. Learning takes place most effectively under conditions in which children are working independently of one another.

_____ 39. Teachers often give students too much freedom of choice in content, methods, and procedures.

_____ 40. Teachers should clearly explain what it is they expect from students.

_____ 41. Students' ideas about content are often better than those ideas found in textbooks.

_____ 42. Classroom discussions are beneficial learning experiences.

EXERCISE 3.4 (*continued*)

_____ 43. A student's education should help the student to become a successful and contributing member of society.

_____ 44. Learning takes place most effectively under conditions in which students are working cooperatively with one another.

_____ 45. Teachers often are too personal with their students.

_____ 46. A teacher should encourage children to disagree with or challenge that teacher in the classroom.

_____ 47. Children have to be able to work effectively with other people to do well in school.

_____ 48. For children to get the most out of school, they must assume at least part of the responsibility for their learning.

_____ 49. Students seem to enjoy discussing their ideas about learning with the teacher and other students.

_____ 50. A child's education should help the child to become a sensitive human being.

Step 2. From the list of 50 items, write the items (by their number) in two columns, those with which you held strong agreement and those with which you strongly disagreed. Ignore those items to which you gave a 2 (were neutral).

Strongly Agreed

Strongly Disagreed

Step 3. In groups of three or four, discuss your lists (in Step 2) with your classmates. From the discussion, you may rerank any items you wish.

EXERCISE 3.4 (continued)

Step 4. You now have a finalized list of those items with which you were in agreement and those with which you disagreed. On the basis of those two lists, write a paragraph that summarizes your philosophy about teaching and learning. It should be no longer than one-half page in length. That statement is a theoretical representation of your present teaching philosophy.

Step 5. Compare your philosophical statement with the three theoretical positions as discussed prior to this exercise. Can you clearly identify your position? Name it:

Explain your rationale:

At the completion of this course, you may wish to revisit your philosophical statement, perhaps even to make revisions to it. It will be useful to have your educational philosophy firmly implanted in your memory for teaching job interviews at a later date (see Chapter 12).

COMMITMENT AND PROFESSIONALISM

The classroom teacher is expected to demonstrate commitment to the school's mission (discussed in Chapter 1) and to the personal and intellectual development of the students (discussed in Chapter 2). Not only do the most effective teachers expect, demand, and receive positive results in learning from their students while in the classroom, they are also interested and involved in students' activities outside the classroom, willing to sacrifice personal time to give them attention and guidance.

Figure 3.1 Noninstructional responsibilities of the classroom teacher

1. Knowledgeable about activities of interest to students
2. Familiar with the school campus and community
3. Acquainted with members of the faculty and support staff
4. Knowledgeable about school and district policies
5. Familiar with the backgrounds of students
6. Knowledgeable about procedures for such routine matters as: planning and scheduling of before- and after-school activities, restroom regulations, distribution and collection of textbooks and other school materials, class dismissal, ordering of supplies, fire drills and severe weather, daily attendance records, school assemblies, sharing of instructional space with other teachers, arranging for and preparing displays for common areas of the school
7. Your expected role in teaching common elements of the curriculum, such as reading, writing, and thinking
8. Your expected role in the advisory program
9. Classroom duties such as: maintaining a cheerful, pleasant, and safe environment; obtaining materials needed for each lesson; keeping supplies orderly; supervising student helpers
10. Your expected role in the parent-teacher organization and other community participation meetings
11. The many conferences that will be needed, such as those between teacher and teacher, teacher and student, teacher and parent or guardian, teacher, student, and parent, teacher and administrator, and teacher and community representative
12. Professional meetings, such as those of the interdisciplinary teaching team, other school and district committees, parent-teacher and community groups, and local, regional, state, and national professional organizations
13. Time to relax and enjoy family and hobbies

Noninstructional Responsibilities

The aspects of the teacher as a decision maker with professional commitments take on a very real dimension when you consider specific noninstruction-related and instruction-related responsibilities of the classroom teacher. Shown in Figure 3.1 are 13 categories of items that should alert you to the many noninstructional matters with which you should become familiar, especially during your first year of teaching. Beginning teachers often underestimate their importance and the amount of time they require.

Instructional Responsibilities

The items listed in Figure 3.2 introduce you to or remind you of the instructional responsibilities you will have as a classroom teacher. These responsibilities are the primary focus of study of the remainder of this resource guide. After you have reviewed the lists of instructional and noninstructional responsibilities of the classroom teacher, complete Exercise 3.5, which is a model of cooperative learning.

Figure 3.2 Instructional responsibilities of the classroom teacher

1. Planning units and daily lessons
2. Learning the interests of students so that lessons will reflect those interests
3. Incorporating the individual learning styles, capacities, and modalities of the students in lesson plans
4. Reading student papers
5. Assessing and recording student progress
6. Preparing the classroom
7. Providing classroom instruction
8. Thinking about professional growth and development, which may include attending university courses, attending workshops and other presentations offered by the school district or professional organizations, and reading professional literature
9. Developing a firm but fair classroom management system
10. Reacquainting yourself with the developmental characteristics of young people
11. Learning the background of students with special problems who might cause concerns in the learning environment
12. Developing techniques and plans for cross-age tutoring, peer coaching, cooperative learning, and other teaching strategies
13. Identifying resources and sources
14. Devoting time to team planning
15. Holding conferences with individual students

EXERCISE 3.5 REVIEWING THE PROFESSIONAL RESPONSIBILITIES OF A FIRST-YEAR TEACHER

INSTRUCTIONS: The purpose of this exercise is to review the responsibilities of a first-year teacher. Have the class of teacher candidates divide into groups of four. Within each group, each member should play one of the following roles: (1) group facilitator; (2) recorder; (3) materials manager; and (4) reporter. The group is to choose one of these six categories of responsibilities:

1. Audiovisual/media
2. Classroom environment
3. Clerical
4. Instructional
5. Professional activities
6. Supervision

The group should then read the responsibilities for their selected category listed on the following cards and arrange them in prioritized order, beginning with the most important. The group facilitator will lead this discussion. Under the guidance of the materials manager, the group may cut the cards apart so that they can be physically manipulated as priorities are discussed. The recorder should take notes of the group's work, which can then be discussed to develop the report that will be made to the class.

After a prearranged discussion time, recall the entire class and ask each reporter to share the group's (1) prioritized order of responsibilities and (2) estimate of the amount of time that a beginning teacher might devote to these responsibilities each week.

As each group reports, all members of the class should enter its list of priorities and time estimate on the Recap Sheet.

After completion of this exercise, the class may wish to discuss the group dynamics of this model of cooperative learning (see Chapter 8). For discussion in either large or small groups, key questions might be:

1. Would you use this form of discussion in your own teaching?
2. How would you divide a class into groups of four?

Other questions may be generated by the group work.

CARDS FOR EXERCISE 3.5

Audiovisual/Media Responsibilities

Selecting, ordering, and returning cassettes, films, videodiscs, and other materials	

Preparing and operating equipment	Reviewing selected materials

Planning class introduction to the audiovisual materials	Other audiovisual responsibilities as determined

Estimated hours a beginning teacher will devote to audiovisual/media responsibilities each week = _____

CARDS FOR EXERCISE 3.5

Classroom Environment Responsibilities

Planning and constructing displays	Preparing bulletin boards

Reading, announcing, and posting class notices	Managing a classroom library

Opening and closing windows, arranging furniture, cleaning the writing board	Other classroom environment responsibilities as determined

Estimated hours a beginning teacher will devote to classroom environment responsibilities each week = _____

CARDS FOR EXERCISE 3.5

Clerical Responsibilities

Maintaining attendance and tardy records	Entering grades, scores, or marks into a record book or onto the computer

Preparing progress and grade reports	Typing, drawing, and duplicating instructional materials

Locating resource ideas and materials to support lessons	Other clerical responsibilities as determined

Estimated hours a beginning teacher will devote to clerical responsibilities each week = _____

CARDS FOR EXERCISE 3.5

Instructional Responsibilities

Giving additional instruction (e.g., to students who need one-to-one attention, those who have been absent, or small review groups)	Correcting student work
Preparing special learning materials	Preparing, reading, and scoring tests; helping students self-evaluate
Writing information on the board	Preparing long-range and daily lesson plans
Grouping for instruction	Other instructional responsibilities as determined

Estimated hours a beginning teacher will devote to clerical responsibilities each week = _____

CARDS FOR EXERCISE 3.5

Professional Activities Responsibilities

Researching and writing teacher reports	Attending teachers' and school district meetings
Planning and attending parent-teacher meetings	Attending local teachers' organization meetings
Attending state, regional, and national professional organizations; taking university classes	Other professional activities responsibilities as determined

Estimated hours a beginning teacher will devote to clerical responsibilities each week = _____

CARDS FOR EXERCISE 3.5

Supervision Responsibilities

Supervising before- or after-school activities	Supervising hallways, lunchrooms, and bathrooms
Supervising student assemblies	Supervising field trips
Supervising laboratory activities	Helping students settle dispute
Other supervision responsibilities as determined	

Estimated hours a beginning teacher will devote to supervision responsibilities each week = _____

EXERCISE 3.5 RECAP SHEET

Audiovisual/Media Responsibilities

1. _____
2. _____
3. _____
4. _____
5. _____

Estimated hours = _____

Classroom Environment Responsibilities

1. _____
2. _____
3. _____
4. _____
5. _____
6. _____

Estimated hours = _____

Clerical Responsibilities

1. _____
2. _____
3. _____
4. _____
5. _____
6. _____

Estimated hours = _____

Instructional Responsibilities

1. _____
2. _____
3. _____
4. _____
5. _____
6. _____
7. _____
8. _____

Estimated hours = _____

EXERCISE 3.5 (continued)

Professional Activities Responsibilities

1. _____

2. _____

3. _____

4. _____

5. _____

6. _____

Estimated hours = _____

Supervision Responsibilities

1. _____

2. _____

3. _____

4. _____

5. _____

6. _____

7. _____

Estimated hours = _____

IDENTIFYING AND BUILDING YOUR INSTRUCTIONAL COMPETENCIES

The overall purpose of this book is to assist you in building your instructional competencies. To do that, we need a starting place and this is it: the identification and presentation of twenty-two specific competencies. You will continue to reflect on and to build upon these competencies through your study of the remaining chapters of this book and, indeed, throughout your professional career.

Characteristics of the Competent Classroom Teacher: An Annotated List

Please do not feel overwhelmed by the following list; it may well be that no teacher expertly models all the characteristics that follow. The characteristics do, however, represent an ideal to strive for.

1. *The teacher is knowledgeable about the subject matter expected to be taught.* You should have both historical understanding and current knowledge of the structure of those subjects you are expected to teach and of the facts, principles, concepts, and skills needed for those subjects. This doesn't mean you need to know everything about the subject, but you should know more than you are likely to teach.

2. *The teacher is an "educational broker."* You will learn where and how to discover information about content you are expected to teach. You cannot know everything there is to know about each subject—indeed, you will not always be able to predict all that is learned—but you should become knowledgeable about where and how to best research it and how to assist your students in developing those same skills. Among other things, this means that you should be computer literate, that is, have the ability to understand and use computers for research and writing, paralleling reading and writing in verbal literacy.

3. *The teacher is an active member of professional organizations, reads professional journals, dialogues with colleagues, and maintains currency in methodology and about the students and subject content he or she is expected to teach.* While this resource guide offers valuable information about teaching and learning, it is much closer to the start of your professional career than it is to the end. As discussed by Art Costa in the Foreword for this resource guide and as explained in Chapter 12, as a teacher you are a learner among learners. Plan to spend your career in a perpetual mode of learning through workshops, advanced course work, coaching and training, reading and study, and collaboration with and role modeling of significant and more experienced colleagues.

4. *The teacher understands the processes of learning.* You will ensure that students understand the lesson objectives, your expectations, and the classroom procedures. They must feel welcome in your classroom and involved in learning activities, and they should have some control over the pacing of their own learning. Furthermore, when preparing your lessons, you will (a) consider the unique learning characteristics of each student; (b) see that content is presented in reasonably small doses—and in a logical and coherent sequence—while using visual, verbal, tactile, and kinesthetic learning activities with opportunities for guided practice and reinforcement, and (c) frequently check for student comprehension to assure the students are learning.

5. *The teacher uses effective modeling behaviors.* Your own behaviors must be consistent with those expected of your students. If, for example, you want your students to demonstrate regular and punctual attendance, to have their work done on time, to have their materials each day for learning, to demonstrate cooperative behavior and respect for others, to maintain an open and inquisitive mind, to demonstrate critical thinking, and to use proper communication skills, then you will do likewise, modeling those same behaviors and attitudes for the students. As a teacher, you serve as a role model for your students. Whether you realize it or not, your behavior sends important messages to students that complement curriculum content. You serve your students well when you model inclusive and collaborative approaches to learning. Specific guidelines for effective modeling are presented later in this chapter.

6. *The teacher is open to change, willing to take risks and to be held accountable.* If there were no difference between what is and what can be, then formal schooling would be of little value. A competent teacher knows not only of historical and traditional values and knowledge, but also of the value of change. He or she thus is willing to plan carefully and experiment, to move between that which is known and that which is not. Realizing that little of value is ever achieved without a certain amount of risk and employing personal strength of convictions, the competent teacher stands ready to be held accountable, as the teacher undoubtedly will be, for assuming such risks.

7. *The teacher is nonprejudiced toward gender, sexual preference, ethnicity, skin color, religion, physical handicaps, socioeconomic status, learning disabilities, or national origin.* Among other things, this means no sexual innuendoes, religious or ethnic jokes, or racial slurs. It means being cognizant of how teachers, male and female, knowingly or unknowingly, historically have mistreated female students and how to avoid those same errors in your own teaching. (Chapter 8 offers specific guidelines.) It means learning about and attending to the needs of individual students in your classroom. It means having high, although not necessarily identical, expectations for all students.

8. *The teacher organizes the classroom and plans lessons carefully.* Long-range plans and daily lessons are prepared thoughtfully, reflected on, revised, and competently implemented with creative, motivating, and effective strategies and skill. Much of this resource guide is devoted to assisting in your development of this competency.

9. *The teacher is a capable communicator.* The competent teacher uses thoughtfully selected words, carefully planned questions, expressive voice inflections, useful pauses, meaningful gestures, and productive and nonconfusing body language. Some of these expressions are carefully and thoughtfully planned during the preactive phase of instruction and others, through practice and reflection, become second-nature skills. Throughout this book you will find useful suggestions for your development of this competency.

10. *The teacher functions effectively as a decision maker.* The classroom is a complex place, busy with fast-paced activities. In a single day you may engage in a thousand or more interpersonal exchanges with students, to say nothing about the numerous exchanges possible with the many adults with whom you will be in contact. The competent teacher is in control of classroom events rather than controlled by them. The teacher initiates, rather than merely reacts, is proactive and in control of her or his interactions, having learned how to manage time to analyze and develop effective interpersonal behaviors. (For this purpose it can be valuable to videotape a class period for later analysis of your interactions.)

11. *The teacher is in a perpetual learning mode, striving to develop further a repertoire of teaching strategies.* As discussed earlier (competency number two) competent teachers are good students, continuing their own learning by reflecting on and assessing their work, attending workshops, studying the work of others, and talking with students, parents and guardians, and colleagues, sometimes over Internet bulletin boards. (The topic of ongoing professional development is the essence of the final chapter of this resource guide.)

12. *The teacher demonstrates concern for the safety and health of the students.* The competent teacher consistently models safety procedures, ensuring precautions necessary to protect the health and psychological and physical safety of the students. The teacher strives to maintain a comfortable room temperature with adequate ventilation and to prevent safety hazards in the classroom. Students who are ill are encouraged to stay home and get well. If a teacher suspects that a student may be ill or may be suffering from neglect or abuse at home (see Chapter 4), the teacher appropriately and promptly acts upon that suspicion by referring the student to the school nurse or an appropriate administrator.

13. *The teacher demonstrates optimism for the learning of every student, while providing a constructive and positive environment for learning.* Much of this resource guide is devoted to the provision of specific guidelines and resources for developing this competency. Both common sense and research tell us clearly that students enjoy and learn better from a teacher who is positive and optimistic, encouraging, nurturing, and happy, rather than from a teacher who is negative and pessimistic, discouraging, uninterested, and grumpy. (See "mood swings" in Chapter 4.)

14. *The teacher demonstrates confidence in every student's ability to learn.* For a student, nothing at school is more satisfying than a teacher who demonstrates confidence in that student's abilities. Unfortunately, for some children, a teacher's show of confidence may be the only positive indicator they ever receive. Each of us can recall with admiration a teacher (or other significant person) who demonstrated confidence in our ability to accomplish seemingly formidable tasks. A competent teacher demonstrates this confidence with each and every student. This doesn't mean you must personally like every student with whom you will ever come into contact; it does mean you must accept each one as a person of dignity worthy of receiving your respect and professional skills.

15. *The teacher is skillful and fair in the employment of strategies for the assessment of student learning.* The competent teacher is knowledgeable about the importance of providing immediate intensive intervention when learning problems become apparent, implementing appropriate learning assessment tools while avoiding the abuse of power afforded by the assessment process. Assessment is the focus of Chapter 11.

16. *The teacher is skillful in working with parents and guardians, colleagues, administrators, and the support staff, and maintains and nurtures friendly and ethical professional relationships.* Teachers, parents and guardians, administrators, cooks, custodians, secretaries, and other adults of the school community all share one common purpose—to serve the education of the students. This is best accomplished when these adults cooperate. An exemplary school and a skillful teacher work together to assure that parents or guardians are involved in their childrens' learning (as discussed in Chapters 1 and 11).

17. *The teacher demonstrates continuing interest in professional responsibilities and opportunities.* Knowing that ultimately each and every school activity has an effect upon the classroom, the competent teacher assumes an active interest in the school community. The purpose of the school is to serve the education of the students, and the classroom is the primary, but not only, place where this occurs. Every committee meeting, school event, team meeting, advisory meeting, faculty meeting, school board meeting, office, program, and any other planned function related to school shares in the ultimate purpose of better serving the education of the students who attend that school.

18. *The teacher exhibits a wide range of interests.* This includes interest in the activities of the students and the many aspects of the school and its surrounding community. The competent teacher is interesting because of his or her interests; a teacher with varied interests more often motivates and captures the attention of more students. A teacher with no interests outside his or her subject and the classroom is likely to be an exceedingly dull teacher.

19. *The teacher shares a healthy sense of humor.* The positive effects of appropriate humor (that is, humor that is not self-deprecating or disrespectful of others) on learning are well established: increased immune system activity and decreased stress-producing hormones; drop in the pulse rate; reduction of feelings of anxiety, tension, and stress; activation of T-cells for the immune system, antibodies that fight against harmful microorganisms, and gamma interferon, a hormone that fights viruses and regulates cell growth; and an increase in blood oxygen. Because of these effects, humor is a stimulant to not only healthy living, but to creativity and higher level thinking. As they should, students appreciate and learn more from a teacher who shares a sense of humor and laughs with the students.

20. *The teacher is quick to recognize a student who may be in need of special attention.* A competent teacher is alert to recognize any student who demonstrates behaviors indicating a need for special attention, guidance, or counseling. The teacher knows how and where to refer the student, doing so with minimal class disruption and without embarrassing the student. For example, a pattern of increasingly poor attendance or of steady negative attention-seeking behaviors are two of the more obvious early signals of the student who is potentially at risk of dropping out of school.

21. *The teacher makes specific and frequent efforts to demonstrate how the subject content may be related to students' lives.* A potentially dry and dull topic is made significant and alive when taught by a competent teacher. Regardless of topic, somewhere competent teachers are teaching that topic, and one of the significant characteristics of their effectiveness is they make the topic alive and relevant to themselves and to their students, helping the students make relevant connections. Time and again studies point out what should be obvious: Students don't learn much from dull, meaningless exercises and assignments. Such uninspired teaching may be one of the root causes of student disaffection with school.[6] Obtaining ideas from professional journals, attending workshops, and communicating with colleagues either personally or via electronic bulletin boards and web sites, and using interdisciplinary thematic instruction are ways of discovering how to make a potentially dry and boring topic interesting and alive for students (and for the teacher).

22. *The teacher is reliable.* The competent teacher can be relied on to fulfill professional responsibilities, promises, and commitments. A teacher who cannot be relied on is quick to lose credibility with the students and with colleagues and administrators. Regardless of his or her potential for effectiveness, an unreliable teacher is an incompetent teacher. For whatever reason, a teacher who is chronically absent from his or her teaching duties is an "at-risk" teacher.

Specific teacher behaviors are discussed in the following section; guidelines and resources to assist you in your development of these competencies permeate this resource guide.

TEACHER BEHAVIORS NECESSARY TO FACILITATE STUDENT LEARNING

Your ability to perform your instructional responsibilities effectively depends directly upon your knowledge of students and how they best learn and your knowledge of and the quality of your teaching skills. Development of your strategy repertoire along with your skills in using specific strategies should be ongoing throughout your teaching career. To be most effective, you need a large repertoire from which to select a specific strategy to attain a particular goal with a distinctive group of students. In addition, you need skill in using that strategy. This section of this chapter is designed to help you begin building your specific strategies repertoire and to develop your skills in using these strategies. As with intelligences, teaching style is neither absolutely inherited nor fixed but continues to develop and emerge throughout one's professional career.

First, you must know why you have selected a particular strategy. An unknowing teacher is likely to use the teaching strategy most common in college classes—the lecture. However, as many student teachers have discovered the hard way, the traditional lecture is seldom an effective or appropriate way to instruct K–12 students. As a rule, unlike many college and university students, not many K–12 students are strong auditory learners by preference and by adeptness. For most of them, learning by sitting and listening is difficult. Instead, they learn best when physically (hands-on) and intellectually (minds-on) active—that is, when using tactile and kinesthetic experiences, touching objects, feeling shapes and textures, moving objects, and talking about and sharing what they are learning.

Second, basic teacher behaviors create the conditions needed to enable students to think and to learn, whether the learning is a further understanding of concepts, the internalization of attitudes and values, the development of cognitive processes, or the actuating of

---

[6]M. Schmoker, *Results: The Key to Continuous School Improvement* (Alexandria, VA: Association for Supervision and Curriculum Development, 1996), p. 99.

the most complex behaviors. The basic teacher behaviors are those that produce the following results: (1) students are physically and mentally engaged in learning activities, (2) instructional time is efficiently used, and (3) classroom distractions and interruptions are minimal.

Third, the effectiveness with which a teacher carries out the basic behaviors can be measured by how well students learn. This last point is the topic of Chapter 11.

The basic teacher behaviors that facilitate student learning are: (1) structuring the learning environment, (2) accepting and sharing instructional accountability, (3) demonstrating withitness and overlapping, (4) providing a variety of motivating and challenging lessons, (5) modeling appropriate behaviors, (6) facilitating student acquisition of data, (7) creating a psychologically safe environment, (8) clarifying whenever necessary, (9) using periods of silence, and (10) questioning thoughtfully.

Facilitating Behaviors and Instructional Strategies: A Clarification

Clearly at least some of the ten behaviors are also instructional strategies. Questioning is one example. The difference is that while the behaviors must be in place for the most effective teaching to occur, strategies—discussed in Part III—are more or less discretionary; that is, they are pedagogical techniques from which you may select but may not be obligated to use. For example, questioning and the use of silence are fundamental teaching behaviors, whereas lecturing and showing videos are not. Thus, you see, your task is two-fold: (1) develop your awareness of and skills in using the fundamental teach-

ing behaviors, and (2) develop your repertoire and skills in selecting and using appropriate instructional strategies.

Starting now and continuing throughout your teaching career, you will want to evaluate your developing competency for each of the ten fundamental facilitating behaviors and improve in areas where you need help. Consider the following descriptions and examples, and discuss them in your class.

Structuring the Learning Environment

Structuring the learning environment means establishing an intellectual, psychological, and physical environment that enables all students to act and react productively. Specifically, you:

- Attend to the organization of the classroom as a learning laboratory to establish a positive, safe, and efficient environment for student learning.
- Establish and maintain clearly understood classroom procedures, definitions, instructions, and expectations. Help students to clarify the learning expectations and to establish clearly understood learning objectives.
- Help students assume tasks and responsibilities, thereby empowering them in their learning.
- Organize the students, helping them to organize their learning. Help students in the identification and their understanding of time and resource constraints. Provide instructional scaffolds, such as building bridges to student learning by helping students connect that which is being learned with what the students already know or think they know and have experienced.

The effective teacher establishes an intellectual, psychological, and physical environment that enables students to act and react productively.

- Plan and implement techniques for schema building, such as providing content and process outlines, visual diagrams, and opportunities for concept mapping.
- Use techniques for students' metacognitive development, such as: *think-pair share*, in which students are asked to think about an idea, share thoughts about it with a partner, and then share the pair's thoughts with the entire class; *think-write-pair-share*, in which each student writes his or her ideas about the new word and then shares in pairs before sharing with the entire class; and *jigsaw*, in which individuals or small groups of students are given responsibilities for separate tasks which lead to a bigger task or understanding, thereby putting together parts to make a whole (as demonstrated by Exercise 3.5).
- Plan units and lessons that have clear and concise beginnings and endings with at least some of the planning done collaboratively with the students.
- Provide frequent summary reviews, often by using student self-assessment of what is being learned. Structure and facilitate ongoing formal and informal discussion based on a shared understanding of rules of discourse.

Accepting and Sharing Instructional Accountability

While holding students accountable for their learning, the teacher is willing to be held accountable for the effectiveness of the learning process and outcomes (the "locus of control" as discussed at the start of this chapter). Specifically, you:

- Assume a responsibility for professional decision making and in the risks associated with that responsibility. Share some responsibility for decision making and risk taking with the students. A primary goal in the education of K–12 students must be to see that they become accountable for themselves as learners and as citizens. To some degree, teachers are advised to work with their students as *partners* in their learning and development. One dimension of the partnership is sharing accountability. One effective way of doing that is by using student portfolios (discussed in Chapters 5 and 11).
- Communicate clearly to parents, administrators, and colleagues.
- Communicate to the students that accomplishment of learning goals and objectives is a responsibility they share with you.
- Plan exploratory activities that engage students in the learning.
- Provide continuous cues for desired learning behaviors and incentives contingent upon desired performance, such as grades, points, rewards, and privileges. Establish a clearly understood and continuous

program of assessment that includes reflection and self-assessment.
- Provide opportunities for the students to demonstrate their learning, to refine and explore their questions, and to share their thinking and results.

Demonstrating Withitness and Overlapping

Withitness and overlapping, first described by Kounin, are separate but closely related behaviors.[7] *Withitness* is your awareness of the whole group. *Overlapping* is your ability to attend to several matters simultaneously. (Further discussion and guidelines for developing these two skills are presented in Chapter 4.) Specifically, you:

- Attend to the entire class while working with one student or with a small group of students, communicating this awareness with eye contact, hand gestures, body position and language, and clear but private verbal cues.
- Continually and simultaneously monitor all classroom activities to keep students at their tasks and to provide students with assistance and resources.
- Continue monitoring the class during any distraction such as when a visitor enters the classroom or while the students are on a field trip.
- Demonstrate an understanding of when comprehension checks and instructional transitions are appropriate or needed.
- Dwell on one topic only as long as necessary for the students' understandings.
- Quickly intervene and redirect potential undesirable student behavior (see Chapter 4).
- Refocus or shift activities for a student when that student's attention begins to fade.

Providing a Variety of Motivating and Challenging Activities

The effective teacher uses a variety of activities that motivate and challenge all students to work to the utmost of their abilities and that engage and challenge the preferred learning styles and learning capacities of more of the students more of the time. Specifically, you:

- Demonstrate optimism toward each student's ability.
- Demonstrate an unwavering expectation that each student will work to the best of his or her ability.
- Show pride, optimism, and enthusiasm in learning, thinking, and teaching.
- View teaching and learning as an organic and reciprocal process that extends well beyond that which can be referred to as the traditional 2 by 4 by 6 curriculum—

---

[7]J. S. Kounin, *Discipline and Group Management in Classrooms* (New York: Holt, Rinehart and Winston, 1970).

that is, a curriculum bound by the two covers of the textbook, the four walls of the classroom, and the six hours of the school day.

- With the students, plan exciting and interesting learning activities, including those that engage the students' natural interest in the mysterious and novel.

Modeling Appropriate Behaviors

Effective teachers model the very behaviors expected of their students. Specifically, you:

- Arrive promptly in the classroom and demonstrate on-task behaviors for the entire class meeting just as is expected of the students.
- Demonstrate respect for all students. For example, you do not interrupt when a student is showing rational thinking, even though you may disagree with or frown upon the words used or the direction of the student's thinking.
- Demonstrate that making "errors" is a natural event in learning and during problem solving, and readily admit and correct mistakes you make.
- Are prompt in returning student papers and offer comments that provide instructive and encouraging feedback.
- Model and emphasize the skills, attitudes, and values of higher-order intellectual processes. Demonstrate rational problem-solving skills and explain to the students the processes engaged in problem solving.[8]
- Model professionalism by spelling correctly, using proper grammar, and writing clearly and legibly.
- Practice communication that is clear, precise, and to the point. For example, use "I" when referring to yourself and "we" when "we" is meant. Rather than responding to student contributions with simply "good" or "okay," tell specifically what about the response was good or what made it okay.
- Practice moments of silence (see section on "Using Periods of Silence" that follows), thus modeling thoughtfulness, reflectiveness, and restraint of impulsiveness.
- Realizing that students are also models for other students, reinforce appropriate student behaviors, and intervene when behaviors are not appropriate (discussed in the next chapter).

Facilitating Student Acquisition of Data

The teacher makes sure that data are accessible to students as input they can process. Specifically, you:

- Ensure that sources of information are readily available for students' use. Select books, media, and materials that facilitate student learning. Assure that equipment and materials are readily available for students to use. Identify and use resources beyond the walls of the classroom and the boundaries of the school campus.
- Create a responsive classroom environment with direct learning experiences.
- Ensure that major ideas receive proper attention and emphasis.
- Provide clear and specific instructions.
- Provide feedback and feedback mechanisms about each student's performance and progress. Encourage students to organize and maintain devices to self-monitor their progress in learning and thinking (discussed in Chapter 11).
- Select anchoring examples that help students bridge what is being learned with what they already know and have experienced.
- Serve as a resource person and use cooperative learning, thus regarding students as resources, too.

Creating a Psychologically Safe Environment

To encourage the positive development of student self-esteem, to provide a psychologically safe learning environment, and to encourage the most creative thought and behavior, the teacher provides an attractive and stimulating classroom environment and appropriate nonevaluative and nonjudgmental responses. Specifically, you:

- Avoid negative criticism. Criticism is often a negative value judgment, and "when a teacher responds to a student's ideas or actions with such negative words as 'poor,' 'incorrect,' or 'wrong,' the response tends to signal inadequacy or disapproval and ends the student's thinking about the task."[9]
- Frequently use minimal reinforcement (that is, nonjudgmental acceptance behaviors, such as nodding head, writing a student's response on the board, or saying "I understand"). Whereas elaborate or strong praise is generally unrelated to student achievement, minimal reinforcement, using words like "right," "okay," "good," "uh-huh," and "thank you," correlates with achievement.

However, be careful with a too frequent and thereby ineffective and even damaging use of the single word "good" following student contributions during a class discussion. Use the word only when the contribution was truly that—good—and better yet, say not only "good" but tell what specifically was good about the contribution. That provides a more powerful reinforcement by demonstrating that you truly heard the student's contribution and thus truly thought it was good.

---

[8]See, for example, J. W. Astington, "Theory of Mind Goes to School," *Educational Leadership* 56(3):46–48 (November 1998).

[9]Costa, *The School as a Home for the Mind*, p. 54.

Serving as a resource person, the competent teacher plans within the lessons activities and behaviors that show respect for the experiences and ideas of individual students, thus regarding students as resources, too.

Statement of Praise	*Statement of Encouragement*
1. Your painting is excellent.	1. It is obvious that you enjoy painting.
2. I am delighted that you behaved so well on our class field trip.	2. I am so delighted that we all enjoyed the class field trip.
3. You did a good job on those word problems.	3. I can tell that you have been working and are enjoying it more.
4. Your oral report on your project was well done.	4. I can tell that you got really interested in your topic for the oral report on your project.
5. Great answer Louise!	5. Louise, your answer shows that you gave a lot of thought to the question.

Figure 3.3   Examples of statements of praise versus encouragement.

- Infrequently use elaborate or strong praise. By the time students are beyond the primary grades, teacher praise, a positive value judgment, has little or no value as a form of positive reinforcement. When praise is used for students in grades four and above, it should be mild, private, and for student accomplishment, rather than for effort; for each student, the frequency in using praise should be gradually reduced. When praise is reduced, a more diffused sociometric pattern develops, that is, more of the students become directly and productively involved in the learning. Authors Good and Brophy emphasize that praise should be simple and direct, delivered in a natural voice without dramatizing. Students see overt theatrics as insincere.[10]

Let us take pause to consider this point. Probably no statement in this resource guide raises more eye-

brows than the statement that praise for most middle and upper grade students has little or no value as a form of positive reinforcement. After all, praise may well motivate some people. However, at what cost? Praise and encouragement are often confused and considered to be the same (see Figure 3.3), but they are not, and they do not have the same long-term results. Consider this explanation:

For many years there has been a great campaign for the virtues of praise in helping children gain a positive self-concept and improve their behavior. This is another time when we must "beware of what works." Praise may inspire some children to improve their behavior. The problem is that they become pleasers and approval "junkies." These children (and later these adults) develop self-concepts that are totally dependent on the opinions of others. Other children resent and rebel against praise, either because they don't want to live up to the expectations of others or because they fear they can't compete with those who seem to get praise so easily. The alternative that considers long-range effects is encouragement. The long-range effect

---

[10]T. L. Good and J. E. Brophy, *Looking in Classrooms,* 7th ed., (New York: Longman, 1977), p. 144–147.

of encouragement is self-confidence. The long-range effect of praise is dependence on others.[11]

- Perceive your classroom as the place where you work and students learn, and make that place of work and the tools available a place of pride, as stimulating and useful as possible.
- Plan within the lessons behaviors that show respect for the experiences and ideas of individual students.
- Provide positive individual student attention as often as possible. Write sincere reinforcing personalized comments on student papers. Provide incentives and rewards for student accomplishments.
- Use nonverbal cues to show awareness and acceptance of individual students. Use paraphrasing and reflective listening. Use empathic acceptance of a student's expression of feelings; demonstrate by words and gestures that you understand the student's position.

Clarifying Whenever Necessary

Your responding behavior seeks further elaboration from a student about that student's idea or comprehension. Specifically, you:

- Help students to connect new content to that previously learned. Help students relate content of a lesson to their other school and nonschool experiences. Help students make learning connections between disciplines.
- Politely invite a student to be more specific, to elaborate on or rephrase an idea, or to provide a concrete illustration of an idea.
- Provide frequent opportunity for summary reviews.
- Repeat or paraphrase a student's response, allowing the student to correct any other person's misinterpretation of what the student said or implied.
- Select instructional strategies that help students correct their prior notions about a topic.

Using Periods of Silence

Use periods of silence in the classroom. Specifically, you:

- Actively listen when a student is talking.
- Keep silent when students are working quietly or are attending to a visual display, and maintain classroom control by using nonverbal signals and indirect intervention strategies.
- Pause while talking to allow for thinking and reflection.
- Use teacher silence to stimulate group discussion.

---

[11]J. Nelsen, *Positive Discipline* (New York: Ballantine Books, 1987), p. 103. See also L. A. Froyen, *Classroom Management: The Reflective Teacher-Leader,* 2d ed. (Upper Saddle River, NJ: Prentice Hall, 1993), pp. 294–298.

- Allow sufficient think-time, as long as nine seconds, after asking a question or posing a problem. (See "wait-time" in Chapter 7.)

Questioning Thoughtfully

Use thoughtfully worded questions to induce learning and to stimulate thinking and the development of students' thinking skills. (Questioning is the topic of Chapter 7.) Specifically, you:

- Encourage student questioning, without judging the quality or relevancy of a student's question. Attend to student questions, and respond and encourage other students to respond, often by building upon the content of a student's questions and student responses.
- Help students develop their own questioning skills and provide opportunities for students to explore their own ideas, to obtain data, and to find answers to their own questions and solutions to their problems.
- Plan questioning sequences that elicit a variety of thinking skills and that maneuver students to higher levels of thinking and doing.
- Use a variety of types of questions.
- Use questions to help students to explore their knowledge, to develop new understandings, and to discover ways of applying their new understandings.

SUMMARY

You have reviewed the realities of the responsibilities of today's teacher. Being a good teacher takes time, commitment, concentrated effort, and plain hard work. Nobody truly knowledgeable about it ever said that good teaching was easy.

You have learned that your professional responsibilities as a classroom teacher will extend well beyond the four walls of the classroom, the six hours of the school day, the five days of the school week, and the 180 days of the school year. You learned of the many expectations: (1) to demonstrate effective decision making; (2) to be committed to young people, to the school's mission, and to the profession; (3) to develop facilitating behaviors and to provide effective instruction; and (4) to fulfill numerous noninstructional responsibilities. As you have read and discussed these responsibilities, you should have begun to comprehend more fully the challenge and reality of being a competent classroom teacher.

Teaching style is the way teachers teach, their distinctive mannerisms complemented by their choices of teaching behaviors and strategies. Style develops from tradition, from one's beliefs and experiences, and from one's knowledge of research findings. You analyzed your own beliefs, observed one teacher and that teacher's style for that lesson, and began the development of your philosophy about teaching and learning, a philosophical statement that should be useful to you during later job interviews (see Chapter 12).

Exciting research findings continue to emerge from several, and related, areas: about learning, conceptual development, thinking styles, and neurophysiology. The findings continue to support the hypothesis that a classroom teacher's best teaching style choice is eclectic with a bent toward the facilitating, at least until the day arrives when students of certain thinking styles can be practically matched to teachers with particular teaching styles. Future research will undoubtedly shed additional light on the relationships among pedagogy, pedagogical styles, and student thinking and learning.

Today, there seems to be much agreement that the essence of the learning process is a combined self-awareness, self-monitoring, and active reflection. Young people learn these skills best when exposed to teachers who themselves effectively model those same behaviors. The most effective teaching and learning is an interactive process that involves not only learning but also thinking about learning and learning how to learn.

The next and final chapter of Part I of this resource guide presents ways of establishing an effective learning environment within which to carry out your professional responsibilities.

QUESTIONS FOR CLASS DISCUSSION

1. Explain the meaning of each of the following two concepts and why you agree or disagree with each. (a) The teacher should hold high, although not necessarily identical, expectations for all students and never waver from those expectations. (b) The teacher should not be controlled by a concern to "cover" the content of the textbook by the end of the school term.

2. More than a third century ago, the publication *Six Areas of Teacher Competencies* (Burlingame, CA: California Teachers Association, 1964) identified six roles of the classroom teacher: director of learning, counselor and guidance worker, mediator of the culture, link with the community, member of the school staff, and member of the profession. When compared with that, have the roles changed for today's classroom teacher? If so, how?

3. Identify a public school teacher you consider to be competent and compare what you recall about that teacher's classroom with the characteristics of competent teachers as presented in this chapter. Share your comparison with others in the class.

4. Before studying this chapter, were you fully aware of the extent of a classroom teacher's responsibilities? Explain your response.

5. Compare the teacher's use of praise and of encouragement for student work; describe specific classroom situations in which each is more appropriate.

6. In *Educating the Reflective Practitioner* (San Francisco: Jossey-Bass, 1987), author Donald Schon speaks of "reflection-on-action," "reflection-in-action," and "reflection-for-action." Read about and compare Schon's three types of reflections with the four phases of decision making and thought processing presented and discussed at the beginning of this chapter.

7. Explain how you now feel about being a classroom teacher. Do you feel motivated, excited, enthusiastic, befuddled, confused, and/or depressed? Explain and discuss your current feelings with your classmates. Sort out common concerns and design avenues for dealing with any negative feelings you might have.

8. Describe any prior concepts you held that changed as a result of your experiences with this chapter. Describe the changes.

9. From your current observations and field work as related to this teacher preparation program, clearly identify one specific example of educational practice that seems contradictory to exemplary practice or theory as presented in this chapter. Present your explanation for the discrepancy.

10. Do you have other questions generated by the content of this chapter? If you do, list them along with ways answers might be found.

FOR FURTHER READING

Bellanca, J. "Teaching for Intelligence: In Search of Best Practices." *Phi Delta Kappan* 79(9):658–660 (May 1998).

Duffy, G. G. "Teaching and the Balancing of Round Stones." *Phi Delta Kappan* 79(10):777–780 (June 1998).

Freiberg, H. J. (Editor). *Perceiving, Behaving, Becoming: Lessons Learned.* Alexandria, VA: Association for Supervision and Curriculum Development, 1999.

Jensen, E. "Emotions and Learning." Chapter 8 of E. Jensen, *Teaching With the Brain in Mind.* Alexandria, VA: Association for Supervision and Curriculum Development, 1998.

Lasley II, T. J. "Paradigm Shifts in the Classroom." *Phi Delta Kappan* 80(1): 84–86 (September 1998).

Mills, R. A. "Expert Teaching and Successful Learning at the Middle Level: One Teacher's Story." *Middle School Journal* 29(1):30–39 (September 1997).

Palmer, P. J. *The Courage to Teach: Exploring the Inner Landscape of a Teacher's Life.* San Francisco: Jossey-Bass, 1998.

Perie, M., et al. *Time Spent Teaching Core Academic Subjects in Elementary Schools. Comparisons across Community, School, Teacher, and Student Characteristics. Statistical Analysis Report.* Washington, DC: National Center for Education Statistics, U.S. Government Printing Office, 1997.

Wassermann, S. "Shazam! You're a Teacher." *Phi Delta Kappa* 80(6):464, 466–468 (February 1999).

Wilson-Saddler, D. "Using Effective Praise to Produce Positive Results in the Classroom." *Teaching and Change* 4(4):338–357 (Summer 1997).

Wubbels, T., Levy, J., and Brekelmans, M. "Paying Attention to Relationships." *Educational Leadership* 54(7):82–86 (April 1997).

Chapter 4

Establishing and Maintaining an Effective, Safe, and Supportive Classroom Learning Environment

To become and to remain an effective teacher with a minimum of distractions in the classroom, you must (1) apply your knowledge of the characteristics and developmental needs of students with whom you work (Chapters 1 and 2), (2) practice the behaviors that facilitate their learning (Chapter 3), and (3) do so in a conducive learning environment. That final requirement is the principal focus of this chapter. The establishment and maintenance of a conducive classroom learning environment derive from one's knowledge about students and how they learn and from careful thought and planning. These responsibilities should not be left for the beginning teacher to learn on the job in a sink-or-swim situation.

A conducive classroom learning environment is one that is psychologically safe, that helps the students to perceive the importance of what is being taught, that helps them realize they can achieve, and that is instructive in the procedures for learning. While it is important that they learn to control impulses and delay their need for gratification (see "characteristics of intelligent behavior" in Chapter 9), students are more willing to spend time on a learning task when they perceive value or reward in doing so, when they possess some ownership in planning and carrying out the task, and when they feel they can accomplish the task. Thoughtful and thorough planning of your procedures for classroom management is as important a part of your preactive phase of instruction (discussed in Chapter 3) as is the preparation of units and lessons (discussed in the chapters that follow in Part II). Indeed, an analysis of fifty years of research studies concludes that classroom management is the single most important factor influencing student learning.[1]

This chapter presents guidelines and resources that will help you to establish and manage a classroom environment that is safe for the students and favorable to their learning. Specifically, upon completion of this chapter you should be able to

1. Identify characteristics of a classroom environment that is both safe for students and favorable to their learning.
2. Describe perceptions that must be in place and why they must be in place.
3. Prepare your written management system.
4. Explain how you will know if you have classroom control and are an effective manager of learning.
5. Explain the difference between direct and indirect intervention to refocus a student and describe situations where you would be most likely to use each, thereby demonstrating that you have begun building your repertoire of understandings of a teacher's options in specific classroom situations.
6. Describe by examples how each of the following contributes to effective classroom control: a positive approach, well-planned lessons, a good start of the school term, classroom procedures and rules, consistency but with professional judgment in enforcing procedures and rules, correction of student misbehavior, and classroom management.

---

[1] M. C. Want, G. D. Haertel, and H. J. Walberg, "What Helps Students Learn?" *Educational Leadership* 51(4):74–79 (December 1993/January 1994).

7. Describe means you can use to help students establish self-control.
8. Demonstrate knowledge of basic legal guidelines for the classroom teacher.

THE IMPORTANCE OF PERCEPTIONS

Unless you believe your students can learn, they will not. Unless you believe you can teach them, you will not. Unless your students believe they can learn and until they want to learn, they will not.

We all know of or have heard of teachers who get the very best from their students, even from those students that many teachers find to be the most challenging to teach. Regardless of individual circumstances, those teachers (a) *know* that, when given adequate support, all students can learn, (b) *expect* the best from each student, (c) establish a classroom environment that motivates students to do their best, and (d) manage their classrooms so class time is efficiently used with the least amount of distraction to the learning process.

Regardless of how well planned you are for the instruction, certain perceptions by students must be in place to support the successful implementation of those plans. Students must perceive (1) the classroom environment as being supportive of their efforts, (2) you care about their learning and they are welcome in your classroom, (3) the expected learning as being challenging but not impossible, and (4) the anticipated learning outcomes as being worthy of their time and effort to try to achieve.

CLASSROOM CONTROL: ITS MEANING—PAST AND PRESENT

Classroom control frequently is of the greatest concern to beginning teachers—and they have good cause to be concerned. Even experienced teachers sometimes find control difficult, particularly at middle and upper grades where so many students come to school with so much psychological baggage and have already become alienated as the result of negative experiences in their lives.

In one respect, being a classroom teacher is much like being a truck driver who must remain alert while going down a steep and winding grade; otherwise, the truck most assuredly will get out of control, veer off the highway, and crash. This chapter has been thoughtfully designed to help you with your concerns about control—and to help you avoid a crash.

Historical Meaning of Classroom Control

To set the stage for your comprehension, consider what the term *classroom control* has meant historically and what it means today. In the 1800s, instead of classroom control, educators spoke of *classroom discipline*, and that meant punishment. Such an interpretation was consistent with the then-popular learning theory that assumed children were innately bad and that inappropriate behavior could be prevented by strictness, or treated with punishment. Schools of the mid-1800s have been described as being "wild and unruly places," and "full of idleness and disorder."[2]

By the early 1900s, educators were asking, "Why are the children still misbehaving?" The accepted answer was that the children were misbehaving *because* of the rigid punitive system. On this point, the era of progressive education began, providing students more freedom to decide what they would learn. The teacher's job, then, became one of providing a rich classroom of resources and materials to stimulate the student's natural curiosity. Since the system no longer would be causing misbehavior, punishment would no longer be necessary. Classes of the 1930s that were highly permissive, however, turned out to cause more anxiety than the restrictive classes of the 1800s.

Today's Meaning of Classroom Control and the Concept of Classroom Management

Today, rather than classroom discipline, educators talk of classroom control, the process of controlling student behavior in the classroom. The most effective teacher is one who is in control of classroom events rather than controlled by them. Classroom control is an important aspect of the broader concept of classroom management. Classroom control is part of a management plan designed to (1) prevent inappropriate student behaviors, (2) help students develop self-control, and (3) suggest procedures for dealing with inappropriate student behaviors.

Effective teaching requires a well-organized, businesslike classroom in which motivated students work diligently at their learning tasks, free from distractions and interruptions. Providing such a setting for learning requires careful thought and preparation and is called effective *classroom management*. Effective classroom management is the process of organizing and conducting a classroom to maximize student learning.

A teacher's procedures for classroom control reflect that teacher's philosophy about how children learn and the teacher's interpretation and commitment to the school's stated mission. In sum, those procedures represent the teacher's concept of classroom management. Although often eclectic in their approaches, today's teachers share a concern for selecting management techniques that enhance student self-esteem and

---

[2] I. A. Hyman and J. D'Allessandro, "Oversimplifying the Discipline Problem," *Education Week* 3(29):24 (April 11, 1984).

Table 4.1   Comparing Approaches to Classroom Management

Authority	To Know What is Going On	To Provide Smooth Transitions
Canter/Jones	Realize that the student has the right to choose how to behave in your class with the understanding of the consequences that will follow his or her choice.	Insist on decent, responsible behavior.
Dreikurs/Nelsen/Albert	Realize that the student wants status, recognition, and a feeling of belonging. Misbehavior is associated with mistaken goals of getting attention, seeking power, getting revenge, and wanting to be left alone.	Identify a mistaken student goal; act in ways that do not reinforce these goals.
Ginott/Kohn	Communicate with the student to find out his/her feelings about a situation and about his/herself.	Invite student cooperation.
Glasser/Gordon	Realize that the student is a rational being; he/she can control his or her own behavior.	Help the student make good choices; good choices produce good behavior, and bad choices produce bad behavior.
Kounin	Develop *withitness,* a skill enabling you to see what is happening in all parts of the classroom at all times.	Avoid jerkiness, which consists of thrusts (giving directions before your group is ready), dangles (leaving one activity dangling in the verbal air, starting another one, and then returning to the first activity), flip-flops (terminating one activity, beginning another one, and then returning to the first activity you terminated).
Skinner	Realize value of nonverbal interaction (i.e., smiles, pats, and handshakes) to communicate to students that you know what is going on.	Realize that smooth transitions may be part of your procedures for awarding reinforcers (i.e., points and tokens) to reward appropriate behavior.

that help students learn how to assume control of their behavior and ownership of their learning.

Although some schools and school districts subscribe heavily to one approach or another, such as the Fred Jones model or Gordon's Teacher Effectiveness Training (TET) model, many others are more eclectic, having evolved from the historical works of several leading authorities. Let's consider what some authorities have said. To assist your understanding, refer to Table 4.1, which illustrates the main ideas of each authority and provides a comparison of their recommended approaches. The guidelines and suggestions

that are presented throughout this chapter represent an eclectic approach, borrowing from many of these authorities.

Classroom Management: Contributions of Some Leading Authorities

You are probably familiar with the term *behavior modification,* which describes several high-control techniques for changing behavior in an observable and predictable way; with **B. F. Skinner's** (1904–1990) ideas about how students learn and how behavior can be

To Maintain Group Alertness	To Involve Students	To Attend to Misbehavior
Set clear limits and consequences; follow through consistently; state what you expect; state the consequences and why the limits are needed.	Use firm tone of voice; keep eye contact; use nonverbal gestures and verbal statements; use hints, questions, and direct messages in requesting student behavior; give and receive compliments.	Follow through with your promises and the reasonable, previously stated consequences that have been established in your class.
Provide firm guidance and leadership.	Allow students to have a say in establishing rules and consequences in your class.	Make it clear that unpleasant consequences will follow inappropriate behavior.
Model the behavior you expect to see in your students.	Build student's self-esteem.	Give a message that addresses the situation and does not attack the student's character.
Understand that class rules are essential.	Realize that classroom meetings are effective means for attending to rules, behavior, and discipline.	Accept no excuses for inappropriate behavior; see that reasonable consequences always follow.
Avoid slowdowns (delays and time wasting) that can be caused by overdwelling (too much time spent on explanations) and by fragmentation (breaking down an activity into several unnecessary steps). Develop a group focus (active participation by all students in the group) through accountability (holding all students accountable for the concept of the lesson) and by attention (seeing all the students and using unison and individual responses).	Avoid boredom by providing a feeling of progress for the students, by offering challenges, by varying class activities, by changing the level of intellectual challenge, by varying lesson presentations, and by using many different learning materials and aids.	Understand that teacher correction influences behavior of other nearby students (the ripple effect).
Set rules, rewards, and consequences; emphasize that responsibility for good behavior rests with each student.	Involve students in "token economies," in contracts, and in charting behavior performance.	Provide tangibles to students who follow the class rules; represent tangibles as "points" for the whole class to use to "purchase" a special activity.

modified by using reinforcers (rewards); and with how his principles of behavior shaping have been extended by others.[3]

Behavior modification begins with four steps: (1) identify the behavior to be modified; (2) record how often and under what conditions that behavior occurs; (3) cause a change by reinforcing a desired behavior with a positive reinforcer (a reward); and (4) choose the type of positive reinforcers to award. Those rewards may include:

- *Activity or privilege reinforcers,* such as choice of playing a game, running the projection equipment for the teacher, caring for a classroom pet, free reading, decorating the classroom, free art time, choice at a learning center, freedom without penalty from doing an assignment or test, or running an errand for the teacher

- *Social reinforcers,* such as verbal attention or praise, nonverbal rewards such as proximity of teacher to student, and facial (such as a wink) or bodily expressions (such as a handshake or pat on the back) of approval

[3] See B. F. Skinner, *The Technology of Teaching* (New York: Appleton-Century-Crofts, 1968) and *Beyond Freedom and Dignity* (New York: Knopf, 1971).

- *Graphic reinforcers,* such as numerals and symbols made by rubber stamps
- *Tangible reinforcers,* such as candy and other edibles, badges, certificates, stickers, and books
- *Token reinforcers,* such as points, stars, or script or tickets that can be accumulated and cashed in later for a tangible reinforcer, such as a trip to the pizza store or ice cream store with the teacher

Lee Canter, a child guidance specialist, and **Marlene Canter,** a specialist in teaching people with learning disabilities, developed their *assertive discipline* model. Using an approach that emphasizes both reinforcement for appropriate behaviors and punishment or consequences for inappropriate behaviors, their model emphasizes four major points. First, as a teacher, you have professional rights in your classroom and should expect appropriate student behavior. Second, your students have rights to choose how to behave in your classroom, and you should plan limits for inappropriate behavior. Third, an assertive discipline approach means you clearly state your expectations in a firm voice and explain the boundaries for behavior. And fourth, you should plan a system of positive consequences (e.g., positive messages home, awards and rewards, special privileges) for appropriate behavior and establish consequences (e.g., time out, withdrawal of privileges, parent conference) for inappropriate student misbehavior. Consistent follow-through is necessary.[4]

With a *logical consequences* approach, **Rudolf Dreikurs** (1897–1972), a psychiatrist specializing in child and family counseling, emphasized six points. First, be fair, firm, and friendly, and involve your students in developing and implementing class rules. Second, students need to clearly understand the rules and the logical consequences for misbehavior. For example, a logical consequence for a student who has painted graffiti on a school wall would be either to clean the wall or pay for a school custodian to do it. Third, allow the students to be responsible not only for their own actions but also for influencing others to maintain appropriate behavior in your classroom. Fourth, encourage students to show respect for themselves and for others, and provide each student with a sense of belonging to the class. Fifth, recognize and encourage student goals of belonging, gaining status, and gaining recognition. Sixth, recognize but do not reinforce correlated student goals of getting attention, seeking power, and taking revenge.[5]

Continuing the work of Dreikurs, **Linda Albert,** a former student of Dreikurs, has developed *cooperative discipline,* a detailed discipline system that is being used in many schools throughout the country. The cooperative discipline model makes use of Dreikurs' fundamental concepts, with emphasis added on Three Cs: capable, connect, and contribute.[6]

Also building upon the work of Dreikurs, psychotherapist **Jane Nelsen** provides guidelines for helping children developing positive feelings of self. Key points made by Nelsen and reflected throughout this resource guide are (a) use natural and logical consequences as a means to inspire a positive classroom atmosphere, (b) understand that children have goals that drive them toward misbehavior (attention, power, revenge, and assumed adequacy), (c) use kindness (student retains dignity) and firmness when administering consequences for a student's misbehavior, (d) establish a climate of mutual respect, (e) use class meetings to give students ownership in problem solving, and (f) offer encouragement as a means of inspiring self-evaluation and focusing on students' behaviors.[7]

Psychiatrist **William Glasser** developed his concept of *reality therapy* (i.e., the condition of the present, rather than of the past, contributes to inappropriate behavior) for the classroom. Glasser emphasizes that students have a responsibility to learn at school and to maintain appropriate behavior while there. He stresses that with the teacher's help, students can make appropriate choices about their behavior in school and can, in fact, learn self-control.[8] Finally, he suggests holding classroom meetings that are devoted to establishing class rules, identifying standards for student behavior, matters of misbehavior, and the consequences of misbehavior. Since the publication of his first book in 1965, Glasser has expanded his message to include the student needs of belonging and love, control, freedom, and fun, asserting that if these needs are ignored and unattended at school, children are bound to fail.[9] Today's commitment to *quality education* (see Chapters 1 and 8) is largely derived from the recent work of Glasser. In schools committed to quality education, stu-

---

[4] See L. Canter and M. Canter, *Assertive Discipline: Positive Behavior Management for Today's Schools,* rev. ed. (Santa Monica, CA: Lee Canter & Associates, 1992).

[5] See R. Dreikurs and P. Cassel, *Discipline Without Tears* (New York: Hawthorne Books, 1972), and R. Dreikurs, B. B. Grunwald, and F. C. Pepper, *Maintaining Sanity in the Classroom: Classroom Management Techniques,* 2d ed. (New York: Harper & Row, 1982).

[6] L. Albert, *A Teacher's Guide to Cooperative Discipline: How to Manage Your Classroom and Promote Self-Esteem* (Circle Pines, MN: American Guidance Service, 1989, revised 1996).

[7] J. Nelsen, *Positive Discipline,* 2d ed. (New York: Ballantine Books, 1987) and J. Nelsen, L. Lott, and H. S. Glenn, *Positive Discipline in the Classroom: How to Effectively Use Class Meetings and Other Positive Discipline Strategies* (Rocklin, CA: Prima Publishing, 1993).

[8] See, for example, W. Glasser, "A New Look at School Failure and School Success," *Phi Delta Kappan* 78(8):597–602 (April 1997).

[9] See W. Glasser, *Reality Therapy: A New Approach to Psychiatry* (New York: Harper & Row, 1965), *Schools Without Failure* (New York: Harper & Row, 1969), *Control Theory in the Classroom* (New York: Harper & Row, 1986), *The Quality School* (New York: Harper & Row, 1990), and *The Quality School Teacher* (New York: HarperPerennial, 1993).

dents feel a sense of belonging, enjoy some degree of power, have fun learning, and experience a sense of freedom in the process.

Psychologist **Haim G. Ginott** (1922–1973) emphasized ways for teacher and student to communicate in his *communication model.* He advised teachers to send a clear message (or messages) about situations rather than about the children. He stressed that teachers must model the behavior they expect from students.[10] Ginott's suggested messages are those that express feelings appropriately, acknowledge students' feelings, give appropriate direction, and invite cooperation.

In his book *Discipline That Works: Promoting Self-Discipline in Children* (New York: Penguin, 1989), clinical psychologist **Thomas Gordon** emphasizes influence over control and decries use of reinforcement (i.e., rewards and punishment) as ineffective tools for achieving a positive influence over a child's behavior. Rather than using reinforcements for appropriate behavior and punishment for inappropriate behaviors, Gordon advocates encouragement and development of student self-control and self-regulated behavior. To have a positive influence and to encourage self-control the teacher (and school) should provide a rich and positive learning environment, with rich and stimulating learning activities. Specific teacher behaviors include active listening, sending I-messages (rather than you-messages), shifting from I-messages to listening when a student resists an I-message, clearly identifying ownership of problems to the student when such is the case (i.e., not assuming ownership if it is a student's problem), and encouraging collaborative problem solving.

Psychologist **Fredric Jones** promotes the idea of helping students support their own self-control by way of a negative reinforcement method in which rewards follow good behavior.[11] Preferred activity time (PAT), for example, is an invention derived from the Jones model. The Jones model makes four recommendations. First, you should properly structure your classroom so students understand the rules and procedures. Second, you maintain control by selecting appropriate instructional strategies. Third, you build patterns of cooperative work. Finally, you develop appropriate backup methods for dealing with inappropriate student behavior.

Jacob Kounin is well known for his identification of the *ripple effect,* or the effect of a teacher's response to one student's misbehavior on students whose behavior was appropriate. Kounin also focused on *withitness,* the teacher's ability to remain alert in the classroom and spot quickly and redirect potential student misbehavior, which is analogous to having "eyes in the back of your head."[12] In addition to being alert to everything going on in the classroom, another characteristic of a "withit" teacher is the ability to attend to the right student.

GUIDELINES FOR DEVELOPING WITHITNESS Consider the following guidelines for developing withitness.

- Avoid spending too much time with any one student or group; longer than 30 seconds may be approaching "too much time."
- Avoid turning your back to all or a portion of the students, such as when writing on the writing board.
- If two or more errant behaviors are occurring simultaneously in different locations, attend to the most serious first, while giving the other(s) a nonverbal gesture showing your awareness (such as by eye contact) and displeasure (such as by a frown).
- Involve all students in the act, not just any one student or group. Avoid concentrating on only those who appear most interested or responsive, sometimes referred to as the "chosen few."
- Keep students alert by calling on them randomly, asking questions and calling on an answerer, circulating from group to group during team learning activities, and frequently checking on the progress of individual students.
- Maintain constant visual surveillance of the entire class, even when talking to or working with an individual or small group of students and when meeting a classroom visitor at the door.
- Move around the room. Be on top of potential misbehavior and quietly redirect student attention before the misbehavior occurs or gets out of control.
- During direct instruction try to establish eye contact with each student about once every minute. It initially may sound impossible to do, but it is not; this skill can be developed with practice.

A prerequisite to being withit is the skill to attend to more than one matter at a time. As discussed in the preceding chapter, this is referred to as the *overlapping ability.* The teacher with overlapping skills uses body language, body position, and hand signals to communicate with students. Consider the following examples of overlapping ability.

- Rather than having students bring their papers and problems to her desk, the teacher expects them to remain seated and to raise their hands as he/she circulates in the room monitoring and attending to individual students.
- The teacher takes care of attendance while visually and/or verbally monitoring the students during their warm-up activity.

[10] See H. G. Ginott, *Teacher and Child* (New York: Macmillan, 1971).

[11] F. Jones, *Positive Classroom Discipline and Positive Classroom Instruction* (both New York: McGraw-Hill, 1987).

[12] J. S. Kounin, *Discipline and Group Management in Classrooms* (New York: Holt, Rinehart & Winston, 1977).

- While attending to a messenger who has walked into the room, the teacher demonstrates verbally or by gestures that students are expected to continue their work.
- While working in a small group, a student raises his hand to get the teacher's attention. The teacher, while continuing to work with another group of students, signals with her hand to tell the student she is aware he wants her attention and will get to him quickly.
- Without missing a beat in his talk, the teacher aborts the potentially disruptive behavior of a student by gesturing, by making eye contact, or by moving closer to the student (proximity control).

Developing Your Own Effective Approach to Classroom Management

As you review these classic contributions to today's approaches to effective classroom management, the expert opinions and research evidence will remind you of the importance of doing the following: (1) concentrating your attention on desirable student behaviors, (2) quickly and appropriately attending to inappropriate behavior, (3) maintaining alertness to all that is happening in your classroom, (4) providing smooth transitions, keeping the entire class on task, and preventing dead time, (5) involving students by providing challenges, class meetings, ways of establishing rules and consequences, opportunities to receive and return compliments, and chances to build self-control and self-esteem.

Using the criteria of your own philosophy, feelings, values, knowledge, and perceptions, you are encouraged to construct a classroom environment and management system that is positive and effective for you and your students and then to apply it consistently.

PROVIDING A SUPPORTIVE LEARNING ENVIRONMENT

It is probably no surprise to hear that teachers whose classrooms are pleasant, positive, and challenging but supportive places to be find that their students learn and behave better than do the students of teachers whose classroom atmospheres are harsh, negative, repressive, and unchallenging. What follows now are specific suggestions for making your classroom a pleasant, positive, and challenging place—an environment that supports the development of meaningful understandings.

Create a Positive Classroom Atmosphere

All students should feel welcome in your classroom and accepted by you as individuals of dignity. Although these feelings and behaviors should be reciprocal—that is, expected of the students as well—they may have to begin with your frequent modeling of the behaviors expected of students. You must help students know that any denial by you of a student's specific behavior is *not* a denial of that individual as a worthwhile person who is still welcome to come to your class to learn as long as the student agrees to follow expected procedures. Specific things you can do to create a positive classroom environment, some of which are repeated from preceding chapters and others that are addressed in later chapters, are

- Admonish behavior, not persons.
- Assure that no prejudice is ever displayed against any student.
- Attend to the classroom's physical appearance and comfort. It is your place of work; show pride in that fact.
- Be an interesting person and an optimistic and enthusiastic teacher.
- Encourage students to set high yet realistic goals for themselves, and then show them how to work in increments toward meeting their goal. Let each know that you are confident in her or his ability to achieve.
- Help students develop their skills in interactive and cooperative learning.
- Involve students in every aspect of their learning, including the planning of learning activities, thereby giving them part ownership and responsibility in their learning.
- Make the learning fun, at least to the extent possible and reasonable.
- Send positive messages home to parents or guardians, even if you have to get help to write the message in the language of the student's home.
- Recognize and reward truly positive behaviors and individual successes, no matter how meager they might seem to you.
- Use interesting and motivating learning activities.

BEHAVIORS TO AVOID
Two items in the preceding list are statements about giving encouragement. When using encouragement to motivate student learning, you should avoid a few important behaviors because they inhibit learning.

- Avoid comparing one student with another, or one class of students with another.
- Avoid encouraging competition among students.
- Avoid giving up or appearing to give up on any student.
- Avoid telling a student how much better he or she could be.
- Avoid using qualifying statements, such as "I like what you did, but . . ." or "It's about time."

Get to Know Students as People to Build Intrinsic Motivation for Learning

For classes to move forward smoothly and efficiently, they should fit the learners' learning styles, learning capacities, developmental needs, and interests. To make the learning meaningful and longest lasting, build curriculum around student interests, capacities, perceptions, and perspectives (as you will learn to do in Part II that follows). Therefore, you need to know your students well enough to be able to provide learning experiences that they will find interesting, valuable, intrinsically motivating, challenging, and rewarding. Knowing your students is as important as knowing your subject. The following paragraphs describe a number of things you can do to get to know your students as people.

QUICKLY LEARN AND USE STUDENT NAMES
Like everyone else, young people appreciate being recognized and addressed by name. Quickly learning and using their names is an important motivating strategy. One technique for learning names quickly is to use a seating chart. Laminate the seating chart onto a neon-colored clipboard that you can carry in class with you. Many teachers prefer to assign permanent seats and then make seating charts from which they can unobtrusively check the roll while students are doing seat work. It is usually best to get your students into the lesson before taking roll and before doing other housekeeping chores. Ways of assigning student seating are discussed later in this chapter (see "The First Day").

Addressing students by name every time you speak to them helps you to learn and remember their names. Be sure to learn to pronounce their names correctly; that helps in making a good impression. Another helpful way to learn student names is to return papers yourself by calling student names and then handing the papers to them, paying careful attention to look at each student and making mental notes that may help you to associate names with faces.

CLASSROOM SHARING DURING
THE FIRST WEEK OF SCHOOL
During the first week of school many teachers take some time each day to have students present information about themselves and/or about the day's assignment. For instance, perhaps five or six students are selected each day to answer questions such as "What name would you like to be called by?" "Where did you attend school last year?" "Tell us about your hobbies and other interests." "What interested you about last night's reading, or yesterday's lesson." You might have your students share information of this sort with each other in groups of three or four, while you visit each group in turn.

Still another approach, good at all age levels including adults, is the "me-in-a-bag" activity. With this, each student is to bring to school a paper bag (limit the size) that contains items brought from home that represent the person. The student then is given time in class to share the items brought.

How the student answers such questions or participates in such activities can be as revealing about the student as is the information (or the lack thereof) that the student shares. From what is revealed during this sharing, you sometimes get clues about additional information you would like to solicit from the student in private or to find out from school sources.

OBSERVE STUDENTS IN THE CLASSROOM—
DEVELOP AND PRACTICE YOUR WITHITNESS
During learning activities the effective teacher is constantly moving around the classroom and is alert to the individual behavior (nonverbal and verbal) of each student in the class, whether the student is on task or gazing off and perhaps thinking about other things. Be cautious, however; just because a child is gazing out the window does not mean that the student is not thinking about the learning task. During group work is a particularly good time to observe students and get to know more about each one's skills and interests.

OBSERVATIONS OF AND CONVERSATIONS
WITH STUDENTS OUTSIDE THE CLASSROOM
Another way to learn more about students is by observing them outside class: at athletic events, on the playground, at dances, at performing arts presentations, over lunch time, at intramural activities, during advisory or homeroom, and at club meetings. Observations outside the classroom can give information about student personalities, friendships, interests, and potentialities. For instance, you may find that a student who seems phlegmatic, lackadaisical, or uninterested in your classroom is a real fireball on the playing field or at some other student gathering.

CONFERENCES AND INTERVIEWS
WITH STUDENTS
Conferences with students, and sometimes with family members as well, afford yet another opportunity to show you are genuinely interested in each child as a person and as a student. Some teachers and teaching teams plan a series of conferences during the first few weeks in which, individually or in small groups of three or four, students are interviewed by the teacher or by the teaching team. Block scheduling is especially conducive to teacher-parent-student conferences. Such conferences and interviews are managed by using open-ended questions. The teacher indicates by the questions, by listening, and by nonjudgmental and

empathic responses (i.e., being able to put her- or himself in the "shoes" of the student, thereby better understanding the student's point of view) a genuine interest in the students. Keep in mind, however, that students who feel they have been betrayed by prior adult associations may at first be distrustful of your sincerity. In such instances, don't force it. Be patient, but do not hesitate to take advantage of the opportunity afforded by talking with individual students outside of class time. Investing a few minutes in a positive conversation with a student, during which you indicate a genuine interest in that student, can pay real dividends when it comes to that student's learning in your classroom.

STUDENT WRITING AND QUESTIONNAIRES

Much can be learned about students by what they write (or draw). It is important to encourage writing in your classroom, (with varying degrees of intensity) read everything that students write (except for personal journals), and ask for clarification when needed. Useful in this strategy are journals and portfolios, discussed in Chapters 5, 9, and 11.

Some teachers use open-ended, interest-discovering, and autobiographical questionnaires. Student responses to these questionnaires can provide ideas about how to tailor assignments for individual students. However, you must assure students that their answers are optional and that you are not invading their privacy.

In an *interest-discovering questionnaire* students are asked to answer questions such as "When at lunch with your friends, what do you usually talk about?" "When you read for fun or pleasure, what do you usually read?" "What are your favorite movies, videos, or TV shows?" "Who are your favorite music video performers?" "Athletes?" "Describe your favorite hobby or other non-school related activity." "What are your favorite sport activities to participate in and as a spectator?"

In an *autobiographical questionnaire* the student is asked to answer questions such as "Where were you born?" "What do you plan to do following high school?" "Do you have a job? If so, what is it? Do you like it?" "How do you like to spend your leisure time?" "Do you like to read?" "What do you like to read?" "Do you have a favorite hobby; what is it?" Many teachers model the process by beginning it with reading their own autobiographical answers to the children.

CUMULATIVE RECORD, DISCUSSIONS WITH COLLEAGUES, AND EXPERIENTIAL BACKGROUNDS

Held in the school office is the cumulative record for each student, containing information recorded from year to year by teachers and other school professionals. The information covers the student's academic background, standardized test scores, and extracurricular activities. However, the Family Educational Rights and Privacy Act (FERPA) of 1974, its subsequent amendments, and local policies may forbid your reviewing the record, except perhaps in collaboration with an administrator or counselor when you have a legitimate educational purpose for doing so. Although you must use discretion before arriving at any conclusion about information contained in the cumulative record, the record may afford information for getting to know a particular student better. Remember, though, a student's past is history and should not be held against that student, but rather used as a means for understanding a student's experiences and current perceptions.

To better understand a student, it is sometimes helpful to talk with the student's other teachers, advisor, or counselor, to learn of their perceptions and experiences with the student. As discussed in Chapter 1, one of the advantages of schools that use looping or that are divided into "houses," or both, is that teachers and students get to know one another better.

Another way of getting to know your students is to spend time in the neighborhoods in which they live. Observe and listen, finding and noting things that you can use as examples or as learning activities.

PREPARATION PROVIDES CONFIDENCE AND SUCCESS

For successful classroom management, beginning the school term may well make all the difference in the world. Remember that you have only one opportunity to make a first and lasting impression. Therefore, you should appear at the first class meeting as well prepared and as confident as possible. In schools genuinely responsive to students, the teachers and administrators hold high expectations for themselves and for one another.

Perhaps in the beginning you will feel nervous and apprehensive, but being ready and well prepared will help you at least to appear to be confident. It is likely that every beginning teacher is to some degree nervous and apprehensive; the secret is to not appear nervous. Being well prepared provides the confidence necessary to cloud feelings of nervousness. A good antiperspirant and a slow under-the-breath counting to 10 at the start can be helpful, too. Then, if you proceed in a businesslike, matter-of-fact way, the impetus of your well-prepared beginning will, most likely, cause the day, week, and year to proceed as desired.

Effective Organization and Administration of Activities and Materials

In a well-managed classroom student movement about the classroom is routinized, controlled, and purposeful to the learning activities. Students know what to do, have the materials needed to do it well, and stay on task while doing it. The classroom atmosphere is supportive, the assignments and procedures for doing them are clear, the materials of instruction are current, interesting, and readily available, and the classroom proceedings are businesslike. At all times, the teacher is in control of events, rather than controlled by them, seeing that students are spending their time on appropriate tasks. For your teaching to be effective you must be skilled in managing the classroom.

Natural Interruptions and Disruptions to Routine

As you plan and prepare to implement your management system, you must also be aware of your own moods and high-stress days and anticipate that your own tolerance levels may vary some. Students, too, are susceptible to personal problems that can be the sources of high stress. As you come to know your students well, you will be able to ascertain when certain students are under an inordinate amount of stress and anxiety.

You must understand that classroom routines may be interrupted occasionally for perfectly natural reasons, especially on certain days and at certain times during the school year. Students will not have the same motivation and energy level on each and every day. Energy level also varies throughout the school day. Your anticipation of—and thoughtful and careful planning for during the preactive phase of instruction—periods of high or low energy levels will preserve your own mental health. Depending on a number of factors, periods of high energy level might include (a) at the beginning of each school day, (b) before a field trip, a holiday, or a school event, such as a dance, picture day, or school assembly, (c) day of a holiday such as Halloween or Valentine's Day, (d) day following a holiday, (e) grade report or parent-conference day, (f) immediately before lunch and immediately after lunch, (g) on a minimum day or the day a substitute teacher is present, (h) toward the end of each school day, toward the end of school each Friday afternoon, and toward the end of the school semester or year.

Although there may be no hard evidence, many experienced teachers will tell you that particular troublesome days for classroom control are those days when there is a strong north wind or a full moon. One teacher jokingly (I suspect) said that on days of both a strong north wind and a full moon, she calls in sick.

How should you prepare for these so-called high energy days? There are probably no specific guidelines that will work for all teachers in all situations in each instance from the list. However, these are days to which you need to pay extra attention during your planning, days that students could possibly be restless and more difficult to control, days when you might need to be especially forceful and consistent in your enforcement of procedures, or even compassionate and more tolerant than usual. Plan instructional activities that might be more readily accepted by the students. In no instance is it my intent to imply that learning ceases and play time takes over. What little instructional time is available to a teacher during a school year is too precious for that to happen.

CLASSROOM PROCEDURES AND GUIDELINES FOR ACCEPTABLE BEHAVIOR

It is impossible to overemphasize the importance of getting the school term off to a good beginning, so let's begin this section by discussing how that is done.

Starting the School Term Well

There are three important keys to getting the school term off to a good beginning. First, be *prepared* and be *fair*. Preparation for the first day of school should include the determination of your classroom procedures and basic expectations for the behavior of students while they are under your supervision. The procedures and expectations must be consistent with school policy and seem reasonable to your students. In enforcing them you must be a fair and consistent professional. However, being coldly consistent is not the same as being fair and professional. As a teacher, you are a professional who deals in matters of human relations and who must exercise professional judgment. You are not a robot, nor is any of your students. Human beings differ from one another, and seemingly similar situations can vary substantially because the people involved are different. Consequently, your response, or lack of response, to each of two separate but similar situations may differ. To be most effective, learning must be enjoyable for students; it cannot be enjoyable when a teacher consistently acts like a marine drill sergeant. If a student infracts upon a rule, rather than assuming why, seeming not to care why, or overreacting to the infraction, find out why before deciding your response. See, for example, "Classroom Vignette: Late Homework Paper From an At-Risk Student" in Chapter 8.

Second, in preparing your classroom management system, remember that too many rules and detailed procedures at the beginning can be a source of trouble. To avoid trouble, it is best at first to present only the minimum number of procedural expectations necessary for an orderly start to the school term. By the time students are in intermediate grades, unless they are recent newcomers, they likely already know the expected procedures (the general rules of expected behavior), although some of their prior teachers may not always have been consistent or even fair about applying these expectations. However, by establishing and sticking to a few explained general expectations (see discussion that follows under "First Day of School") and to those that may be specific to your subject area, you can leave yourself some room for judgments and maneuvering.

Third, consequences for not following established procedures must be reasonable, clearly understood, and fairly applied. The procedures should be quite specific so that students know exactly what is expected and what the consequences are when procedures are not followed.

Procedures Rather than Rules

To encourage a constructive and supportive classroom environment, I encourage you (and your students) to practice thinking in terms of "procedures" (or "standards and guidelines"[13]) rather than of "rules," and of "consequences" rather than "punishment." The rationale is this: to many people, the term *rules* has a more negative connotation than does the term *procedures*. When working with a cohort of students, some rules are necessary but some people feel that using the term *procedures* has a more positive ring to it. For example, a classroom rule might be that when one person is talking we do not interrupt that person until he or she is finished. When that rule is broken, rather than reminding students of the rule, the emphasis can be changed to a procedure simply by reminding the students by asking, "What is our procedure (or expectation) when someone is talking?"

Although some people will disagree, I concur with the contention that thinking in terms of and talking about *procedures* and *consequences* are more likely to contribute to a positive classroom atmosphere than using the terms *rules* and *punishment*. Of course, some argue that by the time students are in the upper grades, you might as well tell it like it is. Especially if your group of students is linguistically and culturally mixed, you will need to be as direct and clear as possible to avoid sending confusing or mixed signals. After considering what experienced others have to say, the final decision is only one of many that you must make and will be influenced by your own thinking and situation. It might be a decision made in collaboration with members of your teaching team. It is, however, important that expectations are communicated clearly to the students and followed consistently by you and other members of your teaching team.

Once you have decided your initial expectations, you are ready to explain them to your students and to begin rehearsing a few of the procedures on the very first day of class. You will want to do this in a positive

way. Students work best in a positive atmosphere, when teacher expectations are clear to them, when procedures are stated in positive terms, when those procedures are clearly understood and agreed upon and have become routine, and when consequences for behaviors that are inappropriate are reasonable, clearly understood, and fairly applied.

The First Day

On the first day you will want to cover certain major points of common interest to you and your students. The following paragraphs offer guidelines and suggestions for meeting your students the first time.

GREETING THE STUDENTS
AND AN INITIAL ASSIGNMENT
Welcome your students with a smile as they arrive, and then the entire class with a friendly but businesslike demeanor. You should not be frowning or off in a corner of the room doing something else as students arrive. As you greet students, tell them to take a seat and start on the first assignment at their desk.

After your greeting, begin the first meeting immediately with some sort of assignment, preferably a written assignment already on each student desk. This assures that students have something to do immediately upon arriving to your classroom. That first assignment might be a questionnaire each student completes. This is a good time to instruct students on the expected standard for heading their papers. After giving instructions on how papers are to be handed in, rehearse the procedure by collecting this first assignment.

STUDENT SEATING
One option for student seating is to have student names on the first assignment paper placed at student seats when students arrive that first class meeting. That allows you to have a seating chart ready on the first day, from which you can quickly take attendance and learn student names. For older children, another option, not exclusive of the first, is to tell students that by the end of the week each should be in a permanent seat (either assigned by you or self-selected), from which you will make a seating chart that will help you to learn their names quickly and to take attendance efficiently each day. Let them know, too, that from time to time you will rearrange seating (if that is true).

INFORMATION ABOUT THE CLASS
After the first assignment has been completed, discussed, and collected, explain to students about the class—what they will be learning and how they will learn it (covering study habits and your expectations regarding the quantity and quality of their work). This is a time you may choose to get student input into the course content (dis-

---

[13] See J. A. Queen et al., *Responsible Classroom Management for Teachers and Students* (Upper Saddle River, NJ: Merrill/Prentice Hall, 1997), especially "Standards and Guidelines Versus Rules" and "Replacing Rules With Standards," pp. 110 and 111–112 respectively.

cussed in Part II) to give students some empowerment. Many teachers of upper grades make a list of expectations or put this information in a course syllabus (Chapter 6), give each student a copy, and review it with them, specifically discussing the teacher's expectations about how books will be used; about student notebooks, journals, portfolios, and assignments; about what students need to furnish; and about the location of resources in the classroom and elsewhere.

CLASSROOM PROCEDURES AND ENDORSED BEHAVIOR

Now discuss in a positive way your expectations regarding classroom behavior, procedures, and routines (discussed next). Students work best when teacher expectations are well understood, with established routines. In the beginning it is important that there be no more procedures than necessary to get the class moving effectively for daily operation. Five or fewer expectations should be enough, such as:

- Arrive promptly and stay on task until excused by the teacher (the teacher, not a bell, excuses students).
- Listen attentively.
- Show mutual respect.
- Use appropriate language.
- Appreciate the rights and property of others.

Too many procedural expectations at first can be restricting and even confusing to students. Most students already know these things so you shouldn't have to spend much time on the topic, except for those items specific to your course, such as dress and safety expectations for laboratory courses, shop and art classes, and physical education. Be patient with yourself, for finding and applying the proper level of control for different groups of students is one of the skills you will develop from experience.

Although many schools traditionally have posted in the halls and in the classrooms a list of prohibited behaviors, exemplary schools tend to focus on the positive, on endorsed attitudes and behaviors. Displaying a list of *do nots* does not encourage a positive school or classroom atmosphere; a list of *dos* does. For example, at Constellation Community Middle School (Long Beach, CA), all students receive regular daily reminders when, after reciting the Pledge of Allegiance, they recite the school's five core principles: (1) Anything that hurts another person is wrong. (2) We are each other's keepers. (3) I am responsible for my own actions. (4) I take pride in myself. (5) Leave it better than when you found it.[14]

---

[14] D. Harrington-Lueker, "Emotional Intelligence," *High Strides* 9(4):1 (March/April 1997).

FIRST HOMEWORK ASSIGNMENT

End the first class meeting with a positive statement about being delighted to be working with them and then give the first homework assignment. The first homework assignment should perhaps be one that will not take too much student time and that each student can achieve a perfect score with minimal effort. Be sure to allow yourself sufficient time to demonstrate where assignments will regularly be posted and to make assignment instructions clearly understood by every student, including a reminder of how you expect students to head their papers.

Establishing Classroom Expectations, Procedures, and Consequences

When establishing classroom behavior expectations and procedures, remember this point: the learning time needs to run efficiently (i.e., with no "dead spots," or time when students have nothing to do), smoothly (i.e., routine procedures are established and transitions between activities are smooth), and with minimum distraction. As discussed in the preceding section, when stating your expectations for student classroom behavior, try to do so in a positive manner, emphasizing procedures and desired attitudes and behaviors, stressing what students should *do* rather than what they should *not do*.

What Students Need to Understand from the Start

As you prepare the guidelines, standards, and expectations for classroom behavior, you (and, if relevant, your teaching team) need to consider some of the specifics about what students need to understand from the start. These specific points, then, should be reviewed and rehearsed with the students, sometimes several times, during the first week of school and then followed *consistently* throughout the school term. Important and specific things that students need to know from the start will vary considerably depending on whether you are working with third graders or high school juniors and whether you are teaching language arts or a shop class, but generally each of the following paragraphs describes things that all students need to understand from the beginning.

SIGNALING THE TEACHER FOR ATTENTION AND HELP

At least at the start of the school term, most teachers who are effective classroom managers expect students to raise their hands until the teacher acknowledges (usually by a nonverbal gesture, such as eye contact and a nod) that the student's hand has been seen. With that acknowledgment, the recommended procedure is that the student should lower his or her hand and return to work.

There are a number of important reasons for expecting students to raise their hands before speaking. Two are that it allows you to (1) control the noise and confusion level and (2) be proactive in deciding who speaks. The latter is important if you (1) are to be in control of classroom events, rather than controlled by them, and (2) are to manage a classroom with equality, with equal attention to individuals regardless of their gender, ethnicity, proximity to the teacher, or another personal characteristic. I am not talking here about students having to raise their hands before talking with their peers during group work; I am talking about disallowing students shouting across the room to get your attention and boisterously talking out freely during whole-class instruction.

Another important reason for expecting students to raise their hands and be recognized before speaking is to discourage impulsive outbursts and to grow intellectually. An instructional responsibility shared by all teachers is to help students develop intelligent behaviors (discussed in Chapter 9). Learning to control impulsivity is an intelligent behavior. Teaching children to control their impulsivity is a highly important responsibility that, in my opinion, is too often neglected by too many teachers (and too many parents). To me, the ramifications of this are frightening.

Some teachers employ the *three-before-me* procedure to avoid dependence on the teacher and having too many students raising their hands for the teacher's attention and to encourage positive interaction among the students. When a student has a question or needs help, the student must quietly ask up to three peers before seeking help from the teacher. Again, as a beginning teacher, you need to try ideas and find what works best for you in your unique situation.

ENTERING AND LEAVING THE CLASSROOM

From the time the class is scheduled to begin and until it officially ends, teachers who are effective classroom managers expect students to be in their assigned seats or at their assigned learning stations and to be attentive to the teacher or to the learning activity until excused by the teacher. And, remember, teachers, not bells, excuse students. This expectation works for college classes, for kindergarten, and for every level in between. For example, students should not be allowed to begin meandering toward the classroom exit in anticipation of the passing bell or the designated passing time; otherwise their meandering toward the door will begin earlier and earlier each day and the teacher will increasingly lose control. Besides, it is a waste of a very valuable and very limited resource—instructional time.

MAINTAINING, OBTAINING, AND USING MATERIALS FOR LEARNING AND ITEMS OF PERSONAL USE

Students need to know where, when, and how to store, retrieve, and care for items such as their coats, backpacks, books, pencils, and medicines; how to get papers and materials; and when to use the pencil sharpener and wastebasket. Classroom control is easiest to maintain when (a) items that students need for class activities and for their personal use are neatly and safely arranged (for example, backpacks stored under tables or chairs rather than in aisles) and located in places that require minimum foot traffic, (b) there are established procedures that students clearly expect and understand, (c) there is the least amount of student off-task time, and (d) students do not have to line up for anything. Therefore, you will want to plan the room arrangement, equipment and materials storage, preparation of equipment and materials, and transitions between activities to avoid needless delays, confusion, and safety hazards. Remember this well: problems in classroom control will most certainly occur whenever some or all students have nothing to do, even if only briefly.

LEAVING CLASS FOR A PERSONAL MATTER

Normally, students should be able to take care of the need for a drink of water or a bathroom break between classes; however, sometimes they do not, or for medical reasons or during long block classes cannot. Reinforce the notion that they should do those things before coming into your classroom or during the scheduled times, but be flexible enough for the occasional student who has an immediate need. Whenever permitting a student to leave class for a personal reason, follow established school procedures, which may, for reasons of personal security, mean that students can only leave the room in pairs, with a hall pass, or when accompanied by an adult.

REACTING TO A VISITOR OR AN INTERCOM ANNOUNCEMENT

Unfortunately, class interruptions do occur, and in some schools they occur far too often and for reasons that are not as important as interrupting a teacher and students' learning would imply. For an important reason the principal or a vice-principal or some other person from the school's office may interrupt the class to see the teacher or a student or to make an announcement to the entire class. Students need to understand what behavior is expected of them during those interruptions. When there is a visitor to the class, the expected procedure should be for students to continue their learning task unless directed otherwise by you. To learn more about class interruptions, complete Exercise 4.1 now.

EXERCISE 4.1 OBSERVING A CLASSROOM FOR FREQUENCY OF EXTERNAL INTERRUPTIONS

INSTRUCTIONS: It is disconcerting how often teachers and student learning in classrooms of some schools are interrupted by announcements from the intercom, a phone call, or a visitor at the door. After all, no one would even consider interrupting a surgeon during the most climatic moments of an open heart operation, nor a defense attorney at the climax of her summation, but it seems far too often that teachers are interrupted just at the moment they have their students at a critical point in a lesson. Once lost because of an interruption, student attention and that teachable moment are nearly impossible to recapture.

School administrators and office personnel must sometimes be reminded that the most important thing going on in the school is that which teachers have been hired to do—teach. The act of teaching must not be frivolously interrupted. In my opinion, except for absolutely critical reasons, teachers should never be interrupted after the first five minutes of a class period and before the last five minutes. That policy should be established and rigidly adhered to. Otherwise, after many years of being a student, the lesson learned is that the least important thing going on at the school is that which is going on in the classroom. No wonder then it is so difficult for teachers in some schools to gain student attention and respect. That respect must be shown starting from the school's central office. Because the turnaround and refocus must somehow begin now, for my effort toward that end I have added this exercise to this resource guide.

Arrange to visit a school classroom and observe for classroom interruptions created from outside the classroom.

1. School and class visited _____

2. Time (start and end of class period) _____

3. Interruptions (tally for each interruption) _____

    3.1 intercom:

    3.2 phone:

    3.3 visitor at door:

    3.4 emergency drill:

    3.5 other (specify):

4. Total number of interruptions _____

5. My conclusion: _____

    _____

    _____

6. Share and compare your results and conclusion with your classmates.

WHEN LATE TO CLASS OR LEAVING EARLY

You must abide by school policies on early dismissals and late arrivals. Make your own procedures routine so students clearly understand what they are to do if they must leave your class early (e.g., for a medical appointment) or when they arrive late. Procedures should be such that late arriving and early dismissal students do not have to disturb you or the learning in progress.

CONSEQUENCES FOR INAPPROPRIATE BEHAVIOR

Most teachers who are effective classroom managers routinize their procedures for handling inappropriate behavior and ensure that students understand the consequences for inappropriate behavior. The consequences are posted in the classroom and, if not counter to school or team policy, may be similar to the following five-step model.

FIRST OFFENSE results in a direct but reasonably unobtrusive (nonverbal) reminder to the student.

SECOND OFFENSE results in a private but direct verbal warning.

THIRD OFFENSE results in the student's being given a time-out in an isolation area (but one that has adult supervision) followed by a private teacher-student conference. (The time-out is discussed in the next section.)

FOURTH OFFENSE results in a suspension from class until there is a student-parent-teacher (and perhaps the counselor) conference.

FIFTH OFFENSE results in the student being referred to the vice-principal, principal, or counselor (depending on school policy), sometimes followed by a limited or permanent suspension from that class or expulsion from school.

Whether offenses subsequent to the first are those that occur on the same day or within a designated period of time, such as one week, is one of the many decisions that must be made by a teacher or by members of a teaching team, department, or the entire faculty.

EMERGENCY DRILLS (PRACTICE) OR REAL EMERGENCIES

Students need to clearly understand what to do, where to go, and how to behave in emergency conditions, such as those that might occur because of a fire, storm, earthquake, or because of a disruptive campus intruder. Students must be expected to behave as well during practice drills as in real emergencies.

Time-Out Procedure

When a time-out is used to deal with a student's inappropriate behavior, the student should have something to do during the time-out. One suggestion is that when instructed to take a time-out the student picks up a form (see Figure 4.1) from a known place near the classroom exit and completes the form while in the time-out area. This procedure is valuable because it (1) gives the student something constructive to do during the time-out, (2) causes the student to reflect and assume ownership for his or her behavior that resulted in the time-out consequence, and (3) provides documentation that might be useful later in conferences

The effective teacher develops a classroom management system *before* meeting the students for the first time. The plan includes procedures that students follow for everything. Students understand the procedures. The teacher is consistent about everyone following the procedures. When procedures are understood by the students and enforced by the teacher, there are fewer problems, students learn, and learning is fun.

with parents, team members, counselors, and school administrative personnel. A second time-out for the same student during the same school day might be cause for a follow-up, such as a conference between the student and members of that student's teaching team and school counselor. A third time-out during the same day may result in a trip to a school administrator and a parent conference before the student is allowed back in school.

To further your understanding of classroom management and to begin the development of your own management system, do Exercises 4.2 and 4.3.

Figure 4.1   Sample time-out form.

TIME-OUT

Your behavior failed to pass our classroom and house expectations and agreements. Those agreements are:

(1) attentive listening
(2) mutual respect of the rights and property of others
(3) right of each student to learn
(4) appreciations of others with no put-downs

Please reflect on your behavior today by answering the following questions.

1. Explain what you did in class that caused you to receive this time-out.

2. What agreement(s) did you fail to honor by your behavior?

3. Did your behavior cause another person to feel embarrassed, angry, or hurt? _____

4. Did your behavior jeopardize the safety of yourself or others? _____

5. Did your behavior keep you or other students from their learning tasks? _____

6. Did your behavior keep another student from being heard by the teacher and class? _____

7. Did your behavior help or hinder the class work? _____ If yes, how?

8. Did your behavior break a school rule?_____ If yes, which one?

9. Explain in your own words what positive behaviors your teacher and classmates will observe from you when you return to class.

When you are ready to honor our class and house agreements, do the following:

1. Return to the classroom and place this completed and signed paper in the appropriate basket on my desk.
2. Return to your assigned seat without disturbing anyone.
3. Rejoin the classroom activity.

Student's signature _____ Date _____

EXERCISE 4.2 TEACHERS' BEHAVIOR MANAGEMENT SYSTEMS

INSTRUCTIONS: The purpose of this exercise is to interview two teachers, from two different grade levels, to discover how they manage their classrooms. Use the outline format that follows, conduct your interviews, and then share the results with your classmates, perhaps in small groups.

1. Teacher interviewed:

2. Date: 4. School:

3. Grade level: 5. Subject(s):

6. Please describe your classroom management system. Specifically, I would like to know your procedures for the following:

   a. How are students to signal that they want your attention and help?

   b. How do you call on students during question and discussion sessions?

   c. How and when are students to enter and exit the classroom?

   d. How are students to obtain the materials for instruction?

   e. How are students to store their personal items?

   f. What are the procedures for students' going to the drinking fountain or bathroom?

   g. What are the procedures during class interruptions?

☞

EXERCISE 4.2 (*continued*)

    h. What are the procedures for tardies or early dismissal?

    i. What are the procedures for turning in homework?

7. Describe your expectations for classroom behavior and the consequences for misbehavior.

In discussion with classmates following the interviews, consider the following.

Many modern teachers advocate the use of a highly structured classroom, and then, as appropriate over time during the school year, they share more of the responsibility with the students. Did you find this to be the case with the majority of teachers interviewed? Was it more or less the case in elementary schools, middle schools, junior highs, or high schools? Was it more or less the case with any particular subject areas?

EXERCISE 4.3: BEGINNING THE DEVELOPMENT OF MY CLASSROOM MANAGEMENT SYSTEM

INSTRUCTIONS: The purpose of this exercise is to begin preparation of the management system that you will explain to your students during the first day or week of school. Answer the questions that follow and share those answers with your peers for their feedback. Then make changes as appropriate. (Upon completion of this chapter, you may want to revisit this exercise to make adjustments to your management plan, as you will from time to time throughout your professional career.)

1. My anticipated grade level and, if relevant, teaching subject:

2. Attention to procedures. Use a statement to explain your procedural expectation for each of the following:

   a. How are students to signal that they want your attention and help?

   b. How do you call on students during question and discussion sessions?

   c. How and when are students to enter and exit the classroom?

   d. How are students to obtain the materials for instruction?

   e. How are students to store their personal items?

   f. What are the procedures for students' going to the drinking fountain or bathroom?

   g. What are the procedures during class interruptions?

   h. What are the procedures for tardies or early dismissal?

EXERCISE 4.3 (*continued*)

    i. What are the procedures for turning in homework?

3. List of student behavior expectations that I will present to my class (no more than five):

Rule 1:

Rule 2:

Rule 3:

Rule 4:

Rule 5:

4. Explanation of consequences for broken rules:

5. How procedures, rules, or consequences may vary (if at all) according to the grade level taught or according to any other criteria, such as in team teaching:

USING POSITIVE REWARDS AS MOTIVATORS

As you probably learned in a psychology course, reinforcement theory contends that a person's gratification derived from receiving a reward strengthens the tendency for that person to continue to act in a certain way, while the lack of a reward (or the promise of a reward) weakens the tendency to act that way. For example, according to the theory, if students are promised a reward of preferred activity time (PAT) on Friday if they work well all week long, then the students are likely to work toward that reward, thus improving their standards of learning. Some educators argue that (1) once the extrinsic reinforcement (i.e., the reward from outside the learner) has been removed, the desired behavior tends to diminish, and (2) rather than extrinsic sources of reinforcement, focus should be on increasing the student's internal sense of accomplishment, an *intrinsic reward*. Perhaps, for the daily work of a teacher in a classroom of many diverse individuals, the practical reality is somewhere between. After all, the reality of classroom teaching is less than ideal, and all activities cannot be intrinsically rewarding. Further, for many children intrinsic rewards are often too remote to be effective.

The promise of extrinsic rewards is not always necessary or beneficial. Students generally will work harder to learn something because they want to learn it (i.e., it is intrinsically motivating) than they will merely to earn PAT, points, grades, candy, or some other form of reward, called an *extrinsic motivator*. In addition, regarding the promise of PAT on Friday, so many children are so preoccupied with "now" that for them the promise on Monday of preferred activity time on Friday probably will have little desired effect on their behavior on Monday. To them on Monday, Friday seems to be a long way off.

Activities that are interesting and intrinsically rewarding are not further served by the addition of extrinsic rewards. This is especially true when working with students who are already highly motivated to learn. Adding extrinsic incentives to learning activities that are already highly motivating tends to reduce student motivation. For most students, the use of extrinsic motivators should be minimal and is probably most useful in skills learning, where there is a lot of repetition and the potential for boredom. If students are working diligently on a highly motivating student-initiated project of study, extrinsic rewards are not necessary and could even have negative effects.

MANAGING CLASS MEETINGS

The guidelines for the first meeting with your students hold true for every meeting thereafter. When it is time for the class period to begin, you should start the learning activities at once, with no delay. By beginning your class meeting without delay you discourage the kind of fooling around and time wasting that might otherwise occur. To minimize problems with classroom control, you must practice this from the very first day of your teaching career.[15]

Once class has begun, the pace of activities should be lively enough to keep students alert and busy, without dead time, but not so fast as to discourage or lose some students. The effective teacher runs a businesslike classroom; at no time does any student sit or stand around with nothing to do. To maintain a smooth and brisk pace and to lessen distractions and prevent dead time, consider the guidelines that follow.

Opening Activities

Although some schools do not use a bell system for the beginning and ending of class periods, many teachers still refer to the initial class activity as the *bell activity*. More frequently, perhaps, it is referred to as the *warm-up activity* or *opener*.

At the beginning of each class, in order to take attendance and to attend to other routine administrative matters, most teachers expect the students to be in their assigned seats. You should greet the students warmly and start their learning quickly. (Unless you really want responses, it perhaps is best to avoid greeting students with a rhetorical question such as "How was your weekend?" See "rhetorical questioning" at the beginning of Chapter 7.) If you are teaching in a school where you must attend to attendance matters at the beginning of each class meeting and are not yet comfortable with your overlapping skill, an effective management procedure is to have the overhead projector on each day when students arrive in class, with the day's agenda and immediate assignment or warm-up activity clearly written on a transparency and displayed on the screen, which then is referred to after your greeting. Once administrative matters are completed (usually in a matter of a minute or two), the day's regular lesson should begin, which could mean that students will move to other stations within the classroom.

When there are no announcements or other administrative matters to cover, you should try to begin the day's first lesson immediately. Then, within a few minutes after the students have begun their lesson activities, attend to attendance matters. Some teachers

---

[15] At the beginning of your student teaching, you may need to follow the opening procedures already established by your cooperating teacher. If your cooperating teacher's procedures for classroom management are largely ineffective, then you should talk with your university supervisor about a different placement.

Many teachers vary the seating arrangement of their classrooms in ways that will accommodate specific types of learning activities and the varying learning modalities of the children.

recommend beginning the day's lesson immediately while giving a reliable classroom aide or student assistant the responsibility of taking attendance and dealing with other routine administrative tasks. However, when another person performs the daily attendance routines, it remains your responsibility to check and sign the relevant attendance forms. Perhaps the best routine, one that requires your practice and overlapping skill, is to do both simultaneously—take attendance while starting a learning activity. Whichever the case, once the class period has begun, routines and lesson activities should move forward briskly and steadily until the official end of the class period, or, in the case of extended class periods or blocks, until a scheduled break.

Warm-up activities include any variety of things, such as a specific topic or question each student responds to by writing in his or her journal or the same topic or question that pairs (dyads) of students discuss and write about in their journals (using the strategy referred to as *think-write-pair-share* that was described in Chapter 3). Other activities include a problem to be solved by each student or student pair, the exchange and discussion of a homework assignment, the completion of the write-up of a laboratory activity, and the writing of individual or student dyad responses to textbook questions.

Now do Exercise 4.4 to learn further how experienced teachers open their class meetings.

EXERCISE 4.4: OBSERVATION AND ANALYSIS OF HOW EXPERIENCED TEACHERS OPEN CLASS MEETINGS

INSTRUCTIONS: Select three experienced teachers, all of the same grade level and (if relevant) subject, to observe for how they begin their class meetings. Observe only the first ten minutes of each class. After collecting these data, share, compile, and discuss the results as follows.

Grade level and subject discipline I observed: _____

1. Make a check for each of the following observations that you make and for each teacher place a number 1, 2, 3, etc., for which of these things the teacher did first, second, third, etc., during that initial ten minutes from time students begin entering the classroom until after the official clock start of class (i.e., when class is supposed to begin).

	✔	Teacher 1	Teacher 2	Teacher 3
Greeting the students	____	____	____	____
Warm and friendly?	____	____	____	____
Giving an assignment (i.e., a warm-up activity)	____	____	____	____
Taking attendance	____	____	____	____
Talking with another adult	____	____	____	____
Talking with one or a few students	____	____	____	____
Readying teaching materials or equipment	____	____	____	____
Working at desk	____	____	____	____
Handing out student papers or materials	____	____	____	____
Other (specify)	____	____	____	____

2. For these three teachers, was there a common way in which they began class?

3. Compile your results with those of your classmates. Write the results here.

☞

EXERCISE 4.4 (*continued*)

4. Compare the results of observations for all subjects and grade levels. What are the similarities and differences?

5. What conclusions can you reach as a class about teachers of particular grade levels and disciplines and how they spent the first ten minutes with their students?

Smooth Implementation of the Lesson

Lessons should move forward briskly and purposefully, with natural transitions from one lesson activity to the next and with each activity starting and ending conclusively, especially when using direct (teacher-centered) instruction. As a beginning teacher, it will take time to develop finesse in your application of this guideline; during your student teaching experience, your cooperating teacher and college or university supervisor will understand that it takes time and will help you develop and hone your skill in the application of this principle. Transitions (discussed below), in particular, are a most troublesome time for many beginning teachers. Transitions are less troublesome when planned carefully during the preactive phase of instruction and written into the lesson plan.

When giving verbal instructions to students, do so quickly and succinctly, without talking too long and giving so much detail that students begin to get restless and bored. Children are quickly bored with long-winded verbal instructions from a teacher.

Once students are busy at their learning tasks, avoid interrupting them with additional verbal instructions, statements, or announcements that get them off task and that could as easily be written on the board or overhead transparency. Also, avoid interventions that could be communicated to a student privately without disturbing the rest of the class. Children are easily distracted; do not be the cause of their distractions.

With whole-class instruction, before starting a new activity, be sure that the present one is satisfactorily completed by most students. Students who finish early can work on an *anchor* or *transitional activity*. End each activity conclusively before beginning a new activity, and with a relevant and carefully prepared transition bridge the new activity with the previous one so students understand the connection. Helping students understand connections is a continuing focus and theme for the classroom teacher.

With your skill in withitness, you will carefully and continuously monitor all students during the entire class period. If one or two students become inattentive and begin to behave inappropriately, quietly (i.e., using indirect intervention) redirect their attention without interrupting the rest of the class.

To help in the prevention of dead time and management problems, especially when using multiple learning tasks and indirect instruction, you will want to establish and rehearse the students in the use of anchor or transitional activities, which are ongoing, relevant tasks that students automatically move to whenever they have completed their individual or small group classroom learning activities. Examples of an anchor activity would be working on their portfolio or writing in their journal.

Transitions: A Difficult Skill for Beginning Teachers

Transitions are the moments in lessons between activities or topics, times of change. It will probably take you a while to master the skill of smooth transitions. Planning and consistency are important to your mastering this important skill. With a dependable schedule and consistent routines, transitions usually occur efficiently and automatically, without disruption. Still, research suggests that the greatest number of discipline problems occur during times of transitions, especially when students must wait for the next activity. To avoid problems during transitions, eliminate wait times by thinking and planning ahead. During the preactive phase of instruction, plan your transitions and write them into your lesson plan.

Transitions in lessons are of two types, and at times both are used. The first is achieved by the teacher's connecting one activity to the next so that students understand the relationship between the two activities. That is a *lesson transition*. The second type of transition occurs when some students have finished a learning activity but must wait for others to catch up before starting the next. This we call an anchor or transitional activity. The transitional activity is one intended to keep all students academically occupied, allowing no time where students have nothing to do but wait. A common example is when a test is given and some students finish while others have not. The effective teacher plans a transitional activity and gives instructions or reminders for that before students start the test.

Teachers who are most effective are those who during the preactive phase of instruction plan and rehearse nearly every move they and the students will make, thinking ahead to anticipate and avoid problems in classroom control. Transitions are planned and students are prepared for them by clearly established transition routines. While in transition and waiting for the start of the next activity students engage in these transitional activities. You can plan a variety of transitional activities relevant and appropriate to the topics being studied, although not necessarily related to the next activity of that particular day's lesson. Transitional activities may include any number of meaningful activities such as journal writing, worksheet activity, lab reports, portfolio work, homework, project work, and even work on an assignment for another class.

As a beginning teacher, it will take time to develop finesse in your application of these guidelines for effective lesson management. During your student teaching experience, your cooperating teacher and college or university supervisor will understand that it takes time and will help you develop and hone your skills.

SELECTED LEGAL GUIDELINES

Among teachers and teacher candidates, the topic of teacher and student rights generates discussions and concerns. You are, or will be, interested in teacher tenure laws, retirement laws, professional organizations, collective bargaining, legal requirements concerning student discipline, teacher liability and insurance, and teacher negligence, topics for which this resource guide cannot pursue or discuss in depth.

Nevertheless, you must be knowledgeable about legal matters regarding teaching and supervising juveniles. Such knowledge can minimize the possibility of making errors that abuse the rights of students, that cause emotional or physical trauma to a student, and that could result in litigation and the end of your teaching career. The content that follows gives only some very basic information.

Title IX: Student Rights

You probably already know that as a result of legislation that occurred more than a quarter century ago—federal law Title IX of the Education Act Amendments of 1972, P.L. 92-318—a teacher is prohibited from discriminating among students on the basis of their gender. In all aspects of school, male and female students must be treated the same. This means, for example, that a teacher must not pit males against females in a subject-content quiz game—or for any other activity or reason. Further, no teacher, student, administrator, or other school employee should make sexual advances toward a student (i.e., touching or speaking in a sexual manner).

Students should be informed by their schools of their rights under Title IX, and they should be encouraged to report any suspected violations of their rights to the school principal or other designated person. Many schools provide students (or parents) with a publication of their rights as students. Each school or district should have a clearly delineated statement of steps to follow in the process of protecting students' rights. For additional resources, see Figure 4.2.

Teacher Liability and Insurance

Credentialed teachers and student teachers in public schools are usually protected by their school districts against personal injury litigation (i.e., a negligence suit filed as the result of a student being injured at school or at a school-sponsored activity). Student teachers and credentialed teachers should investigate carefully the extent of their tort (i.e., any private or civil wrong for which a civil suit can be brought) liability coverage in districts where they work. You may decide that the coverage provided by the district is insufficient. Additional liability coverage can be obtained through private insurance agents and through their affiliations with national teacher's organizations.

Teachers sometimes find themselves in situations where they are tempted to transport students in their own private automobiles, such as for field trips and other off-campus activities. Before ever transporting students in your automobile—or in private automobiles

Figure 4.2 Resources on sexual harassment in schools.

- L. A. Brown, et al., *Student-to-Student Sexual Harassment: A Legal Guide for Schools* (Alexandria, VA: Council of School Attorneys, National School Boards Association, 1998).
- Iowa State Department of Education, *No Big Deal: A Sexual Harassment Training Manual for Middle School and High School Students* (Des Moines, IA: Author, 1998).
- D. L. Siegel, revised by M. Budhos, *Sexual Harassment: Research & Resources*, available from the National Council for Research on Women, 530 Broadway at Spring St., New York, NY 10012-3920, 1995.
- N. Stein and L. Sjostrom, *Flirting or Hurting? A Teacher's Guide on Student-to-Student Sexual Harassment in Schools—Grades 6–12* (Washington, DC: NEA Professional Library, 1994).
- *Stopping Anti-Gay Abuse of Students in Public Schools: A Legal Perspective*, available from the Lambda Legal Defense and Education Fund, 666 Broadway, Suite 12, New York, NY 10012-2317. Phone 212-995-8585.
- *Title IX at 25: Report Card on Gender Equity*, available from the National Women's Law Center, 11 Dupont Circle, NW, Suite 800, Washington, DC 20036, 1997).
- D. H. Wishnietsky, *Establishing School Policies on Sexual Harassment*, Fastback 370. Bloomington, IN: Phi Delta Kappa Educational Foundation, 1994.
- E. Yaffe, "Expensive, Illegal, and Wrong: Sexual Harassment in Our Schools," *Phi Delta Kappan* 77(3):K1–K15 (November 1995).

driven by volunteer adults—you and other drivers should inquire with your insurance agents whether you have adequate automobile insurance liability coverage to do that and if any written permission or release from liability is needed. My advice is to not use private automobiles for transporting students for school events.

Inevitably, teachers take personal items to school—purses, cameras, compact disc players, and so on. It is unlikely that the school's insurance policy covers your personal items if stolen or damaged. A homeowner's or apartment renter's policy might. My advice is to avoid taking valuable personal items to school.

Child Abuse and Neglect

Child abuse and neglect (e.g., physical abuse, incest, malnutrition, improper clothing, and inadequate dental care) has become a grave matter of pressing national concern. *Teachers in all states are legally mandated to report any suspicion of child abuse.* It is a serious moral issue to not report such suspicion; lawsuits have been brought against educators for negligence for not doing so. To report your suspicion of child abuse, you can telephone toll free 1-800-4-A-CHILD. Proof of abuse is not necessary.

Although physical abuse is the easiest to spot, other types of abuse and neglect can be just as serious. General characteristics of children who are abused or neglected are (a) below normal in height and weight, (b) destructive behaviors, (c) hyperactive or aggressive behavior, (d) short attention spans and lack of interest in school activities, (e) sudden and dramatic changes in behavior, (f) fear of everyone and everything, (g) fear of going home after school, (h) fear of their parents and other adults, (i) frequent sickness and absence from school, (j) frequent tiredness, often falling asleep in class, (k) smell of alcohol, (l) poor hygiene, smelling of body wastes, (m) unexpected crying, (n) unexplained lacerations and bruises, (o) withdrawal from adult contact, and (p) withdrawal from peer interaction.[16] A student who comes to your classroom abused or neglected needs to feel welcome and secure while in the classroom. For additional guidance in working with such a student, contact experts from your local school district (e.g., the school psychologist) or seek guidelines from your state department of education or from the local Children's Protective Services (CPS) agency.

First Aid and Medication

Accidents and resulting injuries to students while at school do occur. While doing a laboratory experiment, a student is burned by an acid or a flame. In another class, a student is injured by glass from a falling window pane when the teacher attempts to open a stuck window. While playing on the playground, a student falls and is injured by an automatic sprinkler head that failed to retract into the ground when the system shut down. While on a field trip to the seashore one student falls

---

[16] D. G. Gil, *Violence Against Children: Physical Child Abuse in the United States* (Cambridge, MA: Rand McNally, 1970).

An example of a safe learning environment is the procedural expectation that students wear safety goggles whenever they are doing an activity (such as art, science, or shop) where eye protection if warranted.

and is injured while climbing on rocks. Do you know what you should do when a student is injured in your presence?

First, you should give first aid *only* when necessary to save a limb or life. When life or limb are not at risk, then you should follow school policy by referring the student immediately to professional care. When immediate professional care is unavailable and you believe that immediate first aid is necessary, then you can take prudent action, as if you were that student's parent or legal guardian. But you must always be cautious and knowledgeable about what you are doing, so you do not cause further injury.

Unless you are a licensed medical professional, you should *never* give medication to a minor, whether prescription or over-the-counter. Students who need to take personal medication should bring from home a written parental statement of permission and instructions. Follow school policy on this matter.

STUDENT MISBEHAVIOR

Student behavior in the classroom that is inappropriate can range from minor acts to very serious ones. Sometimes the causes of student misbehavior are the result of problems that originated outside the classroom and spilled over into it. Others are simply misbehaviors that result from the fact that whenever a group of 30 or so young people are grouped together for a period of time, mischief is likely to result. Still others are the result of something the teacher did or did not do. Read on attentively to the guidelines and hints that follow in the remaining pages of this chapter.

Types of Student Misbehavior

Described next are types of student misbehavior that teachers sometimes must contend with, in order of decreasing seriousness.

AGGRESSIVE VIOLENCE
More and more often today, starting as early as kindergarten, teachers are confronted with major problems of misbehavior that have ramifications beyond the classroom or that begin elsewhere and spill over into the classroom. If this happens, you may need to ask for help and should not hesitate to do so. As a teacher, you must stay alert. In the words of Johnson and Johnson,

> Teaching is different from what it used to be. Fifty years ago, the main disciplinary problems were running in halls, talking out of turn, and chewing gum. Today's transgressions include physical and verbal violence, incivility, and in some schools, drug abuse, robbery, assault, and murder. The result is that many teachers spend an inordinate amount of time and energy managing classroom conflicts. When students poorly manage their conflicts with

each other and with faculty, aggression results. Such behavior is usually punished with detentions, suspensions, and expulsions. As violence increases, pressure for safe and orderly schools increases. Schools are struggling with what to do.[17]

Today's schools are adopting a variety of types of schoolwide and classroom instructional programs designed to reduce or eliminate violent, aggressive student behaviors. For example, developed by educators in Seattle, WA, the Second Step Violence Prevention program is a PreK–8 curriculum designed to teach children violence prevention skills of empathy, recognition and creation of options, interpersonal cognitive problem solving, anger management, and impulse control. It is a companion to "Talking About Touching," a personal safety curriculum that teaches children not to be victims of violence, and provides a "second step" in primary prevention by teaching children not to become victimizers. Used in more than 10,000 schools in the United States and Canada since it was developed in 1985, Second Step curriculum consists of photographs, videos, puppet scripts, and role plays. Recent research reported in the prestigious *Journal of the American Medical Association* indicates that the program is effective in reaching its goal.[18]

IMMORALITY
This category includes cheating, lying, and stealing. A student who habitually exhibits any of these behaviors may need to be referred to a specialist. Whenever you have reason to suspect immoral behavior, you should discuss your concerns with members of your teaching team and a school counselor or psychologist.

DEFIANCE OF AUTHORITY
When a student refuses, perhaps hostilely, to do what you say, this defiance is worthy of temporary or permanent removal from the class. Depending upon your judgment of the seriousness of the defiance, you may simply give the student a time-out or you may suspend the student from class until there has been a conference about the situation, which might include you, members of your teaching team, the student, the student's parent or guardian, and a school official.

CLASS DISRUPTIONS
This includes talking out of turn, walking about the room without permission, clowning, and tossing

---

[17] D. W. Johnson and R. T. Johnson, *Reducing School Violence Through Conflict Resolution* (Alexandria, VA: Association for Supervision and Curriculum Development, 1995), p. 1.

[18] D. C. Grossman et al., "Effectiveness of a Violence Prevention Curriculum Among Children in Elementary School," *Journal of the American Medical Association* 277(20):1605-1611 (May 18, 1997). See also the Internet, <http://www.air-dc.org/cecp/resources/success/second_step.htm>.

objects, all of which students know are unacceptable in the classroom. In handling such misbehaviors, it is important that you have explained their consequences to students and then, following your stated procedures, promptly and consistently deal with the violations. Too many beginning teachers (and veteran teachers as well) tend to ignore these class disruptions (seemingly in hope that, if not recognized, they will discontinue). You must *not* ignore minor infractions of this type, for if you do, they most likely will escalate beyond your worst expectations. Without displaying any anger (otherwise students are winning the battle for control), simply and quickly enforce your consequences and keep the focus on the lesson, not the inappropriate behavior. In other words, maintain your control of classroom events rather than become controlled by them.

GOOFING OFF

This least-serious category includes these common misbehaviors: fooling around, not doing assigned tasks, daydreaming, and just generally being off task. Fortunately, in most instances, this type of misbehavior is momentary and sometimes it might even be best if you pretend for a moment or so to not be aware of it.[19] If it persists, all it may take to get the student back on task is a nonobtrusive (silent and private) redirection. If this doesn't work, then go to the second level intervention by calling on the student by name and reminding the student of the correct procedure or of what he or she is supposed to be doing. Avoid asking an off-task student any question, such as a content question, knowing full well the student is not paying attention, or an inquiry, "John, why are you doing that?" Avoid also making a threat such as "John, if you don't turn around and get to work I will send you outside." If you overreact, you could cause more problems than you would resolve. Maintain students' focus on the lesson rather than the off-task behavior.

Examples of trivial misbehaviors that you need not worry about unless they become disruptive are emotionally excited student behavior because the student is really "into the lesson"; brief whispering during a lesson; or short periods of inattentiveness, perhaps accompanied by visual wandering or daydreaming. Teacher responses to student behavior and enforcement of procedures such as raising hands and being recognized before speaking will naturally vary depending on the particular subject, lesson activity, and maturity of the students.

In addition, there is sometimes a tendency among beginning teachers, especially when they have a problem with students goofing off and being disruptive, to assume that the entire class of students is being unruly; in fact, more often it is only one or two or maybe three students. When this is so, you want to avoid saying to the entire class anything that implies that they all are being unruly. That false accusation will only serve to alienate the majority of students who are being attentive to the learning task.

No Short-Term Solutions to Major Problems

Peer pressure and resentment of authority by some students can result in classroom management becoming a major concern of their teachers. Major problems in classroom control may call for extra effort on the part of the teacher in understanding and in dealing with them. There are no short-term solutions for a teacher who is trying to resolve a conflict with a student who causes major problems. Although consequences such as time-out, detention, and suspension may offer short-term relief, long-term efforts and counseling are often called for.[20]

There Are Success Stories

There *are* success stories, examples of which are described in the following paragraphs.

ALTERNATIVE SCHEDULING

After instituting nontraditional flexible scheduling (see Chapter 1) it is not uncommon for schools to report an improved school climate with significant improvement in student behavior, attendance, and academic success.[21]

GUIDANCE AND MENTORING

When teachers, counselors, students, parents, and community representatives work together, it is not uncommon for a school to report improved student attendance and a decline in the dropout rate.[22] A successful effort at helping students make a connection with the value and goals of school has been through school and business partnerships. A special form of partnership called *mentoring* has had success with at-risk students as they become more receptive to schooling. The mentoring component of the partnership movement is a one-on-one commitment by community volunteers to improve the self-esteem, attitudes, and attendance of youngsters. For example, in the Norwalk Public Schools (CN), mentors and students are matched in a one-on-one relationship that may begin

[19] See, for example, T. L. Good and J. E. Brophy, *Looking in Classrooms,* 7th ed. (New York: Addison-Wesley/Longman, 1997), p. 200.

[20] Good and Brophy, *Looking in Classrooms,* p. 178–179.

[21] See examples in Southern Regional Education Board, *1995 Outstanding Practices* (Atlanta, GA: Southern Regional Education Board, 1995).

[22] Southern Regional Education Board, *1995 Outstanding Practices,* p. 30.

as early as kindergarten, where at-risk children are sometimes first identified, and continue through high school. Building self-esteem and preventing school dropout are the primary goals of the Norwalk program. Around the country there are a number of other successful mentoring programs.[23]

HOLDING HIGH EXPECTATIONS FOR ALL STUDENTS AND LINKING LEARNING WITH LIVING

Successful strategies include incorporating modern technology, making classes more student-centered, eliminating the lower curriculum track and raising expectation standards for all students, and linking the school with parents and community representatives. Secondary schools that have used these strategies report a decline in suspensions and an increase in student attendance and academic success, with a decrease in the rate of student dropout and failure.[24]

PRINCIPALS MAKE A DIFFERENCE

In the 1980s, after it had become a run-down school in a run-down neighborhood, the Boston School Committee considered closing Lewenberg Middle School. Then a new principal arrived and, in just twelve years, turned the school around, making it an "exciting, effective, and attractive learning environment." Lewenberg Middle School went from the least-chosen school in the city of Boston to one of the best, to "a school that is 'overchosen' by parents."[25]

SUCCESS FOR ALL INNER-CITY ELEMENTARY SCHOOLS

In 1987, the Success For All (SFA) program for grades preK to five was started by Robert Slavin and others at Johns Hopkins University to keep at-risk inner-city children from falling behind in the early grades. Components of the program include literacy, family support, and teachers' professional development.[26] The SFA program has developed into one of the nation's most successful and extensively researched whole-school restructuring models.

TALENT DEVELOPMENT INNER-CITY MIDDLE AND HIGH SCHOOLS

Building upon the success of the SFA program, the Center for Research on the Education of Students Placed at Risk (CRESPAR) developed the Talent Development School program for secondary schools. TD schools are designed to hold all students to high standards but to provide multiple pathways and research-based practices that ensure their success. The first TD Middle Schools are Evans Junior High School in Washington, DC, and Central East Middle School in Philadelphia, and the first TD High School was established in 1995 at Patterson High School in Baltimore. Early evidence from TD implementation indicates improvement in overall school climate, student attendance, and expected student promotion rates.[27]

Teacher Response to Student Misbehavior: Direct and Indirect Intervention

The goal in responding to student misbehavior is to intervene and redirect the student's focus with the least amount of classroom disturbance. Typically, teachers respond to student classroom misbehaviors in one of three ways: hostile, assertive, and nonassertive. Hostile and nonassertive responses should be avoided. Unlike a hostile response, an assertive response is not abusive or derogatory to the student. Unlike a nonassertive response, an assertive response is a timely and clear communication to the student about the teacher's expectation and an indication that the teacher is prepared to back that expectation with action.[28]

Too often, teachers intervene with verbal commands—direct intervention—when nonverbal gesturing such as eye contact, proximity, facial gesturing, and body language—indirect intervention strategies—are less disruptive and often more effective in redirecting a misbehaving student. Although the offense might be identical, the teacher's intervention for one student might need to be direct while for another student indirect intervention is enough to stop the misbehavior.

[23] S. G. Weinberger, *How to Start a Student Mentor Program*, Fastback 333 (Bloomington, IN: Phi Delta Kappan Educational Foundation, 1992), p. 8. See, for example: *First Step to Success*, a program developed in Oregon for use with at-risk kindergarten children, <http://www.air-dc.org/cecp/resources/success/firstep.htm>, and, *Project Achieve*, a program developed in Florida for use with at-risk elementary school children, <http://www.air-dc.org/cecp/resources/success/project_achieve.htm>.

[24] Southern Regional Education Board, *1995 Outstanding Practices*, p. 3.

[25] M. D. O'Donnell, "Boston's Lewenberg Middle School Delivers Success," *Phi Delta Kappan* 78(7):508–512 (March 1997).

[26] See R. Cooper, R. E. Slavin, and N. A. Madden, *Report 16: Success for All* on the Internet site for the Center for Research on the Education of Students Placed At Risk (CRESPAR), <http://www.csos.jhu.edu/crespar/CRESPAR%20Reports/report16entire.htm>. See also D. Hill, "Success Story," *Teacher Magazine*, pp. 43–49 (August/September 1998).

[27] J. M. McPartland et al., *The Talent Development High School: Early Evidence of Impact on School Climate, Attendance, and Student Promotion. Report No. 2.* (Washington, DC: ED399663, Office of Educational Research and Development, 1996). See also the CRESPAR web site for current reports.

[28] C. H. Edwards, *Classroom Discipline and Management*, 2d ed. (Upper Saddle River, NJ: Prentice Hall, 1997), p. 71–72.

Order of Behavior Intervention Strategies

To redirect a student's attention, your typical *first effort* should be indirect intervention (e.g., proximity, eye contact, gesturing, silence). Your *second effort* could be the simplest (that is, the most private) direct intervention (e.g., "David, please follow procedures"). Your *third effort,* one that in time interval closely follows the second (i.e., within the same class period), should follow your rules and procedures as outlined in your management system, which might mean a time-out or detention and a phone call to the student's parent or guardian (in private, of course). Normally, such a third effort is not necessary. A *fourth effort,* still rarer, is to suspend the student from class (and/or school) for some period of time until decisions about the future of that student in this school are made by school officials in consultation with the student, the parents or guardians, and other professionals such as the school psychologist.

Direct intervention should be reserved for repetitive and serious misbehavior. When using direct intervention, you should give a direct statement, either reminding the student of what he or she is supposed to be doing or telling the student what to do. You should avoid asking a rhetorical question, such as "David, why are you doing that?" When giving students directions about what they are supposed to be doing, a student may ask, "Why do we have to do this?" To that question, you may give a brief academic answer, but do not become defensive or make threats. Rather than spending an inordinate amount of time on the misbehavior, try to focus the student's attention on a desired behavior.

One reason that direct intervention should be held in reserve is because by interrupting the lesson to intervene verbally, you are doing exactly what the student who is being reprimanded was doing—interrupting the lesson. Not only is that improper modeling but it can create a host of management problems beyond your wildest nightmares. Another reason for saving direct intervention is that when used too often, direct intervention loses it effectiveness.

TEACHER-CAUSED STUDENT MISBEHAVIOR: SCENARIOS FOR CASE STUDY REVIEW

As a classroom teacher, one of your major responsibilities is to model appropriate behavior and to *not* contribute to or cause problems in the classroom. Some student misbehaviors and problems in classroom control are caused by, or escalated by, the teacher; these problems could have been prevented or easily rectified had the teacher behaved or acted differently.

In addition to sometimes ignoring minor goofing off, you should also avoid using negative methods of rule enforcement and ineffective forms of punishment, such as exemplified by the following scenarios. You and your classmates might decide to treat these scenarios as case studies for small groups to consider and then discuss before the whole class.

- *Capricious.* Because of her arbitrary and inconsistent enforcement of classroom rules, Fran Fickle has lost the respect and trust of her students and control of her language arts classes. Students are constantly testing Fran to see what they can get away with.
- *Extra Assignments.* When students in Margaret Malopropros's seventh-grade reading class misbehave, she habitually assigns extra reading and written work as punishment, even for the most minor offenses. This behavior has simply reinforced the view of many of her students that school is drudgery, so they no longer look forward to her classes, and behavior problems in her class have steadily increased since the beginning of the school year.
- *Embarrassment.* When eighth-grade social studies teacher Denise Degradini was having difficulty controlling the behavior of one of her students, she got on the classroom phone and called the student's parent. While the entire class of 33 students could hear the conversation, she told the parent about her child's behavior in class and how she was going to have to give the student a referral if the student's behavior did not improve. From that one act Denise lost all respect of her students. Class grades plummeted for the rest of the year.
- *Group Punishment.* Because Fred Flock has not developed his withitness and overlapping skills, he has developed the unfortunate habit of punishing the entire group for every instance of misbehavior. Yesterday, for example, because some students were noisy during a video presentation, he gave the entire class an unannounced quiz on the content of the film. He has lost the respect of the students, who are hostile toward him, and his problems with classroom control are steadily growing worse.
- *Harsh and Humiliating Punishment.* Vince Van Pelt, a physical education teacher, has lost control of his classes and the respect of his students. His thrashing, whipping, tongue-lashing, and use of humiliation are ineffective and indicative of his loss of control. Parents have complained and one is suing him. The district has given Mr. Van Pelt official notice of the nonrenewal of his contract.
- *Loud Talk.* The noisiest person in Steve Shrill's class is Mr. Shrill. His constant and mistaken efforts to talk over the classes have led to his own yelling and screaming, to complaints from neighboring teachers about the noise in his classes, and to a reprimand from the principal.
- *Lowered Marks.* Eunice Erudite, an eighth-grade language arts/social studies core teacher, has a policy of

writing a student's name on the board each time the person is reprimanded for misbehavior. Then, when a student has accumulated five marks on the board, she lowers his or her academic grade by one letter. As a result of her not separating their academic and social behaviors, her students are not doing as well as they were at the start of the year. Parents and students have complained about this policy to the administration, arguing that the grades Ms. Erudite is giving do not reflect the students' academic progress or abilities.

- *Nagging.* Paul Peck's continual and unnecessary scolding and criticizing students upsets the recipient students and arouses resentment from their peers. His nagging resolves nothing and, like a snowball building in size as it rolls down the hill, causes Mr. Peck more and more problems in the classroom.
- *Negative Direct Intervention.* In the seventh-grade humanities block class, Joshua swears more and more frequently and with graphic and startling language. Other students are beginning to behave similarly. Rather than giving Joshua alternative ways of expressing his feelings, Polly Premio, one team teacher, verbally reprimands Joshua each time this happens and threatens to call his parents about it. Ms. Premio doesn't realize that by giving her attention to Joshua's swearing she is rewarding, reinforcing, and causing the increase in Joshua's unacceptable behavior.
- *Negative Touch Control.* When Ezzard, a seventh-grade bully, pushes and shoves other students out of his way for no apparent reason other than to physically manipulate them, his teacher, Tony Trenchant, grabs Ezzard and yanks him into his seat. What "roughneck" Tony the teacher doesn't realize is that he is using the very behavior (physical force) he is trying to stop Ezzard from using. This simply confuses students and teaches them (especially Ezzard) that the use of physical force is okay if you are bigger or older than the recipient of that force. In this situation, unfortunately, hostility begets hostility.
- *Physical Punishment.* Mr. Fit, a history teacher, punishes students by making them go outside and run around the school track when they misbehave in his class. Last week, Sebastian, a student ordered to run four laps for "mouthing off in class," collapsed and died while running. Mr. Fit has been placed on paid leave and is being sued for negligence by Sebastian's parents.
- *Premature Judgments and Actions.* Because of Kathy Kwik's impulsiveness, she does not think clearly before acting, and more than once she has reprimanded the wrong student. Because of her hasty and faulty judgments, students have lost respect for her. For them, her French class has become pure drudgery.

- *Threats and Ultimatums.* Threats and ultimatums from math teacher Bonnie Badger are known to be empty; because she does not follow through, her credibility with the students has been lost. Like wildfire, the word has spread around: "We can do whatever we want in old Badger's class."
- *Too Much Hesitancy.* Because Tim Timideo is too hesitant and slow to intervene when students get off task, his classes have increasingly gotten further and further out of his control, and it is still early in the school year. As a result neighbor teachers are complaining about the noise from his classroom and Tim has been writing more and more referrals.
- *Writing Punishment.* Because they were "too noisy," science teacher Steve Scribe punished his class of 28 students by making each one hand-copy ten pages from encyclopedias. When they submitted this assignment, he tore up the pages in front of the class and said, "Now, I hope you have learned your lesson and from now on will be quiet." Upon hearing about this, all teachers of the school's English department signed and filed a complaint with the principal about Mr. Scribe's use of writing for punishment.

Preventing a Ship from Sinking Is Much Easier than Saving a Sinking One: Fifty Mistakes to Avoid

During your beginning years of teaching, no one, including you, should expect you to be perfect. You should, however, be aware of common mistakes teachers make that often are the causes of student inattention and misbehavior. It is my estimation that as much as ninety-five percent of classroom control problems are teacher-caused and preventable. In this section, you will find descriptions of mistakes commonly made by beginning (and even experienced) teachers. To have a most successful beginning to your career, you will want to develop your skills so as to avoid these mistakes. To avoid making these mistakes requires both knowledge of the potential errors and a reflection upon one's own behaviors in relation to them.

As with all guidelines presented in this resource guide, the items are mostly grade-level and subject-matter neutral, although clearly some may be more relevant to you than others, depending on your own particular teaching situation.

1. *Inadequately attending to long-range and daily planning.* A teacher who inadequately plans ahead is heading for trouble. Inadequate long-term and sketchy daily planning is a precursor to ineffective teaching and, eventually, to teaching failure. Students are motivated best by teachers who clearly are working hard and intelligently for them.

2. *Emphasizing the negative.* Too many warnings to students for their inappropriate behavior—and too little recognition for their positive behaviors—do not help to establish the positive climate needed for the most effective learning to occur. Reminding students of procedures is more positive and will bring you quicker success than reprimanding them when they do not follow procedures.

Too often, teachers try to control students with negative language, such as "There should be no talking," "No gum or candy in class or else you will receive detention," and "No getting out of your seats without my permission." Teachers sometimes allow students, too, to use negative language with each other, such as "Shut up!" Negative language does not help instill a positive classroom climate. To encourage a positive atmosphere, use concise, positive language. Tell students precisely what they are supposed to do rather than what they are not supposed to do. Disallow the use of disrespectful and negative language in your classroom.

3. *Not requiring students to raise hands and be acknowledged before responding.* While ineffective teachers often are ones who are controlled by class events, competent teachers are those who are in control of class events. You cannot be in control of events and your interactions with students if you allow students to shout out their comments, responses, and questions whenever they feel like it. The most successful beginning teacher is one who quickly establishes her control of classroom events.

In addition, indulging their natural impulsivity is not helping students to grow intellectually. When students develop impulse control, they think before acting. Students can be taught to think before acting or shouting out an answer. One of several reasons that teachers should insist on a show of student hands before a student is acknowledged to respond or question is to discourage students from the impulsive, disruptive, and irritating behavior of shouting out in class.[29]

4. *Allowing students' hands to be raised too long.* When students have their hands raised for long periods before you recognize them and attend to their questions or responses, you are providing them with time to fool around. Although you don't have to call on every student as soon as he or she raises a hand, you should acknowledge him or her quickly, such as with a nod or a wave of your hand, so the student can

lower the hand and return to work. Then you should get to the student as quickly as possible. Procedures for this should be clearly understood by the students and consistently practiced by you.

5. *Spending too much with one student or one group and not monitoring the entire group.* Spending too much time with any one student or a small group of students is, in effect, ignoring the rest of the students. As a novice teacher you cannot afford to ignore the rest of the class, even for a moment.

6. *Beginning a new activity before gaining the students' attention.* A teacher who consistently fails to insist that students follow procedures and who does not wait until all students are in compliance before starting a new activity is destined for major problems in classroom control. You must establish and maintain classroom procedures. Starting an activity before all students are in compliance is, in effect, telling the students that they don't have to follow expected procedures. You cannot afford to tell students one thing and then do another. In the classroom, your actions will always speak louder than your words.

7. *Pacing teacher talk and learning activities too fast.* Pacing instructional activities is one of the more difficult skills for beginning teachers to master. Students need time to disengage mentally and physically from one activity before engaging in the next. You must remember that this takes more time for a room of 25 or so students than it does for just one person, you. For this reason transitions need to be planned and written into your lesson plan (discussed in Chapter 6).

8. *Using a voice level that is always either too loud or too soft.* A teacher's voice that is too loud day after day can become irritating to some students, just as one that cannot be heard or understood can become frustrating.

9. *Assigning a journal entry without giving the topic careful thought.* If the question or topic about which students are supposed to write is ambiguous or obviously hurriedly prepared—without your having given thought to how students will interpret and respond to it—students will judge that the task is busywork (e.g., something to keep them busy while you take attendance). If they do it at all, it will be with a great deal of commotion and much less enthusiasm than were they writing on a topic that had meaning to them.

10. *Standing too long in one place.* Most of the time in the classroom, you should be mobile, schmoozing, "working the crowd."

11. *Sitting while teaching.* Unless you are physically unable to stand or you are teaching children of the early grades, in most situations there is no time to sit while teaching. It is difficult to monitor the class while seated. You cannot afford to appear that casual.

12. *Being too serious and no fun.* No doubt, good teaching is serious business. But students are motivated

---

[29] For further reading about the relation between impulse control and intelligence, see D. Goleman, *Emotional Intelligence: Why It Can Matter More Than IQ* (New York: Bantam Books, 1995), and D. Harrington-Lueker, "Emotional Intelligence," *High Strides* 9(4):1, 4–5 (March/April 1997).

by and respond best to teachers who obviously enjoy working with students and helping them learn.

13. *Falling into a rut by using the same teaching strategy or combination of strategies day after day.* A teacher in such a rut is likely to become boring to students. Because of the multitude of differences, students are motivated by and respond best to a variety of well-planned and meaningful learning activities.

14. *Inadequately using silence (wait time) after asking a content question.* When expected to think deeply about a question, students need time to do it. A teacher who consistently gives insufficient time to students to think is teaching only superficially and at the lowest cognitive level and is destined for problems in student motivation and classroom control.

15. *Poorly or inefficiently using instructional tools.* The ineffective use of teaching tools such as books, the overhead projector, writing board, and computer says to students that you are not a competent teacher. Would you want an auto mechanic who did not know how to use the tools of that trade to service your automobile? Would you want a brain surgeon who did not know how to use the tools of the trade to remove your tumor? Working with children in a classroom is no less important. Like a competent automobile mechanic or a competent surgeon, a competent teacher selects and effectively uses the best tools available for the job to be done.

16. *Ineffectively using facial expressions and body language.* Your gestures and body language communicate more to students than your words do. For example, one teacher didn't understand why his class of seventh graders would not respond to his repeated expression of "I need your attention." In one fifteen-minute segment, he used that expression eight times. Studying a videotape of that class period helped him understand the problem. His dress was very casual, and he stood most of the time with his right hand in his pocket. At five foot, eight inches, with a slight build, a rather deadpan facial expression, and a nonexpressive voice, he was not a commanding presence in the classroom. After seeing himself on tape, he returned to the class wearing a tie, and he began using his hands, face, and voice more expressively. Rather than saying "I need your attention," he waited in silence for the students to become attentive. It worked.

17. *Relying too much on teacher talk for classroom control.* Beginning teachers have a tendency to rely too much on teacher talk. Too much teacher talk can be deadly. Unable to discern between the important and the unimportant verbiage, students will quickly tune a teacher out.

Some teachers rely too much on verbal interaction and too little on nonverbal intervention techniques. Verbally reprimanding a student for his or her interruptions of class activities is reinforcing the very behavior you are trying to stop. In addition, verbally reprimanding a student in front of his or her peers can backfire on you. Instead, develop your indirect, silent intervention techniques such as eye contact, mobility, frown, silence, body stance, and proximity.

18. *Inefficiently using teacher time.* During the preactive phase of your instruction (the planning phase), think carefully about what you are going to be doing every minute, and then plan for the most efficient and therefore the most productive use of your time in the classroom. Consider the following example. During a language arts brainstorming session a teacher is recording student contributions on a large sheet of butcher paper that has been taped to the wall. She solicits student responses, acknowledges those responses, holds and manipulates the writing pen, walks to the wall and writes on the paper. Each of those actions requires decisions and movements that consume precious instructional time and that can distract her from her students. An effective alternative should be to have a reliable student helper do the writing while the teacher handles the solicitation and acknowledgment of student contributions. That way she has fewer decisions and fewer actions to distract her, and she does not lose eye contact and proximity with the classroom of students.

19. *Talking to and interacting with only half the class.* While leading a class discussion, there is a tendency among some beginning teachers to favor (by their eye contact and verbal interaction) only 40 to 65 percent of the students, sometimes completely ignoring the others for an entire class period. Knowing that they are being ignored, those students will, in time, become uninterested and perhaps unruly. Remember to spread your interactions and eye contact throughout the entire class.

20. *Collecting and returning student papers before assigning students something to do.* If, while turning in papers or waiting for their return, students have nothing else to do, they get restless and inattentive. Students should have something to do while papers are being collected or returned.

21. *Interrupting while students are on task.* It is not easy to get an entire class of students on task. Once they are on task, you do not want to be the distracter. Try to give all instructions before students begin their work. The detailed instructions should be written in your lesson plan; that way you are sure to not forget anything. Once on task, if there is an important point you wish to make, write it on the board. If you want to return papers while students are working, do it in a way and at a time that is least likely to interrupt them from their learning task.

22. *Using "Shhh" as a means of quieting students.* When you do that, you simply sound like a balloon with a slow leak. The sound should be deleted from your professional vocabulary.

23. *Using poor body positioning.* Develop your skill of withitness by always positioning your body so you can continue to monitor the entire class visually even while talking to and working with one student or a small group. Avoid turning your back to even a portion of the class.

24. *Settling for less when you should be trying for more—not getting the most from student responses.* The most successful schools are those with teachers who expect and get the most from all students. Don't hurry a class discussion; "milk" student responses for all you can, especially when discussing a topic that students are obviously interested in. Ask a student for clarification or reasons for his or her response. Ask for verification. Have another student paraphrase what a student said. Pump students for deeper thought and meaning. Too often, the teacher will ask a question, get an abbreviated (often one word and low cognitive level) response from a student, and then move on to another subject. Instead, follow up a student's response to your question with a sequence of questions, prompting and cueing to elevate the student's thinking to higher levels.

25. *Using threats.* Avoid making threats of any kind. One teacher, for example, told her class that if they continued with their inappropriate talking they would lose their break time. She should have had that consequence as part of the understood procedures and consequences and then taken away the break time for some students if warranted.

26. *Avoid punishing the entire class for the misbehavior of a few.* Although the rationale behind such action is clear (i.e., to get group pressure working for you), often the result is the opposite. Students who have been behaving well are alienated from the teacher because they feel they have been punished unfairly for the misbehavior of others. Those students expect the teacher to be able to handle the misbehaving students without punishing those who are not misbehaving, and they are right!

27. *Using global praise.* Global praise is pretty useless. An example is: "Class, your rough drafts were really wonderful." This is hollow and says nothing. It is simply another instance of useless verbiage from the teacher. Instead, be specific—tell what it was about their drafts that made them so wonderful. As another example, after a student's oral response to the class, rather than simply saying, "Very good," tell what about the student's response was so good.

28. *Using color meaninglessly.* The use of color on transparencies and the writing board is nice but will shortly lose its effectiveness unless the colors have meaning. If, for example, everything in the classroom is color-coded and students understand the meaning of the code, then use of color can serve as an important mnemonic to student learning.

29. *Verbally reprimanding a student from across the room.* This is yet another example of the needless interruption of all students. In addition, because of peer pressure (students tend to support one another), it increases the "you versus them" syndrome. Reprimand when necessary, but do it quietly and as privately as possible.

30. *Interacting with only a "chosen few" students rather than spreading interactions around to all.* As a beginning teacher, especially, it is easy to fall into a habit of interacting with only a few students, especially those who are vocal and who have significant contributions. Your job, however, is to teach all the students. To do that, you must be proactive, not reactive, in your interactions.

31. *Not intervening quickly enough during inappropriate student behavior.* When allowed to continue, inappropriate student behavior only gets worse, not better. It will not go away by itself. It's best to nip it in the bud quickly and resolutely. A teacher who ignores inappropriate behavior, even briefly, is, in effect, approving it. In turn, that approval reinforces the continuation and escalation of inappropriate behaviors.

32. *Not learning and using student names.* To expedite your success, you should quickly learn names and then refer to students by their names. A teacher who does not know or use names when addressing students is viewed by the students as impersonal and uncaring.

33. *Reading student papers only for correct (or incorrect) answers and not for process and student thinking.* Reading student papers only for correct responses reinforces the false notion that the process of arriving at answers or solutions is unimportant and that alternative solutions or answers are impossible or unimportant. It negates the importance of the individual and the very nature and purpose of learning.

34. *Not putting time plans on the board for students.* Yelling out how much time is left for an activity interrupts student thinking; it implies their thinking is unimportant. As I have said before, avoid interrupting students once they are on task. Show respect for their on-task behavior. In this instance, write on the board before the activity begins how much time is allowed for it. Write the time it is to end. If during the activity a decision is made to change the end time, then write the changed time on the board.

35. *Asking global questions that nobody likely will answer.* Examples are "Does everyone understand?" and "Are there any questions?" and "How do you all feel

about . . . ?" It is a brave young soul who in the presence of peers is willing to admit ignorance. It is a waste of precious instructional time to ask such questions. If you truly want to check for student understanding or opinions, then do a spot check by asking specific questions, allowing think time, and then calling on individuals.

36. *Failing to do frequent comprehension checks (every few minutes during most direct instruction situations) to see if students are understanding.* Too often, teachers simply plow through a big chunk of the lesson or the entire lesson, assuming that students are understanding it. Or, in the worst-case scenario, teachers rush through a lesson without even caring if students are getting it. Students are quick to recognize teachers who don't care.

37. *Using poorly worded, ambiguous questions.* Key questions you will ask during a lesson should be planned and written into your lesson plan. Refine and make precise the questions by asking them to yourself or a friend, and try to predict how students will respond to a particular question.

38. *Trying to talk over student noise.* This tells students that their making noise while you are talking is acceptable behavior. When this happens, everyone, teacher included, usually gets increasingly louder during the class period. All that you will accomplish when trying to talk over a high student noise level is a sore throat by the end of the school day and, over a longer period of time, the potential for nodules on your vocal cords.

39. *Wanting to be liked by students.* Forget it. If you are a teacher, then teach. Respect is earned as a result of your effective teaching. Liking you may come later.

40. *Permitting students to be inattentive to an educationally useful media presentation.* This usually happens because the teacher has failed to give the students a written handout of questions or guidelines for what they should acquire from the program. Sometimes students need an additional focus. Furthermore, a media presentation is usually audio and visual. To reinforce student learning, add the kinesthetic such as the writing aspect when a handout of questions is used. This provides minds-on and hands-on activities that enhance learning.

41. *Starting in stutters.* A stutter start is when the teacher begins an activity, is distracted, begins again, is distracted again, tries again to start, and so on. During stutter starts, students become increasingly restless, inattentive, and sometimes even amused by the teacher's futility, making the final start almost impossible for the teacher to achieve. Avoid stutter starts. Begin an activity clearly and decisively. This is most easily accomplished when lesson plans are prepared thoughtfully and in detail.

42. *Introducing too many topics simultaneously.* It is important that you not overload students' capacity to engage mentally by introducing different topics simultaneously. For example, during the first ten minutes of class a teacher started by introducing a warm-up activity, which was journal writing with instructions clearly presented on the overhead. The teacher also verbally explained the activity, although she could have simply pointed to the screen, thereby nonverbally instructing students to begin work on the activity (without disrupting the thinking of those who had already begun). One minute later, the teacher was telling students about their quarter grades and how later in the period they would learn more about those grades. Then she returned to the warm-up activity, explaining it a second time (or third time if one counts the detailed explanation already on the screen). Next she reminded students of the new tardy rules, thereby introducing a third topic. At this time, however, most of the students were still thinking and talking about what she had said about quarter grades, few were working on the warm-up activity, and hardly any were listening to the teacher talking about the new tardy rules. There was a lot of commotion among the students. The teacher had tried to focus student attention on too many topics at once, thus accomplishing little and losing control of the class in the process.

43. *Failing to give students a pleasant greeting on Monday or following a holiday or to remind them to have a pleasant weekend or holiday.* Students are likely to perceive such a teacher as uncaring or impersonal.

44. *Sounding egocentric.* Whether you are or are not egocentric, you want to avoid appearing so. Sometimes the distinction is subtle, although apparent, such as when a teacher says, "What I am going to do now is . . ." rather than "What we are going to do now is . . ." If you want to strive for group cohesiveness—a sense of "we-ness"—then teach not as if you are the leader and your students are the followers, but rather in a manner that empowers your students in their learning.

45. *Taking too much time to give verbal instructions for an activity.* Students become impatient and restless during long verbal instructions from the teacher. It is better to give brief instructions (two or three minutes should do it) and get the students started on the task. For more complicated activities, teach three or four students the instructions and then have those students do workshops with five or six students in each workshop group. This frees you to monitor the progress of each group.

46. *Taking too much time for an activity.* No matter what the activity, during your planning think carefully about how much time students can effectively attend to it. A general rule for most classes (age level and other

factors will dictate variation) is when only one or two learning modalities are involved (e.g., auditory and visual), the activity should not extend beyond about 15 minutes; when more than two modalities are engaged (e.g., add tactile or kinesthetic), then the activity might extend longer, say for 20 or 30 minutes.

47. *Being uptight and anxious.* Consciously or subconsciously, students are quick to detect a teacher who is afraid that events will not go well. It's like a contagious disease: if you are uptight and anxious, your students will likely become the same. To prevent such emotions, at least to the extent they damage your teaching and your students' learning, you must prepare lessons carefully, thoughtfully, and thoroughly. Unless there is something personal going on in your life that is making you anxious, you are more likely to be in control and confident in the classroom when you have lessons that are well prepared. How do you know if your lesson is well-prepared? You will know! It's when you develop a written lesson plan that you are truly excited about and looking forward to implementing; before doing so, review it one more time.

If you have a personal problem that is distracting and making you anxious (and occasionally most of us do), you need to concentrate on ensuring that your anger, hostility, fear, or other negative emotions do not adversely affect your teaching and your interactions with students. Regardless of your personal problems your classes of students will face you each day expecting to be taught reading, mathematics, history, science, physical education, or whatever it is you are supposed to be helping them to learn.

48. *Failing to apply the best of what is known about how children learn.* Too many teachers unrealistically seem to expect success having all 33 students doing the same thing at the same time rather than having several alternative activities simultaneously occurring in the classroom, called *multilevel teaching* or *multitasking.* For example, a student who is not responding well, who is being inattentive and/or disruptive, to a class discussion might behave better if given the choice of moving to a quiet reading center in the classroom or to a learning center to work alone. If after trying an alternative activity, the student continues to be disruptive, then you may have to try still another alternative activity. You may have to send the student to another supervised location out of the classroom, to a place previously arranged by you, until you have time after class or after school to talk with the student about the problem.

49. *Overusing punishment for classroom misbehavior—jumping to the final step without trying alternatives.* Teachers sometimes mistakenly either ignore inappropriate student behavior (see number 31) or they skip steps for intervention, resorting too quickly to punishment. They immediately send the misbehaving student outside to stand in the hall (not a wise choice because the student is not supervised) or too quickly assign detention (a usually ineffective form of punishment). In-between steps to consider include the use of alternative activities in the classroom (as in number 48).

50. *Being inconcise and inconsistent.* Perhaps one of the most frequent causes of problems in classroom control for beginning teachers is when they fail to say what they mean or mean what they say. A teacher who gives only vague instructions or who is inconsistent in his or her behaviors only confuses students (e.g., does not enforce his or her own classroom procedural expectations). A teacher's job is not to confuse students.

Now direct your attention to other specific instances of teacher behaviors, some of which reinforce or cause student misbehavior, by completing Exercise 4.5.

EXERCISE 4.5: IDENTIFYING TEACHER BEHAVIORS THAT CAUSE STUDENT MISBEHAVIOR—A SELF-CHECK EXERCISE

INSTRUCTIONS: The purpose of this exercise is to practice your awareness of the kinds of teacher behaviors to avoid, namely those that tend to reinforce or cause student misbehavior. Place a check next to each of the following situations you believe are teacher behaviors that produce student misbehavior. Then identify what the teacher should do instead. Share your responses with your classmates. An answer key follows.

_____ 1. Ms. Rodriquez is nearly always late for her eighth-grade English class, seldom arriving until at least five minutes past the time class is supposed to start.

_____ 2. Mr. Jones ignores brief whispering between two students during a quiet activity in his sixth-grade social studies class.

_____ 3. While lecturing to her biology class, Ms. Whyte ignores brief talking between two students.

_____ 4. During a class discussion in Mr. Stephen's social studies class, one student appears to be daydreaming and just staring out the window.

☞

EXERCISE 4.5 (*continued*)

_____ 5. During quiet study time in Mr. Orey's sixth-grade reading class, he asks for everyone's attention and then verbally reprimands two students for horsing around. He writes a referral for each of them.

_____

_____

_____

_____

_____

_____ 6. Ms. Fueyo advises her students to pay attention during a film or she will give them a quiz on its content.

_____

_____

_____

_____

_____

_____ 7. Ms. Lee tells a student that because of his behavior in class today he must stay after school with her for ten minutes, the same amount of time that he disturbed the class.

_____

_____

_____

_____

_____

_____ 8. Ms. Murai sees a seventh-grade student cheating on a science test, so he walks over to the student, picks up the test paper, and tears it up in front of the student and the rest of the class.

_____

_____

_____

_____

_____ 9. While Ms. Wong is talking to her second-grade class, the principal walks into the room. She stops her lecture and walks over to greet the principal and to find out what she wants.

_____

_____

_____

_____

☞

EXERCISE 4.5 *(continued)*

_____ 10. While a student learning team is giving its oral report to a third-grade class, Mr. O'Malley, the teacher, begins a conversation with several students in the back of the room.

_____

_____

_____

_____

_____

Answer Key for Exercise 4.5: For reasons explained below, you should have checked situations 1, 3, 5, 6, 7, 8, 9, and 10 as teacher behaviors that reinforce or cause student misbehavior. In some instances, because specific situations may vary, there may be some disagreement about the explanation, but you should talk about these with your classmates and arrive at common understandings.

1. Ms. Rodriquez's behavior is poor modeling for her students. She must model her expectations and those of the school for her students by being on time.

2. Minor infractions such as this are often best ignored as long as the whispering is brief and not disturbing.

3. This should not be ignored. Students are expected to give their attention to the teacher or whomever is speaking; this is common courtesy. By not attending to these students (perhaps by eye contact, proximity, name dropping, or some other form of indirect intervention), Ms. Whyte is saying that it is okay for students to be discourteous. Her failure to follow through with classroom behavioral expectations will cause further and increasingly disturbing management problems.

4. Minor infractions are sometimes best ignored. Perhaps the student is really thinking about ideas presented in the discussion.

5. By his disruption of the class learning activity, Mr. Orey is reinforcing the very behavior he considers inappropriate from his students. This lack of consistency will cause him continued problems in management.

6. Threats are unacceptable, from either students or teachers. In addition, tests should never be administered as punishment. Ms. Fueyo could recommend that students take notes (mental or written) on the film to serve as a focus for discussion and announce that there *will* be a quiz later.

7. By giving the student even more individualized attention after school, Ms. Lee is reinforcing and rewarding the misbehavior. It may also not be safe for her to be alone with the student. Detention, supervised by someone other than Ms. Lee, is a better alternative.

8. Mr. Murai, who has taken no time to diagnose the problem and to prescribe a solution, is reacting too hastily and hostilely. This reinforces the notions that the student is guilty until proven innocent and that due process is more important than the individual student. In addition, Mr. Murai violated this student's right to due process.

9. By stopping her lesson, Ms. Wong has reinforced the idea that the act of teaching is less important than other school business.

10. This is disrespectful and poor modeling. Mr. O'Malley and his entire class should be giving their full attention to the students' report.

SITUATIONAL CASE STUDIES FOR ADDITIONAL REVIEW

To provide further insight into the day-by-day events that occur in K–12 classroom teaching, and to stimulate your thinking about what you might do in similar situations, the following case studies are presented. Each is a situation that actually occurred in recent years. Analyze and discuss these in your class, using the accompanying questions to guide your thinking.

☐ CASE 1. WRONG QUESTIONS ON A TEST

Several teachers have lost their jobs or have been suspended without pay for administering a mathematics worksheet that they were either given by a friend or found on the Internet and that uses drug-questions and ethnic-sounding names. One question, for example, reads, "___ has 2 ounces of cocaine and sells an 8-ball to ___ for $320 and 2 grams to Charlie for $85 per gram. What is the street value of the balance of the cocaine if he doesn't cut it?" Another question reads, "___ is in prison sentenced to six years for murder. He got $10,000 for the hit. If his common-law wife is spending $100 per month, how much money will be left when he is released from prison and how many years will he get after he kills her for spending the money?"

Questions for Discussion

1. After reading this how did you feel? What were you thinking?
2. Does this teacher behavior infringe upon student's rights?
3. Do you know of similar incidents?
4. What do you suppose teachers are thinking when they use such questions?
5. What did you learn from this situation?

☐ CASE 2. STUDENT HAS CRUSH ON TEACHER

During his first year of teaching it had become obvious that one of Mr. Kline's female eighth grade students had developed a serious crush on him. One day, after class was over and all other students had left the room, she approached Mr. Kline and politely asked him if he had a photograph of himself that she could have.

Questions for Discussion

1. Is this a potentially serious situation?
2. How should Mr. Kline respond to the student's request?

☐ CASE 3. FELONIOUS ASSAULTS ON TEACHERS

In the mid 1990s, the following three incidents of students committing felony crimes against teachers were reported in just one month in one state.

- Four elementary school students spiked their teacher's Gatorade™ with rat poison.
- A middle school student allegedly put cleaning fluid in his teacher's water bottle.
- At mid-morning a high school teacher became nauseous and within four hours began to hallucinate with his whole body tingling. While trying to take attendance his students appeared to him to be floating around the classroom. A substitute teacher was called to finish the day for him. While walking to his home he could not step off curbs or climb stairs. He was taken to the hospital. The next day, after hearing of the teacher's problems, some students came forward and reported to the school administrators that the teacher's coffee had been spiked with LSD. A student from the teacher's second-period class, who had been bragging about putting a dose of LSD into her teacher's coffee, was arrested.

Questions for Discussion

1. After reading of these incidents how did you feel? What were you thinking?
2. Do you know of similar incidents?
3. What do you suppose causes students to commit such acts as these against teachers?
4. What precautions, if any, can and should teachers take to protect themselves and their students from such acts.

☐ CASE 4. SCIENCE TEACHER SOLICITS STUDENTS TO PURCHASE MARIJUANA FOR EXPERIMENT

A teacher gave $30 to a student for a quantity of marijuana with the intention of putting the marijuana in a bowl with goldfish so students could study the effects on the fish. Before the experiment ever took place, other students reported the teacher's action to the school principal. The teacher was placed on administrative leave. Subsequently, after pleading guilty to charges of contributing to the delinquency of a minor, the teacher was sentenced to 45 days in jail and two years of probation. Apparently, the experiment was to be a repeat of one done earlier at the school by police officers, but with cutbacks and restraints the teacher decided to use her own money to repeat the experiment.

Questions for Discussion

1. After reading this, what were your thoughts?
2. What, if anything, did you learn from this situation that might be helpful to you during your own teaching career?*

---

* Perhaps the teacher should have searched for an alternative activity. For example, see R. N. Russo and S. Parrish, "Toxicology for the Middle School," *Journal of Chemical Education* 72(1):49–50 (January 1995).

□ CASE 5. STUDENT COMPLAINS TO A STUDENT TEACHER ABOUT CONTINUED SEXUAL HARASSMENT BY A PEER

During the first week after John began his student teaching in eighth-grade history, one of his female students came to him after class and complained that a boy in the class has continued to sexually harass her even after she had reported it to the school vice-principal. She says that the harassment is beyond just verbal abuse and she wants it stopped.

Questions for Discussion

1. After reading this case, what were your thoughts?
2. What, if anything, should John do?
3. What, if anything, did you learn from this situation that might be helpful to you during your own teaching career?

□ CASE 6. STUDENTS USE THE INTERNET FOR EXTRACURRICULAR ACTIVITY

During project work time in a seventh-grade language arts/social studies block, the classroom teacher discovers a group of three students at a computer work station viewing a graphic sex web site.

Questions for Discussion

1. After reading this, what were your immediate thoughts?
2. What should the teacher do?
3. How could the problem have been avoided?
4. What, if anything, did you learn from this case that might be helpful to you during your own teaching career?

□ CASE 7. SIX SEPARATE SCHOOL SHOOTINGS IN LESS THAN NINE MONTHS FOLLOWED ONE YEAR LATER BY THE WORST YET

The chronology of events is as follows:

- October 1, 1997, a 16-year-old stabbed and killed his mother, then shot and killed two students at Pearl High School, Pearl, Mississippi.
- December 1, 1997, a 14-year-old boy shot and killed three students at Heath High School, Paducah, Kentucky.
- March 24, 1998, two boys, ages 11 and 13, shot and killed one teacher and four students at Westside Middle School, Jonesboro, Arkansas.
- April 25, 1998, a 14-year-old middle school student in Edinboro, Pennsylvania, shot and killed a teacher.
- May 19, 1998, a high school senior in Fayetteville, Tennessee, shot and killed another senior student.
- May 21, 1998, two students in Springfield, Oregon, are killed by a 15-year-old high school student.
- April 20, 1999, two high school students in Littleton, Colorado, shoot and kill twelve other students, one

teacher, and themselves, and seriously wound more than a dozen other students.

Questions for Discussion

1. After reading this chronology, how did you feel? What were you thinking?
2. What do you suppose causes students to commit such acts as these against teachers and peers?
3. What precautions, if any, can and should teachers, schools, and communities take to protect themselves and their students from such acts?

SUMMARY

In this chapter, you learned ways to cope with the daily challenges of classroom teaching, guidelines for effectively managing students in the classroom, and some legal rights and responsibilities of students and teachers. Within that framework, your attention was then focused on specific approaches and additional guidelines for effective classroom management and control. You were offered advice for setting up and maintaining a classroom environment that is favorable to student learning and for establishing procedures for efficiently controlling student behavior and encouraging student learning.

This is the end of our overview of teaching and learning. You are now ready for Part II, planning for instruction.

QUESTIONS FOR CLASS DISCUSSION

1. Is it better to be strict with students at first and then relax once your control has been established, or to be relaxed at first and then tighten the reins later if students misbehave? Explain your answer.
2. Explain what your options would be if in your science or shop class students are provided with safety glasses but several students refuse to wear them.
3. Explain why it is important to try to prevent behavior problems before they occur. Describe at least five preventive steps you will take to reduce the number of management problems that you might otherwise have.
4. Explain what you would do if two errant behaviors occurred simultaneously in different locations in your classroom.
5. Explain what you would do if a student from one of your classes came to you and reported that fellow students were harassing him by throwing objects at him, slapping him, pulling his chair out from under him, and pretending to rape him.
6. A historical review of disciplinary practices used in the nation's classrooms shows that corporal punishment has been a consistent and conspicuous part of schooling since the beginning. Many educators are concerned about the increased violence in schools, represented by possession of weapons, harassment, bullying, intimidation, gang or cult activity, arson, and the continued use

of corporal punishment of students. They argue that schools are responsible for turning a child's behavior into an opportunity to teach character and self-control. When self-disciplined adults create a problem, they apologize, accept the consequences, make restitution, and learn from their mistakes. We have a responsibility for teaching children to do the same. An important characteristic of exemplary schooling is that of maintaining respect for a child's dignity even when responding to the child's inappropriate behavior. Saturday School may be an acceptable alternative to more harmful disciplinary practices and a step toward developing more internal rather than external student control methods. Are there any such programs in your geographic area? What is your opinion about using corporal punishment at any level of schooling? Organize a class debate on the issue.

7. You have undoubtedly read and heard much about the importance of your being consistent about implementing the expected classroom procedures and the consequences for inappropriate behavior. When it comes to procedures and consequences, is there a danger in a teacher being too rigid or inflexible? Explain your answer.

8. Compare and contrast your own school experiences with what you have recently observed in schools, especially related to the exercises of the four chapters of Part I of this resource guide. Discuss your conclusions in small groups and then share your group's conclusions with those of the entire class.

9. From your current observations and field work as related to this teacher preparation program, clearly identify one specific example of educational practice that seems contradictory to exemplary practice or theory as presented in this chapter. Present your explanation for the discrepancy.

10. Do you have questions generated by the content of this chapter? If you do, list them along with ways answers might be found.

FOR FURTHER READING

Bodine, R. J., and Crawford, D. K. *The Handbook of Conflict Resolution Education: A Guide to Building Quality Programs in Schools.* San Francisco: Jossey-Bass, 1998.

Curwin, R. L., and Mendler, A. N. *Discipline with Dignity.* Alexandria, VA: Association for Supervision and Curriculum Development, 1988.

Fogarty, R. "The Intelligence-Friendly Classroom." *Phi Delta Kappan* 79(9):655–657 (May 1998).

Foster-Harrison, E. S., and Adams-Bullock, A. *Creating an Inviting Classroom Environment.* Fastback 422. Bloomington, IN: Phi Delta Kappa Educational Foundation, 1998.

Freiberg, H. J. (Ed.). *Beyond Behaviorism: Changing the Classroom Management Paradigm.* Needham Heights: Allyn & Bacon, 1999.

Glasser, W. "A New Look at School Failure and School Success." *Phi Delta Kappan* 78(8):597–602 (April 1997).

Hansen, J. M., and Childs, J. "Creating a School Where People Like to Be." *Educational Leadership* 56(1):14–17 (September 1998).

Jensen, E. "How Threats and Stress Affect Learning." Chapter 6 of E. Jensen, *Teaching With the Brain in Mind.* Alexandria, VA: Association for Supervision and Curriculum Development, 1998.

Kelly, K. "Retention vs. Social Promotion: Schools Search for Alternatives." *The Harvard Education Letter* 15(1):1–3 (January/February 1999).

Middlebrooks, S. *Getting to Know City Kids. Understanding Their Thinking, Imagining, and Socializing* (New York: Teachers College Press, 1998).

Nilges, L. M. "I Thought Only Fairy Tales had Supernatural Power: A Radical Feminist Analysis of Title IX in Physical Education. *Journal of Teaching in Physical Education* 17(2):172–194 (January 1998).

Petrie, G., et al. "Nonverbal Cues: The Key to Classroom Management." *Principal* 77(3):34–36 (January 1998).

Sesno, A. H. *97 Savvy Secrets for Protecting Self and School: A Practical Guide for Today's Teachers and Administrators.* Thousand Oaks, CA: Corwin Press, 1998.

Skiba, R., and Peterson, R. "The Dark Side of Zero Tolerance: Can Punishment Lead to Safe Schools?" *Phi Delta Kappan* 80(5): 372–376, 381–382 (January 1999).

Tomlinson, C. A. *The Differentiated Classroom.* Chapter 4. Alexandria, VA: Association for Supervision and Curriculum Development, 1999.

Urban, V. D. "Eugene's Story: A Case for Caring." *Educational Leadership* 56(6):69–70 (March 1999).

Walters, L. S. "What Makes a Good School Violence Prevention Program?" *The Harvard Education Letter* 15(1):4–5 (January/February 1999).

Part II

PLANNING FOR INSTRUCTION

Part II responds to your needs concerning:

- Collaborative planning
- Curriculum integration and the interdisciplinary thematic unit
- Dealing with content and issues that may be controversial
- Direct and indirect instruction
- Documents that provide guidance for curriculum planning
- Domains of learning
- Goals, objectives, and learning outcomes
- Levels of curriculum planning
- National Educational Goals and national curriculum standards
- Selecting and developing appropriate learning activities
- Selecting and sequencing content
- Using textbooks

REFLECTIVE THOUGHTS

A classroom teacher is responsible for planning at three levels—the year, the units, and the lessons—with critical decisions to be made at each level. Failing to prepare is preparing to fail.

The obsolescence of many past instructional practices has been substantiated repeatedly by those researchers who have made recent studies of exemplary educational practices.

Your challenge is to use performance-based criteria with a teaching style that encourages the development of intrinsic sources of student motivation, and that provides for coincidental learning, which goes beyond what might be considered as predictable, immediately measurable, and minimal expectations.

Teachers must be clear about what they want their students to learn and about the kind of evidence needed to verify their learning. Then they must communicate those things to the students so they are clearly understood.

Curriculum integration refers to a way of thinking, a way of teaching, and a way of planning and organizing the instructional program so the discrete disciplines of subject matter are related to one another in a design that (1) matches the developmental needs of the learners and (2) helps to connect their learning in ways that are meaningful to their current and past experiences.

Experiences afforded by inquiry help students understand the importance of suspending judgment and also the tentativeness of answers and solutions. With those understandings, students grow intellectually and eventually are better able to cope with life's ambiguities.

Chapter 5

Planning: The Curriculum and Its Content

Effective teaching does not just happen; it is produced through the thoughtful planning of each phase of the learning process. Most effective teachers begin their planning months before meeting students for the first time. Daily lessons form parts of a larger scheme designed to accomplish the teacher's long-range goals for the semester or year and to mesh with the school's mission and goals.

If learning is defined only as the accumulation of bits and pieces of information, then we already know everything about how to teach and how students learn. But the accumulation of pieces of information is at the lowest end of a spectrum of types of learning. Discoveries are still being made about the processes involved in higher forms of learning—that is, for meaningful understanding and the reflective use of that understanding. The results of recent research support the use of instructional strategies that help students make connections as they learn. These strategies include the literature-based approach to reading, discovery learning, inquiry, cooperative learning, and interdisciplinary thematic instruction, with a total curriculum that is integrated and connected to students' life experiences.

Like the construction of a bridge, meaningful learning is a gradual and sometimes painstakingly slow process. When compared with traditional instruction, teaching in a constructivist mode is slower, involving more discussion, debate, and the re-creation of ideas. Rather than following clearly defined and previously established steps, the curriculum evolves. Such a curriculum depends heavily on materials, and to a great extent it is determined by the student's interests and questions. Less content is covered, fewer facts are

memorized and tested for, and progress is sometimes tediously slow.[1]

The methodology uses what is referred to as *hands-on* and *minds-on* learning: the learner is learning by doing and is thinking about what she or he is learning and doing. When thoughtfully coupled, these approaches help construct, and often reconstruct, the learner's perceptions. Hands-on learning engages the learner's mind, causing questioning and turning a learner's mind on. Hands-on/minds-on learning encourages students to question and then, with the teacher's guidance, devise ways of investigating satisfactory, although sometimes only tentative, answers to their questions.

As a classroom teacher, your instructional task then is twofold: (1) to plan hands-on experiences, providing the materials and the supportive environment necessary for student's meaningful exploration and discovery, and (2) to know how to facilitate the most meaningful and longest-lasting learning possible once the learner's mind has been engaged by the hands-on learning. To accomplish this requires your knowledge about, and competence in the use of, varied and developmentally appropriate methods of instruction. To assist you in the acquisition of that knowledge and competence is the primary purpose of this book. The two chapters of this part of the book address the planning aspect. As you proceed through these chapters and begin the development of your instructional plans,

---

[1]B. Watson and R. Konicek, "Teaching for Conceptual Change: Confronting Childrens' Experience," *Phi Delta Kappan* 71(9):680–685 (May 1990), p. 685.

from time to time you will want to refer to particular topics in the chapters of Part III and also to the topic of assessment of student learning, Chapter 11. The rationale for careful planning and the components of that planning are the topics of this chapter.

Specifically, upon completion of this chapter you should be able to

1. Explain the difference and the relationship between *hands-on* and *minds-on* learning.
2. Describe the relationship of instructional planning to the preactive and reflective thought-processing phases of instruction.
3. Demonstrate an understanding of the rationale for planning for instruction, the levels of planning, and the components of a total instructional plan.
4. Demonstrate knowledge of the value of various types of documents that can be resources for curriculum and instructional planning.
5. Explain the value and limitations of a syllabus, textbooks, and other resources for student learning.
6. Demonstrate ability to plan the sequence of content for instruction in a particular subject at a specific grade level.
7. Explain both the value and the limitations afforded by using instructional objectives.
8. Prepare instructional objectives for each of the three domains of learning and at various levels within each domain.
9. Explain the relationship between instructional objectives and assessment of student learning.
10. Demonstrate understanding of the difference between conceptual knowledge and procedural knowledge and the role of each in planning for instruction.
11. Differentiate among diagnostic assessment, formative assessment, and summative assessment, and explain the place and use of each in instructional planning.
12. Demonstrate understanding of the value of and tools used for the diagnostic and formative assessment of student learning as related to planning for curriculum and instruction.
13. Anticipate controversial topics and issues that may arise while teaching and what you might do if and when they do arise.
14. Demonstrate understanding of the concept of integrated curriculum and its relevance to curriculum and instruction.
15. Demonstrate understanding of how to help students to develop depth of understanding while still scoring well on mandated standardized tests.

PROVIDING SUCCESSFUL TRANSITIONS

Within the framework of exemplary school organization lie several components that form a comprehensive albeit ever-changing program. Central to the school's purpose and its organizational structure is the concerted effort to see that all students make successful *transitions* from one level to the next, from one grade to the next, from elementary to middle school, from middle school to high school, and from high school to work or postsecondary education. Every aspect of the school program is, in some way, designed to help students to make those transitions. Combining to form the program that students experience are two terms you will frequently encounter, *curriculum* and *instruction*.

Curriculum and Instruction: Clarification of Terms

Curriculum is defined in various ways. Some define it as the planned subject-matter content and skills to be presented to students. Others say curriculum is only that which students actually learn. Still others hold the broad definition that the curriculum is all experiences students encounter, whether planned or unplanned, learned or unlearned.

Four programs are identified that contribute in different ways to student learning, that do, in fact, comprise the broadest definition of curriculum: (1) the program of studies (courses offered), (2) the program of student activities (sports, clubs, and organizations), (3) the program of services (transportation, meals, nurse station, etc.), and (4) the hidden curriculum (i.e., the unplanned and subtle message systems within schools, as discussed in Chapter 1). This working definition considers curriculum as the *entire school program*. Accepting this broad definition, the curriculum embraces every planned aspect of a school's educational program, including the classes that are designed specifically to advance conceptual and procedural knowledge and schoolwide services such as guidance, clubs and interest groups, visual and performing arts productions, student government, and athletic programs.

Instruction, too, has several definitions, some of which are not clearly distinguishable from *curriculum.* Whereas curriculum is usually associated with the content of the learning, instruction is associated with *methods*—that is, with ways of presenting content, conveying information, and facilitating student learning. Obviously, curriculum and instruction must be in tandem to affect student learning.

PLANNING FOR INSTRUCTION

As a classroom teacher, planning for instruction is a major part of your job. You will be responsible for planning at three levels—the school year, the units, and the lessons—with critical decisions to be made at each level.

You need not do all your instructional planning from scratch, and you need not do all your planning alone. In many schools today, as discussed in Chapter 1, the curricula are developed by a team of teachers. Teams of teachers collectively plan special programs for their specific cohorts of students. Team members either plan together or split the responsibilities and then share their individual plans. A final plan is then developed collaboratively.

The heart of good planning is good decision making. For every plan and at each of the three levels, you and your team must make decisions about the goals and objectives to be set, the subject to be introduced, the materials and equipment to be used, the methods to be adopted, and the assessments to be made. This decision-making process is complicated because so many options are available at each level. Decisions made at all three levels result in a total plan.

Although the planning process continues term after term, year after year, the task becomes somewhat easier after the first year as you learn to recycle plans. The process is also made easier via research and communication by reviewing documents and sharing ideas and plans with other teachers.

Teacher-Student Collaborative Team Planning

Classrooms today tend to be more project-oriented and student- and group-centered than the traditional teacher-centered classroom of the past, in which the teacher served as the primary provider of information. Today's students more actively participate in their learning in collaboration with the teacher. The teacher provides some structure and assistance, but the collaborative approach requires that students inquire and interact, generate ideas, seriously listen and talk with one another, and recognize that their thoughts and experiences are valuable and essential to meaningful learning.

Many teachers and teaching teams encourage their students to participate in the planning of some phase of their learning, anywhere from planning an entire course of study to complete interdisciplinary thematic units to specific learning activities within a unit. Such participation tends to give students a proprietary interest in the activities, thereby increasing their motivation for learning. What students have contributed to the plan often seems more meaningful to them than what others have planned for them. Students like to see their own plans succeed. Thus, teacher-student collaboration in planning can be an effective motivational tool. (Collaborative learning will be discussed later in this chapter and in others; in this chapter the discussion focuses on integrated curriculum and planning the course syllabus.)

Reasons for Planning

Planning is done for a number of reasons, perhaps foremost of which is to ensure curriculum coherence. Periodic lesson plans are an integral part of a larger plan represented by course goals and objectives, department goals, and by the school- and district-wide mission and goals. Students' learning experiences are thoughtfully planned in sequence and then orchestrated by teachers who understand the rationale for their respective positions in the curriculum. Of course, such plans do not preclude an occasional diversion from predetermined activities.

Another reason for planning is, as discussed in Chapter 2, to give considerations to students' experiential

Like a good map, good unit and lesson planning facilitates reaching the destination with more confidence and fewer wrong turns.

backgrounds, learning capacities and styles, reading abilities, and special needs.

Planning is necessary to ensure efficient and effective teaching with a minimum of classroom control problems. After deciding *what* to teach, you face the important task of deciding *how* to teach it. To use precious instructional time efficiently, planning should be accomplished with two goals in mind: (1) to not waste anyone's time during the time allotted for instruction and (2) to select strategies that most effectively promote the anticipated student learning.

Planning helps ensure program continuation. The program must continue even if you are absent and a substitute teacher is needed. Planning provides a criterion for reflective practice and self-assessment. After a learning activity and at the end of a school term, you can reflect on and assess what was done and how it affected student learning. Planning provides a means to evaluate your teaching. Your plans represent a criterion recognized and evaluated by administrators. With those experienced in such matters, it is clear that inadequate planning is usually a precursor to incompetent teaching. Put simply, failing to plan is planning to fail.

Components of an Instructional Plan

A total instructional plan has six major components, described as follows.

Rationale component. This is a statement about why the content of the plan is important and about how students will learn it. The statement should be consistent with the school and district mission statement.

Goals and objectives component. The goals and objectives represent the learning target, the procedural and conceptual knowledge to be gained from studying the plan. The plan's stated goals and objectives should be consistent with the rationale statement.

Articulation component. The articulation component shows the plan's relationship to the learning that preceded and the learning that will follow from prekindergarten through twelfth grade, and sometimes beyond in either the workplace or postsecondary education. This is referred to as *vertical articulation.* The plan should also indicate its *horizontal articulation,* which is its connectedness with other activities across grade level. "Writing across the curriculum" is an example of horizontal articulation. Vertical and horizontal articulation are usually represented in curriculum documents and textbook programs by scope and sequence charting.

Learning activities component. This is the presentation of organized and sequential units and lessons appropriate for the subject or grade level and for the age and diversity of the learners.

Resources component. This is a listing of anticipated resources needed, such as books, guest speakers, field trips, and media.

Assessment component. This is the appraisal of student learning and occurs (1) at the start of the instruction (a *preassessment* of what students already know or think they know about the topic), (2) during the instruction to make sure students are learning that which is intended (*formative assessment*), and (3) at the end of the instruction to determine whether and how well students did learn (*summative assessment*).

Planning the Scope of the Curriculum

When planning the scope of a curriculum for a semester or for a school year, you should decide what is to be accomplished in that period of time. To help in setting your goals, you should (a) examine school and other resource documents for mandates and guidelines, (b) communicate with colleagues to learn of common expectations, and (c) probe, analyze, and translate your own convictions, knowledge, and skills into behaviors that foster the intellectual and psychological development of your students.

Documents That Provide Guidance for Content Selection

With the guidance of Exercises 5.1–5.3, you will examine major documents that help guide you in selecting the content of your curriculum. These are: the national curriculum standards, state department of education curriculum documents, school or district courses of study, and school-adopted printed or nonprinted materials. Sources for your examination of these documents include your college or university library, cooperating teachers or administrative personnel at local schools, and sites on the Internet. For sample Internet sites, see Figure 5.1.

National Curriculum Standards

Curriculum standards are a definition of what students should know (content) and be able to do (process and performance). At the national level, curriculum standards did not exist in the United States until those developed and released for mathematics education in 1989. Shortly after the release of the mathematics standards, support for national goals in education was endorsed by the National Governors Association, and the National Council on Education Standards and Testing recommended that in addition to those for mathematics, national standards for subject matter content in K–12 education be developed for the arts, civics/social studies, English/language arts/reading,

Figure 5.1 Internet resources on content standards and frameworks.

General and multiple disciplines
- http://www.mcrel.org
- http://www.enc.org/reform/fworks/index.htm
- http://putwest.boces.org/Standards.html

Discipline specific
- Economics, http://www.ncee.org
- English/reading, http://www.ncte.org
- Mathematics, http://www.nctm.org
- Physical education, http://www.naspe.org
- Science, http://www.nsta.org
- Social studies, http://www.ari.net/online/standards/2.0.html
- Technology, http://www.iste.org/Resources/Projects/TechStandards/NETS/Draft
- Visual and performing arts, http://www.amc-music.com

Figure 5.2 Goals 2000: The National Educational Goals.

By the year 2000—
- All children in America will start school ready to learn.
- The high school graduation rate will increase to at least 90 percent.
- All students will leave grades 4, 8, and 12 having demonstrated competency over challenging subject matter including English, mathematics, science, foreign languages, civics and government, economics, the arts, history, and geography, and every school in America will ensure that all students learn to use their minds well, so they may be prepared for responsible citizenship, further learning, and productive employment in our nation's modern economy.
- U.S. students will be first in the world in mathematics and science achievement.
- Every adult American will be literate and will possess the knowledge and skills necessary to compete in a global economy and exercise the rights and responsibilities of citizenship.
- Every school in the United States will be free of drugs, violence, and the unauthorized presence of firearms and alcohol, and will offer a disciplined environment conducive to learning.
- The nation's teaching force will have access to programs for the continued improvement of their professional skills and the opportunity to acquire the knowledge and skills needed to instruct and prepare all American students for the next century.
- Every school will promote partnerships that will increase parental involvement and participation in promoting the social, emotional, and academic growth of children.

geography, history, and science. Initial funding for the development of national standards was provided by the U.S. Department of Education. In 1994 the United States Congress passed the *Goals 2000: Educate America Act* (see Figure 5.2), amended in 1996 with an Appropriations Act, encouraging states to set standards. Long before, however, as was done for mathematics by the National Council for Teachers of Mathematics, national organizations devoted to various disciplines were already defining standards.

WHAT THE NATIONAL STANDARDS ARE

The national standards represent the best thinking by expert panels, including teachers from the field, about what are the essential elements of a basic core of subject knowledge that all students should acquire. They serve not as national mandates but rather as voluntary guidelines to encourage curriculum development to promote higher student achievement. It is the discretion of state and local curriculum developers in deciding the extent to which the standards are used. Strongly influenced by the national standards, nearly all 50 states have completed or are presently developing state standards for the various disciplines.

By 1992, for example, most states, usually through state curriculum frameworks, were following the 1989 standards for mathematics education to guide what and how mathematics is taught and how student progress is assessed. The essence of many of those recommendations—a hands-on, inquiry-oriented, performance-based approach to learning less but learning it better—can also be found in the standards that were subsequently developed for other disciplines.

STANDARDS BY CONTENT AREA

The following paragraphs describe standards development for content areas of the K–12 curriculum. Many of the standards are available on the Internet (see Figure 5.1).

Arts (visual and performing). Developed jointly by the American Alliance for Theater and Education, the National Art Education Association, the National Dance Association, and the Music Educators National Conference, the National Standards for Arts Education were completed and released in 1994.

Economics. Developed by the National Council on Economic Education, standards for the study of economics were completed and released in 1997.

English/language arts/reading. Developed jointly by the International Reading Association, the National Council of Teachers of English, and the University of Illinois Center for the Study of Reading, standards for English education were completed and released in 1996.

Foreign languages. Standards for Foreign Language Learning: Preparing for the 21st Century was completed and released by the American Council on the Teaching of Foreign Languages (ACTFL) in 1996.[2]

Geography. Developed jointly by the Association of American Geographers, the National Council for Geographic Education, and the National Geographic Society, standards for geography education were completed and released in 1994.[3]

History/civics/social studies. The Center for Civic Education and the National Center for Social Studies developed standards for civics and government, and the National Center for History in the Schools developed the standards for history, all of which were completed and released in 1994.

Health. Developed by the Joint Committee for National School Health Education Standards, *National Health Education Standards: Achieving Health Literacy* was published in 1995.[4]

Mathematics. In 1989, the National Council of Teachers of Mathematics (NCTM) completed and released *Curriculum and Evaluation Standards for School Mathematics.*

Physical education. In 1995, the National Association of Sport and Physical Education (NASPE) published *Moving Into the Future: National Standards for Physical Education.*

Science. With input from the American Association for the Advancement of Science and the National Science Teachers Association, the National Research Council's National Committee on Science Education Standards and Assessment developed standards for science education, which were completed and released in 1996.

Technology. With initial funding from the National Science Foundation and the National Aeronautics and Space Administration, and in collaboration with the International Technology Education Association, National Educational Technology Standards (NETS) are being developed. For an update see the technology site designated in Figure 5.1.

Exercise 5.3 provides guidelines for your examination of national standards in curriculum areas of interest to you.

Now do Exercises 5.1–5.3.

---

[2]Contact ACTFL, Six Executive Plaza, Yonkers, NY 10701-6801.

[3]Contact National Geographic Society, P.O. Box 1640, Washington, DC 20013-1640.

[4]Contact the American Alliance for Health, Physical Education, Recreation and Dance (AAHPRD), 1900 Association Drive, Reston, VA 22091.

EXERCISE 5.1 EXAMINING NATIONAL CURRICULUM STANDARDS

INSTRUCTIONS: The purpose of this exercise is to become familiar with the national curriculum standards for various subjects of the K–12 curriculum. Using the addresses of sources provided in the preceding section, "National Curriculum Standards," and other sources, such as professional journals, review the standards for your subject or subjects. Use the following questions as a guideline for small- or large-group class discussions. Following small subject-area group discussion, share the developments in each field with the rest of the class.

Subject area _____

1. Name of the standards document reviewed

2. Year of document publication

3. Developed by

4. Specific K–12 goals specified by the new standards

5. Are the standards specific as to subject-matter content for each grade level? Explain.

6. Do the standards offer specific strategies for instruction? Describe.

☞

EXERCISE 5.1 (*continued*)

7. Do the standards offer suggestions for teaching children who are different and for children with special needs? Describe.

8. Do the standards offer suggestions or guidelines for dealing with controversial topics?

9. Do the standards offer suggestions for specific resources? Describe.

10. Do the standards refer to assessment? Describe.

11. In summary, compared with what has been taught and how it has been taught in this field, what is new with the standards?

12. Is there anything else about the standards you would like to discuss in your group?

EXERCISE 5.2 EXAMINING STATE CURRICULUM DOCUMENTS

INSTRUCTIONS: The purpose of this exercise is to become familiar with curriculum documents published by your state department of education. You must determine if that department publishes a curriculum framework for various subjects taught in schools. State frameworks provide valuable information about both content and process, and teachers need to be aware of these documents. You may want to duplicate this form so you can use it to evaluate several documents. After examining documents that interest you, use the following questions as a guideline for small- or large-group class discussions.

1. Are there state curriculum documents available to teachers for your state? If so, describe them and explain how they can be obtained.

   Title of document:

   Source:

   Most recent year of publication:

   Other pertinent information:

2. Examine how closely the document follows the eight components presented in this chapter. Are any components omitted? Are there additional components? Specifically, check for these components:

	Yes	*No*
2.1. Statement of philosophy?	_____	_____
2.2. Evidence of a needs assessment?	_____	_____
2.3. Aims, goals, and objectives?	_____	_____
2.4. Schemes for vertical articulation?	_____	_____
2.5. Schemes for horizontal articulation	_____	_____
2.6. Recommended instructional procedures?	_____	_____
2.7. Recommended resources?	_____	_____
2.8. Assessment strategies?	_____	_____

   Other:

3. Are the documents specific as to subject-matter content for each grade level? Describe evidence of both vertical and horizontal articulation schemes.

4. Do the documents offer specific strategies for instruction? If yes, describe.

EXERCISE 5.2 (*continued*)

5. Do the documents offer suggestions and resources for working with students who are culturally different, for students with special needs, and for students who are intellectually gifted and talented? Describe.

6. Do the documents offer suggestions or guidelines for dealing with controversial topics? If so, describe.

7. Do the documents distinguish between what shall be taught (mandated) and what can be taught (permissible)?

8. Do the documents offer suggestions for specific resources?

9. Do the documents refer to assessment strategies? Describe.

10. Is there anything else about the documents you would like to discuss in your group?

EXERCISE 5.3 EXAMINING LOCAL CURRICULUM DOCUMENTS

INSTRUCTIONS: The purpose of this exercise is to become familiar with curriculum documents prepared by local school districts. A primary resource for what to teach is referred to as a *curriculum guide,* or *course of study,* which normally is developed by teachers of a school or district. Samples may be available in your university library or in a local school district resource center. Or perhaps you could borrow them from teachers you visit. Obtain samples from a variety of sources and then examine them using the format of this exercise. (You may duplicate this form for each document examined.) An analysis of several documents will give you a good picture of expectations. If possible, compare documents from several schools districts and states.

Title of document:

District or school:

Date of document:

1. Examine how closely the documents follow the eight components. Does the document contain the following components?

	Yes	No
1.1. Statement of philosophy?	_____	_____
1.2. Evidence of a needs assessment?	_____	_____
1.3. Aims, goals, and objectives?	_____	_____
1.4. Schemes for vertical articulation?	_____	_____
1.5. Schemes for horizontal articulation?	_____	_____
1.6. Recommended instructional procedures?	_____	_____
1.7. Recommended resources?	_____	_____
1.8. Assessment strategies?	_____	_____

2. Does the document list expected learning outcomes? If so, describe what they are.

3. Does the document contain detailed unit plans? If so, describe them by answering the following questions:

   3.1. Do they contain initiating activities (how to begin a unit)?

   3.2. Do they contain specific learning activities?

   3.3. Do they contain suggested enrichment activities (as for gifted and talented students)?

   3.4. Do they contain culminating activities (activities that bring a unit to a climax)?

   3.5. Do they contain assessment procedures (for determining student achievement)?

   3.6. Do they contain activities for learners with special needs? or for learners who are different in other respects?

☞

EXERCISE 5.3 (*continued*)

4. Does it provide bibliographic entries for

   • The teacher?

   • The students?

5. Does it list audiovisual and other materials needed?

6. Does the document clearly help you understand what the teacher is expected to teach?

7. Are there questions not answered by your examination of this document? If so, list them for class discussion.

Books can provide students with important content organization and resources for learning.

Student Textbooks

For several reasons—the recognition of the diversity of learning styles, capacities, and modalities of students, the increasing cost of textbooks, and the availability of nonprinted materials—textbook appearance, content, and use has changed considerably in recent years.

School districts periodically adopt new textbooks (usually every five to eight years). If you are a student teacher or a first-year teacher, this will most likely mean that someone will tell you, "Here are the textbooks you will be using."

BENEFIT OF STUDENT TEXTBOOKS TO STUDENT LEARNING

It is unlikely that anyone could rationally argue that textbooks are of no benefit to student learning. Textbooks can provide (a) an organization of basic or important content for the students, (b) a basis for deciding content emphasis, (c) previously tested activities and suggestions for learning, (d) information about other readings and resources to enhance student learning, and (e) a foundation for building higher-order thinking activities (e.g., inquiry discussions and student research) that help develop critical thinking skills. The textbook, however, should not be the "be all and end all" of the instructional experiences.

PROBLEMS WITH RELIANCE ON A SINGLE TEXTBOOK

The student textbook is only one of many teaching tools, and not the ultimate word. Of the many ways in which you may use textbooks for student learning, the *least* acceptable is to show a complete dependence on a single book and require students simply to memorize material from it. This is the lowest level of learning; furthermore, it implies that you are unaware of other significant printed and nonprinted resources and have nothing more to contribute to student learning.

Another potential problem in relying on a single textbook is that because textbook publishers prepare books for use in a larger market—that is, for national or statewide use—a state- and district-adopted book may not adequately address issues of special interest and importance to the community in which you teach.[5] That is one reason why some teachers and schools provide supplementary printed and nonprinted resources.

Still another problem brought about by reliance upon a single source is that the adopted textbook may not be at the appropriate reading level for many students. For example, a recent study of the readability of high school chemistry textbooks found that 80 percent of the books had reading levels beyond high school. In other words, most high school students would not be able to read and comprehend the majority of books adopted for use in teaching high school chemistry.[6] In today's heterogeneous classrooms, the level of student reading can vary by as much as two-thirds of the chronological age of the students. This means that if the chronological age is twelve years (typical for seventh-graders), the reading-level range would be

---

[5]At least twenty-four states use statewide textbook adoption committees to review books and to then provide local districts with lists of recommended titles from which to choose.

[6]L. Chavkin, "Readability and Reading Ease Revisited: State-Adopted Science Textbooks," *Clearing House* 70(3):151–154 (January–February 1997).

eight years—that is, the class may have some students reading at only the third-grade level while others have eleventh-grade level reading ability.

GUIDELINES FOR TEXTBOOK USE

Generally speaking, students benefit by having their own copies of a textbook in the current edition. However, because of budget constraints, this may not always be possible. The book may be outdated; quantities may be limited. When the latter is the case, students may not be allowed to take the books home or perhaps may only occasionally do so. In other classrooms, there may be no textbook at all. Still other classrooms have *two* sets of the textbook, one set that remains for use in the classroom and another set that is assigned to students to take home to use for home studying. With that arrangement, students don't have to carry around in their backpacks books as heavy as often they are for many subjects taught in school today. The following general guidelines apply to using the textbook as a learning tool.

Progressing through a textbook from the front cover to the back in one school term is not necessarily an indicator of good teaching. The textbook is one resource; to enhance their learning, students should be encouraged to use a variety of resources. Encourage students to search additional sources to update the content of the textbook. This is especially important in certain disciplines such as science and social sciences, where the amount of new information is growing rapidly and students may have textbooks that are several years old. Students should research the library and sources on the Internet for the latest information on certain subjects. Keep supplementary reading materials for student use in the classroom. School and community librarians and resource specialists usually are delighted to cooperate with teachers in the selection and provision of such resources.

Individualize the learning for students of various reading abilities. Consider differentiated reading and workbook assignments in the textbook and several supplementary sources (see multitext and multireadings approaches, a topic that follows). Except to make life simpler for the teacher, there is no advantage in all students working out of the same book and exercises. Some students benefit from the drill, practice, and reinforcement afforded by workbooks that accompany textbooks, but this is not true for all students. Nor do all benefit from the same activity. In fact, the traditional workbook may eventually become extinct, as it is replaced by the modern technology afforded by computer software and laser discs. As the cost of hardware and software programs becomes more realistic for schools, the use of computers by individual students is also becoming more common. Computers

and other interactive media provide students with a psychologically safer learning environment in which they have greater control over the pace of the instruction, can repeat instruction if necessary, and can ask for clarification without the fear of having to do so publicly.

Teachers have invented several methods to help students develop their higher-level thinking skills and their comprehension of expository material:

- **SQ4R** method: *Survey* the chapter, ask *questions* about what was read, *read* to answer the questions, *recite* the answers, *record* important items from the chapter into their notebooks, then *review* it all.
- **SQ3R** method: *Survey* the chapter, ask *questions* about what was read, *read, recite,* and *review.*
- **PQRST** method: *Preview, question, read, state* the main idea, *test* yourself by answering the questions you posed earlier.
- **SRQ2R:** *Survey, read, question, recite,* and *review.* Or, use *reciprocal teaching* where students are taught and practice the reading skills of summarizing, questioning, clarifying, and predicting.[7]

Just because something is in print (or on the Internet, as we discuss in Chapter 10) does not mean it is necessarily accurate or even true.[8] Encourage students to be alert for errors in the textbook, both in content and printing. You might even give them some sort of credit reward, such as points, when they bring an error to your attention. This helps students develop the skills of critical reading, critical thinking, and healthy skepticism. For example, a history book is reported to have stated that the first person to lead a group through the length of the Grand Canyon was John Wesley Powell. Critically thinking students quickly made the point that perhaps Powell was only the first white person to do this, that Native Americans had traveled the length of the Grand Canyon for centuries before Powell's journey.[9]

[7]Source of PQRST: E. B. Kelly, *Memory Enhancement for Educators,* Fastback 365 (Bloomington, IN: Phi Delta Kappa Educational Foundation, 1994), p. 18. Source of SQ3R: F. P. Robinson, *Effective Study* (rev. ed.) (New York: Harper & Brothers, 1961). The original source of SQ4R is unknown. For SRQ2R, see M. L. Walker, "Help for the 'Fourth-Grade Slum'—SRQ2R Plus Instruction in Text Structure or Main Idea," *Reading Horizons* 36(1):38–58 (1995). About reciprocal teaching, see C. J. Carter, "Why Reciprocal Teaching?" *Educational Leadership* 54(6):64–68 (March 1997), and T. L. Good and J. E. Brophy, *Looking in Classrooms* (New York: Longman, 1997), p. 412–414.
[8]See, for example, C. Gauld, "It Must Be True—It's in the Textbook," *Australian Science Teachers Journal* 43(2):21–26 (June 1997).
[9]R. Reinhold, "Class Struggle," *The New York Times Magazine,* September 29, 1991, p. 46.

Multireading Approach

Rather than a single textbook approach, some teachers, especially when using an integrated thematic approach, use a strategy that incorporates many readings that vary in detail and vocabulary but share a common focus. This multiple reading sources strategy gives students a choice in what they read. The various readings allow for differences in reading ability and interest level and stimulate a sharing of what is read and being learned. By using a teacher's guide such as the sample in Figure 5.3, all the students can be directed toward specific information and concepts, but they do not have to all read the same selections.

Now, use Exercise 5.4 to examine student textbooks and accompanying teachers' editions.

Figure 5.3 Sample multiple readings guide and student's book bibliography to assist students in multiple readings about America's revolutionary times in 1776.

- Purpose: To engage students in multiple readings, critical thinking, and problem solving related to America's revolutionary times in 1776.
- Activities:

1. By reading and browsing through several books and by carefully observing several illustrations of people in this particular time period and geographic area, the students can engage in critical thinking and problem solving by working in small groups. The bibliography that follows includes books suitable for a wide range of reading levels related to America in 1776. Students can respond to the following focus questions after multitext reading:
   a. What features of the land (features of government, society, etc.) seem to be important to the people in 1776?
   b. What occupations seem to be most important? What inventions (tools, machines) appear to be most useful?
   c. What do the answers to these questions tell us about the way of life of the people who lived in this time period (geographic area)?
2. Back with the whole group, have the students from each group report on the responses to the questions. Engage students in dictating or writing a paragraph summarizing the responses to the questions.
3. Students can meet with response partners to read their individually written paragraphs aloud to one another and provide suggestions to each other for rewriting the paragraphs.

- Bibliography (*sample only*)

African American

Davis, B. *Black Heroes of the American Revolution.* (San Diego: HarcourtJ, 1976). Nonfictional account depicting contributions of African Americans during the revolutionary war. Includes drawings, etchings, bibliography, and an index.

Hansen, J. *The Captive.* (New York: Scholastic, 1994). Based on a journal written in the late 1700s, this is about Kofi, the twelve-year-old son of an Ashanti chief. Kofi is sold and sent to America after his father is murdered by a family slave. Kofi and others escape from the farmer in Massachusetts and return to Africa. An epilogue relates his good life when he returned to Africa.

Millender, D. H. *Crispus Attucks: Black Leader of Colonial Patriots.* (New York: Macmillan, 1986). Biographical portrayal of the life of a Colonial African American and his contribution to the American Revolution.

European

Wade, M. D. *Benedict Arnold.* (New York: Franklin Watts, 1995). Biographical story of Arnold's life, his heroic deeds, including his leadership at the battle of Saratoga, his later traitorous actions, and his death in London. Includes information about his wife, Peggy Shippen.

Female Image

DePaul, L. G. *Founding Mothers: Women in America in the Revolutionary Era.* (Boston: Houghton Mifflin, 1975). Nonfictional account of the contributions of women during the revolution.

McGovern, A. *Secret Soldier: The Story of Deborah Sampson.* (New York: Scholastic, 1991). Story of a young woman who disguised herself as a boy and joined the army to serve in America's War for Independence.

Latino/Hispanic

Anderson, J. *Spanish Pioneers of the Southwest.* Illustrated by G. Ancona. (New York: Dutton, 1989). Nonfictional account of the lives of the colonists on the east coast contrasted with the lives of the members of a pioneer family in a Spanish community in New Mexico in the 1700s and the family's hard work, harsh living conditions, and traditions.

Native American

Hudson, J. *Dawn Rider.* (New York: Putnam, 1990). Fictional account of 16-year-old Kit Fox, a Blackfoot forbidden to ride horses. She disobeys and her riding skills help her people when their camp is attacked.

Kinsey-Warock, N. *Wilderness Cat.* Illustrated by Mark Graham. (Minneapolis: Cobblehill, 1992). Lives of colonists are contrasted with the lives of Serena's family members when they moved to Canada in the 1700s. Even though the family trades with the Indians, they do not have enough to eat; Papa and Serena's brother leave to find work. Historical fiction.

Religious Minority

Faber, D. *The Perfect Life: The Shakers in America.* (New York: Farrar, Straus, & Giroux, 1974). Escaping from England, Mother Ann and several followers voyage to America and set up the first settlement in New York in 1776. Nonfictional account detailing the Shaker religious beliefs and influence on furniture construction and mechanical inventions.

(*Note:* the bibliography in Figure 5.3 is not intended to be inclusive, only to show how a multiple readings guide might appear.)

EXERCISE 5.4: EXAMINING STUDENT TEXTBOOKS AND TEACHER'S EDITIONS

INSTRUCTIONS: The purpose of this exercise is to become familiar with textbooks that you may be using in your teaching. Student textbooks are usually accompanied by a teacher's edition that contains specific objectives, teaching techniques, learning activities, assessment instruments, test items, and suggested resources. Your university library, local schools, and cooperating teachers are sources for locating and borrowing these enhanced textbooks. For your subject field of interest, select a textbook that is accompanied by a teacher's edition and examine the contents of both using the following format. If there are no standard textbooks available for your teaching field (such as might be the case for art, home economics, industrial arts, music, and physical education), then select a field in which there is a possibility you might teach. Beginning teachers are often assigned to teach in more than one field—sometimes, unfortunately, in fields for which they are untrained or have only minimal training. After completion of this exercise, share the book and your analysis of it with your colleagues.

Title of book:

Author(s):

Publisher:

Date of most recent publication:

1. Analyze the teacher's edition for the following elements.

	Yes	*No*
a. Are its goals consistent with the goals of local and state curriculum documents?	____	____
b. Are there specific objectives for each lesson?	____	____
c. Does the book have scope and sequence charts for teacher reference?	____	____
d. Are the units and lessons sequentially developed, with suggested time allotments?	____	____
e. Are there any suggested provisions for individual differences?	____	____
for reading levels?	____	____
for students with special needs?	____	____
for students who are gifted and talented?	____	____
for students who have limited proficiency in English?	____	____
f. Does it recommend specific techniques and strategies?	____	____
g. Does it have listings of suggested aids, materials, and resources?	____	____
h. Are there suggestions for extension activities (to extend the lessons beyond the usual topic or time)?	____	____
i. Does the book have specific guidelines for assessment of student learning?	____	____

☞

EXERCISE 5.3 (*continued*)

2. Analyze the student textbook for the following elements.

	Yes	No
a. Does it treat the content with adequate depth?	_____	_____
b. Does it treat ethnic minorities and women fairly?	_____	_____
c. Is the format attractive?	_____	_____
d. Does the book have good quality binding with suitable type size?	_____	_____
e. Are illustrations and visuals attractive and useful?	_____	_____
f. Is the reading clear and understandable for the students?	_____	_____

3. Would you like to use this textbook? Give reasons why or why not.

BEGINNING TO THINK ABOUT THE SEQUENCING OF CONTENT

As you have reviewed the rationale and components of instructional planning, and examined state and local curriculum documents, national standards, and student reading materials, you have undoubtedly reflected on your own opinion regarding content that should be included in a subject at a particular grade level. Now it is time to obtain some practical experience in long-range planning. While some authors believe that the first step in preparing to teach is to write the objectives, I believe a more logical starting point is to prepare a sequential topic outline—the next step in this chapter—from which you can then prepare the major target objectives (Chapter 6).

The topic outlines and instructional objectives may be presented to most beginning teachers with the expectation that they will teach from them. For you this may be the case, but someone had to have written those outlines and objectives and that someone was one or more classroom teachers. As a teacher candidate, you must know how this is done, for someday it will be your task. To experience preparing a year-long (or semester-long) content outline for a subject and grade level that you intend to teach, do Exercise 5.5 now.

EXERCISE 5.5: PREPARING A CONTENT OUTLINE

INSTRUCTIONS: The purpose of this exercise is for you to organize your ideas about subject content and the sequencing of content. Unless instructed otherwise by your instructor, you should select the subject (e.g., algebra, science, English/language arts) and the grade level.

With *three levels of headings* (see example that follows), prepare a sequential topic outline (on a separate piece of paper as space is not provided here) for a subject and grade level you intend to teach. Identify the subject by title, and clearly state the grade level. This outline is of topic content only and does *not* need to include student activities associated with the learning of that content (i.e., do not include experiments, assignments, or assessment strategies).

For example, for the study of earth science, three levels of headings might include

I. The Earth's surface

   A. Violent changes in Earth's surface

      1. Earthquakes

      2. Volcanoes

   B. Earth's land surface

      1. Rocks

   etc.

If the study of earth science was just one unit for a grade level's study of the broader area of science, then three levels of headings for that study might include

I. Earth science

   A. The Earth's surface

      1. Violent changes in Earth's surface

   etc.

Share your completed outline to obtain feedback from your colleagues and university instructor. Because content outlines are never to be "carved into stone," make adjustments to your outline when and as appropriate.

Content Outline Assessment Checklist

For the development of your own outline, and for the assessment of outlines by others, here is a content outline assessment checklist:

- Does the outline follow a logical sequence, with each topic logically leading to the next?

   Yes _____ No _____ Comment:

- Does the content assume prerequisite knowledge or skills that the students are likely to have?

   Yes _____ No _____ Comment:

- Is the content inclusive and to an appropriate depth?

   Yes _____ No _____ Comment:

EXERCISE 5.5 (*continued*)

- Does the content consider individual student differences?

  Yes _____ No _____ Comment:

- Does the content allow for interdisciplinary studies?

  Yes _____   No _____ Comment:

- Is the outline complete; are there serious content omissions?

  Yes _____ No _____ Comment:

- Is there content that is of questionable value for this level of instruction?

  Yes _____ No _____ Comment:

Save your content outline and this completed exercise for later when you are working on Exercise 5.11 and exercises in Chapter 6.

PREPARING FOR AND DEALING WITH CONTROVERSY

Controversial content and issues abound in teaching, especially in certain disciplines. For example: in English/language arts, over whole language/phonics and over certain books (see Exercise 5.6B); in social studies, over values and moral issues; in science, over biological evolution and use of animals in research. As a general rule, if you have concern that a particular topic or activity might create controversy, it probably will. During your teaching career, you undoubtedly will have to make decisions about how you will handle such matters. When selecting content that might be controversial, consider the paragraphs that follow as guidelines.

Maintain a perspective with respect to your own goal, which is at the moment to obtain your teaching credential, and then a teaching job, and then tenure. Student teaching is not a good time to become involved in controversy. If you communicate closely with your cooperating teacher and your college or university supervisor, you should be able to prevent major problems dealing with controversial issues.

Sometimes, during normal discussion in the classroom, a controversial subject will emerge spontaneously, catching the teacher off guard. If this happens, think before saying anything. You may wish to postpone further discussion until you have a chance to talk over the issue with members of your teaching team or your supervisors. Controversial topics can seem to arise from nowhere for any teacher, and this is perfectly normal. Young people are in the process of developing their moral and value systems, and they need and want to know how adults feel about issues that are important to them, particularly those adults they hold in esteem—their teachers. Students need to discuss issues that are important to society, and there is absolutely nothing wrong with dealing with those issues as long as certain guidelines are followed.

First, students should learn about all sides of an issue. Controversial issues are open ended and should be treated as such. They do not have "right" answers or "correct" solutions. If they did, there would be no controversy. (As used in this book, an "issue" differs from a "problem" in that a problem generally has a solution, whereas an issue has many opinions and several alternative solutions.) Therefore, the focus should be on both process and content. A major goal is to show students how to deal with controversy and to mediate wise decisions on the basis of carefully considered information. Another goal is to help students learn how to disagree without being disagreeable—how to resolve conflict. To that end students need to learn the difference between conflicts that are destructive and those that can be constructive, in other words, to see that conflict (disagreement) can be healthy, that it can have value. A third goal, of course, is to help students learn about the content of an issue so, when necessary, they can make decisions based on knowledge, not on ignorance.

Second, as with all lesson plans, one dealing with a topic that could lead to controversy should be well thought out ahead of time. Potential problem areas and resources must be carefully considered and prepared for in advance. Problems for the teacher are most likely to occur when the plan has not been well thought out.

Third, at some point all persons directly involved in an issue have a right to input: students, parents and guardians, community representatives, and other faculty. This does not mean, for example, that people outside of the school have the right to censor a teacher's plan, but it does mean that parents or guardians and students should have the right *without penalty* to not participate and to select an alternate activity. Most school districts have written policies that deal with challenges to instructional materials. As a beginning teacher, you should become aware of policies of your school district. In addition, professional associations such as the NCTE, NCSS, NBTA, and NSTA have published guidelines for dealing with controversial topics, materials, and issues.

Fourth, there is nothing wrong with students knowing a teacher's opinion about an issue as long as it is clear that the students may disagree without reprisal or academic penalty. However, it is probably best for a teacher to wait and give her or his opinion only after the students have had full opportunity to study and report on facts and opinions from other sources. Sometimes it is helpful if you assist students in separating facts from opinions on a particular issue being studied by setting up on the overhead or writing board a fact–opinion table, with the issue stated at the top and then two parallel columns, one for facts, the other for related opinions.

A characteristic that has made this nation so great is the freedom for all its people to speak out on issues. This freedom should not be excluded from public school classrooms. Teachers and students should be encouraged to express their opinions about the great issues of today, to study the issues, to suspend judgment while collecting data, and then to form and accept each other's reasoned opinions. We must understand the difference between teaching truth, values, and morals and teaching *about* truth, values, and morals.

As a public school teacher there are limits to your academic freedom, much greater than are the limits on a university professor.[10] You must understand this fact. The primary difference is that the students with

---

[10]For a legal test case regarding the concept of academic freedom in a public secondary school, see D. Lindsay, "Dramatic License," *Teacher Magazine* X(2):24–28 (October 1998).

A major goal for K-12 education should be to show students how to resolve conflict, to deal with controversy, and to mediate wise decisions on the basis of carefully considered information.

whom you will be working are not yet adults; they must be protected from dogma and allowed the freedom to learn and to develop their values and opinions, free from coercion from those who have power and control over their learning.

Now that you have read my opinion and suggested guidelines, what do you think about this topic, which should be important to you as a teacher? Use Exercises 5.6A and 5.6B to develop and express your opinion.

EXERCISE 5.6A: DEALING WITH CONTROVERSIAL CONTENT AND ISSUES

INSTRUCTIONS: The purpose of this exercise is for you to discover controversial content and issues that you may face as a teacher and to consider what you can and will do about them. After completing this exercise, share it with members of your class.

1. After studying current periodicals and talking with colleagues in the schools you visit, list two potentially controversial topics that you are likely to encounter as a teacher. (Two examples are given for you.)

Issue	Source
Use of chimpanzees for medical research	*National Geographic, March 1992*
Human cloning	*Time, March 1997*
Use of calculators in mathematics	*(ongoing)*

2. Take one of these issues, and identify opposing arguments and current resources.

_____

_____

_____

_____

3. Identify your own positions on this issue.

_____

_____

_____

_____

4. How well can you accept students (and parents or guardians) who assume the opposite position?

_____

_____

_____

_____

5. Share the preceding with other teacher candidates. Note comments that you find helpful or enlightening.

_____

_____

_____

_____

EXERCISE 5.6B: CENSORSHIP: BOOKS THAT ARE SOMETIMES CHALLENGED

INSTRUCTIONS: Continuing with the topic introduced in Exercise 5.6A, this exercise concentrates on certain books that, although frequently used in teaching, are sometimes challenged by members of some communities. Book censorship becomes a concern when literature is the base for integrated teaching since there may be attempts to censor books and curricular materials in the schools. Books that have been challenged include

The Adventures of Huckleberry Finn
  (Mark Twain)
Annie on My Mind (Nancy Garden)
The Arizona Kid (Ron Koertge)
The Catcher in the Rye (J. D. Salinger)
The Chocolate War (Robert Cormier)
Christine (Stephen King)
The Clan of the Cave Bear (Jean Auel)
The Color Purple (Alice Walker)
A Day No Pigs Would Die (Robert Newton
  Peck)
Diary of a Young Girl (Anne Frank)
Fallen Angels (Walter Dean Myers)
Flowers in the Attic (V. C. Andrews)
Forever (Judy Blume)

Go Ask Alice (Anonymous)
The Great Santini (Pat Conroy)
Grendel (John Gardner)
The Handmaid's Tale (Margaret Atwood)
I Am the Cheese (Robert Cormier)
I Know Why the Caged Bird Sings (Maya
  Angelou)
Lord of the Flies (William Golding)
Of Mice and Men (John Steinbeck)
The Outsiders (S. E. Hinton)
Romeo and Juliet (William Shakespeare)
Running Loose (Chris Crutcher)
Scary Stories to Tell in the Dark (Alvin
  Schwartz)
Tarzan of the Apes (Edgar Rice Burroughs)

Review one of these books and explain how it might be challenged for censorship and how you would respond to the challenge. We leave the organization of this exercise for your class to decide; we recommend that you assign small groups to review certain books, then report to the entire class so that all the books on the list have been addressed.

_____
_____
_____
_____
_____
_____
_____
_____
_____
_____
_____
_____
_____
_____
_____
_____
_____

AIMS, GOALS, AND OBJECTIVES: THE ANTICIPATED LEARNING OUTCOME

Now that you have examined content typical of the curriculum and have experienced preparing a tentative content outline for a subject that you intend to teach, you are ready to write instructional objectives for that content learning. *Instructional objectives* are statements describing what the student will be able to do upon completion of the instructional experience. Whereas some authors distinguish between *instructional objectives* (hence referring to objectives that are *not* behavior specific) and *behavioral* or *performance objectives* (objectives that *are* behavior specific), the terms are used here as if they are synonymous to emphasize the importance of writing instructional objectives in terms that are measurable. *Terminal objective* is sometimes used to distinguish between instructional objectives that are intermediate and those that are final, or "terminal" to an area of learning.

As a teacher, you frequently will encounter the compound structure that reads "goals and objectives," as you likely found in the curriculum documents that you reviewed (Exercises 5.1–5.4). A distinction needs to be understood. The easiest way to understand the difference between the two words, *goals* and *objectives,* is to consider your *intent*.

Goals are ideals that you intend to reach, that is, ideals that you would like to accomplish. Goals may be stated as teacher goals, as student goals, or, collaboratively, as team goals. Ideally, in all three, the goal is the same. If, for example, the goal is to improve students' reading skills, it could be stated as follows:

"To help students develop   *Teacher or course goal*
  their reading skills"

or

"To improve my reading   *Student goal*
  skills"

Educational goals are general statements of intent and are prepared early in course planning. (*Note*: Some writers use the phrase "general goals and objectives," but that is incorrect usage. Goals *are* general; objectives are specific.) Goals are useful when planned cooperatively with students and/or when shared with students as advance mental organizers to establish a mind-set. The students then know what to expect and will begin to prepare mentally to learn it. From the goals, objectives are prepared. Objectives are *not* intentions. They are the actual behaviors teachers intend to cause students to display. In short, objectives are what students do.

The most general educational objectives are often called *aims;* the objectives of schools, curricula, and courses are called *goals;* the objectives of units and lessons are called *instructional objectives.* Aims are more general than goals, goals are more general than objectives. Instructional objectives are quite specific. Aims, goals, and objectives represent the targets, from general to specific statements of learning expectations, to which curriculum and instruction are designed and aimed.

Instructional Objectives and Their Relationship to Aligned Curriculum and Authentic Assessment

As implied in the preceding paragraphs, goals guide the instructional methods; objectives drive student performance. Assessment of student achievement in learning should be an assessment of that performance. When the assessment procedure matches the instructional objectives, that is sometimes referred to as assessment that is *aligned* or *authentic* (discussed in Chapter 11). When objectives, instruction, and assessment match the stated goals, we have what is referred to as an *aligned curriculum.*

Goals are general statements, usually not even complete sentences, often beginning with the infinitive "to," which identify what the teacher intends the students to learn. Objectives, stated in performance terms, are specific actions and should be written as complete sentences that include the verb "will" to indicate what each student is expected to be able to do as a result of the instructional experience. When writing instructional objectives for their unit and lesson plans, beginning teachers often err by stating what *they* intend to do rather than what the anticipated student performance is. The value of stating learning objectives in terms of student performance is well documented by research.[11]

While instructional goals may not always be quantifiable (that is, readily measurable), instructional objectives should be measurable. Furthermore, those objectives then become the essence of what is measured for in instruments designed to assess student learning; they are the learning targets. Consider the examples shown in Figure 5.4.

LEARNING TARGETS AND GOAL INDICATORS

One purpose for writing objectives in performance terms is to be able to assess with precision whether the instruction has resulted in the desired behavior. In many schools the educational goals are established as *learning targets,* competencies that the students are expected to achieve. These goals are then divided into

---

[11]See, for example, J. C. Baker and F. G. Martin, *A Neural Network Guide to Teaching,* Fastback 431 (Bloomington, IN: Phi Delta Kappa Educational Foundation, 1998), and T. L. Good and J. E. Brophy, *Looking in Classrooms,* 7th ed. (New York: Addison Wesley/Longman, 1997), p. 240.

Figure 5.4   Examples of goals and objectives.

Goals

1. To acquire knowledge about the physical geography of North America.
2. To develop an appreciation for music.
3. To develop enjoyment for reading.

Objectives

1. On a map the student will identify specific mountain ranges of North America.
2. The student will identify ten different musical instruments by listening to a tape recording of the Boston Pops Symphony Orchestra and identify which instrument is being played at specified times as determined by the teacher.
3. The student will read two books, three short stories, and five newspaper articles at home within a two-month period. The student will maintain a daily written log of these activities.

---

performance objectives, sometimes referred to as *goal indicators*. Instruction is designed to teach toward those objectives. When students perform the competencies called for by these objectives, their education is considered successful. As discussed further in Chapters 8 and 11, this is known variously as *criterion-referenced, competency-based, performance-based, results-driven,* or *outcome-based education.* Expecting students to achieve one set of competencies before moving on to the next set is called *mastery learning* (discussed further in Chapter 8.) The success of the student achievement, teacher performance, and the school may each be assessed according to these criteria.

OVERT AND COVERT
PERFORMANCE OUTCOMES

Assessment is not difficult to accomplish when the desired performance outcome is overt behavior, which can be observed directly. Each of the sample objectives of the preceding section is an example of an overt objective. Assessment is more difficult to accomplish when the desired behavior is *covert*, that is, when it is not directly observable. Although certainly no less important, behaviors that call for "appreciation," "discovery," or "understanding," for example, are not directly observable because they occur within a person. Since covert behavior cannot be observed directly, the only way to tell whether the objective has been achieved is to observe behavior that may be indicative of that achievement. The objective, then, is written in overt language, and evaluators can only assume or trust that the observed behavior is, in fact, reasonably close to being indicative of the expected learning outcome.

Furthermore, when assessing whether an objective has been achieved—that learning has occurred—the assessment device must be consistent with the desired learning outcome. Otherwise, the assessment is not aligned; it is invalid. When the measuring device and the learning objective are compatible, we say that the assessment is authentic. For example, a person's competency to teach specific skills in physical education to children in the fourth grade is best (i.e., with highest reliability) measured by directly observing that person *doing* that very thing—teaching specific skills in physical education to fourth graders. Using a standardized paper-and-pencil test of multiple-choice items to determine a person's ability to teach specific physical education skills to fourth grade students is not authentic assessment.

Balance of Behaviorism and Constructivism

While behaviorists assume a definition of learning that deals only with changes in overt behavior, constructivists hold that learning entails the construction or reshaping of mental schemata and that mental processes mediate learning. Thus, people who adhere to constructivism or cognitivism are concerned with both overt and covert behaviors.[12] Does this mean that you must be one or the other, a behaviorist or a constructivist? Probably not. For now, the point is that when writing instructional objectives, you should write most or all of your basic expectations (minimal competency expectations) in overt terms (the topic of the next section). On the other hand, you cannot be expected to foresee all learning that occurs nor to translate all that is learned into performance terms—most certainly not before it occurs.

Teaching toward Multiple Objectives, Understandings, and Appreciations

Any effort to write all learning objectives in performance terms is, in effect, to neglect the individual learner for whom it purports to be concerned. Such an approach does not allow for diversity among learners. Learning that is most meaningful to children is not so neatly or easily predicted or isolated. Rather than

---

[12]See, for example: P. W. Airasian and M. E. Walsh, "Constructivist Cautions," *Phi Delta Kappan* 78(6):444–449 (February 1997); D. R. Geelan, "Epistemological Anarchy and the Many Forms of Constructivism," *Science and Education* 6(1–2):15–28 (January 1997); R. Delay, "Forming Knowledge: Constructivist Learning and Experiential Education," *Journal of Experiential Education* 19(2):76–81 (August/September 1996); J.R. Gentile, "Setbacks in 'The Advancement of Learning'?" *Educational Researcher* 25(7):37–39 (October 1996); and, M. D. Roblyer, "The Constructivist/Objectivist Debate: Implications for Instructional Technology Research," *Learning and Leading with Technology* 24(2):12–16 (October 1996).

teaching one objective at a time, much of the time you should direct your teaching toward the simultaneous learning of multiple objectives, understandings, and appreciations. However, when you assess for learning, assessment is cleaner when objectives are assessed one at a time. More on this matter of objectives and their use in teaching and learning follows later in this chapter. Let's now review how objectives are prepared.

PREPARING INSTRUCTIONAL OBJECTIVES

When preparing instructional objectives, you must ask yourself, "How is the student to demonstrate that the objective has been reached?" The objective must include an action that demonstrates the objective has been achieved. Inherited from behaviorism, this portion of the objective is sometimes called the *anticipated measurable performance*.

Four Key Components

When completely written in performance terms, an instructional objective has four key components. To aid your understanding and remembering, you can refer to these as the ABCDs of writing objectives.

One component is the *audience*. The *A* of the ABCDs refers to the student for whom the objective is intended. To address this, sometimes teachers begin their objectives with the phrase "The student will be able to . . .," or, to personalize the objective, "You will

Figure 5.5 Verbs to avoid when writing overt objectives.

appreciate	enjoy	indicate	like
believe	familiarize	know	realize
comprehend	grasp	learn	understand

be able to . . ." (*Note:* To conserve space and to eliminate useless language, in examples that follow I eliminate use of "be able to," and write simply "The student will . . ." For brevity, writers of objectives sometimes use the abbreviation "TSWBAT . . ." for "The student will be able to . . .")

The second key component is the expected *behavior*, the *B* of the ABCDs. This second component represents the important learning target. The expected behavior (or performance) should be written with verbs that are measurable—that is, with action verbs—so that it is directly observable that the objective, or target, has been reached. As discussed in the preceding section, some verbs are too vague, ambiguous, and not clearly measurable. When writing objectives, you should avoid verbs that are not clearly measurable, covert verbs such as "appreciate," "comprehend," and "understand." (See Figure 5.5.) For the three examples given earlier, for Objectives 1 and 2 the behaviors (action or overt verbs) are "will *identify*," and, for Objective 3, the behaviors are "will *read* and *maintain*."

Now do Exercise 5.7 to assess and further your understanding.

EXERCISE 5.7 RECOGNIZING VERBS THAT ARE ACCEPTABLE FOR OVERT OBJECTIVES— A SELF-CHECK EXERCISE

INSTRUCTIONS: The purpose of this exercise is to check your recognition of verbs that are suitable for use in overt objectives. From the list of verbs below, circle those that *should not* be used in overt objectives—that is, those verbs that describe covert behaviors not directly observable and measurable. Check your answers against the answer key that follows. Discuss any problems with the exercise with your classmates and instructor.

1. apply	11. design	21. know
2. appreciate	12. diagram	22. learn
3. believe	13. enjoy	23. name
4. combine	14. explain	24. outline
5. comprehend	15. familiarize	25. predict
6. compute	16. grasp*	26. realize
7. create	17. identify	27. select
8. define	18. illustrate	28. solve
9. demonstrate	19. indicate	29. state
10. describe	20. infer	30. understand

Answer key: The following verbs should be circled: 2, 3, 5, 13, 15, 16, 21, 22, 26, 30. If you missed more than a couple, then you need to read the previous sections again and discuss your errors with your classmates and instructor. *Note: words in English often have more than one meaning. For example, "grasp," as listed here could mean "to take hold," or it could mean "to comprehend." For the former it would be an acceptable verb for use in overt objectives; for the latter it would not.

EXERCISE 5.8 RECOGNIZING THE PARTS OF CRITERION-REFERENCED INSTRUCTIONAL OBJECTIVES—A SELF-CHECK EXERCISE

INSTRUCTIONS: The purpose of this exercise is to practice your skill in recognizing the four components of an instructional objective. In the following two objectives, identify the parts of the objectives by underlining once the *audience,* twice the *performance (behavior),* three times the *conditions,* and four times the *performance level* (that is, the degree or standard of performance).

Check your answers against the answer key that follows, and discuss any problems with this exercise with your classmates and instructor.

1. Given a metropolitan transit bus schedule, at the end of the lesson the student will be able to read the schedule well enough to determine at what times buses are scheduled to leave randomly selected locations, with at least 90 percent accuracy.

2. Given five rectangular figures, you will correctly compute the area in square centimeters of at least four, by measuring the length and width with a ruler and computing the product using an appropriate calculation method.

Exercise Answer Key:

	Objective 1	*Objective 2*
Audience (underlined once)	The student	You
Behavior (underlined twice)	will be able to read the schedule	will compute
Conditions (underlined three times)	given a metropolitan transit bus schedule	given five rectangular figures
Performance level (underlined four times)	well enough to determine (and) with at least 90 percent accuracy	correctly compute the area in square centimeters of at least four (80 percent accuracy)

Most of the time, when writing objectives for your unit and lesson plans, you will not bother yourself with including the next two components. However, as you will learn, they are important for assessment.

The third ingredient is the *conditions,* the *C* of the ABCDs, the setting in which the behavior will be demonstrated by the student and observed by the teacher. Conditions are forever changing; although the learning target should be clearly recognizable long before the actual instruction occurs, the conditions may not. Thus, conditions are not often included in the objectives teachers write. For the first sample objective, the conditions are: "on a map." For the second sample objective, the conditions are: "by listening to a tape recording of the Boston Pops Symphony Orchestra," and "specified times as determined by the teacher." For the third sample, the conditions are: "at home within a two-month period."

The fourth ingredient, which again is not always included in objectives written by teachers, is the *degree* (or level) of expected performance—the *D* of the ABCDs. This is the ingredient that allows for the assess-

ment of student learning. When mastery learning is expected, the level of expected performance is usually omitted (because it is understood). In teaching for mastery learning, the performance-level expectation is 100 percent. In reality, however, the performance level will most likely be between 85 and 95 percent, particularly when working with a group of students rather than with an individual student. The 5 to 15 percent difference allows for human error, as can occur when using written and oral communication. Like conditions, standards will vary depending on the situation and purpose and thus are not normally included in the unit and lessons that teachers prepare. Now, to reinforce your comprehension, do Exercise 5.8.

Performance level is used to assess student achievement, and sometimes it is used to evaluate the effectiveness of the teaching. Student grades might be based on performance levels; evaluation of teacher effectiveness might be based on the level of student performance.

Now, with Exercise 5.9, try your skill at recognizing student learning objectives that are measurable.

EXERCISE 5.9 RECOGNIZING OBJECTIVES THAT ARE MEASURABLE— A SELF-CHECK EXERCISE

INSTRUCTIONS: The purpose of this exercise is to assess your ability to recognize objectives that are measurable. Place an *X* before each of the following that is an overt, student-centered instructional objective, that is, a clearly measurable learning objective. Although "audience," "conditions," or "performance levels" may be absent, ask yourself, "As stated, is this a student-centered and measurable objective?" If it is, place an *X* in the blank. A self-checking answer key follows. After checking your answers, discuss any problems with the exercise with your classmates and instructor.

_____ 1. To develop an appreciation for literature.

_____ 2. To identify those celestial bodies that are known planets.

_____ 3. To provide meaningful experiences for the students.

_____ 4. To recognize antonym pairs.

_____ 5. To boot up the program on the computer.

_____ 6. To analyze and compare patterns of data or specific quartile maps.

_____ 7. To develop skills in inquiry.

_____ 8. To identify which of the four causes is most relevant to the major events leading up to the Civil War.

_____ 9. To use maps and graphs to identify the major areas of world petroleum production and consumption.

_____ 10. To know the causes for the diminishing ozone concentration.

Exercise Answer Key: You should have marked items 2, 4, 5, 6, 8, and 9.

Items 1, 3, 7, and 10 are inadequate because of their ambiguity. Item 3 is not even a student learning objective; it is a teacher goal. "To develop" and "to know" can have too many interpretations. Although the conditions are not given, items 2, 4, 5, 6, 8, and 9 are clearly measurable. The teacher would have no difficulty recognizing when a learner had reached those objectives. Discuss any problem you had with this exercise with your classmates and instructor.

Classifying Instructional Objectives

When planning instructional objectives, it is useful to consider the three domains of learning objectives:

cognitive domain—involves intellectual operations from the lowest level of the simple recall of information to complex, high-level thinking processes;

affective domain—involves feelings, emotions, attitudes, and values, and ranges from the lower levels of acquisition to the highest level of internalization and action; and

psychomotor domain—ranges from the simple manipulation of materials to the communication of ideas, and finally to the highest level of creative performance.

The Domains of Learning and the Developmental Needs of Children

Educators attempt to design learning experiences to meet the five areas of developmental needs of the total child: intellectual, physical, emotional/psychological, social, and moral/ethical. As a teacher, you must include objectives that address learning within each of these categories of needs. While the intellectual needs are primarily within the cognitive domain and the physical are within the psychomotor, the other needs mostly are within the affective domain.

Too frequently, teachers focus on the cognitive domain while assuming that the psychomotor and affec-

Children are social beings. They like to be with and accepted by their peers. A child will develop a satisfactory self-esteem when given an opportunity to work with others, to offer ideas, and to work out peer relationships. The teacher can help foster not only the learning but also the development of each child's self-esteem.

tive will take care of themselves. Many experts argue that teachers should do just the opposite: that when the affective is directly attended to, the psychomotor and cognitive naturally develop. In any case, you should plan your teaching so your students are guided from the lowest to highest levels of operation within each of the domains, separately or simultaneously.

The three developmental hierarchies are discussed next to guide your understanding of each of the five areas of needs. Notice the illustrative verbs within each hierarchy. These verbs help you fashion objectives when you are developing unit plans and lesson plans. (To see how goals and objectives are fit into one lesson plan, see Figure 6.11, Chapter 6, "Multiple-day, project-centered, interdisciplinary, and transcultural lesson using world-wide communication via the Internet.") However, caution must be urged, for there can be considerable overlap among the levels at which some action verbs may appropriately be used. For example, the verb "identifies" is appropriate in each of the following objectives at different levels (identified in parentheses) within the cognitive domain:

The student will identify the correct definition of the term *osmosis.* (knowledge)

The student will identify examples of the principle of osmosis. (comprehension)

The student will identify the osmotic effect when a cell is immersed into a hypotonic solution. (application)

The student will identify the osmotic effect on turgor pressure when the cell is placed in a hypotonic solution. (analysis)

Cognitive Domain Hierarchy

In a widely accepted taxonomy of objectives, Bloom and his associates arranged cognitive objectives into classifications according to the complexity of the skills and abilities they embodied.[13] The result was a ladder ranging from the simplest to the most complex intellectual processes. Within each domain, prerequisite to a student's ability to function at one particular level of the hierarchy is the ability to function at the preceding level or levels. In other words, when a student is functioning at the third level of the cognitive domain, that student is automatically also functioning at the first and second levels. Rather than an orderly progression from simple to complex mental operations as illustrated by Bloom's taxonomy, other researchers prefer an organization of cognitive abilities that ranges from simple information storage and retrieval, through a higher level of discrimination and concept attainment, to the highest cognitive ability to recognize and solve problems.[14]

The six major categories (or levels) in Bloom's taxonomy of cognitive objectives are (1) *knowledge*—recognizing and recalling information; (2) *comprehension*—understanding the meaning of information; (3) *application*—using information; (4) *analysis*—dissecting information into its component parts to comprehend their relationships; (5) *synthesis*—putting

[13]B. S. Bloom (Ed.), *Taxonomy of Educational Objectives, Book 1, Cognitive Domain* (White Plains, NY: Longman, 1984).

[14]See R. M. Gagné, L. J. Briggs, and W. W. Wager, *Principles of Instructional Design,* 4th ed. (New York: Holt, Rinehart, and Winston, 1994).

components together to generate new ideas; and (6) *evaluation*—judging the worth of an idea, notion, theory, thesis, proposition, information, or opinion. In this taxonomy, the top four categories or levels—application, analysis, synthesis, and evaluation—represent what are called *higher-order cognitive thinking skills.*[15]

Although space does not allow elaboration here, Bloom's taxonomy includes various subcategories within each of these six major categories. It is probably less important that an objective be absolutely classified than it is to be cognizant of hierarchies of thinking and doing and to understand the importance of attending to student intellectual behavior from lower to higher levels of operation in all three domains. Discussion of each of Bloom's six categories follows.

KNOWLEDGE

The basic element in Bloom's taxonomy concerns the acquisition of knowledge—that is, the ability to recognize and recall information. (As discussed in Chapter 8, this is similar to the *input level* of thinking and questioning.) Although this is the lowest of the six categories, the information to be learned may not itself be of a low level. In fact, it may be of an extremely high level. Bloom includes here knowledge of principles, generalizations, theories, structures, and methodology, along with knowledge of facts and ways of dealing with facts.

Action verbs appropriate for this category include "choose," "complete," "cite," "define," "describe," "identify," "indicate," "list," "locate," "match," "name," "outline," "recall," "recognize," "select," and "state."

The following are examples of objectives at the knowledge level. Note especially the verb (in italics) used in each example:

- From memory, the student *will recall* the letters in the English alphabet that are vowels.
- The student *will list* the organelles found in animal cell cytoplasm.
- The student *will identify* the major parts of speech in the sentence.
- The student *will name* the positions of players on a soccer team.

The remaining five categories of Bloom's taxonomy of the cognitive domain deal with the *use* of knowledge. They encompass the educational objectives aimed at developing cognitive skills and abilities, including comprehension, application, analysis, synthesis, and evaluation of knowledge.

COMPREHENSION

Comprehension includes the ability to translate, explain, or interpret knowledge and to extrapolate from it to address new situations. Action verbs appropriate for this category include "change," "classify," "convert," "defend," "describe," "discuss," "estimate," "expand," "explain," "generalize," "infer," "interpret," "paraphrase," "predict," "recognize," "retell," "summarize," and "translate." Examples of objectives in this category are:

- From a sentence, the student *will recognize* the letters that are vowels in the English alphabet.
- The student *will describe* each of the organelles found in animal cell cytoplasm.
- The student *will recognize* the major parts of speech in the sentence.
- The student *will recognize* the positions of players on a soccer team.

APPLICATION

Once learners understand information, they should be able to apply it. Action verbs in this category of operation include "apply," "calculate," "demonstrate," "develop," "discover," "exhibit," "modify," "operate," "participate," "perform," "plan," "predict," "relate," "show," "simulate," "solve," and "use." Examples of objectives in this category are:

- The student *will use* in a sentence a word that contains at least two vowels.
- The student *will predict* the organelles found in plant cell cytoplasm.
- The student *will demonstrate* in a complete sentence each of the major parts of speech.
- The student *will relate* how the positions of players on a soccer team depend upon each other.

ANALYSIS

This category includes objectives that require learners to use the skills of analysis. Action verbs appropriate for this category include "analyze," "arrange," "break down," "categorize," "classify," "compare," "contrast," "debate," "deduce," "diagram," "differentiate," "discover," "discriminate," "group," "identify," "illustrate," "infer," "inquire," "organize," "outline," "relate," "separate," and "subdivide." Examples of objectives in this category include:

- From a list of words, the student *will differentiate* those that contain vowels from those that do not.
- Under the microscope, the student *will identify* the organelles found in animal cell cytoplasm.

---

[15]Compare Bloom's higher-order cognitive thinking skills with R. H. Ennis's "A Taxonomy of Critical Thinking Dispositions and Abilities," and Qellmalz's "Developing Reasoning Skills," both in J. B. Barron and R. J. Sternberg (Eds.), *Teaching Thinking Skills: Theory and Practice* (New York: W. H. Freeman, 1987), and with Marzano's "complex thinking strategies" in R. J. Marzano, *A Different Kind of Classroom: Teaching with Dimensions of Learning* (Alexandria, VA: Association for Supervision and Curriculum Development, 1992).

- The student *will analyze* a paragraph for misuse of major parts of speech.
- The student *will illustrate* on the writing board the different positions of players on a soccer team.

SYNTHESIS

This category includes objectives that involve such skills as designing a plan, proposing a set of operations, and deriving a series of abstract relations. Action verbs appropriate for this category include "arrange," "assemble," "categorize," "classify," "combine," "compile," "compose," "constitute," "create," "design," "develop," "devise," "document," "explain," "formulate," "generate," "hypothesize," "imagine," "invent," "modify," "organize," "originate," "plan," "predict," "produce," "rearrange," "reconstruct," "revise," "rewrite," "summarize," "synthesize," "tell," "transmit," and "write." Examples of objectives in this category are:

- From a list of words, the student *will rearrange* them into several lists according to the vowels contained in each.
- The student *will devise* a classification scheme of the organelles found in animal cell and plant cell cytoplasm according to their functions.
- The student *will write* a paragraph that correctly uses each of the major parts of speech.
- The student *will illustrate* on the chalkboard an offensive plan that uses the different positions of players on a soccer team.

EVALUATION

This, the highest category of Bloom's cognitive taxonomy, includes offering opinions and making value judgments. Action verbs appropriate for this category include "appraise," "argue," "assess," "choose," "compare," "conclude," "consider," "contrast," "criticize," "decide," "discriminate," "estimate," "evaluate," "explain," "interpret," "judge," "justify," "predict," "rank," "rate," "recommend," "relate," "revise," "standardize," "support," and "validate." Examples of objectives in this category are:

- The student *will listen to* and *evaluate* other students' identifications of vowels from sentences written on the board.
- While observing living cytoplasm under the microscope, the student *will justify* his or her interpretation that certain structures are specific organelles of a plant or animal cell.
- The student *will evaluate* a paragraph written by another student for the proper use of major parts of speech.
- The student *will interpret* the reasons for an opposing team's offensive use of the different positions of players on a soccer team.

Affective Domain Hierarchy

Krathwohl, Bloom, and Masia developed a useful taxonomy of the affective domain.[16] The following are their major levels (or categories), from least internalized to most internalized: (1) *receiving*—being aware of the affective stimulus and beginning to have favorable feelings toward it; (2) *responding*—taking an interest in the stimulus and viewing it favorably; (3) *valuing*—showing a tentative belief in the value of the affective stimulus and becoming committed to it; (4) *organizing*—placing values into a system of dominant and supporting values; and, (5) *internalizing*—demonstrating consistent beliefs and behavior that have become a way of life. Although there is considerable overlap from one category to another within the affective domain, these categories do give a basis by which to judge the quality of objectives and the nature of learning within this area. A discussion of each of the five categories follows.

RECEIVING

At this level, which is the least internalized, the learner exhibits willingness to give attention to particular phenomena or stimuli, and the teacher can arouse, sustain, and direct that attention. Action verbs appropriate for this category include "ask," "choose," "describe," "differentiate," "distinguish," "hold," "identify," "locate," "name," "point to," "recall," "recognize," "reply," "select," and "use." Examples of objectives in this category are:

- The student *pays attention* to the directions for enrichment activities.
- The student *listens attentively* to the ideas of others.
- The student *demonstrates sensitivity* to the property, beliefs, and concerns of others.

RESPONDING

At this level, learners respond to the stimulus they have received. They may do so because of some external pressure, or because they find the stimulus interesting, or because responding gives them satisfaction. Action verbs appropriate for this category include "answer," "applaud," "approve," "assist," "command," "comply," "discuss," "greet," "help," "label," "perform," "play," "practice," "present," "read," "recite," "report," "select," "spend (leisure time in)," "tell," and "write." Examples of objectives at this level are:

- The student *reads* for enrichment.
- The student *discusses* what others have said.
- The student *cooperates* with others during group activities.

---

[16]D. R. Krathwohl, B. S. Bloom, and B. B. Masia, *Taxonomy of Educational Goals, Handbook 2, Affective Domain* (New York: David McKay, 1964).

Humans are social beings. Real-world problem solving has become so complex that seldom can any person go it alone. Not all children come to school knowing how to work effectively in groups. Listening, sharing, cooperating, and knowing how to support group efforts are some of the behaviors that should be learned in school.

VALUING

Objectives at the valuing level deal with the learner's beliefs, attitudes, and appreciations. The simplest objectives concern the acceptance of beliefs and values; the higher ones involve learning to prefer certain values and finally becoming committed to them. Action verbs appropriate for this level include "argue," "assist," "complete," "describe," "differentiate," "explain," "follow," "form," "initiate," "invite," "join," "justify," "propose," "protest," "read," "report," "select," "share," "study," "support," and "work." Examples of objectives in this category include:

- The student *protests* against racial or ethnic discrimination.
- The student *synthesizes* a position on biological evolution.
- The student *argues* a position against abortion or pro-choice for women.

ORGANIZING

This fourth level in the affective domain concerns the building of a personal value system. Here the learner is conceptualizing and arranging values into a system that recognizes their relative importance. Action verbs appropriate for this level include "adhere," "alter," "arrange," "balance," "combine," "compare," "defend," "define," "discuss," "explain," "form," "generalize," "identify," "integrate," "modify," "order," "organize," "prepare," "relate," and "synthesize." Examples of objectives in this category are:

- The student *forms judgments* concerning proper behavior in the classroom, school, and community.
- The student *integrates* values into a personal work ethic.

- The student *defends* the important values of a particular subculture.

INTERNALIZING

This is the last and highest category within the affective domain, at which the learner's behaviors have become consistent with his or her beliefs. Action verbs appropriate for this level include "act," "complete," "display," "influence," "listen," "modify," "perform," "practice," "propose," "qualify," "question," "revise," "serve," "solve," and "verify." Examples of objectives in this category are:

- The student's behavior *displays* a well-defined and ethical code of conduct.
- The student *practices* accurate verbal and nonverbal communication.
- The student *performs* independently.

Psychomotor Domain Hierarchy

Whereas identification and classification within the cognitive and affective domains are generally agreed upon, there is less agreement on the classification within the psychomotor domain. Originally, the goal of this domain was simply to develop and categorize proficiency in skills, particularly those dealing with gross and fine muscle control. The classification of the domain presented here follows this lead, but includes at its highest level the most creative and inventive behaviors, thus coordinating skills and knowledge from all three domains. Consequently, the objectives are in a hierarchy ranging from simple gross locomotor control to the most creative and complex, requiring originality and fine locomotor control—for example, from simply turning on a computer to designing a software program. From Harrow we offer the following taxonomy of the psychomotor domain: (1) *moving,* (2) *manipulating,* (3) *communicating,* and (4) *creating.*[17]

MOVING

This level involves gross motor coordination. Action verbs appropriate for this level include "adjust," "carry," "clean," "grasp," "jump," "locate," "obtain," and "walk." Sample objectives for this category are:

- The student *will jump* a rope ten times without missing.
- The student *will correctly grasp* the putter.
- The student *will carry* the microscope to the desk correctly.

MANIPULATING

This level involves fine motor coordination. Action verbs appropriate for this level include "assemble," "build," "calibrate," "connect," "play," "thread," and "turn." Sample objectives for this category are:

- The student *will assemble* a kite.
- The student *will play* the C-scale on the clarinet.
- The student *will turn* the fine adjustment until the microscope is in focus.

COMMUNICATING

This level involves the communication of ideas and feelings. Action verbs appropriate for this level include "analyze," "ask," "describe," "draw," "explain," and "write." Sample objectives for this category are:

- By *asking* appropriate questions the student will demonstrate active listening skills.
- The student *will draw* what he or she observes on a slide through the microscope.
- The student *will describe* his or her feelings about the cloning of humans.

CREATING

Creating is the highest level of this domain and of all domains and represents the student's coordination of thinking, learning, and behaving in all three domains. Action verbs appropriate for this level include "create," "design," and "invent." Sample objectives for this category are:

- The student *will design* a mural.
- The student *will create, choreograph, and perform* a dance pattern.
- The student *will invent* and build a kite pattern.

Now, using Exercise 5.10, assess your recognition of performance objectives according to which domain they belong. Then, with Exercise 5.11, begin writing your own objectives for use in your teaching. You may want to correlate your work on Exercise 5.11 with Exercises 5.5, 6.7, 6.11, and 12.2.

---

[17]A. J. Harrow, *Taxonomy of the Psychomotor Domain* (New York: Longman, 1977). A similar taxonomy for the psychomotor domain is that of E. J. Simpson, *The Classification of Educational Objectives in the Psychomotor Domain. The Psychomotor Domain: Volume 3* (Washington, DC: Gryphon House, 1972).

EXERCISE 5.10 ASSESSING RECOGNITION OF OBJECTIVES ACCORDING TO DOMAIN— A SELF-CHECK EXERCISE

INSTRUCTIONS: The purpose of this exercise is to assess your ability to identify objectives correctly according to their domain. For each of the following instructional objectives, identify by the appropriate letter the domain involved: (*C*) cognitive, (*A*) affective, or (*P*) psychomotor. Check your answers, and discuss the results with your classmates and instructor.

_____ 1. The student will shoot free throws until he or she can complete 80 percent of the attempts.

_____ 2. The student will identify on a map the mountain ranges of the eastern United States.

_____ 3. The student will summarize the historical development of the Democratic Party in the United States.

_____ 4. The student will demonstrate a continuing desire to learn more about using the classroom computer for word processing by volunteering to work at it during free time.

_____ 5. The student will volunteer to tidy up the storage room.

_____ 6. After listening to several recordings, the student will identify their respective composers.

_____ 7. The student will translate a favorite Cambodian poem into English.

_____ 8. The student will calculate the length of the hypotenuse.

_____ 9. The student will indicate an interest in the subject by voluntarily reading additional library books about earthquakes.

_____ 10. The student will successfully stack five blocks.

Exercise Answer Key: 2, 3, 6, 7, 8 = C; 1, 10 = P; 4, 5, 9 = A

EXERCISE 5.11 PREPARING MY OWN INSTRUCTIONAL OBJECTIVES

INSTRUCTIONS: The purpose of this exercise is to begin writing your own behavioral objectives. For a subject and grade level of your choice, prepare ten specific behavioral objectives. Refer to Exercises 5.5, 6.7, 6.11, and 12.2. It is not necessary to include audience, conditions, and performance level unless requested by your course instructor. Exchange completed exercises with your classmates; discuss and make changes where necessary.

Subject _____

Grade level: _____

1. Cognitive knowledge _____

_____

_____

_____

_____

_____

2. Cognitive comprehension _____

_____

_____

_____

_____

_____

3. Cognitive application _____

_____

_____

_____

_____

_____

4. Cognitive analysis _____

_____

_____

_____

_____

_____

5. Cognitive synthesis _____

_____

_____

_____

EXERCISE 5.11 (*continued*)

_____

_____

6. Cognitive evaluation _____

_____

_____

_____

_____

_____

7. Psychomotor (low level) _____

_____

_____

_____

_____

_____

8. Psychomotor (high level) _____

_____

_____

_____

_____

_____

9. Affective (low level) _____

_____

_____

_____

_____

_____

10. Affective (highest level) _____

_____

_____

_____

_____

_____

USING THE TAXONOMIES

Theoretically, the taxonomies are constructed so that students achieve each lower level before being ready to move to the higher levels. However, because categories and behaviors overlap, as they should, this theory does not always hold in practice. Furthermore, as explained by others, feelings and thoughts are inextricably interconnected; they cannot be neatly separated as the taxonomies would imply.[18]

The taxonomies are important in that they emphasize the various levels to which instruction must aspire. For learning to be worthwhile, you must formulate and teach to objectives from both the higher levels of the taxonomies and the lower ones. Student thinking and behaving must be moved from the lowest to the highest levels of thinking and behavior. When all is said and done, it is, perhaps, the highest level of the psychomotor domain (creating) to which we aspire.

In using the taxonomies, remember that the point is to formulate the best objectives for the job to be done. In schools that use outcome-based education (known also as *results-driven education*) models, those models describe levels of mastery standards (*rubrics*) for each outcome. The taxonomies provide the mechanism for assuring that you do not spend a disproportionate amount of time on facts and other low-level learning; they can be of tremendous help where teachers are expected to correlate learning activities to one of the school or district's outcome standards (see Figure 5.6).

Preparing objectives is essential to the preparation of good items for the assessment of student learning. Clearly communicating your performance expectations to students and then specifically assessing student learning against those expectations makes the teaching most efficient and effective, and it makes the assessment of the learning closer to being authentic. This does not mean to imply that you will always write performance objectives for everything taught; nor will you always be able to measure accurately what students have learned. As said earlier, learning that is meaningful to students is not as easily compartmentalized as the taxonomies of educational objectives would imply.

Preparing objectives is essential to the preparation of good items for the assessment of student learning. Clearly communicating your performance expectations to students and then specifically assessing student learning against those expectations makes the teaching most efficient and effective, and it makes the assessment of the learning closer to being authentic. This does not mean to imply that you will always write per-

Figure 5.6   Sample school district-expected learning outcome standards.

Results-driven education helps produce people who are life-long learners, are effective communicators, have high self-esteem, and are:

PROBLEM SOLVERS

- are able to solve problems in their academic and personal lives
- demonstrate higher level analytical thinking skills when they evaluate or make decisions
- are able to set personal and career goals
- can use knowledge, not just display it
- are innovative thinkers

SELF-DIRECTED LEARNERS

- are independent workers
- can read, comprehend, and interact with text
- have self-respect with an accurate view of themselves and their abilities

QUALITY PRODUCERS

- can communicate effectively in a variety of situations (oral, aesthetic/artistic, nonverbal)
- are able to use their knowledge to create intelligent, artistic products that reflect originality
- have high standards

COLLABORATIVE WORKERS

- are able to work interdependently
- show respect for others and their points of view
- have their own values and moral conduct
- have an appreciation of cultural diversity

COMMUNITY CONTRIBUTORS

- have an awareness of civic, individual, national, and international responsibilities
- have an understanding of basic health issues
- have an appreciation of diversity

formance objectives for everything taught; nor will you always be able to measure accurately what students have learned. As said earlier, learning that is meaningful to students is not as easily compartmentalized as the taxonomies of educational objectives would imply.

Observing for Connected (Meaningful) Learning: Logs, Portfolios, and Journals

In learning that is most important and that has the most meaning to students, the domains are inextricably interconnected. Consequently, when assessing for student learning, both during instruction (formative

---

[18]R. N. Caine and G. Caine, *Education on the Edge of Possibility* (Alexandria, VA: Association for Supervision and Curriculum Development, 1997), p. 104–105.

assessment) and at the conclusion of the instruction (summative assessment) you must look for those connections.

Ways of looking for connected learning include (1) maintain a teacher's (or team's) log with daily or nearly daily entries about the progress of each student, and (2) have students maintain individual learning portfolios that document students' thinking, work, and learning experiences. Dated and chronologically organized items that students place in their portfolios can include notes and communications, awards, brainstorming records, photos of bulletin board contributions and of charts, posters, displays, and models made by the student, records of peer coaching, visual maps, learning contract, record of debate contributions, and demonstrations or presentations, mnemonics created by the student, peer evaluations, reading record, other contributions made to the class or to the team, record of service work, and test and grade records.

Another way is to have students maintain a response journal in which they reflect on and respond to their learning, using five categories described as follows:[19]

1. "I never knew that." In this category, student responses are primarily to factual information, responses to their new knowledge, to the bits and pieces of raw information often expected to be memorized regardless of how meaningful to students it might be. However, because this is only fragmented knowledge and merely scratches the surface of meaningful learning, it must not be the end-all of student learning. Learning that is truly meaningful goes beyond the "I never knew that" category, expands upon the bits and pieces, connects them, and allows the learner to make sense out of what he or she is learning. Learning that does not extend beyond the "I never knew that" category is dysfunctional.
2. "I never thought of that." Here, student responses reveal an additional way of perceiving. Their responses may include elements of "I never knew that" but also contain higher-level thinking as a result of their reflection on that knowledge.
3. "I never felt that." In this category, student responses are connected to the affective, eliciting more of an emotional response than a cognitive one. Learning what is truly meaningful is much more than intellectual understanding; it includes a "felt" meaning.[20]
4. "I never appreciated that." Responses in this category reflect a sense of recognition that one's own

life can be enriched by what others have created or done, or that something already known can be valued from an additional perspective.
5. "I never realized that." In this category, student responses indicate an awareness of overall patterns and dynamic ways in which behavior is holistic, establishing meaningful and potentially useful connections among knowledge, values, and purposes.

Still another type of journal is the *double entry journal* where on the left side the student records facts about things learned and on the right side the student writes his or her personal response to the experience.

The use of portfolios and student journals is discussed further in Chapter 11.

Learning That Is Not Immediately Observable

Unlike behaviorists, constructivists do not limit the definition of learning to that which is observable behavior, nor should you. Bits and pieces of new information are stored in short-term memory, where the new information is "rehearsed" until ready to be stored in long-term memory. If the information is not rehearsed, it eventually fades from short-term memory. If it is rehearsed and made meaningful through connections with other stored knowledge, then this new knowledge is transferred to and stored in long-term memory, either by building existing schemata or by forming new schemata. As a teacher, your responsibility is to provide learning experiences that will result in the creation of new schemata and the modification of existing schemata.

To be an effective teacher, the challenge is to use performance-based criteria simultaneously with a teaching style that encourages the development of intrinsic sources of student motivation and that allows, provides, and encourages coincidental learning. That type of learning goes beyond what might be considered predictable, immediately measurable, and representative of minimal expectations.

It has become quite clear to many teachers that to be most effective in helping students to develop meaningful understandings, much of the learning in each discipline can be made more effective and longer lasting when that learning is integrated with the whole curriculum. Learning should be meaningful to the lives of the students rather than simply taught as an unrelated and separate discipline at the same time each day.

As we noted at the start of this chapter, if learning is defined only as being the accumulation of bits and pieces of information, then we already know how that is learned and how to teach it. However, the accumulation of pieces of information is at the lowest end of a spectrum of types of learning. For higher levels of thinking and for learning that is most meaningful and

[19]S. Fersh, *Integrating the Trans-National/Cultural Dimension*, Fastback 361 (Bloomington, IN: Phi Delta Kappa Educational Foundation, 1993), pp. 22–24.
[20]Caine and Caine, *Education on the Edge of Possibility*, p. 113–114.

longest lasting, the results of research support using (1) a curriculum in which disciplines are integrated, and (2) instructional techniques that involve the learners in social interactive learning, such as project-centered learning, cooperative learning, peer tutoring, and cross-age teaching.

INTEGRATED CURRICULUM

When learning about *integrated curriculum* (IC), it is easy to be confused by the plethora of terms that are used, such as *integrated studies, thematic instruction, multidisciplinary teaching, integrated curriculum, interdisciplinary curriculum,* and *interdisciplinary thematic instruction.* In essence, regardless of which of these terms is being used, the reference is to the same thing.

Because it is not always easy to tell where the term *curriculum* leaves off and the term *instruction* begins, let's assume for now that, for the sake of better understanding the meaning of *integrated curriculum,* there is no difference between the two terms. In other words, for the intent of this discussion, whether we use the term *integrated curriculum* or the term *integrated instruction,* we will be referring to the same thing.

Definition of Integrated Curriculum

The term **integrated curriculum** (or any of its synonyms mentioned above) refers to both a way of teaching and a way of planning and organizing the instructional program so the discrete disciplines of subject matter are related to one another in a design that (1) matches the developmental needs of the learners and (2) helps to connect their learning in ways that are meaningful to their current and past experiences. In that respect, IC is the antithesis of traditional disparate subject-matter oriented teaching and curriculum designations.

Integrated Curricula: Past and Present

The reason for the various terminology is, in part, because the concept of an integrated curriculum is not new. In fact, it has had a roller-coaster ride throughout most of the history of education in this country. Over time those efforts to integrate student learning have had varying labels.

Without reviewing that history, suffice to say that prior to now, in some form or another, the most recent popularity stems from the late 1950s, with some of the discovery-oriented, student-centered projects supported by the National Science Foundation. Some of these are *Elementary School Science* (ESS), a hands-on and integrated science program for grades K–6; *Man: A Course of Study* (MACOS), a hands-on, anthropology-based program for fifth graders; and *Environmental Studies* (name later changed to *ESSENCE*), an interdis-

ciplinary program for use at all grades, K–12, regardless of subject-matter orientation. The popularity of integrated curriculum also stems from the middle school movement that began in the 1960s and from the whole-language movement in language arts that had its beginning in the 1980s.

Today's interest in curriculum integration has risen from at least five inextricably connected sources: (1) the success at curriculum integration that has been enjoyed by middle level schools since the beginning of the middle school movement in the 1960s, (2) the literature-based, whole-language movement in reading and language arts that began in the 1980s,[21] (3) the diversity of children in the regular classroom coupled with growing acceptance of the philosophy that a certain percentage of school dropouts is not a viable assumption, (4) needs of the workplace, advances in technology, and a concomitant trend of integrating vocational with academic education in secondary schools, and (5) recent research in cognitive science and neuroscience demonstrating the necessity of helping learners establish bridges between school and life, knowing and doing, content and context, with a parallel rekindled interest in constructivism as opposed to a strictly behaviorist philosophical approach to teaching and learning.

An IC approach may not necessarily be the best approach for every school, nor the best for all learning for every student. Nor is it necessarily the manner by which every teacher should or must always plan and teach. As evidenced by practice, the truth of these statements becomes obvious. You should be well aware now, it is my belief that a teacher's best choice as an approach to instruction—and to classroom management—is one that is eclectic.

The Spectrum of Integrated Curriculum

In attempts to connect students' learning with their experiences, efforts fall at various places on a spectrum or continuum, from the least integrated instruction (level 1) to the most integrated (level 5), as illustrated in Figure 5.7. It is not my intent that this illustration be interpreted as going from "worst case scenario" (far left) to "best case scenario" (far right), although some

---

[21]Various movements and approaches have been used over the years to try to find the most successful approach to teaching English and the language arts—movements with names such as *whole language, integrated language arts, communication arts and skills, literature-based,* and so forth. Whatever the cognomen, certain common elements and goals prevail: student choice in materials to be read, student reading and writing across the curriculum, time for independent and sustained silent reading in the classroom, use of integrated language arts skills across the curriculum, use of nonprint materials, and use of trade books rather than textbooks and basal readers.

Figure 5.7   Levels of curriculum integration.

Least Integrated Level 1	Level 2	Level 3	Level 4	Most Integrated Level 5
Subject-specific topic outline	Subject-specific	Multidisciplinary	Interdisciplinary thematic	Integrated thematic
No student collaboration in planning	Minimal student input	Some student input	Considerable student input in selecting themes and in planning	Maximum student and teacher collaboration
Teacher solo	Solo or teams	Solo or teams	Solo or teams	Solo or teams
Student input into decision making is low.		Student input into decision making is high.		Student input into decision making is very high.

people may interpret it in exactly that way. The fact is that there are various interpretations to curriculum integration and each teacher must make his or her own decisions about the use. Figure 5.7 is meant solely to show how efforts to integrate fall on a continuum of sophistication and complexity. The following is a description of each level of the continuum.

LEVEL 1 CURRICULUM INTEGRATION

Level 1 is the traditional organization of curriculum and classroom instruction, in which teachers plan and arrange the subject-specific scope and sequence in the format of topic outlines, much as you did for Exercise 5.5. If there is an attempt to help students connect their experiences and their learning, then it is up to individual classroom teachers to do it. An elementary or middle school student in a school and classroom that has subject-specific instruction at varying times of the day (e.g., reading and language arts at 8:00, mathematics at 9:00, social studies at 10:30, and so on) from one or more teachers is likely learning at a level 1 instructional environment, especially when what is being learned in one subject has little or no connection with content being learned in another. The same applies for a high school student who moves during the school day from classroom to classroom, teacher to teacher, subject to subject, from one topic to another. A topic in science, for example, might be "earthquakes." A related topic in social studies might be "the social consequences of natural disasters." These two topics may or may not be studied by a student at the same time.

LEVEL 2 CURRICULUM INTEGRATION

If the same students are learning English/language arts, or social studies/history, or mathematics, or science, using a thematic approach rather than a topic outline, then they are learning at level 2. At this level,

themes for one discipline are not necessarily planned and coordinated to correspond or integrate with themes of another or to be taught simultaneously. At level 2, the students may have some input into the decision making involved in planning themes and content from various disciplines. Before going further in our presentation of the levels of curriculum integration, let's stop and consider what is a topic and what is a theme.

Integrated Thematic Unit: Topic Versus Theme. The difference between a topic and a theme is not always clear. For example, whereas "earthquakes" and "social consequences of natural disasters" are topics, "a survival guide to local natural disasters" could be the theme or umbrella under which these two topics could fall. In addition, themes are likely to be problem-based statements or questions; they often result in a product and are longer in duration than are topics. A theme is the point, the message, or the idea that underlies a study. When compared to a topic, a theme is more dynamic; the theme explains the significance of the study. It communicates to the student what the experience means. Although organized around one theme, many topics make up an ITU. Often the theme of a study becomes clearer to students when an overall guiding question is presented and discussed, such as "What could we do to improve our living environment?" or "What happens in our community after natural disasters?"[22]

Some educators say the integrated curriculum of the twenty-first century will be based on broad, unchanging, and unifying concepts (that is, on con-

---

[22]For further delineation between topics and themes in integrated curriculum, see T. Shanahan et al. (Eds.), "Avoiding Some of the Pitfalls of Thematic Units," *The Reading Teacher* 48(8):718–719 (May 1995).

ceptual themes).[23] If so, it would be recycling an approach of the 1960s, as supported by the writings of Jerome Bruner[24] and implemented in some of the National Foundation sponsored curriculum projects of that era. In fact, there is already action in that direction. For example, forming the basis for the national curriculum standards (discussed earlier in this chapter) for social studies are ten "thematic strands," including "people, places, and environments," and "power, authority, and governance." The national standards for science education are centered on unifying conceptual schemes, such as "systems, order, and organization," and "form and function."

LEVEL 3 CURRICULUM INTEGRATION

When the same students are learning two or more of their core subjects (English/language arts, social studies/history, mathematics, and science) around a common theme, such as "natural disasters," from one or more teachers, they are then learning at level 3 integration. At this level, teachers agree on a common theme and *separately* deal with that theme in their individual subject-areas, usually at the same time during the school year. So what the student is learning from a teacher in one class is related to and coordinated with what the student is concurrently learning in another or several others. At level 3, students may have some input into the decision making involved in selecting and planning themes and content. Some authors may refer to levels 2 or 3 as *coordinated* or *parallel curriculum*.

LEVEL 4 CURRICULUM INTEGRATION

When teachers and students collaborate on a common theme and its content and when discipline boundaries begin to disappear as teachers teach about this common theme, either solo or as an *interdisciplinary teaching team*, level 4 integration is achieved.

LEVEL 5 CURRICULUM INTEGRATION

When teachers and their students have collaborated on a common theme and its content, discipline boundaries are truly blurred during instruction, and teachers of several grade levels and of various subjects teach toward student understanding of aspects of the common theme, then this is level 5, an *integrated thematic approach.*

Guidelines for integrating topics and for planning and developing an interdisciplinary thematic unit are presented in the next chapter.

[23]See, for example, E-M. Lolli, "Creating a Concept-Based Curriculum," *Principal* 76(1):26–27 (September 1996), T. L. Riley, "Tools for Discovery: Conceptual Themes in the Classroom," *Gifted Child Today Magazine* 20(1):30–33, 50 (January/February 1997), and C. A. Tomlinson, "For Integration and Differentiation Choose Concepts over Topics," *Middle School Journal* 30(2):3–8 (November 1998).
[24]J. S. Bruner, *Process of Education* (Cambridge, MA: Harvard University Press, 1960).

PLANNING FOR INSTRUCTION: A THREE-LEVEL AND SEVEN-STEP PROCESS

Earlier we noted that complete planning for instruction occurs at three levels: the year, the units, and the lessons. There are seven steps in the process.

1. *Course, grade level, and school goals.* Consider and understand your curriculum goals and their relationship to the mission and goals of the school. Your course is not isolated on Jupiter but is an integral part of the total school curriculum organizational components described earlier in this chapter.

2. *Expectations.* Consider topics and skills you are expected to teach, such as those found in the course of study.

3. *Academic year, semester, or trimester plan.* Think about the goals you want students to reach months from now. Working from your tentative topic outline (Exercise 5.5) and with the school calendar in hand, you will begin by deciding the amount of time (e.g., the number of days) to be devoted to each topic (or unit), penciling those times onto the outline. (Unless you are doing your planning at a computer, you may wish to use pencil because the times are likely to be modified often).

4. *Course schedule.* This schedule becomes a part of the course syllabus that is presented to students (grades four and up) at the beginning of the year. However, the schedule *must* remain flexible to allow for the unexpected, such as the cancellation or interruption of a class meeting, or an extended study of a particular topic.

5. *Plans for each class meeting.* Working from the calendar plan or the course schedule, you are ready to prepare plans for each class meeting, keeping in mind the abilities and interests of your students while making decisions about appropriate strategies and learning experiences. The preparation of daily plans takes considerable time and continues throughout the year as you arrange and prepare instructional notes, demonstrations, discussion topics and questions, and classroom exercises; schedule guest speakers; and arrange for audiovisual materials and media equipment, field trips, and tools for the assessment of student learning. Because the content of each class meeting is often determined by the accomplishments of and your reflections upon the preceding one, your lessons are never "set in concrete" but require your continual revisiting and assessment.

6. *Instructional objectives.* Once you have the finalized schedule, and as you prepare the daily plans, you will complete your preparation of the instructional objectives (begun in Exercise 5.11). Those objectives are critical for proper development of the next and final step.

7. *Assessment.* The final step is that of deciding how to assess student achievement. Included in this component are your decisions about how you will accomplish diagnostic or **preassessment** (that is the assessment of what students know or think they know at the start of a new unit of study or a new topic), **formative assessment** (the ongoing assessment during a unit of study on what the students are learning) and **summative assessment** (the assessment of learning at the conclusion of a unit of study on what the students learned). Also included in the assessment component are your decisions about assignments (discussed in Chapter 8) and the grading procedures (discussed in Chapter 11).

In Chapter 6, you will proceed through these steps as you develop your first instructional plan. However, before starting that, let's consider one more topic—the syllabus.

THE SYLLABUS

A syllabus is a written statement of information about the workings of a particular class or course. As a student in postsecondary education, you have seen a variety of syllabi written by professors, each with their individual ideas about what general and specific logistic information is most important for students to know about a course. Some instructors, however, err in thinking that a course outline constitutes a course syllabus; a course outline is only one component of a syllabus.

Not all teachers use a course syllabus, at least as is described here, but for reasons we will explore in this discussion, I believe they should. Related to that belief are several questions that are answered next: "Why should teachers use a syllabus? What value is it? What use can be made of it? What purpose does it fulfill? How do I develop one? Can students have input into its contents and participate in its development? Where do I start? What information should be included? When should it be distributed? To whom should it be distributed? How rigidly should it be followed?

Use and Development of a Syllabus

The syllabus is printed information about the class or the course which is usually presented to parents of the primary grades, and, for grades four and up, to the students on the first day or during the first week of school. The syllabus may be developed completely by you or in collaboration with members of your teaching team. As you shall learn, it also can be developed collaboratively with students. As always, the final decision about its development is yours to make. However it is developed, the syllabus should be designed so that it helps establish a rapport between students, parents or guardians, and the teacher, helps students feel at ease by providing an understanding of what is expected of them, and helps them to organize, conceptualize, and synthesize their learning experiences.

The syllabus should provide a reference, helping eliminate misunderstandings and misconceptions about the nature of the class—its rules, expectations, procedures, requirements, and other policies. It should provide students with a sense of connectedness (often by allowing students to work collaboratively in groups and actually participate in fashioning *their* course syllabus).

The syllabus should also serve as a plan to be followed by the teacher and the students, and it should serve as a resource for substitute teachers and (when relevant) members of a teaching team. Each team member should have a copy of every other member's syllabus. In essence, the syllabus stands as documentation for what is taking place in the classroom for those outside the classroom (i.e., parents or guardians, school board members, administrators, and other teachers and students). For access by parents and other interested persons, some teachers include at least portions of their course syllabus, such as homework assignment specifications and due dates, with the school's web site on the Internet.

Usually the syllabus, at least portions of it, is prepared by the teacher long before the first class meeting. If you maintain a syllabus template on your computer, then it is a simple task to customize it for each group of students you teach. You may find it is more useful if students participate in the development of the syllabus, thereby having an ownership of it and a commitment to its contents. By having input into the workings of a course and knowing their opinions count, students usually will take more interest in what they are doing and learning. Shown in Figure 5.8 are steps you can use as a collaborative learning experience in which students spend time during the first (or an early) class meeting brainstorming content of their syllabus.

Content of a Syllabus

A syllabus should be concise, matter-of-fact, uncomplicated, and brief—perhaps no more than two pages—and include the following information:

Descriptive information about the course. This includes the teacher's name and, depending on the grade level, the course or class title, class period, days of class meetings, beginning and ending times, and room number.

Importance of the course (for secondary school). This information should describe the course, cite how students will profit from it, tell whether the course is a required course and (if relevant) from which program in the curriculum, such as a core course or elective or vocational, academic, or some other arrangement.

Goals and objectives. This should include the major goals and a few of the major objectives.

Figure 5.8   Steps for involving students in the development of their course syllabus.

Step 1

Sometime during the first few days of the course, arrange students in heterogeneous groups (mixed abilities) of three or four members to brainstorm the development of their syllabus.

Step 2

Instruct each group to spend five minutes listing everything they can think of that they would like to know about the course. Tell students that a group *recorder* must be chosen to write their list of ideas on paper and then, when directed to do so, to transfer the list to the writing board or to sheets of butcher paper to be hung in the classroom for all to see (or on an overhead transparency—a transparency sheet and pen are made available to each group). Tell them to select a group *spokesperson* who will address the class, explaining the group's list. Each group could also appoint a *materials manager,* whose job is to see that the group has the necessary materials (e.g., pen, paper, transparency, chalk), and a *task master,* whose job is to keep the group on task and to report to the teacher when each task is completed.

Step 3

After five minutes, have the recorders prepare their lists. When a transparency or butcher paper is used, the lists can be prepared simultaneously while recorders remain with their groups. If using the writing board, then recorders, one at a time, write their lists on areas of the board that you have designated for each group's list.

Step 4

Have the spokesperson of each group explain the group's list. As this is being done, you should make a master list. If transparencies or butcher paper is being used rather than the writing board, you can ask for either as backup to the master list you have made.

Step 5

After all spokespersons have explained their lists, you ask the class collectively for additional input. "Can anyone think of anything else that should be added?"

Step 6

You now take the master list and design a course syllabus, being careful to address each question and to include items of importance that students may have omitted. However, your guidance during the preceding five steps should ensure that all bases have been covered.

Step 7

At the next class meeting, give each student a copy of the final syllabus. Discuss its content. (Duplicate copies to distribute to colleagues, especially those on your teaching team, interested administrators, and parents and guardians at back-to-school night.)

Materials required. Explain what materials are needed—such as a textbook, notebook, binder, calculator, supplementary readings, apron, and safety goggles—and specify which are supplied by the school, which must be supplied by each student, and what materials must be available each day.

Types of assignments that will be given. These should be clearly explained in as much detail as possible this early in the school term. There should be a statement of your estimate of time required (if any) for homework each night. There should also be a statement about where daily assignments will be posted in the classroom (a regular place each day), the procedures for completing and turning in assignments, and (if relevant) for making corrections to assignments already turned in. Include your policy regarding late work. Also, parents will need to know your expectations of them regarding help with assignments. (Homework is discussed in Chapter 8.)

Attendance expectations. Explain how attendance is related to grades and to promotion (if relevant) and the procedure for making up missed work. Typical school policy allows that for an excused absence, missed work can be completed without penalty if done within a reasonable period of time after the student returns to school. To strongly encourage regular attendance, the policy of Talent Development secondary schools (see Chapter 4) is that a student automatically fails a course when the student accumulates five or more absences per quarter. On the other hand, to encourage students, the policy also includes recovery strategies. For example, each absence can be nullified if the student accumulates five consecutive days of perfect attendance. Policy also provides students with second opportunities for success on assignments, although at some cost to encourage a strong first effort.[25]

Assessment and marking/grading procedures. Explain the assessment procedures and the procedures for determining marks or grades. Will there be quizzes, tests, homework, projects, and group work? What will be their formats, coverage, and weights in the procedure for determining grades? For group work, how will

[25]V. LaPoint et al., *Report 1: The Talent Development High School—Essential Components* (on-line). Available (downloaded June 19, 1998): <http://www.csos.jhu.edu/crespar/CRESPAR%20Reports/report01entire.html>, p. 6.

the contributions and learning of individual students be evaluated?

Other information specific to the course. Field trips? Special privileges? Computer work? Parental expectations? Homework hotline? Classroom procedures and expectations (discussed in Chapter 4) should be included here.

If you are a beginning teacher or are new to the school, you should affirm that your policies as indicated in the first draft of your syllabus are not counter to any existing school policies. You probably should share your first draft of the syllabus with members of your team or the department chairperson for feedback.

Now complete Exercises 5.12 and 5.13.

EXERCISE 5.12 COLLABORATING ON THE CONTENT OF A SYLLABUS

INSTRUCTIONS: The purpose of this exercise is to start developing a syllabus for use in your own teaching. From the following list of items that might appear on a course syllabus, place an (X) before all those you would include in your own syllabus and explain why. Share your list with your classmates, and make any necessary revisions.

Subject _____

Grade _____

_____ 1. Name of the teacher _____

_____ 2. Course title (and/or grade level) _____

_____ 3. Room number _____

_____ 4. Beginning and ending times _____

_____ 5. Times when students may schedule a conference with the teacher _____

_____ 6. Course description _____

_____ 7. Course philosophy or rationale (underline one) _____

_____ 8. Instructional format (such as lecture-discussion, student-centered learning groups, laboratory centered) _____

_____ 9. Absence policy _____

_____ 10. Tardy policy _____

_____ 11. Classroom procedures and behavior rules _____

EXERCISE 5.12 (*continued*)

_____ 12. Goals of the course _____

_____

_____

_____

_____

_____ 13. Objectives of the course _____

_____

_____

_____

_____

_____ 14. Plagiarism policy _____

_____

_____

_____

_____

_____ 15. Name of the textbook and other supplementary materials _____

_____

_____

_____

_____

_____ 16. Policy about use and care of the textbook and other reading materials _____

_____

_____

_____

_____

_____ 17. Materials that the student is to supply_____

_____

_____

_____

_____ 18. Assignments_____

_____

_____

_____

EXERCISE 5.12 (*continued*)

_____ 19. Homework policy (due dates, format, lateness policy, grades) _____

_____

_____

_____

_____ 20. Class relationship to advisor–advisee program, and/or core, co-curricular, exploratories, or some

other aspect of the school curriculum _____

_____

_____

_____

_____ 21. Grading procedure _____

_____

_____

_____

_____ 22. Study skills _____

_____

_____

_____

_____ 23. Themes to be studied _____

_____

_____

_____

_____ 24. Field trips and other special activities _____

_____

_____

_____

_____ 25. Group work policies and types _____

_____

_____

_____

_____ 26. Other members of the teaching team and their roles _____

_____

_____

☞

EXERCISE 5.12 (*continued*)

_____ 27. Tentative daily schedule _____
_____
_____
_____
_____

_____ 28. Other (specify) _____
_____
_____
_____
_____

_____ 29. Other (specify) _____
_____
_____
_____

_____ 30. Other (specify) _____
_____
_____
_____

EXERCISE 5.13 PREPARING A SYLLABUS: AN EXERCISE IN COLLABORATIVE THINKING

INSTRUCTIONS: The purpose of this exercise is to prepare in a group a syllabus for a course, subject, or grade that you intend to teach. Using your results from Exercise 5.12 and working in groups of three or four members, develop one syllabus for a specific class or grade. Grouping may be by subject, grade, or another criterion. Each group's syllabus should be shared with the class. Discuss within each group the pros and cons of having students contribute to their syllabus (see Figure 5.8). Also share the results of this discussion with the class.

SUMMARY

In your comparison and analysis of courses of study and teachers' editions of student textbooks, you probably discovered that many are accompanied by sequentially designed resource units from which the teacher can select and build specific teaching units. A resource unit usually consists of an extensive list of objectives, a large number and variety of activities, suggested materials, and extensive bibliographies for teacher and students.

As you may have also found, some courses of study contain actual teaching units that have been prepared by teachers of the school district. Beginning teachers and student teachers often ask, "How closely must I follow the school's curriculum guide or course of study?" To obtain an answer, you must talk with teachers and administrators of the school before you begin teaching.

In conclusion, your final decisions about what content to teach are guided by (a) discussions with other teachers, (b) review of state curriculum documents, local courses of study, and articles in professional journals, (c) your personal convictions, knowledge, and skills, and (d) the unique characteristics of your students.

In this chapter you learned of the differences between the terms *aims, goals, and objectives*. Regardless of how these terms are defined, the important point is this: *teachers must be clear about what they want their students to learn, what evidence is needed to verify their learning, and how to communicate those things to the students so they are clearly understood.*

Many teachers do not bother to write specific objectives for all the learning activities in their teaching plans. However, when teachers do prepare specific objectives (by writing them themselves or by borrowing them from textbooks and other curriculum documents), teach toward them, and assess students' progress against them, student learning is enhanced. This is called *performance-based teaching* and *criterion-referenced measurement*. It is also known as an *aligned curriculum*. In schools using results-driven education mastery learning models, those models describe levels of mastery standards or rubrics for each outcome or learning target. The taxonomies are of tremendous help in schools where teachers are expected to correlate learning activities to the school's outcome standards.

As a teacher, you will be expected to (1) plan your lessons well, (2) convey specific expectations to your students, and (3) assess their learning against that specificity. However, because it tends toward high objectivity, there is the danger that such performance-based teaching could become too objective, which can have negative consequences. If students are treated as objects, then the relationship between teacher and student becomes impersonal and counterproductive to real learning. Highly specific and impersonal teaching can be discouraging to serendipity, creativity, and the excitement of discovery, to say nothing of its possibly negative impact on the development of students' self-esteem.

Performance-based instruction works well when teaching toward mastery of basic skills, but the concept of mastery learning is inclined to imply that there is some foreseeable end to learning, an assumption that is obviously erroneous. With performance-based instruction, the source of student motivation tends to be extrinsic. Teacher expectations, marks and grades, society, and peer pressures are examples of extrinsic sources that drive student performance. To be a most effective teacher, your challenge is to use performance-based criteria together with a teaching style that encourages the development of intrinsic sources of student motivation and that allows for, provides for, and encourages coincidental learning that goes beyond what might be considered as predictable, immediately measurable, and representative of minimal expectations. With a knowledge of the content of the school curriculum and the value of instructional objectives, you are now ready to prepare detailed instructional plans with sequenced lessons, the subject of the next chapter.

QUESTIONS FOR CLASS DISCUSSION

1. Explore a school library or resource center. Are the student books current? Does this place and its books appear attractive for students and user-friendly? Share your conclusions with your classmates.
2. It is sometimes said that teaching less is better. Explain the meaning and significance of that statement. Explain why you agree or disagree with the concept.
3. Recall your own schooling. What do you really remember? Most likely you remember projects, your presentations, the lengthy research you did, and your extra effort doing art work to accompany your presentation. Maybe you remember a compliment by a teacher or a pat on the back by peers. Most likely you do *not* remember the massive amount of factual content that was covered. Discuss this and your feelings about it with your classmates.
4. Describe the concept of *integrated curriculum.*
5. Some people say it is easier to write performance objectives after a lesson has been taught. What is the significance of that notion?
6. Should a teacher encourage serendipitous (coincidental) learning? If no, why not? If so, describe ways that a teacher can do it.
7. Describe the relationship between goals and objectives. Describe the relationship between scope and sequence, and instructional goals and objectives. At any time during your teaching, should you ignore the planned scope and sequence, goals and objectives? If so, explain why, when, to what extent. If not, explain why not.
8. Some people believe—and some fear—that the national curriculum standards are a first step toward national assessment of student learning. Explain how you feel about this and any concerns you have.

9. From your current observations and field work as related to this teacher preparation program, clearly identify one specific example of educational practice that seems contradictory to exemplary practice or theory as presented in this chapter. Present your explanation for the discrepancy.

10. Do you have questions generated by the content of this chapter? If you do, list them along with ways answers might be found.

FOR FURTHER READING

Airasian, P. W., and Walsh, M. E. "Constructivist Cautions." *Phi Delta Kappan* 78(6):444–449 (February 1997).

Battista, M. T. "The Mathematical Miseducation of America's Youth." *Phi Delta Kappa* 80(6):425–433 (February 1999).

Beane, J. A. *Curriculum Integration: Designing the Core of Democratic Education.* New York: Teachers College Press, 1997.

Caine, R. N., and Caine, G. *Education on the Edge of Possibility.* Alexandria, VA: Association for Supervision and Curriculum Development, 1997.

Clarke, J. H., and Agne, R. M. *Interdisciplinary High School Teaching: Strategies for Integrated Learning.* Boston: Allyn & Bacon, 1997.

Collins, A. "National Science Education Standards: Looking Backward and Forward." *Elementary School Journal* 97(4):299–313 (March 1997).

Connor, M. "Women in United States History: A Thematic Approach." *Social Studies Review* 36(2):88–90 (Spring/Summer 1997).

Costa, A. L., and Liebmann, R. M. (Eds). *Supporting the Spirit of Learning. When Process Is Content.* Thousand Oaks, CA: Corwin Press, 1997.

Darling-Hammond, L., and Falk, B. "Using Standards and Assessments to Support Student Learning." *Phi Delta Kappan* 79(3):190–199 (November 1997).

Fonte, J. D., and Lerner, R. "History Standards Are Not Fixed." *Society* 34(2):20–25 (January–February 1997).

Giffard, S. "Theme Studies and the Arts." *Primary Voices K–6* 5(2):2–5 (April 1997).

Grunert, J. *The Course Syllabus: A Learning-Centered Approach.* Jaffrey, NH: Anker, 1997.

Humphrey, J. W., et al. "Reading Matters: Supporting the Development of Young Adolescent Readers." *Phi Delta Kappan* 79(4):305–311 (December 1997).

Hurley, S. R., and Blake, S. "Animals and Occupations: Why Theme-Based Curricula Work." *Early Childhood News* 9(1):20–25 (January/February 1997).

Hynds, S. *On the Brink: Negotiating Literature and Life with Adolescents.* New York: Teachers College Press, 1997.

Irvin, J. L. "Building Sound Literacy Learning Programs for Young Adolescents." *Middle School Journal* 28(3):4–9 (January 1997).

Jenkins, K. D., and Jenkins, D. M. "Integrating Curriculum in a Total Quality School." *Middle School Journal* 29(4):14–27 (March 1998).

Jensen, E. *Teaching With the Brain in Mind.* Alexandria, VA: Association for Supervision and Curriculum Development, 1998.

Lowery, S. "Censorship: Tactics for Defense." *Phi Delta Kappan* 79(7):546–547 (March 1998).

Martin, B. L., and Briggs, L. J. *The Affective and Cognitive Domains.* Englewood Cliffs, NJ: Educational Technology Publications, 1986.

McMillan, J. H. *Classroom Assessment: Principles and Practice for Effective Instruction,* Chapter 2. Needham Heights, MA: Allyn & Bacon, 1997.

Mee, C. *2000 Voices: Young Adolescents' Perceptions and Curriculum Implications.* Columbus, OH: National Middle Schools Association, 1997.

Morrow, L. M., et al. "The Effect of a Literature-Based Program Integrated in Literacy and Science Instruction With Children from Diverse Backgrounds." *Reading Research Quarterly* 32(1):54–76 (January/March 1997).

Noddings, N. "Thinking About Standards." *Phi Delta Kappan* 79(3):184–189 (November 1997).

Nowicki, J. J., and Meehan, K. F. *Interdisciplinary Strategies for English and Social Studies Classrooms: Toward Collaborative Middle and Secondary School Teaching.* Boston: Allyn & Bacon, 1997.

Page, P. E., et al. *Making Integrated Curriculum Work: Teachers, Students, and the Quest for Coherent Curriculum.* New York: Teachers College Press, 1997.

Perry, P. J. *Guide to Math Materials: Resources to Support the NCTM Standards.* Englewood, CO: Teacher Ideas Press/Libraries Unlimited, 1997.

Post, T. R., et al. *Interdisciplinary Approaches to Curriculum: Themes for Teaching.* Upper Saddle River, NJ: Prentice Hall, 1997.

Powell, R., et al. "Toward an Integrative Multicultural Learning Environment." *Middle School Journal* 29(4):3–13 (March 1998).

Radencich, M. C., and Schumm, J. S. *How to Help Your Child with Homework: Every Caring Parent's Guide to Encouraging Good Study Habits and Ending the Homework Wars (For Parents of Children Ages 6–13).* Revised Edition. Minneapolis: Free Spirit Publishing, 1997.

Reigeluth, C. M. "Educational Standards: To Standardize or to Customize Learning?" *Phi Delta Kappan* 79(3):202–206 (November 1997).

Roberts, P. L. *Literature-Based History Activities for Children, Grades 4–8.* Boston: Allyn & Bacon, 1997.

Roberts, P. L. *Taking Humor Seriously in Children's Literature.* Lanham, MD: Scarecrow, 1997.

Runyan, J. N. "Runyan and Company . . . #1 Because We Think!" *Teaching and Change* 4(4):358–378 (Summer 1997).

Russell, J. F. "Relationships Between the Implementation of Middle-Level Program Concepts and Student Achievement." *Journal of Curriculum and Supervision* 12(2):169–185 (Winter 1997).

Schomoker, M., and Marzano, R. J. "Realizing the Promise of Standards-Based Education." *Educational Leadership* 56(6):17–21 (March 1999).

Suhor, C. (Compiler). *Trends and Issues in English Instruction, 1997—Six Summaries.* Urbana, IL: National Council of Teachers of English, 1997.

Tucker, B., et al. "An Integrated Thematic Curriculum for Gifted Learners." *Roeper Review* 19(4):196–199 (June 1997).

Usnick, V., and McCarthy, J. "Turning Adolescents onto Mathematics through Literature." *Middle School Journal* 29(4):50–54 (March 1998).

Victor, E., and Kellough, R. D. *Science for the Elementary and Middle School.* 9th ed. Upper Saddle River, NJ: Prentice Hall, 2000.

Vossler, J. M. "Beyond Stereotypes: Books About Other Cultures for Middle School Readers." *Middle School Journal* 28(3):54–57 (January 1997).

Watts, S., and Graves, M. F. "Fostering Students' Understanding of Challenging Texts." *Middle School Journal* 29(1):45–51 (September 1997).

Wiggins, G., and McTighe, J. *Understanding by Design.* Alexandria, VA: Association for Supervision and Curriculum Development, 1998.

Wiggins, R., and Wiggins, J. "Integrating Through Conceptual Connections." *Music Educators Journal* 83(4):38–41 (January 1997).

Wraga, W. G. "Patterns of Interdisciplinary Curriculum Organization and Professional Knowledge of the Curriculum Field." *Journal of Curriculum and Supervision* 12(2):98–117 (Winter 1997).

Zeeman, K. L. "Grappling With Grendel or What We Did When the Censors Came." *English Journal* 86(2):46–50 (February 1997).

Chapter 6

Planning: The Instructional Unit

The teacher's edition of the student textbook and other resource materials may expedite your planning but should not substitute for it. You must know how to create a good instructional plan. In this chapter you will learn how it is done. Specifically, upon completion of this chapter you should be able to

1. Complete a unit of instruction with sequential lesson plans.
2. Demonstrate understanding of the significance of the planned unit of instruction and the concept of planning curriculum and instruction as an organic process.
3. Describe the similarities and differences of several types of instructional units.
4. Demonstrate understanding of the place and role of each of the four decision-making and thought-processing phases in unit planning and implementation.
5. Demonstrate understanding of self-reflection as a common thread important to the reciprocal process of teaching and learning.
6. Demonstrate an understanding of the differences between direct and indirect instruction and the advantages and limitations of each.
7. For a discipline and grade level, give examples of learning experiences from each of these categories, and when and why you would use each one: verbal, visual, vicarious, simulated, and direct; and examples of how, why, and when they could be combined.

THE INSTRUCTIONAL UNIT

The instructional unit is a major subdivision of a course (for one course there are several to many units

of instruction) and is comprised of learning activities planned around a central theme, topic, issue, or problem. Organizing the content of the semester or year into units makes the teaching process more manageable than when no plan or only random choices are made by a teacher.

The instructional unit is not unlike a chapter in a book, an act or scene in a play, or a phase of work when undertaking a project such as building a house. Breaking down information or actions into component parts and then grouping the related parts makes sense out of learning and doing. The unit brings a sense of cohesiveness and structure to student learning and avoids the piecemeal approach that might otherwise unfold. You can learn to articulate lessons within, between, and among unit plans and focus on important elements while not ignoring tangential information of importance. Students remember "chunks" of information, especially when those chunks are related to specific units.

Although the steps for developing any type of instructional unit are basically the same, units can be organized in a number of ways. For the purposes of this resource guide, we consider two basic types of units—the standard unit and the integrated thematic unit.

A *standard unit* (known also as a *conventional* or *traditional unit*) consists of a series of lessons centered on a topic, theme, major concept, or block of subject matter. Each lesson builds on the previous lesson by contributing additional subject matter, providing further illustrations, and supplying more practice or other added instruction, all of which are aimed at bringing about mastery of the knowledge and skills on which the unit is centered.

When a standard unit is centered on a central theme (theme versus topic was discussed at the end of Chapter 5), the unit may be referred to as a **thematic unit**. When, by design, the thematic unit integrates disciplines, such as combining the learning of science and mathematics, or combining social studies and English/language arts, or combining all four core (or any other) disciplines, then it is called an *integrated (or interdisciplinary) thematic unit (ITU)*, or simply an integrated unit.

Planning and Developing Any Unit of Instruction

Whether for a standard unit or an integrated thematic unit, steps in planning and developing the unit are the same and are described in the following paragraphs.

1. *Select a suitable theme, topic, issue, or problem.* These may be already laid out in your course of study or textbook or already have been agreed to by members of the teaching team. Many schools change their themes or add new ones from year to year.

2. *Select the goals of the unit and prepare the overview.* The goals are written as an overview or rationale, covering what the unit is about and what the students are to learn. In planning the goals, you should (a) become as familiar as possible with the topic and materials used; (b) consult curriculum documents, such as courses of study, state frameworks, and resource units for ideas; (c) decide the content and procedures (i.e., what the students should learn about the topic and how); (d) write the rationale or overview, where you summarize what you expect the students will learn about the topic; and (e) be sure your goals are congruent with those of the course or grade level program.

3. *Select suitable instructional objectives.* In doing this, you should (a) include understandings, skills, attitudes, appreciations, and ideals, (b) be specific, avoiding vagueness and generalizations, (c) write the objectives in performance terms, and (d) be as certain as possible that the objectives will contribute to the major learning described in the overview.

4. *Detail the instructional procedures.* These procedures include the subject content and learning activities, established as a series of lessons. Proceed with the following steps in your initial planning of the instructional procedures.

   a. By referring to curriculum documents, resource units, and colleagues as resources, gather ideas for learning activities that might be suitable for the unit.

   b. Check the learning activities to make sure that they will actually contribute to the learning designated in your objectives, discarding ideas that do not.

   c. Make sure the learning activities are feasible. Can you afford the time, effort, or expense? Do you have the necessary materials and equipment? If not, can they be obtained? Are the activities suited to the intellectual and maturity levels of your students?

   d. Check resources available to be certain they support the content and learning activities.

   e. Decide how to introduce the unit. Provide *introductory activities* that will: arouse student interest; inform students of what the unit is about; help you learn about your students—their interests, their abilities, and their experiences— and present knowledge of the topic; provide transitions that bridge this topic with that which students have already learned; and involve the students in the planning.

   f. Plan *developmental activities* that will sustain student interest, provide for individual student differences, promote the learning as cited in the specific objectives, and promote a project.

   g. Plan *culminating activities* that will summarize what has been learned, bring together loose ends, apply what has been learned to new situations, provide students with opportunities to demonstrate their learning, and provide transfer to the unit that follows.

5. *Plan for preassessment and assessment of student learning.* Preassess what students already know or think they know. Assessment of student progress in achievement of the learning objectives (formative evaluation) should permeate the entire unit (that is, as often as possible, assessment should be a daily component of lessons). Plan to gather information in several ways, including informal observations, checklist observations of student performance and their portfolios, and paper and pencil tests. As discussed in Chapters 5 and 11, assessment must be congruent with the instructional objectives.

6. *Provide for the materials and tools of instruction.* The unit cannot function without materials. Therefore, you must plan long before the unit begins for media equipment and materials, references, reading materials, reproduced materials, and community resources. Librarians and media center personnel are usually more than willing to assist in finding appropriate materials to support a unit of instruction.

Unit Format, Inclusive Elements, and Time Duration

Follow those six steps to develop any type of unit. In addition, two general points should be made. First, although there is no single best format for a teaching unit, there are minimum inclusions. Particular formats may be best for specific disciplines or grade levels, topics, and types of activities. During your student teaching, your college or university program for teacher preparation and/or your cooperating teacher(s) may have a format that you will be expected to follow. Regardless of the format, the following seven elements should be evident in any unit plan: (1) identification of grade level, subject, topic, and time duration of the unit; (2) statement of rationale and general goals for the unit; (3) major objectives of unit; (4) materials and resources needed; (5) lesson plans; (6) assessment strategies; and (7) a statement of how the unit will attend to variations in students' reading levels, experiential backgrounds, and special needs.

Second, there is no set time duration for a unit plan, although for specific units curriculum guides will recommend certain time spans. Units may extend for a minimum of several days (for example, the Indian Trail Junior High School "prom night" integrated unit discussed in Chapter 8 is a five-day unit) or, as in the case of some interdisciplinary thematic units, for several weeks to an entire school year. However, be aware that when standard units last more than two or three weeks, they tend to lose the character of clearly identifiable units. For any unit of instruction, the exact time duration will be dictated by several factors, including the topic, problem, or theme, the age, interests, and maturity of the students, and the scope of learning activities.

THEORETICAL CONSIDERATIONS FOR THE SELECTION OF INSTRUCTIONAL STRATEGIES

As you prepare to detail your instructional plan, you will be narrowing in on selecting and planning the instructional activities. In Chapter 3, you learned about specific teacher behaviors that must be in place for students to learn: structuring the learning environment, accepting and sharing instructional accountability, demonstrating withitness and overlapping, providing a variety of motivating and challenging activities, modeling appropriate behaviors, facilitating students' acquisition of data, creating a psychologically safe environment, clarifying whenever necessary, using periods of silence, and questioning thoughtfully. In the paragraphs that follow, you will learn more not only about how to implement some of those fundamental behaviors, but also about the large repertoire of other strategies, aids, media, and resources available to you (see Figure 6.1). You will learn how to select and implement from this repertoire.

Decision Making and Strategy Selection

You must make a myriad of decisions to select and implement a particular teaching strategy effectively. The selection of a strategy depends in part upon your decision whether to deliver information directly (direct, expository, or didactic teaching) or to provide students with access to information (indirect or facilitative teaching). Direct teaching tends to be teacher-centered, while indirect teaching is more student-centered. To assist in your selection of strategies, it is important that you understand basic principles of learning summarized starting on page 181.

Direct and Indirect Instruction: A Clarification of Terms

You are probably well aware that professional education is rampant with its own special jargon, which can be confusing to the neophyte. The use of the term **direct teaching** (or its synonym, *direct instruction*) and its antonym **direct experiences** are examples of how con-

Figure 6.1   A list of instructional strategies.

Assignment	Group work	Problem solving
Autotutorial	Guest speaker	Project
Brainstorming	Homework	Questioning
Coaching	Individualized instruction	Review and practice
Collaborative learning	Inquiry	Role play
Cooperative learning	Interactive media	Self-instructional module
Debate	Journal writing	Script writing
Demonstration	Laboratory investigation	Simulation
Diorama	Laser videodisk or compact disc	Study guide
Discovery	Lecture	Symposium
Drama	Library/resource center	Telecommunication
Drill	Metacognition	Term paper
Expository	Mock up	Textbook
Field trip	Multimedia	Think-pair-share
Game	Panel discussion	Tutorial

fusing the jargon can be. The term *direct teaching* (or *direct instruction, expository teaching,* or *teacher-centered instruction*) can also have a variety of definitions, depending on who is doing the defining. For now, you should keep this distinction in mind: do not confuse the term *direct instruction* with the term *direct experience*. The two terms indicate two separate (though not incompatible) instructional modes. The dichotomy of pedagogical opposites shown in Figure 6.2 provides a useful visual distinction of the opposites. While terms in one column are similar if not synonymous, they are near or exact opposites of those across in the other column.

DEGREES OF DIRECTNESS

Rather than thinking and behaving in terms of opposites as may be suggested by Figure 6.2, more likely your teaching will be distinguished by "degrees of directness," or "degrees of indirectness." For example, for a unit of instruction, directions for a culminating project may be given by the teacher in a direct or expository mini-lesson, followed by a student-designed inquiry that leads to the final project.

Rather than focus your attention on the selection of a particular model of teaching (see Figure 6.3), I emphasize the importance of an eclectic model—selecting the best from various models or approaches.

Figure 6.2 Pedagogical opposites.

Delivery mode of instruction	versus Access mode of instruction
Didactic instruction	versus Facilitative teaching
Direct instruction	versus Indirect instruction
Direct teaching	versus Direct experiencing
Expository teaching	versus Discovery learning
Teacher-centered instruction	versus Student-centered instruction

Figure 6.3 Families of instructional models.

As indicated by the example of the preceding paragraph, there will be times when you want to use a direct, teacher-centered approach, perhaps by a mini-lecture or a demonstration. Then there will be many more times when you will want to use an indirect, student-centered or social-interactive approach, such as the use of cooperative learning and investigative projects. And perhaps there will be even more times when you will be doing both at the same time, such as working with a teacher-centered approach with one small group of students, perhaps giving them direct instruction, while another group or several groups of students, in areas of the classroom, are working on their project studies (a student-centered approach). The information in the following sections and specific descriptions in Part III will help you make decisions about when each approach is most appropriate and provide guidelines for their use.

Principles of Classroom Instruction and Learning: A Synopsis

A student does not learn to write by learning to recognize grammatical constructions of sentences. Neither does a person learn to play soccer solely by listening to a lecture on soccer. Learning is superficial unless the instructional methods and learning activities are developmentally and intellectually appropriate, that is, they must be (a) developmentally appropriate for the learners and (b) intellectually appropriate for the understanding, skills, and attitudes desired. Memorizing, for instance, is not the same as understanding. Yet far too often, memorization seems all that is expected of students in many classrooms. The result is low-level learning, a mere verbalism or mouthing of poorly understood words and sentences. The orchestration of short-term memory exercises is not intellectually appropriate and it is not teaching. A mental model of

Information-processing models	*Social models*
• Advance organizer	• Group investigation
• Concept attainment	• Laboratory method
• Inductive thinking	• Roleplay
• Scientific inquiry	• Social inquiry
• Mnemonics	
• Synectics	*Behavioral systems models*
	• Direct teaching
Personal models	• Mastery learning
• Nondirective teaching	• Programmed learning
• Classroom meeting	• Simulation
• Self-actualization	• Social learning

Source: B. R. Joyce and E. F. Calhoun, *Creating Learning Experiences: The Role of Instructional Theory and Research* (Alexandria, VA: Association for Supervision and Curriculum Development, 1996).

learning that assumes a brain is capable of doing only one thing at a time is invidiously incorrect.[1]

When selecting the mode of instruction, you should bear in mind the following six basic principles of classroom instruction and learning.

1. To a great degree, it is the mode of instruction that determines what is learned.
2. Students must be actively involved in their own learning and in the assessment of their learning.
3. You must hold high expectations for the learning of each student (although not necessarily identical expectations for every student) and not waiver from those expectations.
4. Students need constant, steady, understandable, positive, and reliable feedback about their learning.
5. Students should be engaged in both independent study and cooperative learning and give and receive tutorial instruction.
6. No matter what else you are prepared to teach, you are also a teacher of reading, writing, thinking, and study skills.

As discussed in Chapter 5, conceptual knowledge refers to the understanding of relationships, whereas procedural knowledge entails the recording in memory of the meanings of symbols, rules, and procedures needed to accomplish tasks. Unless it is connected in meaningful ways for the formation of conceptual knowledge, the accumulation of memorized procedural knowledge is fragmented and ill-fated and will be maintained in the brain for only a brief time.

To help students establish conceptual knowledge, learning must be meaningful. To help make learning meaningful for your students, you should use direct and real experiences as often as practical and possible. Vicarious experiences are sometimes necessary to provide students with otherwise unattainable knowledge; however, direct experiences that engage all the student's senses and all their learning modalities are more powerful. Students learn to write by writing and by receiving coaching and feedback about their progress in writing. They learn to play soccer by experiencing playing soccer and by receiving coaching and feedback about their developing skills and knowledge in playing the game. They learn these things best when they are actively (hands-on) and mentally (minds-on) engaged in doing them. This is real learning, learning that is meaningful; it is *authentic learning*.

---

[1] See, for example, E. Jensen, *Teaching With the Brain in Mind* (Alexandria, VA: Association for Supervision and Curriculum Development, 1998), and J. C. Baker and F. G. Martin, *A Neural Network Guide to Teaching*, Fastback 431 (Bloomington, IN: Phi Delta Kappa Educational Foundation, 1998).

Direct vs. Indirect Instructional Modes: Strengths and Weaknesses of Each

Selecting an instructional strategy involves two distinct choices (modes): should you deliver information to students directly or should you provide students with access to information? (Refer to the comparison of pedagogical opposites in Figure 6.2.)

The *delivery mode* (known also as the didactic, expository, or traditional style) is to deliver information. Knowledge is passed on from those who know (the teachers, with the aid of textbooks) to those who do not (the students). Within the delivery mode, traditional and time-honored strategies are textbook reading, the lecture (formal teacher talk), questioning, and teacher-centered or teacher-planned discussions.

With the *access mode*, instead of direct delivery of information and direct control over what is learned, you provide students with access to information by working *with* the students. In collaboration with the students, experiences are designed that facilitate their building of their existing schemata and their obtaining new knowledge and skills. Within the access mode, important instructional strategies include cooperative learning, inquiry, and investigative student-centered project learning, each of which most certainly will use questioning, although the questions more frequently will come from the students than from you or the textbook or some other source extrinsic to the student. Discussions and lectures on particular topics also may be involved. But when used in the access mode, discussions and lectures occur during or after (rather than preceding) direct, hands-on learning by the students. In other words, rather than preceding student inquiry, discussions and lectures *result from* student inquiry and then may be followed by further student investigation.

You are probably more experienced with the delivery mode. To be most effective as a classroom teacher, however, you must become knowledgeable and skillful in using access strategies. For young learners, strategies within the access mode clearly facilitate their positive learning and acquisition of conceptual knowledge and help build their self-esteem.

You should appropriately select and effectively use strategies from both modes, but with a strong favor toward access strategies. Thus, from your study of the chapters that follow in Part III, you will become knowledgeable about specific techniques so you can make intelligent decisions for choosing the best strategy for particular goals and objectives for your own discipline and the interests, needs, and maturity level of your own unique group of students.

Figures 6.4 and 6.5 provide an overview of the specific strengths and weaknesses of each mode. By comparing those figures you can see that the strengths and weaknesses of one mode are nearly mirror opposites of

Figure 6.4 Delivery mode: its strengths and weaknesses.

Delivery Mode

Strengths
- Much content can be covered within a short span of time, usually by formal teacher talk, which then may be followed by an experiential activity.
- The teacher is in control of what content is covered.
- The teacher is in control of time allotted to specific content coverage.
- Strategies within the delivery mode are consistent with competency-based instruction.
- Student achievement of specific content is predictable and manageable.

Potential Weaknesses
- The sources of student motivation are mostly extrinsic.
- Students have little control over the pacing of their learning.
- Students make few important decisions about their learning.
- There may be little opportunity for divergent or creative thinking.
- Student self-esteem may be inadequately served.

Figure 6.5 Access mode: its strengths and weaknesses.

Access Mode

Strengths
- Students learn content in more depth.
- The sources of student motivation are more likely intrinsic.
- Students make important decisions about their own learning.
- Students have more control over the pacing of their learning.
- Students develop a sense of personal self-worth.

Potential Weaknesses
- Content coverage may be more limited.
- Strategies are time-consuming.
- The teacher has less control over content and time.
- The specific results of student learning are less predictable.
- The teacher may have less control over class procedures.

the other. As noted earlier, although as a teacher you should be skillful in the use of strategies from both modes, for the most developmentally appropriate teaching of most groups of learners, K–12, you should concentrate more on using strategies from the access mode. Strategies within that mode are more student-centered, hands on, and concrete; students interact with one another and are actually or closer to doing what they are learning to do; that is, the learning is likely more authentic. Learning that occurs from the use of that mode is longer lasting (fixes into long-term memory). And, as the students interact with one another and with their learning, they develop a sense of can-do, which enhances their self-esteem.

SELECTING LEARNING ACTIVITIES THAT ARE DEVELOPMENTALLY APPROPRIATE

Returning to our soccer example, can you imagine a soccer coach teaching students the skills and knowledge needed to play soccer but without ever letting them experience playing the game? Can you imagine a science teacher instructing students on how to read a thermometer without ever letting them actually read a thermometer? Can you imagine a geography teacher teaching students how to read a map without ever letting them put their eyes and hands on a map? Can you imagine a first grade teacher teaching children the let-

ters of the alphabet without ever letting them put the letters together to form words? Can you imagine a piano teacher teaching a child to play piano without ever allowing the child to touch a keyboard? Unfortunately, still today, too many teachers do almost those exact things: they try to teach students to do something without letting the students practice doing it.

In planning and selecting developmentally appropriate learning activities, an important rule to remember is to select activities that are as close to the real thing as possible. In other words, students learn through direct experience. When students are involved in direct experiences, they are using more of their sensory input channels, their learning modalities (i.e., auditory, visual, tactile, and kinesthetic). When all the senses are engaged, learning is more integrated; it is most effective, meaningful, and longest lasting. This learning by doing is called *authentic learning* or *hands-on/minds-on learning*.

The Learning Experiences Ladder

Figure 6.6 depicts what is called the Learning Experiences Ladder, a visual depiction of a range of kinds of learning experiences from which a teacher may select. Hands-on/minds-on learning is at the bottom of the ladder. At the top are abstract experiences, in which the learner is exposed only to symbolization (i.e., letters and numbers) and uses only one or two senses (auditory or visual). The teacher lectures while the students sit and watch and hear. Visual and verbal symbolic experiences, although impossible to avoid when teaching, are less effective in assuring that planned

Learning that is hands on and minds on is longer lasting because it engages more of the sensory input modalities.

Figure 6.6 The Learning Experiences Ladder.

Verbal Experiences
Teacher talk, written words; engaging only one sense; using the most abstract symbolization; students physically inactive. *Examples:* (1) Listening to the teacher talk about tide pools. (2) Listening to a student report about the Grand Canyon. (3) Listening to a guest speaker talk about how the state legislature functions.

Visual Experiences
Still pictures, diagrams, charts; engaging only one sense; typically symbolic; students physically inactive. *Examples:* (1) Viewing slide photographs of tide pools. (2) Viewing drawings and photographs of the Grand Canyon. (3) Listening to a guest speaker talk about the state legislature and show slides of it in action.

Vicarious Experiences
Laser videodisc programs; computer programs; video programs; engaging more than one sense; learner indirectly "doing"; may be some limited physical activity. *Examples:* (1) Interacting with a computer program about wave action and life in tide pools. (2) Viewing and listening to a video program about the Grand Canyon. (3) Taking a field trip to observe the state legislature in action.

Simulated Experiences
Role-playing; experimenting; simulations; mock-up; working models; all or nearly all senses engaged; activity often integrating disciplines; closest to the real thing. *Examples:* (1) Building a classroom working model of a tide pool. (2) Building a classroom working model of the Grand Canyon. (3) Designing a classroom role-play simulation patterned after the operating procedure of the state legislature.

Direct Experiences
Learner actually doing what is being learned; true inquiry; all senses engaged; usually integrates disciplines; the real thing. *Examples:* (1) Visiting and experiencing a tide pool. (2) Visiting and experiencing the Grand Canyon. (3) Designing an elected representative body to oversee the operation of the school-within-the-school program and patterned after the state legislative assembly.

ABSTRACT

↑
↓

CONCRETE

Note: Earlier versions of this concept were Charles F. Hoban Sr. et al., *Visualizing the Curriculum* (New York: Dryden, 1937), p. 39; Edgar Dale, *Audio-Visual Methods in Teaching* (New York: Holt, Rinehart & Winston, 1969), p. 108: and Jerome S. Bruner, *Toward a Theory of Instruction* (Cambridge, MA: Harvard University Press, 1966), p. 49.

The most effective and longest-lasting learning is that which engages most or all of the learner's senses. This is true with adult learners, primary grade children, and students of any age group in between.

and meaningful learning occurs. This is especially so with young children, learners who have special needs, learners with ethnic and cultural differences, and LEP students. Thus, when planning learning experiences and selecting instructional materials, you are advised to select activities that engage the students in the most direct experiences possible and that are developmentally and intellectually appropriate for your specific group of students.

As can be inferred from the Learning Experiences Ladder, when teaching about tide pools (the first example for each step) the most effective mode is to take the students to a tide pool (direct experience), where students can see, hear, touch, smell, and perhaps even taste (if not polluted with toxins) the tide pool. The least effective mode is for the teacher to merely talk about the tide pool (verbal experience, the most abstract and symbolic experience), engaging only the auditory sense.

Of course, for various reasons—such as time, matters of safety, lack of resources, geographic location of your school—you may not be able to take your students to a tide pool. You cannot always use the most direct experience, so sometimes you must select an experience higher on the ladder. Self-discovery teaching is not always appropriate. Sometimes it is more appropriate to build upon what others have discovered and learned. Although learners do not need to "reinvent the wheel," the most effective and longest-lasting learning is that which engages most or all of their senses. On the Learning Experiences Ladder, those are the experiences that fall within the bottom three categories—direct, simulated, and vicarious. This is true with adult learners, primary grade children, and students of any age group in between.

Direct, Simulated, and Vicarious Experiences Help Connect Student Learning

Another value of direct, simulated, and vicarious experiences is that they tend to be interdisciplinary; that is, they blur or bridge subject-content boundaries. That makes those experiences especially useful for teachers who want to help students connect the learning of one discipline with that of others and to bridge what is being learned with their own life experiences. Direct, simulated, and vicarious experiences are more like real life. That means that the learning resulting from those experiences is authentic.

Now do Exercises 6.1 and 6.2.

EXERCISE 6.1 RECALLING MY OWN LEARNING EXPERIENCES IN SCHOOL

INSTRUCTIONS: The purpose of this exercise is to recall and share learning experiences from your own school days. You should reflect upon those with respect to their relationship to the Learning Experiences Ladder and the discussion of the access and delivery modes of instruction.

1. Recall one vivid learning experience from each level of your schooling and identify its position on the Learning Experiences Ladder.

   Elementary or Secondary School Experience:

   Position on Ladder:

   College Experience:

   Position on Ladder:

EXERCISE 6.1 (*continued*)

2. Share with classmates in small groups. After sharing your experiences with others of your group, what, if anything, can your group conclude? Write those conclusions here and then share them with the class.

EXERCISE 6.2 CONVERSION OF AN ABSTRACT LEARNING EXPERIENCE TO A DIRECT ONE

INSTRUCTIONS: This exercise is to tax your creative imagination. Select from your outline a topic that is typically taught by the use of symbolization (at or near the top of the Learning Experiences Ladder); then devise a technique by which, with limited resources, that same content would be taught more directly (at or close to the bottom of the ladder). Upon completion of this exercise, share your proposal with your colleagues for their feedback.

1. Grade level:

2. Topic:

3. Traditional way of teaching this topic:

4. Detailed description of how to teach this topic using direct learning experiences:

5. Statement about why you believe a direct way of teaching this topic is uncommon:

EXERCISE 6.2 (*continued*)

6. Ideas resulting from sharing your proposal with others in your class:

PLANNING AND DEVELOPING AN INTERDISCIPLINARY THEMATIC UNIT

The six steps outlined earlier in this chapter are essential for planning any type of teaching unit, including the interdisciplinary thematic unit (ITU), which may consist of smaller, subject-specific, conventional units developed according to the immediately foregoing guidelines. Because developing interdisciplinary thematic units is an essential task for many of today's teachers, you should learn this process now.

As was discussed in the final section of Chapter 5, the primary responsibility for the development of interdisciplinary thematic units can depend on a single teacher or upon the cooperation of several teachers who represent several disciplines. A teaching team may develop from one to several interdisciplinary thematic units a year. Over time, then, a team will have several units available for implementation. However, the most effective units are often those that are the most current or the most meaningful to students. This means that ever-changing global, national, and local topics provide a smorgasbord from which to choose, and teaching teams must constantly update old units and develop new and exciting ones.

One teaching team's unit should not conflict with others at the same or another grade level. If a school has two or more teams at the same grade level that involve the same disciplines, for example, the teams may want to develop units on different themes and share their products. For example, an eighth grade team must guard against developing a unit quite similar to one that the students had or will have at another grade level. Open lines of communication within, between, and among teams and schools within a school district are critical to the success of interdisciplinary thematic teaching.[2] Consider the steps that follow.

Steps for Developing an Interdisciplinary Thematic Unit

Ten steps to guide you in developing an ITU are:

1. *Agree on the nature or source of the unit.* Team members should view the interdisciplinary approach as a collaborative effort in which all members (and other faculty) can participate if appropriate. Write what you want the students to receive from interdisciplinary instruction. Troubleshoot potential stumbling blocks.

2. *Discuss subject-specific frameworks, goals, and objectives, curriculum guidelines, textbooks and supplemental materials, and units already in place for the school year.* Focus on what you are obligated or mandated to teach, and explain the scope and sequence of the teaching so all team members understand the constraints and limitations.

3. *Choose a theme topic and develop a time line.* From the information provided by each subject-specialist teacher in step 2, start listing possible theme topics that can be drawn from within the existing course outlines. Give-and-take is essential here, as some topics will fit certain subjects better than others. (See "Integrated Thematic Unit: Topic Versus Theme," in Chapter 5.) The chief goal is to find a topic that can be adapted to each subject without detracting from the educational plan already in place. This may require choosing and merging content from two or more other units previously planned. The theme is then drawn from the topic.

Sometimes themes are selected by the teacher or by a teaching team before meeting the students for the first time. Other times they are selected by the teachers in collaboration with students. Even when the theme is preselected, students still should be given major responsibility with guidance from the teacher for deciding the final theme title (name), topics, and corresponding learning activities. Integrated thematic instruction works best when students have ownership in the study, when they have been empowered with major decision-making responsibility.

The basis for theme selection should satisfy two criteria: the theme should (1) fit within the expected scope and sequence of mandated content and (2) be of interest to the students. Regarding the first criterion, many teachers have said that when they and their students embarked on an interdisciplinary thematic study, they did so without truly knowing where the study would go or what the learning outcomes would be—and they were somewhat frightened by that. But when completed, their students had learned everything (or nearly everything) that the teacher would have expected them to learn were the teacher to use a more traditional content-centered approach. And, it was more fun!

When selecting a theme, consider the questions shown in Figure 6.7.

The second criterion is easy to satisfy, as it will most assuredly be when students are truly empowered with major decision-making responsibility for what and how they learn. Once a general theme is selected (one that satisfies the first criterion), its final title, subtopics, and corresponding procedural activities should be finalized in collaboration with the students. (See Step 7.)

4. *Establish two time lines.* The first is for the team only and is to ensure that the deadlines for specific work required in developing the unit will be met by each member. The second time line is for both students and teachers and shows how long the unit should last, when it will start, and in which classes it will be taught.

[2]See G. Quinn and L. N. Restine, "Interdisciplinary Teams: Concerns, Benefits, and Costs," *Journal of School Leadership* 6(5):494–511 (September 1996).

Figure 6.7 Questions to ask when selecting a theme.

- Is the theme within the realm of understanding and experience of the teachers involved?
- Will the theme interest all members of the teaching team?
- Do we have sufficient materials and resources to supply information we might need?
- Does the theme lend itself to active learning experiences?
- Can this theme lead to a unit that is of the proper duration—not too short and not too long?
- Is the theme helpful, worthwhile, and pertinent to the instructional objectives?
- Will the theme be of interest to students, and will it motivate them to do their best?
- Is the theme one with which teachers are not already so familiar that they cannot share in the excitement of the learning?
- Will this theme be of interest to students, and will it motivate them to do their best?

5. *Develop the scope and sequence for content and instruction.* To develop the unit, follow the six steps for planning and developing a unit of instruction outlined earlier in this chapter. This should be done by each team member and by the group during common planning time so members can coordinate dates and activities in logical sequence and depth. This is an organic process and will generate both ideas and anxiety. Under the guidance of the team leader, members should strive to keep this anxiety at a level conducive to learning, experimenting, and arriving at group consensus.

6. *Share goals and objectives.* Each team member should have a copy of the goals and target objectives of every other team member. This helps to refine the unit and lesson plans and to prevent unnecessary overlap and confusion.

7. *Give the unit a name.* The unit has been fashioned and is held together by the chosen theme. Giving the theme a name and using that name tells the students that this unit of study is integrated, important, and meaningful to school and to life.

8. *Share subject-specific units, lesson plans, and printed and nonprinted materials.* Exchange the finalized unit to obtain one another's comments and suggestions. Keep a copy of each teacher's unit(s) as a resource, and see if you could present a lesson using it as your basis (some modification may be necessary). Lesson planning is the topic that follows.

9. *Field test the unit.* Beginning at the scheduled time and date, present the lessons. Team members may trade classes from time to time. Team teaching may take place if and when two or more classes can be combined for instruction (if a classroom space large enough is available).

10. *Reflect, assess, and perhaps adjust and revise the unit.* During planning time, team members should share and discuss their successes and failures and determine what needs to be changed and how and when that should be done to make the unit successful. Adjustments can be made along the way (formative assessments), and revisions for future use can be made after the unit (summative assessment).

The preceding ten steps are not absolutes and should be viewed only as guides. Differing teaching teams and levels of teacher experience and knowledge make the strict adherence to any plan less productive than would be the use of group-generated plans. For instance, some teachers have found that the last point under step 3 could state exactly the opposite; they recommend that the topic for an interdisciplinary unit should be one that a teacher or a teaching team already knows well. In practice, the process that works well—one that results in meaningful learning for the students and in their positive feelings about themselves, learning, and school—is the appropriate process.

Now do Exercises 6.3 and 6.4.

EXERCISE 6.3 GENERATING IDEAS FOR INTERDISCIPLINARY UNITS

INSTRUCTIONS: The purpose of this exercise is to use brainstorming to generate a list of potential topics suitable as interdisciplinary units. Divide your class into groups of three to seven. Each group is to decide the grade or age level for which their unit ideas will be generated. If the group chooses, cooperative learning can be used; group members are then assigned roles such as facilitator, recorder, reporter, monitor of thinking processes, on-task monitor, and so on. Each group is to generate as many topics as possible. One member of each group should record all ideas. Reserve discussion of ideas until no further topics are generated. Lists can be shared in the large group.

Grade level interest of the group _____

1. Existing subject-area content units (as the group knows them to be or as they are predicted to exist)

_____

_____

2. Current topics of
   a. Global interest _____

   _____

   _____

   b. National interest _____

   _____

   _____

   c. Statewide interest _____

   _____

   _____

   d. Local interest _____

   _____

   _____

   e. Interest to the school _____

   _____

   _____

   f. Interest to students of this age _____

   _____

   _____

EXERCISE 6.4 INTEGRATING THE TOPIC

INSTRUCTIONS: The purpose of this exercise is to practice weaving interdisciplinary themes into curricula. In groups of three or four, choose one idea that was generated during Exercise 6.3, and derive a list of suggestions about how that theme could be woven into the curricula of various classes, programs, and activities, as indicated below. It is possible that not all areas listed are relevant to the grade level to which your group is addressing its work. Cooperative learning can be used, with appropriate roles assigned to group members. One person in the group should be the recorder. Upon completion, share your group's work (the process and product of which will be much like that of an actual interdisciplinary teaching team) with the class. Copies should be made available to those who want them.

Unit theme _____

1. In core classes
   a. English _____

   _____

   _____

   b. Social studies _____

   _____

   _____

   c. Mathematics _____

   _____

   _____

   d. Science _____

   _____

   _____

   e. Reading _____

   _____

   _____

   f. Physical education _____

   _____

   _____

   g. Art _____

   _____

   _____

   h. Music _____

   _____

   _____

EXERCISE 6.4 (*continued*)

2. In cocurricular programs and activities
    a. Electives _____

    _____

    _____

    b. Clubs _____

    _____

    _____

    c. School functions _____

    _____

    _____

    d. Assemblies _____

    _____

    _____

    e. Intramurals _____

    _____

    _____

    f. Study skills _____

    _____

    _____

3. In exploratories _____

    _____

    _____

4. In homerooms _____

    _____

    _____

5. Explain how multicultural components could be incorporated into the unit. _____

    _____

    _____

6. As individuals and as a group, how productive was this exercise? _____

    _____

    _____

Developing the Learning Activities: The Heart and Spirit of the ITU

Activities that engage students in meaningful learning constitute the heart and spirit of the ITU: the activities that start a unit into motion are called *initiating activities;* those that comprise the heart of the unit are the

---

INTERDISCIPLINARY THEMATIC UNIT SCENARIO

Learning from Dinosaurs

Once a theme is determined, instruction is planned around a sequence of activities that focus on that theme. Common to many elementary school teachers and to some middle school teachers as well is a theme that centers on the topic of dinosaurs. Whatever its selected title might be in a given situation, a thematic unit on dinosaurs can encompass any number of multidisciplinary activities related to the topic. For example,

- *History.* Students develop a graphic time line showing the long period of time that dinosaurs were dominant on this earth; they visit a museum that features dinosaur exhibits.
- *Mathematics.* Students categorize the types of dinosaurs and create graphs illustrating the variety and proportional sizes of dinosaurs.
- *Reading, writing, and art.* Students create and write illustrated stories about a favorite dinosaur.
- *Science.* Students speculate on both why the dinosaurs were so successful and on the events that led to their rather quick disappearance.

In her self-contained second-grade classroom, Kristie Darras (Elk Grove, CA) guided her students in a thematic unit on dinosaurs. Learning activities integrated science and math, drawing and crafts, music and reading, and publishing original books to support the study. Connecting reading to music, the students listened to a song about each dinosaur being studied. Students read sentence strips with the words of the song. They added sound effects, sang the song several times, and added a rhythmic beat with their fingers and hands. Additionally, students prepared their own dinosaur-shape books, wrote original pages, and created illustrations. To survey favorite dinosaurs, graphing was introduced. The students built their own graph in the classroom by drawing a favorite dinosaur and contributing it to a large graph. Students used individual copies of the graph to record what was added to the large graph and marked Xs with their pencils in the appropriate places. When the class graph was finished, the students read it and talked about the information they had gathered, guided by the teacher.

The culminating event took place at the school's spring Open House. Each student's assignment for Open House was to bring an adult and to explain to that person what he or she had been learning at school. Confidently, the students told their visitors about dinosaurs and proudly displayed their dinosaur books, dinosaur mobiles, dinosaur body shapes made from felt, and dinosaur clay models.

---

ongoing developmental activities; and those that bring the unit to a natural close are *culminating activities.* Although nearly limitless, the list in Figure 6.2 gives you an idea of the many options from which you can choose activities for any of these three categories, some of which, of course, may overlap in some regard or another and some of which might naturally fit one category better than another.

THE COMMON THREAD
Central to the selection and development of learning activities for interdisciplinary thematic instruction is a common thread of four tightly interwoven components: (1) the instruction is centered around a big and meaningful idea (theme) rather than on factitious subject areas, (2) the students and the teacher share in the decision making and responsibility for learning, (3) the learning activities are selected so all students are actively engaged in their learning—that is, they are physically active (hands-on learning) and mentally active (minds-on learning)—and (4) there is steady reflection on and frequent sharing of what is being done and what is being learned.

INITIATING ACTIVITIES
An ITU can be initiated in a limitless variety of ways. You must decide which ways are appropriate for your educational goals and objectives and intended time duration and for your own unique group of students, considering their interests, abilities, and skills. You might start with a current event, a community problem, an artifact, a book, or something interesting found on the Internet. Consider some of these approaches to initiating a unit (Note: the ones in bold type are used to initiate the studies in the examples found in this resource guide.)

display	**learning center**	inquiry
current event	painting	role play
problem focus	questions	social actions
replica	people or places in the community	**outdoor adventure**

You can introduce the unit with a focus on some problem or current event, such as with a video showing a prom night automobile accident (see the Indian Trail Junior High School example in Chapter 8).

You can use outdoor adventures to stimulate interest in a particular unit.[3] Possibilities include

---

[3]See, for example, C. E. Knapp, *Just Beyond the Classroom: Community Adventures for Interdisciplinary Learning* (Charleston, WV: ED388485, ERIC Clearinghouse on Rural Education and Small Schools, 1996).

Fast-food fact finding

Local pollution problems
Nature in the city
Reading the cemetery
   "story"

People, places, and things
   at the shopping center
One city block
Starting a homestead
Urban predator-prey
   relationships

ONGOING DEVELOPMENTAL ACTIVITIES

Once the ITU has been initiated, students become occupied with a variety of ongoing activities such as those listed in Figure 6.2. In working with students in selecting and planning the ongoing learning activities, you will want to keep in mind the concept represented by the Learning Experiences Ladder (Figure 6.7) and the predetermined goals and target objectives (Chapter 5).

Now do Exercises 6.5, 6.6, and 6.7.

EXERCISE 6.5 INITIATING AN ITU WITH A QUESTION MAP

INSTRUCTIONS: The purpose of this exercise is to work with a partner or partners to write questions related to a possible theme for an ITU.

First select a topic that you know is typically taught at a grade level and in a subject area of interest to you and your partners.

Grade level: _____

With your partners taking the role of students, have your partners participate in a discussion about "what we want to know" about the topic. Write their questions on a question map on the writing board. Show the partners how you can group their related questions (main questions and subquestions) together. Ask them to think of headings for the different categories of related questions. Use the following format for recording the input:

1. Topic:

2. Main question:

3. Related subquestions:

   a.

   b.

   c.

Copy the question map from the board to this page so you can use it as a reference.

EXERCISE 6.6 CONNECTING QUESTIONS AND ACTIVITIES FOR AN ITU

INSTRUCTIONS: The purpose of this exercise is to work to connect the questions related to your theme and to ongoing learning activities in specific detail. Learning activities should be planned around some central questions (and subquestions) about the theme. The investigative activities that are needed to inquire about the questions can provide various opportunities for you to respond to the learning styles and needs of your students.

   With your partners, return to the "what we want to know" question map you completed in Exercise 6.5. Use the information to design some learning activities for the unit.

LIST OF LEARNING ACTIVITIES RELATED TO THE QUESTIONS AND SUBQUESTIONS:

1.

2.

3.

4.

5.

6.

EXERCISE 6.7 PUTTING OBJECTIVES, RESOURCES, AND LEARNING ACTIVITIES TOGETHER FOR A TEACHING PLAN

INSTRUCTIONS: The purpose of this exercise is to write a specific teaching plan for a minimum of one day that incorporates what you have done so far: preparing goals, writing objectives, selecting resources, and selecting and planning learning activities. You may want to reference the learning activities to state frameworks, district documents, and local school curriculum. Ask a peer to read and react to your teaching plan. Does your plan convey what you intended to say? What new questions came to mind as you wrote the plan and as it was reviewed by others?

TEACHING PLAN

Interdisciplinary unit theme:

Main focus question:

Related subquestions:

OBJECTIVES

(What will the students learn?)

(What thinking skills, such as observing, communicating, comparing, categorizing, inferring, and applying, will the students develop?)

(What attitudes will be fostered?)

RESOURCES

(Media, display visuals, artifacts, computer, and software)

EXERCISE 6.7 (*continued*)

SPECIFICS OF LEARNING ACTIVITIES

PREASSESSMENT OF STUDENT LEARNING

(How you will determine what students know or think they know about the subject at the start of the unit?)

[Example 1: think-pair-share, where the topic/question is written on the board and students are asked in pairs to think about the topic, discuss it between themselves, and then the pairs share with the whole class what they know or think they already know about it while the teacher writes the major thoughts on the board, perhaps in the form of a concept web.]

[Example 2: using the KWL reading comprehension strategy, with the teacher directing the discussion, three columns are formed on the board or overhead projector. The left-hand column contains what students already KNOW or think they know about the topic; the middle column contains a list of what the students WANT to learn about the topic; the right-hand column is left blank and filled in at the end or during the study with what is and has been LEARNED about the topic.]

EXERCISE 6.7 (*continued*)

FORMATIVE ASSESSMENT

(Techniques used to assess student learning in progress to assure they are on the right track)

Check __ discipline areas drawn upon   Brief description of how

_____ 1. Sciences

_____ 2. Social sciences/history

_____ 3. Mathematics

_____ 4. Reading and language

_____ 5. Poetry and prose

_____ 6. Music and dance

_____ 7. Painting and sculpture

_____ 8. Health and physical education

_____ Other:

FEEDBACK:

_____ 1. What was the reaction of your peer to your teaching plan?

_____ 2. In your opinion, does your plan effectively convey what you originally envisioned?

_____ 3. Does it need more detail or revision?

_____ 4. Do your selected learning activities appropriately address the varied learning styles of your students?

_____ 5. What new questions came to mind as you wrote the plan and as it was reviewed?

CULMINATING ACTIVITY

An ITU is brought to close with a culminating activity. Such an activity often includes an exhibition or sharing of the product of the students' study. You could accept the students' suggestions for a culminating activity if it engages them in summarizing what they have learned with others. A culminating activity that brings closure to a unit can give the students an opportunity for synthesis (by assembling, constructing, creating, inventing, producing, or incorporating something) and even an opportunity to present that synthesis to an audience, such as by establishing an Internet web site or sharing their product on an existing school web site.

With a culminating activity, you can provide opportunity for the students to move from recording information to reporting on their learning. For example, one activity might be for students to take field trips to study something related to the theme and then synthesize their learning after the trip in a way that culminates the study. On field trips, students should be given notepads similar to the ones reporters use and be asked to take notes and make sketches of what they learn. They can discuss what questions they have on the ride to the site. They can discuss what they liked and did not like on the ride back to school. After the trip, each student can choose something he or she saw and then build it to scale, so the students can have a scale model of something they saw on the trip that caught their interest. Teacher and students might devote one full afternoon, or more, to working with rulers, yardsticks, cardboard, clay, and other materials. The students could then invite other classes in to examine the scale models and listen to student reports about why an object caught their interest. Students might also present an art show of drawings about the unit's theme, with a narration that informs others about their study. You might also schedule a culminating activity that asks students to report on individual projects, the aspect each student formerly reserved for individual study.

Examples of actual culminating activities and products of an ITU are endless. As one example, at North Middle School (O'Fallon, MO), an interdisciplinary thematic unit of study about immigrants titled "All Americans" involved four interdisciplinary core teachers. The immigrant experience came alive for students as they assumed an identity and received an official document containing visas for the unit. During the unit students went through processing and naturalization as "immigrants," encountering some of the problems and prejudices faced daily by many immigrants. In the culminating activity for the unit, the "immigrants" became naturalized citizens by completing a required assignment, including a group presentation, a spreadsheet and graph, a fairy tale, and a natural resources map.

From their thematic unit of study about ghost towns, students at a school in Kent, WA, developed an interest in the nearby town of Franklin, located on state park land. As a result of their interdisciplinary study that involved mapping, digging, interviewing former residents, and creating oral histories, the town of Franklin was placed on the National Register of Historic Places.

Culminating activities are opportunities for students to demonstrate and share their learning and creativity proudly in different and individual ways. Now gain further insight about bringing an ITU to closure by doing Exercise 6.8.

Culminating activities are opportunities for students to exhibit, demonstrate, and share their learning and creativity proudly in different and individual ways.

EXERCISE 6.8 PLANNING CULMINATING ACTIVITIES

INSTRUCTIONS: The purpose of this exercise is to plan a closure for the unit (even though you realize that inquiry can be lifelong and has no official closure). In this exercise, you must determine what will affect the length of your unit: the interest of your students in the topic, resources available or unavailable, school holidays, the academic calendar for your school year, and any competing events, such as picture day, assemblies, athletic events, and field trips.

1. What activity/activities could you plan that would permit your students to synthesize what they have learned in the unit and then report the synthesis to a selected audience?

2. Although final decisions about culminating activities are best when made collaboratively with the students, initial thoughts by the teacher are important to be able to offer suggestions. Which of the following might you incorporate into the culmination of a unit? Explain why.

Creating new problems related to the topic and demonstrating a way to resolve them

Designing a chart, map, time line, classroom museum of exhibits, interdisciplinary thematic fair, or classroom "main street" with booths (learning centers); reporting on the data the design represents

An oral and written presentation on an aspect of the topic; using such creative ways to present data as sketches, sculpture works, cartoons, popular songs, a comic strip format, costume props, a story board, puppets, flannel board figures, rhymes, limericks, and other forms of poetry

Creating and producing a drama

☞

EXERCISE 6.8 (*continued*)

Writing and publishing a newsletter or brochure on the topic

Writing and publishing a book

Creating a class or student cohort web page regarding the unit

Other

PREPARING LESSON PLANS: RATIONALE AND ASSUMPTIONS

As described at the beginning of this chapter, step 5 of the seven steps of instructional planning is the preparation for class meetings. The process of designing a lesson is important in learning to provide the most efficient use of valuable and limited instructional time and the most effective learning for the students to meet the unit goals.

Notice the title of this section does not refer to the "*daily* lesson plan," but rather, "the lesson plan." The focus is on how to prepare a lesson plan, which may or may not be a daily plan. In some instances, a lesson plan may extend for more than one class period or days, perhaps two or three. In other instances, the lesson plan is in fact a daily plan and may run for an entire class period. In block scheduling, one lesson plan may run for part of or for an entire two-hour block of time. See "The Problem of Time" later in this chapter.

Effective teachers are always planning for their classes. For the long range, they plan the scope and sequence and develop content. Within this long-range planning, they develop units, and within units they design the activities to be used and the assessments of learning to be done. They familiarize themselves with books, materials, media, and innovations in their fields of interest. Yet, despite all this planning activity, the lesson plan remains pivotal to the planning process.

Consider now the rationale, description, and guidelines for writing detailed lesson plans.

Rationale for Preparing Written Lesson Plans

First, *carefully prepared and written lesson plans show everyone—first and foremost your students, then your colleagues, your administrator, and, if you are a student teacher, your college or university supervisor—that you are a committed professional.* Sometimes, beginning teachers are concerned with being seen by their students using a written plan in class, thinking it may suggest that the teacher has not mastered the material. On the contrary, a lesson plan is tangible evidence that you are working at your job and demonstrates respect for the students, yourself, and the profession. A written lesson plan shows that preactive thinking and planning have taken place. There is absolutely no excuse for appearing before a class without evidence of being prepared.

Written and detailed lesson plans provide an important sense of security, which is especially useful to a beginning teacher. Like a rudder of a ship, it helps keep you on course. Without it, you are likely to drift aimlessly. Sometimes a disturbance in the classroom can distract from the lesson, causing the teacher to get off track or forget an important part of the lesson. A written and detailed lesson plan provides a road map to guide you and help keep you on track.

Written lesson plans help you to be or become a reflective decision maker. Without a written plan, it is difficult or impossible to analyze how something might have been planned or implemented differently after the lesson has been taught. Written lesson plans serve as resources for the next time you teach the same or a similar lesson and are useful for teacher self-evaluation and for the evaluation of student learning and of the curriculum.

Written lesson plans help you organize material and search for "loopholes," "loose ends," or incomplete content. Careful and thorough planning during the preactive phase of instruction includes anticipation of how the lesson activities will develop as the lesson is being taught. During this anticipation you will visualize yourself in the classroom teaching your students, using that visualization to anticipate possible problems.

Written plans help other members of the teaching team understand what you are doing and how you are doing it. This is especially important when implementing an interdisciplinary thematic unit. *Written lesson plans also provide substitute teachers with a guide to follow if you are absent.*

Those reasons clearly express the need to write detailed lesson plans. The list is not exhaustive, however, and you may discover additional reasons why written lesson plans are crucial to effective teaching. In summary, two points must be made: (1) lesson planning is an important and ongoing process, and (2) teachers must take time to plan, reflect, write, test, evaluate, and rewrite their plans to reach optimal performance. In short, preparing written lesson plans is important professional work.

Assumptions about Lesson Planning

Not all teachers need elaborate written plans for every lesson. Sometimes effective and skilled veteran teachers need only a sketchy outline. Sometimes they may not need written plans at all. Veteran teachers who have taught the topic many times in the past may need only the presence of a class of students to stimulate a pattern of presentation that has often been successful (though frequent use of old patterns may lead one into the rut of unimaginative and uninspiring teaching). You probably do not need to be reminded that the obsolescence of many past classroom practices has been substantiated repeatedly by those researchers who have made serious and recent studies of exemplary educational practices.

Considering the diversity among teachers, their instructional styles, and their students and what research has shown, certain assumptions can be made about lesson planning.

1. Although not all teachers need elaborate written plans for all lessons, all effective teachers do have clearly defined goals and objectives in mind and a planned pattern of instruction for every lesson, whether that plan is written out or not.
2. Beginning teachers need to prepare detailed written lesson plans. Failing to prepare is preparing to fail.
3. Some subject-matter fields, topics, or learning activities require more detailed planning than others do.
4. The depth of knowledge a teacher has about a subject or topic influences the amount of planning necessary for the lessons.
5. The skill a teacher has in remaining calm and in following a trend of thought in the presence of distraction will influence the amount of detail necessary when planning activities and writing the lesson plan.
6. A plan is more likely to be carefully and thoughtfully plotted when it is written out.
7. The diversity of students within today's public school classroom necessitates careful and thoughtful consideration about individualizing the instruction; these considerations are best implemented when they have been thoughtfully written into lesson plans.
8. There is no particular pattern or format that all teachers need to follow when writing out plans. Some teacher-preparation programs have agreed on certain lesson-plan formats for their teacher candidates; you need to know if this is the case for your program.

In summary, well-written lesson plans provide many advantages: they give a teacher an agenda or outline to follow in teaching a lesson; they give a substitute teacher a basis for presenting appropriate lessons to a class, thereby retaining lesson continuity in the regular teacher's absence; they are certainly very useful when a teacher is planning to use the same lesson again in the future; they provide the teacher with something to fall back on in case of a memory lapse, an interruption, or some distraction such as a call from the office or a fire drill; using a written plan demonstrates to students that you care and are working for them; and, above all, they provide beginners security because, with a carefully prepared plan, a beginning teacher can walk into a classroom with confidence and professional pride gained from having developed a sensible framework for that day's instruction.

Thus, as a beginning teacher, you should make considerably detailed lesson plans. Naturally, this will require a great deal of work for at least the first year or two, but the reward of knowing that you have prepared and presented effective lessons will compensate for that effort. You can expect a busy first year of teaching.

A Continual Process

Lesson planning is a continual process even for experienced teachers, for there is always a need to keep materials and plans current and relevant. Because no two classes of students are ever identical, today's lesson plan will need to be tailored to the peculiar needs of each classroom of students. Moreover, the content of instruction and learning will change as each group of students with distinct needs and interests give input, as new thematic units are developed, as new developments occur, and as new theories are introduced. Thus, your objectives and the objectives of the students, school, and teaching faculty will change.

For these reasons, lesson plans should be in a constant state of revision. Once the basic framework is developed, however, the task of updating and modifying becomes minimal. If your plans are maintained on a computer, making changes from time to time is even easier.

Well Planned but Open to Last-Minute Change

The lesson plan should provide a tentative outline of the time period given for the lesson but should always remain flexible. A carefully-worked-out plan may have to be set aside because of the unpredictable, serendipitous effect of a "teachable moment" (see the accompanying vignette) or because of unforeseen circumstances, such as a delayed school bus, an impromptu school assembly program, an emergency drill, or the cancellation of school due to inclement weather conditions. Student teachers often are appalled at the frequency of interruptions during a school day and of disruptions to their lesson planning. A daily lesson planned to cover six aspects of a given topic may end with only three of the points having been considered. Although far more frequent than necessary in too many schools, these occurrences are natural in a school setting, and the teacher and the plans must be flexible enough to accommodate this reality.

CLASSROOM VIGNETTE

A Teachable Moment

At Eddy Middle School (Elk Grove, CA) Casey was teaching an eighth grade humanities block, a two-hour block course that integrates student learning in social studies, reading, and language arts. On this particular day while Casey and her students were discussing the topic of manifest destiny, one of the students raised his hand and when acknowledged by Casey, asked, "Why aren't we [referring to the United States] still adding states? [that is, taking more territory into the United States]." Casey immediately replied with "There aren't any more states to add." By responding too quickly, Casey missed one of those "teachable moments," moments when the teacher has the students right where she wants them—thinking and asking questions. What could Casey have done? When was Hawaii added as a state? Why hasn't Puerto Rico become a state? What about Guam? Aren't those possibilities? Why *aren't* more states or territories being added? What are the political and social ramifications today and how do they differ from those of the 1800s?

IMPLEMENTATION OF TODAY'S LESSON MAY NECESSITATE CHANGES IN TOMORROW'S PLAN Although you may have your lesson plans completed for several consecutive lessons, as can be inferred by the vignette involving Casey and her students, what actually transpires during the implementation of today's lesson may necessitate last-minute adjustments to the lesson you had planned for tomorrow. Consequently, during student teaching in particular, it is not uncommon nor unwanted to have last-minute changes penciled in your lesson plan. If, however, penciled-in modifications are substantial and might be confusing to you during implementation of the lesson, then you should rewrite the lesson plan.

The Problem of Time

A lesson plan should provide enough materials and activities to consume the entire class period or time allotted. As mentioned earlier, it should be well understood that in your planning for teaching you need to plan for every minute of every class period. The lesson plan, then, is more than a plan for a lesson to be taught; it is a plan that accounts for the entire class period or time that you and your students are together in the classroom. Since planning is a skill that takes years of experience to master, especially when teaching a block of time that may extend for 90 or more minutes and that involves more than one discipline and perhaps more than one teacher, as a beginning teacher you should overplan rather than run the risk of having too few activities to occupy the time students are in your classroom. One way of assuring that you overplan is to include "if time remains" or alternate activities in your lesson plan (see example in Figure 6.8).

When a lesson plan does not provide sufficient activity to occupy the entire class period or time that the students are available for the lesson, a beginning teacher often loses control of the class as behavior problems mount. Thus, it is best to prepare more than you likely can accomplish in a given period of time. This is not to imply that you should involve the students in meaningless busy work. Students can be very perceptive when it comes to a teacher who has finished the plan and is attempting to bluff through the minutes that remain before dismissal. They are not usually favorably responsive to meaningless busywork.

If you ever do get caught short—as most teachers do at one time or another—one way to avoid embarrassment is to have students work on what is known as an *anchor assignment,* or transitional activity. This is an ongoing assignment, and it is understood by students that whenever they have spare time in class they should be working on it. Example anchor activities include a review of material that has been covered that day or in the past several days, allowing students to work on homework, journal writing, portfolio organization, and long-term project work. Regardless of how you handle time remaining, it works best when you plan for it and write that aspect into your lesson plan. Make sure students understand the purpose and procedures for these anchor assignments.

A Caution about "The Daily Planning Book"

A distinction needs to be made between actual lesson plans and the book for daily planning that many schools require teachers to maintain and even submit to their supervisors a week in advance. Items that a teacher writes into the boxes in a daily planning book (see Figure 6.9) most assuredly are not lesson plans; rather, the pages are a layout by which the teacher writes into the boxes to show what lessons will be taught during the day, week, month, or term. Usually the book provides only a small lined box for time periods for each day of the week. These books are useful for outlining the topics, activities, and assignments projected for the week or term, and supervisors sometimes use them to check the adequacy of teachers' course plans. But they are not lesson plans. Teachers and their supervisors who believe that the notations in the daily planning book are actual lesson plans are fooling themselves. Student teachers should not use these in place of authentic lesson plans.

Figure 6.8 Lesson plan sample with alternative activities.

LESSON PLAN

Descriptive Course Data

Instructor: Michelle Yendrey   *Course:* Western Civilizations   *Period:* 1
Grade level: 9   *Unit:* History of Religion   *Topic:* Persecution of Christians

Objectives

Upon completion of this lesson students will be able to
1. Make connections between persecutions today and persecutions that occurred approximately 2000 years ago.
2. Describe the main teachings of Christianity and how the position of Christianity with the Roman Empire changed over time.
3. Share ideas in a positive and productive manner.

Instructional Components

Activity 1 (Anticipatory Set: 10 minutes) Write on overhead: You have until 8:40 (5 minutes) to write a defense to one of the following statements. (Remember, there are no right or wrong answers. Support your position to the best of your ability.)

• The recent hate crimes in our city can be related to our current unit on the history of religion.
• The recent hate crimes in our city cannot be related to our current unit on the history of religion.

Activity 2 (3–5 minutes) Students will be asked, by a show of hands, how many chose statement A and how many chose statement B. Some reasons for each will be shared orally and then all papers collected.

Activity 3 (3–5 minutes) Return papers of previous assignment. Give students new seat assignments for the activity that follows, and have them assume their new seats.

Activity 4 (15 minutes) The students are now arranged into seven groups. Each group will write a paragraph using the concepts from certain assigned words (for their definition sheets of Section 3 of Chapter 7, "Christianity spread through the empire") to answer the essay question(s) at the end of the definition sheet.

    Each group will select a

Task master to keep members of the group on task.
Recorder to write things down.
Spokesperson to present the results.
Timekeeper to keep group alert so the task is completed on time.

In addition, some groups will have a

Source master to look up or ask about any questions that arise.

Activity 5 (15–20 minutes) Each group's spokesperson will come to the front of the classroom and present the group's result for activity 4.

Alternate Activity (Plan B: 5–10 minutes) Should the activities run more quickly than anticipated, the students will take out their "Religion Comparison Sheets." Using Chapter 2, Section 2, "Jews worshipped a single God," and Chapter 7, Section 3 definition sheets, with the teacher's direction, the students will fill in the boxes for "similar" and "different" with regard to Christianity and Judaism.

Second Alternate Activity (Plan C: 25–30 minutes) In the unlikely event that timing is really off, each student will be given a blank grid and assigned ten vocabulary words from the definition sheets. Students will be directed to create a crossword puzzle using the definitions as clues and the words as answers. After 15–20 minutes, the crosswords will be collected and distributed to different students to solve. If not completed in class, students will finish and hand them in later, along with their essays, for a few points of extra credit. Students will be required to write their names in the appropriate spaces marked "Created By" and "Solved By."

Activity 6 (7–10 minutes) Collect the overhead sheets and pens. Hand out the take-home essay test. Explain and take questions about exactly what is expected from the essay. (This is their first take-home test.)

Materials and Equipment Needed

Overhead projector and transparency sheets (7) and transparency markers (7); 36 copies of the essay question plus directions; 36 copies of the blank grid sheets

Assessment, Reflection, and Plans for Revision

Source: Courtesy of Michelle Yendrey.

CONSTRUCTING A LESSON PLAN: FORMAT, COMPONENTS, AND SAMPLES

Although it is true that each teacher develops a personal system of lesson planning—the system that works best for that teacher in each unique situation—a beginning teacher needs a more substantial framework from which to work. For that, this section provides a "preferred" lesson plan format (Figure 6.10). Nothing is hallowed about this format, however. Review the preferred format and samples and, unless your program of teacher preparation insists otherwise, use it with your own modifications until you find or develop a better model. All else being equal, you are encouraged to begin your teaching following as closely as possible this "preferred" format.

Figure 6.9   Daily planning book.

		DAILY PLANNING BOOK		
Grade _____ Lesson _____ Teacher _____				
Date	*Content*	*Materials*	*Procedure*	*Evaluation*
Monday				
Tuesday				
Wednesday				
Thursday				
Friday				

Figure 6.10 Preferred lesson plan format with seven components*.

---

1. Descriptive Data

Teacher _____ Class _____ Date _____ Grade level _____

Room number _____ Period _____ Unit _____ Lesson Number _____ Topic _____

Anticipated noise level (high, moderate, low)

2. Goals and Objectives
Instructional Goals:

Specific objectives:

[Note: all three domains not always present in every lesson]
Cognitive:

Affective:

Psychomotor:

3. Rationale [Note: rationale not always present in every lesson]

4. Procedure [Procedure with modeling examples, planned transitions, etc.; should usually take up most of the space of lesson plan, often a full page]
Content:
_____ minutes. Activity 1: Set (introduction)

_____ minutes. Activity 2:

_____ minutes. Activity 3: (the exact number of activities in the procedures will vary)

_____ minutes. Final Activity (Lesson Conclusion or Closure):

If time remains:

5. Assignments and Reminders of Assignments
    Special notes and reminders to myself:

---

6. Materials and Equipment Needed
   Audiovisual:

   Other:

7. Assessment, Reflection, and Revision
   Assessment of student learning, how it will be done:

   Reflective thoughts about lesson after taught:

   Suggestions for revision if used again:

   _____

   This blank lesson plan format is placed alone so, if you choose, you may remove it from the book and make copies for use in your teaching.

Figure 6.10 *continued*

The teacher must assure that proper resources and materials are available for the lessons. That takes planning. Students can't use what they don't have.

For Guidance, Reflection, and Reference

While student teaching and during your first few years as a beginning teacher, your lesson plans should be printed from a computer or typewritten or, if that isn't possible, written out in an intelligible style. If you have a spelling problem, I suggest you use a spell check and print your plans from the computer. There is good reason to question teachers who say they have no need for a written plan because they have their lessons planned "in their heads." The hours and periods in a school day range from several to many, as do the numbers of students in each class. When multiplied by the number of school days in a week, a semester, or a year, the task of keeping so many things in one's head becomes mind-boggling. Few persons could effectively do that. Until you have considerable teaching experience, you will need to prepare and maintain detailed lesson plans for guidance, reflection, and reference.

Basic Elements of a Lesson Plan

A written lesson plan should contain the following basic elements: (1) descriptive course data, (2) goals and objectives, (3) rationale, (4) procedure, (5) assignments and assignment reminders, (6) materials and equipment, and (7) a section for assessment of student learning, reflection on the lesson, and ideas for lesson revision.

Those seven components need not be present in every written lesson plan, nor must they be presented in any particular order. Nor are they inclusive or exclusive. You might choose to include additional components or subsections. Figure 6.10 illustrates a format that includes the seven components and sample subsections of those components. Additionally, Figure 6.11 displays a completed multiple-day lesson that incorporates many of the developmentally appropriate learning activities discussed in this resource guide. Following are descriptions of the seven major components of the preferred format, with examples and explanations of why each is important.

Descriptive Data

A lesson plan's descriptive data is demographic and logistical information that identifies details about the class. Anyone reading this information should be able to identify when and where the class meets, who is teaching it, and what is being taught. Although as the teacher you know this information, someone else may not. Members of the teaching team, administrators, and substitute teachers (and, if you are the student teacher, your university supervisor and cooperating teacher) appreciate this information, especially when asked to fill in for you, even if only for a few minutes during a class session. Most teachers find out which items of descriptive data are most beneficial in their situation and then develop their own identifiers. Remember this: The mark of a well-prepared, clearly written lesson plan is the ease with which someone else (such as another member of your teaching team or a substitute teacher) could implement it.

Figure 6.11 Lesson plan sample: multiple-day, project-centered, interdisciplinary, and transcultural lesson using worldwide communication via the Internet.

---

1. Descriptive Data

Teacher _____ Class <u>English/Science</u> Date _____ Grade level <u>6–12</u>

Unit <u>Investigative Research & Generative Writing</u>

Lesson Topic <u>Writing Response and Peer Assessment via Internet</u>

Time duration: <u>several days</u>

2. Goals and Objectives of Unit

Instructional Goals:

2.1. One goal for this lesson is for students to collaborate and prepare response papers to peers from around the world who have shared the results of their own experimental research findings and research paper about ozone concentrations in the atmosphere.

2.2. The ultimate goal of this unit is for students around the world to prepare and publish for worldwide dissemination a final paper about global ozone levels in the atmosphere.

Objectives:

Cognitive:

a. Through cooperative group action, students will conduct experimental research to collect data about the ozone level of air in their environment. (application)
b. In cooperative groups, students will analyze the results of their experiments. (analyze)
c. Students will compile data and infer from their experimental data. (synthesis and evaluation)
d. Through collaborative writing groups, the students will prepare a final paper that summarizes their research study of local atmospheric ozone levels. (evaluation)
e. Through sharing via Internet, students will write response papers to their peers from other locations in the world. (evaluation)
f. From their own collaborative research and worldwide communications with their peers, the students will draw conclusions about global atmospheric ozone levels. (evaluation)

Affective:

a. Students will respond attentively to the response papers of their peers. (attending)
b. Students will willingly cooperate with others during the group activities. (responding)
c. The students will offer opinions about the atmospheric level of ozone. (valuing)
d. The students will form judgments about local, regional, and worldwide ozone levels. (organizing)
e. The students will communicate accurately their findings and attend diligently to the work of their worldwide peers. (internalizing)

Psychomotor:

a. The students will manipulate the computer so that their e-mail communications are transmitted accurately. (manipulating)
b. In a summary to the study students will describe their feelings about atmospheric ozone concentrations. (communicating)
c. The students will ultimately create a proposal for worldwide dissemination. (creating)

3. Rationale

3.1. Important to improvement in one's writing and communication skills are the processes of selecting a topic, decision making, arranging, drafting, proofing, peer review, commenting, revising, editing, rewriting, and publishing the results—processes that are focused on in the writing aspect of this unit.

3.2. Student writers need many readers to respond to their work. Through worldwide communication with peers and dissemination of their final product, this need can be satisfied.

3.3. Students learn best when they are actively pursuing a topic of interest and meaning to them. Resulting from brainstorming potential problems and arriving at their own topic, this unit provides that.

3.4. Real-world problems are interdisciplinary and transcultural; involving writing (English), science, mathematics (data collecting, graphing, etc.), and intercultural communication, this unit is an interdisciplinary transcultural unit.

continued

4. Procedure

Content:

At the start of this unit, collaborative groups were established via Intercultural E-mail Classroom Connections (IECC) (http://www.stolaf.edu/network/iecc) with other classes from schools around the world. These groups of students conducted several scientific research experiments on the ozone level of their local atmospheric air. To obtain relative measurements of ozone concentrations in the air, students set up experiments that involved stretching rubber bands on a board, then observing the number of days until the bands broke. Students maintained daily journal logs of the temperature, barometric pressure, and wind speed/direction, and of the number of days that it took for bands to break.[4] After compiling their data and preparing single-page summaries of their results, via the Internet students exchanged data with other groups. From data collected worldwide students wrote a one-page summary as to what conditions may account for the difference in levels of ozone. Following the exchange of students' written responses and their subsequent revisions based on feedback from the worldwide peers, students are now preparing a final summary report about the world's atmospheric ozone level. The intention is to disseminate worldwide (to newspapers and via the Internet) this final report.

Activity 1: Introduction (____10____ minutes)
Today, in think-share-pairs, you will prepare initial responses to the e-mail responses we have received from other groups from around the world. (Teacher shares the list of places from which e-mail has been received.) Any questions before we get started?

As we discussed earlier, here are the instructions: in your think-share-pairs (each pair is given one response received via e-mail), prepare written responses according to the following outline: (a) note points or information you would like to incorporate in the final paper to be forwarded via Internet; (b) comment on one aspect of the written response you like best; (c) provide questions to the sender to seek clarification or elaboration. I think you should be able to finish this in about 30 minutes, so let's try for that.

Activity 2: (____30____ minutes, if needed)
Preparation of dyad responses

Activity 3: (open)
Let's now hear from each response pair.
Dyad responses are shared with whole class for discussion of inclusion in response paper to be sent via Internet.

Activity 4: (open)
Discussion, conclusion, and preparation of final drafts to be sent to each e-mail corresponder to be done by cooperative groups (the number of groups needed to be decided by the number of e-mail corresponders at this time).

Activity 5: (open)
Later, as students receive e-mail responses from other groups the responses will be printed and reviewed. The class then responds to each using the same criteria as before and returns this response to the e-mail sender.

Closure:

The process continues until all groups (from around the world) have agreed upon and prepared the final report for dissemination.

5. Assignments and Reminders

Remind students of important dates and decisions to be made

6. Materials and Equipment Needed

School computers with Internet access; printers; copies of e-mail responses

7. Assessment, Reflection, and Revision

Assessment of student learning for this lesson is formative: journals, daily checklist of student participation in groups, writing drafts

Reflective thoughts about lesson and suggestions for revision:

---

[4] The source of information about the science experiment is R. J. Ryder and T. Hughes, *Internet for Educators* (Upper Saddle River, NJ: Prentice Hall, 1997), p. 98.

Figure 6.11 *continued*

As shown in the sample plans of Figures 6.8 (social studies), 6.11 (language arts/science), and 6.14 (physical science), the descriptive data include:

1. *Name of course or class.* This heads the plan and facilitates orderly filing of plans.

   Social Studies
   Physical Science
   Language Arts/Science (integrated block course)

2. *Name of the unit.* This facilitates the orderly control of the hundreds of lesson plans a teacher constructs. For example:

Social Studies	Unit: *History of Religion*
Physical Science	Unit: *What's the Matter*
Language Arts/Science	Unit: *Investigative Research and Generative Writing*

3. *Topic to be considered within the unit.* This is also useful for control and identification. For example:

Social Studies	Unit: History of Religion	Topic: *Persecution of Christians*
Physical Science	Unit: What's the Matter	Topic: *Density of Solids*
Language Arts/Science	Unit: Investigative Research and Generative Writing	Topic: *Writing Response and Peer Assessment via the Internet*

ANTICIPATED NOISE LEVEL

Although not included in the sample lesson plans in this resource guide, the teacher might include in the descriptive data the category of "anticipated classroom noise level," such as "high," "moderate," "low." Its inclusion, or at least considering the idea, is useful during the planning phase of instruction in thinking about how active and noisy the students might become during the lesson, how you might prepare for that, and whether you should warn an administrator and teachers of neighboring classrooms.

Goals and Objectives

The instructional goals are general statements of intended accomplishments from that lesson. Teachers and students need to know what the lesson is designed to accomplish. In clear, understandable language, the general goal statement provides that information. From the sample of Figure 6.11, the goals are:

- To collaborate and prepare response papers to peers from around the world who have shared the results of their own experimental research findings and research paper about ozone concentrations in the atmosphere.

- For students worldwide to prepare and publish for worldwide dissemination a final paper about worldwide ozone levels in the atmosphere.

And, from the sample unit of Figure 6.14, goals are:

- Understand that all matter is made of atoms.
- Develop a positive attitude about physical science.

Because the goals are also included in the unit plan, sometimes a teacher may include only the objectives in the daily lesson plan (as done in the lesson plans shown in Figures 6.8 and 6.11), but not the goals. As a beginning teacher, it usually is a good idea to include both.

SETTING THE LEARNING OBJECTIVES

A crucial step in the development of any lesson plan is that of setting the objectives. It is at this point that many lessons go wrong and where many beginning teachers have problems.

A Common Error and How to Avoid It

As we noted in Chapter 5, teachers sometimes confuse "learning activity" (*how* the students will learn it) with the "learning objective" (*what* the student will learn as a result of the learning activity). For example, teachers sometimes mistakenly list what *they* intend to do, such as "lecture on photosynthesis" or "lead a discussion on the causes of the Civil War." They fail to focus on just what the learning objectives in these activities truly are—that is, what the students will be able to do (performance) as a result of the instructional activity. Or, rather than specifying what the student will be able to do as a result of the learning activities, the teacher mistakenly writes what the students will do in class (the learning activity)—such as "in pairs the students will do the 10 problems on page 72"—as if that were the learning objective.

When you approach this step in your lesson planning, to avoid error, ask yourself, "What should students learn from the activities of this lesson?" Your answer to that question is your objective! Objectives of the lesson are included then as specific statements of performance expectations, detailing precisely what students will be able to do as a result of the instructional activities.

No Need to Include All Domains and Hierarchies in Every Lesson

Not all three domains (cognitive, affective, and psychomotor) are necessarily represented in every lesson plan. In fact, any given lesson plan may be directed to only one or two specific objectives. Over the course of a unit of instruction, however, all domains, and most if not all levels within each, should be addressed.

From the lesson shown in Figure 6.11, sample objectives, and the domain and level (in parentheses) within that domain, are:

- Through cooperative group action, students will conduct experimental research to collect data about the ozone level of air in their environment. (cognitive, application)
- Through the Internet students will write and share response papers to their peers from other locations in the world. (cognitive, evaluation)
- Students will form judgments about local, regional, and world ozone levels. (affective, organizing)
- Students will create a proposal for worldwide dissemination. (psychomotor, creating)

From the lesson illustrated in Figure 6.14, sample objectives are:

- Determine the density of a solid cube (cognitive, application)
- Communicate the results of their experiments to others in the class (psychomotor, communicating)

Rationale

The rationale is an explanation of why the lesson is important and why the instructional methods chosen will achieve the objectives. Parents, students, teachers, administrators, and others have the right to know why specific content is being taught and why the methods employed are being used. Prepare yourself well by setting a goal for yourself of always being prepared with intelligent answers to those two questions.

Teachers become reflective decision makers when they challenge themselves to think about *what* (the content) they are teaching, *how* (the learning activities) they are teaching it, and *why* (the rationale) it must be taught. As illustrated in the sample unit of Figure 6.14, sometimes the rationale is included within the unit introduction and goals, but not in every lesson plan of the unit. Some lessons are carryovers or continuations of a lesson; I see no reason to repeat the rationale for a continuing lesson.

Procedure

The procedure consists of the instructional activities for a scheduled period of time. The substance of the lesson—the information to be presented, obtained, and learned—is the *content*. Appropriate information is selected to meet the learning objectives, the level of competence of the students, and the grade level or course requirements. To be sure your lesson actually covers what it should, you should write down exactly what minimum content you intend to cover. This material may be placed in a separate section or combined with the procedure section. The important thing is to be sure your information is written down so you can refer to it quickly and easily when you need to.

If, for instance, you intend to conduct the lesson using discussion, you should write out the key discussion questions. Or, if you are going to introduce new material using a 10-minute lecture, then you need to outline the content of that lecture. The word "outline" is not used casually. You need not have pages of notes to sift through; nor should you ever read declarative statements to your students. You should be familiar enough with the content so that an outline (in as much detail as you believe necessary) will be sufficient to carry on the lesson, as in the following example of a content outline

Causes of Civil War
    A. Primary causes
        1. Economics
        2. Abolitionist pressure
        3. Slavery
        4. etc.
    B. Secondary causes
        1. North-South friction
        2. Southern economic dependence
        3. etc.

The procedure or procedures to be used, sometimes referred to as the *instructional components*, comprise the *procedure* component of the lesson plan. It is the section that outlines what you and your students will do during the lesson. Appropriate instructional activities are chosen to meet the objectives, to match the students' learning styles and special needs, and to assure that all students have an equal opportunity to learn. Ordinarily, you should plan this section of your lesson as an organized entity with a beginning (an introduction or set), a middle, and an end (called the *closure*) to be completed during the lesson. This structure is not always needed, because some lessons are parts of units or long-term plans and merely carry on activities spelled out in those long-term plans. Still, most lessons need to include in the procedure: (1) an *introduction*, the process used to prepare the students mentally for the lesson, sometimes referred to as the set, or initiating activity; (2) *lesson development*, the detailing of *activities* that occur between the beginning and the end of the lesson, including the transitions that connect activities (see discussion regarding transitions in Chapter 4), (3) plans for *practice*, sometimes referred to as the follow-up, ways you intend having students interacting in the classroom, such as individual practice, dyads, or small groups receiving guidance or coaching from each other and from you, (4) the *lesson conclusion* (or closure), the planned process of bringing the lesson to an end, thereby providing students with a sense of completeness and, with effective teaching, accomplishment and comprehension by helping students to synthesize the information learned from the lesson, (5) a *timetable* that serves simply as a planning and implementation guide, (6) a plan for what to do if you finish the lesson and time remains, and (7) *assignments* on what students are instructed to do as follow-up to the lesson, either as homework or as in-class work, providing students an opportunity to practice and enhance what is being learned. Let's now consider some of those elements in detail.

INTRODUCTION TO THE LESSON

Like any good performance, a lesson needs an effective beginning. In many respects the introduction sets the tone for the rest of the lesson by alerting the students that the business of learning is to begin. The introduction should be an attention-getter. If it is exciting, interesting, or innovative, it can create a favorable mood for the lesson. In any case, a thoughtful introduction serves as a solid indicator that you are well prepared. Although it is difficult to develop an exciting introduction to every lesson taught each day, a variety of options is available by which to spice up the launching of a lesson. You might, for instance, begin the lesson by briefly reviewing the previous lesson, thereby helping students connect the learning. Another possibility is to review vocabulary words from previous lessons and to introduce new ones. Still another possibility is to use the key point of the day's lesson as an introduction and then again as the conclusion. Sometimes teachers begin a lesson by demonstrating a discrepant event (i.e., an event that is contrary to what one might expect), sometimes referred to as a "hook." Yet another possibility is to begin the lesson with a writing activity on some controversial aspect of the ensuing lesson. Sample introductions are:

For U.S. history, study of westward expansion:

The teacher asks "Who has lived somewhere else other than *(name of your state)*?" After students show hands and answer, the teacher asks individuals why they moved to *(name of your state)*. The teacher then asks students to recall why the first European settlers came to the United States, then moves into the next activity.

For science, study of the science process skill of predicting:

The teacher takes a glass filled to the brim with colored water (colored so it is more visible) and asks students to discuss and predict (in dyads) how many pennies can be added to the glass before any water spills over the rim of the glass.

In short, you can use the introduction of the lesson to review past learning, tie the new lesson to the previous lesson, introduce new material, point out the objectives of the new lesson, help students connect their learning with other disciplines or with real life (such as with the Indian Trail Junior High School "prom night" unit in Chapter 9), or—by showing what will be learned and why the learning is important—induce in students motivation and a mindset favorable to the new lesson.

LESSON DEVELOPMENT

The developmental activities that comprise the bulk of the plan are the specifics by which you intend to achieve your lesson objectives. They include activities that present information, demonstrate skills, provide reinforcement of previously learned material, and provide other opportunities to develop understanding and skill. Furthermore, by actions and words, during lesson development the teacher models the behaviors expected of the students. Students need such modeling. By effective modeling, the teacher can exemplify the anticipated learning outcomes. Activities of this section of the lesson plan should be described in some detail so (1) you will know exactly what it is you plan to do and (2) during the intensity of the class meeting, you do not forget important details and content. For this reason you should consider, for example, noting answers (if known) to questions you intend to ask and solutions (if known) to problems you intend to have students solve.

LESSON CONCLUSION

Having a concise closure to the lesson is as important as having a strong introduction. The concluding activity should summarize and bind together what has ensued in the developmental stage and should reinforce the principal points of the lesson. One way to accomplish these ends is to restate the key points of the lesson. Another is to briefly outline the major points. Still another is to review the major concept. Sometimes the closure is not only a review of what was learned but the summarizing of a question left unanswered that signals a change in your plan of activities for the next day. In other words, it becomes a transitional closure.

TIMETABLE

To estimate the time factors in any lesson can be very difficult, especially for the beginning teacher. A good procedure is to gauge the amount of time needed for each learning activity and note that alongside the activity and strategy in your plan, as shown in the preferred sample lesson plan format. Placing too much faith in your time estimate may be foolish; an estimate is more for your guidance during the preactive phase of instruction than for anything else. Beginning teachers frequently find that their planned discussions and presentations do not last as long as was expected. To avoid being embarrassed by running out of material, try to make sure you have planned enough meaningful work to consume the entire class period. Another important reason for including a time plan in your lesson is to give information to students about how much time they have for a particular activity, such as a quiz or a group activity.

Assignments

When an assignment is to be given, it should be noted in your lesson plan. When to present an assignment to the students is optional, but it should never be yelled as an afterthought as the students are exiting the classroom at the end of the period. Whether they are to be begun and completed during class time or done out of school, assignments should be written on the writing board, in a special place on the bulletin board, in each student's assignment log maintained in a binder, or on a handout. Take extra care to be sure that assignment specifications are clear to the students. Many teachers give assignments to their students on a weekly or other periodic basis. When given on a periodic basis, rather than daily, assignments should still show in your daily lesson plans so to remind yourself to remind students of them.

Once assignment specifications and due dates are given, it is a good idea to not make major modifications to them, and it is especially important not to change assignment specifications several days after an assignment has been given. Last-minute changes in assignment specifications can be very frustrating to students who have already begun or completed the assignment; it shows little respect to those students. (See also "assignments and homework" in Chapter 8.)

ASSIGNMENT VERSUS PROCEDURE

Understand the difference between assignments and procedures. An assignment tells students *what* is to be done, while procedures explain *how* to do it. Although an assignment may include procedures, spelling out procedures alone is not the same thing as giving an academic assignment. When students are given an assignment, they need to understand the reasons for doing it and have some notion of ways the assignment might be done.

BENEFITS OF COACHED PRACTICE

Allowing time in class for students to begin work on homework assignments and long-term projects is highly recommended; it affords an opportunity for the teacher to provide individual attention to students. Being able to coach students is the reason for in-class time to begin assignments. The benefits of *coached practice* include being able to (a) monitor student work so a student doesn't go too far in a wrong direction, (b) help students to reflect on their thinking, (c) assess the progress of individual students, (d) provide for peer tutoring, and (e) discover or create a "teachable moment." For the latter, for example, while observing and monitoring student practice the teacher might discover a commonly shared student misconception. The teacher then stops and discusses that and attempts to clarify the misconception or collaboratively with students plans a subsequent lesson focusing on the common misconception.

Special Notes and Reminders

In their lesson plan format many teachers have a regular place for special notes and reminders. In that spe-

cial section that can be referred to quickly, you can place reminders concerning such things as announcements to be made, school programs, long-term assignment due dates, and makeup work for certain students.

Materials and Equipment to Be Used

Materials of instruction include books, media, handouts, and other supplies necessary to accomplish the lesson objectives. You must be *certain* that the proper and necessary materials and equipment are available for the lesson; to be certain requires planning. Teachers who, for one reason or another, have to busy themselves during class looking for materials or equipment that should have been readied before class began are likely to experience classroom control problems.

Assessment, Reflection, and Revision

Details of how you will assess how well students *are* learning (formative assessment) and how well they *have learned* (summative assessment) should be included in your lesson plan. This does not mean to imply that both types of assessment will be in every daily plan. Comprehension checks for formative assessment can be in the form of questions you ask and students ask during the lesson (in the procedural section), and in various kinds of checklists.

For summative assessment, teachers typically use review questions at the end of a lesson (as a closure) or the beginning of the next lesson (as a review or transfer introduction), in independent practice or summary activities at the completion of a lesson, and in tests.

In most lesson plan formats, a section is reserved for the teacher to make notes or reflective comments about the lesson. Many student teachers seem to prefer to write their reflections at the end or on the reverse page of their lesson plans. Reflections about the lesson are useful for you and those who are supervising you if you are a student teacher or a teacher being mentored or considered for tenure. Sample reflective questions you might ask yourself are shown in Figure 6.12.

As shown in Figure 6.13, both writing and later reading your reflections can provide not only ideas that may be useful if you plan to use the lesson again at some later date, but offer catharsis, easing the tension caused from teaching. To continue working effectively at a challenging task (that is, to prevent intellectual downshifting, or reverting to earlier learned, lower cognitive level behaviors) requires significant amounts of reflection.

After you have reviewed the sample lesson plan formats (Figures 6.10, 6.11, and the unit plan of Figure 6.14), proceed to Exercise 6.9, where you will analyze a lesson that failed; then, as instructed by your course instructor, do Exercises 6.10 and 6.11.

Figure 6.12   Questions for lesson self-reflection.

- What is my overall feeling about today's lesson—good, fair, or bad? What made me feel this way?
- Did students seem to enjoy the lesson? What makes me think so?
- Did the objectives seem to be met? What evidence do I have?
- What aspects of the lesson went well? What makes me believe so?
- Were I to repeat the lesson, what changes might I make?
- Which students seemed to do well? Which ones need more attention? Why and how?
- To what extent was this lesson individualized according to student learning styles, abilities, interests, talents, and needs? Could I do more in this regard? Why or why not?
- Did the students seem to have sufficient time to think and apply? Why or why not?
- Would I have been proud had the school superintendent been present to observe this lesson? Why or why not?

The ability to reflect on one's work is the mark of a true professional. Both writing and later reading your reflections on your teaching can provide not only ideas that may be useful if you plan to use the lesson again, but offer catharsis, easing the tension caused from teaching.

Figure 6.13   Reflective thoughts as recorded by a middle school language arts teacher on six consecutive lesson plans after teaching each lesson.

Date	Reflection
May 9	Yesterday was interesting in that I didn't notice the absence of the VCR until it was too late. I had known it was going away and that I would have to get one from the school, but had totally forgotten. Fortunately, I had overplanned for that day and there was no lack of activity. I got everyone in their groups and found, as usual, mostly off-task behavior taking place, even when the advent of my brilliant student accountability form. I am still trying desperately for ways to get these sixth graders to stay on task in small groups. Better do more research.
May 10	Yesterday we mainly watched the film, and so of course the kids were pretty well behaved. Most are making progress on their stories, and today I held an optional after-school workshop for students who wanted some help. I was surprised at the number of students who showed up. It was a good day.
May 11	I'm still having trouble with small-group management, but at least I got them all to remain seated and stay with their groups. They're just so loud, and when there are five groups all talking in one room, the volume keeps rising. They did pretty much stay on task though; my constant circulating and sitting in on groups helps, I think.
May 12	Yesterday the students vociferously demanded that I show more of *Star Wars* since I seemingly promised I would. I told them they had to earn it, though, and write silently for 20 minutes on their stories. It worked! Score one for teacher (and the students).
May 15	We broke into groups to read "My Journey," but I'm afraid they thought it was boring. Oh well. My bizarre life holds no fascination for them whatsoever. You definitely leave your ego home in this job. It's good for you.
May 16	It's taking too long to show *Star Wars,* and I'm losing some of the girls. They are not all that interested, and I can't say I blame them. When I teach this unit again, I will be more mindful of showing, reading myths, reading stories that have broad appeal across gender, ethnicity, etc. Although the film does have a female hero as well as a male hero, some of the girls in the class just aren't interested in science fiction.

Figure 6.14 Sample of a unit plan with one daily lesson for lab science.

UNIT PLAN SAMPLE WITH A DAILY LESSON

Course _Science_

Teacher _____ **Duration of Unit** _Ten days_

Unit Title _What's the Matter?_ **Grade Level** _Grades 5–12_

Purpose of the Unit
This unit is designed to develop students' understanding of the concept of matter. At the completion of the unit, students should have a clearer understanding of matter and its properties, of the basic units of matter, and of the source of matter.

Rationale of the Unit
This unit topic is important for building a foundation of knowledge for subsequent courses in science. This can increase students' chances of success in those courses, and thereby improve their self-confidence and self-esteem. A basic understanding of matter and its properties is important because of daily decisions that affect the manipulation of matter. It is more likely that students will make correct and safe decisions when they understand what matter is, how it changes form, and how its properties determine its use.

Goals of the Unit
The goals of this unit are for students to

1. Understand that all matter is made of atoms.
2. Understand that matter stays constant and that it is neither created nor destroyed.
3. Develop certain basic physical science laboratory skills.
4. Develop a positive attitude about physical science.
5. Look forward to taking other science courses.
6. Understand how science is relevant to their daily lives.

Instructional Objectives of the Unit
Upon completion of this unit of study, students should be able to

1. List at least ten examples of matter.
2. List the four states of matter, with one example of each.
3. Calculate the density of an object when given its mass and volume.
4. Describe the properties of solids, liquids, and gases.
5. Demonstrate an understanding that matter is made of elements and that elements are made of atoms.
6. Identify and explain one way the knowledge of matter is important to their daily lives.
7. Demonstrate increased self-confidence in pursuing laboratory investigations in physical science.
8. Demonstrate skill in communicating within the cooperative learning group.
9. Demonstrate skill in working with the triple-beam balance.

Unit Overview
Throughout this unit, students will be developing a concept map of matter. Information for the map will be derived from laboratory work, class discussions, lectures, student readings, and research. The overall instructional model is that of concept attainment. Important to this is an assessment of students' concepts about matter at the beginning of the unit. The preassessment and the continuing assessment of their concepts will center on the following:

1. What is matter and what are its properties? Students will develop the concept of matter by discovering the properties that all matter contains (that is, it has mass and takes up space).
2. Students will continue to build upon their understanding of the concept of matter by organizing matter into its four major states (that is, solid, liquid, gas, plasma). The concept development will be used to define the attributes of each state of matter, and students will gather information by participating in laboratory activities and class discussions.
3. What are some of the physical properties of matter that make certain kinds of matter unique? Students will experiment with properties of matter such as elasticity, brittleness, and density. Laboratory activities will allow student to contribute their observations and information to the further development of their concept of matter. Density activities enable students to practice their lab and math skills.
4. What are the basic units of matter, and where did matter come from? Students will continue to develop their concept of matter by working on this understanding of mixtures, compounds, elements, and atoms.

continued

Assessment of Student Achievement

For this unit, assessment of student achievement will be both formative and summative. Formative evaluation will be done daily by checklists of student behavior, knowledge, and skills. Summative evaluation will be based on the following criteria:

1. Student participation as evidenced by completion of daily homework, classwork, laboratory activities, and class discussions, and by the information on the student behavior checklists.
2. Weekly quizzes on content.
3. Unit test.

Lesson Number _____   **Duration of Lesson** _1–2 hours_ _____

Unit Title _What's the Matter?_ _____   **Teacher** _____

Lesson Title _Mission Impossible_ _____   **Lesson Topic** _Density of Solids_ _____

Objectives of the Lesson

Upon completion of this lesson, students should be able to

1. Determine the density of a solid cube.
2. Based on data gathered in class, develop their own definition of density.
3. Prepare and interpret graphs of data.
4. Communicate the results of their experiments to others in the class.

Materials Needed

1. Two large boxes of cereal and two snack-size boxes of the same cereal.
2. Four brownies (two whole and two cut in halves).
3. Four sandboxes (two large plastic boxes and two small boxes, each filled with sand).
4. Two triple-beam balances.
5. Several rulers.
6. Six hand-held calculators.
7. Eighteen colored pencils (six sets with three different colors per set).
8. Copies of lab instructions (one copy for each statement).

Instructional Procedure with Approximate Time Line

ANTICIPATORY SET (10–15 MINUTES)

Begin class by brainstorming to find what students already know about density. Place the word on the board or overhead, and ask students if they have heard of it. Write down their definitions and examples. Hold up a large box of cereal in one hand and the snack-size box in the other. Ask students which is more dense. Allow them time to explain their responses. Then tell them that by the end of this lesson they will know the answer to the question and that they will develop their own definition of density.

LABORATORY INVESTIGATION (30–60 MINUTES)

Students are divided into teams of four students of mixed abilities. Each member has a role:

1. *Measure master:* In charge of the group's ruler and ruler measurements.
2. *Mass master:* In charge of the group's weighings.
3. *Engineer:* In charge of the group's calculator and calculations.
4. *Graph master:* In charge of plotting the group's data on the graph paper.

Each team has eight minutes before switching stations. Each team completes three stations and then meets to make their graphs and to discuss results.

Station 1: **Cereal Box Density.** Students calculate the density of a large and a small box of cereal to determine if a larger and heavier object is more dense. The masses versus the volumes of the two boxes are plotted on graph paper using one of the pencil colors.

Figure 6.14   *continued*

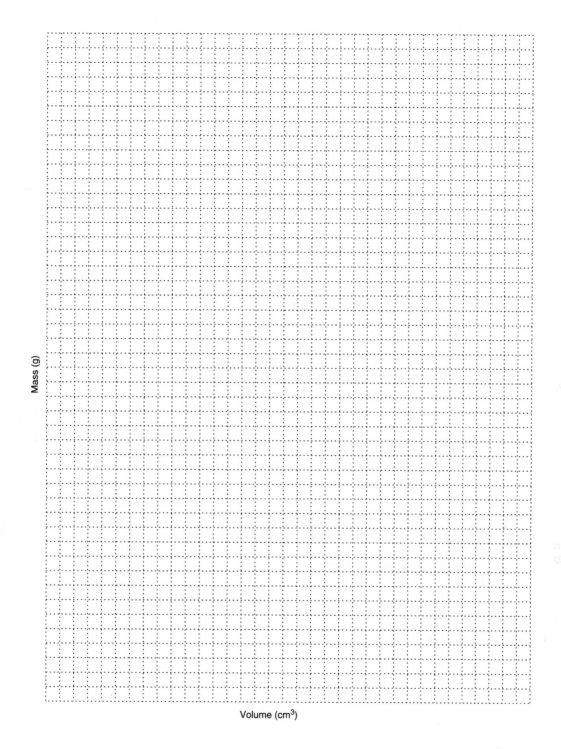

Instructions

1. The density of any object is determined by dividing its mass by its volume. Density in grams is divided by volume in cubic centimeters. Example: 20 g/10 cm^3 ÷ 2 g/cm^3.
2. Measure the volume of the small cereal box (length × width × height), and use the balance to determine its mass in grams. The engineer can do the calculations on the calculator. The graph master should graph the results of each trial and connect two points with a straight line.
3. Repeat the procedure using the large box of cereal.
4. The engineer computes the density of both cereal boxes with the calculator and records the results on the proper blank below the graph.

Figure 6.14 *continued*

a. Density of large box of cereal _____

b. Density of small box of cereal _____

c. Density of large brownie _____

d. Density of small brownie _____

e. Density of large sandbox _____

f. Density of small sandbox _____

***Station 2:* Brownie Density.** Students calculate the density of a full-size brownie and a half-size brownie. Results are plotted on the same graph as in Station 1, but with the second color.
Instructions

1. The density of any object is determined by dividing its mass by its volume. Density in grams is divided by volume in cubic centimeters. Example: 20 g/10 cm^3 ÷ 2 g/cm^3.
2. Measure the volume of a small brownie (length × width × height), and use the balance to determine its mass in grams. The engineer can do the calculations on the calculator. The graph master should graph the results of each trial and connect two points with a straight line.
3. Repeat the procedure using the large brownie.
4. The engineer computes the density of both brownies and records the result on the proper blank.

***Station 3:* Sandbox Density.** Students calculate the density of a large and a small box filled with sand. Results are plotted on the graph, but with the third color.
Instructions

1. The density of any object is determined by dividing its mass by its volume. Density in grams is divided by volume in cubic centimeters. Example: 20 g/10 cm^3 ÷ 2 g/cm^3.
2. Measure the volume of the small sandbox (length × width × height), and use the balance to determine its mass in grams. The engineer can do the calculations on the calculator. The graph master should graph the results of each trial and connect two points with a straight line.
3. Repeat the procedure using the large sandbox.
4. The engineer computes the density of both boxes and records the result on the proper blank.

Lab Worksheet. Teams return to their seats to do the graphing, analyze the results, and answer the following questions from their lab sheets:

1. Is a larger, heavier object more dense than its smaller counterpart? Explain your evidence.
2. What is your definition of density?
3. Which is more dense, a pound of feathers or a pound of gold? Explain your answer.

LESSON CLOSURE (10 MINUTES OR MORE)
When all teams are finished, teams should display their graphs, and share and discuss the results.

Concepts

1. Density is one of the properties of matter.
2. Mass and volume are related.
3. Density is determined by dividing mass by volume.

Extension Activities

1. Use a density graph to calculate the mass and volume of a smaller brownie.
2. Explore the story of Archimedes and the king's crown.

Evaluation, Reflection, and Revision of Lesson
Upon completion of this lesson and of the unit, revision in this lesson may be made on the basis of teacher observations and student achievement.

Figure 6.14 *continued*

Source: Courtesy of Will Hightower.

EXERCISE 6.9 ANALYSIS OF A LESSON THAT FAILED

INSTRUCTIONS: The planning and structure of a lesson are often predictors of the success of its implementation. The purpose of this exercise is to read the following synopsis of the implementation of a lesson, answer the discussion questions individually, and use your responses as a basis for class discussion in small groups about the lesson.

The Setting: Seventh-grade life science class; 1:12–2:07 P.M., spring semester

SYNOPSIS OF EVENTS

1:12	Bell rings.
1:12–1:21	Teacher directs students to read from their texts, while he takes attendance.
1:21–1:31	Teacher distributes a ditto to each student; students are now to label the parts of a flower shown on the handout.
1:31–1:37	Silent reading and labeling of ditto.
1:37–1:39	Teacher verbally gives instructions for working on a real flower, e.g., by comparing it with the drawing on the handout. Students may use the microscopes if they want.
1:39–1:45	Teacher walks around room, giving each student a real flower.
1:45–2:05	Chaos erupts. There is much confusion, with students wandering around, throwing flower parts at each other. Teacher begins writing referrals and sends two students to the office for their misbehavior. Teacher is flustered, directs students to spend remainder of period quietly reading from their texts. Two more referrals are written.
2:05–2:07	A few students begin meandering toward the exit.
2:07	End of period (much to the delight of the teacher).

QUESTIONS FOR CLASS DISCUSSION

1. Do you think the teacher had a lesson plan? If so, what (if any) were its good points? Its problems?

   _____

   _____

   _____

2. If you believed that the teacher had a lesson plan, do you believe that it was written and detailed? Explain your response. What is your evidence? _____

   _____

   _____

   _____

3. How might the lesson have been prepared and implemented to avoid the chaos? _____

   _____

   _____

   _____

4. Was the format of the lesson traditional? Explain. _____

   _____

   _____

   _____

EXERCISE 6.9 *(continued)*

5. Have you experienced a class such as this? Explain. _____

   _____

   _____

   _____

6. Which teacher behaviors were probable causes of much of the chaos? (Hint: See Chapter 4.) _____

   _____

   _____

   _____

7. What teacher behaviors could have prevented the chaos and made the lesson more effective? _____

   _____

   _____

   _____

8. Within the 55-minute class period, students were expected to operate rather high on the Learning Experiences Ladder (see Figure 6.6). Consider this analysis: 9 minutes of silent reading; 10 minutes of listening; 6 minutes of silent reading and labeling; 2 minutes of listening; 6 minutes of action (the only direct experience); and an additional 22 minutes of silent reading. In all, there were approximately 49 minutes (89 percent of the class time) of abstract verbal and visual symbolization. Is this a problem? _____

   _____

   _____

   _____

9. What have you learned from this exercise? _____

   _____

   _____

   _____

EXERCISE 6.10A PREPARING A LESSON PLAN

INSTRUCTIONS: Use the model lesson format or an alternative format that is approved by your instructor to prepare a _____-minute lesson plan (length to be decided in your class) for a grade and course of your choice. After completing your lesson plan, evaluate it yourself, modify it, and then have your modified version evaluated by at least three peers, using Exercise 6.10b for the evaluation, before turning it in for your instructor's evaluation. This exercise may be connected with Exercise 6.11.

EXERCISE 6.10B SELF AND PEER ASSESSMENT OF MY LESSON PLAN

INSTRUCTIONS: You may duplicate blank copies of this form for evaluation of the lesson you developed for Exercise 6.10a. Have your lesson plan evaluated by two of your peers and yourself. For each of the items below, evaluators should check either "yes" or "no," and write instructive comments. Compare the results of your self-evaluation with the other evaluations.

	No	*Yes*	*Comments*
1. Are descriptive data adequately provided?			
2. Are the goals clearly stated?			
3. Are the objectives specific and measurable?			
4. Are objectives correctly classified?			
5. Are objectives only low-order or is higher-order thinking expected?			
6. Is the rationale clear and justifiable?			
7. Is the plan's content appropriate?			
8. Is the content likely to contribute to achievement of the objectives?			
9. Given the time frame and other logistical considerations, is the plan workable?			
10. Will the opening (set) likely engage the students?			
11. Is there a preassessment strategy?			
12. Is there a proper mix of learning activities for the time frame of the lesson?			
13. Are the activities developmentally appropriate for the intended students?			
14. Are transitions planned?			

EXERCISE 6.10B (*continued*)

15. If relevant, are key questions written out
    and key ideas noted in the plan?

16. Does the plan indicate how coached
    practice will be provided for each student?

17. Is adequate closure provided in plan?

18. Are materials and equipment needed
    identified and are they appropriate?

19. Is there a planned formative assessment,
    formal or informal?

20. Is there a planned summative assessment?

21. Is the lesson coordinated in any way with
    other aspects of the curriculum?

22. Is the lesson likely to provide a sense of
    meaning for the students by helping
    bridge their learning?

23. Is an adequate amount of time allotted to
    address the information presented?

24. Is a thoughtfully prepared and relevant
    student assignment planned?

25. Could a substitute who is knowledgeable
    follow the plan?

Additional comments:

EXERCISE 6.11 PREPARING AN INSTRUCTIONAL UNIT: BRINGING IT ALL TOGETHER

INSTRUCTIONS: The purpose of this exercise is threefold, to (1) give you experience in preparing an instructional unit, (2) assist you in preparing an instructional unit that you can use in your teaching, and (3) start your collection of instructional units that you may be able to use later in your teaching. This is an assignment that will take several hours to complete, and you will need to read ahead in this resource guide. My advice, therefore, is that the assignment be started early, with a due date much later in the course. Your course instructor may have specific guidelines for your completion of this exercise; what follows is the essence of what you are to do.

First, divide your class into two teams, each with a different assignment pertaining to this exercise. The units completed by these teams are to be shared with all members of the class for feedback and possible use later.

TEAM 1

Members of this team, individually or in dyads, will develop standard teaching units, perhaps with different grade levels in mind. (You will need to review the content of Chapters 7–11.) Using a format that is practical, *each member or pair of this team* will develop a minimum two-week (10-day) unit for a particular grade level, subject, and topic. Regardless of format chosen, each unit plan should include the following elements:

1. Identification of (a) grade level, (b) subject, (c) topic, and (d) time duration.
2. Statement of rationale and general goals.
3. Separate listing of instructional objectives for each daily lesson. Wherever possible, the unit should include objectives from all three domains—cognitive, affective, and psychomotor.
4. List of the materials and resources needed and where they can be obtained (if you have that information). These should be listed for each daily lesson.
5. Ten consecutive daily lesson plans (see Exercise 6.10a).
6. List all items that will be used to assess student learning *during* and at *completion* of the unit of study.
7. Statement of how the unit will attend to variations in students' reading levels, socioethnic backgrounds, and special needs.

TEAM 2

In collaboration, members of this team will develop interdisciplinary thematic units. Depending upon the number of students in your class, Team 2 may actually comprise several teams, with each team developing an ITU. Each team should be comprised of no less than two members (e.g., a math specialist and a science specialist) and no more than four (e.g., social studies, language arts/reading, mathematics, and science).

SUMMARY

You have learned of the importance of learning modalities and instructional modes. You have learned about youth, their needs, the importance of providing an accepting and supportive learning environment, and teacher behaviors that are necessary to facilitate student learning beyond that of procedural knowledge.

With this chapter in particular you continued building your knowledge base about why planning is important and how units with lessons are useful pedagogical tools. Developing units of instruction that integrate student learning and provide a sense of meaning for the students requires coordination throughout the curriculum. Hence, for students, learning is a process of discovering how information, knowledge, and ideas are interrelated so they can make sense out of self, school, and life. Preparing chunks of information into units and units into lessons helps students to process and understand knowledge. You have developed your first unit of instruction and are well on your way to becoming a competent planner of instruction.

In Part II, you have been guided through the processes necessary to prepare yourself to teach in a classroom. Later, after you have studied Part III on specific instructional strategies, aids, media, and resources to supplement your instruction, you may choose to revisit this chapter and make revisions to your completed unit and lessons. In Part III your attention is directed to the selection and implementation of specific strategies, aids, and resources from which you may select to facilitate students learning of particular skills and content, beginning with the use of questioning.

QUESTIONS FOR CLASS DISCUSSION

1. In grade level and subject field discussion groups, list and describe specific considerations you should give to student safety when preparing instructional plans. Share your lists with other groups.

2. Explain the importance of the notion that all teachers are teachers of reading, writing, studying, and thinking. Do you agree or disagree with the notion? Why?

3. Give several reasons why both a student teacher and a first-year teacher need to prepare detailed lesson plans. Describe when, if ever, the teacher can or should divert from the written lesson plan.

4. Divide your class into subject area and grade level groups. Have each group devise two separate lesson plans to teach the same topic to the same group of students (identified), but where one plan uses direct instruction while the other uses indirect. Have groups share the outcomes of this activity with one another.

5. Explain why, when taught by access strategies, students learn less content but learn it more effectively? For a teacher, could this be a problem? Explain.

6. Which mode, access or delivery, do you believe better encourages student thinking? Explain. Can you find research evidence to support your conclusion? Do you believe use of either mode, access or delivery, does more to enhance the development of student self-esteem? Explain. Can you find research evidence to support your conclusion?

7. Describe observable behaviors that would enable you to tell whether a child is learning to think critically. Describe where, specifically, in a unit plan one would expect to find these observable behaviors.

8. Describe any prior concepts you held that changed as a result of your experiences with this chapter. Describe the changes.

9. From your current observations and field work as related to this teacher preparation program, clearly identify one specific example of educational practice that seems contradictory to exemplary practice or theory as presented in this chapter. Present your explanation for the discrepancy.

10. Do you have questions generated by the content of this chapter? If you do, list them along with ways answers might be found.

FOR FURTHER READING

Barab, S. A., and Landa, A. "Designing Effective Interdisciplinary Anchors." *Educational Leadership* 54(6):52–55 (March 1997).

Bass, J. A. F., et al. "Teaching About Rural Life Through Literature-Based Thematic Units." *Rural Educator* 19(2):30–35 (Winter 1997).

Butzow, C. M., and Butzow, J. W. *More Science through Children's Literature: An Integrated Approach.* Englewood, CO: Teacher Ideas Press, 1998.

Carnine, D. W., et al. *Direct Instruction Reading,* 3rd ed. Upper Saddle River, NJ: Prentice Hall, 1997.

Giffard, S. "Theme Studies and the Arts." *Primary Voices K–6* 5(2):2–5 (April 1997).

Herzberg, C. K. "Trees in Art, Literature, and Nature." *Book Links* 6(4):9–13 (March 1997).

Holt, E. *Using Primary Sources in the Primary Grades.* Bloomington, IN: ED419773, Clearinghouse for Social Studies/Social Science Education, 1998.

Howe, A. C., and Bell, J. "Factors Associated with Successful Implementation of Interdisciplinary Curriculum Units." *Research in Middle Level Education Quarterly* 21(2):39–52 (Winter 1998).

Jensen, E. "Getting the Brain's Attention." Chapter 5 of E. Jensen, *Teaching With the Brain in Mind.* Alexandria, VA: Association for Supervision and Curriculum Development, 1998.

Muir, M. "Planning Integrative Curriculum with Skeptical Students." *Middle School Journal* 30(2):9–17 (November 1998).

Phillips, P., and Bickley-Green, C. "Integrating Art and Mathematics." *Principal* 77(4):46–49 (March 1998).

Roberts, P. L., and Kellough, R. D. *A Guide for Developing an Interdisciplinary Thematic Unit,* 2d. ed. Upper Saddle River, NJ: Prentice Hall, 2000.

Schiro, M. *Integrating Children's Literature and Mathematics in the Classroom: Children as Meaning Makers, Problem Solvers, and Literary Critics.* New York: Teachers College Press, 1997.

Stein, M., et al. "Direct Instruction: Integrating Curriculum Design and Effective Teaching Practice." *Intervention in School and Clinic* 33(4):227–233 (March 1998).

Wiggins, G., and McTighe, J. *Understanding by Design.* Chapter 8. Alexandria, VA: Association for Supervision and Curriculum Development, 1998.

Part III

STRATEGIES, AIDS, MEDIA, AND RESOURCES FOR EFFECTIVE INSTRUCTION

Part III responds to your needs concerning:

- Assuring equality in the classroom
- Ensuring academic success for each student
- Helping students develop a repertoire of skills for lifelong learning
- Making homework and assignments
- Developing ideas for lessons and projects
- Individualizing (personalizing) student learning
- Preparing and implementing a lesson for feedback
- Planning project-centered learning and student exhibitions and presentations
- Finding resources for free and inexpensive instructional materials
- Employing service learning
- Teaching for thinking

- Teaching toward mastery
- Using electronic media and the Internet
- Using games and simulations
- Using inquiry and discovery learning
- Using learning activity centers, lectures, and demonstrations
- Using peer teaching and small group and cooperative learning
- Using questioning and discussions
- Using student writing and journals
- Using the writing board, the bulletin board, guest speakers, and field trips

REFLECTIVE THOUGHTS

Your goals should include helping students to learn how to solve problems, to make decisions, to think creatively and critically, and to feel good about themselves and their learning. To do this, you will:

1. *Involve students in direct experiences, both hands on and minds on, so they use more of their sensory modalities and develop their learning capacities. When all the senses are engaged, learning is the most effective and longest lasting.*

2. *Use questioning in a way designed to guide students to higher levels of thinking and doing.*

3. *Share in the responsibility for teaching reading, writing, thinking, and study skills.*

Experiences afforded by inquiry help students understand the importance of suspending judgment and also the tentativeness of answers and solutions. With those understandings, students eventually are better able to deal with life's ambiguities.

Teaching all students how to access and assess Internet sites adds to their repertoire of skills for lifelong learning.

Chapter 7

Strategies for Teaching: Questioning

A strategy of fundamental importance to any mode of instruction is, as introduced in Chapter 3, questioning. You will use questioning for so many purposes that you must be skilled in its use to teach effectively. Because it is so important and because it is so frequently used and abused, this chapter is devoted to assisting you in the development of your skills in using questioning.

Specifically, upon completion of this chapter you should be able to

1. Identify five categories of purposes for which questioning can be used as an instructional strategy.
2. Demonstrate understanding of the types of cognitive questions.
3. Demonstrate ways of helping students to develop their metacognitive skills.
4. Contrast the three levels of questioning and compare those with levels of thinking.
5. Demonstrate skill in the use of questioning.
6. Explain the value and use of students' questions.

PURPOSES FOR USING QUESTIONING

You will adapt the type and form of each question to the purpose for which it is asked. The purposes questions can serve can be separated into five categories, as follows.

1. *To give instructions politely.* An example is, "Josephine, would you please turn out the lights so we can show the slides?" Although they probably should avoid doing so, teachers sometimes also use rhetorical questions for the purpose of regaining student attention and maintaining classroom control, as in, "Marcello, would you please attend to your work?" Rhetori-

cal questions can sometimes backfire on the teacher. In this case, for example, Marcello might say "No;" then the teacher would have a problem that could perhaps have been avoided had the teacher at first been more direct and simply told Marcello to attend to his work, rather than asking him if he would. Consider the scenario that follows.

CLASSROOM SCENARIO

Kindergarten Teacher Asks a Rhetorical Question

At the completion of an opening reading lesson, Jennifer, a kindergarten teacher, asked the children, "Shall we do our math lesson now?" One of the children in the class, Mario, answered "No, I don't like math." Ignoring Mario's response Jennifer began the math lesson. It is likely that the lesson learned here by Mario was not the lesson intended by Jennifer if indeed she intended one at all. The lesson learned by Mario probably is that the teacher didn't really care what his answer to her question was. The next time Jennifer asks a question Mario may be reluctant to answer at all.

---

2. *To review and remind students of classroom procedures.* For example, if students continue to talk when they shouldn't, you can stop the lesson and ask, "Class, I think we need to review the procedure for listening when someone else is talking. Who can tell me, what is the procedure that we agreed upon?"

3. *To gather information.* Examples are: "How many of you have finished the assignment?" or, to find out whether a student knows something, "Charlie, can you please tell us the difference between a synonym and antonym?"

4. *To discover student knowledge, interests, or experiences.* Examples might be: "How many of you think you know the process by which water in our city is made potable?" or "How many of you have visited the local water treatment plant?"

5. *To guide student thinking and learning.* It is this category of questioning that is the focus here. In teaching, questions in this category are used to:

- *Develop appreciation.* For example, "Do you now understand the ecological relationship between that particular root fungus, voles, and the survival of the large conifers of the forests of the Pacific Northwest?"

- *Develop student thinking.* For example, "What do you suppose the effects to the ecology are when standing water is sprayed with an insecticide that is designed to kill all mosquito larvae?"

- *Diagnose learning difficulty.* For example, "What part of the formula don't you understand, Sally?"

- *Emphasize major points.* For example, "If we have never been to the sun, how do we know what it is made of?"

- *Encourage students.* For example, "OK, so you didn't remember the formula for glucose. What really impressed me in your essay is what you did understand about photosynthesis. Do you know what part impressed me?"

- *Establish rapport.* For example, "We have a problem here, but I think we can solve it if we put our heads together. What do you think ought to be our first step?"

- *Evaluate learning.* For example, "Sean, what is the effect when two rough surfaces are rubbed together?"

- *Give practice in expression.* For example, "Yvonne, would you please share with us the examples of impressionism you found?"

- *Help students in their own metacognition.* For example, "Yes, something did go wrong in the experiment. Do you still think your original hypothesis is correct? If not, then where was the error in your thinking? Or if you still think your hypothesis is correct, then where might the error have been in the design of your experiment? How might we find out?"

- *Help students interpret materials.* For example, "Something seems to be wrong with this compass. How do you suppose we can find out what is wrong with it? For example, if the needle is marked N and S in reverse, how can we find out if that is the problem?"

- *Help students organize materials.* For example, "If you really want to carry out your proposed experiment, then we are going to need certain materials. We are going to have to deal with some strategic questions here, such as, what do you think we will need, where can we find those things, who will be responsible for getting them, and how will we store and arrange

them once we are ready to start the investigation?"

- *Provide drill and practice.* For example, "Team A has prepared some questions that they would like to use as practice questions for our unit exam, and they are suggesting that we use them to play the game of Jeopardy on Friday. Is everyone in agreement with their idea?"

- *Provide review.* For example, "Today, in your groups, you are going to study the unit review questions I have prepared. After each group has studied and prepared its answers to these written questions, your group will pick another group and ask them your set of review questions. Each group has a different set of questions. Members of Team A are going to keep score, and the group that has the highest score from this review session will receive free pizza at tomorrow's lunch. Ready?"

- *Show agreement or disagreement.* For example, "Some scientists fear that the Antarctic ice shelf is breaking up and melting and that there will be worldwide flooding. With evidence that you have collected from recent articles, do you agree with this conclusion? Explain why or why not."

- *Show relationships, such as cause and effect.* For example, "What do you suppose would be the global effect if just one inch of the total Antarctic ice shelf were to melt rather suddenly?"

- *Build the curriculum.* It is the students' questions that provide the basis for the learning that occurs in an effective program that is inquiry based and project centered. More on this subject follows later beginning on page 247.

Questions to Avoid Asking

Before going further, while it is important to avoid asking rhetorical questions for which you do not want a response, you should also avoid asking questions that call for little or no student thinking, such as those that can be answered with a simple yes or no or some other sort of alternative answer response. Unless followed up with questions calling for clarification, questions that call for simple responses such as yes or no have little or no diagnostic value; they encourage guessing and inappropriate student responses that can cause classroom control problems for the teacher.

It is even more important to avoid using questions that embarrass a student, punish a student, or in any way deny the student's dignity. Questions that embarrass or punish tend to damage the student's developing self-esteem and serve no meaningful academic or instructional purpose. Questioning is an important instructional tool that teachers should use only for academic reasons. Although it is not always possible to predict when a student might be embarrassed by a question, a teacher should *never* deliberately ask questions for the purpose of embarrassment or punishment. In other words, avoid asking a student a content question when you know the student was not paying attention and/or does not know the answer. When done deliberately to punish or embarrass, such questions border on abuse!

TYPES OF COGNITIVE QUESTIONS: A GLOSSARY

Let us now define, describe, and provide examples for each of the types of cognitive (or mental) questions that you will use in teaching. Please note that although we refer to these in the traditional fashion as cognitive questions, any question type could relate to any of the three domains of learning (cognitive, affective, or psychomotor). In the section that follows, your attention is focused on the levels of cognitive questions.

CLARIFYING QUESTION

The clarifying question is used to gain more information from a student to help the teacher better understand a student's ideas, feelings, and thought processes. Often, asking a student to elaborate on an initial response will lead him or her to think more deeply, restructure his or her thinking, and while doing so, discover a fallacy in the original response. Examples of clarifying questions are "What I hear you saying is that you would rather work alone than in your group. Is that correct?" "So, Patrick, you think the poem is a sad one, is that right?" Research has shown a strong positive correlation between student learning and development of metacognitive skills (that is, their thinking about thinking) and the teacher's use of questions that ask for clarification.[1] In addition, by seeking clarification, you are likely to be demonstrating an interest in the student and her or his thinking.

CONVERGENT-THINKING QUESTION

Convergent-thinking questions, also called *narrow questions,* are low-order thinking questions that have a single correct answer (such as recall questions, discussed further in the next section). Examples of convergent questions are "How would you classify the word spelled *c-l-o-s-e,* as a homophone or homograph?" "If the radius of a circle is 20 meters, what is its circumference?" "What is the name of the first battle of the Civil War?" When using questions of this type, try to come back with follow-up questions so the student answering can demonstrate thinking beyond rote memory.

CUEING QUESTION

If you ask a question to which, after sufficient **wait time** (longer than two seconds), no students respond or to

which their inadequate responses indicate they need more information, then you can ask a question that cues the answer or response you are seeking.[2] In essence, you are going backward in your questioning sequence, to cue the students. For example, as an introduction to a lesson on the study of prefixes, a teacher asks her students, "How many legs each do crayfish, lobsters, and shrimp have?" and there is no accurate response. She might then cue the answer with the following information and question, "The class to which those animals belong is class Decapoda. Does that give you a clue about the number of legs they have?" If that clue is not enough, and after allowing sufficient time for students to think (longer than 2 seconds), then she might ask, "What is a decathlon?" or "What is the decimal system?" or "What is a decimeter?" or "What is a decibel?" or "What is a decade?" or "What is the Decalogue?"

When questioning students over reading material, researchers recommend the **question answer relationship (QAR)** strategy.[3] QAR involves asking a question and, if a student is unable to respond, providing one of three types of cues. "Right there" is used for questions for which the answer can be found explicitly stated in the sentence or paragraph. "Search and think" means the answer is not directly stated and therefore must be inferred. "On your own" is used for critical thinking questions for which the answers are neither explicit nor inferred in the text.[4]

DIVERGENT-THINKING QUESTION

Divergent-thinking questions (also known as *broad, reflective,* or *thought questions*) are open-ended in that they usually have no singularly correct answer. These high-order thinking questions require analysis, synthesis, or evaluation. Students must think creatively, leave the comfortable confines of the known, and reach out into the unknown. Examples of questions that require divergent thinking are "What measures could be taken to reduce crime in our neighborhood?" and "What measures could be taken to improve the post-lunchtime trash problem on our campus?"

---

[1]A. L. Costa, *The School as a Home for the Mind* (Palatine, IL: Skylight Publishing, 1991), p. 63.

[2]Studies in wait time began with the classic study of M. B. Rowe, "Wait Time And Reward As Instructional Variables, Their Influence On Language, Logic And Fate Control: Part I. Wait Time," *Journal of Research in Science Teaching* 11(2):81–94 (1974). See also M. B. Rowe, "Science, Silence, and Sanctions," *Science and Children* 34(1):35–37 (September 1996).

[3]See, for example, H. K. Ezell, et al., "Use of Peer-Assisted Procedures to Teach QAR Reading Comprehension Strategies to Third-Grade Children," *Education and Treatment of Children* 15(3):205–227 (August 1992), and M. E. McIntosh and R. J. Draper, "Using the Question-Answer Relationship Strategy to Improve Students' Reading of Mathematics Texts," *Clearing House* 69(3):154–162 (January/February 1996).

[4]J. S. Choate and T. A. Rakes, *Inclusive Instruction for Struggling Readers* (Bloomington, IN: Fastback 434, Phi Delta Kappa Educational Foundation, 1998), p. 27.

EVALUATIVE QUESTION

Whether convergent or divergent, some questions require students to place a value on something or to take a stance on some issue; these are referred to as *evaluative questions*. If the teacher and students all agree on certain premises, then the evaluative question would also be a convergent question. If original assumptions differ, then the response to the evaluative question would be more subjective, and therefore that evaluative question would be divergent. Examples of evaluative questions are "Should the United States allow clear-cutting in its national forests?" and "Should women have the right to choose whether or not to have abortions?" and "Is it an impeachable offense?"

FOCUS QUESTION

This is any question that is designed to focus student thinking. For example, the first question of the preceding paragraph is a focus question when the teacher asking it is attempting to focus student attention on the economic issues involved in clear-cutting.

PROBING QUESTION

Similar to a clarifying question, the probing question requires student thinking to go beyond superficial first-answer or single-word responses. Examples of probing questions are "Why, Antoine, do you think it to be the case that every citizen has the right to have a gun?"

Socratic Questioning

In the fifth century B.C., Socrates, the great Athenian teacher, used the art of questioning so successfully that to this day we still hear of the Socratic method.[5] What, exactly, is the Socratic method? Socrates' strategy was to ask his students a series of leading questions that gradually snarled them up to the point where they had to look carefully at their own ideas and to think rigorously for themselves. Today that strategy is referred to as the Socratic approach or method.

Socratic discussions were informal dialogues taking place in a natural, pleasant environment. Although Socrates sometimes had to go to considerable lengths to ignite his students' intrinsic interest, their response was natural and spontaneous. In his dialogues, Socrates tried to aid students in developing ideas. He did not impose his own notions on students. Rather, he encouraged them to develop their own conclusions and draw their own inferences. Of course, Socrates may have had pre-conceived notions about what the final learning should

be and carefully aimed his questions so that the students would arrive at the desired conclusions. Still, his questions were open-ended, causing divergent rather than convergent thinking. The students were free to go mentally wherever the facts and their thinking led them.

Throughout history, teachers have tried to adapt the methods of Socrates to the classroom. In some situations, they have been quite successful and are a major mode of instruction.[6] However, we must remember that Socrates used this method in the context of a one-to-one relationship between the student and himself. Some teachers have adapted it for whole-class direct instruction by asking questions first of one student and then of another, moving slowly about the class. This technique may work, but it is difficult because the essence of the Socratic technique is to build question on question in a logical fashion so that each question leads the student a step further toward the understanding sought. When you spread the questions around the classroom, you may find it difficult to build up the desired sequence and to keep all the students involved in the discussion. Sometimes you may be able to use the Socratic method by directing all the questions at one student—at least for several minutes—while other students look on and listen in. That is how Socrates did it. When the topic is interesting enough, this technique can be quite successful and even exciting, but in the long run, the Socratic method works best when the teacher is working in one-on-one coaching situations or with small groups of students, rather than in whole-class direct instruction.

In using Socratic questioning the focus is on the questions, not answers, and thinking is valued as the quintessential activity.[7] In essence, to conduct Socratic questioning, with the student or class identify a problem (either student- or teacher-posed) and then ask students a series of probing questions designed to cause them to examine critically the problem and potential solutions. The main thrust of the questioning and the key questions must be planned in advance so that the questioning will proceed logically. To think of quality probing questions on the spur of the moment is too difficult. It is the Socratic method that you will be using in a micro peer teaching exercise later in this chapter (Exercise 7.5).

LEVELS OF COGNITIVE QUESTIONS AND STUDENT THINKING

The questions you pose are cues to your students to the level of thinking expected of them, ranging from the lowest level of mental operation, requiring simple

[5]See, for example, V. C. Polite and A. H. Adams, *Improving Critical Thinking through Socratic Seminars*. Spotlight on Student Success, No. 110 (Philadelphia, PA: Mid-Atlantic Laboratory for Student Success, 1996), and S. Schoeman, "Using the Socratic Method in Secondary Teaching," *NASSP Bulletin* 81(587):19–21 (March 1997).

[6]See, for example, the Atheneum Middle School home page at <http://www.atheneum@alaska.net>.

[7]B. R. Brogan and W. A. Brogan, "The Socratic Questioner: Teaching and Learning in the Dialogical Classroom," *Educational Forum* 59(3):288–296 (Spring 1995).

recall of knowledge (convergent thinking), to the highest, requiring divergent thought and application of that thought. It is important that you are aware of the levels of thinking, that you understand the importance of attending to student thinking from low to higher levels of operation, and that you understand what for one student may be a matter of simple recall of information may for another require a higher-order mental activity, such as figuring something out by deduction.

You should structure and sequence your questions (and assist students in developing their own skill in structuring and sequencing their questions) in a way that is designed to guide students to higher levels of thinking. For example, when students respond to questions in complete sentences that provide supportive evidence for their ideas, it is fairly safe to assume that their thinking is at a higher level than were the response an imprecise and nondescriptive single-word answer.

To help your understanding, three levels of questioning and thinking are described as follows.[8] You should recognize the similarity between these three levels of questions and the six levels of thinking from Bloom's taxonomy of cognitive objectives (Chapter 5). For your daily use of questioning it is just as useful but more practical to think and behave in terms of these three levels, rather than of six.

1. *Lowest level (the data input phase): Gathering and recalling information.* At this level questions are designed to solicit from students concepts, information, feelings, or experiences that were gained in the past and stored in memory. Sample key words and desired behaviors are:

complete, count, define, describe, identify, list, match, name, observe, recall, recite, select

Thinking involves receiving data through the senses, followed by the processing of those data. Inputting without processing is brain-dysfunctional. Information that has not been processed is stored only in short-term memory.

2. *Intermediate level (the data processing phase): Processing information.* At this level questions are designed to draw relationships of cause and effect, to synthesize, analyze, summarize, compare, contrast, or classify data. Sample key words and desired behaviors are:

analyze, classify, compare, contrast, distinguish, explain, group, infer, make an analogy, organize, plan, synthesize

Thinking and questioning that involve processing of information can be conscious or unconscious. When

students observe the teacher thinking aloud, and when they are urged to think aloud, to think about their thinking, and to analyze it as it occurs, they are in the process of developing their intellectual skills.

At the processing level, this internal analysis of new data may challenge a learner's preconceptions (and misconceptions) about a phenomenon. The learner's brain will naturally resist this challenge to existing beliefs. The greater the mental challenge, the greater will be the brain's effort to draw upon data already in storage. With increasing data, the mind will gradually examine existing concepts and ultimately, as necessary, develop new mental concepts.

If there is a match between new input and existing mental concepts, no problem exists. Piaget called this process *assimilation.*[9] If, however, in processing new data there is no match with existing mental concepts, then the situation is what Piaget called *cognitive disequilibrium.* The brain does not "like" this disequilibrium and will drive the learner to search for an explanation for the discrepancy. Piaget called this process *accommodation.* However, although learning is enhanced by challenge, the brain is less flexible in accommodating new ideas in threatening situations. As discussed in Chapter 4, that is why each student must feel welcomed in the classroom, and learners must perceive the classroom environment as challenging but nonthreatening, an environment of *relaxed alertness.*[10]

Questions and experiences must be designed to elicit more than merely recall memory responses (assimilation). Many teachers find it useful to use discrepant events to introduce concepts. *Discrepant events* are phenomena that cause cognitive disequilibrium, thus stimulating higher-level mental functioning. However, merely exposing students to a discrepant event will not in itself cause them to develop new conceptual understandings. It simply stirs the mind into processing, without which mental development does not occur (see Figure 7.1.)

3. *Highest level (the data output phase): Applying and evaluating in new situations.* Questions at the highest level encourage learners to think intuitively, creatively, and hypothetically, to use their imagination, to expose a value system, or to make a judgment. Sample key words and desired behaviors are:

apply a principle, build a model, evaluate, extrapolate, forecast, generalize, hypothesize, imagine, judge, predict, speculate

You must use questions at the level best suited for the purpose, use questions of a variety of different lev-

---

[8]This three-tiered model of thinking has been described variously by others. For example, in E. Eisner's *The Educational Imagination* (Upper Saddle River, NJ: Prentice Hall, 1979), the levels are referred to as "descriptive," "interpretive," and "evaluative." For a comparison of thinking models, see Costa, *The School as a Home for the Mind,* p. 44.

[9]See, for example, J. Piaget, *The Development of Thought: Elaboration of Cognitive Structures* (New York: Viking, 1977).

[10]R. N. Caine and G. Caine, *Education on the Edge of Possibility* (Alexandria, VA: Association for Supervision and Curriculum Development, 1997), p. 107.

Figure 7.1 Example of a discrepant event demonstration.

BALLOON WILL NOT POP

Practice this first. Partially blow up a balloon, tie it off. Take a large but sharp sewing needle and slowly push it into the balloon. Because the needle immediately plugs the hole, the balloon remains filled. Sure, you say, students have seen this done by magicians or birthday party clowns. But wait. Now for the real discrepant event: slowly remove the needle, and Voila! The balloon does not collapse. The balloon material expands to plug the hole. Make several holes. Take a long needle (as used in doll making) and push it through the balloon and out through the other side, keeping the needle in both holes. The balloon stays filled. (Hint: push the needle into the thickest portion of the balloon, opposite the opening.) If students believe you are using a fake balloon, take the same needle and quickly puncture the balloon, popping it.

---

els, and structure questions in a way intended to move student thinking to higher levels. When teachers use higher-level questions, their students tend to score higher on tests of critical thinking and on standardized tests of achievement.[11]

With the use of questions as a strategy to move student thinking to higher levels, the teacher is facilitating students' intellectual development.

Developing your skill in using questioning requires attention to detail and practice. The following guidelines will provide that detail and some practice, but first, complete Exercise 7.1 to check your understanding of the levels of questions.

---

[11]See, for example, B. Newton, "Theoretical Basis for Higher Cognitive Questioning—An Avenue to Critical Thinking," *Education* 98(3):286–290 (March–April 1978); and D. Redfield and E. Rousseau, "A Meta-Analysis of Experimental Research on Teacher Questioning Behavior," *Review of Educational Research* 51(2):237–245 (Summer 1981).

EXERCISE 7.1: IDENTIFYING THE COGNITIVE LEVELS OF QUESTIONS— A SELF-CHECK EXERCISE

INSTRUCTIONS: The purpose of this exercise is to test your understanding and recognition of the levels of questions. Mark each of the following questions with a:

1, if it is at the lowest level of mental operation, gathering and recalling data.
2, if it is at a middle level, processing data.
3, if it is at the highest level, applying or evaluating data in a new situation.

Check your answers against the key that follows. Resolve problems by discussing them with your classmates and instructor.

_____ 1. Do you recall the differences between an Asian elephant and an African elephant?

_____ 2. How are the natural habitats of the Asian and African elephants similar? How are they different?

_____ 3. Which of the elephants do you think is the more interesting?

_____ 4. For what do you think the elephant uses its tusks?

_____ 5. Do all elephants have tusks?

_____ 6. Did the trick ending make the story more interesting for you?

_____ 7. How might these evergreen needles be grouped?

_____ 8. How do these two types of pine needles differ?

_____ 9. For how many years was the Soviet Union a communist-dominated nation?

_____ 10. How many republics do you believe will be in the new Commonwealth of Independent States (the former Soviet Union) by the year 2010?

_____ 11. Why do you think the city decided to move the zoo?

_____ 12. How would the park be different today had the zoo been left there?

_____ 13. How do zoos today differ from those of the mid-nineteenth century?

_____ 14. Should a teacher be entitled to unemployment benefits during the summer or when school is not in session?

_____ 15. If $4X + 40 = 44$, what is X?

_____ 16. What happens when I spin this egg?

_____ 17. How does this poem make you feel?

_____ 18. What will happen when we mix equal amounts of the red and yellow solutions?

_____ 19. What is the capital of West Virginia?

_____ 20. What will be the long-term global effects if the rain forests continue to be removed at the present rate?

Answer Key: 1 = 1 (recall); 2 = 2 (compare); 3 = 3 (judge); 4 = 3 (imagine); 5 = 3 (extrapolate); 6 = 3 (evaluate); 7 = 2 (classify); 8 = 2 (contrast); 9 = 1 (recall); 10 = 3 (predict); 11 = 2 (explain cause and effect); 12 = 3 (speculate); 13 = 2 (contrast); 14 = 3 (judge); 15 = 1 (recall of how to work the problem); 16 = 1 (observe); 17 = 1 (describe); 18 = 3 (hypothesize); 19 = 1 (recall); 20 = 3 (speculate or generalize)

Figure 7.2 Examples of questions that use appropriate cognitive terminology

Instead of	*Say*
"How else might it be done?"	"How could you apply . . .? "
"Are you going to get quiet?"	"If we are going to hear what Joan has to say, what do you need to do?"
"How do you know that is so?"	"What evidence do you have?"

GUIDELINES FOR USING QUESTIONING

As emphasized many times in several ways throughout this book, your goals are to help your students learn how to solve problems, to make decisions and value judgments, to think creatively and critically, and to feel good about themselves, their schools, and their learning. You must go beyond filling their minds with bits and pieces of information that will likely last only a brief time in the students' short-term memory. How you construe your questions and how you carry out your questioning strategy is important to the realization of these goals.

Preparing Questions

When preparing questions, consider the following guidelines.

Key cognitive questions should be planned, thoughtfully worded, and written into your lesson plan. Thoughtful preparation of questions helps to assure that they are clear and specific, not ambiguous, that the vocabulary is appropriate, and that each question matches its purpose. Incorporate questions into your lessons as instructional devices, welcomed pauses, attention grabbers, and checks for student comprehension. Thoughtful teachers even plan questions they intend to ask specific students, targeting questions to the readiness level, interest, or learning profile of a student.

Match questions with their target purposes. Carefully planned questions are sequenced and worded to match the levels of cognitive thinking expected of students. To help students in developing their thinking skills, you need to demonstrate how to do this. To demonstrate, you must use terminology that is specific and provides students with examples of experiences consonant with the meanings of the cognitive words. You should demonstrate this every day so students learn the cognitive terminology. As stated by Brooks and Brooks, "framing tasks around cognitive activities such as analysis, interpretation, and prediction—and explicitly using those terms with students—fosters the

construction of new understandings."[12] See the three examples in Figure 7.2.

Implementing Questioning

Careful preparation of questions is one part of the skill in questioning. Implementation is the other part. The following are guidelines for effective implementation.

Ask your well-worded question before calling on a student for a response. A common error made is when the teacher first calls on a student and then asks the question, such as "Sean, would you please tell us what you believe the author meant by the title 'we are one'?" Although probably not intended by the teacher, as soon as the teacher called on Sean, that signaled to the rest of the class that they were released from having to think about the question. The preferred strategy is to phrase the question, allow time for all students to think, and then call on Sean and other students for their interpretations of the author's meaning of the title.

Avoid bombarding students with too much teacher talk. Sometimes teachers talk too much. This could be especially true for teachers who are nervous, as might be the case for many during initial weeks of their student teaching. Knowing the guidelines presented here will help you avoid that syndrome. Remind yourself to be quiet after you ask a question that you have carefully formulated. Sometimes, due to lack of confidence, and especially when a question hasn't been carefully planned, the teacher asks the question and then, with a slight change in wording, asks it again, or asks several questions, one after another. That is too much verbiage. It's called "shotgun questioning" and only confuses students, allowing too little time for them to think.

After asking a question, provide students with adequate time to think. The pause after asking a question is called *wait time* (or *think time*). Knowing the subject better than the students know it and having given prior thought to the subject, too many teachers fail to allow students sufficient time to think after asking a question. In addition, by the time they have reached the intermediate grades, students have learned pretty well how to play the "game"—that is, they know that if they remain silent long enough, the teacher will probably answer his or her own question. After asking a well-worded question you should remain quiet for awhile, allowing students time to think and to respond. If you

---

[12]J. G. Brooks and M. G. Brooks, *In Search of Understanding: The Case for Constructivist Classrooms* (Alexandria, VA: Association for Supervision and Curriculum Development, 1993), p. 105.

wait long enough, they usually will. You may need to rehearse your students on this procedure.

After asking a question, how long should you wait before you do something? You should wait at least two seconds, and as long as nine. Stop reading now and look at your watch or a clock to get a feeling for how long two seconds is. Then, observe how long nine seconds is. Did nine seconds seem a long time? Because most of us are not used to silence in the classroom, two seconds of silence can seem quite long, while nine seconds may seem eternal. If, for some reason, students have not responded after a period of two to nine sec-

onds of wait time, then you can ask the question again (but don't reword an already carefully worded question, or else students are likely to think it is a new question). Pause for several seconds; then if you still haven't received a response you can call on a student, then another, if necessary, after sufficient wait time. Soon you will get a response that can be built upon. Avoid answering your own question!

Now, to better understand the art of questioning, the importance of well-worded questions and well-prepared and clear instructions, and the need to allow students time to think, do Exercise 7.2.

EXERCISE 7.2: THINK TIME AND THE ART OF QUESTIONING: AN IN-CLASS EXERCISE

INSTRUCTIONS: The purpose of this exercise is to further your understanding of the art and power of questioning, the importance of well-worded questions with well-prepared and clear instructions, and the need to give students time to think.

1. Roleplay simulation: From your class ask for three volunteers. One volunteer will read the lines of Estella, a second will read the one line of the student, while the third volunteer uses a stop watch to direct Estella and the student to speak their lines at the designated times. The rest of your class can pretend to be students in Estella's English class.

   1:00:   *Estella:* "Think of a man whom you admire, perhaps a father figure, and write a three-sentence paragraph describing that person." Students begin their writing.

   1:00:05:   *Estella:* "Only three sentences about someone you look up to. It might be your father, uncle, anyone."

   1:00:07:   *Student:* "Does it have to be about a man?"
   Estella: "No, it can be a man or a woman, but someone you truly admire."

   1:01:   Estella works the rows, seeing that students are on task.

   1:01:10:   *Estella:* "Three sentences are all you need to write."

   1:01:15:   *Estella:* "Think of someone you really look up to, and write three sentences in a paragraph that describes that person."

   1:01:30:   *Estella:* "Someone you would like to be like."

   1:02:   Estella continues walking around helping students who are having difficulty. All students are on task.

   1:04:   *Estella:* "Now I want you to exchange papers with the person behind or beside you, read that person's description of the person they admire, and describe a setting that you see their person in. Write a paragraph that describes that setting."

   1:04–1:05: Students exchange papers; teacher walks around seeing that everyone has received another student's paper.

   1:05:   *Estella:* "Where do you see that person being? Below the paragraph I want you to write a new paragraph describing where you see this person, perhaps in an easy chair watching a ball game, on a porch, in a car, or in the kitchen cooking."

   1:05:10:   *Estella:* "Describe a scene you see this person in."

   1:05:15:   *Estella:* "After you read the description I want you to create a setting for the person described."

   1:05:18:   Students seem confused either about what they are reading (e.g., asking the writer what a word is or means) or what they are supposed to do.

   1:05:19:   *Estella:* "Anything is fine. Use your imagination to describe the setting."

   1:05:22:   *Estella:* "Describe a setting for this person."

   1:09:   *Estella:* "Now I want you to exchange papers with yet someone else, and after reading the previous two paragraphs written by two other students, write a third paragraph describing a problem you think this admired person has."

2. After the roleplay simulation, hold a whole-class discussion or small group discussions and use the following as a springboard for your discussion: Describe what you believe are the good points and weak points of this portion of Estella's lesson and her implementation of it.

Practice gender equity. To practice gender equity, here are four rules to follow when using questioning: (1) Avoid going to a boy to bail out a girl who fails to answer a question, and (2) avoid going to a boy to improve upon a girl's answer. For the first, without seeming to badger, try to give the student clues until she can answer with success. For the second, hold and demonstrate high expectations for all students. (3) Allow equal wait time regardless of student gender. (4) Call on boys and girls equally.

Practice calling on all students. Related to Rule 4 of the preceding paragraph, you must call on not just the bright or the slow, not just the boys or the girls, not only those in the front or middle of the room, but all of them. To do these things takes concentrated effort on your part, but it is important. To ensure that students are called on equally, some teachers have in hand laminated copies of their seating charts, perhaps on bright neon-colored clipboards (gives students a visual focus), and, with a wax pencil or water soluble marker, make a mark next to the name of the student each time he or she is called on. With the seating chart laminated, and using erasable markers, the marks can be erased at the end of the day and the seating chart used over and over. Additional suggestions for practicing equity in the classroom are in Chapter 8.

Give the same minimum amount of wait time (think time) to all students. This, too, will require concentrated effort on your part but is important to do. A teacher who waits for less time when calling on a slow student or students of one gender, is showing a prejudice or a lack of confidence in certain students, both of which are detrimental when a teacher is striving to establish for all students a positive, equal, and safe environment for classroom learning. Show confidence in all students, and never discriminate by expecting less or more from some than from others. Although some students may take longer to respond, it is not necessarily because they are not thinking or have less ability. There may be cultural differences to think about, in that some cultures simply allow more wait time than others. The important point here is to individualize to allow students who need more time to have it. Variation in wait time allowed should not be used to single out some students and to lead to lower expectations but rather to allow for higher expectations.

Require students to raise their hands and be called on. This is true for kindergarten teachers and for all teachers thereafter. When you ask questions, instead of allowing students to randomly shout out their answers, require them to raise their hands and to be called on before they respond. Establish that procedure and stick with it. This helps to assure both that you call on all students equally, fairly distributing your interactions with the students, and that girls are not interacted with less because boys tend to be more obstreperous (see Exer-

cise 8.4). Even in college classrooms, male students tend to be more vocal than female students and, when allowed by the instructor, tend to outtalk and interrupt their female peers. Every teacher has the responsibility to guarantee a nonbiased classroom and an equal distribution of interaction time in the classroom. That is impossible to do if students are allowed to talk at will.

Another important reason for this advice is to aid students in their learning to control their impulsivity. Controlling one's impulsivity is a characteristic of intelligent behavior presented and discussed in Chapter 10. One of your many instructional responsibilities is to help students develop this skill.

Actively involve as many students as possible in the questioning-answering discussion session. The traditional method of the teacher asking a question and then calling on a student to respond is essentially a one-on-one interaction. Many students, those not called on, are likely to view that as their opportunity to disengage in the lesson at hand. Even though you call on one student you want the other students to stay mentally engaged. There are many effective ways to keep all engaged. Consider the following.

To keep all students mentally engaged, you will want to call on students who are sitting quietly and have not raised their hands along with those who have, but avoid badgering or humiliating an unwilling participant. When a student has no response, you might suggest he or she think about it and you will come back to the student to assure the student eventually understands or has an answer to the original question.

By dividing a single question into several parts, the number of students involved can be increased. For example, "What are the causes of the Civil War? Who can give one reason?" followed then by "Who can give another?" Or, you can involve several students in answering a single question. For example, ask one student for an answer such as to the question "What was the first battle of the Civil War?", a second to read the text aloud to verify the student's answer, and sometimes a third to explore the reason or thinking that makes it the accepted answer.

Carefully gauge your responses to students' responses to your questions. The way you respond to students' answers influences students' subsequent participation. Responses by the teacher that encourage student participation include probing for elaboration, discussing student answers, requesting justification, asking how answers were arrived at, and providing positive reinforcement.[13]

Use strong praise sparingly. A teacher's use of strong praise is sometimes okay, especially with kindergarten and early primary grade children. But for older students and when you want students to think divergently

---

[13]J. S. Choate and T. A. Rakes, *Inclusive Instruction for Struggling Readers*, p. 26.

Students can be taught the skills in the use of questioning and can practice those skills while peer coaching.

and creatively, you should be stingy with use of strong praise to student responses. Strong praise from a teacher tends to terminate divergent and creative thinking. Strong praise can also cause children to become dependent on external sources of praise—to become "praise junkies." (See discussion and Figure 3.3 in Chapter 3 about praise versus encouragement.)

One of your goals is to help students find intrinsic sources for motivation, an inner drive of intent or desire that causes them to want to learn. Use of strong praise tends to build conformity, causing students to depend on outside forces—the giver of praise—for their worth rather than upon themselves. An example of a strong praise response is "That's right! Very good." On the other hand, passive acceptance responses, such as "Okay, that seems to be one possibility," keep the door open for further thinking, particularly for higher-level, divergent thinking.

Another example of a passive acceptance response is one used in brainstorming sessions, when the teacher says, "After asking the question and giving you time to think about it, I will hear your ideas and record them on the board." Only after all student responses have been heard and recorded does the class begin its consideration of each. That kind of nonjudgmental acceptance of all ideas in the classroom will generate a great deal of expression of high-level thought.[14]

---

[14]For further discussion of the use of praise and rewards in teaching, see C. H. Edwards, *Classroom Discipline and Management*, 2d ed. (Upper Saddle River, NJ: Prentice Hall, 1997).

QUESTIONS FROM STUDENTS: THE QUESTION-DRIVEN CLASSROOM

Student questions can and should be used as springboards for further questioning, discussions, and investigations. Indeed, in a constructivist learning environment, student questions often drive content. Students should be encouraged to ask questions that challenge the textbook, the process, or other persons' statements, and they should be encouraged to seek the supporting evidence for a statement.

Being able to ask questions may be more important than having right answers. Knowledge is derived from asking questions. Being able to recognize problems and to formulate questions is a skill and the key to problem solving and critical thinking skill development. You have a responsibility to encourage students to formulate questions and to help them word their questions in such a way that tentative answers can be sought. That is the process necessary to build a base of knowledge that can be drawn upon whenever necessary to link, interpret, and explain new information in new situations.

Questioning: The Cornerstone of Critical Thinking, Real-World Problem Solving, and Meaningful Learning

Real-world problem solving usually offers no absolute right answers. Rather than "correct" answers, some are better than others. The student with a problem needs to learn how to: (1) recognize the problem, (2) formulate a question about that problem (e.g., Should I date this person or not? Should I take this after-school job or not? Should I abuse drugs or not? To which colleges should I apply?), (3) collect data, and (4) arrive at a temporarily acceptable answer to the problem, while realizing that at some later time, new data may dictate a review of the former conclusion. For example, if a biochemist believes she has discovered a new enzyme, no textbook, teacher, or any other outside authoritative source can tell her if she is correct. Rather, on the basis of her self-confidence in identifying problems, asking questions, collecting enough data, and arriving at a tentative conclusion based on those data, she assumes that for now her conclusion is safe.

Encourage students to ask questions about content and process. As emphasized in *Tried and True,* from the U.S. Department of Education, question asking often indicates that the inquirer is curious, puzzled, and uncertain; it is a sign of being engaged in thinking about a topic. And, yet, in too many classrooms too few students ask questions.[15] Students should be encouraged to ask questions. From students, there is no such thing as a "dumb" question. Sometimes students, like everyone else, ask questions that could just as easily have been looked up or are irrelevant or show lack of thought or sensitivity. Those questions can consume precious class time. For a teacher, they can be frustrating. A teacher's initial reaction may be quickly and mistakenly to brush off that type of question with sarcasm, while assuming that the student is too lazy to look up an answer. In such instances, you are advised to think before responding and to respond kindly and professionally, although in the busy life of a classroom teacher that may not always be so easy to remember. Be assured, there is a reason for a student's question. Perhaps the student is signaling a need for recognition or simply demanding attention.

In large schools, it is sometimes easy for a student to feel alone and insignificant (although this seems less the case with schools that use a school-within-a-school plan and where teachers and students work together in interdisciplinary teams, or, as in looping, where one cadre of teachers remains with the same cohort of students for two or more years). When a student makes an effort to interact with you, that can be a positive sign, so gauge carefully your responses to those efforts. If a student's question is really off track, off the wall, out of order, and out of context with the content of the lesson, consider this as a possible response: "That is an interesting question (or comment), and I would very much like to talk with you more about it. Could we meet at lunch time or before or after school or at some other time that is mutually convenient?"

Avoid bluffing an answer to a question for which you do not have an answer. Nothing will cause you to lose credibility with students any faster than faking an answer. There is nothing wrong with admitting you do not know. It helps students realize you are human. It helps them maintain an adequate self-esteem, realizing they are okay. What is important is that you know where and how to find possible answers and that you help students develop that same knowledge and those same process skills.

Now, to reinforce your understanding, do Exercises 7.3 through 7.8.

---

[15]United States Department of Education, *Tried and True: Tested Ideas for Teaching and Learning from the Regional Educational Laboratories* (Washington, DC: Office of Educational Research and Improvement, U.S. Department of Education, 1997), p. 53.

EXERCISE 7.3 EXAMINING COURSE MATERIALS FOR LEVEL OF QUESTIONING

INSTRUCTIONS: It is often reported that when evaluating the levels of questions found in teacher guides, student workbooks, and tests, a very high percentage of the questions are low level, or devoted to factual recall. Examine course materials for the levels of questions presented to students. For a subject and grade level you intend to teach, examine a textbook (or other instructional material) for the questions posed to students, perhaps at the ends of the chapters. Also examine workbooks, examinations, instructional packages, and any other printed or electronic material used by students. Complete the exercise that follows; then share your findings with your classmates.

1. Materials examined (include date of publication and target students) _____

   _____

2. Questions at the recall (lowest) level: _____

   _____

   _____

   _____

   _____

3. Questions at the processing (intermediate) level: _____

   _____

   _____

   _____

   _____

4. Questions at the application (highest) level: _____

   _____

   _____

   _____

   _____

5. Approximate percentages of questions at each level: _____

   a. Recall = ____%

   b. Processing = ____ %

   c. Application = ____ %

6. Did you find evidence of question-level sequencing? If so, describe it. _____

   _____

   _____

   _____

   _____

EXERCISE 7.3 (*continued*)

7. After sharing and discussing your results with your classmates, what do you conclude from this exercise?

_____

_____

_____

_____

8. When using instructional materials that you believe have a disproportionately high percentage of questions at the input (or recall) level, in addition to the two examples provided, what should or could you do?

Example 1: Have students scan chapter subheadings and develop higher-level cognitive questions based on the subheadings, which they would then answer through their reading.

Example 2: Require students to defend their answers to low-level cognitive chapter review and end-of-chapter questions with textual information and experience.

_____

_____

_____

EXERCISE 7.4 OBSERVING THE COGNITIVE LEVELS OF CLASSROOM VERBAL INTERACTION

INSTRUCTIONS: The purpose of this exercise is to develop your skill in recognizing the levels of classroom questions. Arrange to visit a classroom in any school of your choice that has been approved by your instructor. On the form below, record each instance of a teacher question (or statement) that causes students to gather or recall data, to process data, or to apply or evaluate data. Reword by writing in each question or statement. In the left-hand column, you may want to write in additional key words to assist your memory. After your observation, compare and discuss the results with your colleagues.

School and class visited _____

Date _____

QUESTION OR STATEMENT

RECALL LEVEL

(Key words: "complete," "count," "define," "describe")

PROCESSING LEVEL

(Key words: "analyze," "classify," "compare")

APPLICATION LEVEL

(Key words: "apply," "build," "evaluate")

EXERCISE 7.5 PRACTICE IN RAISING QUESTIONS TO HIGHER LEVELS

INSTRUCTIONS: The purpose of this exercise is to develop your skill in raising questions from one level to the next higher level. Fill in the blanks below with questions at the appropriate levels. Share and discuss your responses with your classmates.

RECALL LEVEL	PROCESSING LEVEL	APPLICATION LEVEL
1. How many of you read a newspaper today?	Why did you read a newspaper today?	What do you think would happen if nobody ever read a newspaper again?
2. What was today's top newspaper headline?	Why was the news item important enough to be the top headline?	Do you think that the news items will be in tomorrow's paper?
3. Who is the president of the United States?	How does the work he has done compare with that done by the previous president?	
4. How many presidents has the United States had?		
5. (Create your own questions)		

EXERCISE 7.6 PRACTICE IN CREATING COGNITIVE QUESTIONS

INSTRUCTIONS: The purpose of this exercise is to provide practice in writing cognitive questions. Read the following passage. Then compose three questions about it that cause students to identify, list, and recall; three that cause students to analyze, compare, and explain; and three that cause students to predict, apply, and hypothesize. Share and check your questions with your peers.

WE ARE ONE

Truth, love, peace, and beauty,
We have sought apart
   but will find within, as our
Moods—explored, shared,
    questioned, and accepted—
Together become one and all.

Through life my friends
We can travel together,
for we now know
each could go it alone.

To assimilate our efforts into one,
While growing in accepting,
and trusting, and sharing the
   individuality of the other,
Is truly to enjoy God's greatest gift—
Feeling—knowing love and compassion.

Through life my friends
We are together,
for we must know
we are one.

         —R. D. Kellough

RECALL QUESTIONS

1. to identify _____

_____

_____

_____

2. to list _____

_____

_____

_____

3. to recall _____

_____

_____

_____

EXERCISE 7.6 (*continued*)

PROCESSING QUESTIONS

1. to analyze _____

_____

_____

_____

2. to compare _____

_____

_____

_____

3. to explain _____

_____

_____

_____

APPLICATION QUESTIONS

1. to predict _____

_____

_____

_____

2. to apply _____

_____

_____

_____

3. to hypothesize _____

_____

_____

_____

EXERCISE 7.7 A COOPERATIVE LEARNING AND MICRO PEER TEACHING EXERCISE IN THE USE OF SOCRATIC QUESTIONING—MICRO PEER TEACHING I

INSTRUCTIONS: The purpose of this exercise is to practice preparing and asking questions that are designed to lead student thinking from the lowest level to the highest. Before class, prepare a five-minute lesson for posing questions that will guide the learner from lowest to highest levels of thinking. Teaching will be one-on-one, in groups of four, with each member of the group assuming a particular role—teacher, student, judge, or recorder. Each of the four members of your group will assume each of those roles once for five minutes. (If there are only three members in a group, the roles of judge and recorder can be combined during each five-minute lesson; or, if there are five members in the group, one member can sit out each round, or two can work together as judge.) Each member of the group should have his or her own tally sheet.

SUGGESTED LESSON TOPICS

- Teaching styles
- Characteristics of youngsters of a particular age
- Learning styles of students
- Evaluation of learning achievement
- A skill or hobby
- Teaching competencies
- A particular teaching strategy
- Student teaching and what it will really be like

Each of your group members should keep the following role descriptions in mind:

- *Teacher (sender).* Pose recall (input), processing, and application (output) questions related to one of the topics above or to any topic you choose.
- *Student (receiver).* Respond to the questions of the teacher.
- *Judge.* Identify the level of each question or statement used by the teacher *and* the level of the student's response.
- *Recorder.* Tally the number of each level of question or statement used by the teacher (S = sender) as indicated by the judge; also tally the level of student responses (R = receiver). Record any problems encountered by your group.

TALLY SHEET				
	Minute	**Input**	**Processing**	**Output**
Sender _____	1 S			
Receiver _____	R			
	2 S			
	R			
	3 S			
	R			
	4 S			
	R			
	5 S			
	R			

☞

EXERCISE 7.7 (*continued*)

	Minute	Input	Processing	Output
TALLY SHEET				
Sender _____	1 S			
Receiver _____	R			
	2 S			
	R			
	3 S			
	R			
	4 S			
	R			
	5 S			
	R			

EXERCISE 7.8 IDENTIFYING TEACHING BEHAVIORS IN CLASSROOM INTERACTION— A SELF-CHECK EXERCISE*

INSTRUCTIONS: The purpose of this exercise is to assess your understanding of the teacher's use of certain facilitative behaviors, including the use of questioning. It is a synthesis of what you have learned not only from this chapter but from previous chapters as well. (You may want to refer to Chapter 3.) The following is a sample classroom interaction, which includes examples of various levels of questions and structuring and responsive behaviors. See if you can identify them. Your answers should be from this list: *structuring, facilitating, active acceptance, passive acceptance, clarifying, input questioning, process questioning,* and *application questioning*. (An answer key is found at the end of this exercise.) Discuss and resolve any problems with your classmates and instructor.

INTERACTION		TEACHER'S BEHAVIOR
Joyce:	Ms. Clarion, here's a picture that shows how a magnet works.	
Teacher:	Okay, Joyce, would you please share this with the rest of the group? Tell us what you think is happening.	1. _____
Joyce:	Well, this girl is in the garage using a magnet to pick up things, and over here it shows all the things a magnet will pick up.	
Teacher:	What kind of things are they, Joyce?	2. _____
Joyce:	Nails, paper clips, spoons, screws, screwdr—	
Molly:	It will not pick up spoons, Joyce. I've tried it.	
Joyce:	It will too. It shows right here.	
Olivia:	I picked up a spoon with a magnet that my uncle gave me.	
Joyce:	Sure it will.	
Sarah:	No it won't, 'cause—	
Teacher:	Just a minute. We'd like to hear everyone's idea, but we can't if we all talk at once. If you'll raise your hand, then I'll know who to call on next.	3. _____
Teacher:	Now, Joyce says a magnet will pick up spoons. Sarah says that a magnet can't pick it up.	4. _____
Teacher:	Yes, Sarah, what do you think?	5. _____
Sarah:	I'm not sure, but I think it has to be metal.	
Linda:	I think it depends upon the kind of spoon. Some spoons have metal, and some are plastic and other stuff.	
Teacher:	That's another possibility.	6. _____
Teacher:	How can we solve this problem as to whether a magnet will pick up the spoons?	7. _____
Molly:	We can get some spoons and try it with our magnet.	
Teacher:	All right. Anybody know where we can get some spoons?	8. _____
José:	There's a spoon in my lunch bag.	
Olivia:	There are some spoons in the lunchroom. Can we go get them?	
Teacher:	Yes, José, would you get yours? Olivia, would you get some from the lunchroom? Be sure you ask the cook. Joyce, would you get the magnet?	9. _____

☞

EXERCISE 7.8 (*continued*)

[*Later*]

Teacher:	Now, because this is José's spoon, what do you think would be the fair thing to do?	10. _____
David:	Let him try the magnet on his own spoon.	
Teacher:	All right, José, what do you think will happen when we touch the magnet to your spoon?	11. _____
José:	It probably won't pick it up because it's not the right kind of stuff for a magnet to pick up.	
Teacher:	What do you mean, "the right kind of stuff"?	12. _____
Sarah:	He means the right kind of metal.	
Teacher:	José, would you try it? Let's all watch.	13. _____
Molly:	See, I told you a magnet wouldn't pick up a spoon.	
Raul:	But it does pick up some spoons.	
Joyce:	I don't mean all spoons, only those made of metal. The spoon in the book is made of metal.	
Linda:	Is this pin made out of steel?	
Teacher:	No, Linda it isn't.	14. _____
Linda:	I thought it was steel or stuff like that—like a piece of car.	
Teacher:	I don't understand what you mean, Linda. What do you mean, "a piece of car"?	15. _____
Linda:	When Dad banged up our car, you could see the shining metal under the paint. He said it was steel.	
Sarah:	I think the most powerful magnet in the world might be able to pick it up.	
David:	An electromagnet, I think, is the strongest magnet that was ever invented.	
Teacher:	Are you saying, David, that you think a stronger magnet would pick up the spoon?	16. _____
David:	Um-hm. I think so.	
Teacher:	What would you want to do to find out?	17. _____
David:	We could set up our electromagnet and try it.	
Teacher:	Okay.	18. _____

Answer Key: 1. Structuring; 2. Input questioning; 3. Structuring (listening); 4 Active acceptance; 5. Process questioning (explaining); 6. Passive acceptance; 7. Process question (problem solving); 8. Input question (locating); 9. Data acquisition (this might also be interpreted as a structuring behavior since the teacher directs the students to perform a task); 10. Application question (evaluation); 11. Application question (predicting); 12. Clarifying; 13. Data acquisition; 14. Data acquisition; 15. Clarifying; 16. Clarifying; 17. Process question (planning); 18. Passive acceptance.

*Adapted and modified from A. L. Costa, *The Enabling Behaviors* (Orangevale, CA: Search Models Unlimited 1989) pp. 75–78. By permission of Arthur L. Costa.

SUMMARY

This chapter presented a great deal of information about one teaching strategy, which will be perhaps the most important one in your teaching repertoire. Questioning is the cornerstone to meaningful learning, thinking, communication, and real-world problem solving. The art of its use is something you will continue to develop throughout your teaching career.

In the next two chapters, your attention is directed to how teachers group students and to the selection and implementation of specific instructional strategies to facilitate students' meaningful learning of skills and content of the curriculum.

QUESTIONS FOR CLASS DISCUSSION

1. Have you ever noticed that some teachers seem to anticipate a lower-level response to their questions from particular students? Discuss your answer with your peers.

2. Should a teacher verbally respond to every student's verbal comment or inquiry? Explain why or why not. If not, on what basis does the teacher decide when and how to respond?

3. Describe when, if ever, and how strong praise could be used by a teacher. Explain the difference, if any, between strong praise and positive reinforcement.

4. Explain why it is important to wait after asking students a content question. How long should you wait? What should you do if after waiting a certain amount of time there is no student response?

5. To what extent should (or can) a classroom teacher allow student questions to determine content studied? To what extent should students' initial interest, or lack of interest, in a topic determine whether the topic gets taught?

6. Explain the meaning of the following statement: We should look not for what students can reiterate but for what they can demonstrate and produce. Explain why you agree or disagree with the concept.

7. How many teachers can members of your class find during a designated period of time who actually plan and write the questions they ask children during a lesson? Discuss the results of your investigation.

8. Describe any prior concepts you held that changed as a result of your experiences with this chapter. Describe the changes.

9. From your current observations and field work as related to this teacher preparation program, clearly identify one specific example of educational practice that seems contradictory to exemplary practice or theory as presented in this chapter. Present your explanation for the discrepancy.

10. Do you have questions generated by the content of this chapter? If you do, list them along with ways answers might be found.

FOR FURTHER READING

Brualdi, A. C. *Classroom Questions*. Washington, DC: ED422407, ERIC Clearinghouse on Assessment and Evaluation, 1998.

Cardellichio, T., and Field, W. "Seven Strategies That Encourage Neural Branching." *Educational Leadership* 54(6):33–36 (March 1997).

Deal, D., and Sterling, D. "Kids Ask the Best Questions." *Educational Leadership* 54(6):61–63 (March 1997).

Gibson, J. "Any Questions, Any Answers?" *Primary Science Review* 51:20–21 (January/February 1998).

Good, T. L., and Brophy, J. E. *Looking in Classrooms,* 7th ed. Chapter 9. New York: Longman, 1997.

Grambo, G. "Questions in Your Classroom." *Gifted Child Today Magazine* 20(3):42–43 (May/June 1997).

Kligman, P. S., and Aihara, K. A. "Observing Student-Based Questions in a Whole Language Second-Grade Classroom." *Indiana Reading Journal* 29(3):17–22 (Summer 1997).

Latham, A. "Asking Students the Right Questions." *Educational Leadership* 54(6):84–85 (March 1997).

Martinello, M. L. "Learning to Question for Inquiry." *Educational Forum* 62(2):164–171 (Winter 1998).

Ostergard, S. A. "Asking Good Questions in Mathematics Class: How Long Does It Take to Learn How?" *Clearing House* 71(1):48–50 (September/October 1997).

Sole, D. "Johari's Window for Generating Questions." *Journal of Adolescent & Adult Literacy* 40(6):481–483 (March 1997).

Spargo, P. E., and Enderstein, L. G. "What Questions Do They Ask? Ausubel Rephrased." *Science and Children* 34(6):43–45 (March 1997).

Tanner, M. L., and Casados, L. "Promoting and Studying Discussions in Math Classes." *Journal of Adolescent & Adult Literacy* 41(5):342–350 (February 1998).

Traver, R. "What Is a Good Guiding Question?" *Educational Leadership* 55(6): 70–73 (March 1998).

Watts, M., et al. "Children's Questions in the Classroom." *Primary Science Review* 49:6–8 (September/October 1997).

Wiggins, G., and McTighe, J. *Understanding by Design.* Chapter 2. Alexandria, VA: Association for Supervision and Curriculum Development, 1998.

Chapter 8

Strategies for Teaching: Grouping and Assignments for Positive Interaction and Quality Learning

Rather than diluting standards and expectations, exemplary schools and teachers believe in the learning potential of every student. To foster that potential, they effectively modify the key variables of time, methodology, and grouping to help individual students achieve mastery of the curriculum. In Chapter 1 we discussed ways in which time is modified. Throughout the book we talk of ways of varying the methodology. In this chapter we focus on ways of grouping students to enhance positive interaction and quality learning.

In the most effective instructional environments, during any given week or even day of school, a student might experience a succession of group settings. Ways of grouping children for instruction is the initial topic of this chapter, from individualized instruction to working with dyads, small groups, and large groups. You also will learn how to ensure equality in the classroom, how to use assignments and homework, and how to coordinate various forms of independent and small-group project-based study.

Specifically, upon completion of this chapter you should be able to

1. Describe the meaning of *mastery learning* and its implications for the classroom teacher.
2. Explain the advantages and disadvantages of various ways of grouping students for quality learning.
3. Explain how the teacher can personalize the instruction to ensure success for each student.
4. Demonstrate an understanding of the meaning and importance of classroom equity and how it can be achieved.
5. Demonstrate a theoretical and practical understanding of how to use each of these instructional

strategies effectively: assignments, homework, written and oral reports, cooperative learning, learning centers, and problem-based learning and projects.

MASTERY LEARNING AND PERSONALIZED INSTRUCTION

Learning is an individual or personal experience. Yet as a classroom teacher you will be expected to work effectively with students on other than an individual basis—often 35 or more at a time. Much has been written of the importance of individualizing the instruction for learners. Virtually all the research concerning better instructional practice emphasizes greater individualization, or personalization, of instruction.[1] We know of the individuality of the learning experience. We know that while some children are primarily verbal learners, many more are primarily visual, tactile, or kinesthetic learners. As the teacher, though, you find yourself in the difficult position of simultaneously "treating" many separate and individual learners with individual learning capacities, styles, and preferences.

In lieu of academic tracking, to individualize the learning, schools use exploratory programs, cooperative learning groups, project-based learning, and independent study to respond to the variety of individual student competencies, interests, needs, and abilities. They also use nonconventional scheduling so that teaching teams can vary the length of time in periods

---

[1] J. M. Carroll, "The Copernican Plan Evaluated," *Phi Delta Kappan* 76(2):105–113 (October 1994).

and also vary the size of instructional groups and the learning strategies within a given time period.

Common sense tells us that student achievement in learning is related to both the quality of attention and the length of time given to learning tasks. In 1968, Benjamin Bloom, building upon a model developed earlier by John Carroll, developed the concept of individualized instruction called **mastery learning,** which suggests that students need sufficient time on task (i.e., engaged time) to master content before moving on to new content.[2] From that concept Fred Keller developed an instructional plan called the Personalized System of Instruction (PSI), or the Keller Plan, which by the early 1970s enjoyed popularity and success, especially at many two-year colleges. PSI involves the student's learning from printed modules of instruction (which today would likely be presented as computer software programs) that allow the student greater control over the learning pace. The instruction is mastery oriented; that is, the student demonstrates mastery of the content of one module before proceeding to the next.

Today's Emphasis: Quality Learning for All Students

Emphasis today is on mastery of content, or quality learning, rather than coverage of content, or quantity of learning. Because of that emphasis and research indicating that quality learning programs positively effect achievement, the importance of the concept of mastery learning has resurfaced. For example, in today's efforts to restructure schools, two approaches—Results-Driven Education (RDE), also known as Outcome-Based Education (OBE), and the Coalition of Essential Schools (CES), use a goal-driven curriculum model with instruction that focuses on the construction of individual knowledge through mastery and assessment of student learning against the anticipated outcomes.[3]

In some instances, unfortunately, attention may only be on the mastery of minimum competencies; thus, students are not encouraged to work and learn to the maximum of their talents and abilities. By mastery of content, we mean that the student demonstrates his or her use of what has been learned. In some schools using

the mastery approach, the final demonstration by a student is what is known as "graduation by exhibition."[4]

Assumptions about Mastery, or Quality, Learning

Today's concept of mastery, or quality, learning is based on six assumptions:

1. Mastery learning can ensure that students experience success at each level of the instructional process. Experiencing success at each level provides incentive and motivation for further learning.
2. Mastery of content, or quality learning, is possible for all students.
3. Although all students can achieve mastery, to master a particular content, some students may require more time than others. The teacher and the school must provide for this difference in time needed to complete a task successfully.
4. For quality learning to occur, instruction must be modified and adapted, not the students. Tracking and ability grouping do not fit with the concept of mastery learning.
5. Most learning is sequential and logical.
6. Most desired learning outcomes can be specified in terms of observable and measurable performance.[5]

Components of Any Mastery Learning Model

Any instructional model designed to teach toward mastery (quality) learning will contain the following five components: (1) a clearly defined instructional objectives, (2) a preassessment of the learner's present knowledge, (3) an instructional component with choices and options for students, (4) practice, reinforcement, frequent comprehension checks (both diagnostic and formative assessment), and corrective instruction at each step to keep the learner on track, and (5) a postassessment to determine the extent of student mastery of the objectives.

Strategies for Personalizing the Instruction

You can immediately provide personalized instruction by (1) starting study of a topic from where the children are in terms of what they know (or think they know) and what they want to know about the topic (see

---

[2]See B. Bloom, *Human Characteristics and School Learning* (New York: McGraw-Hill, 1987, and J. Carroll, "A Model of School Learning," *Teachers College Record* 64(8):723–733 (May 1963).

[3]See, for example, T. R. Guskey, "Defining the Differences Between Outcome-Based Education and Mastery Learning," *School Administrator* 51(8):34–37 (September 1994). Information about CES, such as a directory of participating schools, can be obtained from <http://www.essentialschools.org>. See also W. Malloy, "Essential Schools and Inclusion: A Responsive Partnership," *Educational Forum* 60(3):228–236 (Spring 1996).

[4]See, for example, J. P. McDonald et al., *Graduation by Exhibition: Assessing Genuine Achievement* (Providence, RI: Coalition of Essential Schools, 1993).

[5]See J. Battistini, *From Theory to Practice: Classroom Application of Outcome-Based Education* (Bloomington, IN: ERIC Clearinghouse on Reading, English, and Communication, 1995), and L. Horton, *Mastery Learning*, Fastback 154 (Bloomington, IN: Phi Delta Kappa Educational Foundation, 1981).

To a great degree, student achievement in learning is determined by two factors: (1) how well students understand and follow procedures, and (2) the mode of instruction. Both of these factors are under the control of the teacher.

"think-pair-share" discussed in a section that follows titled "learning in pairs"), (2) providing students with choices from a rich variety of pathways and hands-on experiences to learn more about the topic, (3) providing multiple instructional approaches (that is, using multilevel instruction in a variety of settings, from learning alone to whole-class instruction), and (4) empowering students with responsibility for decision making, reflection, and self-assessment.

LEARNING ALONE

Some students learn well in pairs (dyads), others learn well with their peers in groups—collaboratively, cooperatively, or competitively—or collaboratively with adults, and still others learn well in combinations of these patterns. However, researchers tell us that more than 10 percent of students learn best alone. Learning-alone students often are gifted, nonconforming, able to work at their own pace successfully, and comfortable using media. Or they may be seemingly underachieving but potentially able students for whom unconventional instructional strategies, such as *contract learning packages* (agreements between the teacher and individual students to proceed with tasks appropriate to their readiness, interests, or learning profiles in a sequence and at a pace each student selects) or multisensory instructional packages, encourage academic success.[6]

LEARNING IN PAIRS

It is sometimes advantageous to pair students (dyads) for learning. Four types of dyads are described as follows.

Peer tutoring, mentoring, and cross-age coaching. Peer mentoring, tutoring, or peer-assisted learning (PAL) is a strategy whereby one classmate tutors another. It is useful, for example, when one student helps another who has limited proficiency in English or when a student skilled in math helps another who is less skilled. For many years, it has been demonstrated repeatedly that peer tutoring is a significant strategy for promoting active learning.[7] Cross-age coaching is a strategy whereby one student is coached by another from a different, and usually higher, grade level. This is similar to peer tutoring, except that the coach is from a different age level than the student being coached.[8] As discussed in Chapter 1 and in the last section of this chapter, many schools have service learning projects that involve older students mentoring younger children.

Paired team learning. Paired team learning is a strategy whereby students study and learn in teams of two. Students identified as gifted work and learn especially

[6]R. Dunn, *Strategies for Diverse Learners,* Fastback 384 (Bloomington, IN: Phi Delta Kappa Educational Foundation, 1995), p. 15.

[7]See, for example, E. S. Foster-Harrison, *Peer Tutoring for K—12 Success,* Fastback 415 (Bloomington, IN: Phi Delta Kappa Educational Foundation, 1997).

[8]See, for example, R. B. Schneider and D. Barone, "Cross-Age Tutoring," *Childhood Education* 73(3):136–143 (Spring 1997), describing a project that involved third and fourth graders reading books to younger children, and T. G. Jones et al., "Show-and-Tell Physics," *Science Teacher* 63(8):24–27 (November 1996), describing how teams of fifth graders and high school students work together to explore physical science.

Students can learn and practice useful learning skills such as brainstorming, think-pair-share, and reciprocal teaching.

The learning center is a special station located in the classroom where an individual student (or a pair of students, if student interaction is necessary for the center) can quietly work and learn at his or her own pace.

well when paired. Specific uses for paired team learning include drill partners, reading buddies, book report pairs, summary pairs, homework partners,[9] project assignment pairs, and elaborating and relating pairs.

Think-pair-share. Think-pair-share is a strategy in which students in pairs examine a new concept or topic about to be studied. After the students of each dyad discuss what they already know or think they know about the concept, they present their percep-

tions to the whole group. This is an excellent technique for discovering student's misconceptions, also called **naïve theories,** about a topic. Introducing a writing step, the modification called *think-write-pair-share,* is when the dyad thinks and writes their ideas or conclusions before sharing with the larger group.

The Learning Center

Another significantly beneficial way of pairing students for instruction (and of individualizing the instruction and learning alone and integrating the learning) is by

---

[9]See, for example, C. Kaplan, "Homework Partners," *Mathematics Teaching in the Middle School* 2(3):168–169 (January 1997).

using the learning center (LC). The LC is a special station located in the classroom where one student (or two, if student interaction is necessary or preferred at the center) can quietly work and learn at his or her own pace more about a special topic or improve specific skills. All materials needed are provided at that station, including clear instructions for operation of the center. Whereas the LC used to be thought of as belonging to the domain of elementary school teachers with self-contained classrooms, now, with block scheduling and longer class periods, the LC has special relevance for all teachers, regardless of grade level. Familiar examples are the personal computer station and the reading center.

The value of learning centers as instructional devices undoubtedly lies in the following facts. LCs can provide instructional diversity. While working at a center, the student is giving time and quality attention to the learning task (learning toward mastery) and is likely to be engaging her or his most effective learning modality, or integrating several or all modalities. To adapt instruction to students' individual needs and preferences, it is possible to design a learning environment that includes several learning centers, each of which uses a different medium and modality or focuses on a special aspect of the curriculum. Students then rotate through the various learning centers according to their needs and preferences.[10]

Learning centers are of three types. In the *direct-learning center*, performance expectations for cognitive learning are quite specific and the focus is on mastery of content. In the *open-learning center*, the goal is to provide opportunity for exploration, enrichment, motivation, and creative discovery. In the *skill center*, as in a direct-learning center, performance expectations are quite specific but the focus is on the development of a particular skill or process.

In all instances the primary reason for using a learning center is to individualize—to provide collections of materials and activities adjusted to the various readiness levels, interests, and learning profiles of students. Other reasons to use an LC are to provide (a) a mechanism for learning that crosses discipline boundaries, (b) a special place for a student with special needs, (c) opportunities for creative work, enrichment experiences, and multisensory experiences, and (d) an opportunity to learn from learning packages that use special equipment or media of which only one or a limited supply may be available in your classroom (e.g., science materials, a microscope, a computer, a laser videodisc player, or some combination of these).

To construct an LC, you can be as elaborate and as creative as your time, imagination, and resources allow. Students can even help you plan and set up learning centers, which will relieve some of the burden from your busy schedule. The following paragraphs present guidelines for setting up and using this valuable instructional tool.

The center should be designed with a theme in mind, preferably one that integrates the student's learning by providing activities that cross discipline boundaries. Decide the purpose of the center and give the center a name, such as "the center for the study of wetlands," "walking tour of Florence," "traveling to Quebec City," "structure and function," "patterns in nature," "the United Nations," "patterns of discrimination," "editing a video," "the center for worldwide communication," and so on. The purpose of the center should be clearly understood by the students. Centers should always be used for educational purposes, *never* for punishment.

The center should be designed to be attractive, purposeful, and uncluttered. It should be identified with an attractive sign. Learning centers should be activity-oriented (i.e., dependent on the student's manipulation of materials, not just paper-and-pencil tasks).

Topics for the center should be related to the instructional program for review and reinforcement, remediation, or enrichment. The center should be self-directing; thus, specific instructional objectives and procedures for using the center should be clearly posted and understandable to the student user. An audio or videocassette or a computer program is sometimes used for this purpose. The center should also be self-correcting: student users should be able to tell by the way they have completed the task whether or not they have done it correctly and have learned.

The center should contain a variety of activities geared to the varying abilities and interest levels of the students. A choice of two or more activities at a center is one way to provide for this.

Materials to be used at the center should be maintained at the center, with descriptions for use provided to the students. Materials should be safe for student use, and the center should be easily supervised by you or another adult. Some centers may become more or less permanent centers and remain for the school term or longer, whereas other centers may change according to what is being studied at the time.

LEARNING IN SMALL GROUPS

Small groups are those involving three to eight students, in either a teacher- or a student-directed setting. Using small groups for instruction, including the cooperative learning group (CLG), enhances opportunities

---

[10]A. A. Glatthorn, *Developing A Quality Curriculum* (Alexandria, VA: Association for Supervision and Curriculum Development, 1994), p. 105.

for students to assume greater control over their own learning, sometimes referred to as *empowerment*.

Purposes for Using Small Groups

Small groups can be formed to serve a number of purposes. They might be useful for a specific learning activity (e.g., reciprocal reading groups, where students take turns asking questions, summarizing, making predictions about, and clarifying a story). Or they might be formed to complete an activity that requires materials in short supply, to complete a science experiment or a project only lasting as long as the project does. Teachers have various rationales for assigning students to groups. Groups can be formed by grouping students according to (a) personality type (e.g., sometimes a teacher may want to team less-assertive students together to give them the opportunity for greater management of their own learning), (b) social pattern (e.g., sometimes it may be necessary to break up a group of rowdy friends, or it may be desirable to broaden the association among students), (c) common interest, (d) learning styles (e.g., forming groups of either mixed styles or of styles in common), or (e) according to their abilities in a particular skill or their knowledge in a particular area. One specific type of small group instruction is the cooperative learning group.

COOPERATIVE LEARNING

Lev Vygotsky (1896–1934) studied the importance of a learner's social interactions in learning situations. Vygotsky argued that learning is most effective when learners cooperate with one another in a supportive learning environment under the careful guidance of a teacher. Cooperative learning, group problem solving, problem-based learning, and cross-age tutoring are instructional strategies used by teachers that have grown in popularity as a result of research evolving from Vygotsky's work.

The Cooperative Learning Group (CLG)

The *cooperative learning group* is a heterogeneous group (i.e., mixed according to one or more criteria, such as ability or skill level, ethnicity, learning style, learning capacity, gender, and language proficiency) of three to six students who work together in a teacher- or student-directed setting, emphasizing support for one another. Often times, a CLG consists of four students of mixed ability, learning styles, gender, and ethnicity, with each member of the group assuming a particular role. Teachers usually change the membership of each group several to many times during the year.

THE THEORY AND USE OF COOPERATIVE LEARNING

The theory of cooperative learning is that when small groups of students of mixed backgrounds and capabilities work together toward a common goal, members of the group increase their friendship and respect for one another. As a consequence, each individual's self-esteem is enhanced, students are more motivated to participate in higher-order thinking, and academic achievement is accomplished.[11]

There are several techniques for using cooperative learning. Of special interest to teachers are general methods of cooperative learning, such as student team–achievement division (STAD) in which the teacher presents a lesson, students work together in teams to help each other learn the material, individuals take quizzes, and team rewards are earned based on the individual scores on the quizzes. Another method is teams-games-tournaments (TGT) in which tournaments (rather than quizzes) are held and students compete against others of similar academic achievements; winners contribute toward their team's score. Group investigations are a third option.[12] Yet the primary purpose of each is for the groups to learn—which means, of course, that individuals within a group must learn. Group achievement in learning, then, is dependent upon the learning of individuals within the group. Rather than competing for rewards for achievement, members of the group cooperate with one another by helping one another learn, so that the group reward will be a good one. Normally, the group is rewarded on the basis of group achievement, though individual members within the group can later be rewarded for individual contributions. Because of peer pressure, when using CLGs you must be cautious about using group grading. For grading purposes, bonus points can be given to all members of a group; individuals can add to their own scores when everyone in the group has reached preset standards. The preset standards must be appropriate for all members of a group. Lower standards or improvement criteria could be set for students with

[11]See, for example: J. D. Laney et al., "The Effect of Cooperative and Mastery Learning Methods on Primary Grade Students' Learning and Retention of Economic Concepts," *Early Education and Development* 7(3):253–274 (July 1996); and, R. E. Slavin, "Cooperative Learning in Middle and Secondary Schools, *Clearing House* 69(4): 200–204 (March/April 1996).

[12]For details about these CLG strategies and others, see R. E. Slavin, *Student Team Learning: A Practical Guide for Cooperative Learning*, 3rd ed. (Washington, DC: National Education Association, 1991); E. Coelho, *Learning Together in the Multicultural Classroom* (Portsmouth, NH: Heinemann, 1994); and Y. Sharan and S. Sharan, *Expanding Cooperative Learning through Group Investigation* (New York: Teachers College Press, 1992).

lower ability so everyone feels rewarded and successful. To determine each student's term grades, individual student achievement is measured later through individual students' results on tests and other criteria, and through each student's performance in the group work.

ROLES WITHIN THE COOPERATIVE LEARNING GROUP

It is advisable to assign roles (specific functions) to each member of the CLG. (The lesson plan shown in the unit plan of Figure 6.14, Chapter 6, shows the use of a CLG activity using assigned roles for a lesson in lab science.) These roles should be rotated, either during the activity or from one time to the next. Although titles may vary, five typical roles are

- *Group facilitator*—role is to keep the group on task.
- *Materials manager*—role is to obtain, maintain, and return materials needed for the group to function.
- *Recorder*—role is to record all group activities and processes and perhaps to assess periodically how the group is doing.
- *Reporter*—role is to report group processes and accomplishments to the teacher and/or to the entire class. When using groups of four members, the roles of recorder and reporter can easily be combined.
- *Thinking monitor*—role is to identify and record the sequence and processes of the group's thinking. This role encourages metacognition and the development of thinking skills.

It is important that students understand and perform their individual roles and that each member of the CLG performs her or his tasks as expected. No student should be allowed to ride on the coattails of the group. To emphasize significance and to reinforce the importance of each role, and to be able to recognize readily the role any student is playing during CLG activity, one teacher made a trip to an office supplier and had permanent badges made for the various CLG roles. During CLGs, then, each student attaches the appropriate badge to her or his clothing.

WHAT STUDENTS AND THE TEACHER DO WHEN USING COOPERATIVE LEARNING GROUPS

Actually, for learning by CLGs to work, each member of the CLG must understand and assume two roles or responsibilities: the role he or she is assigned as a member of the group and that of seeing that all others in the group are performing their roles. Sometimes this requires interpersonal skills that students have yet to learn or to learn well. This is where the teacher must assume some responsibility. Simply placing students into CLGs and expecting each member

and each group to function and to learn the expected outcomes may not work. In other words, skills of cooperation must be taught. If all your students have not yet learned the skills of cooperation, then you will have to teach them. This doesn't mean that if a group is not functioning you immediately break up the group and reassign members to new groups. Part of group learning is learning the process of how to work out conflict. A group may require your assistance to work out a conflict. With your guidance the group should be able to discover what problem is causing the conflict, identify some options, and mediate at least a temporary solution. If a particular skill is needed, then with your guidance students identify and learn that skill.

WHEN TO USE COOPERATIVE LEARNING GROUPS

CLGs can be used for problem solving, investigations, opinion surveys, experiments, review, project work, test making, or almost any other instructional purpose. Just as you would for small group work in general, you can use CLGs for most any purpose at any time, but as with any other type of instructional strategy, it should not be overused.

OUTCOMES OF USING COOPERATIVE LEARNING GROUPS

When the process is well planned and managed, the outcomes of cooperative learning include (a) improved communication and relationships of acceptance among students of differences, (b) quality learning with fewer off-task behaviors, and (c) increased academic achievement. For example, for the latter, students who practice in cooperative groups demonstrate greater long-term memory of problem-solving strategies in mathematics.[13] In the words of Good and Brophy,

> Cooperative learning arrangements promote friendships and prosocial interaction among students who differ in achievement, sex, race, or ethnicity, and they promote the acceptance of mainstreamed handicapped students by their nonhandicapped classmates. Cooperative methods also frequently have positive effects, and rarely have negative effects, on affective outcomes such as self-esteem, academic self-confidence, liking for the class, liking and feeling liked by classmates, and various measures of empathy and social cooperation.[14]

---

[13]See, for example, P. E. Duren and A. Cherrington, "The Effects of Cooperative Group Work versus Independent Practice on the Learning of Some Problem-Solving Strategies," *School Science and Mathematics* 92(2):80–83 (February 1992).

[14]T. L. Good and J. E. Brophy, *Looking in Classrooms*, 7th ed. (New York: Longman, 1997), p. 278.

WHY SOME TEACHERS HAVE DIFFICULTY
USING CLGS

Sometimes, when they think they are using CLGs, teachers have difficulty and either give up trying to use the strategy or simply tell students to divide into groups for an activity and call it cooperative learning.[15] For the strategy to work, each student must be given training in and have acquired basic skills in interaction and group processing. Students must realize that individual achievement rests with that of their group. And, as true for any other strategy, the use of CLGs must not be overused. Teachers must vary their strategies.

For CLGs to work well, advance planning and effective management are a must. Students must be instructed in the necessary skills for group learning. Each student must be assigned a responsible role within the group and be held accountable for fulfilling that responsibility. When a CLG activity is in process, groups must be continually monitored by the teacher for possible breakdown of this process within a group. In other words, while students are working in groups the teacher must exercise his or her skills of withitness. When a potential breakdown is noticed, the teacher quickly intervenes to help the group get back on track.

LEARNING IN LARGE GROUPS

Large groups are those that involve more than eight students, usually the entire class. Most often, they are teacher-directed. Student presentations and whole-class discussions are two techniques that involve the use of large groups.

Student Presentations

Students should be encouraged to be presenters for discussion of the ideas, opinions, and knowledge obtained from their own independent and small-group study. Several techniques encourage the development of certain skills, such as studying and organizing material, discovery, discussion, rebuttal, listening, analysis, suspending judgment, and critical thinking. Possible forms of discussions involving student presentations are described in the following paragraphs.

- *Debate.* The debate is an arrangement in which formal speeches are made by members of two opposing teams, on topics preassigned and researched. The speeches are followed by rebuttals from each team.
- *Jury trial.* The jury trial is a discussion approach in which the class simulates a courtroom, with class members playing various roles of judge, attorneys, jury members, bailiff, and court recorder.[16]
- *Panel.* The panel is a setting in which from four to six students, with one designated as the chairperson or moderator, discuss a topic about which they have studied, followed by a question-and-answer period involving the entire class. The panel usually begins with each panel member giving a brief opening statement.
- *Research report.* One or two students or a small group of students gives a report on a topic they investigated, followed by questions and discussions by the entire class.
- *Roundtable.* The roundtable is a small group of three to five students, who sit around a table and discuss among themselves (or with the rest of the class listening and perhaps later asking questions) a problem or issue they have studied. One member of the panel may serve as moderator.
- *Symposium.* Similar to a roundtable discussion but more formal, the symposium is an arrangement in which each student participant presents an explanation of his or her position on a preassigned topic researched by the student. Again, one student should serve as moderator. After the presentations, questions are accepted from the rest of the class.

To use these techniques effectively, students may need to be coached by you—individually, in small groups, or in whole class sessions—on: how and where to gather information; how to listen, take notes, select major points, organize material, and present a position succinctly and convincingly (see Figure 8.1); how to play roles; and how to engage in dialogue and debate with one another.

Whole Class Discussion

Direct whole-class discussion is a teaching technique used frequently by most or all teachers. On this topic, you should consider yourself an expert. Having been a student in formal learning for at least fifteen years, you are undoubtedly knowledgeable about the advantages and disadvantages of whole-class discussions, at least from your personal vantage point. Explore your knowledge and share your experiences by responding to Exercise 8.1. Then do Exercise 8.2, in which guidelines for using whole-class discussion will be generated.

---

[15]See, for example, C. A. Tomlinson et al., "Use of Cooperative Learning at the Middle Level: Insights from a National Survey," *Research in Middle Level Education Quarterly* 20(4):37–55 (Summer 1997).

[16]See, for example, M. A. Jones, "Use of a Classroom Jury Trial to Enhance Students' Perceptions of Science as Part of Their Lives," *Journal of Chemical Education* 74(5):537 (May 1997).

Figure 8.1 Sample scoring rubric for group presentations.
(Can be adapted for individual presentations).

GROUP PRESENTATION SCORING RUBRIC

5. Presentation was excellent. Clear understanding of their project and organized in delivery.

- Made eye contact throughout presentation
- Spoke loud enough for all to hear
- Spoke clearly
- Spoke for time allotted
- Stood straight and confidently
- Covered at least five pieces of important information
- Introduced project
- All members spoke

4. Presentation was well thought out and planned.

- Made eye contact throughout most of presentation
- Spoke loud enough and clearly most of the time
- Spoke nearly for time allotted
- Covered at least four pieces of important information
- Introduced project
- All members spoke

3. Adequate presentation. Mostly organized.

- Made eye contact at times
- Some of audience could hear the presentation
- Audience could understand most of what was said
- Spoke for about half of time allotted
- At least half of team spoke
- Covered at least three pieces of important information
- Project was vaguely introduced

2–1. Underprepared presentation. Disorganized and incomplete information.

- No eye contact during presentation
- Most of audience was unable to hear presentation
- Information presented was unclear
- Spoke for only brief time
- Covered less than three pieces of information
- Project was not introduced or only vaguely introduced

EXERCISE 8.1 WHOLE-CLASS DISCUSSION AS A TEACHING STRATEGY: WHAT DO I ALREADY KNOW?

INSTRUCTIONS: Answer the following questions, and then share your responses with your class, perhaps in discussion groups organized by subject field or grade level.

1. Your grade-level interest or subject field: _____

2. For what reasons would you hold a whole-class discussion? _____

   _____

   _____

   _____

3. Assuming that your classroom has movable seats, how would you arrange them? _____

   _____

   _____

   _____

4. What would you do if the seats were not movable? _____

   _____

   _____

   _____

5. What rules would you establish before starting the discussion? _____

   _____

   _____

   _____

6. Should student participation be forced? Why or why not? If so, how? _____

   _____

   _____

   _____

7. How would you discourage a few students from dominating the discussion? _____

   _____

   _____

   _____

8. What preparation should the students and teacher be expected to make before beginning the discussion?

   _____

   _____

   _____

☞

EXERCISE 8.1 (*continued*)

9. How would you handle digression from the topic? _____

_____

_____

_____

10. Should students be discussion leaders? Why or why not? If so, what training, if any, should they receive,

and how? _____

_____

_____

_____

_____

11. What teacher roles are options during a class discussion? _____

_____

_____

_____

_____

12. When is each of these roles most appropriate? _____

_____

_____

_____

13. When, if ever, is it appropriate to hold a class meeting for discussing class procedures, not subject matter?

_____

_____

_____

14. Can brainstorming be a form of whole-class discussion? Why or why not? _____

_____

_____

_____

_____

15. What follow-up activities would be appropriate after a whole-class discussion? On what basis would you

decide to use each? _____

_____

_____

_____

EXERCISE 8.1 (*continued*)

16. What sorts of activities should precede a class discussion? _____

_____

_____

_____

_____

17. Should a discussion be given a set length? Why or why not? If so, how long? How is the length to be

decided? _____

_____

_____

_____

_____

18. Should students be graded for their participation in class discussion? Why or why not? If so, how? On

what basis? By whom? _____

_____

_____

_____

_____

19. For effective discussions, 10 to 12 feet is the maximum recommended distance between participants.

During a teacher-led discussion, what can a teacher do to keep within this limit? _____

_____

_____

_____

20. Are there any pitfalls or other points of importance that a teacher should be aware of when planning

and implementing a whole-class discussion? If so, explain them and how to guard against them. _____

_____

_____

_____

EXERCISE 8.2 WHOLE-CLASS DISCUSSION AS A TEACHING STRATEGY: BUILDING UPON WHAT I ALREADY KNOW

INSTRUCTIONS: Share your responses to Exercise 8.1 with your colleagues. Then individually answer the first two questions below. Next, as a group, use all three questions to guide you as you generate a list of five general guidelines for the use of whole-class discussion as a strategy in teaching. Share your group's guidelines with the entire class. Then, as a class, derive a final list of general guidelines.

1. How effective was your small-group discussion in sharing Exercise 8.1? _____

_____

_____

_____

_____

_____

_____

_____

_____

2. What allowed for or inhibited the effectiveness of that small-group discussion? _____

_____

_____

_____

_____

_____

_____

_____

_____

_____

3. How effective was this small-group discussion? Why? _____

_____

_____

_____

_____

_____

_____

_____

_____

_____

EXERCISE 8.2 (continued)

General Guidelines Generated from Small-Group Discussion

1. _____

    _____

2. _____

    _____

3. _____

    _____

4. _____

    _____

5. _____

    _____

General Guidelines: Final List Derived from Whole Class

_____

_____

_____

_____

_____

_____

_____

_____

_____

_____

_____

_____

_____

_____

_____

_____

_____

_____

_____

EQUALITY IN THE CLASSROOM

Especially when conducting direct whole-group discussions, it is easy for a teacher to fall into the trap of interacting with only "the stars," or only those in the front of the room or on one side, or only the most vocal and assertive. You must exercise caution and avoid falling into that trap. To ensure a psychologically safe and effective environment for learning for every person in your classroom, you must attend to all students and try to involve all students equally in all class activities. You must avoid any biased expectations about certain students, and you must avoid discriminating against students according to their gender or some other personal characteristic.

Research has identified the unintentional tendency of teachers of *both* sexes to discriminate on the basis of gender. For example, teachers, along with the rest of society, tend to have lower expectations for girls than for boys in mathematics and science. They tend to call on and encourage boys more than girls. They often let boys interrupt girls but praise girls for being polite and waiting their turn. To avoid such discrimination may take special effort on your part, no matter how aware of the problem you may be. Some researchers believe the problem is so insidious that separate courses about gender bias are needed in teacher training.[17]

To guarantee equity in interaction with students, many teachers have found it helpful to ask someone secretly to tally classroom interactions between the teacher and students during a class discussion. After an analysis of the results, the teacher arrives at decisions about his or her own attending and facilitating behaviors. Such an analysis is the purpose of Exercise 8.3. You are welcome to make blank copies and share them with your teaching colleagues.

In addition to the variables mentioned at the beginning of Exercise 8.3, the exercise can be modified to include responses and their frequencies according to other teacher-student interactions, such as your calling on all students equally for responses to your questions, calling on students equally to assist you with classroom helping jobs, chastising students for inappropriate behavior, or asking questions to assume classroom leadership roles.

Ensuring Equity

In addition to the advice given in Chapter 7 about using questioning, many other strategies can help ensure that students are treated fairly in the classroom, including the following:

- Encourage students to demonstrate an appreciation for one another by applauding all individual and group presentations.
- Have and maintain high expectations, although not necessarily identical expectations, for all students.
- Insist on politeness in the classroom. For example, a student can be shown appreciation with a sincere "thank you" or "I appreciate your contribution," or with a genuine smile for her or his contribution to the learning process.
- Insist that students be allowed to finish what they are saying without being interrupted by others. Be certain you model this behavior yourself.
- During whole-class instruction, insist that students raise their hands and be called on by you before they are allowed to speak.
- Keep a stopwatch handy to control unobtrusively the wait time given for each student. Although at first this idea may sound impractical, it works.
- Use a seating chart attached to a clipboard, and next to each student's name, make a tally for each interaction you have with a student. This also is a good way to maintain records to reward students for their contributions to class discussion. Again, it is workable at any grade level. The seating chart can be laminated so it can be used day after day simply by erasing the marks of the previous day.

Now complete Exercise 8.3, through which you will examine a teacher's behavior with students according to gender.

---

[17]See, for example, S. Zaher, "Gender and Curriculum in the School Room," *Education Canada* 36(1):26–29 (Spring 1996), and S. M. Bailey, "Shortchanging Girls and Boys," *Educational Leadership* 53(8):75–79 (May 1996). For information on how to identify equity problems and develop programs to help school achieve academic excellence for all students contact EQUITY 2000, 1233 20th St. NW, Washington, DC 20056-2304; 202-822-5930.

EXERCISE 8.3 TEACHER INTERACTION WITH STUDENTS ACCORDING TO STUDENT GENDER

INSTRUCTIONS: The purpose of this exercise is to provide a tool for analysis of your own interactions with students according to gender. To become accustomed to the exercise, you should do a trial run in one of your university classes, then use it during your student teaching and again during your first years of teaching. The exercise can be modified to include (1 the amount of time given for each interaction, (2) the response time given by teacher according to student gender, and (3) other student characteristics, such as ethnicity.

Prior to class, select a student (this will be you during the trial run recommended above) or an outside observer, such as a colleague, to do the tallying and calculations, as follows. Ask the person to tally secretly the interactions between you and students by placing a mark after the name of each student (or on the student's position on a seating chart) with whom you have verbal interaction. If a student does the tallying, he or she should not be counted in any of the calculations.

Exact time at start _____

Exact time at end _____

Total time in minutes _____

CALCULATIONS BEFORE TALLYING

a. Total number of students _____

b. Number of female students _____

c. Number of male students _____

d. Percentage of students who are female _____ (= b divided by a)

e. Percentage of students who are male _____ (= c divided by a)

(Check: d + e should = 100%)

CALCULATIONS AFTER TALLYING

f. Total females interacting _____

g. Total males interacting _____

h. Percentage of students interacting _____ (f + g divided by a)

i. Total female tallies _____

j. Total male tallies _____

k. Total of all tallies (i + j) _____

l. Percentage interacting students who are female _____ (i divided by k)

m. Percentabe interacting students who are male _____ (j divided by k)

n. Most tallies for any one male _____

o. Percentage of class interactions directed to most frequently addressed male _____ (n divided by k)

p. Most tallies for any female _____

q. Percentage of class interactions directed to most frequently addressed female _____ (p divided by k)

EXERCISE 8.3 (*continued*)

TEACHER CONCLUSIONS

_____
_____
_____
_____
_____
_____
_____
_____
_____
_____
_____
_____
_____
_____
_____
_____
_____
_____
_____
_____
_____
_____
_____
_____
_____
_____
_____
_____
_____
_____
_____
_____

LEARNING FROM ASSIGNMENTS AND HOMEWORK

An assignment is a statement of *what* the student is to accomplish and is tied to a specific instructional objective. Assignments, whether completed at home or at school, can ease student learning in many ways, but when poorly planned they can discourage the student and upset an entire family. *Homework* can be defined as any out-of-class task a student is assigned as an extension of classroom learning. Like all else you do as a teacher, it is your professional responsibility to think about and plan carefully any and all homework assignments you give to students. Consider how you would feel were you given the assignment and about how much out-of-class time you expect the assignment to take.

Purposes for Assignments

Purposes for giving homework assignments can be any of the following: to extend constructively the time students are engaged in learning, to help students to develop personal learning, to help students to develop their research skills, to help students to develop their study skills, to help students to organize their learning, to individualize the learning, to involve parents and guardians in their children's' learning,[18] to provide a mechanism by which students receive constructive feedback, to provide students with opportunity to review and practice what has been learned, to reinforce classroom experiences, and to teach new content.

Guidelines for Using Assignments

To use assignments, consider the guidelines in the following paragraphs. While an assignment is a statement of *what* the student is to accomplish, procedures are statements of *how* to do something. Although students may need some procedural guidelines, especially with respect to your expectations on an assignment, generally you will want to avoid supplying too much detail on how to accomplish an assignment.

Plan early and thoughtfully the types of assignments you will give (e.g., daily and long-range; minor and major; in class, at home, or both; individual, paired, or group[19]), and prepare assignment specifications. Assignments must correlate with specific instructional objectives and should *never* be given as busy work or as punishment. For each assignment, let students know the purpose, for example, whether the assignment is to prepare the student for what is to come in class, to practice what has been learned in class, or to extend the learning of class activities.

Use caution in giving assignments that could be controversial or pose a hazard to the safety of students. In such cases (especially if you are new to the community), before giving the assignment it is probably a good idea to talk it over with members of your teaching team, the departmental chair, or an administrator. Also, for a particular assignment, you may need to have parental or guardian permission and even support for students to do it or be prepared to give an alternate assignment for some students.

Provide differentiated, tiered, or optional assignments, variations given to students or selected by them on the basis of their interests and learning capacities.[20] Students can select or be assigned different activities to accomplish the same objective, such as read and discuss, or they can participate with others in a more direct learning experience. After their study, as a portion of the assignment, students share what they have learned. This is an example of using multilevel teaching.

The time a student needs to complete assignments beyond school time will vary according to grade level and school policy. There is considerable debate about the value of homework, especially for the elementary grades.[21] Very generally, children in lower elementary grades may be expected to spend from none to about 15 minutes each school night on homework, while children in the upper elementary and middle school grades may spend 40 minutes to an hour or so, while students in high school may have two or more hours of homework each school night.

Teachers have found it beneficial to prepare individualized study guides with questions to be answered and activities to be done by the student while reading textbook chapters as homework. One advantage of a study guide is that it can make the reading more than a visual experience. A study guide can help to organize student learning by accenting instructional objectives, emphasizing important points to be learned, providing a guide for studying for tests, and encouraging the student to read the homework assignment.

As a general rule, homework assignments should stimulate thinking by arousing a student's curiosity, raising questions for further study, and encouraging and supporting the self-discipline required for independent study.

---

[18] A useful reference for teachers and parents is M. C. Radencich and J. S. Schumm, *How to Help Your Child with Homework: Every Caring Parents' Guide to Encouraging Good Study Habits and Ending the Homework Wars* (For Parents of Children Ages 6–13), rev. ed. (Minneapolis, MN: Free Spirit, 1997).

[19] See, for example, C. Kaplan, "Homework Partners," *Mathematics Teaching in the Middle School* 2(3):168–169 (January 1997).

[20] See, for example, M. H. Sullivan and P. V. Sequeira, "The Impact of Purposeful Homework on Learning," *Clearing House* 69(6):346–348 (July/August 1996).

[21] See, for example, S. Black, "The Truth about Homework," *American School Board Journal* 183(10):48–51 (October 1996).

Determine the resources students will need to complete assignments, and check the availability of these resources. This is important; students can't be expected to use that which is unavailable to them. Many will not use that which is not readily available.

Avoid yelling out assignments as students are leaving your classroom. When giving assignments in class, you should write them on a special place on the writing board, give a copy to each student, require that each student write the assignment into his or her assignment folder, or include them in the course syllabus. Take extra care to be sure that assignment specifications are clear to students and allow time for students to ask questions about an assignment. It's important that your procedure for giving and collecting assignments be consistent throughout the school year.

Students should be given sufficient time to complete their assignments. In other words, avoid announcing an assignment that is due the very next day. As a general rule, all assignments should be given much sooner than the day before they are due. Try to avoid changing assignment specifications after they are given. Especially avoid changing them at the last minute. Changing specifications at the last minute can be frustrating to students who have already completed the assignment, and it shows little respect for those students.

Allow time in class for students to begin work on homework assignments, so you can give them individual attention (guided or coached practice). Your ability to coach students is *the reason* for in-class time to begin work on assignments. As you have learned, many secondary schools have extended the length of class periods to allow more in-class time for teacher guidance on assignments. The benefits of this coached practice include being able to (1) monitor student work so that a student does not go too far in a wrong direction, (2) help students reflect on their thinking, (3) assess the progress of individual students, and (4) discover or create a "teachable moment." For example, while monitoring students doing their work, you might discover a commonly shared student misconception. Then, taking advantage of this teachable moment, you stop and talk about that and attempt to clarify the misconception.

Timely, constructive, and corrective feedback from the teacher on the homework—and grading of homework—increases the positive contributions of homework.[22] If the assignment is important for students to do, then you must give your full and immediate attention to the product of their efforts. Read almost everything that students write. Students are much more willing to do homework when they believe it is useful, when it is treated as an integral part of instruction, when it is read and evaluated by the teacher, and when it counts as part of the grade.

Provide feedback about each student's work, and be positive and constructive in your comments. Always think about the written comments that you make to be relatively certain they will convey your intended message to the student. When writing comments on student papers, consider using a color other than red, such as green or blue. Although to you this may sound unimportant, to many people, red brings with it a host of negative connotations (e.g., blood, hurt, danger, stop).

Rather than grading by giving a percentage or numerical grade, with its negative connotations, teachers sometimes prefer to score assignments with constructive and reinforcing comments and symbols they have created for this purpose.

Regardless of grade level or subject taught, you must give attention to the development of students' reading, listening, speaking, and writing skills. Attention to these skills must also be obvious in your assignment specifications and your assignment grading policy. Reading is crucial to the development of a person's ability to write. For example, to foster high-order thinking, students in any subject can and should be encouraged to write (in their journals, as discussed in Chapter 5 and later in this chapter), or draw representations of their thoughts and feelings about the material they have read.

Strategies for Student Recovery

Although it is important to encourage good initial efforts by students, sometimes, for a multitude of reasons, a student's first effort is inadequate or is lacking entirely. Perhaps the student is absent from school without legitimate excuse, or the student does poorly on an assignment or fails to turn in an assignment on time, or at all. Although accepting late work from students is extra work for the teacher, and although allowing the resubmission of a marked or tentative-graded paper increases the amount of paperwork, many teachers report that it is worthwhile to give students opportunity for recovery and a day or so to make corrections and resubmit an assignment for an improved score. However, out of regard for students who do well from the start you are advised against allowing a resubmitted paper to receive an *A* grade (unless, of course, it was an *A* paper originally).

Talent Development schools (discussed in Chapter 4) provide recovery methods that encourage students by recognizing both achievement and improvement on report cards and by providing students with second opportunities for success on assignments, although at some cost to encourage a good first effort. For example, although the school's policy is that a student automatically fails a course when the student accumulates

---

[22]H. J. Walberg, "Productive Teaching and Instruction: Assessing the Knowledge Base," *Phi Delta Kappan* 71(6):472 (February 1990).

five or more absences per quarter, each absence can be nullified if the student accumulates perfect school attendance for five consecutive days.[23]

Students sometimes have legitimate reasons for not completing an assignment by the due date. (Consider the classroom vignette "Late Homework Paper from an At-Risk Student.") It is my opinion that the teacher should listen and exercise professional judgment in each instance. As someone once said, there is nothing democratic about treating unequals as equals. The provision of recovery options seems a sensible and scholastic tactic.

CLASSROOM VIGNETTE

Late Homework Paper from an At-Risk Student

An eleventh grade student turned in an English class assignment several days late and the paper was accepted by the teacher without penalty although the teacher's policy was that late papers would be severely penalized. During the week that the assignment was due, the student had suffered a miscarriage. In this instance her teacher accepted the paper late sans penalty because the student carried a great deal of psychological baggage and the teacher felt that turning in the paper at all was a positive act. If the paper had not been accepted or had been accepted only with severe penalty to her grade, then, in the teacher's opinion, the student would have simply quit trying and probably dropped out of school altogether.

How to Avoid Having So Many Papers to Grade That Time for Effective Planning Is Restricted

A downfall for some beginning teachers is that of being buried under mounds of homework to be read and graded, leaving less and less time for effective planning. To keep this from happening to you, consider the following suggestions. Although in my opinion the teacher should read almost everything that students write, papers can be read with varying degrees of intensity and scrutiny, depending on the purpose of the assignment. For assignments that are designed for learning, understanding, and practice, you can allow students to check them themselves using either self-checking or peer checking. During the peer or self-checking, you can walk around the room, monitor the activity, and record whether a student did the assignment or not. Or, after the checking, you can collect the papers and do your recording. In addition to reducing the amount of paperwork for you, student peer or self-

checking provides other advantages: (1) it allows students to see and understand their errors, (2) it encourages productive peer dialogue, and (3) it helps them develop self-assessment techniques and standards. If the purpose of the assignment is to assess mastery competence, then the papers should be read, marked, and graded only by you.

PROJECT-CENTERED LEARNING: GUIDING LEARNING FROM INDEPENDENT AND GROUP INVESTIGATIONS, PAPERS, AND ORAL REPORTS

For the most meaningful student learning to occur, independent study, individual writing, student-centered projects, and oral reports should be major features of your instruction. There will be times when students are interested in an in-depth inquiry of a topic and will want to pursue a particular topic for study. This undertaking of a learning project can be flexible: the investigation can be done by an individual student, a team of two, a small group, or the entire class. The *project* is a relatively long-term investigative study from which students produce something called the *culminating presentation*. It is a way for students to apply what they are learning. The culminating presentation is a final presentation that usually includes an oral and written report accompanied by a hands-on item of some kind (e.g., a display, play or skit, book, song or poem, multimedia presentation, diorama, poster, maps, charts, and so on.)

Values and Purposes of Project-Centered Learning

The values and purposes of encouraging project-centered learning are to:

- Develop individual skills in cooperation and social interaction.
- Develop student skills in writing, communication, and higher-level thinking and doing.
- Foster student engagement, independent learning, and thinking skills.
- Optimize personal meaning of the learning to each student by considering, valuing, and accommodating individual interests, learning styles, learning capacities, and life experiences.
- Provide opportunity for each student to become especially knowledgeable and experienced in one area of subject content or in one process skill, thus adding to the student's knowledge and experience base and sense of importance and self-worth.
- Provide opportunity for students to become intrinsically motivated to learn because they are working on

[23] V. LaPoint et al., *Report 1: The Talent Development High School—Essential Components* [Online]. Available (Downloaded June 19, 1998): <http://www.csos.jhu.edu/crespar/CRESPAR%20Reports/report01entire.html>, 6.

topics of personal meaning, with outcomes and even time lines that are relatively open ended.

- Provide opportunity for students to make decisions about their own learning and to develop their skills in managing time and materials.
- Provide opportunity for students to make some sort of a real contribution.

As has been demonstrated time and again, when students choose their own projects, integrating knowledge as the need arises, motivation and learning follow naturally.[24]

GUIDELINES FOR GUIDING STUDENTS IN PROJECT-CENTERED LEARNING

In collaboration with the teacher, students select a topic for the project. What you can do is to stimulate ideas and provide anchor studies. You can stimulate ideas by providing lists of things students might do, by mentioning each time an idea comes up in class that this would be a good idea for an independent, small group, or class project, by having former students tell about their projects, by showing the results of other students' projects (anchor studies), by suggesting Internet resources and readings that are likely to give students ideas, and by using class discussions to brainstorm ideas.

Sometimes a teacher will write the general problem or topic in the center of a graphic web and ask the students to brainstorm some questions. The questions will lead to ways for students to investigate, draw sketches, construct models, record findings, predict items, compare and contrast, and discuss understandings. In essence, brainstorming is the technique often used by teachers in collaboration with students for the selection of an interdisciplinary thematic unit of study.

Allow students to choose individually whether they will work alone, in pairs, or in small groups. If they choose to work in groups, then help them delineate job descriptions for each member of the group. For project work, groups of four or less students usually work better than groups of more than four. Even if the project is one the whole class is pursuing, the project should be broken down into parts with individuals or small groups of students undertaking independent study of these parts.

You can keep track of the students' progress by reviewing weekly updates of their work. Set deadlines with the groups. Meet with groups daily to discuss any

With coaching from the teacher, as investigators and presenters, students learn and develop important skills such as studying, organizing, analyzing, synthesizing, and presenting.

questions or problems they have. Based on their investigations, the students will prepare and present their findings in culminating presentations.

Provide coaching and guidance. Work with each student or student team in topic selection and in the processes of written and oral reporting. Allow students to develop their own procedures, but guide their preparation of work outlines and preliminary drafts, giving them constructive feedback and encouragement along the way. Aid students in their identification of potential resources and in research techniques. Your coordination with the library and other resource centers is central to the success of project-centered teaching. Frequent drafts and progress reports from the students are a must. With each of these stages, provide students with constructive feedback and encouragement. Provide written guidelines and negotiate time lines for the outlines, drafts, and completed project.

Promote sharing. Insist that students share both the progress and the results of their study with the rest of the class. The amount of time allowed for this sharing will, of course, depend upon many variables. The value of this type of instructional strategy comes not

[24]See, for example, M. Tassinari, "Hands-On Projects Take Students Beyond the Book," *Social Studies Review* 34(3):16–20 (Spring 1996); D. K. Meyer et al., "Challenge in a Mathematics Classroom: Students' Motivation and Strategies in Project-Based Learning," *Elementary School Journal* 97(5):501–521 (May 1997); and, "Lilian Katz on the Project Approach," *Scholastic Early Childhood Today* (10(6):20–21 (March 1996).

only from individual contributions but also from the learning that results from the experience and the communication of that experience with others.

Without careful planning and unless students are given steady guidance, project-based teaching can be a frustrating experience, for both students and the teacher, especially for a beginning teacher who is inexperienced in such an undertaking. Students should do projects because they want to and because the project seems meaningful. Therefore, students with guidance from you should decide *what* project to do and *how* to do it. Your role is to advise and guide students so they experience success. If a project is laid out in too much detail by the teacher, that project is a procedure rather than a student-centered project. There must be a balance between structure and opportunities for student choices and decision making. Without frequent progress reporting by the student and guidance and reinforcement from the teacher, a student can get frustrated and quickly lose interest in the project.

WRITING SHOULD BE A REQUIRED
COMPONENT OF PROJECT-CENTERED LEARNING
Provide options but insist that writing (or drawing) be a part of each student's work. Research examining the links among writing, thinking, and learning has helped emphasize the importance of writing. Writing is a complex intellectual behavior and process that helps the learner create and record his or her understanding—that is, to construct meaning. Insist that writing be a part of the student's work (see section that follows).

When teachers use project-centered teaching with upper elementary and older students, a paper and an oral presentation are usually automatically required of all students. It is recommended that you use the *I-Search paper* instead of the traditional research paper. Under your careful guidance, the students (1) lists things they would like to know and from the list select one that becomes the research topic, (2) conduct the study while maintaining a log of activities and findings, which, in fact, becomes a process journal, (3) prepare a booklet of paragraphs and visual representations that presents their findings, (4) prepare a summary of the findings, including the significance of the study and their personal feelings, and (5) share the project as a final oral report with the teacher and classmates.

ASSESS THE FINAL PRODUCT
The final product of the project, including papers, oral reports, and presentations, should be graded. The method of determining the grade should be clear to students from the beginning, along with the weight of the project grade toward the term grade. Provide students with clear descriptions (rubrics) of how evaluation and grading will be done. Evaluation should include meeting deadlines for drafts and progress reports. The final grade for the study should be based on four criteria: (a) organization, including meeting draft deadlines; (b) the quality and quantity of both content and procedural knowledge gained from the experience; (c) the quality of the student's sharing of that learning experience with the rest of the class; and (d) the quality of the student's final written or oral report. For oral presentations, a sample scoring rubric and a checklist are shown in Figures 8.1 and 11.4, respectively; for scoring rubrics for research papers and other aspects of project study, see Figures 11.10 and 11.11.

WRITING ACROSS THE CURRICULUM

Because writing is a discrete representation of thinking, every teacher should consider himself or herself to be a teacher of writing. In exemplary schools, student writing is encouraged in all subjects, across the curriculum.

Kinds of Writing

A student should experience a variety of kinds of writing rather than the same form, class after class, year after year. Perhaps most important is that writing should be emphasized as a process that illustrates one's thinking, rather than solely as a product completed as an assignment. Writing and thinking develop best when students experience during any school day various forms of writing to express their ideas, such as the following.

Analysis—speculation about effects. The writer conjectures about the causes and effects of a specific event.

Autobiographical incident. The writer narrates a specific event in his or her life and states or implies the significance of the event.

Evaluation. The writer presents a judgment on the worth of an item—book, movie, artwork, consumer product—and supports this with reasons and evidence.

Eyewitness account. The writer tells about a person, group, or event that was objectively observed from the outside.

Firsthand biographical sketch. Through incident and description, the writer characterizes a person he or she knows well.

Problem solving. The writer describes and analyzes a specific problem and then proposes and argues for a solution.

Report of information. The writer collects data from observation and research and chooses material that best represents a phenomenon or concept.

Story. Using dialogue and description, the writer shows conflict between characters or between a character and the environment.

Student Journals

Many teachers across the curriculum have their students maintain journals in which the students keep a log of their activities, findings, and thoughts (i.e., *process journals,* as discussed above) and write their thoughts about what it is they are studying (*response journals,* as discussed in Chapter 5). Actually, commonly used are two types of response journals: dialogue journals and reading-response journals. *Dialogue journals* are used for students to write anything that is on their minds, usually on the right side of a page, while peers, teachers, and parents or guardians respond on the left side of a page, thereby "talking with" the journal writer. *Response journals* are used for students to write (and perhaps draw—a "visual learning log") their reactions to what is being studied. (See also "double-entry response journal" in Chapter 5.)

Purpose and Assessment of Student Journal Writing

Normally, academic journals are *not* the personal diaries of the writer's recollection of daily events and the writer's thoughts about the events. Rather, the purpose of journal writing is to encourage students to write, to think about their writing, to record their creative thoughts about *what they are learning,* and to share their written thoughts with an audience—all of which help in the development of their thinking skills, in their learning, and in their development as writers. Students are encouraged to write about experiences, both in school and out, that are related to the topics being studied. They should be encouraged to record their feelings about what and how they are learning.

Journal writing provides practice in expression and should not be graded by the teacher. Negative comments and evaluations from the teacher will discourage creative and spontaneous expression by students. Teachers should read the journal writing and then offer constructive and positive feedback, but teachers should avoid negative comments or grading the journals. For grading purposes, most teachers simply record whether or not a student does, in fact, maintain the required journal.

The National Council of Teachers of English (NCTE) has developed guidelines for journal writing. Your school English/language arts department will likely have a copy of these guidelines, or you can contact NCTE directly or via the Internet. Resources on writing across the curriculum are shown in Figure 8.2.

Figure 8.2 Resources for writing across the curriculum.

- The American Literacy Council at 212-781-0099, e-mail to *amspell@aol.com,* or web page at <http://www.under.org/alc/welcome.htm>.
- International Reading Association, 800 Barksdale Road, Newark, DE 19711.
- Maxwell, R. J. *Writing Across the Curriculum in Middle and High Schools* (Des Moines, IA: Allyn and Bacon, 1996).
- National Center for the Study of Writing and Literature (NCSWL), School of Education, University of California—Berkeley, Berkeley, CA 94720. (Having completed its mission the NCSWL no longer functions as an independent entity; its publications may be obtained from the NWP headquarters.)
- National Council of Teachers of English, 1111 Kenyon Road, Urbana, IL 61801, <http://www.ncte.org>.
- National Writing Project (NWP), 5627 Tolman Hall, University of California—Berkeley, Berkeley, CA 94720. Web page at <http://www-gse.berkeley.edu/research/nwp/nwp.html>. E-mail to *writ@violet.berkeley.edu.*
- Pugalee, D. K. "Connecting Writing to the Mathematics Curriculum." *Mathematics Teacher* 90(4):308–310 (April 1997).
- Whole Language Umbrella, Unit 6-846, Marion Street, Winnipeg, Manitoba, Canada R2JOK4.
- Writing to Learn, Council for Basic Education, 725 15th Street, NW, Washington, DC 20005.

A COLLECTION OF ANNOTATED MOTIVATIONAL TEACHING STRATEGIES WITH IDEAS FOR LESSONS, INTERDISCIPLINARY TEACHING, TRANSCULTURAL STUDIES, AND STUDENT PROJECTS

Today's youth are used to multimillion-dollar productions on television, videodiscs, arcade games, and the movie screen. When they come into a classroom and are subjected each day to something short of a high-budget production, it is little wonder that they sometimes react in a less than highly motivated fashion. No doubt, today's youth are growing up in a highly stimulated instant-action society, a society that has learned to expect instant headache relief, instant meals, instant gratification, and perhaps, in the minds of many youth, instant high-paying employment for jobs that entail more fun than hard work. In light of this cultural phenomenon, I am on your side: the classroom teacher is on the firing line each day and is expected to perform—perhaps instantly and entertainingly, but most certainly in a highly competent and professional manner—in situations that are far from ideal. In any case, you must gain your students' attention before you can teach them.

In this final section of this chapter, you will find the presentation of an annotated list of ideas, many of which have been offered over recent years by classroom teachers (see also Figure 8.3). Although the ideas are organized according to discipline, and some may be more appropriate at one grade level than another, you may profit from reading all entries for each field. Although a particular entry might be identified as

Figure 8.3 Internet sites for teaching ideas.

All subjects and grade levels, lessons, units, and project ideas

- Columbia Education Center Lesson Plans at <http://www.col-ed.org/cur/>
- eDscape, at <http://www.edscape.com>
- Global Schoolhouse at <http://www.gsh.org>
- K–12 Projects <http://www.eagle.ca/~matink/projects.html>
- Teachers Net Lesson Exchange at <http://www.teachers.net/lessons>

Art

- Crayola Art Education <http://www.crayola.com/art_education>
- Eyes on Art <http://www.kn.pacbell.com/wired/art/art.html>
- Incredible Art Department <http://www.in.net/~kenroar>
- Kinder Art <http://www.bconnex.net/~jarea/lessons.htm>
- World Wide Arts Resources <http://wwar.com/>

Dance

- CyberDance <http://www.thepoint.net/~raw/dance.htm>
- Dance Directory <http://www.cyberspace.com/vandehey/dance.html>
- Dance links <http://www.SapphireSwan.com/dance/>

Drama and Film

- Performing Arts Resources <http://www.educationindex.com/theater/>
- Screensite at <http://www.tcf.ua.edu/screensite>

Environmental Issues

- Environmental links <http://www.nceet.snre.umich.edu/>
- World Bank's site <http://www.worldbank.org/depweb>
- World Resources <http://www.wri.org>

History/Social Studies

- K–12 Africa Guide <http://www.sas.upenn.edu/African_Studies/Home_Page/AFR_GIDE.html>
- Amigo! Mexico Web Center <http://www.mexonline.com/>
- FedWorld <http://www.fedworld.gov>
- Historical Text Archive <http://www.msstate.edu/Archives/History/index.html>
- The History Net <http://www.thehistorynet.com>
- History/social studies resources <http://www.execpc.com/~dboals/boals.html>
- Houghton Mifflin Social Studies Center <http://www.eduplace.com/ss/>
- Links to lesson plans, unit plans, thematic units, and resources <http://www.csun.edu/~hcedu013/index.html>

- Medieval Life <http://www.pastforward.co.uk/>
- Native American resources <http://hanksville.phast.umass.edu/misc/NAresources.html>
- Scrolls from the Dead Sea <http://sunsite.unc.edu/expo/deadsea.scrolls.exhibit/intro.html>
- Social Sciences Research Network Online <http://www.ssrn.com/index.html>
- Social Science Resources Home Page <http://www.nde.state.ne.us/SS/ss.html>
- U.S. History, From Revolution to Reconstruction <http://grid.let.rug.nl/~welling/usa/usa.html>
- Women's History <http://frank.mtsu.edu/~kmiddlet/history/women.html>

Language and Literacy

- The Encyclopedia Mythica <http://www.pantheon.org/mythica/>
- ESL/EFL links <http://www.pacificnet.net/~sperling/eslcafe.html>
- Foreign language links <http://polyglot.lss.wisc.edu/lss/lang/langlink.html>
- Galaxy <http://galaxy.einet.net/galaxy.Humanities/Literature.html>
- Language and Literacy Project <http://www.uis.edu/~cook/langlit/index.html>
- Literature and humanities links <http://galaxy.einet.net/galaxy/Humanities/Literature.html>
- Mandel's Internet site <http://www.pacificnet.net/~mandel/LanguageArts.html>

Mathematics

- Math Archives <http://archives.math.utk.edu/>
- The Math Forum <http://forum.swarthmore.edu/>
- More math project ideas <http://www.luc.edu/schools/education/csimath/zmathed.htm>
- Math resources <http://www-personal.umd.umich.edu/~jobrown/math.html>
- MathSource <http://mathsource.wri.com/>
- PBS Mathline <http://www.pbs.org/learn/mathline/>
- Plane Math <http://www.planemath.com/>
- Schoolnet: Math Department <http://www.schoolnet.ca/math/\sci/math/>

Music

- American Music Conference <http://www.amc'music.com>
- Music Education Resource Links (MERL) <http://www.isd77.k12.mn.us/resources/staffpages/shirk/k12.music.html>
- Music Educator's Home Page <http://www.athenet.net/~wslow/>

(continued)

- Music, The Universal Language
  <http://www.jumpoint/com/bluesman/>
- Music lesson plans and other resource links
  <http://www.csun.edu/~vceed009/music.html>
- Virtual Library on music <http://syy.oulu.fi/music>

Science

- Animal diversity web
  <http://www.oit.itd.umich.edu/projects/ADW>
- BioRap <http://www.biorap.org.>
- Chemistry Teaching Resources
  <http://www.anachem.umu.se/eks/pointers.htm>
- Chemistry tutorial site <http://dbhs.wvusd.k12.ca.us/ChemTeamIndex.html>
- Cody's Science Education Zone <http://www.ousd.k12.ca.us/~codypren/CSEZ_Home>
- Co-Vis Project
  <http://www.nwu.edu/mentors/welcome.html>

- Cyberspace Middle School
  <http://www.scri.fsu.edu/~dennisl/CMS.html>
- Earthshots <http://edcwww.cr.usgs.gov/Earthshots>
- Electronic Zoo <http://netvet.wustl.edu/e-zoo.html>
- Mandel's web site
  <http://www.pacificnet.net/~mandel/Science.html>
- NASA Spacelink <http://spacelink.nasa/gov/.index.html>
- Science and Mathematics Education Resources
  <http://www.hpec.astro.washington.edu/scied/science.html>
- Stanford Solar Center <http://solar-center.stanford.edu>
- Weather Underground
  <http://groundhog.sprl.umich.edu/>
- Windows to the Universe Project
  <http://www.windows.umich.edu>

Figure 8.3 (*Continued*)

specific to one discipline, it might also be useful in others; many of these strategies can be used in interdisciplinary teaching—for example number one can clearly be combined with mathematics, science, and art. Or it might stimulate a creative thought for your own stock of motivational techniques, such as an idea for a way to use the theory of multiple learning capacities or to emphasize the multicultural aspect of a lesson in math, social studies, or whatever the central discipline or theme of an instruction unit.

The Visual and Performing Arts

1. As part of a unit combining design or creativity with science, have students construct, design, and decorate their own kite. When the projects are complete, designate a time to fly them.

2. Use lyrics from popular music to influence class work, such as by putting the lyrics into pictures.

3. Use the outdoors or another environment for a free drawing experience.

4. Invite a local artist who has created a community mural to speak to the class about the mural. Plan and create a class mural, perhaps on a large sheet of plywood or some other location approved by the school administration. For example, at Chartiers Valley Intermediate School (Pittsburgh, PA), for more than a decade, each fifth grade class has contributed its own section to a growing mural in the school cafeteria as the culminating project to the school's visual art education program.

5. Use a mandala to demonstrate the importance of individual experience, as in interpreting paintings and in interpreting poetry.

6. Collect books/magazines/posters/films/videos/computer software programs and so forth that

show different kinds of masks people around the world wear. Ask students to identify the similarities and differences in the masks. Have them research the meanings that mask characters have in various cultures. Have students design and create their own masks to illustrate their own personalities, cultures, and so forth.

7. As part of a unit on the creative process, have each student draw or sketch on a piece of paper and then pass it on to the next person who makes additions to the drawing. Instructions could include "improve the drawing," "make the drawing ugly," and "add what you think would be necessary to complete the composition."

8. Imagine that you're a bird flying over the largest city you have visited. What do you see, hear, smell, feel, taste? Draw a "sensory" map.

9. Assign a different color to each student. Have them arrange themselves into warm and cool colors and explain their decisions (why blue is cool, etc.). Discuss people's emotional responses to each of the colors.

10. Watch videos of dances from various countries and cultures. Have students identify similarities and differences. Have students research meanings and occasions of particular dances.

11. Have students discover ways in which music, art, and dance are used around them and in their community.

12. Find a popular song that students like. Transpose the melody into unfamiliar keys for each instrument. This makes the student want to learn the song, but in the process the student will have to become more familiar with his or her instrument.

13. Set aside one weekend morning a month and hold small informal recitals (workshops) allowing students to participate/observe the performance situation(s) among their peers and themselves. (Students

might be told previously about these "special days" and encouraged to prepare a selection of their own choosing.)

14. Play a group-activity rhythm game, such as Dutch Shoe Game, to get students to cooperate, work together, and enjoy themselves using rhythm. Dutch Shoe Game participants sit in a circle and, as the song is sung, each person passes one of his or her shoes to the person on the right in rhythm to the music. Shoes continue to be passed as long as verses are sung. Those with poor rhythm will end up with a pile of shoes in front of them!

15. Choose a rhythmical, humorous poem or verse to conduct. The students read the poem in chorus, while the teacher stands before them and conducts the poem as if it were a musical work. Students must be sensitive to the intonation, speed, inflection, mood, and dynamics that the teacher wants them to convey in their reading.

16. Start a Retired Senior Citizens Volunteer Program (RSCVP). Senior citizens can present folk art workshops with students, and the students and seniors can work together to create artwork for the school. For example, students at one school make tray favors, napkin rings, place mats, door decorations, and cards and treat cups for the residents of the local veterans home.

Family and Consumer Economics, Foods, and Textiles

17. Often the foods we like originated from another part of our country or the world. Have the children identify such foods and from where they came, foods such as spaghetti, enchiladas, fajitas, wontons, tacos, quiches, croissants, teriyaki, fried rice, pizza, hot dog, hamburger, noodle, tomato, chocolate, potato, hoagy, chop suey, ice cream cone, submarine, poor boy. Have them list the names and origins, and place pictures of the food in place on a large world map.

18. Take still photos of class members at special events such as dinners, fashion shows, field trips, and special projects. Build a scrapbook or bulletin board with these and display on campus.

19. Plan thematic units on cultural foods, using the traditions, costumes, and music of a particular culture. Have the students decorate the room. Invite the principal and perhaps community representatives for a meal and visit.

20. Have students plan and create a bulletin board displaying pictures of 100-calorie portions of basic nutritional foods and popular fad foods that contain only empty calories. The display can motivate a discussion on foods with calories and nutrients versus foods with empty calories.

21. Pin the names of different garments on the backs of students. The students are then to sort themselves into different wash loads.

22. For a clothing unit hold an "idea day." Ask each student to bring in an idea of something that can be done to give clothes a new look, a fun touch, or an extended wearing life. Ideas they may come up with include: appliqués, embroidery, tie-dye, batik, colorful patches, and restyling old clothes into current or creative fashions.

23. Have the students write, practice, and present skits for videotape presentations on consumer fraud.

24. Once a month have students plan a menu, prepare the food, and serve it to invited senior citizens from the community.

25. Organize a program with senior citizens and students working together on a community garden.

26. Plan a program at a senior citizens center whereby students and seniors work together on planning and decorating the center for special occasions and holidays.

27. With your students, plan a community service program. For example, at Discovery Middle School (Vancouver, WA), students provide child care, cross-age tutoring, and companionship to preschool, elementary, and elderly clients at off-campus locations.

English, Languages, and the Language Arts

28. Organize a letter-writing activity between senior citizens and your students.

29. For a unit on the Renaissance, creation of a wall-to-wall mural depicting a village of the times may be a total team project. Some students can research customs, costumes, and architecture. Others may paint or draw.

30. On a U.S. road map, have students find the names of places that sound "foreign," and categorize the names according to nationality or culture.

31. To enhance understanding of parts of speech, set up this problem: Provide several boxes containing different parts of speech. Each student is to form one sentence from the fragments chosen from each box, being allowed to discard only at a penalty. The students then nonverbally make trades with other students to make coherent and perhaps meaningfully amusing sentences. A student may trade a noun for a verb but will have to keep in mind what parts of speech are essential for a sentence. Results may be read aloud as a culmination to this activity.

32. Have students match American English and British English words (or any other combination of languages), such as: cookies and biscuits; hood and bonnet; canned meat and tinned meat; elevator and lift; flashlight and torch; subway and tube; garbage collector and dustman; undershirt and vest; sweater and jumper; gasoline and petrol. Or, have students compare pronunciations and spellings.

33. English words derive from many other languages. Have students research and list some, such as

ketchup (Malay), alcohol (Arabic), kindergarten (German), menu (French), shampoo (Hindi), bonanza (Spanish), piano (Italian), kosher (Yiddish), and smorgasbord (Swedish).

34. Try this for an exercise in objective versus subjective writing: After a lesson on descriptive writing, bring to the class a nondescript object, such as a potato, and place it before the class. Ask them to write a paragraph either describing the potato in detail—its color, size, markings, and other characteristics—or describing how the potato feels about them.

35. Read to the class a story without an ending, then ask the students (as individuals or in think-write-share-pairs) to create and write their own endings or conclusions.

36. Ask students to create in groups of no more than three students each an advertisement using a propaganda device of their choice. Videotape their presentations.

37. Ask students to (individually or in dyads) create and design an invention and then write a "patent description" for the invention.

38. Using think-write-pair-share, have students write a physical description of some well-known (but unnamed) public figure, such as a movie star, politician, athlete, or musician. Other class members may enjoy trying to identify the "mystery" personality from the written description.

39. A bulletin board may be designated for current events and news in the world of writers. Included may be new books and recording releases and reviews. News of poets and authors (student authors and poets, too) may also be displayed.

40. Everyone has heard of or experienced stereotyping. For example: Girls are not as athletic as boys, boys are insensitive, women are better cooks than men, men are more mechanical. Ask students to list some stereotypes they have heard and examples they find in newspapers, magazines, movies, and television. Have students discuss these questions: How do you suppose these stereotypes came to be? Does stereotyping have any useful value? Is it sometimes harmful?

41. Remove the text from a Sunday newspaper comic strip and have the students work in pairs to create a story line; or, give each pair a picture from a magazine and have the pair create a story about the picture.

42. Use newspaper want ads to locate jobs as a base for completing job application forms and creating letters of inquiry. Use videotape equipment to record employer–employee role-play situations and interviews for jobs to develop language and listening skills. Child-parent situations are also good fodder for role plays.

43. Have students choose a short story from a text and write it into a play and perform the play for parents.

44. When beginning a poetry unit, ask students to bring in the words to their favorite songs. Show how these fit into the genre of poetry.

45. Have students look for commercial examples of advertisements that might be classified as "eco-pornographic," i.e., ads that push a product that is potentially damaging to our environment. Or have students analyze advertisements for the emotions they appeal to, techniques used, and their integrity. Try the same thing with radio, teen magazines, the Internet, and other media.

46. Change the environment by moving to an outdoor location, and ask students to write poetry to see if the change in surroundings stimulates or discourages their creativeness. Discuss the results. For example, take your class to a large supermarket to write, to a lake, into a forest, or to the school athletic stadium.

47. To introduce the concept of interpretations, use your state's seal to start the study. Have students analyze the seal for its history and the meaning of its various symbols.

48. When learning a second language, provide puppets in native costume for students to use while practicing dialogue.

49. Use the Internet to establish communication with students from another area of the country or world; establish a web page for your school.

50. Use drama to build children's language arts and thinking skills. Have students write dialogue, set scenes, and communicate emotions through expressive language and mime.

51. Establish a community-service learning literacy project. For example: students from Greenville High School (Greenville, TN) serve as mentors to local elementary school students to help the children develop their reading and comprehension skills. Students from Urbana High School (Urbana, IL) are trained to give one-on-one tutoring in reading to students from a local elementary school.

Mathematics

52. Collaboratively plan with students a simulation in which members role-play the solar system. Students calculate their weights, set up a proportion system, find a large field, and on the final day actually simulate the solar system, using their own bodies to represent the sun, planets, and moons. Arrange to have the event photographed.

53. Encourage students to look for evidence of Fibonacci number series (i.e., 1, 1, 2, 3, 5, 8, 13, 21, etc.), outside of mathematics, such as in nature and in manufactured objects. Here are examples of where evidence may be found: piano keyboard, petals on flowers, spermatogenesis and oogenesis. Perhaps your students might like to organize a Fibonacci Club and through the Internet establish communication with other clubs around the world.

54. Have students research the history of cost of a first-class U.S. postage stamp and ask them to devise

ways of predicting its cost by the year they graduate, or are grandparents, or some other target year.

55. Give students a list of the frequencies of each of the 88 keys and strings of a piano (a local music store can provide the information). Challenge students to derive an equation to express the relation between key position and frequency. After they have does this, research and tell them about the Bösendorfer piano (Germany) with its nine extra keys at the lower end of the keyboard. See if students can predict the frequencies of those extra keys.

56. Using a light sensor to measure the intensity of a light source from various distances, have students graph the data points and then, with their scientific calculators, find the relevant equation.

57. Establish a service-learning project at your school. For example, at Sunset Elementary School (Airway Heights, WA), while helping students develop skills in leadership and communication, the students are trained by adults to tutor other children in mathematics.

Physical Education

58. Have students choose individually (or in dyads) a famous athlete they most (or least) admire. A short report will be written about the athlete. Students will then discuss the attributes and/or characteristics that they admire (or dislike) in the athlete and how they feel they can emulate (or avoid) those qualities. After all pairs of students have made their presentations, as a class devise two lists, one of common attributes admired, the other of qualities to avoid.

59. Have students in cooperative learning groups make up an exercise routine to their favorite music recording and share it with the class, and discuss how they arrived at decisions along the way.

60. Have the class divide into groups. Given the basic nonlocomotor skills, have each group come up with a "people machine." Each student within the group is hooked up to another demonstrating a nonlocomotor skill and adding some sort of noise to it. Have a contest for the most creative people machine.

61. Give students a chance to design a balance-beam routine that has two passes on the beam and must include: front support mount, forward roll, leap, low or high turn, visit, chassé, and cross support dismount. Post these routines to show the variety of ways the different maneuvers can be put together.

62. Divide the class into groups. Have them create a new game or activity for the class, using only the equipment they are given. Let the class play their newly created games.

63. Have the children plan ways of educating the school and local community about general nutrition and exercise.

Science

64. Have students create and test their own microscopes using bamboo rods with a drop of water in each end.

65. Have students create and test litmus indicators using the petals of flowers.

66. Use cassette-tape recorders to record sounds of the environment. Compare and write about day and night sounds.

67. For a life science class, give each student on the first day of class one live guppy in a test tube and one live cactus plant in a 3-inch pot. Tell the students that the minimum they each need to pass the course is to bring their pet plant and fish back to you during the final week of school, alive.

68. Plan a year-long project in which each student, or small group of students, must develop knowledge and understanding of some specific piece of technology. Each project culmination presentation must have five components: visual, oral, written, artistic, and creative.

69. If you are a life science teacher, make sure your classroom looks like a place for studying life rather than a place of death.

70. Use landlord-tenant situations to develop a simulation of predator-prey relationships.

71. With each student playing the role of a cell part, have students set up and perform a role-play simulation of cells.

72. Divide your class into groups and ask each group to create an environment for an imaginary animal, using discarded items from the environment. By asking questions each group will try to learn about other groups' "mystery" animals.

73. Have each student, or student pair, "adopt" a chemical element. The student then researches that element and becomes the class expert whenever that particular substance comes up in discussion. There could be a special bulletin board for putting up questions on interesting or little-known facts about the elements.

74. Milk can be precipitated, separated, and the solid product dried to form a very hard substance that was, in the days before plastic, used to make buttons. Help students make their own buttons from milk.

75. As a class or interdisciplinary team project, obtain permission and "adopt" a wetlands area near the school.

76. Have students research the composition and development of familiar objects. For example, a standard pencil is made of cedar wood from the forests of the Pacific Northwest. The graphite is often from Montana or Mexico and is reinforced with clays from Georgia and Kentucky. The eraser is made from soybean oil, latex from trees in South America, reinforced with pumice from California or New Mexico, and sulfur, calcium, and barium. The metal band is aluminum or brass, made

from copper and zinc, mined in no fewer than 13 states and nine provinces of Canada. The paint to color the wood and the lacquer to make it shine are made from a variety of different minerals and metals, as is the glue that holds the wood together.

77. Have students locate and design large posters to hang on the classroom walls that show the meaning of words used in science that are not typical of their meaning in everyday language usage—the word *theory*, for example.

78. To bridge cross-cultural differences have students design large posters to hang on the classroom walls showing potential differences in perceptions or views according to ethnoscience and formal science.

79. With your students, plan a community service project. For example, elementary children of the Powder River County School District (Broadus, MT) adopted community flower beds and conduct an annual food drive for the needy. At Great Falls Middle School (Montague, MA), students research and produce television documentaries on subjects related to energy. The documentaries are broadcast on the local cable channel to promote energy literacy in the school and community. Students at Baldwyn Middle School (Baldwyn, MS) plan and care for the landscaping of the local battlefield/museum; students from classes at Hollidaysburg Area Senior High School (Hollidaysburg, PA) joined to refurbish a local cemetery.

80. Sometimes projects become ongoing permanent endeavors with many spin-off projects of shorter duration. For example, what began as a science classroom project at W. H. English Middle School (Scottsburg, IN) has become the largest animal refuge shelter in the Midwest. While nursing animals back to health, the students study them and learn about environmental policies. Over the years, students in the program have shared their work by making presentations in ten states and as guests of the International Animal Rights Convention in Russia.[25]

Social Sciences

81. Organize an Intergenerational Advocacy program, in which students and senior citizens work together to make a better society for both groups.[26] For example, at Morgantown Elementary School (Morgantown, KY), in a unit of instruction titled "Young

Friends, Old Friends," students team with residents of a local health care center to provide compassionate friendships while learning about the problems associated with aging. At Burns Middle School (Owensboro, KY) students work in collaboration with a retired senior volunteer program to develop their understanding of personal and social responsibilities.

82. Initiate a service-learning project, where for an extended period of time students work directly with community organizations and agencies. For example, at Columbia Elementary School (Champaign, IL) primary grade students do art work for local hospitals, and students of grades four and five interview senior citizens and explore background experiences. At John Ford Middle School (St. Matthews, SC) students incorporate The Constitutional Right Foundation "City Youth" program into the curriculum, helping to make decisions about areas of the community that need improvement.

83. Develop a year-long, three-stage project. During the first stage students individually research the question "Who Am I?"; during the second stage, "Who Are They?"; third stage, "Who Are We?" Multimedia presentations should be part of the culminating presentations.

84. During their study of ancient Egypt, have students create and build their own model pyramids.

85. Let your students devise ways they would improve their living environment, beginning with the classroom, then moving out to the school, home, community, and world. See, for example, the instructional scenario on "An Interdisciplinary Thematic Unit for Children in the Primary Grades."

86. Start a pictorial essay on the development and/or changes of a given area in your community, such as a major corner or block adjacent to the school. This is a study project that could continue for years and that has many social, political, and economic implications.

87. Start a folk hero study. Each year ask, "What prominent human being who has lived (during a particular period of time) do you most (and/or least) admire?" Collect individual responses to the question, tally, and discuss. After you have done this for several years you may wish to share with your class for discussion purposes the results of your surveys of previous years.

88. Start a sister school program. Establish a class relationship with a similar class from another school from elsewhere in the country or the world, perhaps by using the Internet.

89. Role-play a simulated family movement to the West in the 1800s. What items would they take? What would they throw out of the wagon to lighten the load?

90. Have students collect music, art, or athletic records from a particular period of history. Have them compare with today and predict the future.

[25] Source: J. Arnold, "High Expectations For All: Perspective and Practice," *Middle School Journal* 28(3):52 (January 1997).

[26] See, for example, J. M. Halford, "For Significant Support, Turn to Seniors," and J. Smith, "It Takes 100 Grandparents," both in *Educational Leadership* 58(8):52–53 and pp. 49–51, respectively (May 1998). Additional information about intergenerational programs can be obtained from the Center for Intergenerational Learning, Temple University, 1601 N. Broad St., Room 206, Philadelphia, PA 19122 (http://www/temple.edu/departments/CIL).

CLASSROOM SCENARIO

An Interdisciplinary Thematic Unit for Children in the Primary Grades

Perhaps influenced in some way by *Keepers of the Earth: Native American Stories and Environmental Activities for Children* by M. J. Caduto and J. Bruchac (Golden, CO: Fulcrum, 1988), two primary-grade teachers developed a thematic unit that they titled "Keepers of the Earth." To begin, they located various resources, including children's books related to different aspects of the main topic, the environment. They also found useful poetry and prose in books related to the subtopics of daily lessons, such as *Learning from Our Mistakes, Action Plans for the Environment, Animals and Plants, Recycling,* and *Nature's Balance, Recovery, and Interconnections.*

After sharing information about nature with the students, the teachers let the students take the lead in devising activities related to the main topic. A few students proposed a fund raiser to raise money to buy trees to plant in the woods behind their school, an idea that developed into a used-toy sale at the local country fair. After some discussion, the students decided to create a bird sanctuary near the school, because nearby construction was encroaching on the wooded area. The money raised was designated for the purchase of several bird feeders and trees and shrubs that would attract the birds. The students advertised, gathered used toys, priced them, and worked at a booth at the fair. Another group of students showed an interest in plants, and these young "landscape architects," supported by their teachers, studied plant types and shopped for good prices.

The students prepared and presented the sanctuary proposal to the school principal, a district administrator, and the head of the school grounds crew, and to representatives of a local chemical company, the school's community partner, which had offered to help fund the project. Once given the go-ahead, the students planted the newly purchased trees and shrubs for the bird sanctuary. Other classes helped mulch around the new plants. Interestingly, what had started as an idea of a few students in one class had turned into a project "owned" by the school and its community partner. Others in the school and community made contributions as well. Another class of students planted flowers, the parent-teacher organization purchased picnic tables for use as an outdoor classroom, and a local garden club donated bulbs.

91. Using play money, establish a capitalistic economic system within your classroom. Salaries may be paid for attendance and bonus income for work well done, taxes may be collected for poor work, and a welfare section established in a corner of the room.

92. Divide your class into small groups and ask that each group make predictions as to what world governments, world geography, world social issues, or some other related topic will be like some time in the future. Let each group give its report, followed by debate and discussion. Plant the predictions in some secret location on the school grounds for a future discovery.

93. As an opener to a unit on the U.S. Constitution, have students design their own classroom or team "bill of rights."

94. One day treat your students in class as if your class were a socialist society; the next day treat them as if they were a fascist society; on another day as a communist society; etc. At the end of the simulation have students discuss and compare their feelings about each day.

95. Using Legos™ as construction blocks, assign roles for students to simulate the building of the Great Wall of China or the Great Pyramids of Egypt.

96. At Indian Trail Junior High School (Addison, IL) all eighth graders and teachers from not only social studies but various other content areas, including English, mathematics, physical education, and science, work together on a real-world, problem-based project titled the "Inspector Red Ribbon Unit," which focuses on a social problem that has occurred too many times, the prom night automobile accident. During the study, under guidance from teachers of the various classes, students interview witnesses, visit and assess the scene of the accident, review medical reports, and make their recommendations in a press conference.[27]

97. Establish a caring anti-violence program. For example, in Lynn Haven, FL, high school students work as tutors/mentors with elementary school students to help boost confidence and self-esteem among both groups of students.

98. Students at Northern Wayne Vocational-Technical School (WV) study castles and build model castles that are shared with students at Wayne High School who are in an interdisciplinary thematic unit of study (the history and literature of the medieval period of Europe).

99. At Davis Senior High School (Davis, CA), students in U.S. History are given this assignment for an activity titled "Creating a Candidate." The assignment is done in pairs. Research electronic and print media about the progressive movement in early California history. Determine relevant issues a candidate for governor of the state in 1910 would need to address. Create a fictitious candidate. Your exhibition must include (a) an election poster, (b) a slogan, (c) a theme song that you must sing, and (d) a five-minute platform speech addressing the issues, your solutions, and the position of your opponents.

[27]K. Rasmussen, "Using Real-Life Problems to Make Real-World Connections," *ASCD Curriculum Update* (Summer 1997), p. 2.

Vocational-Career Education

100. At Bell County High School (Pineville, KY), students operate an on-campus bank where fellow students can actually make deposits, earn interest, and borrow money.

101. At North Penn High School (Lansdale, PA), students designed and built equipment for the school's child development playground.

SUMMARY

This chapter has continued the development of your repertoire of teaching strategies. As you know, young people can be quite peer-conscious, can have relatively short attention spans for experiences in which they are uninterested, and prefer active experiences that engage many or all of their senses. Most are intensely curious about things of interest to them. Cooperative learning, student-centered projects, and teaching strategies that emphasize shared discovery and inquiry (discussed in the next chapter) within a psychologically safe environment encourage the most positive aspects of thinking and learning. Central to your strategy selection should be those strategies that encourage students to become independent thinkers and skilled learners who can help in the planning, structuring, regulating, and assessing of their own learning and learning activities.

QUESTIONS FOR CLASS DISCUSSION

1. Describe research that you can find on the use of cooperation (cooperative learning groups) vs. competition (competitive learning groups) in teaching. Explain why you would or would not use cooperative learning groups as they were discussed in this chapter.

2. Do you have concerns about using project-centered teaching and not being able to cover all the content you believe should be covered? Think back to your own schooling. What do you really remember? Most likely you remember projects, yours and other students' presentations, the lengthy research you did and your extra effort for the artwork to accompany your presentation. Maybe you remember a compliment by a teacher or a pat on the back by peers. Most likely you do not remember the massive amount of content that was covered. Discuss your feelings about this with your classmates. Share common experiences and concerns.

3. It is an aphorism that to learn something well students need time to practice it. There is a difference, however, between solitary practice and coached practice. Describe the difference and conditions in which you would use each.

4. Divide into teams of four, and have each team develop one learning center. Set up and share the LCs in your classroom.

5. Explain how a teacher can tell when he or she is truly using cooperative learning groups for instruction as opposed to traditional small group learning.

6. When a student is said to be on task, does that necessarily imply that the student is mentally engaged? Is it possible for a student to be mentally engaged although not on task? Explain your answers.

7. Identify and describe instructional strategies that encourage students to become independent thinkers and skilled learners. How, specifically, can a teacher determine when a child has become an independent thinker and a skilled learner? What behaviors does one look for?

8. Describe any prior concepts you held that changed as a result of your experiences with this chapter. Describe the changes.

9. From your current observations and field work as related to this teacher preparation program, clearly identify one specific example of educational practice that seems contradictory to exemplary practice or theory as presented in this chapter. Present your explanation for the discrepancy.

10. Do you have questions generated by the content of this chapter? If you do, list them along with ways answers might be found.

FOR FURTHER READING

Bingen, M. "Exhibitions of Mastery: The Tail That Wags the Dog." *English Journal* 86(1):32–36 (January 1997).

Bouas, M. J.; Thompson, P.; and Farlow, N. "Self-Selected Journal Writing in the Kindergarten Classroom: Five Conditions That Foster Literacy Development." *Reading Horizons* 38(1): 3–12 (1997).

Bower, B., and Lobdell, J. "History Alive! Six Powerful Constructivist Strategies." *Social Education* 62(1): 50–53 (January 1998).

Chesser, W. D., et al. "Do Paideia Seminars Explain Higher Writing Scores?" *Middle School Journal* 29(1):40–44 (September 1997).

Choate, J. S., and Rakes, T. A. *Inclusive Instruction for Struggling Readers.* Fastback 434. Bloomington, IN: Phi Delta Kappa Educational Foundation, 1998.

Cohen, E. G. "Making Cooperative Learning Equitable." *Educational Leadership* 56(1):18–21 (September 1998).

Cummings, L., and Winston, M. "Service-Based Solutions." *Science Teacher* 65(1): 39–41 (January 1998).

Finkel, L., et al. "Freshwater Ecology." *Science Teacher* 65(5): 42–43 (May 1998).

Gorman, M. E., et al. "Turning Students into Inventors: Active Learning Modules for Secondary Students." *Phi Delta Kappan* 79(7):530–537 (March 1998).

Heller, N. *Technology Connections for Grades 3–5. Research Projects and Activities.* Englewood, CO: Libraries Unlimited, 1998.

Holt, P. W. "The Oregon Trail: Wyoming Students Construct a CD-ROM." *Social Education* 62(1):41–45 (January 1998).

Harmelink, K. "Learning the Write Way." *Science Teacher* 65(1):36–38 (January 1998).

Johnson, D. W., and Johnson, F. P. *Joining Together: Group Theory and Group Skills.* 6th ed. Boston: Allyn & Bacon, 1997.

Kaldhusdal, T.; Wood, S.,; and Truesdale, J. "Virtualville Votes: An Interdisciplinary Project." *Multimedia Schools* 5(1): 30–35 (January/February 1998).

Latham, A S. "Gender Differences on Assessments." *Educational Leadership* 55(4):88–89 (December 1997/January 1998).

Matthews, C. E., et al. "Challenging Gender Bias in Fifth Grade." *Educational Leadership* 55(4):54–57 (December 1997/January 1998).

Metzger, M. "Teaching Reading: Beyond the Plot." *Phi Delta Kappan* 80(3):240–246, 256 (November 1998).

Murphey, C. E. "Using the Five Themes of Geography to Explore a School Site." *Social Studies Review* 37(2):49–52 (Spring/Summer 1998).

Pilger, M. A. *Multicultural Projects Index: Things To Make and Do To Celebrate Festivals, Cultures, and Holidays Around the World.* Second Edition. (Englewood, CO: Libraries Unlimited, 1998).

Punch, K. F., and Moriarty, B. "Cooperative and Competitive Learning Environments and Their Effects on Behavior, Self-Efficacy, and Achievement." *Alberta Journal of Educational Research* 43(2–3):158–160 (Summer–Fall 1997).

Tomlinson, C. A. *The Differentiated Classroom.* Alexandria, VA: Association for Supervision and Curriculum Development, 1999.

Tomlinson, C. A., and Kalbfleisch, M. L. "Teach Me, Teach My Brain: A Call for Differentiated Classrooms." *Educational Leadership* 56(3):52–55 (November 1998).

Weinman, J., and Haag, P. "Gender Equity in Cyberspace." *Educational Leadership* 56(5):44–49 (February 1999).

Chapter 9

Strategies for Teaching: Teacher Talk, Demonstrations, Thinking, Inquiry, and Games

Perhaps no other strategy is used more by teachers than is teacher talk, so this chapter begins with a presentation of guidelines for using that vital and significant instructional strategy. A strategy related to teacher talk is the demonstration, which is addressed later in the chapter, followed by guidelines for other important strategies for thinking, inquiry and discovery, and games.

Specifically, upon your completion of this chapter you should be able to demonstrate

1. When and how to use teacher talk for instruction.
2. An effective demonstration.
3. How to help students learn to think and behave intelligently.
4. Understanding of the relationship between thinking, problem solving, discovery, and inquiry.
5. How and when to use student inquiry.
6. Ways of integrating strategies for integrated learning.
7. Your knowledge of advantages and disadvantages of each of seven categories of games for learning.

TEACHER TALK: FORMAL AND INFORMAL

Teacher talk encompasses both lecturing *to* students and talking *with* students. A lecture is considered formal teacher talk, whereas a discussion with students is considered informal teacher talk.

Cautions in Using Teacher Talk

Whether your talk is formal or informal, you should keep in mind certain cautions. Perhaps the most

---

TEACHING VIGNETTE

A Precious Moment in Teaching with Advice to Beginning Teachers

I share with you this teaching vignette which is both humorous and indicative of creative thinking. While teaching a history class, a high school teacher began a lesson with the question, "What comes to mind when you hear the words 'Puritan' and 'Pilgrim'?" Without hesitation, a rather quiet student voice from near the rear of the room replied, "Cooking oil and John Wayne." To me, that represented one of those rare and precious moments in teaching, reaffirming my belief that every teacher is well advised to maintain throughout his or her teaching career a journal in which such intrinsically rewarding moments can be recorded so to be reviewed and enjoyed again years later.

---

important is that of talking too much. If a teacher talks too much, the significance of his or her words may be lost because some students will tune the teacher out.

Another caution is to avoid talking too fast. Children can hear faster than they can understand what they hear. It is a good idea to remind yourself to talk slowly and to check frequently for student comprehension of what you are talking about. It is also important to remember that your one brain is communicating with many student brains, each of which responds to sensory input (auditory in this instance) at different rates. Because of this, you will need to pause to let words sink in, and you will need to pause during transitions from one point or activity to the next.

A third caution is to be sure you are being heard and understood. Sometimes teachers talk in too low a pitch or use words that are not understood by many students. You should vary the pitch of your voice, and you should stop and help students with their understanding of vocabulary that may be new to them. If you have students in your class who have only limited English-language proficiency, then you need to help them learn what is essentially two new vocabularies—the vocabulary of the English language in general and the vocabulary that is unique to the subject you teach.

A fourth caution is to remember that just because students have heard something before does not necessarily mean that they understand it or learned it. From our earlier discussions of learning experiences (such as The Learning Experiences Ladder in Chapter 6, Figure 6.6), remember that although verbal communication is an important form of communication, because of its reliance on the use of abstract symbols it is not a very reliable form of communication. Teacher talk relies on words and on skill in listening, a skill that is not mastered by many children (or for that matter, many adults). For that and other reasons, to ensure student understanding, it is good to reinforce your teacher talk with either direct or simulated learning experiences.

A related caution is to resist believing that students have attained a skill or have learned something that was taught previously by you or by another teacher. During any discussion (formal or informal), rather than assuming that your students know something, you should ensure they know it. For example, if the discussion and a student activity involve a particular thinking skill, then you will want to make sure that students know how to use that skill (thinking skills are discussed later in this chapter).

Still another problem is talking in a humdrum monotone. Students need teachers whose voices exude enthusiasm and excitement (although not to be overdone) about the subject and about teaching and learning. Such enthusiasm and excitement for learning are contagious. A voice that demonstrates enthusiasm for teaching and learning is more likely to motivate children to learn.

Keep those cautions in mind as you study the general principles and specific guidelines for the productive and effective use of teacher talk.

Teacher Talk: General Guidelines

Certain general guidelines should be followed whether your talk is formal or informal. First, begin the talk with an advance organizer. Advance organizers are introductions that mentally prepare students for a study by helping them make connections with material already learned or experienced—a *comparative organizer*—or by providing students with a conceptual arrangement of what is to be learned—an *expository*

organizer.[1] The value of using advance organizers is well documented by research.[2] An advance organizer can be a brief introduction or statement about the main idea you intend to convey and how it is related to other aspects of the students' learning (an expository organizer), or it can be a presentation of a discrepancy to arouse curiosity (a comparative organizer, in this instance causing students to compare what they have observed with what they already knew or thought they knew). Preparing an organizer helps you plan and organize the sequence of ideas, and its presentation helps students organize their own learning and become motivated about it. An advance organizer can also make their learning meaningful by providing important connections between what they already know and what is being learned.

Second, your talk should be planned so that it has a beginning and an end, with a logical order between. During your talk, you should reinforce your words with visuals (discussed in the specific guidelines that follow). These visuals may include writing unfamiliar terms on the board (helping students learn new vocabulary), visual organizers, and prepared graphs, charts, photographs, and various audiovisuals.

Third, pacing is important. Your talk should move briskly, but not too fast. The ability to pace the instruction is a difficult skill for many beginning teachers (the tendency is to talk too fast and too much), but one that will improve with experience. Until you have developed your skill in pacing lessons, you probably will need to remind yourself constantly during lessons to slow down and provide silent pauses (allowing for think time) and frequent checks for student comprehension. Specifically, your talk should:

- Be brisk, though not too fast, but with occasional slowdowns to change the pace and to check for student comprehension. Allow students time to think, ask questions, and make notes.
- Have a time plan. A talk planned for 10 minutes, if interesting to students, will probably take longer. If not interesting to them, it will probably take less time.
- Always be planned with careful consideration to the characteristics of the students. For example, if you have a fairly high percentage of LEP students or of students with special needs, then your teacher talk may be less brisk, sprinkled with even more visuals and repeated statements, and frequent checks for student comprehension.

Fourth, encourage student participation. Their active participation enhances their learning. This

[1]D. P. Ausubel, *The Psychology of Meaningful Learning* (New York: Grune & Stratton, 1963).
[2]T. L. Good and J. E. Brophy, *Looking in Classrooms,* 7th ed. (New York: Addison-Wesley/Longman, 1997), p. 240.

encouragement can be planned as questions that you ask, as time allowed for students to comment and ask questions, or as some sort of a visual and conceptual outline that students complete during the talk.

Fifth, plan a clear ending (closure). Be sure your talk has a clear ending, followed by another activity (during the same or next class period) that will help secure the learning. As for all lessons, you want to strive for planning a clear and mesmerizing beginning, an involving lesson body, and a firm and meaningful closure.

Teacher Talk: Specific Guidelines

Specific guidelines for using teacher talk are presented in the following paragraphs.

Understand the various purposes for using teacher talk. Teacher talk, formal or informal, can be useful to discuss the progress of a unit of study, explain an inquiry, introduce a unit of study, present a problem, promote student inquiry or critical thinking, provide a transition from one unit of study to the next, provide information otherwise unobtainable to students, share the teacher's experiences, share the teacher's thinking, summarize a problem, summarize a unit of study, and teach a thinking skill by modeling that skill.

Clarify the objectives of the talk. Your talk should center on one idea. The learning objectives, which should not be too numerous for one talk, should be clearly understood by the students.

Choose between informal and formal talk. Although an occasional formal "cutting edge" lecture may be appropriate for some classes, spontaneous interactive informal talks of 5 to 12 minutes are preferred. You should *never* give long lectures with no teacher-student interaction. Remember, though, a formal period-long noninteractive lecture, common in some college teaching, is developmentally inappropriate when teaching most groups of K–12 learners. (Some experts believe that its appropriateness is questionable for most learning even at the college level). On the other hand, to arouse student interest and to provide new information in relatively small and intellectually digestible chunks, the lecture may be appropriate. If during your student teaching you have doubt or questions about your selection and use of a particular instructional strategy, discuss it with your cooperating teacher or your university supervisor, or both. When you have doubt about the appropriateness of a particular strategy, trust your intuition: without some modification, the strategy probably is inappropriate.

Remember also, today's youth are of the "media," or "light," generation; they are accustomed to video interactions and "commercial breaks." For many lessons, especially those that are teacher-centered, after about ten minutes student attention is likely to begin to stray. For that eventuality you need elements planned to recapture student attention. These planned elements can include: analogies to help connect the topic to students' experiences; verbal cues, such as voice inflections; pauses to allow information to sink in; humor; visual cues, such as the use of slides, overhead transparencies, charts, board drawings, excerpts from videodiscs, real objects (realia), or body gestures; and sensory cues, such as eye contact and proximity (as in moving around the room, or casually and gently touching a student on the shoulder without interrupting your talk).

Vary strategies and activities frequently. Perhaps most useful as a strategy for recapturing student attention is to change to an entirely different strategy or learning modality. For example, from teacher talk (a teacher-centered strategy) you would change to a student activity (a student-centered strategy). Notice that changing from a lecture (mostly teacher talk) to a teacher-led discussion (mostly more teacher talk) would not be changing to an entirely different modality. Figure 9.1 provides a comparison of different changes.

As a generalization, when using teacher-centered direct instruction, with most classes you will want to change the learning activities about every 10 to 15 minutes. (That is one reason that in the sample lesson plan format of Chapter 6, you find space for at least four activities, including the introduction and closure.) This means that in a 60-minute time block, for example, you should probably plan three or four sequenced learning activities, with some that are teacher-centered and many others that are more student-centered. In a 90-minute block, plan five or six learning activities. At all age levels, in exemplary classrooms teachers often have several activities *concurrently* being performed by individuals, dyads, and small groups of students (that is, using multitasking or multilevel instruction).

Prepare and use notes as a guide for your talk. Planning your talk and preparing notes to be used during formal and informal teacher talk is as important as implementing the talk with visuals. There is absolutely nothing wrong with using notes during your teaching. You can carry them on a clipboard, perhaps a brightly colored one that gives students a visual focus, as you move around the room. Your notes for a formal talk can first be prepared in narrative form; for class use, though, they should be reduced to an outline form. *Talks to students should always be from an outline, never read from prose.* The only time a teacher's reading from prose aloud to students is appropriate is when reading a brief published article (such as in science or social studies) or portions of a story or a poem (such as in reading/English/language arts).

In your outline, use color coding with abbreviated visual cues to yourself. You will eventually develop your own coding system; keep whatever coding system you

Figure 9.1 Comparison of recapturing student attention by changing the instructional strategy.

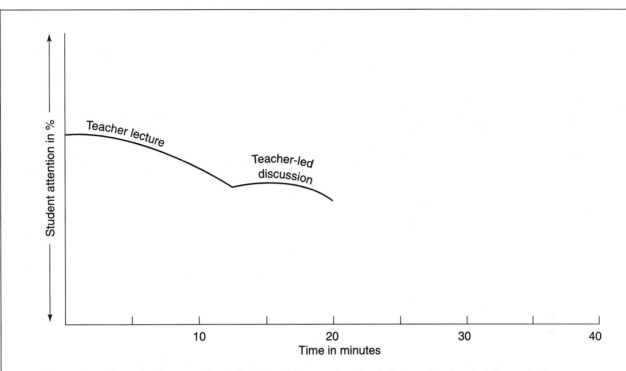

Example 1: Changing from teacher talk (lecture) to more teacher talk (e.g., teacher-led discussion).

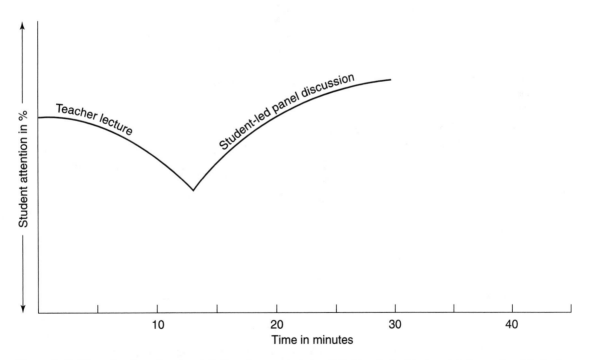

Example 2: Changing from teacher talk (teacher-centered activity) to student-led panel discussion (student-centered activity).

Figure 9.1 *(continued)*

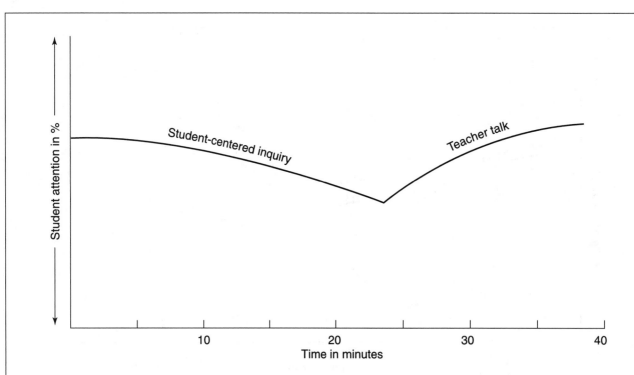

Example 3: Changing from inquiry (student-centered) to teacher-talk fueled by student questions from inquiry.

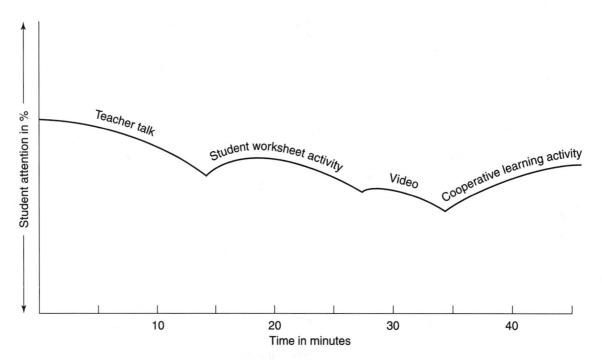

Example 4: Changing from teacher talk (teacher-centered activity) to cooperative learning activity (student-centered activity).

use simple lest you forget what the codes are for. Consider these examples of coding: where transition of ideas occur and you want to allow silent moments for ideas to sink in, mark *P* for *pause,* *T* for a *transition,* and *S* for moments of *silence;* where a slide or other visual aid will be used, mark *AV* for *audiovisual;* where you intend to stop and ask a question, mark *TQ* for *teacher question,* and mark *SQ* or *?* where you want to stop and allow time for *student questions;* where you plan to have a discussion, mark *D;* or mark *SG* where you plan *small-group work* and *L* where you plan to switch to a *laboratory* investigation; for *reviews* and *comprehension checks,* mark *R* and *CS.*

Share your note organization with your students. Teach the students how to take notes and what kinds of things they should write down. Use colored chalk to outline and highlight your talk; have your students use colored pencils for notetaking, so their notes can be color-coded to match your chalkboard notes.

Rehearse your talk. Rehearsing your planned talk is important. Using your lesson plan as your guide, rehearse your talk using a camcorder or an audiorecorder, or rehearse it while talking into a mirror or to a roommate. (For example, when we see professors walking across the campus mumbling to themselves, we like to think they are rehearsing their lecture.) You may want to include a time plan for each subtopic to allow you to gauge your timing during implementation of the talk.

Avoid racing through the talk solely to complete it by a certain time. It is more important that students understand some of what you say than that you cover it all and they understand none of it. If you do not finish, continue it later.

Augment your talk with multisensory stimulation and allow for think time. Your presentation should not overly rely on verbal communication. When using visuals, such as video excerpts or overhead transparencies, do not think that you must be constantly talking. After clearly explaining the purpose of a visual, give students sufficient time to look at it, think about it, and ask questions about it. The visual is new to the students, so give them time to take it in.

Carefully plan the content of your talk. The content of your talk should supplement and enhance that found in the student textbook rather than simply rehash content from the textbook. Students may never read their book if you tell them in an interesting and condensed fashion everything they need to know from it.

Monitor your delivery. Your voice should be pleasant and interesting to listen to rather than a steady, boring monotone or a constantly shrieking, irritating, high pitch. It is good to show enthusiasm for what you are talking about, for teaching and learning. Occasionally use dramatic voice inflections to emphasize important points and meaningful body language to give students

a visual focus. So not to appear phony, practice these skills so they become second nature.

As is always the case when teaching, *avoid standing in the same spot for long periods of time.* Even during direct instruction, you need to monitor student behavior and to use proximity as a means of keeping students on task.

View the vocabulary of the talk as an opportunity to help students with their word morphology. Words you use should be easily understood by the students, though you should still model professionalism and help students develop their vocabulary—both the vocabulary of your special discipline and the more general vocabulary of the English language. During your lesson planning, predict when you are likely to use a word that is new to most students, and plan to stop to ask a student to help explain its meaning and perhaps demonstrate its derivation. Help students with word meaning. This helps students with their remembering. Regardless of subject or grade level, *all teachers are language arts teachers.* Knowledge of word morphology is an important component of skilled reading and includes the ability to generate new words from prefixes, roots, and suffixes. For some students, nearly every subject in the curriculum is like a foreign language. That is certainly true for some LEP students, for whom teacher talk, especially formal teacher talk, should be used sparingly, if at all. Every teacher has the responsibility of helping students learn how to learn, and that includes helping students develop their word comprehension skills, reading skills, thinking and memory skills, and their motivation for learning.

For example, if introducing to students the word *hermaphrodite,* the science teacher has the opportunity to teach a bit of Greek mythology in the process of helping the students with the meaning of that important term in biology, through showing students the origin of the word's two roots (Hermes, or Mercury, the messenger of the gods, and Aphrodite, or Venus, goddess of love and beauty). Taking time to teach a bit of Greek mythology affords the science teacher an opportunity to cross disciplines and capture the interest of a few more students.

Give thoughtful and intelligent consideration to student diversity. During the preactive phase of planning, while preparing your talk, consider students in your classroom who are culturally and linguistically different and those who have special needs. Personalize the talk for them by choosing your vocabulary carefully and appropriately, speaking slowly and methodically, repeating often, and by planning meaningful analogies and examples and relevant audio and visual displays.

Use familiar examples and analogies to help students make relevant connections (bridges). Although this sometimes takes a great deal of creative thinking and action during the preactive planning phase, it is important that you attempt to connect the talk with ideas and events with which the students are already familiar. The most effective talk is one that makes frequent and meaningful connections between what students already know and what they are learning, which bridges what they are learning with what they have experienced in their lives. Of course, this means you need to "know" your students. (See section of Chapter 4 titled, "Get to Know the Students as People So as to Build Intrinsic Motivation for Learning.")

Establish eye contact frequently. Your primary eye contact should be with your students—always! That important point cannot be overemphasized. Only momentarily should you look at your notes, your visuals, the projection screen, the writing board, and other adults or objects in the classroom. Although you will probably raise your eyebrows when you read this, it is true and it is important that with practice you can learn to scan a classroom of 30 students, establishing eye contact with each student about once a minute. To "establish" eye contact means that the student is aware that you are looking at him or her. Frequent eye contact can have two major benefits. First, as you "read" a student's body posture and facial expressions, you obtain clues about that student's attentiveness and comprehension. Second, eye contact helps to establish rapport between you and a student. Be alert, though, for students who are from cultures where eye contact is infrequent or unwanted and could have negative consequences. In other words, don't push it!

Frequent eye contact is easier when using an overhead projector than when using the writing board. When using a writing board, you have to turn at least partially away from your audience, and you may also have to pace back and forth from the board to the students to retain that important proximity to them.

Remember our discussions in Chapters 3 and 4 about "overlapping" as an important teaching skill? This is one of those times when its importance really comes into play. While lecturing on a topic you must remain aware and attentive to everything that is happening in the classroom (that is, to student behavior as well as the content of your lecture). No one ever said that good teaching is easy, or if they did, they didn't know what they were talking about. But don't dismay; with the knowledge of the preceding guidelines and with practice, experience, and intelligent reflection, you will develop the necessary skills.

DEMONSTRATION

Most students like demonstrations because the demonstrator is actively engaged in a learning activity rather than merely talking about it. Demonstrations can be used in teaching at any grade level in any subject and for a variety of purposes. The teacher demonstrates

role playing in preparation for a social studies simulation. A teacher demonstrates the steps in solving a mathematics problem. A language arts/English teacher demonstrates clustering to students ready for a creative writing assignment. A science teacher demonstrates the result of combining an acid and a base. The physical education teacher demonstrates the proper way to serve in volleyball.

Purposes of Demonstrations

A demonstration can be designed to serve any of the following purposes: to assist in recognizing a solution to an existing problem; to bring an unusual closure to a lesson or unit of study; to demonstrate a thinking skill; to model a skill used in conflict resolution; to establish problem recognition; to give students opportunity for vicarious participation in active learning; to illustrate a particular point of content; to introduce a lesson or unit of study in a way that grabs the students' attention; to reduce potential safety hazards (where the teacher demonstrates with materials that are too dangerous for students to handle); to review; to save time and resources (as opposed to the entire class doing that which is being demonstrated); and to set up a discrepancy recognition.

Guidelines for Using Demonstrations

When planning a demonstration, you should consider the following guidelines.

Decide what is the most effective way to conduct the demonstration. It might be a verbal or silent demonstration, by a student or by the teacher, by the teacher with a student helper, to the entire class or to small groups, or by some combination of these such as first by the teacher followed then by a repeat of the demonstration by a student or a succession of students.

Be sure that the demonstration is visible to all students. For this purpose, some classrooms use overhead mirrors or, where demonstrations are frequent and where financial resources have been available, video cameras that are connected to large-screen television monitors.

Practice with the materials and procedure before demonstrating to the students. During your practice, try to prepare for anything that could go wrong during the real demonstration; if you don't, as Murphy's Law states, if anything can go wrong, it probably will. Then, if something does go wrong during the live demonstration, use that as an opportunity for a teachable moment: engage the students in working with you to try to figure out what went wrong or, if that isn't feasible, then go to Plan B (see Chapter 10).

Consider your pacing of the demonstration, allowing for enough student wait-see and think time. At the start of the demonstration, explain its purpose and the learning objectives. Remember this adage: tell them what you are going to do, show them, and then tell them what they saw. As with any lesson, plan your closure and allow time for questions and discussion. During the demonstration, as in other types of teacher talk, use frequent stops to check for student understanding.

Consider the use of special lighting to highlight the demonstration. For example, a slide projector can be set up and used as a spotlight.

Be sure that the demonstration table and area are free of unnecessary objects that could distract, obstruct view, or pose a safety hazard. With potentially hazardous demonstrations, such as might occur in physical education, science, or vocational classes, you should *model* proper safety precautions. Wear safety goggles, have fire-safety equipment at hand, and position a protective shield between the demonstration table and nearby students.

TEACHING THINKING FOR INTELLIGENT BEHAVIOR

Pulling together what has been learned about learning and brain functioning, teachers are encouraged to integrate explicit thinking instruction into daily lessons. In other words, teachers should help students develop their thinking skills. In teaching for thinking, we are interested not only in what students know but also in how students behave when they don't know. Gathering evidence of the performance and growth of intelligent behavior requires "kid-watching," or observing students as they try to solve the day-to-day academic and real-life problems they encounter. By collecting anecdotes and examples of written, oral, and visual expressions, we can see students' increasingly voluntary and spontaneous performance of intelligent behaviors.

Characteristics of Intelligent Behavior

Characteristics of intelligent behavior that you should model, teach, and observe developing in your students, as identified by Costa,[3] are described in the following paragraphs.

Persistence. Persistence is sticking to a task until it is completed. Consider the following examples.

- Nearly single-handedly and against formidable odds, Clara Barton persevered to form the American Red Cross in 1882.
- Refusing to be intimidated by the chemical industry, powerful politicians, and the media, Rachel Carson was persistent in her pursuit to educate society about the ill effects of pesticides on humans and the natural world. She refused to accept the premise that damage to nature was the inevitable cost of technological and scientific progress. Her book *Silent Spring*, published in 1963, was the seed for the beginning of the development of today's more responsible ecological attitude.
- Amelia Earhart, born in 1898, demonstrated from the time she was a young girl that she was creative, curious, and persistent. Learning to fly in 1920, in just eight more years Earhart became the first woman to fly the Atlantic Ocean, thereby paving the way for other women to become active in aviation.
- As the result of childhood diseases, Wilma Rudolf, at the age of 10, could not walk without the aid of leg braces. Just ten years later, at the age of 20, she was declared to be the fastest running woman in the world, having won three gold medals in the 1960 World Olympics.

Decreasing impulsivity. When students develop impulse control, they think before acting. Impulsive behavior can worsen conflict and can inhibit effective problem solving.[4] Students can be taught to think before shouting out an answer, before beginning a project or task, and before arriving at conclusions with insufficient data. One of several reasons that teachers should usually insist on a show of student hands before a student is acknowledged to respond or question is to help students develop control over the impulsive behavior of shouting out in class.[5]

Listening to others with understanding and empathy. Some psychologists believe the ability to listen to others, to empathize with and to understand their point of view, is one of the highest forms of intelligent behavior. Empathic behavior is considered an important skill for conflict resolution. Piaget refers to this behavior as *overcoming egocentrism.* In class meetings, brainstorming sessions, think tanks, town meetings, advisory councils, board meetings, and legislative bodies, people from various walks of life convene to share their thinking, to explore their ideas, and to broaden their perspectives by listening to the ideas and reactions of others.

[3]A. L. Costa, *The School as a Home for the Mind* (Palatine, IL: Skylight Publishing, 1991), pp. 20–31. See also Armstrong's twelve qualities of genius—curiosity, playfulness, imagination, creativity, wonderment, wisdom, inventiveness, vitality, sensitivity, flexibility, humor, and joy—in T. Armstrong, *Awakening Genius in the Classroom* (Alexandria, VA: Association for Supervision and Curriculum Development, 1998), pp. 2–15.

[4]See, for example, M. Goos and P. Galbraith, "Do It This Way! Metacognitive Strategies in Collaborative Mathematics Problem Solving," *Educational Studies in Mathematics* 30(3):229–260 (April 1996).

[5]For further reading about the relation of impulse control to intelligence, see D. Goleman, *Emotional Intelligence: Why It Can Matter More Than IQ* (New York: Bantam Books, 1995), and D. Harrington-Lueker, "Emotional Intelligence," *High Strides* 9(4):1, 4–5 (March/April 1997).

Cooperative thinking-social intelligence. Humans are social beings. Real-world problem solving has become so complex that seldom can any person go it alone. Not all students come to school knowing how to work effectively in groups. They may exhibit competitiveness, narrow-mindedness, egocentrism, ethnocentrism, or criticism of others' values, emotions, and beliefs. Listening, consensus seeking, giving up an idea to work on someone else's, empathy, compassion, group leadership, cooperative learning, knowing how to support group efforts, altruism—those behaviors are indicative of intelligent human beings, and they can be learned by students at school and in the classroom.

Flexibility in thinking. Sometimes referred to as *lateral thinking,* flexibility in thinking is the ability to approach a problem from a new angle using a novel approach. With modeling by the teacher, students can develop this behavior as they learn to consider alternative points of view and to deal with several sources of information simultaneously.

Metacognition. Learning to plan, monitor, assess, and reflect on one's own thinking is another characteristic of intelligent behavior. Cooperative learning groups, journals, portfolio conferences, self-assessment, and thinking aloud in dyads are strategies that can be used to help students develop this intelligent behavior. Thinking aloud is good modeling for your students, helping them to develop their own cognitive skills of thinking, learning, and reasoning.[6]

Striving for accuracy and precision. Teachers can observe students growing in this behavior when students take time to check over their work, review the procedures, refuse to draw conclusions with only limited data, and use concise and descriptive language.

Sense of humor. The positive effects of humor on the body's physiological functions are well established: a drop in the pulse rate, an increase of oxygen in the blood, the activation of antibodies that fight against harmful microorganisms and gamma interferon, and the release of gamma interferon, a hormone that fights viruses and regulates cell growth. Humor liberates creativity and provides high-level thinking skills, such as anticipation, finding novel relationships, and visual imagery. The acquisition of a sense of humor follows a developmental sequence similar to that described by Piaget[7] and Kohlberg.[8] Initially, young children may find humor in all the wrong things—human frailty, ethnic humor, sacrilegious riddles, ribald profanities. Later, creative children thrive on finding incongruity and will demonstrate a whimsical frame of mind during problem solving.

Questioning and problem posing. Children are usually full of questions, and, unless discouraged, they ask them. We want students to be alert to and recognize discrepancies and phenomena in their environment and to freely inquire about their causes. In exemplary educational programs, students are encouraged to ask questions (see Chapter 7) and then from those questions to develop a problem-solving strategy to investigate their questions.

Drawing on knowledge and applying it to new situations. A major goal of formal education is for students to apply school-learned knowledge to real-life situations. To develop skills in drawing on past knowledge and applying that knowledge to new situations, students must be given opportunity to practice doing that very thing. Problem recognition, problem solving, and project-based learning are ways of providing that opportunity.

Taking risks. Students should be encouraged to venture forth and explore their ideas. Teachers should model this behavior and can provide opportunities for students to develop this intelligent behavior by using techniques such as brainstorming, exploratory investigations, projects, and cooperative learning.

Using all the senses. As discussed in previous chapters, especially Chapter 6, as often as is appropriate and feasible, students should be encouraged to learn to use and develop all their sensory input channels to learn (i.e., verbal, visual, tactile, and kinesthetic).

Ingenuity, originality, insightfulness: creativity. All students must be encouraged to do and discouraged from saying "I can't." Students must be taught in such a way as to encourage intrinsic motivation rather than reliance on extrinsic sources. Teachers must be able to offer criticism so the student understands that the criticism is not a criticism of self. In exemplary programs, students learn the value of feedback. They learn the value of their own intuition, of guessing—they learn "I can."

Wonderment, inquisitiveness, curiosity, and the enjoyment of problem solving: a sense of efficacy as a thinker. Young children express wonderment, an expression that should never be stifled. Through effective teaching, adolescents can recapture that sense of wonderment as they are guided by an effective teacher into a feeling of "I can." They can express a feeling of "I enjoy."

We should strive to help our own students develop these characteristics of intelligent behavior. In Chapter 3 you learned of specific teacher behaviors that facilitate this development. Now, let's review additional research findings that offer important considerations in the facilitation of student learning and intelligent behaving.

---

[6]See, for example, J. W. Astington, "Theory of Mind Goes to School," *Educational Leadership* 56(3):46–48 (November 1998).

[7]J. Piaget, *The Psychology of Intelligence* (Totowa, NJ: Littlefield Adams, 1972).

[8]I. Kohlberg, *The Meaning and Measurement of Moral Development* (Worcester, MA: Clark University Press, 1981).

Direct Teaching for Thinking and Intelligent Behavior

The curriculum of any school includes the development of skills that are used in thinking. Because the academic achievement of students increases when they are taught thinking skills directly, many researchers and educators concur that direct instruction should be given to all students on how to think and to behave intelligently.[9]

Research Imperatives for the Teaching of Thinking

The direct teaching of thinking has been influenced by four research perspectives. The *cognitive view of intelligence* asserts that intellectual ability is not fixed but can be developed. The *constructivist approach to learning* maintains that learners actively and independently construct knowledge by creating and coordinating relationships in their mental repertoire. The *social psychology view of classroom experience* focuses on the learner as an individual who is a member of various peer groups and a society. The *perspective of information processing* deals with the acquisition, elaboration, and management of information.[10]

Direct Teaching of Skills Used in Thinking

Rather than assuming that students have developed thinking skills (such as classifying, comparing, concluding, generalizing, inferring, and others—see Figure 9.3), teachers should devote classroom time to teaching them directly. When teaching a thinking skill directly, the subject content becomes the vehicle for thinking. For example, a social studies lesson can teach students how to distinguish fact and opinion; a language arts lesson instructs students how to compare and analyze; a science lesson can teach students how to set up a problem for their inquiry.

Inquiry teaching and discovery learning are both useful tools for learning and for teaching thinking skills. For further insight and additional strategies and for the many programs concerned with teaching thinking, see the resources in this chapter's footnotes and the list of readings at the end of the chapter.[11]

INQUIRY TEACHING AND DISCOVERY LEARNING

Intrinsic to the effectiveness of both inquiry and discovery is the assumption that students would rather actively seek knowledge than receive it through traditional expository (i.e., information delivery) methods such as lectures, demonstrations, and textbook reading. Although inquiry and discovery are important teaching tools, there is sometimes confusion about exactly what inquiry teaching is and how it differs from discovery learning. The distinction should become clear as you study the following descriptions of these two important tools for teaching and learning.

Problem Solving

Perhaps a major reason why inquiry and discovery are sometimes confused is that in both, students are actively engaged in problem solving. Problem solving is the ability to define or describe a problem, determine the desired outcome, select possible solutions, choose strategies, test trial solutions, evaluate outcomes, and revise these steps where necessary.[12]

Inquiry vs. Discovery

Problem solving is *not* a teaching strategy but a high-order intellectual behavior that facilitates learning. What a teacher can and should do is to provide opportunities for students to identify and tentatively solve problems. Experiences in inquiry and discovery can provide those opportunities. With the processes involved in inquiry and discovery, teachers can help students develop the skills necessary for effective problem solving. Two major differences between discovery and inquiry are (1) who identifies the problem and (2) the percentage of decisions that are made by the students. Table 9.1 shows three levels of inquiry, each level defined according to what the student does and decides.

It should be evident from Table 9.1 that what is called *Level I inquiry* is actually traditional, didactic, "cookbook" teaching, where both the problem and the process for resolving it are defined for the student. The student then works through the process to its inevitable resolution. If the process is well designed, the result is inevitable, because the student "discovers" what was intended by the writers of the program. This level is also called *guided inquiry* or *discovery*, because the students are carefully guided through the investigation to (the predictable) "discovery."

[9]See, for example, A. Whimbey, "Test Results From Teaching Thinking," in A. L. Costa (Ed.) *Developing Minds: A Resource Book for Teaching Thinking* (Alexandria, VA: Association for Supervision and Curriculum Development, 1985), pp. 269–271.

[10]B. Z. Presseisen, *Implementing Thinking in the School's Curriculum*, unpublished paper presented at the third Annual Meeting of the International Association for Cognitive Education, Riverside, CA, on February 9, 1992.

[11]For products for teaching thinking, contact Critical Thinking Press & Software, P.O. Box 448, Pacific Grove, CA 93950. Phone 800-458-4849.

[12]A. L. Costa (Ed.), *Developing Minds: A Resource for Teaching Thinking* (Alexandria, VA: Association for Supervision and Curriculum Development, 1985), p. 312.

Table 9.1   Levels of Inquiry.

	Level I	Level II	Level III
Problem identification	By teacher or textbook	By teacher or textbook	By student
Process of solving the problem	Decided by teacher or text	Decided by student	Decided by student
Indentification of tentative solution	Resolved by student	Resolved by student	Resolved by student

Figure 9.2   The inquiry cycle.

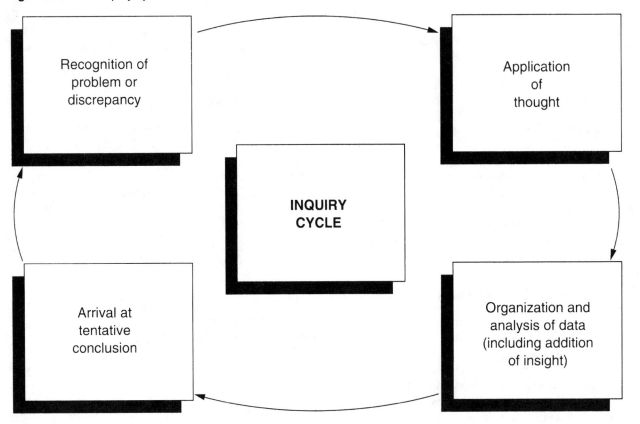

Level I is in reality a strategy within the *delivery mode,* the advantages of which were described in Chapter 6. Because Level I "inquiry" is highly manageable and the learning outcome is predictable, it is probably best for teaching basic concepts and principles. Students who never experience learning beyond Level I are missing an opportunity to engage their highest mental operations, and they seldom (or never) get to experience more motivating, real-life problem solving. Furthermore, those students may come away with the false notion that problem solving is a linear process, which it is not. As illustrated in Figure 9.2, true inquiry is cyclical rather than linear. For that reason, Level I is *not* true inquiry, because it is a linear process. Real-world problem solving is a cyclical rather than linear process. One enters the cycle whenever a discrepancy or problem is observed and recognized, and that can occur at any point in the cycle.

True Inquiry

By the time children are in the intermediate grades, they should be provided experiences for true inquiry, which begins with *Level II,* where students actually decide and design processes for their inquiry. True inquiry emphasizes the tentative nature of conclusions, which makes the activity more like real-life problem solving in which decisions are always subject to revision if and when new data so prescribe.

At *Level III* inquiry students recognize and identify the problem, decide the processes, and reach a conclusion. In project-centered teaching, which has been discussed and described throughout this resource guide, especially in Chapter 8, students are usually engaged at this level of inquiry. By the time students are in middle grades, Level III inquiry should be a major strategy for instruction, which is often the case in schools that use

REAL-LIFE SCENARIO

Problem Solving and Decision Making in the Real World Is an Integrated and Interdisciplinary Inquiry Activity

On any given day or specified time period, teacher and students can look at a problem or subject of study from the point of view of many separate disciplines. Such an interdisciplinary approach to some matter of concern has been adopted not only by educators but by other professionals as well. It is the mode of meaningful learning and real-life problem solving.

For example, consider the fact-finding and decision-making approach of public officials in Colorado when confronted with the task of making decisions about projects proposed for watersheds in their state. While gathering information, the officials brought in Dave Rosgen, a state hydrologist. Rosgen led the officials into the field to demonstrate specific strategies to help control erosion and rehabilitate damaged streams. He took the officials to Wolf Creek, where they donned high waders. Rosgen led the group down the creek to examine various features of that complex natural stream. He pointed out evidence of the creek's past meanders, patterns that he had incorporated into his rehabilitation projects. In addition to listening to this scientist's point of view, the public officials listened to other experts to consider related economic and political issues before making final decisions about projects that had been proposed for watersheds in that state.

During interdisciplinary thematic units, students study a topic, its underlying ideas, and related knowledge from various disciplines on an ongoing basis. The teacher, sometimes with the help of students and other teachers and adults, presents experiences designed to illustrate ideas and skills from various disciplines, just as Rosgen introduced information from hydrology, to develop literacy skills through the unit. For instance, the teacher might stimulate communication skills through creative writing and other projects. Throughout the unit, the students are guided in exploring ideas related to different disciplines to integrate their knowledge.

cross-age teaching and interdisciplinary thematic instruction. Using this strategy is not easy; like most good teaching practices it is a lot of work. But as in all good teaching, the intrinsic rewards make the effort worthwhile. One teacher using interdisciplinary thematic instruction with student-centered inquiry exclaimed, "I've never worked harder in my life, but I've never had this much fun, either."

The Critical Thinking Skills of Discovery and Inquiry

In true inquiry, students generate ideas and then design ways to test those ideas. The various processes used represent the many critical thinking skills. Some of those skills are concerned with generating and organizing data; others are concerned with building and using ideas. Figure 9.3 provides four main categories of these thinking processes and illustrates the place of each within the inquiry cycle.

Some processes in the cycle are discovery processes, and others are inquiry processes. Inquiry processes include the more complex mental operations, including all of those in the idea-using category. Project-centered teaching provides an avenue for doing that, as does problem-centered teaching.

Inquiry learning is a higher-level mental operation that introduces the concept of the discrepant event, something that establishes cognitive disequilibrium (using the element of surprise to challenge prior notions) to help students develop skills in observing and being alert for discrepancies. Such a strategy provides opportunities for students to investigate their own ideas about explanations. Inquiry, like discovery, depends upon skill in problem solving; the difference between the two is in the amount of decision-making responsibility given to students. Experiences afforded by inquiry help students understand the importance of suspending judgment and also the tentativeness of answers and solutions. With those understandings, students eventually can better deal with life's ambiguities. When students are not provided these important educational experiences, their education is incomplete.

One of the most effective ways of stimulating inquiry is to use materials that provoke students' interest. These materials should be presented in a non-threatening, noncompetitive context, so students think and hypothesize freely. The teacher's role is to encourage students to form as many hypotheses as possible and then support their hypotheses with reasons. After the students suggest several ideas, the teacher should begin to move on to higher-order, more abstract questions that involve the development of generalizations and evaluations. True inquiry problems have a special advantage in that they can be used with almost any group of students. Members of a group approach the problem as an adventure in thinking and apply it to whatever background they can muster. Background experience may enrich a student's approach to the problem but is not crucial to the use or understanding of the evidence presented to him or her. Locating a colony, the activity presented in Figure 9.4, is a Level II inquiry. As a class, do the inquiry now.

Figure 9.3 Inquiry cycle processes.

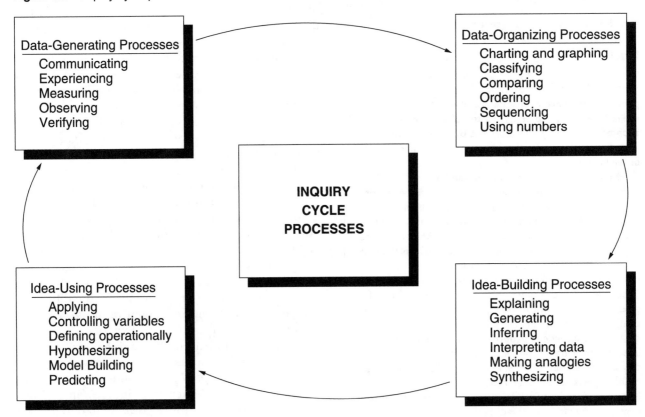

INTEGRATING STRATEGIES FOR INTEGRATED LEARNING

In today's exemplary classrooms, instructional strategies are combined to establish the most effective teaching-learning experience. For example, in an integrated language arts program, teachers are interested in their students' speaking, reading, listening, thinking, study, and writing skills. These skills (and not textbooks) form a holistic process that is the primary aspect of integrated language arts.

In the area of speaking skills, oral discourse (discussion) in the classroom has a growing research base that promotes methods of teaching and learning through oral language. These methods include cooperative learning, instructional scaffolding, and inquiry teaching.

In cooperative learning groups, students discuss and use language for learning that benefits both their content learning and skills in social interaction. Working in heterogeneous groups, students participate in their own learning and can extend their knowledge base and cultural awareness with students of different backgrounds. When students share information and ideas, they are completing difficult learning tasks, using divergent thinking and decision making, and developing their understanding of concepts. As issues

are presented and responses are challenged, student thinking is clarified. Students assume the responsibility for planning within the group and for carrying out their assignments. When needed, the teacher models an activity with one group in front of the class and, when integrated with student questions, the modeling can become inquiry teaching. Activities can include any from a variety of heuristics (a heuristic is a tool used in solving a problem or understanding an idea), such as the following:

Brainstorming. Members generate ideas related to a key word and record them. Clustering or chunking, mapping, and the Venn diagram (all discussed below) are variations of brainstorming.

Think-pair-share. A concept is presented by the teacher, and students are paired to discuss the concept. They share what they already know or have experienced about that concept and then share that information with the rest of the class. This strategy is an excellent technique for preassessing and discovering students' prior notions.

Chunking or clustering. Groups of students apply mental organizers by clustering information into chunks for easier manipulation and remembering.

Memory strategies. The teacher and students model the use of acronyms, mnemonics, rhymes, or clustering

Figure 9.4 Locating a colony: a Level II inquiry.
(*Source:* Adapted by permission from unpublished material provided by Jennifer Devine and Dennis Devine.)

Presentation of the Problem. In groups of three or four, students receive the following information.

Background. You (your group is considered as one person) are one of 120 passengers on the ship, the *Prince Charles.* You left England 12 weeks ago. You have experienced many hardships, including a stormy passage, limited rations, sickness, cold and damp weather, and hot, foul air below deck. Ten of your fellow immigrants to the New World, including three children, have died and been buried at sea. You are now anchored at an uncertain place, off the coast of the New World, which your captain believes to be somewhere north of the Virginia Grants. Seas are so rough and food so scarce that you and your fellow passengers have decided to settle here. A landing party has returned with a map they made of the area. You, as one of the elders, must decide at once where the settlement is to be located. The tradesmen want to settle along the river, which is deep, even though this seems to be the season of low water levels. Within ten months they expect deep-water ships from England with more colonists and merchants. Those within your group who are farmers say they must have fertile, workable land. The officer in charge of the landing party reported seeing a group of armed natives who fled when approached. He feels the settlement must be located so that it can be defended from the natives and from the sea.

Directions, step one: You (your group) are to select a site on the attached map that you feel is best suited for a colony. Your site must satisfy the different factions aboard the ship. A number of possible sites are already marked on the map (letters *A–G*). You may select one of these locations or use them as reference points to show the location of your colony. When your group has selected its site, list and explain the reasons for your choice. When each group has arrived at its tentative decision, these will be shared with the whole class.

Directions, step two: After each group has made its presentation and argument, a class debate is held about where the colony should be located.

Notes to teacher: For the debate, have a large map drawn on the writing board or on an overhead transparency, where each group's mark can be made for all to see and discuss. After each group has presented its argument for its location and against the others, we suggest that you then mark on the large map the two, three, or more hypothetical locations (assuming that, as a class, there is no single favorite location yet). Then take a straw vote of the students, allowing each to vote independently rather than as members of groups. At this time you can terminate the activity by saying that if the majority of students favor one location, then that, in fact, is the solution to the problem—that is, the colony is located wherever the majority of class members believe it should be. No sooner will that statement be made by you than someone will ask, "Are we correct?" or "What is the right answer?" They will ask such questions because, as students in school, they are used to solving problems that have right answers (Level I inquiry teaching). In real-world problems, however, there are no "right" answers, though some answers may seem better than others. It is the process of problem solving that is important. You want your students to develop confidence in their ability to solve problems and understand the tentativeness of "answers" to real-life problems.

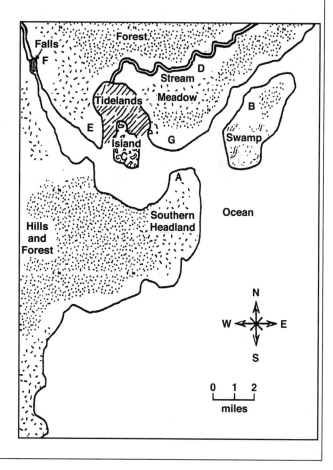

of information into categories to promote learning. Sometimes, such as in memorizing a social security number, one must learn by rote information that is not connected to any prior knowledge. To do that it is helpful to break the information to be learned into smaller chunks, such as dividing the nine digit social security number into smaller chunks of information (with, in this instance, each chunk separated by a hyphen). Learning by rote is also easier if one can connect that which is to be memorized to some prior knowledge. Strategies such as these are used to bridge the gap between rote learning and meaningful learning and are known as *mnemonics*.[13] Sample mnemonics are:

- The notes on a treble staff are *FACE* for the space notes and *Empty Garbage Before Dad Flips* (*EGBDF*) for the line notes. The notes on the bass staff are *All Cows Eat Granola Bars* or *Grizzly Bears Don't Fly Airplanes* (*GBDFA*).
- The order of the planets from the Sun are *My Very Educated Mother Just Served Us Nine Pizzas* (*Mercury, Venus, Earth, Mars, Jupiter, Saturn, Uranus, Neptune, and Pluto*—although, in reality, Pluto and Neptune alternate in this order because of their elliptical orbits).
- The names of the Great Lakes: *HOMES* for *Huron, Ontario, Michigan, Erie,* and *Superior*.
- Visual mnemonics are useful too, such as remembering that Italy is shaped in the form of a boot.

Comparing and contrasting. Similarities and differences between items are found and recorded.

Concept mapping. A variety of terms for the visual tools useful for learning have been invented—some of which are synonymous—terms such as brainstorming web, mindmapping web, spider map, cluster, concept map, cognitive map, semantic map, Venn diagram, visual scaffold, and graphic organizer. Hyerle separates these visual tools into three categories, according to purpose: (1) *brainstorming tools* (such as mind mapping, webbing, and clustering) for the purpose of developing one's knowledge and creativity; (2) *task-specific organizers* (such as life cycle diagrams used in biology, decision trees used in mathematics, and text structures in reading); and (3) *thinking process maps* (such as concept mapping) for encouraging cognitive development across disciplines.[14] It is the latter in which we are interested here.

Based on Ausubel's theory of meaningful learning,[15] concept mapping has been found useful for helping students in changing prior notions or misconceptions, sometimes referred to as *naïve views*. Concept mapping can help students develop their ability to organize, represent their thoughts, and connect new knowledge to their past experiences and precepts.[16] Simply put, concepts can be thought of as classifications that attempt to organize the world of objects and events into a smaller number of categories. In everyday use, the term *concept* means idea, as when someone says, "My concept of love is not the same as yours." Concepts embody a meaning that develops in complexity with experience and learning over time. For example, the concept of love held by a second grader is unlikely to be as complex as that held by a ninth grader. Concept mapping is a graphical way of demonstrating the relationship between and among concepts.

Typically, a concept map refers to a visual or graphic representation of concepts with bridges (connections) that show relationships. Figure 9.5 shows a partially complete concept map in social studies, where students have made connections of concept relationships between fruit farming and marketing. The general procedure for concept mapping is to have the students: (1) identify important concepts in materials being studied, often by circling those concepts, (2) rank order the concepts from the most general to the most specific, and (3) arrange the concepts on a sheet of paper, connect related ideas with lines, and define the connections between the related ideas.

Inferring. For instance, students assume the roles of people (real or fictional) and infer their motives, personalities, and thoughts.

Outlining. Each group completes an outline that contains some of the main ideas but with subtopics omitted.

Paraphrasing. In a brief summary, each student restates a short selection of what was read or heard.

Reciprocal teaching. In classroom dialogue, students take turns at generating questions, summarizing, clarifying, and predicting.[17]

Study strategies. Important strategies that should be taught explicitly include vocabulary expansion,

[13]See, for example, M. A. Mastropieri et al., "Using Mnemonic Strategies to Teach Information about U.S. Presidents: A Classroom-Based Investigation," *Learning Disability Quarterly* 20(1):13–21 (Winter 1997), and J. G. van Hell and A. C. Mahn, "Keyword Mnemonics Versus Rote Rehearsal: Learning Concrete and Abstract Foreign Words by Experienced and Inexperienced Learners," *Language Learning* 47(3):507–546 (September 1997).

[14]D. Hyerle, *Visual Tools for Constructing Knowledge* (Alexandria, VA: Association for Supervision and Curriculum Development, 1996)

[15]D. P. Ausubel, *The Psychology of Meaningful Learning* (New York: Grune & Stratton, 1963).

[16]About concept mapping, see: J. D. Novak, "Concept Maps and Vee Diagrams: Two Metacognitive Tools to Facilitate Meaningful Learning," *Instructional Science* 19(1):29–52 (1990); J. D. Novak and B. D. Gowin, *Learning How to Learn* (Cambridge, England: Cambridge University Press, 1984); and E. Plotnick, *Concept Mapping: A Graphical System for Understanding the Relationship Between Concepts.* ED407938, Syracuse, NY: ERIC Clearinghouse on Information and Technology, 1997.

[17]See C. J. Carter, "Why Reciprocal Teaching?" *Educational Leadership* 54(6):64–68 (March 1997).

Figure 9.5 Sample partially completed concept map.

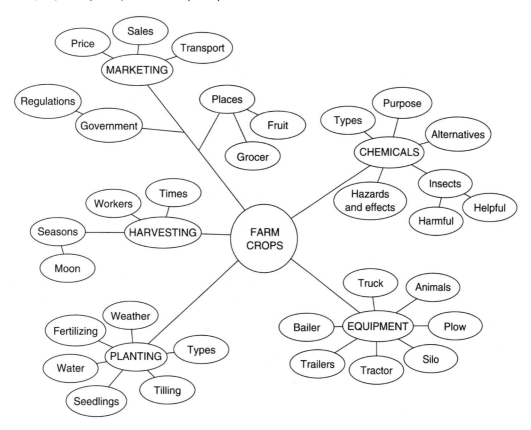

reading and interpreting graphic information, locating resources, using advance organizers, adjusting one's reading rate, and skimming, scanning, and study reading.[18]

Textbook study strategies. Students use the *SQ4R* or related study strategies (see Chapter 5).

Vee mapping. This road map is completed by students as they learn, showing the route they follow from prior knowledge to new and future knowledge.

Venn diagramming. This technique compares two concepts or, for example, two stories, to show similarities and differences. Using stories as an example, a student draws two circles that intersect and marks the circles one and two and the area where they intersect

three. In circle one, the student lists characteristics of one story, and in circle two she or he lists the characteristics of the second story. In the area of the intersection, marked three, the student lists characteristics common to both stories.

Visual learning log (VLL). This variation of the road map is completed by students showing the route they follow from prior knowledge to new and future knowledge, except that the VLL consists of pictograms (freeform drawings) that each student makes and that are maintained in a journal.

To further explore inquiry teaching and integrated learning, do Exercise 9.1.

---

[18]J. S. Choate, and T. A. Rakes, *Inclusive Instruction for Struggling Readers,* Fastback 434 (Bloomington, IN: Phi Delta Kappa Educational Foundation, 1998.

EXERCISE 9.1 A STUDY OF INQUIRY AND STRATEGY INTEGRATION

INSTRUCTIONS: The purpose of this exercise is to analyze the Locating a Colony inquiry (the Level II inquiry of Figure 9.4 that you did with your classmates) and the discussion in the text about integrating strategies and then to synthesize that information for use in your own teaching. We suggest that you first answer the questions of this exercise and then share your answers with others in your discipline (in groups of about four). Finally, share your group's collective responses with the entire class.

1. My subject field and/or grade level interest: _____

    _____

2a. How I could use the Locating a Colony inquiry (for what purpose, goals, or objectives): _____

    _____

    _____

2b. Content in my class that students might be expected to learn from doing the Locating a Colony

    inquiry: _____

    _____

3. In what way could I involve my students in cooperative learning while doing the Locating a Colony

    inquiry: _____

    _____

    _____

4. How brainstorming could be used while doing the Locating a Colony inquiry: _____

    _____

    _____

5. How clustering could be used while doing the Locating a Colony inquiry: _____

    _____

    _____

6. How concept mapping could be used while doing the Locating a Colony inquiry: _____

    _____

7. How comparing and contrasting could be used while doing the Locating a Colony inquiry: _____

    _____

8. How outlining could be used while doing the Locating a Colony inquiry: _____

    _____

    _____

9. How paraphrasing could be used while doing the Locating a Colony inquiry: _____

    _____

    _____

☞

EXERCISE 9.1 (*continued*)

10. How summarizing could be used while doing the Locating a Colony inquiry: _____

_____

_____

11. How memory strategies could be used while doing the Locating a Colony inquiry: _____

_____

_____

12. How inferring could be used while doing the Locating a Colony inquiry: _____

_____

_____

13. What other skills could be taught while doing the Locating a Colony inquiry? For each, describe how.

_____

_____

LEARNING BY EDUCATIONAL GAMES

Devices classified as educational games include a wide variety of learning activities, such as simulations, role-play and sociodrama activities, mind games, board games, computer games, and sporting games, all of which provide valuable learning experiences for participants. These experiences tend to involve several senses and several learning modalities, tend to engage higher-order thinking skills, and tend to be quite effective as learning tools.

Of all the arts, drama involves the learner-participant most fully—intellectually, emotionally, physically, verbally, and socially. Interactive drama, which is roleplaying, is a simplified form of drama, a method by which children can become involved with literature. Studies show that children's comprehension increases and they are highly motivated to read if they are involved in analyzing and actively responding to the characters, plot, and setting of the story being read.[19]

Simulations, a more complex form of drama, serve many of the developmental needs of young people. They provide interaction with peers and allow students of different backgrounds and talents to work together on a common project. They engage students in physical activity and give them opportunity to try out different roles, which help them to understand themselves better. Role-play simulations, like the *Redwood Controversy,* for example, can provide concrete experiences that help students to understand complex concepts

and issues, and they provide opportunities to explore values and develop skill in decision making.

Educational games can play an integral role in interdisciplinary teaching and serve as valuable resources for enriching the effectiveness of students' learning. As with any other instructional strategy, the use of games should follow a clear educational purpose, have a careful plan, and be congruent with the instructional objectives.

Classification of Educational Games

What are educational games? Seven types of games fall under the general heading of "educational games." Table 9.2 shows the seven types, with characteristics and examples of each. Certain types have greater educational value than do others. Games that do not emphasize the element of competition—that are not "contest"—are particularly recommended for use in the academic classroom (types 1, 3, and 5 in Table 9.2).

Purposes of Educational Games

Games can be powerful tools for teaching and learning. A game can have one to several of the following purposes: (a) add variety and change of pace, (b) assess student learning, (c) enhance student self-esteem, (d) motivate students, (e) offer a break from the usual rigors of learning, (f) provide learning about real-life issues through simulation and role-playing, (g) provide learning through tactile and kinesthetic modalities, (h) provide problem-solving situations and experiences, (i) provide skill development and motivation through computer usage, (j) provide skill development in inductive thinking, (k) provide skill development in verbal

---

[19]R. Coney and S. Kanel, "Opening the World of Literature to Children through Interactive Drama Experiences," paper presented at the Annual International Conference and Exhibition of the Association for Childhood Education (Portland, OR, April 9–12, 1997).

Table 9.2 Classification of Educational Games.

Type	Characteristics	Examples
1. Pure game*	Fun	*Ungame, New Games*
2. Pure contest	Stimulates competition; built-in inefficiency[‡]	Political contests, e.g. U.S. presidential race
3. Pure simulation*	Models reality	Toddler play
4. Contest/game	Stimulates competition; fun; built-in inefficiency	Golf; bowling; *Trivial Pursuit*
5. Simulation/game*	Models reality; fun	*SIMCITY; Our Town's Planning Commission Meeting*[§]
6. Contest/simulation	Stimulates competition; models reality; built-in inefficiency	Boxcar Derby of Akron, OH
7. Simulation/game/contest	Models reality; fun; stimulates competition; built-in inefficiency	*Monopoly, Life, Careers*

*These game types do not emphasize competition and thus are particularly recommended for use in the classroom as learning tools.

[‡] Rules for accomplishing the game objective make accomplishment of that objective less than efficient. For example, in golf the objective is to get the ball into the hole with the least amount of effort, but to do that, one has to take a peculiarly shaped stick (the club) and hit the ball, find it, and hit it again, continuing that sequence until the ball is in the hole. Yet, common sense tells us that the best way to get the ball into the hole with the least amount of effort would be simply to pick up the ball and place it by hand into the hole.

[§] See J. V. Vort, "Our Town's Planning Commission Meeting," *Journal of Geography* 96(4):183–190 (July–August 1997).

communication and debate, (l) reinforce convergent thinking, (m) review and reinforce subject matter learning, (n) encourage learning through peer interaction, (o) stimulate critical thinking, (p) stimulate deductive thinking, (q) stimulate divergent and creative thinking, and (r) teach both content and process.

Sources of Educational Games

Sources for useful educational games include professional journals (see Figure 9.6) and the Internet. Sources of commercially available educational games for use in teaching are shown in Figure 9.7. Now do Exercise 9.2.

Figure 9.6 Sample professional journals with educational games.

- J. Bassett, "The Pullman Strike of 1894," *OAH Magazine of History* 11(2):34–41 (Winter 1997). Role-play simulation.
- D. Bogan and D. Wood, "Simulating Sun, Moon, and Earth Patterns," *Science Scope* 21(2):46, 48 (October 1997). Role-play for middle school.
- C. Collyer, "Winter Secrets: An Instant Lesson Plan," *Pathways: The Ontario Journal of Outdoor Education* 9(2):18–20 (April 1997). Instructions for two games about predator-prey relationships.
- P. Cunningham, "Reading Clinic. Making Decoding Fun with This Cross-Checking Game," *Instructor* 107(2):74–75 (September 1997). For teaching K–3.
- S. A. Farin, "Acting Atoms," *Science Scope* 21(3):46 (November/December 1997). Role play for middle school.
- J. Gorman, "Strategy Games: Treasures from Ancient Times," *Mathematics Teaching in the Middle School* 3(2):110–116 (October 1997). Presents several games for integrating history and mathematics.
- S. Hightshoe, "Sifting Through the Sands of Time: A Simulated Archaeological Special Feature," *Social Studies and the Young Learner* 9(3):28–30 (January/February, 1997). For elementary and middle school.
- M. J. Howle, "Play-Party Games in the Modern Classroom," *Music Educators Journal* 83(5):24–28 (March 1997). Introduces games that were popular on the 19th-century American frontier.
- T. Levy, "The Amistad Incident: A Classroom Reenactment," *Social Education* 59(5):303–308 (September 1995).
- T. M. McCann, "A Pioneer Simulation for Writing and for the Study of Literature," *English Journal* 85(3):62–67 (March 1996).
- H. Morris, "Universal Games from A to Z," *Mathematics in School* 26(4):35–40 (September 1997). See also F. Tapson, "Mathematical Games," pp. 2–6 of same issue.
- K. D. Owens et al., "Playing to Learn: Science Games in the Classroom," *Science Scope* 20(5):31–33 (February 1997). Games for middle school that encourage abstract thinking.

Figure 9.7 Sources of educational games.

- Ampersand Press, 750 Lake St., Port Townsend, WA 98368, 800-624-4263.
- Aristoplay, 450 S. Wagner Rd., Ann Arbor, MI 48103., 800-GR8-GAME.
- Carolina Biological Supply Company, 2700 York Road, Burlington, NC 27215, 800-334-5551.
- Creative Teaching Associates, P.O. Box 7766, Fresno, CA 93747, 800-767-4282.
- Dawn Publications, 14618 Tyler-Foote Rd., Nevada City, CA 95959, 800-545-7475.
- Delta Educational, 5 Hudson Park Dr., P.O. Box 915, Hudson, NH 03051, 800-258-1302.
- Harcourt Brace School Publishers, 6277 Sea Harbor Dr., Orlando, FL 32887, 800-346-8648.
- Higher-Order Thinking Company, 1733 N.E. Patterson Dr., Lee's Summit, MO 64086, 816-524-2701.
- Latz Chance Games, P.O. Box 72308, Marietta, GA 30007-2308, 888-LCH-GAME.
- Novostar Designs, 317 S. Main St., P.O. Box 1328, Burlington, NC 27216-1328, 800-659-3197.
- Optical Data School Media, 512 Means St., NW, Atlanta, GA 30318, 800-524-2481.
- Other Worlds Educational Enterprises, P.O. Box 6193, Woodland Park, CO 80866-6193, 719-687-3840.
- Summit Learning, P.O. Box 493, Fort Collins, CO 80522, 800-777-8817.
- Teacher Created Materials, 6421 Industry Way, Westminster, CA 92683, 800-662-4321.
- Young Naturalist Company, 1900 N. Main St., Newton, KS 67114, 316-283-9108.

EXERCISE 9.2 DEVELOPING A LESSON USING INQUIRY LEVEL II, THINKING SKILL DEVELOPMENT, A DEMONSTRATION, OR AN INTERACTIVE LECTURE— MICRO PEER TEACHING II

INSTRUCTIONS: The purpose of this exercise is to provide the opportunity for you to create a brief lesson (about 20 minutes of instructional time but to be specified by your instructor) designed for a specific grade level and subject and to try it out on your peers for their feedback in an informal (i.e., nongraded) micro peer teaching demonstration.

Divide your class into four groups. The task of members of each group is to prepare lessons (individually) that fall into one of the four categories: Level II inquiry, thinking level, demonstration, or interactive lecture. Schedule class presentations so that each class member has the opportunity to present her or his lesson and to obtain feedback from class members about it. For feedback, class members who are the "teacher's" audience can complete the assessment rubric shown after this exercise (by circling one of the three choices for each of the 10 categories) and give their completed form to the teacher for use in analysis and self-assessment. Before your class starts this exercise you may want to review the scoring rubric and make modifications to it with the class's input.

To structure your lesson plan, use one of the sample lesson plan formats presented in Chapter 6; however, each lesson should be centered around one major theme or concept and be planned for about 20 minutes of instructional time.

Group 1: Develop a Level II inquiry lesson.

Group 2: Develop a lesson designed to raise the level of student thinking.

Group 3: Develop a lesson that involves a demonstration.

Group 4: Develop a lesson that is an interactive lecture.

☞

EXERCISE 9.2 (*continued*)

PEER AND SELF-ASSESSMENT RUBRIC FOR USE WITH EXERCISE 9.2

For: _____   Group: _____

	1	0.5	0
1. Lesson beginning	effective	less effective	not effective
Comment:			
2. Sequencing	effective	less effective	rambling
Comment:			
3. Pacing of lesson	effective	less effective	too slow or too fast
Comment:			
4. Audience involvement	effective	less effective	none
Comment:			
5. Motivators (e.g., analogies, verbal cues, humor, visual cues, sensory cues)	effective	less effective	not apparent
Comment:			
6. Content of lesson	well chosen	interesting	boring or inappropriate
Comment:			
7. Voice of teacher	stimulating	minor problem	major problems
Comment:			
8. Vocabulary used	well chosen	appropriate	inappropriate
Comment:			
9. Eye contact	excellent	average	problems
Comment:			
10. Closure	effective	less effective	unclear/none
Comment:			

OTHER COMMENTS:

SUMMARY

Central to your selection of instructional strategies should be those strategies that encourage students to become independent thinkers and skilled learners who can help in the planning, structuring, regulating, and assessing of their own learning and learning activities.

Important to helping students construct their understandings are the cognitive tools that are available for their use. There is a large variety of useful and effective aids, media, and resources from which to draw as you plan your instructional experiences, the topic of the next and final chapter of Part III.

QUESTIONS FOR CLASS DISCUSSION

1. Many cognitive researchers agree that students should spend more time actively using knowledge to solve problems and less time reading introductory material and listening to teachers lecture. Describe the meaning of this statement and how you feel about it with respect to your decision to become a teacher.
2. Explain why you would or would not like to teach by inquiry (Level II or III).
3. Explain the meaning of integrating strategies for integrated learning.
4. Are there any cautions that teachers need to be aware of when using games for teaching? If there are, describe them.
5. Explain some specific ways you can help students develop their skills in thinking and learning. Explain how you will determine that students have raised their skill level in thinking and learning.
6. Select one of the characteristics of intelligent behavior and (for a grade level of your choice and time limit as decided by your class) and write a lesson plan for helping students develop that behavior. Share or teach your lesson to others in your class for their analysis and suggestions.
7. Describe one teacher demonstration that is typically done by teachers of a particular grade level and subject. Describe ways that you might try and improve on the way the demonstration is typically done.
8. Describe any prior concepts you held that changed as a result of your experiences with this chapter. Describe the changes.
9. From your current observations and field work as related to this teacher preparation program, clearly identify one specific example of educational practice that seems contradictory to exemplary practice or theory as presented in this chapter. Present your explanation for the discrepancy.
10. Do you have questions generated by the content of this chapter? If you do, list them along with ways answers might be found.

FOR FURTHER READING

Blackey, R. "New Wine in Old Bottles: Revitalizing the Traditional History Lecture." *Teaching History: A Journal of Methods* 22(1):3–25 (Spring 1997).

Cardellichio, T., and Field, W. "Seven Strategies That Encourage Neural Branching." *Educational Leadership* 54(6):33–36 (March 1997).

Checkley, K. "Problem-Based Learning: The Search for Solutions to Life's Messy Problems." *ASCD Curriculum Update* (Summer 1997).

Choate, J. S., and Rakes, T. A. *Inclusive Instruction for Struggling Readers.* Fastback 434. Bloomington, IN: Phi Delta Kappa Educational Foundation, 1998.

Chuoke, M., and Eyman, B. "Play Fair—And Not Just at Recess." *Educational Leadership* 54(8):53–55 (May 1997).

Clemens-Walatka, B. "Amusement Park Inquiry." *Science Teacher* 65(1):20–23 (January 1998).

Geocaris, C. "Increasing Student Engagement: A Mystery Solved." *Educational Leadership* 54(4):72–75 (December 1996/January 1997).

Lacy, C. "Entrepreneurial Earth Science." *Science Teacher* 64(1):54–58 (January 1997).

Morris, H. "Resources for Games and Puzzles in the Math Classroom." *Mathematics in School* 26(4):44–45 (September 1997).

Myers, R. E. *Mind Sparklers. Fireworks for Igniting Creativity in Young Minds.* Book 1 for Grades K–3. Waco, TX: Prufrock Press, 1998.

Myers, R. E. *Mind Sparklers. Fireworks for Igniting Creativity in Young Minds.* Book 2 for Grades 4–8. Waco, TX: Prufrock Press, 1998.

Novak, J. D. *Learning, Creating, and Using Knowledge: Concept Maps as Facilitative Tools in Schools and Corporations.* Mahwah, NJ: Lawrence Erlbaum, 1998.

Owens, K. D., et al. "Playing to Learn: Science Games in the Classroom." *Science Scope* 20(5):31–33 (February 1997).

Petit, M., and Zawojewski, J. S. "Teachers and Students Learning Together about Assessing Problem Solving." *Mathematics Teacher* 90(6):472–477 (September 1997).

Rosenthal, M., and Andrea, L. "Stop and Think!? Using Metacognitive Strategies To Teach Students Social Skills." *Teaching Exceptional Children* 29(3):29–31 (January/February 1997).

Sternberg, R. J. "What Does It Mean to Be Smart?" *Educational Leadership* 54(6):20–24 (March 1997).

Tarquin, P., and Walker, S. *Creating Success in the Classroom! Visual Organizers and How to Use Them.* Englewood, CO: Teachers Ideas Press/Libraries Unlimited, 1997.

Taylor, L. M., and King, J. L. "A Popcorn Project for All Students." *Mathematics Teacher* 90(3):194–200 (March 1997).

Verran, J., et al. "The Body Game: Developed by Undergraduates for Key Stage 2 National Curriculum Science." *Journal of Biological Education* 31(3):181–184 (Autumn 1997).

Wilhelm, J. D. *"You Gotta BE the Book": Teaching Engaged and Reflective Reading with Adolescents.* New York: Teachers College Press, 1997.

Young, A. C. "Higher-Order Learning and Thinking: What Is It and How Is It Taught?" *Educational Technology* 37(4):38–41 (July/August 1997).

Chapter 10

Strategies for Teaching: Aids, Media, and Resources

Important to helping students construct their understandings are the cognitive tools available for their use. You will be pleased to know that you can draw from a large variety of useful and effective media, aids, and resources as you plan your instructional experiences. On the other hand, you could also become overwhelmed by the sheer quantity of different materials available: textbooks, supplementary texts, pamphlets, anthologies, paperbacks, encyclopedias, tests, programmed instructional systems, dictionaries, reference books, classroom periodicals, newspapers, films, records and cassettes, computer software, transparencies, realia, games, filmstrips, audio- and videotapes, slides, globes, manipulatives, CD-ROMs, DVDs, videodiscs, and graphics. You could spend a great deal of time reviewing, sorting, selecting, and practicing with the materials and tools for your use. Although nobody can make the job easier for you, information in this chapter may expedite the process.

Specifically, upon completion of this chapter, you should be able to

1. Demonstrate an awareness of the variety of materials and resources for use in your teaching.
2. Demonstrate knowledge of copyright laws for using printed and media materials for teaching.
3. Demonstrate an understanding about using community resources, speakers, and field trips.
4. Demonstrate an awareness of electronic media available for teaching your subject field, how they can be used, and how and where they can be obtained.
5. Demonstrate competency in using standard classroom tools for teaching.

PRINTED MATERIALS, VISUAL DISPLAYS, AND THE INTERNET

Historically, of all the materials available for instruction, the printed textbook has had, and still has, the most influence on teaching and learning (discussed in Chapter 5). In addition to the student textbook and perhaps an accompanying workbook, there is a vast array of other printed materials available for use in teaching, many of which are available without cost. Printed materials include books, workbooks, pamphlets, magazines, brochures, newspapers, professional journals, periodicals, and duplicated materials including those materials copied from Internet sources.

In reviewing printed materials, factors to be alert for include (1) appropriateness of the material in both content and in reading level, (2) articles in newspapers, magazines, and periodicals, related to the content your students will be studying or to the skills they will be learning, (3) assorted workbooks available from tradebook publishers that emphasize thinking and problem solving rather than rote memorization, with an assortment of workbooks you can have students working on similar but different assignments depending upon their interests and abilities (an example of multilevel teaching), (4) pamphlets, brochures, and other duplicated materials that students can read for specific information and viewpoints about particular topics, and (5) inexpensive paperback books that would provide multiple book readings for your class and make it possible for students to read primary sources.

Sources of Free and Inexpensive Printed Materials

For free and inexpensive printed materials look for sources in your college or university, or public library, or the resource center at a local school district, sources such as those listed in Figure 10.1. Additionally, teachers obtain free and inexpensive teaching materials through connections on the Internet. When considering using materials that you have obtained free or inexpensively, you will want to ensure that the materials are appropriate for use with the age group with whom you work, and that they are free of bias or an unwanted message. The National Education Association (NEA) has published guidelines for teachers to consider before purchasing or using commercial materials; for a free copy contact NEA Communications, 1201 16th STREET, NW, Washington, DC 20036; phone 202-822-7200.

The Internet

Originating from a Department of Defense project in 1969 (called ARPANET) to establish a computer network of military researchers, its successor, the federally funded Internet, has become an enormous, steadily expanding, worldwide system of connected computer networks. The Internet provides literally millions of resources to explore, with thousands more added nearly every day. When the previous edition of this resource guide was published, it was difficult to find any published information about the Internet. Today you can surf the Internet and find many sources about how to use it, and you can walk into most any bookstore and find hundreds of recent titles, most of which give their authors' favorite web sites. However, new technologies are steadily emerging and the Internet

Figure 10.1 Resources for free and inexpensive printed materials.

- *A Guide to Print and Nonprint Materials Available from Organizations, Industry, Governmental Agencies and Specialized Publishers.* New York: Neal Schuman.
- Civil Aeronautics Administration, *Sources of Free and Low-Cost Materials.* Washington, DC: U.S. Department of Commerce.
- Educators Progress Service, Inc., 214 Center Street, Randolph, WI 53956. 414-326-3126. *Educator's Guide to Free Materials; Educator's Guide to Free Teaching Aids.*
- *Freebies for Teachers.* Los Angeles: Lowell House, 1994.
- *Freebies: The Magazine with Something for Nothing.* PO Box 5025, Carpinteria, CA 93014-5025.
- *Video Placement Worldwide (VPW).* Source of free sponsored educational videos and print materials on Internet at <http://www.vpw.com>.

changes every day, with some sites and resources disappearing or not kept current, others changing their location and undergoing reconstruction, and new ones appearing; it would be superfluous for me in this book, which will be around for a few years, to make too much of sites that I personally have viewed and can recommend as teacher resources. Nevertheless, Figure 10.2 includes available Internet resources that I have surfed and can recommend. Other web sites have been mentioned in the text throughout this resource guide, and still others are listed in Figures 1.9 and 8.4 of Chapters 1 and 8 respectively. Perhaps you have found others that you can share with your classmates (and with me). To that end, complete Exercise 10.1.

Figure 10.2 Additional Internet sites: materials and technology.

- *Beyond the MLA Handbook: Documenting Electronic Sources on the Internet* <http://falcon.eku.edu/honors/beyond-mla>. See also *Citing Internet Addresses* <http://www.classroom.net/classroom/CitingNetResources.htm>, and J. Walker's *MLA-Style Citations of Electronic Sources* <http://www.cas.usf.edu/english/walker/mla.html>.
- *Big Page of School Internet Projects and Educational Technology* <http://www.mts.net/~jgreenco/internet.html#Index>.
- *California Instructional Technology Clearinghouse* <http://clearinghouse.k12.ca.us>.
- *Education Resource Organizations Directory* <http://oeri.edu.gov:8888/STATES/direct/SF>.
- *Education World* <http://www.educational-world.com>.
- *Epicenter* <http://www.epicent.com>. *Information resource of software, textbooks, research journal articles, professional conference listings.*
- *ERIC Documents Online* <http://ericir.syr.edu>.
- *Geometry Center* <http://www.geom.umn.edu/welcome.html>.
- *Hewlett Packard E-mail Mentor Program* <http://www.telementor.org>.
- *Interactive Frog Dissection* <http://teach.virginia.edu/go/frog>.
- *Learn the Net* <http://www.learnthenet.com>.
- *Map Resources* <http://www.gsn.org/cf/maps.html>.
- *Mathematics Archives* <http://archives.math.utk.edu/>.
- *Middle School Home Pages Around the World* <http://www.deltanet.com/hewes/middle.html>.
- *National Archives and Records Administration* <http://www.nara.gov>.
- *National Education Association (NEA)* <http://www.nea.org/resources/refs.html>.
- *National Endowment for the Arts Home Page* <http://www.arts.endow.org>.
- *National Geographic Map Machine* <http://www.nationalgeographic.com>.
- *School Match* <http://schoolmatch.com>. Directory of U.S. schools.
- *School Page* <http://www.eyesoftime.com/teacher/index.html>. A teacher's exchange.
- *Science Stuff* <http://www.sciencestuff.com>.
- *Telementoring Young Women in Science, Engineering, and Computing* <http://www.edc.org/CCT/telementoring>.
- *Teachers Network* <http://www.teachnet.org>. A teacher's exchange.
- *The 21st Century Teachers Network* <http://www.21ct.org>. For help in using technology.
- *United States Copyright Office* <http://lcweb.loc.gov/copyright>.
- *WWW4Teachers* <http://4teachers.org>. A source about using educational technology.

EXERCISE 10.1 INTERNET SITES OF USE TO TEACHERS

INSTRUCTIONS: The purpose of this exercise is to search the Internet for sites that you find interesting and useful, or useless, for teaching and to share those sites with your classmates (and, if you want, with the author of this resource guide). Make copies of this page for each site visited; then share your results with your classmates.

Web site I investigated: http:// _____

I consider the site   *highly useful*   *moderately useful*   *of no use*

Specifically for teachers of (grade level and/or subject field):

 Sponsor of site:

Features of interest and usefulness to teachers:

CAUTIONS AND GUIDELINES FOR USING
THE INTERNET

If you have yet to learn to use the Internet, I shall leave the mechanics of that to the many resources available to you, including the experts that can be found among your peers, on your college or university staff, and among members of any public school faculty. The remaining pages of this section address the "how" of using the Internet from an academic perspective. Let's begin with the fictitious although feasible teaching scenario illustrated in Figure 10.3.

Figure 10.3   Teaching scenario: natural disasters.

Let us suppose that the students from your "house" have been working nearly all year on an interdisciplinary thematic unit titled "surviving natural disasters" (returning to the example in Chapter 5 regarding ITU themes). As a culmination to their study they "published" a document titled "Natural Disaster Preparation and Survival Guide for *(name of their community)*" and proudly distributed the guide to their parents and members of the community.

Long before preparing the guide, however, the students had to do research. To learn about the history of various kinds of natural disasters that had occurred or might occur locally and about the sorts of preparations a community should take for each kind of disaster, students searched sources on the Internet, such as federal documents, scientific articles, and articles from newspapers from around the world where natural disasters had occurred. They also searched in the local library and the local newspaper's archives to learn of floods, tornadoes, and fires that had occurred during the past 200 years. Much to their surprise, they also learned that their community is located very near the New Madrid Fault and did, in fact, experience a serious earthquake in 1811, although none since. As a result of that earthquake, two nearby towns completely disappeared; the Mississippi River flowed in reverse, and its course changed and even caused the formation of a new lake in Tennessee.

From published and copyrighted sources, including web sites, the students found many useful photographs, graphics, and articles, which they included in whole or in part in their "Natural Disaster Preparation and Survival Guide." They did so without obtaining permission from the original copyright holders or even citing those sources.

You and the other members of your teaching team and other people were so impressed with the student's work that students were encouraged to offer the document for publication on the school's web site. In addition, the document was received with so much acclaim that the students decided to sell it in local stores. This would help defray the original cost of duplication and enable them to continue the supply of guides.

To the scenario in Figure 10.3, there is a good aspect and there is a not-so-good aspect. The good aspect is that the children used a good technological tool (the Internet) to research a variety of sources, including many primary ones. The not-so-good aspect is that when they published their document on the Internet and when they made copies of their guide to be sold, they did so without permission from original copyright holders. They were infringing copyright law. Although it would take an attorney to say for sure, with this scenario it is probable that the students, teacher, school, and the school district would be liable. As is true for other documents (such as published photos, graphics, and text), unless there is a *clear statement* that materials taken from the Internet are "public domain," it is best to assume that they are copyrighted and should not be republished for profit or on another web site.[1]

There is such a proliferation of information today, from both printed materials and from information on the Internet. Except for the obvious reliable sites such as the *New York Times* and the Library of Congress, how can a person determine the validity and currency of a particular piece of information? When searching for useful and reliable information on a particular topic, how can one be protected from wasting valuable time sifting through all the information? Children need to know that just because information is found on a printed page or is published on the Internet doesn't necessarily mean that the information is accurate or current. Using a checklist such as the one shown in Figure 10.4, and provided with examples of materials that meet and do not meet the criteria of the checklist, students can learn how to assess materials and information on the Internet.

Teaching all students how to access and assess web sites adds to their repertoire of skills for lifelong learning. Consider allowing each student or teams of students to become experts on specific sites during particular units of study. It might be useful to start a chronicle of student-recorded log entries about particular web sites to provide comprehensive long-term data about those sites.

When students use information from the Internet, require that they print copies of sources of citations and materials so you can check for accuracy. These copies may be maintained in their portfolios.

Student work published on the Internet should be considered as intellectual material and protected from plagiarism by others. Most school districts now post a copyright notice on their home page. Someone at the school usually is assigned to supervise the school web

---

[1]J. McKenzie, "Keeping It Legal: Questions Arising Out of Web Site Management," *From Now On* 5(7):5 (June 1996) <http:www.pacifi-crim.net/~mckenzie/jun96/legal.html> (August 13, 1997).

Figure 10.4 Checklist for evaluating Internet information. *Source:* R. J. Ryder and T. Hughes, *Internet for Teachers* (Upper Saddle River, NJ: Merrill/Prentice Hall, 1997), pp. 185–186. By permission of Prentice Hall Publishing Company.

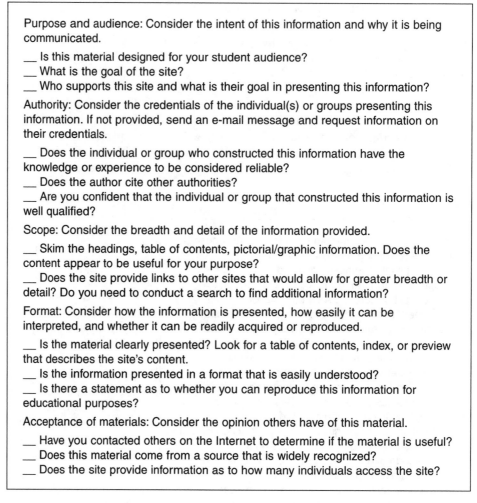

Purpose and audience: Consider the intent of this information and why it is being communicated.

__ Is this material designed for your student audience?
__ What is the goal of the site?
__ Who supports this site and what is their goal in presenting this information?

Authority: Consider the credentials of the individual(s) or groups presenting this information. If not provided, send an e-mail message and request information on their credentials.

__ Does the individual or group who constructed this information have the knowledge or experience to be considered reliable?
__ Does the author cite other authorities?
__ Are you confident that the individual or group that constructed this information is well qualified?

Scope: Consider the breadth and detail of the information provided.

__ Skim the headings, table of contents, pictorial/graphic information. Does the content appear to be useful for your purpose?
__ Does the site provide links to other sites that would allow for greater breadth or detail? Do you need to conduct a search to find additional information?

Format: Consider how the information is presented, how easily it can be interpreted, and whether it can be readily acquired or reproduced.

__ Is the material clearly presented? Look for a table of contents, index, or preview that describes the site's content.
__ Is the information presented in a format that is easily understood?
__ Is there a statement as to whether you can reproduce this information for educational purposes?

Acceptance of materials: Consider the opinion others have of this material.

__ Have you contacted others on the Internet to determine if the material is useful?
__ Does this material come from a source that is widely recognized?
__ Does the site provide information as to how many individuals access the site?

site to see that district and school policy and legal requirements are observed.

For additional and more specific and the most current information on using the Internet, refer to the many sources available, such as reliable sources on the Internet, professional journals and periodicals (see Figure 10.5), and books, some of which are listed at the end of this chapter.[2]

Professional Journals and Periodicals

Figure 10.5 lists examples of the many professional periodicals and journals that can provide useful teaching ideas and web site information and that carry information about instructional materials and how to get them. Some of these may be in your university or college library and accessible through Internet sources. Check there for these and other titles of interest to you.

---

[2]See, for example, C. Caruso, "Before You Cite a Site," *Educational Leadership* 55(3):24–25 (November 1997), and, on the Internet, *Evaluating Internet Resources: A Checklist* at: <http://infopeople. berkeley.edu:8000/bkmk/select.html>.

The ERIC Information Network

The Educational Resources Information Center (ERIC) system, established by the U.S. Department of Education, is a widely used network providing access to information and research in education. Selected clearinghouses and their addresses are shown in Figure 10.6.

Copying Printed Materials

As a teacher you must be familiar with the laws about the use of copyrighted materials, printed and nonprinted, including those obtained from sources on the Internet. Remember that just because there is no notice on a web page that the material is copyrighted, original material is still protected by copyright law; that is just as true for the intellectual property created by a minor as it is for that of an adult.

Although space here prohibits full inclusion of United States legal guidelines, your local school district should be able to provide a copy of current district policies for compliance with copyright laws. District policies should include guidelines for teachers and students in publishing materials on the Internet. If no district

Figure 10.5   Professional journals and periodicals for teachers.

The American Biology Teacher	*Mathematics Teaching in the Middle School*
American Educational Research Quarterly	*The Middle School Journal*
The American Music Teacher	*Modern Language Journal*
American Teacher	*Music Educators Journal*
The Arithmetic Teacher	*NEA Today*
The Art Teacher	*The Negro Educational Review*
Childhood Education	*The New Advocate*
The Computing Teacher	*OAH Magazine of History*
Creative Classroom	*Phi Delta Kappan*
The Earth Scientist	*Physical Education*
Educational Horizons	*Primary Voices K–6*
Educational Leadership	*The Reading Teacher*
English Journal	*Reading Today*
English Language Teaching Journal	*School Arts*
The Good Apple Newspaper	*School Library Journal*
Hispania	*The School Musician*
The History Teacher	*School Science and Mathematics*
The Horn Book	*School Shop*
Instructor	*Science*
Journal of Business Education	*Science Activities*
Journal of Chemical Education	*Science and Children*
Journal of Economic Education	*Science Scope*
Journal of Geography	*Social Education*
Journal of Home Economics	*The Science Teacher*
Journal of Learning Disabilities	*The Social Studies*
Journal of the National Association of Bilingual Educators	*Social Studies and the Young Learner*
	Social Studies Review
Journal of Physical Education and Recreation	*Teacher Magazine*
Journal of Reading	*Teaching K–8*
Journal of Teaching in Physical Education	*Theory and Research in Social Education*
Language Arts	*TESOL Quarterly*
Language Learning	*Voices from the Middle*
Learning	*Writing Teacher*
The Mathematics Teacher	*Young Children*

guidelines are available, when using printed materials adhere to the guidelines shown in Figure 10.7.[3]

When preparing to make a copy, you must find out whether the copying is permitted by law under the category of "permitted use." If not allowed under "permitted use," then you must get written permission to reproduce the material from the holder of the copyright. If the address of the source is not given on the material, addresses may be obtained from various references, such as *Literary Market Place, Audio-Visual Market Place,* and *Ulrich's International Periodical's Directory.*

The Classroom Writing Board

As is true for an auto mechanic or a brain surgeon or any other professional, a teacher needs to know when and how to use the tools of the trade. One of the tools

available to most every classroom teacher is the writing board. Can you imagine a classroom without a writing board? In this section you will find guidelines for using this important tool.

They used to be, and in some schools still are, slate blackboards. In today's classroom, however, the writing board is more likely to be either a board that is painted plywood (chalkboard); a magnetic chalkboard (plywood with a magnetic backing); or a white or colored (light green and light blue are common) *multipurpose board* on which you write with special marking pens. In addition to providing a surface upon which you can write and draw, the multipurpose board can be used as a projection screen and as a surface to which figures cut from colored transparency film will stick. It may also have a magnetic backing.

Extending the purposes of the multipurpose board and correlated with modern technology is an *electronic whiteboard* that can transfer information that is written on it to a connected computer monitor; the computer

---

[3]See also the *Copyright and Fair Use* web site of Stanford University, at <http://fairuse.stanford.edu/>.

Figure 10.6 Selected ERIC addresses.

- *Assessment and Evaluation.* The Catholic University of America, 210 O'Boyle Hall, Washington, DC 20064-4035. <http://ericae2.educ.cua.edu>
- *Counseling and Student Services.* School of Education, 201 Ferguson Building, University of North Carolina at Greensboro, Greensboro, NC 27412-5001. <http://www.unicg.edu/~ericcas2>
- *Handicapped and Gifted Children.* Council for Exceptional Children, 1920 Association Drive, Reston, VA 22191-1589. <http://www.cec.sped.org/ericed.htm>
- *Information and Technology.* Center for Science and Technology, Syracuse University, Syracuse, NY 13244-4100. <http://eric.r.syr.edu/ithame>
- *Languages and Linguistics.* Center for Applied Linguistics, 1118 22nd Street, NW, Washington, DC 20037-1214. <http://www.cal.org/ericcll>
- *Reading, English, and Communication Skills.* Indiana University, 2805 East 10th Street, Smith Research Center, Suite 150, Bloomington, IN 47408-2698. <http://www.indiana.edu/~eric_rec>
- *Rural Education and Small Schools.* Appalachia Educational Laboratory, 1031 Quarrier Street, PO Box 1348, Charleston, WV 25325-1348. <http://aelvira.ael.org/erichp.htm>
- *Science, Mathematics, and Environmental Education.* Ohio State University, 1929 Kenny Road, Columbus, OH 43210-1080. <http://www.ericse.org.>
- *Service Learning.* University of Minnesota, College of Education and Human Development, 1954 Bufford Ave., VoTech Building, St. Paul, MN 55108. <http://www.nicsl.coled.um.educ>
- *Social Studies/Social Science Education.* Indiana University, Social Studies Development Center, 2805 East 10th Street, Bloomington, IN 47408-2698. <http://www.indiana.edu/~ssac/eric_chess.html>
- *Urban Education.* Teachers College, Columbia University, Institute for Urban and Minority Education, Main Hall, Rm. 303, Box 40, New York, NY 10027-6696. <http://eric_web.tc.columbia.edu>

Figure 10.7 Guidelines for copying printed materials that are copyrighted.
Source: Section 107 of the 1976 Federal Omnibus Copyright Revision Act.

PERMITTED USES: YOU MAY MAKE

1. Single copies of:
   - A chapter of a book
   - An article from a periodical, magazine, or newspaper
   - A short story, short essay, or short poem whether or not from a collected work
   - A chart, graph, diagram, drawing, cartoon
   - An illustration from a book, magazine, or newspaper

2. Multiple copies for classroom use (not to exceed one copy per student in a course) of:
   - A complete poem if less than 250 words
   - An excerpt from a longer poem, but not to exceed 250 words
   - A complete article, story, or essay of less than 2,500 words
   - An excerpt from a larger printed work not to exceed 10 percent of the whole or 1,000 words
   - One chart, graph, diagram, cartoon, or picture per book or magazine issue

PROHIBITED USES: YOU MAY *NOT*

1. Copy more than one work or two excerpts from a single author during one class term (semester or year).
2. Copy more than three works from a collective work or periodical volume during one class term.
3. Reproduce more than nine sets of multiple copies for distribution to students in one class term.
4. Copy to create, replace, or substitute for anthologies or collective works.
5. Copy "consumable" works, e.g., workbooks, standardized tests, or answer sheets.
6. Copy the same work year after year.

Bulletin boards can be designed as decorative, motivational, and instructional tools that invite student participation by establishing a theme and then asking questions and providing means by which students manipulate parts of the display to verify their answers, such as pockets or movable parts. Students are often more interested in bulletin boards when they take an active part in deciding the purpose of the bulletin board and its design and construction.

in turn can save the material as a file. The electronic whiteboard uses dry-erase markers and special erasers that have optically encoded sleeves that enable the device to track their position on the board. The data are then converted into a display for the computer monitor, which may then be printed, cut and pasted into other applications, sent as an e-mail or fax message, or networked to other sites.[4]

Each day, each class, and even each new idea should begin with a clean board, except for announcements that have been placed there by you or another teacher. At the end of each class, clean the board, especially if another teacher follows you in that room, as a simple professional courtesy.

Use colored chalk or marking pens to highlight your "board talk." This is especially helpful for students with learning difficulties. Beginning at the top left of the board, print or write neatly and clearly, with the writing intentionally positioned to indicate content relationships (e.g., causal, oppositional, numerical, comparative, categorical, and so on).

Use the writing board to acknowledge acceptance and to record student contributions. Print instructions for an activity on the board in addition to giving them orally. At the top of the board frame you may find clips for hanging posters, maps, and charts.

Learn to use the board without having to turn your back entirely on students and without blocking their view of the board. When you have a lot of material to

put on the board, do it before class and then cover it, or better yet, put the material on transparencies and use the overhead projector rather than the board, or use both. Be careful not to write too much information. When using the writing board to complement your lesson and teacher talk, write only key words and simple diagrams, thereby making it possible for the student's right brain hemisphere to process what is seen, while the left hemisphere processes the elaboration provided by your words.

The Classroom Bulletin Board

Bulletin boards also are found in nearly every classroom. Although sometimes poorly used or not used at all, they can be relatively inexpensively transformed into attractive and valuable instructional tools. Among other uses, the bulletin board is a convenient location for posting reminders, assignments and schedules, and commercially produced materials, and to celebrate and display model student work and anchor papers.

To plan, design, and prepare bulletin board displays, some teachers use student assistants or committees, giving those students guidance and responsibility for planning, preparing, and maintaining bulletin board displays. When preparing a bulletin board display, keep these guidelines in mind: the display should be simple, emphasizing one main idea, concept, topic, or theme, and captions should be short and concise; illustrations can accent learning topics; verbs can vitalize the captions; phrases can punctuate a student's thoughts; and alliteration can announce anything you wish on the board. Finally, as in all other aspects of the classroom learning environment, remember to ensure that the board display reflects gender and ethnic equity.

---

[4]Sources of electronic whiteboards include: MicroTouch, Tewksbury, MA (800-642-7686); Numonics, Montgomeryville, PA (215-362-2766); Smart Technologies, Calgary, AB, Canada (403-245-0333); SoftBoard, Portland, OR (888-763-8262); and TEGRITY, San Jose, CA (408-369-5150).

One of the richest educational resources is the local community and the people and places in it.

THE COMMUNITY AS A RESOURCE

One of the richest resources for learning is the local community and the people and places in it. You will want to build your own file of community resources: speakers, sources for free materials, and field trip locations. Your school may already have a community resource file available for your use. However, it may need updating. A community resource file (see Figure 10.8) should contain information about (1) possible field trip locations, (2) community resource people who could serve as guest speakers or mentors, and (3) local agencies that can provide information and instructional materials.

There are many ways of using community resources, and quite a variety have been demonstrated by the schools specifically mentioned throughout this resource guide (see "Schools" in index). Here, the discussion is limited to two often used, although sometimes abused, instructional tools: (1) guest speakers

and (2) out-of-classroom and off-campus excursions, commonly called field trips.

Guest Speaker

Bringing outside speakers into your classroom can be for students a valuable educational experience, but not automatically so. In essence, guest speakers can be classified within a spectrum of four types, two of which should not be considered. (1) Ideally, a speaker is both informative and inspiring. (2) A speaker may be inspiring but with nothing substantive to offer, except for the possible diversion it might offer from the usual rigors of classroom work. (3) A speaker may be informative but boring to students. (4) At the worst end of this spectrum is the guest speaker who is both boring and uninformative. As with any other instructional experience, to make the experience most effective takes careful planning on your part. To make sure that the experience is beneficial to student learning, consider the following guidelines.

- If at all possible, meet and talk with the guest speaker in advance to inform the speaker about your students and your expectations for the presentation and to gauge how motivational and informative the speaker might be. If you believe the speaker might be informative but boring, then perhaps you can help structure the presentation in some way to make the presentation a bit more inspiring. For example, stop the speaker every few minutes and involve the students in questioning and discussions of points made.
- Prepare students in advance with key points of information that you expect students to obtain.
- Prepare students with questions to ask the speaker, things the students want to find out, and information you want them to inquire about.
- Follow up the presentation with a thank you letter to the guest speaker and perhaps further questions that developed during class discussions after the speaker's presentation.

Field Trips

What is the most memorable field trip that you were ever on as a student? What made it memorable? You may want to discuss these questions and others like them with your students.

Today's schools often have very limited funds for the transportation and liability costs for field trips. In some cases, there are no funds at all. At times, parent-teacher groups, business, and civic organizations help by providing financial resources so that students get valuable first-hand experiences that field trips so often can offer.

To prepare for and implement a successful field trip, there are three important stages of planning—

Figure 10.8 Community resources for speakers, materials, and field trips.

Airport	Highway patrol station
Apiary	Historical sites and monuments
Aquarium	Industrial plant
Archeological site	Legislature session
Art gallery	Levee and water reservoir
Assembly plant	Library and archive
Bakery	Native American Indian reservation
Bird and wildlife sanctuary	Mass transit authority
Book publisher	Military installation
Bookstore	Mine
Broadcasting and TV station	Museum
Building being razed	Newspaper plant
Building under construction	Observatory
Canal lock	Oil refinery
Cemetery	Park
Chemical plant	Poetry reading
City or county planning commission	Post office and package delivery company
Courthouse	Police station
Dairy	Recycling center
Dam and flood plain	Retail store
Dock and harbor	Sanitation department
Factory	Sawmill or lumber company
Farm	Shopping mall
Fire department	Shoreline (stream, lake, wetland, ocean)
Fish hatchery	Telecommunications center
Flea market	Town meeting
Foreign embassy	Utility company
Forest and forest preserve	Universities and colleges
Freeway under construction	Warehouse
Gas company	Water reservoir and treatment plant
Geological site	Wildlife park and preserve
Health department and hospital	Weather bureau and storm center
Highway construction site	Zoo

before, during, and after—and critical decisions to be made at each stage. Consider the following guidelines.

BEFORE THE FIELD TRIP

When the field trip is your idea (and not the students), discuss the idea with your teaching team, principal, or department chair, especially when transportation will be needed, *before* mentioning the idea to your students. There is no cause served by getting students excited about a trip before you know if it is feasible.

Once you have obtained the necessary, but tentative, approval from school officials, take the trip yourself (or with team members), if possible. A previsit allows you to determine how to make the field trip most productive and what arrangements will be necessary. For this previsit you might consider taking a couple of your students along for their ideas and help. If a previsit is not possible, you still will need to arrange for travel directions, arrival and departure times, parking, briefing by the host, if there is one, storage of students'

personal items, such as coats and lunches, provisions for eating and restrooms, and fees, if any.

If there are fees, you need to talk with your administration about who will pay the fees. If the trip is worth taking, the school should cover the costs. If that is not possible, perhaps students can plan a fund-raising activity or financial assistance can be obtained from some other source. If this does not work, you might consider an alternative that does not involve costs.

Arrange for official permission from the school administration. This usually requires a form for requesting, planning, and reporting field trips. After permission has been obtained, you can discuss the field trip with your students and arrange for permissions from their parents or guardians. You need to realize that although parents or guardians sign official permission forms allowing their children to participate in the trip, these only show that the parents or guardians are aware of what will take place and give their permission for their child to participate. Although the permission form should include a statement that the parent or guardian absolves the teacher and the school from liability should an accident occur, it *does not* lessen the teacher's and the school's responsibilities should there be negligence by a teacher, driver, or chaperone.

Arrange for students to be excused from their other classes while on the field trip. Using an information form prepared and signed by you and perhaps by the principal, the students should then assume responsibility for notifying their other teachers of the planned absence from classes and assure them that they will make up whatever work is missed. In addition, you will need to make arrangements for your own teaching duties to be covered. In some schools, teachers cooperate by filling in for those who will be gone. In other schools, substitute teachers are hired. Sometimes teachers have to hire their own substitute.

Arrange for whatever transportation is needed. Your principal, or the principal's designee, will help you with the details. In many schools, this task is handled by someone else. In any case, the use of private automobiles is ill-advised, because you and the school could be liable for the acts of the drivers.

Arrange for the collection of money that is needed for fees. If there are out-of-pocket costs to be paid by students, this information needs to be included on the permission form. No students should ever be excluded from the field trip because of a lack of money. This can be a tricky issue, because there may be some students who would rather steal the money for a field trip than admit they don't have it. Try to anticipate problems; hopefully the school or some organization can pay for the trip so that fees need not be collected from students and potential problems of this sort are avoided.

Plan details for student safety and the monitoring of their safety from departure to return. Included should be a first-aid kit and a system of student control, such as a "buddy system" whereby students must remain paired (and even hold hands in the case of young children) throughout the trip. The pairs sometimes are given numbers that are recorded and kept by the teacher and the chaperones, and then checked at departure time, periodically during the trip, at the time of return, and again upon return. Use adult chaperones. As a very general rule, there should be one adult chaperone for every ten students. Some districts have a policy regarding this. While on a field trip, at all times all students should be under the direct supervision of an adult.

Plan the complete route and schedule, including any stops along the way. If transportation is being provided, you will need to discuss the plans with the provider.

Establish and discuss rules of behavior with your students to the extent you believe necessary. Included in this might be details of the trip, its purpose, direc-

tions, instructions about what they should wear and bring, academic expectations (consider, for example, giving each student a study guide), and follow-up activities. Also included should be information about what to do if anything should go awry, for example, if a student is late for the departure or return, loses a personal possession along the way, gets lost, is injured, becomes sick, or misbehaves. For the latter, *never* send a misbehaving student back to school alone. Involve the adult chaperones in the previsit discussion. All of this information should also be included on the parental permission form.

If a field trip is supposed to promote some kind of learning, as is probably the case, then to avoid leaving the learning to happen by chance, the learning expectations need to be clearly defined and the students given an explanation of how and where they may encounter the learning experience. Before the field trip, students should be asked questions such as, "What do we already know about _____?" "What do we want to find out about _____?" "How can we find out?" and then, with their assistance, an appropriate guide can be prepared for the students to use during the field trip.

To further ensure learning and individual student responsibility for that learning, you may want to assign different roles and responsibilities to students, just as would be done in cooperative learning (see, for example, the lesson plan of Figure 6.14 in Chapter 6), assuring that each student has a role with responsibility.

You may want to take recorders and cameras so the field trip experience can be relived and shared in class upon return. If so, roles and responsibilities for the equipment and its care and use can be assigned to students as well.

DURING THE FIELD TRIP

If your field trip has been carefully planned according to the preceding guidelines, it should be a valuable and safe experience for all. En route, while at the trip location, and on the return to school, you and the adult chaperones should monitor student behavior and learning just as you do in the classroom.

AFTER THE FIELD TRIP

Plan the follow-up activities. As with any other lesson plan, the field trip lesson is complete only when there is both a proper introduction and a well-planned closure. All sorts of follow-up activities can be planned as an educational wrap-up to this educational experience. For example, a bulletin board committee can plan and prepare an attractive display summarizing the trip. Students can write about their experiences in their journals or as papers. Small groups can give oral reports to the class about what they did and learned. Their reports can then serve as springboards for further class discussion and perhaps further investigations. Finally, for future planning, all who were involved should contribute to an assessment of the experience.

MEDIA TOOLS

Your attention is now focused on teaching tools that depend upon electricity to project light and sound and to focus images on screens. Included are projectors of various sorts, computers, CD-ROMs, sound recorders, video recorders, and laser videodisc players. The aim here is *not* to provide instruction on how to operate modern equipment but to help you develop a philosophy for using it and to provide strategies for using media tools in your teaching. Consequently, to conserve space in this book, I devote no attention to traditional AV equipment, such as 16mm film, opaque, overhead, and slide projectors. There are staff members on any school faculty who gladly will assist you in locating and using those tools.

It is important to remember that the role of media tools is to aid student learning, not to teach for you. You must still select the objectives, orchestrate the instructional plan, assess the results, and follow up the lessons, just as you have learned to do with various other instructional strategies. If you use media tools prudently, your teaching and students' learning will benefit. As we have noted, like a competent brain surgeon or a competent auto mechanic, a competent teacher knows when and how to select and use the right tool at the right time. Would you want a surgeon who was unfamiliar with the tools used in surgery handling your child's operation? The education of a child should be no less important.

When Equipment Malfunctions

When using media equipment, it is nearly always best to set up the equipment and have it ready to go before students arrive. That helps avoid problems in classroom management that can occur during a delay to set up equipment. After all, if you were a surgeon ready to begin an operation and your tools and equipment weren't ready, your patient's life would likely be placed in extra danger. Like any other competent professional, a competent teacher is ready when the work is to begin.

Of course, delays may be unavoidable when equipment breaks down or if a videotape breaks. Remember Murphy's law, which says if anything can go wrong, it will? It is particularly relevant when using audiovisual equipment. You need to be prepared for such emergencies. Effectively planning for and responding to this eventuality is a part of your system of movement management and takes place during the preactive stage of your planning (see Chapter 3). That preparation includes consideration of a number of factors.

When equipment malfunctions, three principles should be kept in mind: (1) you want to avoid dead time in the classroom, (2) you want to avoid causing permanent damage to equipment, and (3) you want to avoid losing content continuity of a lesson. What do you do when equipment breaks down? Again, the answer is: Be prepared for the eventuality.

If a projector bulb goes out, quickly insert another. That means you should have an extra bulb on hand. If a tape breaks, you can do a quick temporary splice with cellophane tape. That means that tape should be readily available. If you must do a temporary splice, do it on the film or videotape that has already run through the machine rather than on the end yet to go through, so as not to mess up the machine or the film. Then, after class or after school, be sure to notify the person in charge of the tape that a temporary splice was made, so the tape can be permanently repaired before its next use.

If a patient's brain artery suddenly and unexpectedly breaks during surgery, the surgeon and the surgical team is ready for that eventuality and makes the necessary repair. If while working on an automobile a part breaks, the mechanic gets a replacement part. If, while teaching, a computer program freezes or aborts on the screen, or if a fuse blows or for some other reason you lose power, and you feel there will be too much dead time before the equipment is working again, it's time to go to an alternate lesson plan. You have probably heard the expression "go to Plan B." It is a useful phrase; what it means is that without missing a beat in the lesson, to accomplish the same instructional objective or another objective, you immediately and smoothly switch to an alternate learning activity. It does not mean you must plan two lessons for every one, but when planning a lesson that uses media equipment, you should plan in your lesson an alternative activity, just in case. Then, you move your students into the planned alternative activity quickly and smoothly.

Multimedia Program

A multimedia program is a collection of teaching/learning materials involving more than one type of medium and organized around a single theme or topic. The types of media involved vary from rather simple kits—perhaps a videotape, a game, activity cards, student worksheets, and a manual of instructions for the teacher—to very sophisticated packages involving building-level site licensed computer software, student handbooks, reproducible activity worksheets, classroom wall hangings, and an on-line subscription to a telecommunication network. Some kits are designed for teacher's use, others by individual or small groups of students, and many more for the collaborative use of students and teachers. Teachers sometimes incorporate multimedia programs with learning activity centers.

Table 10.1   Selected Multimedia Programs with Sources

Title	Source (Computer: D = DOS, M = Macintosh, W = Windows)	Phone/Internet
Age of Discovery	Society for Visual Education (M,W)	(800-829-1900)
Atlas of the Ancient World	Maris Multimedia (M,W)	(415-492-2819)
Battles of the World	SoftKey Multimedia (M,W)	(510-792-2101)
Chronicle of the 20th Century	DK Multimedia (M,W)	(212-213-4800); www.dk.com
Civil War II	Entrex Software (M,W)	(800-667-0007)
Civilization II	Spectrum HoloByte, Inc. (W)	(510-522-3584)
Culture & Technology	The Learning Team (M)	(800-793-8326)
Decisions, Decisions 5.0	Tom Snyder Productions (M,W)	(800-342-0236); www.teachtsp.com
Discovering America	Lawrence Productions (M,W)	(800-421-4157)
Exploring Ancient Cities	Sumeria, Inc. (M,W)	(415-904-0800)
Go West!	Steck-Vaughn (M,W)	(800-531-5015); www.steck-vaughn.com
Greatest Moments of Our Time	E.M.M.E. Interactive (M,W)	(800-424-3663)
History CD-ROMs	CLEARVUE/eav (M,W)	(800-253-2788); www.clearvue.com
Ideas That Changed the World	Integrated Communications & Entertainment	(416-868-6423)
IDIOM History	Chadwyck-Healey (W)	(800-752-0515)
Klondike Gold	DNA Multimedia (W)	(800-797-3303)
Multicultural CD	UXL (D,M)	(800-877-4253)
Oregon Trail II	Learning Company, The (M,W)	(800-685-6322)
Paths to Freedom	Encyclopedia Britannica (M)	(800-554-9862)
Robert E. Lee: Civil War General	Sierra On-Line (W)	(800-853-7788)
Social Science 2000	Decision Development Corp. (M,W)	(800-835-4332)
The American Journals CD	K–12 Micromedia Publishing (M)	(800-292-1997)
The Balkan Odyssey	Chelsea House Publishers (M,W)	(800-848-2665)
The Native Americans	Philips Media Software (M,W)	(800-883-3767)
The Voyages of the Mimi	Sunburst Communications (M,W)	(800-321-7511); www.SUNBURST.com
Time Travel to the 18th Century	Folkus Atlantic (M,W)	(800-780-8266)
Vital Links	Davidson & Associates (M,W)	(800-545-7677)
Who Built America?	Voyager (M)	(800-446-2001)
World History Interactive Library	Thynx (M,W)	(609-514-1600)
World War II	FlagTower Multimedia (W)	(617-338-8720)

Many multimedia programs are available on CD-ROM; they are designed principally as reference resources for students and teachers but include other aspects as well. One example is National Geographic's *Mammals: A Multimedia Encyclopedia,* which provides a lesson-planning guide, facts on more than 200 animals, 700 still color photos, range maps, animal vocalizations, full-motion movie clips, an animal classification game, glossary, and a printing capability. A brief selection of additional multimedia programs is shown in Table 10.1.

Television, Videos, and Videodiscs

Everyone knows that television, videos, and videodiscs represent a powerful medium. Their use as teaching aids, however, may present scheduling, curriculum, and physical problems that some school systems are yet unable to handle adequately.

TELEVISION
For purposes of professional discussion, television programming can be divided into three categories: instructional television, educational television, and general commercial television. Instructional television refers to programs specifically designed as classroom instruction. Educational television refers to programs of cable television and public broadcasting designed to educate in general, but not aimed at classroom instruction. Commercial television programs include the entertainment and public service programs of the television networks and local stations.

Watch for announcements for special educational programs in professional journals. And, of course, television program listings can be obtained from your local commercial, educational, or cable companies or by writing directly to network stations. Addresses for national networks are shown in Figure 10.9. Some networks sponsor Internet websites. For those, see <http://www.flnet.com/~tw/media/televisn.htm>.

VIDEOS AND VIDEODISCS
Combined with a television monitor, the VCR (videocassette recorder) is one of the most popular and frequently used tools in today's classroom. Videotaped programs can do nearly everything that the former

Figure 10.9 Addresses for national television networks.

- American Broadcasting Company, Inc. (ABC), 77 West 66th Street, New York, NY 10023, 212-456-7777.
- Arts & Entertainment Network (A&E), 235 East 45th Street, New York, NY 10017, 212-661-4500.
- AMC, BRV-American Movie Classics, Bravo, Rainbow Programming Holdings, Inc., 150 Crossways PK. W, Woodbury, NY 11797, 516-364-2222.
- Black Entertainment Television (BET), 1232 31st Street, NW, Washington, DC 20007, 202-636-2400.
- Cable News Network (CNN), One CNN Center, Box 105366, Atlanta, GA 30348-5366, 404-827-1500.
- Columbia Broadcasting System (CBS), 51 West 52nd Street, New York, NY 10019, 212-975-4321.
- Consumer News and Business Channel (CNBC), 2200 Fletcher Avenue, Fort Lee, NJ 07024, 201-585-2622.
- Cable-Satellite Public Affairs Network (C-Span), 400 North Capitol Street, NW, Suite 650, Washington, DC 20001, 202-737-3220.
- The Discovery Channel, 7700 Wisconsin Avenue, Bethesda, MD 20814-3522, 301-986-0444.
- The Disney Channel, 3800 West Alameda Avenue, Burbank, CA 91505, 818-569-7500.
- ESPN, ESPN Plaza, 935 Middle Street, Bristol, CT 06010-9454, 860-585-2000.
- Fox Television, 205 East 67th Street, New York, NY 10021, 212-452-5555.
- The Learning Channel, 7700 Wisconsin Avenue, Bethesda, MD 20815-3579, 301-986-0444.
- Lifetime, 309 West 49th Street, New York, NY 10019, 212-424-7000.
- Music Television (MTV), 1515 Networks, Inc., 1515 Broadway, New York, NY 10036, 212-258-8000.
- National Broadcasting Company (NBC), 30 Rockefeller Plaza, New York, NY 10112, 212-664-4444.
- Nickelodeon/Nick at Nite, MTV Networks, Inc., 1515 Broadway, New York, NY 10036, 212-258-8000.
- Public Broadcasting Service (PBS), 1320 Braddock Place, Alexandria, VA 22314-1698, 703-739-5000, <http://www.pbs.org>.
- Turner Broadcasting (TBS), One CNN Center, Atlanta, GA 30348-5366, 404-827-1647.
- United Paramount Network, 5555 Melrose Avenue, MOB 1200, Los Angeles, CA 90038, 213-956-5000.
- USA Network, 1230 Avenue of the Americas, New York, NY 10020, 212-408-9100.
- Warner Brothers Television Network, 4000 Warner Boulevard, Building 34R, Burbank, CA 91522, 818-954-6000.

16-mm films could do. In addition, the VCR, combined with a video camera, makes it possible to record student activities, practice, projects, and student demonstrations and your own teaching. It gives students a marvelous opportunity to self-assess as they see and hear themselves in action.

Entire course packages and supplements are now available on videocassettes or on computer software programs. The schools where you student teach and where you eventually are employed may have a collection of such programs. Some teachers make their own.

Laser videodiscs and players for classroom use are reasonably priced, with a large variety of disc topics for classroom use. There are two formats of laser videodisc: (1) freeze-frame format (CAV—Constant Angular Velocity, or Standard Play) and (2) non-freeze-frame format (CLV—Constant Linear Velocity, or Extended Play). Both will play on all laser disc players. Laser videodisc players are quite similar to VCRs and just as easy to operate. The discs are visual archives or visual databases that contain large amounts of information that can be easily retrieved, reorganized, filed, and controlled by the user with the remote control that accompanies the player. Each side of a double-sided disc stores 54,000 separate frames of information—whether pictures, printed text, diagrams, films, or any combination of these. Visuals, both still and motion sequences, can be stored and then selected for showing on a televi-

sion monitor or programmed onto a computer disc for a special presentation. Several thousand videodisc titles are available for educational use (see Table 10.2 for a few sample titles). Your school or district audiovisual or curriculum resource center probably has many titles; for additional titles refer to the latest annual edition of *Videodisc Compendium.*[5]

Carefully selected programs, tapes, discs, films, and slides enhance student learning. For example, laser videodiscs and CD-ROMs offer quick and efficient accessibility of thousands of visuals, thus providing an appreciated boost to teachers of students with limited language proficiency. With the use of frame control, students can observe phenomena in detail previous students only read about.

Check school supply catalogs and Internet resources for additional titles and sources for videodiscs. Generally, companies that sell computer software and CD-ROMs also sell videodiscs. Figure 10.10 provides sample addresses from which you may obtain catalogs of information.

---

[5] Published and sold by Emerging Technology Consultants Inc., 2819 Hamline Avenue North, St. Paul, MN 55113. Phone 612-639-3973, fax 612-639-0110.

Table 10.2 Selected Videodisc Titles and Sources

Subject	Title	Source (phone or see Figure 10.10)
Art	*The Louvre*	Voyager
Earth Science	*Restless Earth*	National Geographic
English	*Treasure Island*	Pioneer Laserdisc Corporation
Environmental	*Global Warning: Hot Times Ahead?*	Churchill Media
Foreign Languages	*Basic French by Video*	Pioneer Laserdisc Corporation
Health	*AIDS—What Everyone Needs to Know*	Churchill Media
History	*Set on Freedom*	CEL Educational Resources
Life Science	*Rain Forest*	National Geographic
Physical Science	*Principles of Physical Science*	Optical Data School Media
Social Studies	*Visual Experiences: Social Studies*	Optical Data School Media

Figure 10.10 Selected resources for videodiscs, videotapes, computer software, CD-ROMs, and interactive multimedia.

- A.D.A.M. Software, Inc., 1600 River Edge Pkwy., Ste. 800, Atlanta, GA 30328, 800-755-2326, ext. 3018, <http://www.adam.com>
- Agency for Instructional Technology, Box A, Bloomington, IN 47402-0120, 800-457-4509, <http://www.ait.net>
- AIMS Multimedia, 9710 DeSoto Ave., Chatsworth, CA 91311, 800-367-2467, <http://www.aims-multimedia.com>
- Broderbund Software, 500 Redwood Blvd., Novato, CA 94948, 800-474-8840.
- Central Scientific Co., 3300 CENCO Parkway, Franklin Park, IL 60131, 800-262-3625, <http://www.cenconet.com>
- Cuisenaire Dale Seymour, 10 Banks St., Box 5026, White Plains, NY 10602-5026, 800-872-1100/800-237-0338, <http://www.cuisenaire.com>
- DK Publishing & Multimedia, 95 Madison Ave., New York, NY 10016, 212-213-4800, <http://www.dk.com>
- Educational Software Institute, 4213 S. 94th St., Omaha, NE 68127, 800-955-5570, <http://www.edsoft.com>
- Environmental Media Corp., P.O. Box 99, Beaufort, SC 29901-0099, 800-368-3382, <http://www.envmedia.com>
- ETA, 620 Lakeview Parkway, Vernon Hills, IL 60061-9923, 800-445-5985, <http://www.eta.universe.com>
- Fisher Science Education, 485 S. Frontage Rd., Burr Ridge, IL 60521, 800-955-1177, <http://www.fisheredu.com>
- Harcourt Brace School Publishers, 6277 Sea Harbor Dr., Orlando, FL 32887, 800-346-8648, <http://www.hbschool.com>
- Higher-Order Thinking Co., 1733 N.E. Patterson Dr., Lee's Summit, MO 64086, 816-524-2701.
- IBM Global Education, 4111 Northside Parkway, Atlanta, GA 30301-2150, 800-426-4968, <http://www.solutions.ibm.com/k12>
- Mindscape, 88 Rowland Way, Novata, CA 94945, 800-231-3088, <http://www.mindscape.com>
- Modern School Supplies, P.O. Box 958, Hartford, CT 06143, 800-243-2329, <http://www.tiac.net/users/modern>
- NASCO-Modesto, 4825 Stoddard Road, P.O. Box 3837, Modesto, CA 95352-3837, 800-558-9595, <http://www.nascofa.com>
- Optical Data School Media, 512 Means Street, NW, Atlanta, GA 30318, 800-524-2481, <http://www.opticaldata.com>
- Pitsco, Inc., 912 East Jefferson St., Pittsburg, KS 66762, 800-835-0686, <http://www.pitsco.com>
- Sargent-Welch/VWR Scientific, P.O. Box 5229, Buffalo Grove, IL 60089-5229, 800-727-4368, <http://www.SargentWelch.com>
- Schoolmasters Science, 745 State Circle, P.O. Box 1941, Ann Arbor, MI 48106, 800-521-2832, <http://www.schoolmasters.com>
- Science Kit and Boreal Laboratories, 777 E. Park Dr., Tonawanda, NY 14150, 800-828-7777, <http://sciencekit.com>
- Sunburst Communications, 101 Castleton Street, Pleasantville, NY 10570-0100, 800-321-7511, <http://www.SUNBURST.com>
- SVE & Churchill Media, 6677 N. Northwest Highway, Chicago, IL 60631, 800-829-1900, <http://www.svemedia.com>
- Tom Snyder Productions, Inc., 80 Coolidge Hill Road, Watertown, MA 02472, 800-342-0236, <http://www.teachtsp.com>
- Troll School & Library L.L.C., 100 Corporate Drive, Mahway, NJ 07430, 800-979-8765, <http://www.troll.com>

COMPUTERS AND COMPUTER-BASED INSTRUCTIONAL TOOLS

As a teacher of the twenty-first century, you must be computer literate. You must understand and be able to use computers as well as you can read and write. As a matter of fact, some K–12 public school districts have added computer literacy as a requirement for student matriculation, as have programs for teacher certification.

The computer can be valuable to a classroom teacher in several ways. For example, the computer can help you manage the instruction by obtaining information, storing and preparing test materials, maintaining attendance and grade records, and preparing programs to aid in the academic development of individual students. This category of uses of the computer is referred to as *computer-managed instruction* (CMI). The computer can also be used for instruction by employing various instructional software programs. In some schools, *computer-assisted instruction* (CAI) using integrated learning systems (individualized academic tutorials) has shown impressive gains.[6] The computer can be used to teach about computers and to help students develop their metacognitive skills along with their skills in computer use.[7]

The Placement and Use of Computers: The On-Line Classroom

Teachers looking to make their classrooms more student-centered, collaborative, and interactive are turning increasingly to telecommunications networks. Webs of connected computers allow teachers and students from around the world to reach each other directly and gain access to quantities of information previously unimaginable. Students using networks learn new inquiry and analytical skills in a stimulating environment, and they can also gain an increased awareness of their role as world citizens.[8]

The way you use the computer for instruction is determined by several factors, including your knowledge of and skills in its use, the number of computers you have available for instructional use, the location of computers and printers in the school, available software, and telecommunications capabilities (that is, wiring, phone lines, modems, and servers).

Schools continue to purchase or lease computers and upgrade their telecommunications capabilities. Regarding computer placement and equipment available, here are some possible scenarios and how classroom teachers work within each.

Scenario 1. With the assistance of a computer lab and the lab technician, computers are integrated into the whole curriculum. In collaboration with members of interdisciplinary teaching teams, in a computer lab students use computers, software, and sources on the Internet as tools to build their knowledge, write stories with word processors, illustrate diagrams with paint utilities, create interactive reports with hypermedia, and graph data they have gathered using spreadsheets.

Scenario 2. In some schools, students take "computer" as an elective or exploratory course. You may give students in your classes who are simultaneously enrolled in such a course special computer assignments they can then share with the rest of the class.

Scenario 3. Some classrooms have a computer connected to a large-screen video monitor. The teacher or a student works the computer, and the monitor screen can be seen by the entire class. As they view the screen, students can verbally respond to and interact with what is happening on the computer.

Scenario 4. You may be fortunate to have one or more computers in your classroom for all or for a part of the school year, computers with Internet connections, with CD-ROM playing capabilities, a videodisc player, an overhead projector, and a LCD (liquid crystal display) projection system. Coupled with the overhead projector, the LCD projection system allows you to project onto your large wall screen (and TV monitor at the same time) any image from computer software or a videodisc. With this system, all students can see and verbally interact with the multimedia instruction.

Scenario 5. Many classrooms have at least one computer with telecommunications capability, and some have many. When this is the case in your classroom, then you most likely will have one or two students working at the computer while others are doing other learning activities (multilevel teaching). Computers can be an integral part of a learning activity center and an important aid in your overall effort to personalize the instruction within your classroom. Unfortunately, however, many school computers are old systems for which software is no longer made and for which multimedia software and computer networks are not available.

---

[6] V. Hancock and F. Betts, "From the Lagging to the Leading Edge," *Educational Leadership* 51(7):25 (April 1994).
[7] See, for example, X. Bornas et al., "Preventing Impulsivity in the Classroom: How Computers Can Help Teachers," *Computers in the Schools* 13(1–2):27–40 (1997).
[8] See, for example, articles by K. Rasmussen and L. Mann in "Making Connections Through Global Education," Summer 1998 theme issue of *Curriculum Update* (a quarterly publication of the Association for Supervision and Curriculum Development).

Selecting Computer Software

When selecting software programs, you and your colleagues need to choose those that are compatible with your brand of computer(s) and with your instructional objectives.

Programs are continually being developed and enhanced to meet the new and more powerful computers being made available. (Videodiscs, computer software, and CD-ROMs are usually available from the same companies, addresses of which are listed in Figure 10.10.) For evaluating computer software programs and testing them for their compatibility with your instructional objectives, many forms are available from the local school district, the state department of education, and professional associations.

The CD-ROM

Personal computers have three types of storage disks: floppy disks of various storage capacities, the hard disk, and the CD-ROM, which is an abbreviation for "compact disc—read only memory." Use of a CD-ROM disc requires a computer and a CD-ROM drive. Newer computers may have built-in CD-ROM drives, while others may be connected to one. As with floppy and hard disks, CD-ROMs are used for storing characters in a digital format, while images on a videodisc are stored in an analog format. The CD-ROM is capable of storing some 20,000 images or the equivalent of approximately 250,000 pages of text—the capacity of 1,520 360K floppy disks or eight 70MB hard disks; therefore, CD-ROMs are ideal for storing large amounts of information such as dictionaries, encyclopedias, and general reference works full of graphic images you can copy and modify.

The same material is used for both CD-ROM disks and videodiscs, but the videodisc platter is 12 inches across, while the CD-ROM disk is just 4.5 inches. Newer CD-ROM discs include video segments, just like those of videodiscs. Any information stored on a CD-ROM disk or a videodisc can be found and retrieved within a few seconds. CD-ROMs are available from the distributors of videodiscs and will likely ultimately replace videodiscs, or both the CD-ROM and videodisc may be replaced by even more advanced technology, such as the DVD (digital video disc).

Researchers found that students who read selections on interactive CD-ROMs scored higher on longer and more difficult comprehension passages on tests than their peers who read the same selections in print.[9] The researchers suggest that the reason is that the CD-ROMs provide instant help for students confronting new vocabulary. Students can click on a word and hear it pronounced, defined, and used in context. Additionally, students enjoy the music, special effects, and interactive approach.

With superior sound and visual performance, the DVD may replace CDs, VCR tapes, videodiscs, and computer CD-ROMs. Although in appearance it resembles the CD-ROM, the DVD can store nearly 17 gigabytes of information and provide a faster retrieval of data; in addition, DVD can be made interactive. Information about CD-ROM titles for education is available from the sources shown in Figure 10.11.

Sources of Free and Inexpensive Audiovisual Materials

For free and inexpensive audiovisual materials, check Internet sources and your college or university library for sources listed in Figure 10.12.

Figure 10.11   Resources of information about CD-ROM titles.

- *CD-ROM Finder*, 5th ed., J. Shelton, Ed. (Medford, NJ: Learned Information, 1993).
- *CD-ROM for Librarians and Educators: A Book to Over 300 Instructional Programs*, by B. H. Sorrow and B. S. Lumpkin (Jefferson, NC: McFarland, 1993).
- *CD-ROMs in Print*, Meckler Publishing, 11 Ferry Lane West, Westport, CT 06880.
- *The Directory of Video, Computer, and Audio-Visual Products*, published annually by the International Communications Industries Association, Fairfax, VA.
- Educational Software Institute catalog, 4213 South 94th Street, Omaha, NE 68127, 800-955-5570.

Figure 10.12   Resources for free and inexpensive audiovisual materials.

- Best freeware and shareware at <http://wwwl.zdnet.com/pccomp/1001dl/html/1001.html>
- Professional periodicals and journals
- *Catalog of Audiovisual Materials: A Guide to Government Sources* (ED 198 822), Arlington, VA: ERIC Documents Reproduction Service
- Educator's Progress Service, Inc., 214 Center Street, Randolph, WI 53956 (414-326-3126): *Educator's Guide to Free Audio and Video Materials; Educator's Guide to Free Films; Educator's Guide to Free Filmstrips; Guide to Free Computer Materials; Educator's Guide to Free Science Materials*
- *Video Placement Worldwide (VPW):* Source of free sponsored educational videos on Internet at <http://www.vpw.com>

[9]R. Olson and R. Meyer, "News: Survey Says CD-ROMs Boost Reading Scores," *School Library Journal* 41(9):108 (September 1995).

Using Copyrighted Video, Computer, and Multimedia Programs

You must be knowledgeable about the laws on the use of copyrighted videos and computer software materials. Although space here prohibits full inclusion of United States legal guidelines, your local school district undoubtedly can provide a copy of current district policies to ensure compliance with all copyright laws. As noted earlier in the discussion about the use of printed materials that are copyrighted, when preparing to make any copy you must find out whether the copying is permitted by law under the category of "per-

mitted use." If not allowed under "permitted use," then you must get written permission to reproduce the material from the holder of the copyright. Figures 10.13 and 10.14 present guidelines for the copying of videotapes and of computer software.

Usually, when purchasing CD-ROMs and other multimedia software packages intended for use by schools, you are also paying for a license to modify and use its contents for instructional purposes. However, not all CD-ROMs include copyright permission, so always check the copyright notice on any disk you purchase and use. Whenever in doubt, don't use it until you have asked your district media specialists about

---

PERMITTED USES

You may

1. Request your media center or audiovisual coordinator to record a program for you if you cannot or if you lack the equipment.
2. Keep a videotaped copy of a broadcast (including cable transmission) for forty-five calendar days, after which the program must be erased.
3. Use the program in class once during the first ten school days of the forty-five calendar days, and a second time if instruction needs to be reinforced.
4. Have professional staff view the program several times for evaluation purposes during the full forty-five day period.
5. Make a few copies to meet legitimate needs, but these copies must be erased when the original videotape is erased.
6. Use only a part of the program if instructional needs warrant.
7. Enter into a licensing agreement with the copyright holder to continue use of the program.

PROHIBITED USES

You may not

1. Videotape premium cable services such as HBO without express permission.
2. Alter the original content of the program.
3. Exclude the copyright notice on the program.
4. Videorecord before a request for use is granted—the request to record must come from an instructor.
5. Keep the program, and any copies, after forty-five days.

Figure 10.13 Copyright law for off-air videotaping.
Source: R. Heinich, M. Molenda, J.D. Russell, and S. E. Smaldino, *Instructional Media and Technologies for Learning,* 6th ed. (Upper Saddle River, NJ: Merrill/Prentice Hall, 1999), p. 389. By permission of Prentice Hall.

PERMITTED USES

You may

1. Make a single back-up or archival copy of the computer program.
2. Adapt the computer program to another language if the program is unavailable in the target language.
3. Add features to make better use of the computer program.

PROHIBITED USES

You may not

1. Make multiple copies.
2. Make replacement copies from an archival or back-up copy.
3. Make copies of copyrighted programs to be sold, leased, loaned, transmitted, or given away.

Figure 10.14 Copyright law for use of computer software.
Source: December 1980 Congressional amendment to the 1976 Copyright Act.

Figure 10.15 Fair use guidelines for using multimedia programs.

1. For portions of copyrighted works used in your own multimedia production for use in teaching, follow normal copyright guidelines (e.g., the limitations on the amount of material used, whether it be motion media, text, music, illustrations, photographs, or computer software).
2. You may display your own multimedia work using copyrighted works to other teachers, such as in workshops. However, you may *not* make and distribute copies to colleagues without obtaining permission from copyright holders.
3. You may use your own multimedia production for instruction over an electronic network (e.g., distance learning) provided there are limits to access and to the number of students enrolled. You may *not* distribute such work over any electronic network (local area or wide area) without expressed permission from copyright holders.
4. You must obtain permissions from copyright holders before using any copyrighted materials in educational multimedia productions for commercial reproduction and distribution or before replicating more than one copy, distributing copies to others, or for use beyond your own classroom.

copyrights or have obtained necessary permissions from the original source.

As yet, there are no guidelines for fair use of films, filmstrips, slides, and multimedia programs. A general rule of thumb for use of any copyrighted material is to treat the work of others as you would want your own material treated were it protected by a copyright (see Figure 10.15).

SUMMARY

You have learned of the variety of tools available to supplement your instruction. When used wisely, these tools will help you to reach more of your students more of the time. As you know, teachers must meet the needs of a diversity of students, many of whom are linguistically and culturally different. The material selected and presented in this chapter should be of help in doing that. The future will undoubtedly continue bringing technological innovations that will be even more helpful; compact discs, computers, and telecommunications equipment have only marked the beginning of a revolution in teaching. As we enter a new millennium, new instructional delivery systems made possible by microcomputers and multimedia workstations will likely fundamentally alter what had become the traditional role of the classroom teacher during the twentieth century.

You should remain alert to developing technologies for your teaching. Laser videodiscs, digital videodiscs (DVDs), CD-ROMs interfaced with computers (i.e., the use of multimedia), and telecommunications offer exciting technologies for learning. New instructional technologies are advancing at an increasingly rapid rate. You and your colleagues must maintain vigilance over new developments, constantly looking for those that will not only help make student

learning meaningful and interesting—and your teaching effective—but that are cost-effective as well.

QUESTIONS FOR CLASS DISCUSSION

1. Explain how your effective use of the writing board and bulletin board can help students see relationships among verbal concepts or information.
2. Describe what you should look for when deciding whether material that you have obtained free or inexpensively is appropriate for use in your teaching.
3. Meet with a peer and tell each other how you would respond to a parent who questioned you about the benefit of using CD-ROM material in teaching.
4. Share with others in your class your knowledge, observations, and feelings about the use of multimedia and telecommunications for teaching. From your discussion, what more would you like to know about the use of multimedia and telecommunications for teaching? How might you learn more about these things?
5. In 1922 Thomas Edison predicted that "the motion picture is destined to revolutionize our educational system and . . . in a few years it will supplant largely, if not entirely, the use of textbooks." In 1945 William Levenson of the Cleveland public schools' radio station claimed that "the time may come when a portable radio receiver will be as common in the classroom as is the blackboard." In the early 1960s B. F. Skinner believed that with the help of the new teaching machines and programmed instruction, students could learn twice as much in the same time and with the same effort as in a standard classroom. Did motion pictures, radio, programmed instruction, and television revolutionize education? Will computers become as much a part of the classroom as writing boards? What do you predict the public school classroom of the year 2050 will be like? Will the role of a teacher be different in any way than it is today?
6. Select and identify one instructional tool that is *not* discussed in this chapter and explain to your classmates its

advantages and disadvantages for use in teaching a subject and grade level of your choice.

7. Has the purchase of new textbooks and library books become stagnated as schools increase their spending on leading-edge technology? Have traditional shop classes given way to technology education programs? Have music and art programs suffered as a result of increased expenditures on technology? How are school districts finding funds necessary for the cost of technology, such as for the cost of wiring classrooms for networking and for updated computers, for the planning, installation, and maintenance of complex computer networks? Or are districts finding the necessary funds? In this respect, are some districts worse off or better off than others? Is this an issue? An issue for which every classroom teacher need be aware?

8. Describe any prior concepts you held that changed as a result of your experiences with this chapter. Describe the changes.

9. From your current observations and field work as related to this teacher preparation program, clearly identify one specific example of educational practice that seems contradictory to exemplary practice or theory as presented in this chapter. Present your explanation for the discrepancy.

10. Do you have questions generated by the content of this chapter? If you do, list them along with ways answers might be found.

FOR FURTHER READING

Barron, A. E., and Ivers, K. S. *The Internet and Instruction: Activities and Ideas.* 2d ed. Englewood, CO: Libraries Unlimited, 1998.

Cotton, E. G. *The Online Classroom: Teaching with the Internet.* 3d ed. Bloomington, IN: EDINFO Press, 1998.

Curchy, C., and Kyker, K. *Educator's Survival Guide to TV Production Equipment and Setup.* Englewood, CO: Libraries Unlimited, 1998.

Harris, J. *Design Tools for the Internet-Supported Classroom.* Alexandria, VA: Association for Supervision and Curriculum Development, 1998.

Heide, A., and Stillborne, L. *The Teacher's Complete & Easy Guide to the Internet.* 2d ed. New York: Teachers College Press, 1999.

Leu, D. J., Jr.; Leu, D. D.; and Leu, K. R. *Teaching with the Internet: Lessons from the Classroom.* Norwood, MA: Christopher-Gordon, 1999.

Miller, E. B. *The Internet Resource Directory for K–12 Teachers and Librarians, 97/98 Edition.* Englewood, CO: Libraries Unlimited, 1998.

Talab, R. S. "An Educational Use Checklist for Copyright and Multimedia." *TechTrends* 42(1):9–11 (January/February 1997).

Tapscott, D. "Educating the Net Generation." *Educational Leadership* 56(5):6–11 (February 1999).

Tarquin, P., and Walker, S. *Creating Success in the Classroom! Visual Organizers and How to Use Them.* Englewood, CO: Teacher Ideas Press/Libraries Unlimited, 1997.

Teicher, J. "An Action Plan for Smart Internet Use." *Educational Leadership* 56(5):70–74 (February 1999).

Virginia Space Grant Consortium. *The Educator's Guide to the Internet: A Handbook with Resources and Activities,* 3d ed. Palo Alto, CA: Dale Seymour Publications, 1997.

Weinman, J., and Haag, P. "Gender Equity in Cyberspace." *Educational Leadership* 56(5):44–49 (February 1999).

Woody, R. H., III, and Woody, R. H., II. *Music Copyright Law in Education.* Fastback 368. Bloomington, IN: Phi Delta Kappa Educational Foundation, 1994.

Part IV

ASSESSMENT AND PROFESSIONAL DEVELOPMENT

Part IV responds to your needs concerning:

- Assessing student learning
- Finding a teaching job
- Grading and reporting student achievement
- Meeting with parents and guardians
- Assessing your performance
- Remaining an alert and effective teacher
- Scoring rubrics
- Self-assessing through micro-peer teaching
- Student teaching

REFLECTIVE THOUGHTS

When assessing for student achievement, it is important to use procedures that are compatible with the instructional objectives.

Performance-based assessment procedures require students to produce rather than to select responses.

That which separates the professional teacher from "anyone off the street" is the teacher's ability to go beyond mere description of a student's behavior.

For students' continued intellectual and emotional development, your comments about their work should be useful, productive, analytical, diagnostic, and prescriptive.

You must provide opportunities for students to think about what they are learning, how they are learning it, and how far they have progressed in learning it.

It is unprofessional to place a student teacher into a "sink-or-swim" situation.

Teaching is such an electrifying profession that it is not easy to remain energetic and stay abreast of changes and trends in research and practice.

A teacher's concern should not be with deciding which students are better than others but helping all of them succeed.

Chapter 11

Assessing and Reporting Student Achievement

While preceding parts of this resource guide addressed the *why* (Part I), *what* (Part II), and *how* (Part III) of teaching, Part IV focuses on the fourth and final component—the *how well*, or assessment, component. Together, these four components are the essentials of effective instruction.

Teaching and learning are reciprocal processes that depend on and affect one another. Thus, the assessment component deals with both how well students are learning and how well the teacher is teaching. This chapter addresses the first.

Assessment is an integral part and ongoing process in the educational arena. Curricula, buildings, materials, specific courses, teachers, supervisors, administrators, equipment—all must be periodically assessed in relation to student learning, the purpose of the school. When gaps between anticipated results and student achievement exist, efforts are made to eliminate those factors that seem to be limiting the educational output or in some other way to improve the situation. Thus, educational progress occurs.

To learn effectively, students need to know how they are doing. Similarly, to be an effective teacher, you must be informed about what the student knows, feels, and can do so that you can help the student build on her or his skills, knowledge, and attitudes. Therefore you and your students need continuous feedback on their progress and problems to plan appropriate learning activities and to make adjustments to those already planned. If this feedback says that progress is slow, you can provide alternative activities; if it indicates that some or all of the students have already mastered the desired learning, you can eliminate unnecessary activi-

ties and practice for some or for all children. In short, assessment provides a key for both effective teaching and learning.

The importance of continuous assessment mandates that you know various principles and techniques of assessment. This chapter explains some of those and shows you how to construct and use assessment instruments. It defines terms related to assessment, suggests procedures to use in the construction of assessment items, points out the advantages and disadvantages of different types of assessment items and procedures, and explains the construction and use of alternative assessment devices.

In addition, this chapter discusses grading (or marking) and reporting of student achievement, two responsibilities that can consume much of a teacher's valuable time. Grading is time-consuming and frustrating for many teachers. What should be graded? Should grades or marks represent student growth, level of achievement in a group, effort, attitude, general behavior, or a combination of these? What should determine grades—homework, tests, projects, class participation and group work, or some combination of these? And, what should be their relative weights? These are just a few of the questions that plague teachers, parents, and, indeed, the profession; they have persisted for a century or more of education in this country.

Still today, in too many schools, the grade progress report and final report card are about the only communication between the school and the student's home. Unless the teacher and the school have clearly determined what grades or marks represent and unless such understanding is periodically reviewed with each set of new parents or guardians, these reports may create unrest and dissatisfaction on the parts of parents, guardians, and students and prove to be alienating devices. The grading system and reporting scheme, then, instead of informing parents and guardians, may separate even further the home and the school, which do have a common concern—the intellectual, physical, social, and emotional development of the student.

The development of the student encompasses growth in the cognitive, affective, and psychomotor domains. Traditional objective paper-and-pencil tests provide only a portion of the data needed to indicate student progress in those domains. Many experts today, as indeed they have in the past, question the traditional sources of data and encourage the search for, development of, and use of alternative means to assess more authentically the students' development of thinking and higher-level learning. Although best practices in assessment continue to evolve, one point that is clear is that various techniques of assessment must be used to determine how the student works, what the student is learning, and what the student can produce as a result of that learning. As teacher, you must develop a repertoire of means of assessing learner behavior and academic progress.

Although marks and grades have been a part of school for about 100 years, it is clear to many experts that the conventional report card with marks or grades falls short of being a developmentally appropriate procedure for reporting the academic performance or progress of learners. Some schools are experimenting with other ways of reporting student achievement in learning, but letter grades for older students still seem firmly entrenched. Parents, students, colleges, and employers have come to expect grades as evaluations. Some critics suggest that the emphasis in schools is on getting a high grade rather than on learning, arguing that, as traditionally measured, the two do not necessarily go hand in hand. Today's interest is (or should be) more on what the student can do (performance testing) as a result of learning than merely on what the student can recall (memory testing) from the experience.

In addition, there have been complaints about subjectivity and unfair practices. As a result of these concerns, a variety of systems of assessment and reporting have evolved, are still evolving, and will likely continue to evolve throughout your professional career.

When teachers are aware of alternative systems, they may be able to develop assessment and reporting processes that are fair and effective for particular situations. After beginning with assessment, the final focus in this chapter considers today's principles and practices in grading and reporting student achievement.

Specifically, upon completion of this chapter you should be able to

1. Demonstrate an understanding of the importance of assessment in teaching and learning.

2. Explain the concept of authentic assessment.
3. Explain the value of and give an example of a performance assessment that could be used at a particular grade level or discipline.
4. Explain why criterion-referenced grading is preferred over norm-referenced grading.
5. Explain how rubrics, checklists, portfolios, and journals are used in the assessment of student learning.
6. Differentiate between diagnostic assessment, summative assessment, and formative assessment, with examples of when and how each can be used at a particular grade level or discipline.
7. Describe the importance of self-assessment in teaching and learning.
8. Describe the importance of and manner by which parents can be involved in the education of their children.

PURPOSES AND PRINCIPLES OF ASSESSMENT

Assessment of achievement in student learning is designed to serve several purposes:

1. *To assist in student learning.* This is the purpose usually first thought of when speaking of assessment, and it is the principal topic of this chapter. For the classroom teacher it is (or should be) the most important purpose.

2. *To identify children's strengths and weaknesses.* Identification and assessment of children's strengths and weaknesses are necessary for two reasons: to structure and restructure the learning activities and to restructure the curriculum. Concerning the first, for example, data on student strengths and weaknesses in content and process skills are important in planning activities appropriate for both skill development and intellectual development. This is *diagnostic assessment* (known also as preassessment). For the second, data on student strengths and weaknesses in content and skills are useful for making appropriate modifications to the curriculum.

3. *To assess the effectiveness of a particular instructional strategy.* It is important for you to know how well a particular strategy helped accomplish a goal or objective. Competent teachers continually reflect on and evaluate their strategy choices, using a number of sources: student achievement as measured by assessment instruments, their own intuition, informal feedback given by the students, and, sometimes, informal feedback given by colleagues, such as members of a teaching team or mentor teachers. (Mentor teachers are discussed in Chapter 12).

4. *To assess and improve the effectiveness of curriculum programs.* Components of the curriculum are continually assessed by committees composed of teachers and

administrators and sometimes parents, students, and other members of the school and community. The assessment is done while students are learning (i.e., formative assessment) and afterward (summative assessment).

5. *To assess and improve teaching effectiveness.* To improve student learning, teachers are periodically evaluated on the basis of (a) their commitment to working with students at a particular level, (b) their ability to cope with students at a particular age, developmental, or grade level, and (c) their mastery of the appropriate instructional techniques articulated throughout this resource guide.

6. *To provide data that assist in decision making about a student's future.* Assessment of student achievement is important in guiding decision making about course and program placement, promotion, school transfer, class standing, eligibility for honors and scholarships, and career planning.

7. *To provide data to help communicate with and involve parents and guardians in their children's learning.* Parents, communities, and school boards all share accountability for the effectiveness of students' learning. Today's schools at all levels are reaching out more than ever before and engaging parents, guardians, and the community in their children's education. All teachers play an important role in the process of communicating with, reaching out to, and involving parents and the community.

Because the welfare and, indeed, the future of so many people depend on the outcomes of assessment, it is impossible to overemphasize its importance. For a learning endeavor to be successful, the learner must have answers to basic questions: Where am I going? Where am I now? How do I get where I am going? How will I know when I get there? Am I on the right track for getting there? These questions are integral to a good program of assessment. Of course, in the process of teaching and learning, the answers may be ever-changing, and the teacher and students continue to assess and adjust plans as appropriate and necessary. As you have been reminded many times in this resource guide, the exemplary school is in a mode of continuous change and progress.

Based on the preceding questions are the following principles that guide the assessment program and that are reflected in the discussions in this chapter.

- Teachers need to know how well they are doing.
- Students need to know how well they are doing.
- Assessment is a reciprocal process, which includes assessment of teacher performance and student achievement.
- The program of assessment should aid teaching effectiveness and contribute to the intellectual and psychological growth of children.

- Evidence and input data for knowing how well the teacher and students are doing should come from a variety of sources and types of data-collecting devices.
- Assessment is a continuous process. The selection and implementation of plans and activities require continuing monitoring and assessment to check on progress and to change or adopt strategies to promote desired behavior.
- Reflection and self-assessment are important components of any successful assessment program. Reflection and self-assessment are important if students are to develop the skills necessary for them to assume increasingly greater ownership of their own learning.
- A teacher's responsibility is to facilitate student learning and to assess student progress in that learning; for that, the teacher is, or should be, held accountable.

TERMS USED IN ASSESSMENT

When discussing the assessment component of teaching and learning it is easy to be confused by the terminology. The following clarification of terms is offered to aid your reading and comprehension.

Assessment and Evaluation

Although some authors distinguish between the terms **assessment** (the process of finding out what students are learning, a relatively neutral process) and **evaluation** (making sense of what was found out, a subjective process), in this text I do not. I consider the difference too slight to matter; I consider the terms to be synonymous.

Measurement and Assessment

Measurement refers to quantifiable data about specific behaviors. Tests and the statistical procedures used to analyze the results are examples. Measurement is a descriptive and objective process; that is, it is relatively free from human value judgments.

Assessment includes objective data from measurement but also other types of information, some of which are more subjective, such as information from anecdotal records, teacher observations, and ratings of student performance. In addition to the use of objective data (data from measurement), assessment also includes arriving at value judgments made on the basis of subjective information.

An example of the use of these terms is as follows. A teacher may share the information that Penny Brown received a score in the 90th percentile on the seventh-grade statewide achievement test in reading (a statement of measurement) but may add that "according to my assessment of her work in my language arts class, she has not been an outstanding student" (a statement of assessment).

Validity and Reliability

The degree to which a measuring instrument actually measures that which it is intended to measure is the instrument's **validity.** For example, when we ask if an instrument (such as a performance assessment instrument) has validity, key questions concerning that instrument are:

- Does the instrument adequately sample the intended content?
- Does it measure the cognitive, affective, and psychomotor knowledge and skills that are important to the unit of content being tested?
- Does it sample all the instructional objectives of that unit?

The accuracy with which a technique consistently measures that which it does measure is its **reliability.** If, for example, you know that you weigh 114 pounds, and a scale consistently records 114 pounds when you stand on it, then that scale has reliability. If the same scale consistently records 100 pounds when you stand on it, we can still say the scale has reliability. By this example, then, it should be clear to you that an instrument could be reliable (it produces similar results when used again and again) although not necessarily valid. In this second instance, the scale is not measuring what it is supposed to measure, so although it is reliable, it is not valid. Although a technique might be reliable but not valid, a technique must have reliability before it can have validity. The greater the number of test items or situations on a particular content objective, the higher the reliability. The higher the reliability, the more consistency there will be in students' scores measuring their understanding of that particular objective.

Authentic Assessment: Advantages and Disadvantages

When assessing for student achievement, it is important that you use procedures that are compatible with the instructional objectives. This is referred to as **authentic assessment.** Other terms used for authentic assessment are *accurate, active, aligned, alternative,* and *direct.* Although performance assessment is sometimes used, performance assessment refers to the type of student response being assessed, whereas authentic assessment refers to the assessment situation. Although not all performance assessments are authentic, assessments that are authentic are most assuredly performance assessments.

In English/language arts, for example, although it may seem fairly easy to develop a criterion-referenced

test, administer it, and grade it, tests often measure language skills rather than language use. It is extremely difficult to measure students' communicative competence with a test. Tests do not measure listening and talking very well, and a test on punctuation marks, for example, does not indicate students' ability to use punctuation marks correctly in their own writing. Instead, tests typically evaluate students' ability to add punctuation marks to a set of sentences created by someone else or to proofread and spot punctuation errors in someone else's writing. An alternative and far better approach is to examine how students use punctuation marks in their own writing.[1] An authentic assessment of punctuation, then, would be an assessment of a performance item that involves students in writing and punctuating their own writing. For the authentic assessment of the student's understanding of that which the student has been learning, you would use a performance-based assessment procedure.

Consider another example. "If students have been actively involved in classifying objects using multiple characteristics, it sends them a confusing message if they are then required to take a paper-and-pencil test that asks them to 'define classification' or recite a memorized list of characteristics of good classifications schemes."[2] An authentic assessment technique would be a performance item that actually involves the students in classifying objects. In other words, to obtain an accurate assessment of a student's learning, the teacher uses a performance-based assessment procedure that requires students to produce rather than to select a response.

Advantages claimed for the use of authentic assessment include (1) the direct (also known as performance-based, criterion-referenced, or outcome-based) measurement of what students should know and can do and (2) an emphasis on higher-order thinking. On the other hand, disadvantages of authentic assessment include a higher cost, difficulty in making results consistent and usable, and problems with validity, reliability, and comparability.

Unfortunately, a teacher may never see a particular student again after a given school semester or year is over, and thus the teacher may never observe the effects he or she has had on a student's values and attitudes. In schools where groups or teams of teachers remain with the same cohort of students—as in the house concept and looping programs—those teachers often do have opportunity to observe the positive changes in their students' values and attitudes.

---

[1]G. E. Tompkins and K. Hoskisson, *Language Arts: Content and Teaching Strategies* (Upper Saddle River, NJ: Prentice Hall, 1991), p. 63.
[2]S. J. Rakow, "Assessment: A Driving Force," *Science Scope* 15(6):3 (March 1992).

Figure 11.1   Sample form for evaluating and recording student verbal and nonverbal behaviors.

Student _____	Course _____	School _____
Observer	Date	Period
Objective	Desired behavior	What student did, said, or wrote
Teacher's (observer's) comments:		

Diagnostic, Formative, and Summative Assessment

As you learned in Part II of this resource guide, assessing a student's achievement is a three-stage process, involving:

Diagnostic assessment (sometimes called *preassessment*)—the assessment of the student's knowledge and skills before the new instruction;

Formative assessment—the assessment of learning during the instruction; and

Summative assessment—the assessment of learning after the instruction, ultimately represented by the student's final term, semester, or year's achievement grade.

Grades or marks shown on unit tests, progress reports, deficiency notices, and interim reports are examples of formative evaluation reports. However, an end-of-chapter test or a unit test is summative when the test represents the absolute end of the student's learning of material for that instructional unit.

ASSESSING STUDENT LEARNING: THREE AVENUES

There are three general avenues for assessing a student's achievement in learning. You can assess:

1. What the student *says*—for example, the quantity and quality of a student's contributions to class discussions
2. What the student *does*—for example, a student's performance (e.g., the amount and quality of a student's participation in the learning activities)
3. What the student *writes*—for example, as shown by items in the student's portfolio (e.g., homework assignments, checklists, project work, and written tests).

Importance and Weight of Each Avenue

Although your own situation and personal philosophy will dictate the levels of importance and weight you give to each avenue of assessment, you should have a strong rationale if you value and weigh the three avenues for assessment differently than one-third each.

Assessing What a Student Says and Does

When evaluating what a student says, you should (1) listen to the student's oral reports, questions, responses, and interactions with others and (2) observe the student's attentiveness, involvement in class activities, creativeness, and responses to challenges. Notice that I say you should *listen* and *observe*. While listening to what the student is saying, you should also be observing the student's nonverbal behaviors. For this you can use narrative observation forms (see Figure 11.1) and you can use observations with checklists and scoring rubrics (see sample checklists in Figures 11.2, 11.5, and 11.6, and sample scoring rubrics in Figures 8.1, 11.2, 11.3, 11.4, 11.10, 11.11, and 11.12) and periodic conferences with the student.

With each technique used, you must proceed from your awareness of anticipated learning outcomes (the instructional objectives), and you must assess a student's progress toward meeting those objectives. That is referred to as **criterion-referenced** assessment.

OBSERVATION FORM

Figure 11.1 illustrates a sample generic form for recording and evaluating teacher observations of a student's verbal and nonverbal behaviors. With modern technology, such as is afforded, for example, by the software program *Learner Profile*, a teacher can record observations electronically anywhere at any time.[3]

CHECKLIST VERSUS SCORING RUBRIC

As you can see from the sample rubric and sample checklist shown in Figure 11.2, there is little difference between a checklist and a rubric: the difference is that

---

[3]For information about *Learner Profile*, contact Sunburst, 101 Castleton Street, P.O. Box 100, Pleasantville, NY 10570-0100. Phone 800-321-7511.

Figure 11.2 Checklist and rubric compared.

Sample rubric for assessing a student's skill in listening.

Score Point 3—Strong listener:
    Responds immediately to oral directions
    Focuses on speaker
    Maintains appropriate attention span
    Listens to what others are saying
    Is interactive
Score Point 2—Capable listener:
    Follows oral directions
    Usually attentive to speaker and to discussions
    Listens to others without interrupting
Score Point 1—Developing listener:
    Has difficulty following directions
    Relies on repetition
    Often inattentive
    Has short attention span
    Often interrupts the speaker

Sample checklist for assessing a student's skill in map work:

    Check each item if the map comes up to standard in this particular category.

    _____ 1. Accuracy

    _____ 2. Neatness

    _____ 3. Attention to details

rubrics show the degrees for the desired characteristics while checklists usually show only the desired characteristics. The checklist could easily be made into a scoring rubric, and the rubric could easily be made into a checklist.

GUIDELINES FOR ASSESSING WHAT A STUDENT SAYS AND DOES

When assessing a student's verbal and nonverbal behaviors in the classroom you should:

1. Maintain an anecdotal record (teacher's log) book or folder, with a separate section in it for your records of each student.
2. For a specific activity, list the desirable behaviors.
3. Check the list against the specific instructional objectives.
4. Record your observations as quickly as possible following the occurrence. Audio or video recordings and computer software programs can help you maintain records and check the accuracy of your memory but, if this is inconvenient, you should spend time during school, immediately after school, or later that evening recording your observations while they are still fresh in your memory.
5. Record your professional judgment about the student's progress toward the desired behavior, but

think it through before transferring it to a permanent record.
6. Write comments that are reminders to yourself, such as, "Discuss observation with the student," "Check validity of observation by further testing," "Discuss observations with student's mentor" (e.g., an adult representative from the community), and "Discuss observations with other teachers on the teaching team."

Assessing What a Student Writes

When assessing what a student writes, you can use worksheets, written homework and papers, student journal writing, student writing projects, student portfolios, and tests (all discussed later in this chapter). In many schools, portfolios, worksheets, and homework assignments are the tools typically used for the formative evaluation of each student's achievement. Tests, too, should be a part of this evaluation, but tests are also used for summative evaluation at the end of a unit and for diagnostic purposes.

Your summative evaluation of a student's achievement and any other final judgment you make about a student can have impact upon the emotional and intellectual development of that student. Special attention is given to this later in the section titled "Recording Teacher Observations and Judgments."

Figure 11.3   Sample scoring rubric for assessing student writing.
Source: Texas Education Agency, *Writing Inservice Guide for English Language Arts and TAAS*
(Austin, TX: Author, 1993).

Score Point 4—correct purpose, mode, audience; effective elaboration; consistent organization; clear sense of order and completeness; fluent

Score Point 3—correct purpose, mode, audience; moderately well elaborated; organized but possible brief digressions; clear, effective language

Score Point 2—correct purpose, mode, audience; some elaboration; some specific details; gaps in organization; limited language control

Score Point 1—attempts to address audience; brief, vague, unelaborated; wanders off topic; lack of language control; little or no organization; wrong purpose and mode

---

GUIDELINES FOR ASSESSING STUDENT WRITING
Use the following guidelines when assessing what a student writes.

Student writing assignments, test items, and scoring rubrics (see Figure 11.3) *should be criterion-referenced;* that is, they should correlate with and be compatible with specific instructional objectives. Regardless of the avenue chosen and the relative weights you assign, you must evaluate against the instructional objectives. Any given objective may be checked by using more than one method and by using more than one instrument. Subjectivity, inherent in the assessment process, may be reduced as you check for validity, comparing results of one measuring strategy against those of another.

Read nearly everything a student writes (except, of course, for personal writing in a student's journal). If it is important for the student to do the work, then it is equally important that you give your professional attention to the product of the student's efforts. Of course, papers can be read with varying degrees of intensity and scrutiny, depending on the purpose of the assignment.

Provide written or verbal comments about the student's work, and be positive in those comments. Rather than just writing "good" on a student's paper, briefly state what made it good. Rather than simply saying or pointing out that the student didn't do it right, tell or show the student what is acceptable and how to achieve it. For reinforcement, use positive rewards and encouragement as frequently as possible.

Think before writing a comment on a student's paper, asking yourself how you think the student (or a parent or guardian) will interpret and react to the comment and if that is a correct interpretation or reaction to your intended meaning.

Avoid writing evaluative comments or grades in student journals.[4] Student journals are for encouraging students to write, to think about their thinking, and to record their creative thoughts. In journal writing, students should be encouraged to write about their experiences in school and out of school and especially about their experiences related to what is being learned. They should be encouraged to write their feelings about what is being learned and about how they are learning it. Writing in journals gives them practice in expressing themselves in written form and in connecting their learning and should provide nonthreatening freedom to do it. Comments and evaluations from teachers might discourage creative and spontaneous expression.

Gibbs and Earley suggest that the following "don'ts" may be more important than any "do's." Don't correct spelling or grammar. Don't probe. Resist the temptation to ask for more than the student chooses to share. Don't respond with value judgments. Simple empathic statements, such as "I understand your point of view" and "Thanks for sharing your thoughts," can be used to avoid making value judgments. Don't require students to share their entries with you or their peers. Pages that students do not want the teacher to read may be folded shut and marked "Personal."[5]

When reading student journals, talk individually with students to seek clarification about their expressions. Student journals are useful to the teacher (of any subject) in understanding the student's thought processes and writing skills (diagnostic evaluation) and should not be graded. For grading purposes, teachers may simply record whether the student is maintaining a journal and, perhaps, a judgment about the quantity of writing in it, but no judgment should be made about the quality.

When reviewing student portfolios, discuss with students individually the progress in their learning as shown by the materials in their portfolios. As with student journals, the portfolio should not be graded or

---

[4]See, for example, A. Chandler, "Is This for a Grade? A Personal Look at Journals," *English Journal* 86(1):45–49 (January 1997).

[5]L. J. Gibbs and E. J. Earley, *Using Children's Literature to Develop Core Values,* Fastback 362 (Bloomington, IN: Phi Delta Kappa Educational Foundation, 1994).

compared in any way with those of other students. Its purpose is for student self-assessment and to show progress in learning. For this to happen, students should keep in their portfolios all or major samples of papers related to the course. (Student journals and portfolios are discussed later in this chapter.)

Assessment for Affective and Psychomotor Domain Learning

While assessment of cognitive domain learning lends itself to traditional written tests of achievement, the assessment of learning within the affective and psychomotor domains is best suited by the use of performance checklists where student behaviors can be observed in action. However, many educators today are encouraging the use of alternative assessment procedures (i.e., alternatives to traditional paper-and-pencil written testing). After all, in learning that is most important and that has the most meaning to students, the domains are inextricably interconnected. Learning that is meaningful to students is not as easily compartmentalized as the taxonomies of educational objectives would imply. Alternative assessment strategies include the use of group projects, portfolios, skits, papers, oral presentations, and performance tests.

COOPERATIVE GROUP LEARNING AND ASSESSMENT

As you learned in Chapter 8, the purpose of a cooperative learning group is for the group to learn, which means that individuals within the group must learn. Group achievement in learning, then, depends on the learning of individuals within the group. Rather than competing for rewards for achievement, members of the group cooperate with each other by helping each other to learn so the group reward will be a good one. Theoretically, when small groups of students of mixed backgrounds, skills, and capabilities work together toward a common goal, they increase their liking and respect for one another. As a result, there is an increase in each student's self-esteem and academic achievement.

When the achievement of a cooperative learning group is recognized, group achievement is rewarded along with individual achievement. Remembering that the emphasis must be on peer support rather than peer pressure, you must be cautious about ever giving group grades.[6] Some teachers give bonus points to all

members of a group to add to their individual scores when everyone in the group has reached preset criteria. In establishing preset standards, the standards can be different for individuals within a group, depending on each member's ability and past performance. It is important that each member of a group feel rewarded and successful. Some teachers also give subjective grades to individual students on their role performances within the group (see Figure 11.4). For determination of students' report card grades, individual student achievement is measured later through individual results on tests and other sources of data. The final grade is based on those sources and on the student's performance in the group.

STUDENT INVOLVEMENT IN ASSESSMENT

Students' continuous self-assessment should be planned as an important component of the assessment program.[7] If students are to progress in their understanding of their own thinking (*metacognition*) and in their intellectual development, then they must receive instruction and guidance in how to become more responsible for their own learning. During that empowerment process they learn to think better of themselves and of their individual capabilities. To achieve this self-understanding and improved self-esteem requires the experiences afforded by successes, along with guidance in self-understanding and self-assessment.

To meet these goals, teachers provide opportunities for students to think about what they are learning, about how they are learning it, and about how far they have progressed. One procedure is for students to maintain portfolios of their work, using rating scales or checklists periodically to self-assess their progress.

Using Student Portfolios

Portfolios are used by teachers as a means of instruction and by teachers and students as one means of assessing student learning. Although there is little research evidence to support or to refute the claim, educators believe the instructional value comes from the process of the student's assembling and maintaining a personal portfolio. During that creative process the student is expected to self-reflect and to think critically about what has and is being learned. The student is assuming some responsibility for his or her own learning.

---

[6]See S. Kagan, "Group Grades Miss the Mark," *Educational Leadership* 52(8):68–71 (May 1995), and D. W. Johnson and R. T. Johnson, "The Role of Cooperative Learning in Assessing and Communicating Student Learning," Chapter 4 in T. R. Guskey (Ed.), *Communicating Student Learning* (Alexandria, VA: 1996 Yearbook, Association for Supervision and Curriculum Development, 1996).

[7]See, for example, D. Rothenberg, "Student Involvement in the Assessment of Learning," *Middle School Journal* 25(4):54–57 (March 1997).

Figure 11.4 Sample scoring rubric for assessing individual students in cooperative learning group project. Possible score = 50. Scorer marks a relevant square in each of the five categories (horizontal rows), and the student's score for that category is the small number in the top right corner within that square.

	9–10	8	7	1–6
Goals	Consistently and actively helps identify group goals; works effectively to meet goals.	Consistently communicates commitment to group goals; carries out assigned roles.	Sporadically communicates commitment to group goals; carries out assigned role.	Rarely, if ever, works toward group goals or may work against them.
Interpersonal Skills	Cooperates with group members by encouraging, compromising, and/or taking a leadership role without dominating; shows sensitivity to feelings and knowledge of others.	Cooperates with group members by encouraging, compromising, and/or taking a leadership role.	Participates with group, but has own agenda; may not be willing to compromise or to make significant contributions.	May discourage others, harass group members, or encourage off-task behavior. Makes significant changes to others' work without their knowledge or permission.
Quality Producer	Contributes significant information, ideas, time, and/or talent to produce a quality product.	Contributes information, ideas, time, and/or talent to produce a quality product.	Contributes some ideas, though not significant; may be more supportive than contributive; shows willingness to complete assignment but has no desire to go beyond average expectations.	Does little or no work toward the completion of group product; shows little or no interest in contributing to the task; produces work that fails to meet minimum standards for quality.
Participation	Attends daily; consistently and actively utilizes class time by working on the task.	Attends consistently; sends in work to group if absent; utilizes class time by working on the task.	Attends sporadically; absences/tardies may hinder group involvement; may send in work when absent; utilizes some time; may be off task by talking to others, interrupting other groups, or watching others do the majority of the work.	Frequent absences or tardies hinder group involvement; fails to send in work when absent; wastes class time by talking, doing other work, or avoiding tasks; group has asked that member be reproved by teacher or removed from the group.
Commitment	Consistently contributes time out of class to produce a quality product; attends all group meetings as evidenced by the group meeting log.	Contributes time out of class to produce a quality product; attends a majority of group meetings as evidenced by the group meeting log.	Willing to work toward completion of task during class time; attends some of the group meetings; may arrive late or leave early; may keep inconsistent meeting log.	Rarely, if ever, attends group meetings outside of class or may attend and hinder progress by the group; fails to keep meeting log.

Source: Courtesy of Susan Abbott and Pam Benedetti, Elk Grove School District, Elk Grove, CA.

Student portfolios fall into three general categories, and the purpose in a given situation may transcend some combination of all three. The categories are (1) *selected works portfolio,* in which students maintain samples of their work as prompted by the teacher, (2) *longitudinal or growth portfolio,* which is oriented toward outcome-driven goals and includes samples of student work from the beginning and from the end of the school term (or thematic unit of study) to exemplify achievement toward the goals, and (3) *passport or career portfolio,* which contains samples of student work that will enable the student to make transitions, such as from one school grade level to the next.

Student portfolios should be well organized and, depending on the purpose (or category) should contain assignment sheets, class worksheets, the results of homework, project binders, forms for student self-assessment and reflection on their work, and other class materials thought important by the students and teacher.[8] As a model of a real-life portfolio, you can show students your personal career portfolio (see Chapter 12).

PORTFOLIO ASSESSMENT: DEALING
WITH ITS LIMITATIONS
Although portfolio assessment as an alternative to traditional methods of evaluating student progress has gained momentum in recent years, establishing standards has been difficult. Research on the use of portfolios for assessment indicate that validity and reliability of teacher evaluation are often quite low. In addition, portfolio assessment is not always practical for use by every teacher. For example, if you are the sole art teacher for an elementary school and are responsible for teaching art to 700 children in the school, you are unlikely to have the time or storage capacity for 700 portfolios. For your assessment of student learning, the use of checklists, rubrics, and student self-assessment may be more practical.

Before using portfolios as an alternative to traditional testing, you are advised to consider carefully and understand clearly the reasons for doing it and its practicality in your situation. Then decide carefully portfolio content, establish rubrics or expectation standards, anticipate grading problems, and consider and prepare for parent reactions.

While emphasizing the criteria for assessment, rating scales and checklists provide students with means of expressing their feelings and give the teacher still another source of input data for use in assessment. To provide students with reinforcement and guidance to improve their learning and development, teachers can meet with individual students to discuss their self-assessments. Such conferences should provide students with understandable and achievable short-term goals and help them develop and maintain an adequate self-esteem.[9]

Although almost any instrument used for assessing student work can be used for student self-assessment, in some cases it might be better to construct specific instruments with the student's understanding of the instrument in mind. Student self-assessment and self-reflection should be done on a regular and continuing basis so comparisons can be made periodically by the student. You will need to help students learn how to analyze these comparisons. Comparisons should provide a student with information previously not recognized about his or her own progress and growth.

Using Checklists

One of the items that can be maintained by students in their portfolios is a series of checklists. Checklist items can be used easily by a student to compare with previous self-assessments. Items on the checklist will vary depending on your purpose, subject, and grade level. (See sample forms, Figures 11.5 and 11.6.) Open-ended questions allow the student to provide additional information and to do some expressive writing. After a student has demonstrated each of the skills satisfactorily, a check is made next to the student's name, either by the teacher alone or in conference with the student.

GUIDELINES FOR USING PORTFOLIOS
FOR ASSESSMENT
Here are general guidelines for using student portfolios in the assessment of learning.

- Contents of the portfolio should reflect course aims and objectives.
- Students should date everything that goes into their portfolios.
- Determine what materials should be kept in the portfolio and announce clearly (post schedule in room) when, how, and by what criteria you will review portfolios.
- Give responsibility for maintenance of the portfolios to the students.
- Portfolios should be kept in the classroom.
- The portfolio should not be graded or compared in any way with those of other students. Its purpose is for student self-assessment and for showing progress in learning. For this to happen, students should

---

[8]Software packages for the development of student electronic portfolios are available, such as *Classroom Manager* from CTB Macmillan/McGraw-Hill (Monterey, CA), *Electronic Portfolio* from Learning Quest (Corvallis, OR), and *Grady Profile* from Aurbach and Associates (St. Louis, MO).

[9]For a discussion of the biological importance and educational benefits of positive feedback, student portfolios, and group learning, see R. Sylwester, "The Neurobiology of Self-Esteem and Aggression," *Educational Leadership* 54(5):75–79 (February 1997).

Figure 11.5 Sample checklist: assessing a student's oral report.

Checklist: Oral Report Assessment

Student _____ Date _____

Teacher _____ Time _____

Did the student	Yes	No	Comments
1. Speak so that everyone could hear?	_____	_____	_____
2. Finish sentences?	_____	_____	_____
3. Seem comfortable in front of the group?	_____	_____	_____
4. Give a good introduction?	_____	_____	_____
5. Seem well informed about the topic?	_____	_____	_____
6. Explain ideas clearly?	_____	_____	_____
7. Stay on the topic?	_____	_____	_____
8. Give a good conclusion?	_____	_____	_____
9. Use effective visuals to make the presentation interesting?	_____	_____	_____
10. Give good answers to questions from the audience?	_____	_____	_____

Figure 11.6 Sample checklist: student learning assessment for use with interdisciplinary thematic instruction.

Checklist: Interdisciplinary Thematic Unit Learning

Student _____ Date _____

Teacher _____ Time _____

Did the student	Yes	No	Comments/Evidence
1. Can identify theme, topic, main idea of the unit	_____	_____	_____
2. Can identify contributions of others to the theme	_____	_____	_____
3. Can identify problems related to the unit study	_____	_____	_____
4. Has developed skills in:	_____	_____	_____
Applying knowledge	_____	_____	_____
Assuming responsibility	_____	_____	_____
Classifying	_____	_____	_____
Categorizing	_____	_____	_____
Decision making	_____	_____	_____
Discussing	_____	_____	_____
Gathering resources	_____	_____	_____
Impulse control	_____	_____	_____
Inquiry	_____	_____	_____
Justifying choices	_____	_____	_____
Listening to others	_____	_____	_____
Locating information	_____	_____	_____
Metacognition	_____	_____	_____

(continued)

Figure 11.6 (*continued*)

Did the student	Yes	No	Comments/Evidence
Ordering	_____	_____	_____
Organizing information	_____	_____	_____
Problem recognition/identification	_____	_____	_____
Problem solving	_____	_____	_____
Reading text	_____	_____	_____
Reading maps and globes	_____	_____	_____
Reasoning	_____	_____	_____
Reflecting	_____	_____	_____
Reporting to others	_____	_____	_____
Self-assessing	_____	_____	_____
Sharing	_____	_____	_____
Studying	_____	_____	_____
Summarizing	_____	_____	_____
Thinking	_____	_____	_____
Using resources	_____	_____	_____
Working with others	_____	_____	_____
Working independently	_____	_____	_____
(Others unique to the unit)	_____	_____	_____

Additional teacher and student comments:

keep in their portfolio all papers, or major sample papers, related to the course. For grading purposes, you can simply record whether or not the portfolio was maintained and by checklist whether all required materials are in the portfolio.

MAINTAINING RECORDS OF STUDENT ACHIEVEMENT

You must maintain well-organized and complete records of student achievement. You may do this in a written record book or on an electronic record book. At the very least, the record book should include attendance records and all records of scores on tests, homework, projects, and other assignments.

Daily interactions and events occur in the classroom that may provide informative data about a student's intellectual, emotional, and physical development. Maintaining a dated log of your observations of these interactions and events can provide important information that might otherwise be forgotten. At the end of a unit and again at the conclusion of a grading

term, you will want to review your records. During the course of the school year, your anecdotal records (and those of other members of your teaching team) will provide important information about the intellectual, psychological, and physical development of each student and ideas for attention to be given to individual students.

Recording Teacher Observations and Judgments

You must think carefully about any written comments that you intend to make about a student. Children can be quite sensitive to what others say about them, and most particularly to comments about them made by a teacher.

Additionally, we have seen anecdotal comments in students' permanent records that said more about their teachers who made the comments than about the recipient students. Comments that have been carelessly, hurriedly, and thoughtlessly made can be detrimental to a student's welfare and progress in school. Teacher comments must be professional; that is, they must be diagnostically useful to the continued intellectual and psychological development of the student. This is true for any comment you make or write, whether on a student's paper, or on the student's permanent school record, or on a message sent to the student's home.

As an example, consider the following unprofessional comment observed in one student's permanent record. A teacher wrote, "John is lazy." Describing John as "lazy" is nonproductive, and it is certainly not a professional diagnosis. How many times do you suppose John needs to receive such negative descriptions of his behavior before he begins to believe he is lazy and as a result acts that way even more often? Written comments like that can also be damaging because they may be read by the teacher who next has John in class and lead that teacher to perpetuate the same expectation of John. To say that John is lazy merely describes behavior as judged by the teacher who wrote the comment. More important, and more professional, would be for the teacher to try to analyze why John is behaving that way, then to *prescribe* activities that are likely to motivate John to assume more constructive charge of his own learning behavior.

For students' continued intellectual and emotional development, your comments should be useful, productive, analytical, diagnostic, and prescriptive. The professional teacher makes diagnoses and prepares descriptions; a professional teacher does not label students as "lazy," "vulgar," "slow," "stupid," "difficult," or "dumb." The professional teacher sees the behavior of a student as being goal-directed. Perhaps "lazy" John found that particular behavioral pattern won him attention. John's goal, then, was attention (don't we all need attention?), and John assumed negative, perhaps even self-destructive, behavioral patterns to reach that goal. The professional task of any teacher is to facilitate the learner's understanding (perception) of a goal and help the student identify acceptable behaviors positively designed to achieve that goal.

That which separates the professional teacher from "anyone off the street" is the teacher's ability to go beyond mere description of behavior. Keep that in mind always when you write comments that will be read by students, by their parents or guardians, and by other teachers. Let us reinforce this concept by focusing your attention on Exercise 11.1.

EXERCISE 11.1 EVALUATING WRITTEN TEACHER COMMENTS—A SELF-CHECK EXERCISE

INSTRUCTIONS: The purpose of this exercise is to reinforce the importance of teacher comments about student behavior that go beyond that of merely describing behavior. The following comments were written by teachers on student records. Check those you consider to be professionally useful and those that are not. Then compare your responses against the key that follows. Discuss the results with your classmates and instructor.

	Yes	No
1. Sonja performs her writing assignments much better when done in class than when done as homework.	( )	( )
2. Lucretia was very disruptive in class during our unit on westward expansion.	( )	( )
3. Aram has a lot of difficulty staying in his seat.	( )	( )
4. Arthur seems more responsible during science experiments than during my lectures.	( )	( )
5. Razmik seems to have an excess of nervous energy, and I am concerned about his nutrition.	( )	( )
6. Su Chin did very well this year in laboratory activities but seems to have reading difficulties.	( )	( )
7. Catalina does not get along well with her peers during group learning activities.	( )	( )
8. Angela seems unable to understand my verbal instructions.	( )	( )
9. I am recommending special remediation for José, perhaps through tutoring.	( )	( )
10. I do not appreciate Dan's use of vulgarity.	( )	( )

Note: It can be argued that those comments identified as not useful, although not prescriptive, could be signals that the student might benefit from a session with the school counselor.

Exercise Answer Key: Answer Key to Exercise 11.1

1. Useful.
2. Not useful, because there are no helpful specifics. "Disruptive" is merely descriptive, not prescriptive. Also, it could cause Lucretia's future teachers to be biased against her.
3. Useful.
4. Useful.
5. Useful.
6. Useful, although additional specifics would be helpful.
7. Useful, although additional specifics would be helpful.
8. Not very useful; it may tell more about the teacher than it does Angela.
9. Useful.
10. Not useful.

GRADING AND MARKING STUDENT ACHIEVEMENT

If conditions were ideal (which they are not) and teachers did their job perfectly (which many of us do not), then all students would receive top marks (the ultimate in mastery or quality learning) and there would be less of a need to talk about grading and marking. (Believing that letter grades do not reflect the nature of the developmental progress of young children, many school districts hold off using letter grades until children are in at least third grade or even the sixth grade; instead, they favor using developmental checklists and narratives.[10]) Mastery learning implies that some end point of learning is attainable, but there probably isn't an end point. In any case, because conditions for teaching are never ideal and we teachers are mere humans, let us continue with this topic of grading, which is undoubtedly of special interest to you, your students, their parents or guardians, school counselors, administrators and school boards, potential employers, providers of scholarships, and college admissions officers.

The term *achievement* is used frequently throughout this resource guide. What is the meaning of the term? Achievement means accomplishment, but is it accomplishment of the instructional objectives against preset standards, or is it simply accomplishment? Most teachers probably choose the former, where the teacher subjectively establishes a standard that must be met for a student to receive a certain grade for an assignment, project, test, quarter, semester, or course. Achievement, then, is decided by degrees of accomplishment.

Preset standards are usually expressed in percentages (degrees of accomplishment) needed for marks or *ABC* grades. If no student achieves the standard required for an *A* grade, for example, then no student receives an *A*. On the other hand, if all students meet the preset standard for the *A* grade, then all receive *A*s. Determining student grades on the basis of preset standards is referred to as *criterion-referenced grading*.

Criterion-Referenced vs. Norm-Referenced Grading

While criterion-referenced (or competency-based) grading is based on preset standards, norm-referenced grading measures the relative accomplishment of individuals in the group (e.g., one classroom of fourth graders or one classroom of high school chemistry students) or in a larger group (e.g., all fourth graders or all students enrolled in high school chemistry) by comparing and ranking students. Norm-referenced grading is commonly known as "grading on a curve." Because it encourages competition and discourages cooperative learning, for the determination of student grades norm-referenced grading is not recommended. Norm-referenced grading is educationally dysfunctional. For your personal interest, after several years of teaching, you can produce frequency-distribution studies of grades you have given over a period of time, but do not give students grades that are based on a curve. That grading and reporting should always be done in reference to learning criteria and never on a curve is well supported by research studies and authorities on the matter.[11] Grades for student achievement should be tied to performance levels and determined on the basis of each student's achievement toward preset standards.

In criterion-referenced grading, the aim is to communicate information about an individual student's progress in knowledge and work skills in comparison to that student's previous attainment or in the pursuit of an absolute, such as content mastery. Criterion-referenced grading is featured in **continuous-progress** curricula, competency-based curricula, and other programs that focus on individualized education.

Criterion-referenced grading is based on the level at which each student meets the specified objectives (standards) for the course or grade level. The objectives must be clearly stated to represent important student learning outcomes. This approach implies that effective teaching and learning result in high grades (*A*s) or marks for most students. In fact, when a mastery concept is used, the student must accomplish the objectives before being allowed to proceed to the next learning task. The philosophy of teachers who favor criterion-referenced procedures recognizes individual potential. Such teachers accept the challenge of finding teaching strategies to help students progress from where they are to the next designated level. Instead of wondering how Juanita compares with Sally, the comparison is between what Juanita could do yesterday and what she can do today and how well these performances compare to the preset standard.

Most school systems use some sort of combination of both norm-referenced and criterion-referenced data usage. Sometimes both kinds of information are useful. For example, a report card for a student in the eighth grade might indicate how that student is meeting certain criteria, such as an *A* grade for addition of fractions. Another entry might show that this mastery is expected, however, in the sixth grade. Both criterion- and norm-referenced data may be communicated to

---

[10]K. Lake and K. Kafka, "Reporting Methods in Grades K-8," Chapter 9 in T. R. Guskey (Ed.), *Communicating Student Learning.*

[11]See, for example, T. R. Guskey (Ed.) *Communicating Student Learning,* pp. 18–19, and R. J. Stiggins, *Student-Centered Classroom Assessment,* 2d ed. (Upper Saddle River, NJ: Prentice Hall, 1997), pp. 436–437.

the parents or guardians and the student. Appropriate procedures should be used: a criterion-referenced approach to show whether or not the student can accomplish the task, and if so, to what degree, and a norm-referenced approach to show how well that student performs compared to the larger group to which the child belongs. The latter is important data for college admissions officers and for committees that appropriate academic scholarships.

Determining Grades

Once entered onto school transcripts, grades have significant impacts upon the futures of students. When determining achievement grades for student performance, you must make several important and professional decisions. Although in a few schools, and for certain classes or assignments, only marks such as *E, S,* and *I* or pass/no pass, are used, percentages of accomplishment and letter grades are used for most intermediate grades and higher.[12]

GUIDELINES FOR DETERMINING GRADES
For determining student grades, consider the guidelines presented in the following paragraphs.

At the start of the school term, explain your marking and grading policies first to yourself, then to your students and to their parents or guardians at back-to-school night, or by a written explanation that is sent home, or both. Share sample scoring and grading rubrics with students and parents. In addition, include your grading policy in the course syllabus (Chapter 5).

When converting your interpretation of a student's accomplishments to a letter grade, be as objective as possible. For the selection of criteria for ABC grades, select a percentage standard, such as 92 percent for an *A,* 85 percent for a *B,* 75 percent for a *C,* and 65 percent for a *D.* Cutoff percentages used are your decision, although the district, school, program area, or department may have established guidelines you are expected to follow.

For the determination of students' final grades, many teachers use a point system, in which work that students write, say, and do are given points (but not for journals or portfolios, except, perhaps, simply for whether the student does one or not); then the possible point total is the factor for grade determination. For example, if 92 percent is the cutoff for an *A* and 500 points are possible, then any student with 460 points or more (500 × 0.92) has achieved an *A.* Likewise, for a test or any other assignment, if the value is 100 points, the cutoff for an *A* is 92 (100 × 0.92). With a point system and preset standards, the teacher and students, at any time during the grading period, always know the current points possible and can easily calculate a student's current grade standing. Then, as far as a current grade is concerned, students always know where they stand in the course.

Build your grading policy around degrees of accomplishment rather than failure by fostering a learning environment where students proceed from one accomplishment to the next. This is *continuous promotion,* not necessarily the promotion of the student from one grade level to the next, but within the classroom. (However, some schools have eliminated grade-level designation and, in its place, use the concept of continuous promotion from the time of student entry into the school through the student's graduation or exit from it).

Remember that *assessment* and *grading* are not synonymous. As you learned earlier, assessment implies the collection of information from a variety of sources, including measurement techniques and subjective observations. These data, then, become the basis for arriving at a final grade, which in effect is a final value judgment. Grades are one aspect of evaluation and are intended to communicate educational progress to students and to their parents or guardians. To be valid as an indicator of that progress, you must use a variety of sources of data for determination of a student's final grade.

Decide beforehand your policy about makeup work. Students will be absent and will miss assignments and tests, so it is best that your policies about late assignments and missed tests be clearly communicated to students and to their parents or guardians. For makeup work, please consider the following.

Homework Assignments. As discussed earlier (in Chapter 8), I recommend that after due dates have been negotiated or set for assignments no credit or reduced credit be given for work that is turned in late. Sometimes, however, a student has legitimate reasons why he or she could not get an assignment done by the due date, and the teacher must exercise a professional judgment in each instance. Although it is important that teachers have rules and procedures—and that they consistently apply those—the teacher is a professional who must consider all aspects of a student's situation and, after doing so, show compassion, caring, and understanding of the human situation. (Refer to Figure 8.2 and the discussion titled "Strategies for Student Recovery" in Chapter 8.)

Tests. If students are absent when tests are given, you have several options. Some teachers allow students to miss or discount one test per grading period. Another technique is to allow each student to substitute a written homework assignment or project for one missed test.

---

[12]For other methods used to report student achievement, see K. Lake and K. Kafka, "Reporting Methods in Grades K-8," and J. Bailey and J. McTighe, "Reporting Achievement at the Secondary Level: What and How," Chapters 9 and 10 (respectively) in T. R. Guskey, *Communicating Student Learning.*

Still another option is to give the absent student the choice of either taking a makeup test or having the next test count double. When makeup tests are given, the makeup test should be taken within a week of the regular test unless there is a compelling reason (e.g., medical or family problem) why this cannot happen.

Sometimes students miss a testing period, not because of being absent from school but because of involvement in other school activities. In those instances, the student may be able to arrange to take the test during another of your class periods or your prep period on that day or the next. If a student is absent during performance testing, the logistics and possible diminished reliability of having to readminister the test for one student may necessitate giving the student an alternate paper-and-pencil test or some other option.

Quizzes. Many teachers give frequent and brief quizzes, as often as every day. As opposed to tests (see next section), quizzes are usually brief (perhaps taking only five minutes of class time) and intended to reinforce the importance of frequent study and review. (However, quizzes should be prepared using the same care and precision as presented in the guidelines that follow in the sections for testing and preparation of assessment items). When quizzes are given at frequent intervals, no single quiz should count very much toward the student's final grade; therefore, you will probably want to avoid having to schedule and give makeup quizzes for students who were absent during a quiz period. The following are reasonable options to administering makeup quizzes, and are presented here in order of our preference, number one being our first choice. (1) Give a certain number of quizzes during a grading period, say ten, but allow a student to discount a few quiz scores, say two of the ten, thereby allowing the student to discount a low score or a missed quiz due to absence or both. (2) Count the next quiz double for a student who missed one due to absence. About the only problem with this option is when a student misses several quizzes. If that happens, (3) count the unit test a certain and relative percentage greater for any student who missed a quiz during that unit. By the way, I see absolutely no educational value in giving "pop" or unannounced graded quizzes.

TESTING FOR ACHIEVEMENT

One source of information used for determining grades is data obtained from testing for student achievement. There are two kinds of tests, those that are standardized and those that are not.

Standardized and Nonstandardized Tests

Standardized tests have been constructed and published by commercial testing bureaus and used by states and districts to determine and compare student achievement, principally in the core subjects. Standardized norm-referenced tests are best for diagnostic purposes and should not be used for determining student grades. Space in this book does not allow a consideration of standardized achievement testing. Rather, our focus is on non-standardized tests that you design for your own unique group of students.

Textbook publisher's tests, test item pools, and standardized tests are available from a variety of sources, but because schools, teachers, and students are different, most of the time you will be designing (or collaboratively participating in the designing) and preparing tests for your own purposes for your distinct group of students.

Competent planning, preparing, administering, and scoring of tests is an important professional skill. You may want to refer to the guidelines that follow while you are student teaching and again occasionally during your initial years as an employed teacher.

Purposes for Testing

Tests can be designed for several purposes, and a variety of kinds of tests and alternate test items will keep your testing program interesting, useful, and reliable. As a college student, you are probably most experienced with testing for measuring for achievement, but you will use tests for other reasons as well. Tests are also used to assess and aid in curriculum development; help determine teaching effectiveness; help students develop positive attitudes, appreciations, and values; help students increase their understanding and retention of facts, principles, skills, and concepts; motivate students; provide diagnostic information for planning for individualization of the instruction; provide review and drill to enhance teaching and learning; and serve as informational data for students and parents.

Frequency of Testing

First of all, assessment for student learning should be continual; that is, it should be going on every minute of every class day. For grading or marking purposes, it is difficult to generalize about how often to test formally for student achievement, but I believe that testing should be cumulative and frequent. By "cumulative," I mean that each assessment should assess for the student's understanding of previously learned material and for the current unit of study; that is, it should assess for connected learning. By "frequent," for self-sustained classes I mean as often as daily and for classes that meet for an hour or so each day I mean as often as once a week. Advantages of assessment that is cumulative include the review, reinforcement, and articulation of old material with the most recent.

Advantages of frequent assessment include a reduction in student anxiety over tests and an increase in the validity of the summative assessment.

Test Construction

After determining the reasons for which you are designing and administering a test, you need to identify the specific instructional objectives the test is being designed to measure. (As you learned in Chapter 5, your written instructional objectives are specific so that you can write assessment items to measure against those objectives in keeping with criterion-referenced assessment.) Thus, the first step in test construction is identification of the purpose(s) for the test. The second step is to identify the objectives to be measured, and the third step is to prepare the test items. The best time to prepare draft items is after you have prepared your instructional objectives—while the objectives are fresh in your mind, which means before the lessons are taught. After a lesson is taught you will then want to rework your first draft of the test items that are related to that lesson to make any modifications to the draft items as a result of the instruction that occurred.

Administering Tests

For many students, test taking can be a time of high anxiety. Children demonstrate test anxiety in various ways. Just before and during testing some are quiet and thoughtful, while others are noisy and disruptive. To measure student achievement more accurately, you will want to take steps to reduce their anxiety. To control or reduce student anxieties, consider the following discussion as guidelines for administering tests.

Since many people respond best to familiar routine, plan your formative assessment program so tests are given at regular intervals and administered at the same time and in the same way. In some secondary schools in particular, days of the week are assigned to departments for administering major tests. For example, Tuesdays might be assigned for language arts and mathematics testing, while Wednesday is the day for social studies and science testing.

Avoid tests that are too long and that will take too much time. Sometimes beginning teachers have unreasonable expectations of children about their attention spans during testing. Frequent testing with frequent sampling of student knowledge is preferred over infrequent and long tests that attempt to cover everything.

Attend to creature comforts. Try to arrange the classroom so it is well-ventilated, the temperature is comfortable, and, when giving paper-and-pencil tests individually, the seats are well spaced. If spacing is a problem, then consider group testing or using alternate forms of the test, where students seated adjacent to one another have different forms of the same test (for example, multiple choice answer alternatives are arranged in different order).

Before distributing the test, explain to students what they are to do when finished, such as quietly begin a homework or reading assignment, because not all of the students will finish at the same time. It is unreasonable to expect most students to sit quietly after finishing a test; they need something to do.

When ready to test, don't drag it out. Distribute tests quickly and efficiently. Once testing has begun, avoid interrupting the students. Items or announcements of important information can be written on the board or, if unrelated to the test, held until all are finished with the test. Stay in the room and visually monitor the students. If the test is not going to take an entire class period (and most shouldn't) and it's a major test, then give it at the beginning of the period, if possible, unless you are planning a test review just prior to it (although that seems rather late to conduct a meaningful review). It's improbable that any teacher can effectively teach a lesson with a reasonable degree of student interest in it just prior to or immediately after a major test.

Controlling Cheating

Cheating on tests does occur, but you can take steps to discourage it or reduce the opportunity and pressure that cause students to cheat.

Preventing cheating. Space students or use alternate forms of the test. Frequent testing and not allowing a single test to count too much toward a term grade reduce test anxiety and the pressure that can cause cheating, and increase student learning by "stimulating greater effort and providing intermittent feedback" to the student.[13] Prepare test questions that are clear and not ambiguous, thereby reducing student frustration caused by a question or instructions they do not understand. Avoid tests that are too long and that will take too much time. During long tests, some students get discouraged and restless, and that is a time when classroom management problems can occur.

By their sheer nature, performance tests can cause even greater pressure on students and can also provide greater opportunity for cheating. When administering performance tests to an entire class, it is best to have several monitors, such as members of your teaching team. If that isn't possible, consider testing groups of students, such as cooperative learning groups, rather than individuals. Evaluation of test performance, then, would be based on group rather than individual achievement.

---

[13]H. J. Walberg, "Productive Teaching and Instruction: Assessing the Knowledge Base," *Phi Delta Kappan* 71(6):472 (February 1990).

Consider using open-text and open-notebook tests or allowing each student to prepare a page of notes to use during the test. When students can use their books and notes, that not only reduces anxiety but it helps them with the organization of information and the retention of what has been learned.

Stopping cheating. The preceding paragraphs provide hints to prevent student cheating. If you suspect cheating is occurring, move and stand in the area of the suspected student. Usually that will stop it.

Dealing with cheating. When you suspect cheating has occurred, you are faced with a dilemma. Unless your suspicion is backed by solid proof, you are advised to forget it, but keep a close watch on the student the next time to prevent cheating from happening. Your job is not to catch students being dishonest but to discourage dishonesty. If you have absolute proof that a student has cheated, then you are obligated to proceed with school policy on student cheating, which may call for a session with the counselor or the student and the student's parent or guardian, perhaps an automatic *F* grade on the test, and even a temporary suspension from class.

Determining the Time Needed to Take a Test

Again, avoid giving tests that are too long and that will take too much time. Preparing and administering good tests is a skill you will develop over time. In the meantime, it is best to test frequently and to use tests that sample student achievement rather than try for a comprehensive measure of that achievement.

Some students take more time on the same test than do others. You want to avoid giving too much time, or classroom management problems will result. On the other hand, you don't want to cut short the time needed by students who can do well but need more time to think and to write. As a very general guide, use the table of time needed for different types of test items (Table 11.1). This is only a guide for determining the approximate amount of time to allow students to complete a test. For example, for a test made up of 10 multiple-choice items, five arrangement items, and two short-explanation items, you would want to plan for about 30 minutes for students to complete the test.

PREPARING ASSESSMENT ITEMS

Preparing and writing good assessment items is yet another professional skill, and to become proficient at it takes study, time, practice, and reflection. Because of the importance of an assessment program, please assume this professional charge seriously and responsibly. Although poorly prepared items take no time at all to construct, they will cause you more trouble than you can ever imagine. As a professional you should take time to study different types of assessment items that can be used and how best to write them, and then practice writing them. Remember, when preparing assessment items, ensure that they match and sufficiently cover the instructional objectives. In addition, you should prepare each item carefully enough to be reasonably confident that each item will be understood by students in the manner that you anticipate its being understood. With the diversity of students in today's school classroom, especially with respect to their proficiency in oral and written English language and students with special needs, this is an especially important point. Finally, after administering a test, you must take time to analyze the results and reflect on the value of each item before ever using that item again.

Classification of Assessment Items

Assessment items can be classified as verbal (oral or written words), visual (pictures and diagrams), and manipulative or performance (handling of materials and equipment, performing). Written verbal items have traditionally been most frequently used in testing. However, visual items and visual tests are useful, for example, when working with students who lack fluency with the written word or when testing students who have limited or no proficiency in English language.

Performance items and tests are useful when measuring for psychomotor skill development. Common examples are performance testing of a student's

Table 11.1 Approximate Time to Allow for Testing as Determined by the Types of Items*.

Type of Test Item	Time Needed per Item
Matching	1 minute per matching item
Multiple-choice	1 minute
Completion	1 minute
Completion drawing	2–3 minutes
Arrangement	2–3 minutes
Identification	2–3 minutes
Short explanation	2–3 minutes
Essay and performance	10 or more minutes

*Students with disabilities or LEP students may need more time per item.

ability to carry a microscope or hold a jumping rope in place (gross motor skill) or to focus a microscope or to jump rope (fine motor skill). Performance testing also can and should be a part of a wider testing program that includes testing for higher-level thinking skills and knowledge, as, for example, when a student or small group of students are given the problem of creating from discarded materials a habitat for an imaginary animal and then instructed to display, write about, and orally present their product to the rest of the class.

As noted often throughout this book, educators have rekindled their interest in this last described form of performance testing as a means of assessment that is closer to measuring for authentic learning. In a program for teacher preparation, micro peer teaching and the student teaching experience are examples of performance assessment; that is, assessment practices used to assess the teacher candidate's ability to teach (to perform). It seems axiomatic that assessment of student teaching is a more authentic assessment of a candidate's ability to teach than would be a written (paper-and-pencil test) or verbal (oral test) form of assessment. Although less direct and perhaps less reliable than a checklist observation and analysis of a student teacher actually teaching, an observation of a student teacher's analysis of a video recorded episode (that is, with pictures) of another teacher's performance would be another way to assess more authentically a teacher's ability to teach than would be a paper-and-pencil response item test.

Performance Testing Can Be Expensive and Time-Intensive

Performance testing is usually more expensive and time-consuming than is verbal testing, which in turn is more time demanding and expensive than is written testing. However, a good program of assessment will use alternate forms of assessment and not rely solely on one form (such as written) and one type of written item (such as multiple-choice).

The type of test and items you use depend upon your purpose and objectives. Carefully consider the alternatives within that framework. To provide validity checks and to account for the individual differences of students, a good assessment program should include items from all three types. That is what writers of articles in professional journals are referring to when they talk about **alternative assessment.** They are encouraging the use of multiple assessment items, as opposed to the traditional heavy reliance on objective items such as multiple-choice questions.

General Guidelines for Preparing for Assessment

Consider the following six general guidelines when preparing for assessment. (1) Include several kinds of items and assessment instruments (see twelve types that follow). (2) Assure that content coverage is complete (i.e., that all objectives are being measured). (3) Assure that each item is reliable—that is, that it measures the intended objective. One way to check item reliability is to have more than one item measuring for the same objective. (4) Assure that each item is clear and unambiguous to all students. (5) Plan each item to be difficult enough for the poorly prepared student but easy enough for the student who is well prepared. (6) Because it is time-consuming to write good assessment items, you are advised to maintain a bank of items, with each item coded according to its matching instructional objective, domain of learning (cognitive, affective, or psychomotor), and perhaps level within the hierarchy of a particular domain. Another code could indicate whether the item requires thinking that is recall, processing, or application. Computer software programs are available for this. Ready-made test item banks are available on computer disks and accompany many programs or textbooks. If you use them, be certain the items are well written and match your course objectives. It doesn't follow that because they were published, they are well written and match what students were supposed to have learned. When preparing items for your test bank, use your creative thinking and best writing skills. Prepare items that match your objectives, put them aside, think about them, then work them over again.

Every test you administer to your students should represent your best professional effort. It should be clean and sans spelling and grammar errors. A quickly and poorly prepared test can cause you more grief than you can imagine. One that is obviously prepared hurriedly and wrought with spelling and grammar errors will quickly be frowned upon by discerning parents or guardians. If you are a student teacher, such sloppiness will certainly bring about an admonishment from your university supervisor and, if it continues, your speedy dismissal from the teacher preparation program.

Attaining Content Validity

To ensure that your test measures what you intend to measure, you can construct a table of specifications. A two-way grid indicates behavior in one dimension and content in the other (see Figures 11.7 and 11.8).

Figure 11.7   Table of specifications I.

CONTENT	BEHAVIORS								TOTAL
Social Studies Grade 6	*Cognitive*						Affective	Psychomotor	
Ancient Greece	Knowledge	Comprehension	Application	Analysis	Synthesis	Evaluation			
I. Vocabulary Development		2 (1, 2)	1 (2)						3
II. Concepts		2 (3, 4)	2 (4)						4
III. Applications	1 (5)	1 (5)	1 (5)	1 (5)	1 (5)	1 (5)			6
IV. Problem-solving		1 (6)		1 (6)					2
TOTAL	1	6	4	2	1	1			15

Figure 11.8   Table of specifications II.

CONTENT	BEHAVIORS							TOTAL
	Cognitive			*Affective*		*Psychomotor*		
	Input	Processing	Application	Low	High	Low	High	
I.								
II.								
III.								
IV.								
TOTAL								

In this grid, behavior relates to the three domains: cognitive, affective, and psychomotor. In Figure 11.7, the cognitive domain is divided, according to Bloom's taxonomy (Chapter 5), into six categories: knowledge or simple recall, comprehension, application, analysis, synthesis (often involving an original product in oral or written form), and evaluation. The specifications table of Figure 11.7 does not specify levels within the affective and psychomotor domains.

To use a table of specifications, the teacher examining objectives for the unit decides what emphasis should be given to the behavior and to the content. For instance, if vocabulary development is a concern for this sixth-grade study of Ancient Greece, then probably 20 percent of the test on vocabulary would be appropriate, but 50 percent would be unsuitable. This planning enables the teacher to design a test to fit the situation rather than a haphazard test that does not correspond to the objectives either in content or behavior emphasis. Since knowledge questions are easy to write, tests often fail to go beyond that level even though the objectives state that the student will analyze and evaluate. The sample table of specifications for a sixth-grade social studies unit on Ancient Greece indicates a distribution of questions on a test. Since this test is to be an objective test and it is so difficult to write objective items to test affective and psychomotor behaviors, this table of specifications calls for no test items in these areas. If these categories are included in the unit objectives, some other assessment devices must be used to test learning in these domains. The teacher could also show the objectives tested, as indicated within parentheses in Figure 11.7. Then, a check later on inclusion of all objectives is easy.

Preferred by some teachers is the alternative table shown in Figure 11.8. Rather than differentiating among all six of Bloom's cognitive levels, this table separates cognitive objectives into just three levels: those that require simple low-level recall of knowledge, those that require information processing, and those that require application of the new knowledge (refer to Chapter 7, "Levels of Cognitive Questions and Student Thinking"). In addition, the affective and psychomotor domains each are divided into low- and high-level behaviors. A third alternative, not illustrated here, is a table of specifications that shows all levels of each of the three domains.

TYPES OF ASSESSMENT ITEMS: DESCRIPTIONS, EXAMPLES, AND GUIDELINES FOR PREPARING AND USING

This section presents descriptions, advantages and disadvantages, and guidelines for preparing and using twelve types of assessment items. When reading about the advantages and disadvantages of each, you will notice that some types are appropriate for use in direct or performance assessment, while others are not.

Arrangement

Description: Terms or real objects (realia) are to be arranged in a specified order.

Example 1: Arrange the following list of events on a timeline in order of their occurrence: Maximilian I elected King of Germany; Maximilian I becomes Holy Roman Emperor; Diet of Augsburg establishes Council of Regency, divides Germany into six regions; Charles I of Spain becomes Holy Roman Emperor; Ferdinand I assumes the title of Holy Roman Emperor.

Example 2: The assortment of balls on the table represents the planets in our solar system. (*Note:* The balls are of various sizes, such as marbles, tennis balls, basketballs, and so on, each labeled with a planetary name, with a large sphere in the center labeled the sun.) Arrange the balls in their proper order around the sun.

Advantages: This type of item tests for knowledge of sequence and order and is good for review, for starting discussions, and for performance assessment. Example 2 is also an example of a performance test item.

Disadvantages: Scoring could be difficult, so be cautious and meticulous when using this type for grading purposes.

Guideline for use: To enhance reliability, you may need to include instructions to students to include the rationale for their arrangement, making it a combined arrangement and short-explanation type of assessment, allowing space for explanations on an answer sheet. Useful for small, heterogeneous group assessment to allow students to share and learn from their collaborative thinking and reasoning.

Completion Drawing

Description: An incomplete drawing is presented and the student is to complete it.

Example 1: Connect the following items with arrow lines to show the stages from introduction of a new bill until it becomes law (items not included here).

Example 2: In the following food web (not included here), draw arrow lines indicating which organisms are consumers and which are producers.

Advantages: This type requires less time than would a complete drawing that might be required in an essay item. Scoring is relatively easy.

Disadvantages: Care needs to be exercised in the instructions so students do not misinterpret the expectation.

Guidelines for use: Use occasionally for diversion, but take care in preparing. This type can be instructive when assessing for student thinking and reasoning as it can measure conceptual knowledge. Consider making the item a combined completion-drawing, short-explanation type by having students include their rationales for the thinking behind their drawing completion. Be sure to allow space for their explanations. Useful for small, heterogeneous group assessment to allow students to share and learn from their collaborative thinking and reasoning.

Completion Statement

Description: Sometimes called a "fill-in" item, an incomplete sentence is presented and the student is to complete it by filling in the blank space(s).

Example 1: A group of words that have a special meaning, such as "a skeleton in the closet," is called a(n) _____.

Example 2: To test their hypotheses, scientists and social scientists conduct _____.

Advantages: This type is easy to devise, take, and score.

Disadvantages: When using this type, there is a tendency to emphasize rote memory and measure procedural knowledge only. Provision of a word bank of possible answers is sometimes useful, especially with mainstreamed students, to reduce dependency on rote memory. It is difficult to write this type of item to measure for conceptual knowledge and higher levels of cognition. You must be alert for a correct response different from the expected. For example, in Example 2, although the teacher's key has "experiments" as the correct answer, a student might answer the question with "investigations" or "tests" or some other response that is equally valid.

Guideline for use: Use occasionally for review or for preassessment of student knowledge. Avoid using this type for grading unless you can write quality items that extend student thinking beyond mere recall. In all instances, avoid copying items verbatim from the student book. As with all types, be sure to provide adequate space for students' answers, and large spaces for students with motor control difficulties. Try to use only one blank per item. Try also to keep the blanks equal in length. Useful for small, heterogeneous group assessment to allow students to share and learn from their collaborative thinking and reasoning.

Correction

Description: This is similar to the completion type except that sentences or paragraphs are complete but with italicized or underlined words that can be changed to make the sentences correct.

Example 1: The work of the TVA was started by building *sand castles*. A *sand castle* is a wall built across a *kid* to stop its flow. The *sand castle* holds back the *football* so the *kids* do not overflow their *backpacks* and cause *tears*.

Example 2: 1, 1, 2, 3, 5, 8, *12*, 21, 34, *87*, 89

Advantages: Writing this type can be fun for the teacher for the purpose of preassessment of student knowledge or for review. Students may enjoy this type, especially when used only occasionally, for the tension relief afforded by incorrect absurdities. This type is useful for introducing words with multiple meanings.

Disadvantages: As with the completion type, the correction type tends to measure for low level recall and rote memory (although this is not necessarily the case in Example 2; if a student is unfamiliar with the Fibonacci number series in mathematics, it would be a relatively high-level question). The underlined incorrect items could be so whimsical that they might cause more classroom disturbance than you want.

Guidelines for use: Use occasionally for diversion and discussion. Try to write items that measure for higher-level cognition. Consider making it a combined correction, short-explanation type. Be sure to allow space for student explanations.

Essay

Description: A question or problem is presented, and the student is to compose a response in the form of sustained prose, using the student's own words, phrases, and ideas, within the limits of the question or problem.

Example 1: In the story just read, does the author elaborate the setting in great detail or barely sketch it? Explain your response.

Example 2: A healthy green coleus plant sitting in front of you has been planted in fertile soil and sealed in a glass jar. If we place the jar on the window sill where it will receive strong sunlight and the temperature inside the jar is maintained between 60 and 80 degrees Fahrenheit, how long do you predict the plant will live? Justify your prediction.

Advantages: This type measures conceptual knowledge and higher mental processes, such as the ability to synthesize material and to express ideas in clear and precise written language. It is especially useful in integrated thematic teaching. It provides practice in written expression and can be used in performance assessment, as is the case for Example 2.

Disadvantages: Essay items require a good deal of time to read and to score. They tend to provide an unreliable sampling of achievement and are vulnerable to teacher subjectivity and unreliable scoring. Furthermore, they tend to punish the student who writes slowly and laboriously, who has limited proficiency in the written language but who may have achieved as well as a student who writes faster and is more proficient in the language. Essay items tend to favor students who have fluency with words but whose achievement may not necessarily be better. In addition, unless the students have been given instruction in the meaning of key directive verbs and in how to respond to them, the teacher should not assume that all students understand such verbs (such as *explain* in the first example and *justify* in the second).

GUIDELINES FOR USING AN ESSAY ITEM

1. When preparing an essay-only test, many questions, each requiring a relatively short prose response (see the short-explanation type, page 370), are preferable to a smaller number of questions requiring long prose responses. Briefer answers tend to be more precise, and the use of many items provides a more reliable sampling of student achievement. When preparing short prose response, be sure to avoid using words verbatim from the student textbook.

2. Allow students adequate test time for a full response.

3. Different qualities of achievement are more likely comparable when all students must answer the same questions, as opposed to providing a list of essay items from which students may select those they answer.

4. After preparing essay items, make a tentative scoring key, deciding the key ideas you expect students to identify and how many points will be allotted to each.

5. Students should be informed about the relative test value for each item. Point values, if different for each item, can be listed in the margin of the test next to each item.

6. Inform students of the role of spelling, grammar, and sentence structure in your scoring of their essay items.

7. When reading student essay responses, read all student papers for one item at a time in one sitting, and, while doing that, make notes to yourself; then repeat and while reading that item again, score each student's paper for that item. Repeat the process for the next item but change or alter the order of the pile of papers so you are not reading them in the same order by student. While scoring essay responses, keep in mind the nature of the objective being measured, which may or may not include the qualities of handwriting, grammar, spelling, punctuation, and neatness.

8. To nullify the "halo effect" that can occur when you know whose paper you are reading, have students put their name on the back of the paper or use a number code rather than having students put their names on essay papers, so while reading the papers, you are unaware of whose paper is being read.

9. While having some understanding of a concept, many students are not yet facile with written expression, so you must remember to be patient, tolerant, positive, and prescriptive. Mark papers with positive and constructive comments, showing students how they could have explained or responded better.

10. Prior to using this type of test item, give instruction and practice to students in responding to key directive verbs that will be used (see Figure 11.9).

Figure 11.9 Meaning of key directive verbs for essay item responses.

Compare asks for an analysis of similarity and difference, but with a greater emphasis on similarities or likenesses.

Contrast asks more for differences than for similarities.

Criticize asks for the good and bad of an idea or situation.

Define means to express clearly and concisely the meaning of a term, as from a dictionary or in the student's own words.

Diagram means to put quantities or numerical values into the form of a chart, graph, or drawing.

Discuss means to explain or argue, presenting various sides of events, ideas, or situations.

Enumerate means to name or list one after another, which is different from "explain briefly" or "tell in a few words."

Evaluate means to express worth, value, and judgment.

Explain means to describe, with emphasis on cause and effect.

Generalize means to arrive at a valid generalization from provided specific information.

Identify means to state recognizable or identifiable characteristics.

Infer means to forecast what is likely to happen as a result of information provided.

Illustrate means to describe by means of examples, figures, pictures, or diagrams.

Interpret means to describe or explain a given fact, theory, principle, or doctrine within a specific context.

Justify means to show reasons, with an emphasis on correct, positive, and advantageous.

List means just that, to simply name items in a category or to include them in a list, without much description.

Outline means to give a short summary with headings and subheadings.

Prove means to present materials as witnesses, proof, and evidence.

Relate means to tell how specified things are connected or brought into some kind of relationship.

Summarize means to recapitulate the main points without examples or illustrations.

Trace means to follow a history or series of events, step by step, by going backward over the evidence.

Grouping

Description: Several items are presented, and the student is to select and group those that are in some way related.

Example 1: Separate the following words into two groups (words are not included here); those that are homonyms, place in group A, and those that are not homonyms, place in group B.

Example 2: Circle the figure that is least like the others (showing a wrench, screwdriver, saw, and swing).

Advantages: This type of item tests knowledge of grouping and can be used to measure conceptual knowledge, for higher levels of cognition, and to stimulate discussion. As Example 2 shows, it can be similar to a multiple-choice item.

Disadvantage: Remain alert for the student who has an alternative but valid rationale for her or his grouping.

Guideline for use: To allow for an alternative correct response, consider making the item a combination grouping, short-explanation type, being certain to allow adequate space to encourage student explanations.

Identification

Description: Unknown "specimens" are to be identified by name or some other criterion.

Example 1: Identify each plant specimen on the table by its common name.

Example 2: Identify by style each of the three poems shown on the screen.

Advantages: Verbalization (i.e., the use of abstract symbolization) is less significant, as the student is working with real materials; should be measuring for higher level learning than simple recall. The item can also be written to measure for procedural understanding, such as for identification of steps in booting up a computer program. This is another useful type for authentic and performance assessments.

Disadvantages: Because of a special familiarity with the material, some students may have an advantage over others; to be fair, "specimens" used should be equally familiar or unfamiliar to all students. This type takes more time than many of the other types, both for the teacher to prepare and for students to do.

Guidelines for use: Whatever "specimens" are used, they must be familiar to all or to none of the students, and they must be clear, not confusing. For example, fuzzy photographs or unclear photocopies, dried and incomplete plant specimens, and garbled music recordings can be confusing and frustrating to try to discern. Consider using dyad or team rather than individual testing.

Matching

Description: Students are to match related items from a list of numbered items to a list of lettered choices or in some way to connect those items that are the same or are related. Or, to eliminate the paper-and-pencil aspect and make the item more direct, use an item such as, "Of the materials on the table, pair up those that are most alike."

Example 1: In the blank space next to each description in Column A (stem or premises column) put the letter of the correct answer from Column B (answer or response column).

A (stem column)	**B (answer column)**
_____ 1. Current president of the U.S.	A. Bill Clinton
_____ 2. Most recent past president of the U.S.	B. Jessie Jackson
_____ 3. U.S. president during the Persian Gulf War	C. Thomas Jefferson
_____ 4. First president of the U.S.	D. George Washington
	E. etc.

Example 2: Match items in Column A (stem column) to those of Column B (answer column) by drawing lines connecting the matched pairs.

Column A	**Column B**
ann/enn	conquer
auto	large
min	self
vic/vinc	small
(etc.)	year
	(etc.)

Advantages: Matching items can measure for ability to judge relationships and to differentiate between similar facts, ideas, definitions, and concepts. They are easy to score and can test a broad range of content. They reduce guessing, especially if one group (e.g., answer column) contains more items than the other, are interesting to students, and are adaptable for performance assessment.

Disadvantages: Although the matching item is adaptable for performance assessment, items are not easily adapted to measuring for higher cognition. Because all parts must be homogeneous, it is possible that clues will be given, thus reducing item validity.

Guidelines for use: The number of items in the response or answer column should exceed the number in the stem column. The number of items in the stem column to be matched should not exceed ten. Less is better. Matching sets should have high homogeneity (i.e., items in both columns or groups should be of the same general category; avoid, for example, mixing dates, events, and names). Answers in the response column should be kept short, to one or two words each, and should be ordered logically, such as alphabetically. If answers from the response column can be used more than once—and that is suggested to avoid guessing by elimination—the directions should so state. Be prepared for the student who can legitimately defend an "incorrect" response. To eliminate the paper-and-pencil aspect and make the item more direct, use an item such as "of the materials on the table, pair up those that are most alike."

Multiple-Choice

Description: This type is similar to the completion item in that statements are presented (the stem), sometimes in incomplete form, but with several options or alternatives, requiring recognition or even higher cognitive processes rather than mere recall.

Example 1: Of four cylinders with the following dimensions, the one that would cause the highest-pitched sound would be

(a) 4 inches long and 3 inches in diameter
(b) 4 inches long and 1 inch in diameter
(c) 8 inches long and 3 inches diameter
(d) 8 inches long and 1 inch in diameter

Example 2: Which one of the following is a pair of antonyms?

(a) loud—soft
(b) halt—finish
(c) absolve—vindicate
(d) procure—purchase

Advantages: Items can be answered and scored quickly. A wide range of content and higher levels of cognition can be tested in a relatively short time. This type is excellent for all testing purposes—motivation, review, and assessment of learning.

Disadvantages: Unfortunately, because multiple-choice items are relatively easy to write, there is a tendency to write items measuring only for low levels of cognition. Multiple-choice items are excellent for major testing, but it takes care and time to write quality questions that measure higher levels of thinking and learning.

GUIDELINES FOR USING MULTIPLE-CHOICE ITEMS

1. If the item is in the form of an incomplete statement, it should be meaningful in itself and imply a direct question rather than merely lead into a collection of unrelated true and false statements.

2. Use a level of language that is easy enough for even the poorest readers and those with limited proficiency in English to understand; avoid unnecessary wordiness.

3. If there is much variation in the length of alternatives, arrange the alternatives in order from shortest to longest (i.e., first alternative is the shortest, last alternative is the longest). For single-word alternatives, consistent use of arrangement of alternatives is recommended, such as by length of answer or alphabetically.

4. Arrangement of alternatives should be uniform throughout the test and listed in vertical (column) form rather than in horizontal (paragraph) form.

5. Incorrect responses (distracters) should be plausible and related to the same concept as the correct alternative. Although an occasional humorous distracter may help relieve text anxiety, along with absurd distracters they should generally be avoided. They offer no measuring value and increase the likelihood of the student guessing the correct response.

6. It is not necessary to maintain a fixed number of alternatives for every item, but the use of less than three is not recommended. Although it is not always possible to come up with four or five plausible responses, the use of four or five reduces chance responses and guessing, thereby increasing reliability for the item. If you cannot think of enough plausible distracters, include the item on a test the first time as a completion item. As students respond, wrong answers will provide you with a number of plausible distracters that you can use the next time to make the item a multiple-choice type item.

7. Some mainstreamed students may work better when allowed to circle their selected response rather than writing its letter or number in a blank space.

8. Responses such as "all of these" or "none of these" should be used only when they will contribute more than another plausible distracter. Care must be taken that such responses answer or complete the item. "All of the above" is a poorer alternative than "none of the above" because items that use it as a correct response need to have four or five correct answers; also, if it is the right answer, knowledge of any two of the distracters will cue it.

9. Every item should be grammatically consistent. For example, if the stem is in the form of an incomplete sentence, it should be possible to complete the sentence by attaching any of the alternatives to it.

10. The stem should state a single and specific point.

11. The stem must mean the same thing to every student.

12. The item should be expressed in positive form. A negative form can present a psychological disad-

vantage to students. Negative items are those that ask what is not characteristic of something, or what is the least useful. Discard the item if you cannot express it in positive terminology.

13. The stem must not include clues that would indicate the correct alternative. For example, "A four-sided figure whose opposite sides are parallel is called _____.

    (a) an octagon
    (b) a parallelogram
    (c) a trapezoid
    (d) a triangle."

    Use of the word "parallel" clues the answer.

14. There must be only one correct or best response. This is easier said than done (refer to guideline 19).

15. Measuring for understanding of definitions is better tested by furnishing the name or word and requiring choice between alternative definitions than by presenting the definition and requiring choice between alternative words.

16. Avoid using alternatives that include absolute terms such as *never* and *always*.

17. Multiple-choice items need not be entirely verbal. Consider the use of realia, charts, diagrams, videos, and other visuals. They will make the test more interesting, especially to students with low verbal abilities or to those who have limited proficiency in English. Consequently, they will make the assessment more direct.

18. Once you have composed a series of multiple-choice items or a test comprised completely of this item type, tally the position of answers to be sure they are evenly distributed, to avoid the common psychological habit (when there are four alternatives) of having the correct alternative in the third position. In other words, when alternative choices are A, B, C, and D, or 1, 2, 3, and 4, unless the test designer is aware and avoids it, more correct answers will be in the "C" or "3" position than in any other.

19. Consider providing space between test items for students to include their rationales for their response selections, thus making the test a combination multiple-choice and short-explanation item type. This provides for the measurement of higher levels of cognition and encourages writing. It provides for the student who can rationalize an alternative that you had not considered plausible, especially possible today with the diversity of cultural experiences represented by students. For example, we recall the story of the math question on a test which asked if a farmer saw eight crows sitting on a fence and shot three of them, how many would be left. Of course, the "correct" response on the answer key was "5." However, one critical thinking student chose "none" as his response, an answer that was marked "wrong" by the teacher. However, the student was thinking that those crows that weren't shot would be frightened and would all fly away.

20. While scoring, on a blank copy of the test, for each item tally the incorrect responses. Analyze incorrect responses for each item to discover potential errors in your scoring key. If, for example, many students select B for an item for which your key says the correct answer is A, you may have made a mistake on your scoring key, in teaching the lesson, or in providing a second response students could interpret as correct.

21. Sometimes teachers attempt to discourage cheating by preparing several versions of the multiple-choice exam with the questions in different order. This could be giving one group of students an unfair advantage if the order of their questions are in the same sequence in which the information was originally presented and learned and for another group of students the questions are in a random order. To avoid this, questions should be in random order on every version of the exam.

Performance

Description: Provided with certain conditions or materials, the student solves a problem or accomplishes some other action.

Example 1: Write a retelling of your favorite fable and create a diorama to go along with it.

Example 2: As a culminating project for a unit on sound, groups of students were challenged to design and make their own musical instruments. The performance assessment included:

1. Play your instrument for the class.
2. Show us the part of the instrument that makes the sound.
3. Describe the function of other parts of your instrument.
4. Demonstrate how you change the pitch of the sound.
5. Share with us how you made your instrument.

Example 3: Demonstrate your understanding of diffusion by designing and completing an experiment using only those chemicals and materials located at this learning station.

Example 4: Measure and calculate the square footage of our gymnasium playing floor to the nearest centimeter.

Advantages: Performance test item types come closer to direct measurement (authentic assessment) of certain expected outcomes than do most other types. As has been indicated in discussions of the preceding question types, other types of questions

Figure 11.10   Procedure for setting up a performance assessment situation.

```
1. Specify the performance objective.
2. Specify the test conditions.
3. Establish the standards or criteria (scoring rubric)
   for judging the quality of the process and/or
   product.
4. Prepare directions in writing, outlining the
   situation, with instructions that the students are to
   follow.
5. Share the procedure with a colleague for feedback
   before using it with students.
```

can be prepared as performance-type items, in which the student actually does what he or she is being tested for.

Disadvantages: This type can be difficult and time consuming to administer to a group of students. Adequate supply of materials could be a problem. Scoring may tend to be subjective. It could be difficult to give makeup tests to students who were absent.

Guidelines for use: Use your creativity to design and use performance tests, as they tend to measure well the important objectives. To reduce subjectivity in scoring, prepare distinct scoring guidelines (rubrics), as was discussed in scoring essay-type items and as shown in examples in Figures 11.11 and 11.12. To set up a performance assessment situation, see instructions in Figure 11.10.

Short Explanation

Description: The short explanation question is like the essay-type but requires a shorter answer.

Example 1: Briefly explain in a paragraph how you would end the story.

Example 2: Briefly explain why organ pipes are made to vary in length.

Advantages: As with the essay type, student understanding is assessed, but this type takes less time for the teacher to read and to score. By using several questions of this type, a greater amount of content can be covered than with a lesser number of essay questions. This type of question is good practice for students to learn to express themselves succinctly in writing.

Disadvantages: Some students will have difficulty expressing themselves in a limited fashion or in writing. They need practice, coaching, and time.

Guidelines for use: This type is useful for occasional reviews and quizzes and as an alternative to other types of questions. For scoring, establish a scoring rubric and follow the same guidelines as for the essay-type item.

True-False

Description: A statement is presented that students are to judge as being accurate or not.

Example 1: A suffix is any bound morpheme added to the end of a root word. T or F?

Example 2: Christopher Columbus discovered America in 1492. T or F?

Advantages: Many items can be answered in a relatively short time, making broad content coverage possible. Scoring is quick and simple. True-false items are good as discussion starters, for review, and for diagnostic evaluation (preassessment) of what students already know or think they know.

Disadvantages: It is sometimes difficult to write true-false items that are purely true or false or without qualifying them in such a way that clues the answer. In the second sample question, for example, the student may question whether Columbus really did discover America or misunderstand the meaning of "discovering America." Weren't there people already there when he landed? Where, in fact, did he land? What is meant by "America?" Example 2 is poor also because it tests for more than one idea—Columbus, America, and 1492.

Much of the content that most easily lends itself to the true-false type of test item is trivial. Students have a 50-percent chance of guessing the correct answer, thus giving this item type both poor validity and poor reliability. Scoring and grading give no clue about why the student missed an item. Consequently, the disadvantages of true-false items far outweigh the advantages; pure true-false items should not be used for arriving at grades. For grading purposes, you may use modified true-false items (see guideline 11 below), where space is provided between items for students to write in their explanations, thus making the item a combined true-false, short-explanation type.

GUIDELINE FOR PREPARING TRUE-FALSE ITEMS

1. For preparing a false statement, first write the statement as a true statement, then make it false by changing a word or phrase.

2. Try to avoid using negative statements since they tend to confuse students.

3. A true-false statement should include only one idea.

4. Use close to an equal number of true and false answers.

5. Try to avoid using specific determiners (e.g., "always," "all," or "none"), because they usually clue that the statement is false. Avoid also words that may clue that the statement is true (e.g., "often," "probably," and "sometimes").

6. Avoid words that may have different meanings for different students.

Figure 11.11 Sample scoring rubric for student research project paper. Possible score = 100. Scorer marks a relevant square in each of the six categories (the horizontal rows), and the student's score for that category is the number within that square.

	14–15	12–13	11	1–10
Parenthetical References	All documented correctly. Paper's references document a wide variety of sources cited—at least five from bibliography.	Most documented correctly. Few minor errors. At least three sources from bibliography are cited.	Some documented correctly. Some show no documentation at all. May not correlate to the bibliography.	Few to none are documented. Does not correlate to the bibliography. May be totally absent.
Bibliography and Sources	Strong use of library research. Exceeds minimum of five sources. Bibliography is correctly formatted.	Good use of library research. Exceeds minimum of five sources. Bibliography has few or no errors in format.	Some use of library research. Meets minimum of five sources. Bibliography is present but may be problematic.	Fails to meet minimum standards for library research. Bibliography has major flaws or may be missing.
Mechanics/Format	Correct format and pagination. Neat title page, near-perfect spelling, punctuation, and grammar.	Mostly correct format and pagination. Neat. Few errors in title page, spellings, punctuation, and grammar.	Errors in format and pagination. Flawed title page. Distracting errors in spelling, punctuation, and grammar.	Incorrect format. Title page is flawed or missing. Many errors in spelling, punctuation, and grammar. Lack of planning is obvious. Paper is difficult to read.
	9–10	8	7	1–6
Thesis	An original and comprehensive thesis that is clear and well thought out. All sections work to support it.	Comprehensive and well-focused thesis, which is clearly stated. All sections work to support it.	Adequate thesis that is understandable but may be neither clear nor focused. It covers the majority of the issues found in the sections.	Inadequate thesis that is disconnected from the research or may be too broad to support. May be convoluted, confusing, or absent.
	18–20	16–17	14–15	1–13
Completeness/ Coherence	Paper reads as a unified whole. There is no repetition of information. All sections are in place, and transitions between them are clearly developed.	Paper reads as a unified whole with no repetition. All sections are in place, but transitions between them are not as smooth.	Paper has required sections. Repetitions may be evident. The paper does not present a unified whole. Transitions are missing or inadequate.	Paper lacks one or more sections and makes no attempt to connect sections as a whole unit. Sections may be grossly repetitive or contradictory.
	23–25	20–22	18–19	1–16
Thinking/Analyzing	Strong understanding of the topic. Knowledge is factually relevant, accurate, and consistent. Solutions show analysis of research discussed in paper.	Good understanding of the topic. Uses main points of information researched. Solutions build on examination of research discussed in paper.	General understanding of topic. Uses research and attempts to add to it; solutions refer to some of the research discussed.	Little understanding of topic. Uses little basic information researched. Minimal examination of the topic. Solutions may be based solely on own opinions, without support.

Source: Elk Grove School District, Elk Grove, California.

Figure 11.12 Sample scoring rubric for student project presentation. Possible score = 100. Scorer marks a relevant square in each of the six categories (the horizontal rows), and the student's score for that category is the number within that square.

Professional Presentation	**14–15** Well organized; smooth transitions between sections; all enthusiastically participate and share responsibility.	**12–13** Well organized with transitions, students confer/present ideas; group shows ability to interact; attentive discussion of research.	**11** Shows basic organization; lacks transitions; some interaction; discussion focuses mostly on research.	**1–10** Unorganized, lacks planning; no transitions; reliance on spokesperson; little interaction; disinterest; too brief.
Engagement of Audience	**14–15** Successfully and actively engages audience in more than one pertinent activity; maintains interest throughout.	**12–13** Engages audience in at least one related activity; maintains attention through most of presentation.	**11** Attempts to engage audience in at least one activity; no attempt to involve entire audience. May not relate in significant way.	**1–10** Fails to involve audience; does not maintain audience's attention; no connection with audience. No relationship between activity and topic.
Use of Literature	**18–20** Strong connection between literature and topic; significant, perceptive explanation of literature; pertinent to topic. At least two pieces used.	**16–17** Clear connection between literature and topic; clear explanation; appropriate to topic. Two pieces used.	**14–15** Weak connection to topic; unclear explanation; one genre; one piece used.	**1–13** No connection to topic; no explanation; inappropriate literature; no literature.
Knowledge of Subject	**18–20** Strong understanding of topic; knowledge factually relevant, accurate, and consistent; solution shows analysis of evidence.	**16–17** Good understanding of topic; uses main points of information researched; builds solution or examination of major evidence.	**14–15** Shows general understanding; focuses on one aspect, discusses at least one other idea; uses research, attempts to add to it; solution refers to evidence.	**1–13** Little understanding or comprehension of topic; uses little basic information researched; forms minimal solution; relies on solely own opinions without support.
Use of Media	**18–20** Effectively combines and integrates three distinct forms with one original piece; enhances understanding; offers insight into topic.	**16–17** Combines two forms with one original piece; relates to topic; connection between media and topic is explained.	**14–15** Includes two or three forms but no original piece; media relates to topic. Explanation may be vague or missing.	**1–13** On form; no original piece; connection between media and topic is unclear.
Speaking Skills	**9–10** Clear enunciation; strong projection; vocal variety; eye contact with entire audience; presentation posture; solid focus with no interruptions.	**8** Good enunciation; adequate projection; partial audience eye contact; appropriate posture.	**7** Inconsistent enunciation; low projection with little vocal variety; inconsistent posture.	**1–6** Difficult to understand; inaudible; monotonous; no eye contact; inappropriate posture; interruptions and distractions.

Source: Elk Grove School District, Elk Grove, California.

7. Avoid using verbatim language from the student textbook.

8. Avoid trick items, such as a slight reversal of numbers in a date.

9. Rather than using symbols for the words *true* and *false* (sometimes teachers use symbols such as + and -) that might be confusing, or having students write the letters *T* and *F* (sometimes a student does not write the letters clearly enough for the teacher to be able to distinguish which it is), have students either write out the words *true* and *false* or, better yet, have students simply circle *T* or *F* in the left margin of each item as indicated by the sample in guideline number eleven.

10. Proofread your items (or have a friend do it) to be sure that the sentences are well constructed and are free from typographical errors.

11. To avoid "wrong" answers, caused by variations in thinking, and to make the item more valid and reliable, students should be encouraged to write in their rationale for selecting true or false, making the item a modified true-false item. For example,

T or F? When a farmer saw 8 crows sitting on the fence surrounding his corn field, he shot 3 of them. Five were left on the fence.

Explanation: _____

For grading purposes, you may use modified true-false items, thus making the item a combined true-false, short-explanation type, and allowing for divergent and critical thinking. Another form of modified true-false item is the "sometimes-always-never" item, where a third alternative, "sometimes," is introduced to reduce the chance for guessing.

Now do Exercise 11.2 to start the development of your skill in writing assessment items. As you work on Exercise 11.2 you may want to correlate it with your previous work on Exercises 5.5 and 6.7, 6.11.

EXERCISE 11.2 PREPARING ASSESSMENT ITEMS

INSTRUCTIONS: The purpose of this exercise is to practice your skill in preparing the different types of assessment items discussed above. For use in your own teaching, select one specific instructional objective and write assessment items for it. When completed, share this exercise with your colleagues for their feedback.

Objective _____

Grade and subject _____

  1. Arrangement item _____

  _____

  _____

  _____

  _____

  2. Completion drawing item _____

  _____

  _____

  _____

  _____

  3. Completion statement item _____

  _____

  _____

  _____

  _____

  _____

  4. Correction item _____

  _____

  _____

  _____

  _____

  5. Essay item _____

  _____

  _____

  _____

  _____

☞

EXERCISE 11.2 (*continued*)

6. Grouping item _____

_____

_____

_____

_____

7. Identification item _____

_____

_____

_____

_____

8. Matching item _____

_____

_____

_____

_____

9. Multiple-choice item _____

_____

_____

_____

_____

10. Performance item _____

_____

_____

_____

_____

11. Short-explanation item _____

_____

_____

_____

12. Modified true-false item _____

_____

_____

_____

REPORTING STUDENT ACHIEVEMENT

One of your responsibilities as a classroom teacher is to report student progress in achievement to parents or guardians and to the school administration for record keeping. In some schools the reporting is of student progress and effort as well as of achievement. As described in the discussions that follow, reporting is done in two, and sometimes more, ways. However, for secondary schools, letter grades on report cards are still the most widely used method for reporting student learning.[14]

The Grade Report

Periodically a grade report (report card) is issued (generally from four to six times a year, depending upon the school, its purpose, and its type of scheduling). Grade reports may be distributed during an advisory period or they may be mailed to the student's home. This grade report represents an achievement grade (formative evaluation). The final report of the semester is also the semester grade, and for courses that are only one semester long, it also is the final grade (summative evaluation). In essence, the first and sometimes second reports are progress notices, with the semester grade being the one that is transferred to the student's transcript of records.

In addition to the student's academic achievement, you must report the student's social behaviors (classroom conduct) while in your classroom. Whichever reporting form is used, you must separate your assessments of a student's social behaviors from his or her academic achievement. Academic achievement (or accomplishment) is represented by a letter (sometimes a number) grade (A through E or F, or E, S, and U, or 1 to 5, and sometimes with minuses and pluses), and the social behavior by a "satisfactory" or an "unsatisfactory," by more specific items, or supplemented by teacher-written or computer-generated comments. In some instances, there may be a location on the reporting form for teachers to check whether basic grade-level standards have been met in the core subjects.

MORE ABOUT PARENTAL INVOLVEMENT AND HOME-SCHOOL CONNECTIONS

Study after study shows that when parents get involved in their child's school and school work, students learn better and earn better grades, and teachers experience more positive feelings about teaching. As a result, many schools increasingly are searching for new and better ways to involve parents. What follows are additional suggestions and resources.

Contacting Parents

Although it is not always obligatory, some teachers make a point to contact parents or guardians by telephone or by e-mail, especially when a student has shown a sudden turn for either the worse or the better in academic achievement or in classroom behavior. That initiative and contact by the teacher are usually welcomed by parents and can lead to productive conferences with the teacher. A telephone conference can save valuable time for both the teacher and the parent.

Another way of contacting parents is by letter. Contacting a parent by letter gives you time to think and to make clear your thoughts and concerns to that parent and to invite the parent to respond at her or his convenience by letter, by phone, or by arranging to have a conference with you.

Progress Reporting to Parents

In the absence of a computer-link assignment/progress report hotline, most schools have a progress report form that, upon request by a parent, can be sent home with the student as often as weekly. It may be similar to the one shown in Figure 11.13 to show the student's progress in each of the core subjects or perhaps like the one in Figure 11.14 that requires student self-evaluation, teacher assessment, office signature, and parental response and signature.

Meeting Parents

You will meet some of the parents or guardians early in the school year during "Back To School" or "Meet the Teacher" or "Curriculum" night, throughout the year in individual parent conferences, and later in the year during spring open house. For the beginning teacher, these meetings with parents can be anxious times. It is also a time to celebrate your work and to solicit help from parents. The following paragraphs provide guidelines to help you with those experiences.[15]

Back to School or Meet the Teacher night is the evening early in the school year when parents and guardians come to the school and meet their children's teachers. The parents arrive at the student's homeroom and then proceed through a simulation of their sons' or daughters' school day; as a group, they meet each class and each teacher for a few minutes.

---

[14]T. R. Guskey, *Communicating Student Learning*, p. 121.

[15]For suggestions from a school administrator for delivering powerful presentations to parents at Back to School Night, see W. B. Ribas, "Tips for Reaching Parents," *Educational Leadership* 56(1):83–85 (September 1998).

Figure 11.13 Weekly assessment checklist: sample with teacher input only.

WEEKLY ASSESSMENT CHECKLIST For _____

	Math	Social Studies	Science	Language Arts
Number of tardies				
Number of absences				
Academic grade				
Citizenship grade				

	Usually	Sometimes	Rarely	Never
Homework turned in on time				
Class work satisfactorily completed				
Exhibits acceptable classroom behavior				
Exhibits acceptable use of time in class				
Skill level is adequate to do work				
Participates orally in class discussions				
Participates in classroom learning activities				
Assumes responsibilities for own actions				
Avoids talking excessively or out of turn				
Comes to class prepared with supplies				
Is ready to start working when class begins				
Performs well on quizzes and tests				
Is attentive and focused during class				
Shows good listening skills				
Shows good organizational skills				
Shows for assigned detentions				
Respects the property of others and of the school				
Respects the rights of others				

Other comments or concerns

Figure 11.14 Progress report: subject-specific with student and parent input.

PROGRESS REPORT: MARINA DEL REY SCHOOL

Student: <u>Anthony von Hauser</u>   Course: <u>Algebra I</u>   Date: <u>September 14, 2000</u>

This progress report form incorporates evaluation by student, teacher, and parent. The form will be completed by the student on Wednesday and by the teacher on Thursday and reviewed by the office and returned to the student on Friday. The student will take the form home for parental review, comments, and signature.

Section I: Self-Assessment: The student is asked to evaluate progress in the course in terms of goals and how closely these goals are being achieved. Do you feel you have made progress since the last progress report?
     <u>By taking this algebra class I achieved a greater understanding of it. I feel I have made a lot of progress since I took the class in 8th grade. It is also taught much better which makes it easier.</u>

Section II: Teacher Assessment: The teacher is asked to assess the student's entry, competency, and achievement to date and make recommendations.
     <u>Anthony is doing quite well. He has had to make some adjustments from previous work habits (i.e., showing work), but he has made an excellent transition. Anthony has great skills and strong understanding of concepts.</u>

PRESENT STATUS (Rated A–F)		*WHAT IS NEEDED*
<u>B+</u> Class work/participation	A = Excellent	_<u>✓</u>_ Emphasis on homework
<u>C+</u> Homework	B = Above Average	_____ Improve class participation
<u>A</u> Portfolio	C = Average	_____ More careful preparation for tests
<u>A</u> Quizzes	D = Below Average	_<u>✓</u>_ Keep up the good work
<u>A-</u> Tests	F = Failing	_____ Contact teacher
<u>A-</u> Overall		_____ Improve portfolio
		_____ Other _____
		Office Initial <u>CM</u>

Section III: Parent Evaluation and Comments: Parents are asked to respond and sign this progress report.
     <u>I thank you for this timely report. I am delighted that Anthony has started off well and is liking the class. He talks at home a lot about the class and the interesting activities; a tribute to good teaching. I can tell from our conversations at home that he is feeling much better about his math capability. I thank you.</u>
                                                                                        Eric von Hauser

---

Later, in the spring, many schools host an open house where parents may have more time to talk individually with teachers, although the major purpose of the open house is for the school and teachers to celebrate and display the work and progress of the students for that year. Throughout the school year, there will be opportunities for you and parents to meet and to talk about their child.

At Back To School Night, parents are anxious to learn as much as they can about their children's teachers. You will meet each group of parents for a brief time, perhaps about ten minutes. During that meeting you should provide them with a copy of the course syllabus, make some straightforward remarks about yourself, and talk about the course, its requirements, your expectations of the students, and how parents might help.

Although there will be precious little time for questions from the parents, during your introduction the parents will be delighted to learn that you have your program well planned, are a "task master," appreciate their interest, and welcome their participation. They will be happy to hear your willingness to communicate with them. Parents and guardians will be pleased to know that you are "from the school of the three Fs"—that is, that you are firm, friendly, and fair.

Specifically, depending upon the grade level, parents will expect to learn about your curriculum—goals and objectives, any long-term projects, class size, schedules for tests, and grading procedures. They will want to know what you expect of them: Will there be homework, and if so, should they help their children with it? How can they contact you? Try to anticipate other questions. Your principal, department chair, or colleagues can be of aid in helping you anticipate and prepare for these questions. Of course, you can never prepare for the question that comes from left field. Just remain calm and avoid being flustered (or at least appear so). Ten minutes will fly by quickly, and parents will be reassured to know you are an in-control person.

Parent Conferences

When meeting parents for conferences, you should be as specific as possible when explaining student progress in your class. Again, express your appreciation for parents' interest. Be helpful to their understanding, and don't saturate parents with more information than they need. Resist any tendency to talk too much. Allow time for parents to ask questions. Keep your answers succinct. Never compare one student with another or with the rest of the class. If parents ask a question for which you do not have an answer, tell them you will try to find an answer and will phone them as quickly as you can. Then do it. Have students' portfolios and other work with you during the parent conference so you can show examples of what is being discussed. Also, have your grade book on hand, or a computer printout of it, but be prepared to protect from parents the names and records of other students.

Sometimes it is helpful to have a three-way conference, a conference with the parent, the student, and you, or a conference with the parent, the principal or counselor, and several or all of the student's teachers. If, especially as a beginning teacher, you would like the presence of an administrator at a parent-teacher conference as backup, don't be hesitant to arrange that.

Some educators prefer a student-led conference, arguing that "placing students in charge of the conference makes them individually accountable, encourages them to take pride in their work, and encourages student-parent communication about school performance."[16] But, like most innovations in education, the concept of student-led conferences has its limitations—the most important of which perhaps is the matter of time.[17]

When a parent asks how she or he may help in the child's learning, the paragraphs that follow offer sug-

gestions for your consideration. Many schools have made special and successful efforts to link home and school. At some schools, through homework hotlines, parents have phone access to their children's assignment specifications and to their progress in their schoolwork, and parents with a personal computer and a modem have access to tutorial services to assist students with assignments.

Helping students become critical thinkers is one of the aims of education and one that parents can help with by reinforcing the strategies being used in the classroom. Ways to do this are to ask "what if" questions; think aloud as a model for the child's thinking development; encourage the child's own metacognition by asking questions such as, "How did you arrive at that conclusion?" or "How do you feel about your conclusion now?" Parents should ask these questions about the child's everyday social interactions and topics that are important to the child. They can ask their child to elaborate on his or her ideas, accepting the fact that the child may make mistakes but encouraging the child to learn from them.

Many resources are available for parents to use at home. The United States government, for example, has a variety of free or low-cost booklets available. For information, contact the Consumer Information Center, Department BEST, Pueblo, CO 81009, or the web site <http://www.pueblo.gsa.gov>. Figure 11.15 presents addresses for additional ideas and resources for home-school partnerships.

Figure 11.15 Resources for developing home-school partnerships.

- Alliance for Parental Involvement in Education, P.O. Box 59, East Chatham, NY 12060-0059, 518-392-6900.
- Center on Families, Communities, Schools & Children's Learning, 3505 N. Charles St., Baltimore, MD 21218, 410-516-8800.
- *How to Help Your Child with Homework: Every Caring Parents' Guide to Encouraging Good Study Habits and Ending the Homework Wars (For Parents of Children Ages 6-13)*, by M. C. Radencich and J. S. Schumm. 1997 edition. Free Spirit Publishing, 400 First Avenue North, Suite 616, Minneapolis, MN.
- National Coalition for Parent Involvement in Education, Box 39, 1201 16th St., NW, Washington, DC 20036.
- National Community Education Association, 3929 Old Lee Highway, Suite 91A, Fairfax, VA 22030-2401, 703-359-8973.
- National PTA, 330 North Wabash Ave., Ste 2100, Chicago, IL 60611-3690, 312-670-6782.
- Parents for Public Schools, PO Box 12807, Jackson, MS 39236-2807, 800-880-1222.

---

[16]D. W. Johnson and R. T. Johnson, "The Role of Cooperative Learning in Assessing and Communicating Student Learning," p. 43 in T. R. Guskey, *Communicating Student Learning.*

[17]For a discussion of the pros and cons of using the student-led conference and for a conference organizer tool, see J. Bailey and J. McTighe, "Reporting Achievement at the Secondary Level: What and How," pp. 137–139 of T. R. Guskey, *Communicating Student Learning.* See also L. Countryman and M. Schroeder, "When Students Lead Parent-Teacher Conferences," *Educational Leadership* 53(7):64–68 (April 1996), and D. G. Hackmann, *Student-Led Conferences at the Middle Level* (Champaign, IL: ED407171, ERIC Clearinghouse on Elementary and Early Childhood Education, 1997).

Dealing with an Angry Parent or Guardian

If a parent or guardian is angry or hostile toward you and the school, the paragraphs that follow offer guidelines for dealing with that hostility.

Remain calm in your discussion with the parent, allowing the parent to talk out his or her hostility while you say very little; usually, the less you say the better off you will be. What you do say must be objective and to the point of the child's work in your classroom. The parent may just need to vent frustrations that might have very little to do with you, the school, or even the child.

Do not allow yourself to be intimidated, put on the defensive, or backed into a verbal corner. If the parent tries to do so by attacking you personally, do not press your defense at this point. Perhaps the parent has made a point that you should take time to consider, and now is a good time to arrange for another conference with the parent for about a week later. In a follow-up conference, if the parent agrees, you may want to consider bringing in a mediator, such as another member of your teaching team, an administrator, or a school counselor.

You must *not* talk about other students; keep the conversation focused on the progress of this parent's child. The parent is *not* your rival or should not be. You both share a concern for the academic and emotional well-being of the child. Use your best skills in critical thinking and problem solving, trying to focus the discussion by identifying the problem, defining it, and then arriving at some decision about how mutually to go about solving it. To this end you may need to ask for help from a third party, such as the child's school counselor. If agreed to by the parent, please take that step.

Parents do *not* need to hear about how busy you are, about your personal problems, or about how many other students you are dealing with on a daily basis, unless, of course, a parent asks. Parents expect you to be a capable professional who knows what to do and is doing it.

SUMMARY

Whereas preceding parts of this resource guide addressed the *why, what,* and *how* components of teaching, this chapter has focused your attention on the fourth and final component—*how well*—and on the first of two aspects of that component. Assessment is an integral, ongoing factor in the teaching-learning process; consequently, this chapter has emphasized the importance of your including the following in your teaching performance:

- Use a variety of instruments to collect a body of evidence to most reliably assess the learning of students that focus on their individual development.

- Involve students in the assessment process; keep students informed of their progress. Return tests promptly, review answers to all questions, and respond to inquiries about marks given.
- Consider your assessment and grading procedures carefully, plan them, and explain your policies to the students.
- Make sure to explain any ambiguities that result from the terminology used, and base your assessments on the material that has been taught.
- Strive for objective and impartial assessment as you put your assessment plan into operation.
- Try to minimize arguments about grades, cheating, and teacher subjectivity by involving students in the planning, reinforcing individual student development, and providing an accepting, stimulating learning environment.
- Maintain accurate and clear records of assessment results so that you will have an adequate supply of data on which to base your judgmental decisions about achievement.

Because teaching and learning work hand in hand and because they are reciprocal processes in that one depends on and affects the other, the *how well* component deals with the assessment of both how well the students are learning and how well the teacher is teaching. This chapter has dealt with the first. In the next and final chapter of this resource guide, your attention is directed to techniques designed to help you develop your teaching skills and assess that development, a process that will continue throughout your teaching career.

QUESTIONS FOR CLASS DISCUSSION

1. Identify a problem in grading that you personally experienced as a student in school. What was your perceived cause of the problem? How might it have been avoided? What was the resolution and how was that resolution arrived at? Was the resolution satisfactory to all concerned? Why or why not?
2. Other than a paper-and-pencil test, identify three alternative techniques for assessing student learning during or at completion of an instructional unit.
3. Investigate various ways that schools are experimenting today with assessing and reporting student achievement. Share what you find with your classmates. Analyze the pros and cons of various systems of assessing and reporting.
4. When using a point system for determining student grades, is it educationally defensible to give a student a higher grade than that student's points call for? a lower grade? Give your rationale for your answers.
5. Describe any student learning activities or situations that you believe should *not* be graded but should or could be used for assessment of student learning.
6. Research the practice of student-led parent-teacher-student conferences, and report to your class what you find out about the practice.

7. Describe the roles and limitations of objectivity and subjectivity in the assessment of student learning.
8. Describe any prior concepts you held that changed as a result of your experiences with this chapter. Describe the changes.
9. From your current observations and field work as related to this teacher preparation program, clearly identify one specific example of educational practice that seems contradictory to exemplary practice or theory as presented in this chapter. Present your explanation for the discrepancy.
10. Do you have questions generated by the content of this chapter? If you do, list them along with ways answers might be found.

FOR FURTHER READING

Allen, D. (Ed.) *Assessing Student Learning: From Grading to Understanding.* New York: Teachers College Press, 1998.

Bingen, M. "Exhibitions of Mastery: The Tail That Wags the Dog." *English Journal* 86(1):32–36 (January 1997).

Bishop, J. E., and Fransen, S. "Building Community: An Alternative Assessment." *Phi Delta Kappan* 80(1):39–40, 57–58 (September 1998).

Black, P., and Dylan, W. "Inside the Black Box: Raising Standards Through Classroom Assessment." *Phi Delta Kappan* 80(2):139–144, 146–148 (October 1998).

Colby, S. A. "Grading in a Standards-Based System." *Educational Leadership* 56(6):17–21 (March 1999).

Crockett, T. *The Portfolio Journey: A Creative Guide to Keeping Student-Managed Portfolios in the Classroom.* Englewood, CO: Teachers Ideas Press/Libraries Unlimited, 1998.

Doran, R., Chan, F., and Tamir, P. *Science Educator's Guide to Assessment.* Arlington, VA: National Science Teachers Association, 1998.

Ensign, J. "Parents, Portfolios, and Personal Mathematics." *Teaching Children Mathematics* 4(6): 346–351 (February 1998).

Gustafson, C. "Phone Home." *Educational Leadership* 56(2):31–32 (October 1998).

Haladyna, T. M. *Writing Test Items to Evaluate Higher Order Thinking.* Needham Heights, MA: Allyn & Bacon, 1997.

Kelly, K. "Retention vs. Social Promotion: Schools Search for Alternatives." *The Harvard Education Letter* 15(1):1–3 (January/February 1999).

Leuder, D. C. *Creating Partnerships with Parents: An Educator's Guide.* Lancaster, PA: Technomic Publishing Company, 1998.

Mehrens, W. A., et al. "How To Prepare Students for Performance Assessments." *Educational Measurement: Issues and Practice* 17(1):18–22 (Spring 1998).

Mitchell, J. P., et al. "Making Sense of Literacy Portfolios: A Four-Step Plan." *Journal of Adolescent & Adult Literacy* 41(5):384–386 (February 1998).

National PTA. *National Standards for Parent/Family Involvement Programs.* Chicago: Author, 1997.

Roe, M. F., and Vukelich, C. "Literacy Portfolios: Challenges that Affect Change." *Childhood Education* 74(3):148–153 (Spring 1998).

Schurr, S. L. "Teaching, Enlightening: A Guide to Student Assessment." *Schools in the Middle* 7(3):22–27, 30–31 (January/February 1998).

Shafer, S. *Writing Effective Report Card Comments.* Jefferson City, MO: Scholastic, 1997.

Shaklee, B D., et al. *Designing and Using Portfolios.* Needham Heights, MA: Allyn & Bacon, 1997.

Steinberg, A. "The Human Cost of Over-Reliance on Tests." *Harvard Education Letter* 15(2):8 (March/April 1999).

Stiggins, R. J. *Student-Centered Classroom Assessment.* 2d ed. Upper Saddle River, NJ: Prentice Hall, 1997.

Taggart, G. L. et al. *Rubrics: A Handbook for Construction and Use.* Lancaster, PA: Technomic, 1998.

Upham, D. A., et al. "What Do Teachers and Parents Want in Their Communication Patterns?" *Middle School Journal* 29(5):48–55 (May 1998).

Walker, M. "Authentic Assessment in the Literature Classroom." *English Journal* 86(1):69–73 (January 1997).

Wiggins, G., and McTighe, J. *Understanding by Design.* Alexandria, VA: Association for Supervision and Curriculum Development, 1998.

Zmuda, A., and Tomaino, M. "A Contract for the High School Classroom." *Educational Leadership* 56(6):59–61 (March 1999).

Chapter 12

Assessing Teaching Effectiveness and Continued Professional Development

Although most of us are not born with innate teaching skills, the good news is that teaching skills can be learned and steadily improved. Teachers who wish to improve their teaching can do so with help from many resources (in addition to this resource guide).

This chapter addresses the assessment and development of your effectiveness as a classroom teacher, a process that continues throughout your professional career. Teaching is such an electrifying profession that it is not easy to remain energetic and to stay abreast of changes and trends that result from research and practice. You will need to make a continuous and determined effort to remain an alert and effective teacher.

Whether you are a beginning or experienced teacher, one way to collect data and improve your effectiveness is through periodic assessment of your teaching performance, either by an evaluation of your teaching in the real classroom or, if you are in a program of teacher preparation, by a technique called *micro peer teaching*. The latter is the focus of the final section of this chapter and is an example of a final performance (authentic) assessment for this resource guide.

Specifically, upon completion of this chapter you should be able to

1. Demonstrate knowledge about the field components of teacher preparation.
2. Demonstrate knowledge of how to find a teaching job.
3. Demonstrate knowledge of how to remain an alert and effective classroom teacher throughout your teaching career.

PROFESSIONAL DEVELOPMENT THROUGH STUDENT TEACHING

You are excited about the prospect of being assigned as a student teacher to your first classroom, but you are also concerned. Questions linger in your mind. Will your host (cooperating) teacher(s) like you? Will you get along? Will the students accept you? Will you be assigned to the school, grade level, and subjects you want? What will the students be like? Will there be many classroom management problems? What about mainstreamed students and students with only limited proficiency in English? Your questions will be unending.

Indeed, you *should* be excited and concerned, for this experience of student teaching is one of the most significant and important facets of your program of teacher preparation. In some programs, this practical field experience is planned as a coexperience with the college or university theory classes. In other programs, student teaching is the culminating experience. Different sequences are represented in different programs. For example, at some colleges, field teaching extends over two or three semesters. In other programs, teacher candidates first take a theory followed by a full second semester of student teaching. Regardless of when and how your student teaching occurs, the experience is a bright and shining opportunity to hone your teaching skills in a real classroom. During this time, you will be supported by an experienced college or university supervisor and by carefully selected cooperating teachers who will share their expertise.

Everyone concerned in the teacher preparation program—your cooperating teacher, university instructors, school administrators, and university supervisor—

Student teaching is perhaps the most significant and important facet of your training.

realize this is your practicum in learning how to teach. During your student teaching, you will no doubt make errors, and with the understanding and guidance of those supervising your work, you will benefit and learn from those errors. Sometimes your fresh approach to motivation, your creative ideas for learning activities, and your energy and enthusiasm make it possible for the cooperating teacher to learn from you. After all, teaching and learning are always reciprocal processes. What is most important is that the students who are involved with you in the process of learning to teach will benefit from your role as the teacher candidate in the classroom. The following guidelines are offered to help make this practical experience beneficial to everyone involved.

Student Teaching Is the Real Thing

Because you have a classroom setting for practicing and honing your teaching skills with active, responsive, young people, student teaching *is* the real thing. On the other hand, student teaching is *not* real in the sense that your cooperating teacher, not you, has the ultimate responsibility and authority for the classroom.

Getting Ready for Student Teaching

To prepare yourself for student teaching, you must study, plan, practice, and reflect. You should become knowledgeable about your students and their develop-

mental backgrounds. In your theory classes, you learned a great deal about students. Review your class notes and textbooks from those courses, or select some readings suggested in Part I. Perhaps some of the topics will have more meaning for you now.

First Impressions

First impressions are often lasting impressions. You have heard that statement before, and now, as you get ready for this important phase of your professional preparation, you hear it again because it is crucial to your success. Remember it as you prepare to meet your school principal and cooperating teacher for the first time, remember it again as you prepare to meet your students for the first time, and remember it again as you prepare for your university supervisor's first observation of your teaching. In each case, you have only one opportunity to make a first impression.

Continuing to Get Ready for Student Teaching

In addition to the aforementioned preparations, you will need to be knowledgeable about your assigned school and the community that surrounds it. Review the subject areas you will be teaching and the curriculum content and standards in those areas. Carefully discuss with your cooperating teacher (or teachers, as you may have more than one) and your university supervisor all responsibilities that you will be expected to assume.

As a student teacher you may want to run through each lesson verbally, perhaps in front of a mirror, the night before teaching your lesson. Some student teachers read through each lesson, audiorecording the lesson, playing it back, and evaluating whether the directions are clear, the instruction is mind-grabbing (or at least interesting), the sequence is logical, and the lesson closure is concise. Still another student teacher always has a "Plan B" in mind in case "Plan A" turns out to be inappropriate.

Student Teaching from the Cooperating Teacher's Point of View

For your consideration, information about student teaching from the viewpoint of a cooperating teacher is presented here in a question-and-answer format. You may wish to share this section with your cooperating teacher.

What is my role? As the cooperating teacher, your role is to assist when necessary: to provide guidance, to review lesson plans before they are taught, to facilitate the learning and skill development of your student teacher, and to help your student teacher become and feel like a member of the school faculty and of the profession.

How can I prepare for the experience? Get to know your student teacher before he or she begins teaching. Develop a collegial rapport with the student teacher.

Who is my student teacher? Your student teacher is a person who is making the transition from another career or from the life of a college student to the profession of teaching. Your student teacher may be your age, or older, or younger. In any case, your student teacher may be scared to death, anxious, knowledgeable, and, when it comes to teaching philosophy, somewhere between being a romantic idealist and a pragmatic realist. Do not destroy the idealism—help the student teacher to understand and deal with the realism of everyday teaching.

It is important that you learn about the kinds of teaching experiences that your student teacher has had prior to this assignment so the student teacher and you may build from those experiences. For example, this may be your student teacher's very first teaching experience, or he or she may have substitute teaching experience, experience teaching in another country, or student teaching at another school prior to this term.

What kind of support, criticism, and supervision should I give? Much of this you will have to decide for yourself. On the other hand, some teacher preparation programs include seminars that train cooperating teachers in techniques for supervising student teachers. Cooperating teachers are often selected not only because of their effectiveness in teaching but also because of their skill in working with other adults. You will likely be working as a member of a team that includes you, the student teacher, and the university supervisor. Your student teacher may have more than one cooperating teacher, who should then also be included as a member of this professional team. Whatever the situation, your student teacher needs support, helpful suggestions, and productive monitoring. It is unprofessional to place a student teacher into a sink-or-swim situation.

What danger signs should I be alert for? Your student teacher may be quite different from you in both appearance and style of teaching but may be potentially just as effective a teacher. Be slow and cautious in judging your student teacher's effectiveness. Offer suggestions but do not make demands.

A student teacher who is not preparing well is likely to be heading for trouble. The saying stands: Failing to prepare is preparing to fail. Be certain to ask for and to receive lesson plans before they are taught, especially in the beginning and whenever you feel the student teacher is not preparing well.

Another danger signal is when the student teacher seems to show no real interest in the school and the students beyond the classroom. The student teacher should be prompt, eager to spend extra time with you and attend faculty meetings, and aware of the necessity of performing school clerical tasks. If you suspect a lurking problem, then let the student teacher or the university supervisor know immediately. Trust your intuition. Poor communication between members of the teaching team is another danger signal.

What else should I know? Your student teacher may be employed elsewhere and have other demands on his or her time. Become aware of these other demands, but keep the educational welfare of your students paramount in your mind.

See that your student teacher is treated as a member of the faculty and invited to faculty functions. Your student teacher should have a personal mailbox (or share yours, with his or her name on it as well) and should understand school policies, procedures, and curriculum documents.

Once your student teacher is well grounded, he or she should be ready to be gradually alone with the students for increasingly longer periods of time. For a specified time, a student teacher's goal is to work toward a competency level that enables him or her to assume increasing responsibility for everything. This means you are nearby and on call in case of an emergency, but out of sight of the students.

Comments from the University Supervisor

When is the supervisor coming? Is the supervisor going to be here today? Do you see a university or a college supervisor's observation of your student teaching as a pleasant experience or a painful one? Do you realize that classroom observations of your teaching continue during your beginning years of teaching? Being observed and evaluated does not have to be a painful, nerve-racking experience for you. You don't have to become a bundle of raw nerve endings when you realize the supervisor is coming to see you. Whether you are a student teacher being observed by your university supervisor, or a probationary teacher being evaluated by your principal, some professional suggestions may help you turn an evaluating observation into a useful, professionally satisfying experience.

What to Do before an Observation

Successful teachers seem to be able to ameliorate tension and get through an evaluation with skill and tact. Prepare for your evaluative visit by deciding what you do well and plan to demonstrate your best skills. Decorate your room and bulletin boards, especially by displaying student work, make sure your work area is orderly (this shows good organization), and select an academic aspect of the teaching day that demonstrates some of your best teaching skills. If your university supervisor has previously targeted some of your weak areas, plan to demonstrate growth in those teaching abilities.

What to Do during an Observation

Some supervisors and administrators choose to preannounce their visits. This is certainly true for *clinical supervision* practices. Clinical supervision is based on shared decision making between the supervisor and teacher, and focused on improving, rather than evaluating, teaching behaviors. With the use of clinical supervision, you know when the supervisor or administrator is coming, and you will probably look forward to the visit because of the rapport that has been established between members of your triad (in student teaching situations, your triad is composed of you, your cooperating teacher, and your university or college supervisor).

Features of effective clinical supervision include a preobservation conference, observation of teaching, and a postobservation conference. In the preobservation conference, the student teacher, cooperating teacher, and supervisor meet to discuss goals, objectives, teaching strategies, and the evaluation process. During the observation of teaching, the supervisor collects data on the classroom students' performance of objectives and on the student teacher's performance of the teaching strategies. In the postobservation conference, the student teacher, cooperating teacher, and supervisor discuss the performances. They may compare what happened with what was expected, make inferences about students' achievement of objectives,

and discuss relationships between teaching performance and student achievement. The supervisor and cooperating teacher act as educational consultants and may discuss alternative strategies for teaching at this conference or at a later one.

Sometimes your supervisor or administrator may drop in unannounced. When that happens you can take a deep breath, count to ten (quietly), and then proceed with your lesson. You will undoubtedly do just fine if you have been following the guidelines set forth in this book. Additional guidelines for a classroom observation are: allow the observer to sit wherever he or she wishes; do not interrupt your lesson to introduce the observer, unless the observer requests it, but *do* prepare your students in advance by letting them know who may be visiting and why; do not put the observer on the spot by suddenly involving him or her in the lesson, but *do* try to discern in advance the level of participation desired by your observer.

If you have been assigned to a classroom for a student teaching experience, your university supervisor will meet with you and explain some of the tasks you should attend to when the supervisor visits your class. These may vary from the list presented. For instance, some supervisors prefer to walk into a classroom quietly and not interrupt the learning activities. Some prefer not to be introduced to the class or to participate in the activities. Some supervisors are already well known by the students and teaching staff from prior visits to the school. Other supervisors may give you a special form to be completed before they arrive for the visit. This form often resembles a lesson plan format and includes space for your objectives, lesson procedures, motivational strategies, related activities, and method of assessing how well the students learned from the lesson. Remember, keep the line of communication open with your supervisor so you have a clear understanding of what is expected of you when she or he visits your classroom to observe your teaching. Without missing a beat in your lesson, you may walk over and quietly hand the observer a copy of the lesson plan and the textbook (or any other materials being used), opened to the appropriate page.

In some teacher preparation programs the student teacher is expected to maintain a student teaching binder in the classroom. The binder is kept in a particular location so that the cooperating teacher may refer to it and so that the college or university supervisor can pick it up upon entering the classroom and refer to it during the observation. Organized in the binder are the current lesson plan, the current unit plan, previous lessons with reflections, tests and their results, assignments, classroom management plan, and a current seating chart with the students' names. The student teaching binder can, in fact, represent the start of your professional portfolio (discussed later in this chapter).

Soon after the observational visit, there should be a conference in which observations are discussed in a nonjudgmental atmosphere. It might be necessary for you to make sure that a conference is scheduled. The purposes of this postobservation conference are for you and the observer(s) to discuss, rather than to evaluate, your teaching, and for you to exit the conference with agreements about areas for improvement and how to accomplish those improvements.

What to Do during an Observation Conference

Some supervisors will arrange to have a conference with you to discuss the classroom observation and to begin to resolve any classroom teaching problems. As a teacher or teacher candidate, you should be quite professional during this conference. For instance, one student teacher asks for additional help by requesting resources. Another takes notes and suggests developing a cooperative plan with the supervisor to improve teaching competencies. Still another discusses visiting other classrooms to observe exemplary teachers.

During other conferences, student teachers may ask for assistance in scheduling additional meetings with the supervisor. At such meetings, the teacher (or teacher candidate) views videos of selected teaching styles or methods, listens to audiotapes, or visits an outside educational consultant or nearby resource center.

Almost all supervisors conclude their conferences by leaving something in writing with the teacher or teacher candidate. This written record usually includes a summary of teaching strengths or weaknesses, with a review of classroom management, the supervisor's recommendations, and, perhaps, steps in an overall plan for the teacher's (or student teacher's) continued professional growth and development.

What to Do after the Supervisor Leaves

In addition to observing the classes of other teachers, attending workshops and conferences, and conferring with college and university authorities, you can take other steps to implement your plan for improvement. Be sure you debug your lesson plans by walking through them in advance of implementing them in the classroom. Do what you and your supervisor have agreed on. Document your activities with a record or diary with dated entries. If you maintain a supervisor's binder, this documentation may be kept in the binder along with the supervisor's written comments. If you have a problem with classroom management or organization, review your written classroom management plan and procedures, comparing your plan with the guidelines presented in Chapter 4. Review your plan and procedures with your cooperating teacher, a trusted teaching colleague, or your university supervisor. Obtain help when you need it. Write comments to parents or guardians about students' progress, and leave space for a return message from the adult (see, for example Figure 11.11 of Chapter 11). Keep positive responses that you receive from these adults and share them with your supervisor at your next conference.

FINDING A TEACHING POSITION

As your successful student-teaching experience draws to a close, you will embark upon finding your first paid teaching job. Your goal of finding that first job should be encouraged by the fact that the projected need for new teachers for the next several years is great. The guidelines that follow are provided to help you accomplish your goal.

Guidelines for Locating a Teaching Position

To prepare for finding the position you want, you should focus on (1) letters of recommendation from your cooperating teacher(s), your college or university supervisor, and, in some instances, the school principal, (2) your professional preparation as evidenced by your letters of recommendation and other items in your professional portfolio (discussed next), and (3) your job-interviewing skills.

First, consider the recommendations about your teaching. Most colleges and universities have a career center, usually called a job (or career) placement center, where there is probably a counselor who can advise you on how to open the job placement file that will hold your professional recommendations. This enables prospective personnel directors or district personnel who are expecting to employ new teachers to review your recommendations. Sometimes there are special forms for writing these recommendations. It is your responsibility to request letters of recommendation and, when appropriate, to supply the person writing the recommendation with the blank form and an appropriately addressed stamped envelope. Sometimes the job placement files are confidential, so your recommendations will be mailed directly to the placement office. The confidentiality of recommendations may be optional, and, when possible, you may want to maintain your own copies of letters of recommendation and include them in your professional portfolio.

The letters of recommendation from educators at the school(s) where you did your student teaching should include the following information: the name of the school and district where you did your student teaching, the grade levels and subjects you taught, your proven skills in managing students of diversity in the classroom, your ability to teach the relevant subject(s), your skills in assessing student learning and in reflecting on your teaching performance and learning from that reflection, and your skills in communicating and interacting with students and adults.

Second, consider your preparation as a teacher. Teachers, as you have learned, represent a myriad of specialties. Hiring personnel will want to know how you see yourself—for example, as a primary grade teacher, a specialist in middle school core, or an elementary or high school music teacher. Perhaps your interest is in teaching children at any level of elementary school or only in chemistry at the secondary level. You may indicate a special interest or skill, such as competency in teaching English as a foreign language. Or, perhaps, although your teaching field is mathematics, you also are bilingual and have had rich and varied crosscultural experiences. Have you had a rich and varied background of experience so that you will feel comfortable when you are hired and placed in the one assignment in which you were least interested? The hiring personnel who consider your application will be interested in your sincerity and will want to see that you are academically and socially impressive.

Last, consider your in-person interview with a district official. Sometimes, you will have several interviews or you will be interviewed simultaneously with other candidates. In some districts an initial screening interview by an administrative panel from the district is followed by an interview by a department chairperson, a school principal, or a school team composed of one or more teachers and administrators from the interested school or district. In all interviews, your verbal and nonverbal behaviors will be observed as you respond to various questions, including (1) factual questions about your student teaching or about particular curriculum programs with which you would be expected to work, and (2) hypothetical questions, such as "What would you do if . . .?" Often these are questions that relate to your philosophy of education, your reasons for wanting to be a teacher, your approach to handling a particular classroom situation, and perhaps specifically your reasons for wanting to teach at this particular school and in this district. Interview guidelines follow later in this section.

The Professional Career Portfolio

A way to be proactive in your job search is to create a personal professional portfolio to be shared with persons who are considering your application for employment. That is the objective of Exercise 12.1.

The professional career portfolio is organized to provide clear evidence of your teaching skills and to make you professionally desirable to a hiring committee. A professional portfolio is not simply a collection of your accomplishments randomly tossed into a folder. It is a deliberate, current, and organized collection of your skills, attributes, experiences, and accomplishments.

Because it would be impractical to send a complete portfolio with every application you submit, it might be advisable to have a minimum portfolio (portfolio B) that could be sent with each application, in addition to a complete portfolio (portfolio A) that you could make available upon request and take with you to an interview. However it is done, the actual contents of the portfolio will vary depending on the specific job being sought; you will continually add to and delete materials from your portfolio. Exercise 12.1 suggests categories and subcategories, listed in the order that they may be best presented in portfolios A and B.[1]

---

[1]For further information, see K. Wolf, "Developing an Effective Teaching Portfolio," *Educational Leadership* 53(6):34–37 (March 1996), and Chapter 4, "Creating a Professional Portfolio," in C. Danielson, *Enhancing Professional Practice: A Framework for Teaching* (Alexandria, VA: Association for Supervision and Curriculum Development, 1996). See also the Internet at <http://www.teachnet.com/> Preservice teachers in particular may be interested in several articles about portfolios in the theme issue of Teacher Education Quarterly, 25(1): (Winter 1998).

EXERCISE 12.1 DEVELOPMENT OF A PROFESSIONAL PORTFOLIO

INSTRUCTIONS: The purpose of this exercise is to guide you in the creation of a personal professional portfolio that will be shared with persons who are considering your application for employment as a credentialed teacher.

Because it would be impractical to send a complete portfolio with every application you submit, you should consider developing a minimum portfolio (portfolio B) that could be sent with each application, in addition to a complete portfolio (portfolio A) that you could make available upon request and take with you to an interview. However it is done, the actual contents of the portfolio will vary depending on the specific job being sought; you will continually add to and delete materials from your portfolio. Suggested categories and subcategories, listed in the order that they may be best presented in portfolios A and B are as follows.

1. Table of contents of portfolio (not too lengthy)—portfolio A only.
2. Your professional résumé—both portfolios.
3. Evidence of your language and communication skills (evidence of your use of English and of other languages, including American Sign)—portfolio A. (Also state this information briefly in your letter of application. See the résumé section that follows.)
    a. Your teaching philosophy (written in your own handwriting so to demonstrate your handwriting). (See Exercise 3.4.)
    b. Other evidence to support this category.
4. Evidence of teaching skills—portfolio A.
    a. For planning skills, include instructional objectives, a syllabus, and a unit plan. (See Exercises 5.11, 5.13, and 6.7.)
    b. For teaching skills, include a sample lesson plan and a video of your actual teaching. (See Exercises 6.10A, 9.2, and 12.2.)
    c. For assessment skills, include a sample personal assessment and samples of student assessment. (See Exercises 9.2, 11.2, and 12.2.)
5. Letters of recommendation and other documentation to support your teaching skills—both portfolios.
6. Other (for example, personal interests related to the position for which you are applying)—portfolio A.

Resources for Locating Teaching Vacancies

To locate teaching vacancies, you can establish contact with any of the following resources.

1. *Academic employment network.* A network employment page on the Internet <http://www.acad employ.com/>. Contact AEN, 2665 Gray Road, Windham, ME 04062, 800-890-8283. E-mail: info @academploy.com.
2. *College or university placement office.* Establishing a career placement file with your local college or university placement service is an excellent way to begin the process of locating teaching vacancies.
3. *Local school or district personnel office.* You can contact school personnel offices to obtain information about teaching vacancies and sometimes about open job interviews.
4. *County educational agency.* Contact local county offices of education about job openings.
5. *State departments of education.* Some state departments of education maintain information about job openings statewide. See listing in Figure 12.1.

6. *Independent schools.* You can contact private schools that interest you either directly or through educational placement services such as:
    - IES (Independent Educational Services), 20 Nassau Street, Princeton, NJ 08540, 800-257-5102.
    - European Council of Independent Schools, 21B Lavant St., Petersfield, Hampshire, GU32 3EL, England.
7. *Commercial placement agencies.* Nationwide job listings and placement services are available from such agencies as:
    - Carney, Sandoe & Associates, 136 Boylston Street, Boston, MA 02116, 800-225-7986.
    - National Education Service Center, P.O. Box 1279, Department NS, Riverton, WY 82501-1279, 307-856-0170.
    - National Teachers Clearinghouse-SE, P.O. Box 267, Boston, MA 02118-0267, 617-267-3204.
8. *Out-of-country teaching opportunities.* Information regarding teaching positions outside the United States can be obtained from:

- American Field Services Intercultural Programs, 313 East 43rd St., New York, NY 10017.
- Department of Defense Dependent Schools, 4040 N. Fairfax Dr., Arlington, VA 22203-1634.
- European Council of Independent Schools, 21B Lavant St., Petersfield, Hampshire, GU32 3EL, England.
- International Schools Service, P.O. Box 5910, Princeton, NJ 08543.
- Peace Corps, Recruitment Office, 806 Connecticut Ave., NW, Washington, DC 20526.
- Teachers Overseas Recruitment Centers, National Teacher Placement Bureaus of America, Inc., P.O. Box 09027, 4190 Pearl Rd., Cleveland, OH 44109.
- YMCA of the USA, Attn: Teaching in Japan and Taiwan, 101 N. Wacker Dr., Chicago, IL 60606.

9. *Professional educational journals and other publications.* Professional teaching journals (as found in Figure 10.3, Chapter 10) often run advertisements of teaching vacancies, as do education newspapers such as *Education Week* or Web site http://www.edweek.org. These can be found in your college or university library.

State and Territorial Sources for Information about Credential Requirements

If you are interested in the credential requirements for other states and U.S. territories, check at the appropriate office of your own college or university teacher preparation program. Find out what information is available about requirements for states of interest to you and whether the credential that you are about to receive has reciprocity with other states. Addresses and contact numbers for information about state credentials are available at <http://www.ed.gov/Programs/bastmp/SEA.htm>.

The Professional Résumé

Résumé preparation is the subject of how-to books, computer programs, and commercial services, but a teacher's résumé is specific. Although no one can tell you exactly what résumé will work best for you, a few basic guidelines are especially helpful to prepare a teacher's résumé:

- The résumé should be no more than *two pages* in length. If it is any longer, it becomes a life history rather than a professional résumé.
- The presentation should be neat and uncluttered.
- Page size should be standard 8 1/2 × 11 inches. Oversized and undersized pages can get lost.
- Stationery color should be white or off-white.
- Do not give information such as your age, height, weight, marital status, number or names of your children, or a photograph of yourself, because including

personal data may make it appear that you are trying to prejudice members of the hiring committee, which is simply unprofessional.
- Sentences should be clear and concise; avoid educational jargon, awkward phrases, abbreviations, or unfamiliar words.
- Organize the information carefully, in this order: your name, address, and telephone number, followed by your education, professional experience, credential status, location of placement file, professional affiliations, and honors.
- When identifying your experiences—academic, teaching, and life—do so in reverse chronological order, listing your most recent degree or your current position first. (See sample résumé in Figure 12.1.)
- Be absolutely truthful; avoid any distortions of facts about your degrees, experiences, or any other information that you provide on your résumé.
- Take time to develop your résumé, and then keep it current. Do not duplicate hundreds of copies; produce a new copy each time you apply for a job. If you maintain your résumé on a computer disc, then it is easy to make modifications and print a current copy each time one is needed.
- Prepare a cover letter to accompany your résumé that is written specifically for the position for which you are applying. Address the letter personally but formally to the personnel director. Limit the cover letter to one page, and emphasize yourself, your teaching experiences and interests, and reasons that you are best qualified for the position. Show a familiarity with the particular school or district. Again, if you maintain a generic application letter on a computer disc, you can easily modify it to make it specific for each position.
- Have your résumé and cover letter edited by someone familiar with résumé writing and editing, perhaps an English-teaching friend. A poorly written, poorly typed, or poorly copied résumé fraught with spelling and grammar errors will guarantee that you will not be considered for the job.
- Be sure that your application reaches the personnel director by the announced deadline. If for some reason it will be late, then telephone the director, explain the circumstances, and request permission to submit your application late.

The In-Person Interview

If your application and résumé are attractive to the personnel director, you will be notified and scheduled for a personal or small-group interview, although in some instances the hiring interview may precede the request for your personal papers. Whichever the case, during the interview you should be honest, and you should be yourself. Practice an interview, perhaps with

Figure 12.1 Sample professional résumé.

Lee Roberson
10 Main St, Weaverville, CA 96093
(916) 552-8996; e-mail Lrob@aol.com

CREDENTIAL

January 2000   California Preliminary Single Subject Credential in English
                         Supplemental authorizations in Social Studies and Physical Education
May 2000   CLAD (Culture and Language Academic Development) Certificate
                         California State University, Sacramento

EDUCATION

May 1994   Bachelor of Arts Degree in English Literature
                         Saint Olaf College, Northfield, Minnesota

TEACHING EXPERIENCE

Fall 2000
(Student Teaching III)   **Douglass Junior High School (Woodland, CA).** *Two 7th grade 2-hour block*
                         Language Arts and Social Studies core classes
                         • Worked with a team to develop interdisciplinary thematic lessons

Spring 2000
(Student Teaching II)   **Davis High School (Davis, CA).** *One period of Jr. Lit*
                         • Developed book clubs, small group forums for discussing three novels
                         • Developed poetry unit in which students published their poems

Fall 1999
(Student Teaching I)   **Los Cerros Middle School.** *One period ESL—13 culturally diverse 7th and 8th*
                         graders.
                         • Bilingual stories and activities; reader's theater presentations

RELATED EXPERIENCE

Summer of 1999   • Developed and taught a Summer Writing Workshop for small groups of students,
                            grades 3–10. Met with students and parents to establish goals.
1997–1998   • Reader for English department of Valley High School.

the aid of a videocamera. Ask someone to role-play an interview with you and to ask you some tough questions. Plan your interview wardrobe and get it ready the night before. Leave early for your interview so that you arrive in plenty of time. If possible, long before your scheduled interview, locate someone who works in the school district and discuss curriculum, classroom management policies, popular programs, and district demographics with that person.

If you anticipate a professionally embarrassing question during the interview, think of diplomatic ways to respond. This means that you should think of ways to turn your weaknesses into strengths. For instance, if your cooperating teacher has mentioned that you need to continue to develop your room environment skills (meaning that you were sloppy), admit that you realize that you need to be more conscientious about keeping supplies and materials neat and tidy, but mention your concern about the students and the learning and that you realize you have a tendency to interact with students more than with objects. Assure someone that you will work on this skill, and then do it.

The paragraphs that follow offer additional specific guidelines for preparing for and handling the in-person interview. As you peruse these guidelines please know that what may seem trite and obvious to one reader is not necessarily obvious to another.

You will be given a specific time, date, and place for the interview. Regardless of your other activities, accept the time, date, and location suggested rather than trying to manipulate the interviewer around a schedule more convenient for you.

As a part of the interview you may be expected to do a formal but abbreviated (10–15 minutes) teaching demonstration. You may or may not be told in advance of this expectation. It is a good idea to develop and rehearse a model demonstration that you could perform on immediate request. Just in case it might be useful, some candidates carry to the interview a videotape of one of their best real teaching episodes made during student teaching.

Dress for success. Regardless of what else you may be doing for a living, take the time necessary to make a professional and proud appearance.

Avoid coming to the interview with small children. If necessary, arrange to have them cared for by a friend, relative, or child care professional.

Arrive promptly, shake your dry hands firmly with members of the committee, and initiate conversation with a friendly comment, based on your personal knowledge about the school or district.

Be prepared to answer standard interview questions. Sometimes school districts will send candidates the questions that will be asked during the interview; at other times, these questions are handed to the candidate upon arrival at the interview. The questions that are likely to be asked will cover the following topics:

- *Your experiences with students of the relevant age.* The committee wants to be reasonably certain that you can effectively manage and teach at this level. You should answer this question by sharing specific successes that demonstrate you are a decisive and competent teacher.
- *Hobbies and travels.* The committee wants to know more about you as a person to ensure that you will be an interesting and energetic teacher and a congenial member of the faculty.
- *Extracurricular interests and experiences.* The committee wants to know about all the ways in which you might be helpful in the school and that you will promote the interests and cocurricular activities of students and the school community.
- *Classroom management techniques.* You must convince the committee that you can effectively manage a classroom of diverse learners in a manner that will help the students to develop their self-esteem.
- *Knowledge of the curriculum standards and the subject taught at the grade for which you are being considered.* The committee needs to be reasonably certain that you have command of the subject and its place within the developmental stages of students at this level. This is where you should show your knowledge of national standards and of state and local curriculum documents.
- *Knowledge of assessment strategies relevant for use in teaching at this level.* This is your place to shine with your professional knowledge about using rubrics and performance assessment.
- *Commitment to teaching at this level.* The committee wants to be assured that you are knowledgeable about and committed to teaching and learning at this level and are not just seeking this job until something better comes along.
- *Your ability to reflect on experience and to grow from that reflection.* Demonstrate that you are a reflective decision maker and a life-long learner.
- *Your perceived weaknesses.* If you are asked about your weaknesses, you have an opportunity to show that you can effectively reflect and self-assess, that you can think reflectively and critically, and that you know the value of learning from your own errors and how to do it. Be prepared for this question by identifying a specific error that you have made, perhaps while student teaching, and explain how you turned that error into a profitable learning experience.

Throughout the interview you should maintain eye contact with the interviewer while demonstrating interest, enthusiasm, and self-confidence. When an opportunity arises, ask one or two planned questions that demonstrate your knowledge of and interest in this position and this community and school or district.

When the interview has obviously been brought to a close by the interviewer, that is your signal to leave. Do not hang around; this is a sign of lacking confidence. Follow the interview with a thank-you letter addressed to the personnel director or interviewer; even if you do not get the job, you will be better remembered for future reference.[2]

Once you are employed as a teacher, your professional development continues. The sections that follow demonstrate ways in which that can happen.

PROFESSIONAL DEVELOPMENT THROUGH REFLECTION AND SELF-ASSESSMENT

Beginning now and continuing throughout your career, you will reflect on your teaching (reflection is inevitable) and you will want to continue to grow as a professional as a result of those reflections (growth is not so inevitable unless self-initiated and systematically planned). The most competent professional is one who is proactive, who takes charge and initiates his or her own continuing professional development. One useful way of continuing to reflect, self-assess, and grow professionally is by maintaining a professional journal, much as your students do when they maintain journals reflecting on what they are learning. Another is by continuing to maintain the professional career portfolio that you began assembling early in your preservice program and finalized for your job search. Some teachers maintain professional logbooks, which serve not only as documentations of their specific professional contributions and activities but also of the breadth of their professional involvement. Some teachers maintain research logs as a way of recording questions that come up during the busy teaching day, and of establishing a plan for finding answers.[3] The research log

---

[2]For additional suggestions for preparing for a teaching job interview, see Internet Web site <http://www.teachnet.com/>.

[3]For more on the professional portfolio and logs, see Chapter 4, "Creating a Professional Portfolio," of C. Danielson, *Enhancing Professional Practice: A Framework for Teaching* (Alexandria, VA: Association for Supervision and Curriculum Development, 1996), pp. 38–50.

strategy can be of tremendous benefit to you in actively researching and improving your classroom work but also can be of interest to colleagues. Finally, working in teams and sharing your work with team members is still another way of continuing to reflect, self-assess, and grow as a teacher.

PROFESSIONAL DEVELOPMENT THROUGH MENTORING

Mentoring, one teacher facilitating the learning of another teacher, can aid in professional development.[4] In what is sometimes called *peer coaching,* a mentor teacher volunteers or is selected by the teacher who wishes to improve or is selected by a school administrator, formally or informally. The mentor observes and coaches the teacher to help him or her to improve in teaching. Sometimes the teacher simply wants to learn a new skill. In other instances, the teacher being coached remains with the mentor teacher for an entire school year, developing and improving old and new skills or learning how to teach with a new program. In many districts, new teachers are automatically assigned to mentor teachers for their first, and sometimes second, year as a program of induction.

PROFESSIONAL DEVELOPMENT THROUGH IN-SERVICE AND GRADUATE STUDY

In-service workshops and programs are offered for teachers at the school level, by the district, and by other agencies such as a county office of education or a nearby college or university. In-service workshops and programs are usually designed for specific purposes, such as to train teachers in new teaching skills, to update their knowledge in content, and to introduce them to new teaching materials or programs. For example, Baltimore City Public School provides a systemwide professional development program for teachers of grades 6–8, administrators, and staff at its Lombard Learning Academy Demonstration Center. The Lombard Learning Academy is a school-within-a-school located at Lombard Middle School. Cohorts of five to ten teachers from other schools in the district visit the Academy for five-day periods to observe instruction, practice strategies, and hone their skills in the use of technology.

---

[4]For additional information, see "The International Center for Information About New Teacher Mentoring and Induction" at <http://www.teachermentors.com/MCenter%20Site/Advice BegTchr.html> and a description of California's Beginning Teacher Support and Assessment (BSTA) Program at <http://www.ccoe.k12.ca.us/coe/curins.sbtsa/description>.

University graduate study is yet another way of continuing your professional development. Some teachers pursue master's degrees in academic teaching fields, while many others pursue master's degrees in curriculum and methods of instruction or in educational administration or counseling. Some universities offer a Master of Arts in Teaching (MAT), a program of courses in specific academic fields that are especially designed for teachers.

PROFESSIONAL DEVELOPMENT THROUGH PARTICIPATION IN PROFESSIONAL ORGANIZATIONS

There are many professional organizations, local, statewide, national, and international. The organizations are usually discipline-specific, such as the International Reading Association, the National Council of Teachers of Mathematics, the National Council for the Social Studies, and the National Science Teachers Association (see footnotes for Chapter 5). In most states there is a statewide organization, probably affiliated with a national organization. In addition, the National Education Association (NEA), the Association of American Educators (AAE), and the American Federation of Teachers (AFT) offer professional development opportunities for members.

Local, district, state, and national organizations have meetings that include guest speakers, workshops, and publishers' displays. Professional meetings of teachers are educational, enriching, and fulfilling for those who attend. In addition, many other professional associations, such as those for reading teachers, supply speakers and publish articles in their journals that are often of interest to teachers in addition to the target audience.

Professional organizations publish newsletters and journals for their members, and these will likely be found in your college or university library. Sample periodicals were listed in Figure 10.3 (Chapter 10). Many professional organizations have special membership prices for teachers who are still college or university students, a courtesy that allows for an inexpensive beginning affiliation with a professional association. For information on special membership prices and association services, contact those of interest to you.

PROFESSIONAL DEVELOPMENT THROUGH COMMUNICATIONS WITH OTHER TEACHERS

Valuable experiences can be gained by visiting teachers at other schools, attending in-service workshops and graduate seminars and programs, participating in teacher study groups[5] and meetings of professional organizations, participation in teacher networks,[6] and sharing with teachers by means of electronic bulletin boards. Talking and sharing with teachers from across the country and around the world can provide helpful and refreshing perspectives. These discussions include not only a sharing of "war stories" but of ideas and descriptions of new programs, books, materials, and techniques that work.

As in other process skills, the teacher practices and models skill in communication, in and out of the classroom. This includes communicating with other teachers to improve one's own repertoire of strategies and knowledge about teaching and sharing one's experiences with others. Teaching other teachers about your own special skills and sharing your experiences are important components of the communication and professional development processes.

PROFESSIONAL DEVELOPMENT THROUGH SUMMER AND OFF-TEACHING WORK EXPERIENCE

In many areas of the country, special programs of short-term employment are available to interested teachers. Public agencies, private industry, foundations, and research institutes offer these opportunities especially, although not exclusively, to teachers of physical education, mathematics, science, and social studies. These institutions are interested in disseminating information and providing opportunities for teachers to update their skills and knowledge, with an ultimate hope that the teachers will stimulate in more students a desire to develop their physical fitness, to understand civic responsibilities, and to consider careers in science and technology. Participating industries, foundations, governments, and institutes provide on-the-job training with salaries or stipends to teachers who are selected to participate. During the program of employment and depending on the nature of that work, a variety of people (e.g., scientists, technicians, politicians, businesspeople, social workers, and sometimes university educators) meet with teachers to share experiences and discuss what is being learned and its implications for teaching and curriculum development.

Some of the programs for teachers are government sponsored, field centered, and content specific. For example, a program may concentrate on geology, anthropology, mathematics, or reading. At another location, a program may concentrate on teaching, using a specific new or experimental curriculum. These programs located around the country may have university affiliation, which means that university credit may be available. Room and board, travel, and a stipend are sometimes granted to participating teachers.

Sources of information about the availability of programs include professional journals, the local chamber of commerce, and meetings of the local or regional teachers' organization. In areas with few or no organized programs of part-time work experience for teachers, some teachers have had success in initiating their own by establishing contact with management personnel of local businesses or companies.

PROFESSIONAL DEVELOPMENT THROUGH MICRO PEER TEACHING

Micro peer teaching (MPT) is a skill-development strategy used for professional development by both preservice (prior to credentialing) and in-service (credentialed and employed) teachers. Micro peer teaching (to which you were introduced in Exercises 7.7 and 9.2) is a scaled-down teaching experience involving a:

- Limited objective
- Brief interval for teaching a lesson
- Lesson taught to a few (8–10) peers (as your students)
- Lesson that focuses on the use of one or several instructional strategies

Micro peer teaching can be a predictor of later teaching effectiveness in a regular classroom. More importantly, it can provide an opportunity to develop and improve specific teaching behaviors. A videotaped MPT allows you to see yourself in action for self-evaluation and diagnosis. Evaluation of an MPT session is based on:

- The quality of the teacher's preparation and lesson implementation
- The quality of the planned and implemented student involvement
- Relative success in attaining instructional objective(s)
- The appropriateness of the cognitive level of the lesson

Whether a preservice or in-service teacher, you are urged to participate in one or more MPT experiences. Formatted differently from previous exercises in this resource guide, Exercise 12.2 can represent a summative performance assessment for the course for which this book is being used.

---

[5]See, for example, G. Cramer et al., *Teacher Study Groups for Professional Development*, Fastback 406 (Bloomington, IN: Phi Delta Kappa Educational Foundation, 1996).

[6]See, for example, A. Lieberman and M. Grolnick, "Networks, Reform, and the Professional Development of Teachers," Chapter 10 (pp. 192–215) of A. Hargreaves (Ed.), *Rethinking Educational Change With Heart and Mind* (Alexandria, VA: ASCD 1997 Yearbook, Association for Supervision and Curriculum Development, 1997).

EXERCISE 12.2 PULLING IT ALL TOGETHER—MICRO PEER TEACHING III

INSTRUCTIONS: The purpose of this exercise is to learn how to develop your own MPT experiences. You will prepare and teach a lesson that is prepared as a lesson presentation for your peers, at their level of intellectual maturity and understanding (i.e., as opposed to teaching the lesson to peers pretending that they are public school students).

This experience has two components:

1. Your preparation and implementation of a demonstration lesson
2. Your completion of an analysis of the summative peer assessment and the self-assessment, with statements of how you would change the lesson and your teaching of it were you to repeat the lesson

You should prepare and carry out a 15- to 20-minute lesson to a group of peers. The exact time limit for the lesson should be set by your group, based on the size of the group and the amount of time available. When the time limit has been set, complete the time-allowed entry (item 1) of Form A of this exercise. Some of your peers will serve as your students; others will be evaluating your teaching. (The process works best when "students" do not evaluate while being students.) Your teaching should be videotaped for self-evaluation.

For your lesson, identify one concept and develop your lesson to teach toward an understanding of that concept. Within the time allowed, your lesson should include both teacher talk and a hands-on activity for the students. Use Form A for the initial planning of your lesson. Then complete a lesson plan, selecting a lesson plan format as discussed in Chapter 6. Then present the lesson to the "students." The peers who are evaluating your presentation should use Form B of this exercise.

After your presentation, collect your peer evaluations (the Form B copies that you gave to the evaluators). Then review your presentation by viewing the videotape. After viewing the tape, prepare:

- A tabulation and statistical analysis of peer evaluations of your lesson
- A self-evaluation based on your analysis of the peer evaluations, your feelings having taught the lesson, and your thoughts after viewing the videotape
- A summary analysis that includes your selection and description of your teaching strengths and weaknesses, as indicated by this peer-teaching experience, and how you would improve were you to repeat the lesson.

TABULATION OF PEER EVALUATIONS

The procedure for tabulating the completed evaluations received from your peers is as follows:

1. *Use a blank copy of Form B for tabulating.* In the left margin of that copy, place the letters N (number) and σ (total) to prepare for two columns of numbers that will fall below each of those letters. In the far right margin, place the word *Score*.
2. *For each item (A through Y) on the peer evaluation form, count the number of evaluators who gave a rating (from 1 to 5) on the item.* Sometimes an evaluator may not rate a particular item, so although there may have been ten peers evaluating your micro peer teaching, the number of evaluators giving you a rating on any one particular item could be less than ten. For each item, the number of evaluators rating that item we call N. Place this number in the N column at the far left margin on your blank copy of Form B, next to the relevant item.
3. *Using a calculator, obtain the sum of the peer ratings for each item.* For example, for item A, Lesson Preparation, you add the numbers given by each evaluator for that item. If there were ten evaluators who gave you a number rating on that item, then your sum on that item will not be more than 50 (5×10). Because individual evaluators will make their X marks differently, you sometimes must estimate an individual evaluator's number rating; that is, rather than a clear rating of 3 or 3.5 on an item, you may have to estimate it as being a 3.2 or a 3.9. In the left-hand margin of your blank copy of Form B, in the σ column, place the sum for each item.
4. *Now obtain a score for each item, A through Y.* The score for each item is obtained by dividing σ by N. Your score for each item will range between 1 and 5. Write this dividend in the column in the right-hand margin under the word *Score* on a line parallel to the relevant item. This is the number you will use in the analysis phase.

☞

EXERCISE 12.2 (*continued*)

PROCEDURE FOR ANALYZING THE TABULATIONS

Having completed the tabulation of the peer evaluations of your teaching, you are ready to proceed with your analysis of those tabulations.

1. To proceed, you need a blank copy of Form C of this exercise, your self-analysis form.
2. On the blank copy of Form C are five items: Implementation, Personal, Voice, Materials, and Strategies.
3. In the far left margin of Form C, place the letter σ for the sum. To its right, and parallel with it, place the word *Average.* You now have arranged for two columns of five numbers each—a σ column and an *Average* column.
4. For each of the five items, get the total score for that item, as follows:
   a. *Implementation.* Add all scores (from the right-hand margin of blank Form B) for the four items a, c, x, and y. The total should be 20 or less (4 × 5). Place this total in the left-hand margin under σ (to the left of "1. Implementation").
   b. *Personal.* Add all scores (from the right-hand margin of blank Form B) for the nine items f, g, m, n, o, p, q, s, and t. The total should be 45 or less (9 × 5). Place this total in the left-hand margin under σ (to the left of "2. Personal").
   c. *Voice.* Add all scores (from the right-hand margin of blank Form B) for the three items h, i, and j. The total should be 15 or less (3 × 5). Place this total in the left-hand margin under σ (to the left of "3. Voice").
   d. *Materials.* Add all scores (from the right-hand margin of blank Form B) for item k. The total should be 5 or less (1 × 5). Place this total in the left-hand margin under σ (to the left of "4. Materials").
   e. *Strategies.* Add all "scores" (from the right-hand margin of blank Form B) for the eight items b, d, e, l, r, u, v, and w. The total should be 40 or less (8× 5). Place this total in the left-hand margin under σ (to the left of "5. Strategies").
5. Now, for each of the five categories, divide the sum by the number of items in the category to get your peer evaluation average score for that category. For item 1 you will divide by 4; for item 2, by 9; for item 3, by 3; for item 4, by 1; and for item 5, by 8. For each category you should then have a final average peer evaluation score of a number between 1 and 5. If correctly done, you now have average scores for each of the five categories: Implementation, Personal, Voice, Materials, and Strategies. With those scores and evaluator's comments you can prepare your final summary analysis.

The following table includes three sample analyses of MPT lessons based *only* on the scores—that is, without reference to comments made by individual evaluators, although peer evaluator's comments are important considerations for actual analyses.

Sample Analyses of MPTs Based Only on Peer Evaluation Scores

	Category/Rating					
Teacher	**1**	**2**	**3**	**4**	**5**	**Possible Strengths and Weaknesses**
A	4.2	2.5	2.8	4.5	4.5	Good lesson, weakened by personal items and voice
B	4.5	4.6	5.0	5.0	5.0	Excellent teaching, perhaps needing a stronger start
C	2.5	3.0	3.5	1.0	1.5	Poor strategy choice, lack of student involvement

EXERCISE 12.2 FORM A MPT PREPARATION

INSTRUCTIONS: Form A is to be used for initial preparation of your MPT lesson. (For preparation of your lesson, study Form B.) After completing Form A, proceed with the preparation of your MPT lesson using a lesson plan format as discussed in Chapter 6. A copy of the final lesson plan should be presented to the evaluators at the start of your MPT presentation.

1. Time allowed _____

2. Title or topic of lesson I will teach _____

3. Concept _____

4. Specific instructional objectives for the lesson:

Cognitive _____

_____

Affective _____

_____

Psychomotor _____

_____

5. Strategies to be used, including approximate time plan: _____

Set introduction _____

_____

Transitions _____

_____

Closure _____

_____

Others _____

_____

6. Student experiences to be provided (i.e., specify for each—visual, verbal, kinesthetic, and tactile experiences):

_____

_____

7. Materials, equipment, and resources needed:

_____

_____

EXERCISE 12.2 FORM B PEER EVALUATION

INSTRUCTIONS: Evaluators use Form B, making an *X* on the continuum between 5 and 1. Far left (5) is the highest rating; far right (1) is the lowest. Completed forms are collected and given to the teacher upon completion of that teacher's MPT and are reviewed by the teacher prior to reviewing his or her videotaped lesson.

To evaluators: Comments as well as marks are useful to the teacher.

To teacher: Give one copy of your lesson plan to the evaluators at the start of your MPT. (*Note:* It is best if evaluators can be together at a table at the rear of the room.)

Teacher _____ Date _____

Topic _____

Concept _____

1. Organization of Lesson	5	4	3	2	1
a. Lesson preparation evident	very		somewhat		no
b. Lesson beginning effective	yes		somewhat		poor
c. Subject-matter knowledge apparent	yes		somewhat		no
d. Strategies selection effective	yes		somewhat		poor
e. Closure effective	yes		somewhat		poor

Comments _____

_____

_____

_____

_____

_____

_____

_____

_____

_____

_____

_____

2. Lesson Implementation	5	4	3	2	1
f. Eye contact excellent	yes		somewhat		poor
g. Enthusiasm evident	yes		somewhat		no
h. Speech delivery	articulate		minor problems		poor
i. Voice inflection; cueing	effective		minor problems		poor
j. Vocabulary use	well-chosen		minor problems		poor
k. Aids, props, and materials	effective		okay		none

☞

EXERCISE 12.2 FORM B (*continued*)

l. Use of examples and analogies	effective	need improvement	none
m. Student involvement	effective	okay	none
n. Use of overlapping skills	good	okay	poor
o. Nonverbal communication	effective	a bit confusing	distracting
p. Use of active listening	effective	okay	poor
q. Responses to students	personal and accepting	passive or indifferent	impersonal and antagonistic
r. Use of questions	effective	okay	poor
s. Use of student names	effective	okay	no
t. Use of humor	effective	okay	poor
u. Directions and refocusing	succinct	a bit vague	confusing
v. Teacher mobility	effective	okay	none
w. Use of transitions	smooth	a bit rough	unclear
x. Motivating presentation	very	somewhat	not at all
y. Momentum (pacing) of lesson	smooth and brisk	okay	too slow or too fast

Comments _____

_____

_____

_____

_____

_____

_____

_____

_____

_____

_____

_____

_____

_____

_____

_____

EXERCISE 12.2 FORM C TEACHER'S SUMMATIVE PEER EVALUATION

See instructions within Exercise 12.2 for completing this form.

1. Implementation (items a, c, x, y)	5	4	3	2	1
2. Personal (items f, g, m, n, o, p, q, s, t)	5	4	3	2	1
3. Voice (items h, i, j)	5	4	3	2	1
4. Materials (item k)	5	4	3	2	1
5. Strategies (items b, d, e, l, r, u, v, w)	5	4	3	2	1

Total = _____

Comments _____

_____

_____

_____

_____

_____

_____

_____

_____

_____

_____

_____

_____

_____

_____

_____

_____

_____

_____

_____

_____

_____

_____

_____

_____

SUMMARY

Because teaching and learning go hand in hand and the effectiveness of one affects that of the other, the final two chapters of this resource guide have dealt with both aspects of the *how well* component of teacher preparation—how well the students are learning and how well the teacher is teaching.

In addition, you have been presented with guidelines about how to obtain your first teaching job and how to continue your professional development. Throughout your teaching career you will continue improving your knowledge and skills in all aspects of teaching and learning.

I wish you the very best in your new career. Be the very best teacher you can be. The nation and its youth need you.

—Richard Kellough

QUESTIONS FOR CLASS DISCUSSION

1. Discover what professional teacher organizations are located in your geographical area. Share what you find with others in your class. Attend a local, regional, or national meeting of a professional teachers' association, and report to your class what it was like and what you learned. Share with your class any free or inexpensive teaching materials you obtained.
2. Talk with experienced teachers and find out how they remain current in their teaching fields. Share what you find with others in your class.
3. Describe any prior concepts you held that changed as a result of your experiences with this chapter. Describe the changes.
4. From your current observations and field work related to this teacher preparation program, clearly identify one specific example of educational practice that seems contradictory to exemplary practice or theory presented in this chapter. Present your explanation for the discrepancy.
5. Congratulations! You have reached the end of this resource guide, but there may be questions lingering in your mind. As before, list them and try to find answers.

FOR FURTHER READING

Cambell, D. M., et al. *How to Develop a Professional Portfolio: A Manual for Teachers.* Needham Heights, MA: Allyn & Bacon, 1997.

Good, T. L., and Brophy, J. E. Chapter 11. *Looking in Classrooms.* New York: Longman, 1997.

Graham, P., et al. (Eds.) *Teacher/Mentor.* New York: Teachers College Press, 1999.

Kellough, R. D. *Surviving Your First Year of Teaching: Guidelines for Success.* New Jersey: Merrill/Prentice Hall, 1999.

Lowenhaupt, M. A., and Stephanik, C. E. *Making Student Teaching Work: Creating a Partnership.* Fastback 447. Bloomington, IN: Phi Delta Kappa Educational Foundation, 1999.

Lyons, N. (Ed.). *With Portfolio in Hand.* New York: Teachers College Press, 1998.

Newman, J. M., et al. *Tensions of Teaching: Beyond Tips to Critical Reflection.* New York: Teachers College Press, 1998.

Van Wagenen, L., and Hibbard, K. M. "Building Teacher Portfolios." *Educational Leadership* 55(5):26–29 (February 1998).

Glossary

ability grouping The assignment of students to separate classrooms or to separate activities within a classroom according to their perceived academic abilities. Homogeneous grouping is the grouping of students of similar abilities, whereas heterogeneous grouping is the grouping of students of mixed abilities.

accommodation The cognitive process of modifying a schema or creating new schemata.

accountability Reference to the concept that an individual is responsible for his or her behaviors and should be able to demonstrate publicly the worth of the activities carried out.

advance organizer Preinstructional cues that encourage a mind-set, used to enhance retention of materials to be studied.

advisor-advisee A homeroom or advisory program that provides each student the opportunity to interact with peers about school and personal concerns and to develop a meaningful relationship with at least one member of the school staff.

affective domain The area of learning related to interests, attitudes, feelings, values, and personal adjustment.

alternative assessment Assessment of learning that is different from traditional paper-and-pencil objective testing. See *authentic assessment.*

American Federation of Teachers (AFT) A national professional organization of teachers founded in 1916 and currently affiliated with the American Federation of Labor and Congress of Industrial Organizations (AFL-CIO).

anticipatory set See *advance organizer.*

assessment The relatively neutral process of finding out what students are learning or have learned as a result of instruction.

assignment A statement telling the student what he or she is to accomplish.

assimilation The cognitive process by which a learner integrates new information into an existing schema.

at risk General term applied to students who show a high potential for not completing school.

authentic assessment Assessment that is highly compatible with the instructional objectives. Also referred to as *accurate, active, aligned, alternative, direct,* and *performance assessment.*

behavioral objective A statement of expectation describing what the learner should be able to do upon completion of the instruction, with four components: the audience (learner), the overt behavior, the conditions, and the level or degree of performance. Also referred to as *performance* and *terminal* objective.

behaviorism A theory that equates learning with changes in observable behavior.

block scheduling The school programming procedure that provides large blocks of time (e.g., two hours) in which individual teachers or teacher teams can arrange groupings of students for varied periods of time, thereby more effectively individualizing the instruction for students with various needs and abilities.

brainstorming An instructional strategy used to create a flow of new ideas, during which the judgments of the ideas of others are forbidden.

CD-ROM (compact disc, read-only memory) Digitally encoded information permanently recorded on a compact disc (CD).

classroom control The process of influencing student behavior in the classroom.

classroom management The teacher's system of establishing a climate for learning, including techniques for preventing and handling student misbehavior.

closure In a lesson, the means by which a teacher brings the lesson to an end.

coaching See *mentoring.*

cognitive disequilibrium The mental state of not yet having made sense out of a perplexing (discrepant) situation.

cognitive domain   The area of learning related to intellectual skills, such as retention and assimilation of knowledge.

cognitive psychology   A branch of psychology devoted to the study of how individuals acquire, process, and use information.

cognitivism   A theory that holds that learning entails the construction or reshaping of mental schemata and that mental processes mediate learning. Also known as *constructivism.*

common planning time   A regularly scheduled time during the school day when teachers who teach the same students meet for joint planning, parent conferences, materials preparation, and student evaluation.

competency-based instruction   See *performance-based instruction.*

comprehension   A level of cognition that refers to the skill of understanding.

computer-assisted instruction (CAI)   Instruction received by a student when interacting with lessons programmed into a computer system.

computer literacy   The ability at some level to understand and use computers.

computer-managed instruction (CMI)   The use of a computer system to manage information about learner performance and learning-resources options to prescribe and control individual lessons.

concept map   A visual or graphic representation of concepts and their relationships; words related to a key word are written in categories around the key word, and the categories are labeled.

constructivism   See *cognitivism.*

continuous progress   An instructional procedure that allows students to progress at their own pace through a sequenced curriculum.

convergent thinking   Thinking that is directed to a preset conclusion.

cooperative learning   A genre of instructional strategies that use small groups of students working together and helping one another on learning tasks, with an emphasis on support among group members rather than on competition.

core curriculum   Subject or discipline components of the curriculum considered as being absolutely necessary, including English/language arts, mathematics, science, and history/social studies.

covert behavior   A learner behavior that is not outwardly observable.

criterion   A standard by which behavioral performance is judged.

criterion-referenced measurement   The measurement of behaviors against preset standards rather than against the behaviors of others.

critical thinking   The ability to recognize and identify problems and discrepancies, to propose and test solutions, and to arrive at tentative conclusions based on the data collected.

curriculum   What is planned and encouraged for teaching and learning, including both school and non-school environments, overt (formal) and hidden (informal) curricula, and both broad and narrow notions of content (its development, acquisition, and consequences).

deductive learning   Learning that proceeds from the general to the specific. See *expository learning.*

detracking   An effort to minimize or eliminate separate classes or programs for students according to their differing abilities.

developmental characteristics   A set of common intellectual, psychological, physical, social, and moral and ethical characteristics that, when considered as a whole, indicate an individual's development relative to others during a particular age span.

developmental needs   A set of needs unique and appropriate to the developmental characteristics of a particular age span.

diagnostic assessment   See *preassessment.*

didactic teaching   See *direct teaching.*

direct experience   Learning by doing (applying) that which is being learned.

direct intervention   Teacher use of verbal reminders or verbal commands to redirect student behavior, as opposed to the use of nonverbal gestures or cues.

direct teaching   Teacher-centered expository instruction.

discipline   The process of controlling student behavior in the classroom. The term has been largely supplanted by the terms *classroom control* and *classroom management.* The term is also used in reference to the subject taught (e.g., the disciplines of language arts, science, mathematics, etc.).

discovery learning   Learning that proceeds from identification of a problem, through the development and testing of hypotheses, to the arrival at a conclusion. See *critical thinking.*

divergent thinking   Thinking that expands beyond original thought.

early adolescence   The developmental stage young people go through as they approach and begin to experience puberty, usually occurring between ages ten and fourteen.

eclectic   Using the best from a variety of sources.

effective school   A school where students master basic skills, seek academic excellence in all subjects, demonstrate achievement, and display good behavior and attendance.

elective   High-interest or special-needs courses that are based on student selection from various options.

empathy   The ability to understand the feelings of another person.

equality   Considered to be same in status or competency level.

equilibration   The mental process of moving from disequilibrium to equilibrium.

equilibrium   The balance between assimilation and accommodation.

equity   Fairness and justice, with impartiality.

evaluation   See *assesment.*

exceptional child   See *special-needs student.*

expository learning   The traditional classroom instructional approach that proceeds as follows: presentation of information to the learners, reference to particular examples, application of the information to the learner's experiences.

extrinsic motivators   Rewards from outside the learner, such as parent and teacher expectations, gifts, certificates, and grades.

facilitating behavior   Teacher behaviors that make student learning possible.

facilitative teaching   See *indirect teaching.*

family   See *school-within-a-school.*

feedback Information sent from the receiver to the originator that provides disclosure about the reception of the intended message.

flexible scheduling Organization of classes and activities in a way that allows for variation from day to day, as opposed to the traditional fixed schedule that does not vary from day to day.

formative assessment Evaluation of learning in progress.

full inclusion The commitment to education of each special-needs student, to the maximum extent appropriate, in the school and classroom that he or she would otherwise attend.

goal, course A broad generalized statement telling about the expected outcomes of the course.

goal, educational A desired instructional outcome that is broad in scope.

goal, teacher A statement telling what the teacher hopes to accomplish.

hands-on learning Learning by doing, or active learning.

heterogeneous grouping A grouping pattern that does not separate students into groups based on their intelligence, learning achievement, or physical characteristics.

high school A school that houses students in any combination of grades 9–12.

holistic learning Learning that incorporates emotions with thinking.

homogeneous grouping A grouping pattern that usually separates students into groups based on their intelligence and past school achievement, or physical characteristics.

house See *school-within-a-school*.

independent study An instructional strategy that allows a student to select a topic, set the goals, and work alone to attain them.

indirect teaching Student-centered teaching using discovery and inquiry instructional strategies.

individualized instruction See *individualized learning*.

individualized learning The self-paced process whereby individual students assume responsibility for learning through study, practice, feedback, and reinforcement, with appropriately designed instructional packages or modules.

inductive learning Learning that proceeds from specifics to the general. See *discovery learning*.

inquiry learning Like discovery learning, except the learner designs the processes to be used in resolving the problem, thereby requiring higher levels of cognition.

instruction Planned arrangement of experiences to help a learner develop understanding and to achieve a desirable change in behavior.

instructional module Any free standing instructional unit that includes these components: rationale, objectives, pretest, learning activities, comprehension checks with instructive feedback, posttest.

instructional scaffolding See *concept map*.

integrated (interdisciplinary) curriculum Curriculum organization that combines subject matter traditionally taught separately.

interdisciplinary team An organizational pattern of two or more teachers representing different subject areas; the team shares the same students, schedule, areas of the school, and the opportunity for teaching more than one subject.

interdisciplinary thematic unit (ITU) A thematic unit that crosses boundaries of two or more disciplines.

internalization The extent to which an attitude or value becomes a part of the learner; that is, without having to think about it, the learner's behavior reflects the attitude or value.

interscholastic sports Athletic competition between teams from two or more schools.

intervention The teacher interrupts to redirect a student's behavior, either by direct intervention (e.g., a verbal command) or by indirect intervention (e.g., eye contact or physical proximity).

intramural program Organized activity program that features events between individuals or teams from within the school.

intrinsic motivation Rewards from within a person, such as a student's internal sense of accomplishment.

intuition Knowing without conscious reasoning.

junior high school A school that houses grades 7–9 or 7–8 and that has a schedule and curriculum that resembles that of the (senior) high school (grades 9–12 or 10–12) more than that of the elementary school.

lead teacher The teacher in a teaching team who is designated to facilitate the work and planning of that team.

learning The development of understandings and the change in behavior resulting from experiences; see *behaviorism* and *cognitivism* for different interpretations of learning.

learning center (LC) An instructional strategy that uses activities and materials located at a special place in the classroom and that is designed to allow a student to work independently at his or her own pace to learn one area of content.

learning modality The way a person receives information; four modalities are recognized: visual, auditory, tactile (touch), and kinesthetic (movement).

learning resource center The central location in the school where instructional materials and media are stored, organized, and accessed by students and staff.

learning style The way a person learns best in a given situation.

looping An arrangement in which the cohort of students and teachers remain together as a group for several or for all the years a student is at a particular school; used at all levels of schooling, but especially in the primary grades and in some middle schools. Also referred to as multiyear grouping, multiyear instruction, multiyear placement, and teacher–student progression.

magnet school A school that specializes in a particular academic area, such as science, mathematics, and technology, or the arts; also referred to as a *theme school*.

mainstreaming Placing a special-needs student in regular education classrooms for all (full inclusion) or part (partial inclusion) of the school day.

mastery learning The concept that a student should master the content of one lesson before moving on to the content of the next.

measurement The process of collecting and interpreting data.

mentoring One-on-one coaching, tutoring, or guidance to facilitate learning.

metacognition   The ability to plan, monitor, and evaluate one's own thinking.

micro peer teaching (MPT)   Teaching a limited objective for a brief period of time to a small group of peers, for the purpose of evaluation and improvement of particular teaching skills.

middle grades   Grades 5–8.

middle level education   Any school unit between elementary and high school.

middle school   A school that has been planned and organized especially for students of ages ten through fourteen and that generally has grades 5–8, with grades 6–8 being the most popular grade-span organization. There are many variations, though; for example, a school might include only grades 7 and 8 and still be called a middle school.

minds-on learning   Learning in which the learner is intellectually active, thinking about what is being learned.

misconception   Faulty understanding of a major idea or concept; also known as *naive theory* and *conceptual misunderstanding*.

modeling   The teacher's direct and indirect demonstration, by actions and by words, of the behaviors expected of students.

multicultural education   A deliberate attempt to help students understand facts, generalizations, attitudes, and behaviors derived from their own ethnic roots as well as others. In this process, students unlearn racism and ethnic prejudices and recognize the interdependent fabric of society, giving due acknowledgment for contributions made by its members.

multilevel instruction   See *multitasking*.

multimedia   The combined use of sound, video, and graphics for instruction.

multiple intelligences   A theory of several different intelligences, as opposed to just one general intelligence; other intelligences that have been described are linguistic, musical, logical-mathematical, spatial, kinesthetic, interpersonal, and intrapersonal.

multipurpose board   A writing board with a smooth plastic surface used with special marking pens rather than chalk; sometimes called a *visual aid panel*. A multipurpose board may have a steel backing, which allows it to be used as a magnetic board and a screen for projecting visuals.

multitasking   When several levels of teaching and learning are going on simultaneously in the same classroom, when students are working on different objectives, or when different students are doing various tasks leading to the same objective; also called *multilevel instruction*.

naïve theory   See *misconception*.

National Education Association (NEA)   The nation's oldest professional organization of teachers, founded in 1857 as the National Teachers Association and changed in 1879 to its present name.

norm-referenced   Individual performance is judged relative to overall performance of the group (e.g., grading on a curve), as opposed to criterion-referenced.

orientation set   See *advance organizer*.

overlapping   A teacher behavior whereby the teacher is able to attend to more than one matter at once.

overt behavior   A learner behavior that is outwardly observable.

paraprofessional   An adult who is a credentialed teacher but who works with children in the classroom with and under the supervision of a credentialed person.

partial inclusion   Placing special-needs students in a regular education classroom part of the day.

peer tutoring   An instructional strategy that places students in a tutorial role, whereby one student helps another learn.

performance assessment   See *authentic assessment*.

performance-based instruction   Instruction designed around assessment of student achievement against specified and predetermined objectives.

performance objective   See *behavioral objective*.

portfolio assessment   An alternative approach to assessment that assembles representative samples of a student's work over time as a basis for assessment.

positive reinforcement   Encouraging desired student behavior by rewarding those behaviors when they occur.

PQRST   A study strategy whereby students review the reading to identify the main parts, create questions, read the material, state the main theme or idea, and test themselves by answering the questions they posed earlier.

preassessment   Diagnostic assessment, or assessment of what students know or think they know prior to the instruction.

probationary teacher   An untenured teacher. After a designated number of years in the same district (usually three), the probationary teacher receives a tenure contract upon rehire.

procedure   A statement telling the student how to accomplish a task.

psychomotor domain   The domain of learning that involves locomotor behaviors.

realia   Real objects used as visual props during instruction, such as political campaign buttons, plants, memorabilia, artwork, balls, and so forth.

reciprocal teaching   A form of collaborative teaching, whereby the teacher and the students share the teaching responsibility and all are involved in asking questions, clarifying, predicting, and summarizing.

reflection   The conscious process of mentally replaying experiences.

reflective abstraction   See *metacognition*.

reliability   In measurement, the accuracy with which a technique consistently measures that which it does measure.

schema   A mental construct by which the learner organizes his or her perceptions of situations and knowledge (plural: schemata).

school-within-a-school   Where one team of teachers is assigned to work with the same group of about 125 students for a common block of time, the entire school day, or, in some instances, for all the years those students are at that school; sometimes referred to as a *house, cluster, village, pod,* or *family*.

secondary school   Traditionally, any school housing students for any combination of grades 7–12.

self-contained classroom   A grouping pattern where one teacher teaches all or almost all subjects to one group of children; commonly used in the primary grades.

self-paced learning   See *individualized learning*.

senior high school   See *high school*.

sequencing   Arranging ideas in logical order.

simulation   An abstraction or simplification of a real-life situation.

special-needs student   A student who deviates from the average in any of the following ways: mental characteristics, sensory ability, neuromotor or physical characteristics, social behavior, communication ability, or in multiple handicaps. Also known as *exceptional child* and *special education student*.

SQ3R   A study strategy whereby students survey the reading, create questions, read to answer the questions, recite the answers, and review the original material.

SQ4R   Similar to SQ3R, but with the addition of recording. The students survey the reading, ask questions about what was read, read to answer the questions, recite the answers, record important items into their notebooks, then review it all.

student teaching   The field-experience component of teacher preparation, often the culminating experience, in which the teacher candidate practices teaching children while under the supervision of a credentialed teacher and a university supervisor.

summative assessment   Evaluation of learning after instruction is completed.

teacher leader   See *lead teacher*.

teaching   See *instruction*.

teaching style   The way a teacher teaches, including any distinctive mannerisms and personal choices of teaching behaviors and strategies.

teaching team   A team of two or more teachers who work together to provide instruction to the same group of students, either alternating the instruction or simultaneously team teaching.

team teaching   Two or more teachers working together to provide instruction to a group of students.

tenured teacher   A teacher with a tenure contract, which means that the teacher is automatically rehired each year thereafter unless the contract is revoked by either the district or the teacher and for specific and legal reasons; see *probationary teacher*.

terminal behavior   What has been learned as a direct result of instruction.

thematic unit   A unit of instruction built on a central theme or concept.

theme school   See *magnet school*.

think time   See *wait time*.

tracking   The practice of students' voluntary or involuntary placement in different programs or courses according to their ability and prior academic performance.

transescence   The stage of human development, usually thought of as ages ten through fourteen, which begins before the onset of puberty and extends through the early stages of adolescence. Students in this stage of development are referred to variously as the *transescent, preadolescent, preteen, in-betweenager,* and *tweenager*.

transition   In a lesson, the planned procedures that move student thinking from one idea to the next, or that move their actions from one activity to the next.

untracking   See *detracking*.

validity   In measurement, the degree to which an item or instrument measures that which it is intended to measure.

village   See *school-within-a-school*.

wait time   In the use of questioning, the period of silence between the time a question is asked and the questioner (teacher) does something, such as repeating the question, rephrasing the question, calling on a particular student, answering the question him- or herself, or asking another question.

whole-language learning   A point of view with a focus on seeking or creating meaning that encourages language production, taking risks, independence in producing language, and using a wide variety of print materials in authentic reading and writing situations.

withitness   The teacher's ability to intervene in a timely way and redirect a student's inappropriate behavior.

young adolescent   The 10- to 14-year-old who is experiencing the developmental stage of early adolescence.

Name Index

Subject Index